Pedagogical Use of Color

Throughout the Ninth Edition of **Fundamentals of Corporate Finance**, we make color a functional dimension of the discussion. In almost every chapter, color plays an extensive and largely self-evident role. Color in these chapters alerts students to the relationship between numbers in a discussion and an accompanying table or figure

Chapter 2
Section 2.4
Blue: Identifies net captial spending and change in net working capital
Green: Identifies cash flow numbers

Chapters 3 and 4
Throughout the chapter
Blue: Identifies income statements
Green: Identifies balance sheets
(Also see all 23 ratios in Chapter 3)

Chapter 7
Section 7.1
Blue: Identifies key numbers that combine to determine the value of a bond
Green: Identifies the bond value
Section 7.4
Blue: Identifies the implicit interest expense
Green: Identifies the straight interest expense

Chapter 9
Section 9.5
Blue: Identifies Project A
Green: Identifies Project B

Chapter 12
Section 12.5 (See Figure 12.11)
Blue, Green and **Bold Black**: Identify the three normal distribution ranges and use them to illustrate from which range each number has been derived

Chapter 13
Sections 13.1 and 13.2
Blue: Identifies Stock L
Green: Identifies Stock U
Section 13.7
Blue: Identifies Asset B
Green: Identifies Asset A

Chapter 14
Section 14.2
Blue: Identifies dollar and percentage changes in dividends
Green: Identifies dividends

Chapter 15
Section 15.9
Blue: Identifies values of shares with and without dilution
Green: Identifies original values of shares

Chapter 16
Section 16.2
Blue: Identifies the propsed capital structure
Green: Identifies the original capital structure
Sections 16.4 and 16.6
Blue: Identifies Firm L
Green: Identifies Firm U

Chapter 17
Section 17.6 (See Table 17.2 and Figure 17.3)
Blue: Identifies large dividend payouts
Green: Identifies small dividend payouts

Chapter 18
Throughout the chapter
Blue: Identifies income statements
Green: Identifies balance sheets
Section 18.4
Blue: Identifies total cash collections
Green: Identifies total cash disbursements
Bold Black: Identifies the net cash inflows

Chapter 19
End-of-chapter Appendix
Blue: Identifies contributing costs
Green: Identifies the opportunity trading and total costs

Chapter 20
Throughout the chapter
Blue: Identifies numbers exceeding the cost-minimizing restock quantity
Green: Identifies numbers falling below the cost-minimizing restock quantity
Bold Black: Identifies cost-minimizing quantity

Chapter 21
Section 21.5
Blue: Identifies cash flows
Green: Identifies expected exchange rates

Alternate Edition – Additional Chapters

Chapter 23
Sections 23.2, 23.3, and 23.6
Blue: Identifies the payoff profile
Green: Identifies the risk profile
Bold Black: Identifies the hedge position

Chapter 24
Section 24.1
Blue: Identifies puts
Green: Identifies calls
Section 24.2
Blue: Identifies stock value
Green: Identifies portfolio value
Section 24.5
Blue: Identifies calls
Green: Identifies warrants

Chapter 26
Section 26.1 (See Tables 26.1, 26.2, and 26.3)
Blue: Identifies Firm A and Global Resources
Green: Identifies Firm B and Regional Enterprises
Bold Black: Identifies the merged firm, Firm AB, and the merged

Green: Identifies total cash flow

New for the 9th edition!

Ross, Westerfield, and Jordan introduce an important and substantial innovation in financial education: **Excel Master for Corporate Finance**. This new supplement goes far beyond existing spreadsheet tutorials. It expertly demonstrates to students how to use the most powerful tools in Excel to do professional quality financial analysis. Excel Master is fully integrated with the textbook such that every suitable topic in the text is covered in depth. The result is that students end up learning corporate finance **and** spreadsheet techniques at the same time.

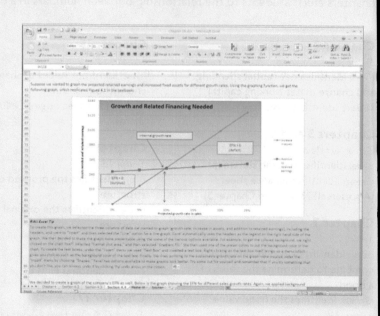

The screen captures here only hint at the depth of this new learning tool. Access the complete tutorial from the Online Learning Center and find out how students can become RWJ Excel Masters!

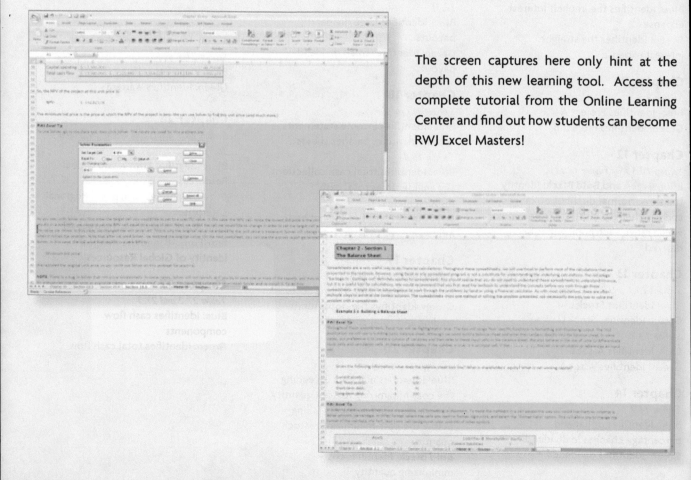

exam to explore the OLC.
udy tools on DAY ONE!

For Students:

Excel Master: Created by the authors and aligned with specific chapter content, this tutorial will expertly guide you through solving problems using spreadsheets.

Self-Study Quizzes: Revised by the Test Bank author, these automatically graded quizzes are representative of the types of questions you'll see on the exams.

Excel Templates: Solve specific end-of chapter problems by using these pre-created excel templates.

Premium Content: Additional study tools are available for purchase.
  Narrated PowerPoint Presentations: Expanded for the 9th edition, these chapter presentations cover key concepts and walk (and talk!) you through how to solve problems from the text.
  iPod Content: Download the NPPTs and quizzes onto your iPod for studying on the go!

For Instructors:

Teaching Materials:
  Instructor's Manual and Expanded PowerPoint Presentations: Annotations such as Real-World Examples, Lecture Tips, and Ethics Notes have been updated and incorporated into the PPT slides and the IM.
  Solutions: Discover detailed answers to end-of-chapter questions, problems, Excel templates, and cases.

Homework Manager Options: McGraw-Hill's homework manager options allow you to choose from an infinite number of homework questions, post assignments digitally, and automatically grade students' work.

Visit the Ross/Westerfield/Jordan Online Learning Center for even more student and instructor support.

Fundamentals of Corporate Finance,
9e offers a robust supplements package. Valuable tutorials, study tools, and course preparation materials are all conveniently located on the **Online Learning Center (OLC)** www.mhhe.com/rwj.

Alternate Edition

FUNDAMENTALS OF CORPORATE FINANCE

The McGraw-Hill/Irwin Series in Finance, Insurance, and Real Estate

Stephen A. Ross
Franco Modigliani Professor of Finance and Economics
Sloan School of Management, Massachusetts Institute of Technology, Consulting Editor

Financial Management

Adair
Excel Applications for Corporate Finance
First Edition

Block, Hirt, and Danielsen
Foundations of Financial Management
Thirteenth Edition

Brealey, Myers, and Allen
Principles of Corporate Finance
Ninth Edition

Brealey, Myers, and Allen
Principles of Corporate Finance, Concise
First Edition

Brealey, Myers, and Marcus
Fundamentals of Corporate Finance
Sixth Edition

Brooks
FinGame Online 5.0

Bruner
Case Studies in Finance: Managing for Corporate Value Creation
Sixth Edition

Chew
The New Corporate Finance: Where Theory Meets Practice
Third Edition

Cornett, Adair, and Nofsinger
Finance: Applications and Theory
First Edition

DeMello
Cases in Finance
Second Edition

Grinblatt (editor)
Stephen A. Ross, Mentor: Influence through Generations

Grinblatt and Titman
Financial Markets and Corporate Strategy
Second Edition

Higgins
Analysis for Financial Management
Ninth Edition

Kellison
Theory of Interest
Third Edition

Kester, Ruback, and Tufano
Case Problems in Finance
Twelfth Edition

Ross, Westerfield, and Jaffe
Corporate Finance
Ninth Edition

Ross, Westerfield, Jaffe, and Jordan
Corporate Finance: Core Principles and Applications
Second Edition

Ross, Westerfield, and Jordan
Essentials of Corporate Finance
Sixth Edition

Ross, Westerfield, and Jordan
Fundamentals of Corporate Finance
Ninth Edition

Shefrin
Behavioral Corporate Finance: Decisions that Create Value
First Edition

White
Financial Analysis with an Electronic Calculator
Sixth Edition

Investments

Bodie, Kane, and Marcus
Essentials of Investments
Eighth Edition

Bodie, Kane, and Marcus
Investments
Eighth Edition

Hirt and Block
Fundamentals of Investment Management
Ninth Edition

Hirschey and Nofsinger
Investments: Analysis and Behavior
Second Edition

Jordan and Miller
Fundamentals of Investments: Valuation and Management
Fifth Edition

Financial Institutions and Markets

Rose and Hudgins
Bank Management and Financial Services
Eighth Edition

Rose and Marquis
Money and Capital Markets: Financial Institutions and Instruments in a Global Marketplace
Tenth Edition

Saunders and Cornett
Financial Institutions Management: A Risk Management Approach
Sixth Edition

Saunders and Cornett
Financial Markets and Institutions
Fourth Edition

International Finance

Eun and Resnick
International Financial Management
Fifth Edition

Kuemmerle
Case Studies in International Entrepreneurship: Managing and Financing Ventures in the Global Economy
First Edition

Real Estate

Brueggeman and Fisher
Real Estate Finance and Investments
Thirteenth Edition

Ling and Archer
Real Estate Principles: A Value Approach
Third Edition

Financial Planning and Insurance

Allen, Melone, Rosenbloom, and Mahoney
Retirement Plans: 401(k)s, IRAs, and Other Deferred Compensation Approaches
Tenth Edition

Altfest
Personal Financial Planning
First Edition

Harrington and Niehaus
Risk Management and Insurance
Second Edition

Kapoor, Dlabay, and Hughes
Focus on Personal Finance: An Active Approach to Help You Develop Successful Financial Skills
Third Edition

Kapoor, Dlabay, and Hughes
Personal Finance
Ninth Edition

FUNDAMENTALS OF
CORPORATE FINANCE

NINTH EDITION
ALTERNATE EDITION

Stephen A. Ross
Massachusetts Institute of Technology

Randolph W. Westerfield
University of Southern California

Bradford D. Jordan
University of Kentucky

with additional material from
Fundamentals of Investments
Valuation and Management

Fifth Edition

Bradford D. Jordan
University of Kentucky

Thomas W. Miller, Jr.
Saint Louis University

FE 323 | Financial Management

 **Learning Solutions**

Boston   Burr Ridge, IL   Dubuque, IA   New York   San Francisco   St. Louis
Bangkok   Bogotá   Caracas   Lisbon   London   Madrid
Mexico City   Milan   New Delhi   Seoul   Singapore   Sydney   Taipei   Toronto

Fundamentals of Corporate Finance, Ninth Edition, Alternate Edition
FE 323 | Financial Management

This book is a McGraw-Hill Learning Solutions textbook and contains select material from the following sources:
Fundamentals of Corporate Finance, Ninth Edition by Stephen A. Ross, Randolph W. Westerfield and Bradford D. Jordan. Copyright © 2010, 2008, 2006, 2003, 2000, 1998, 1995, 1993, 1991 by The McGraw-Hill Companies, Inc.
Fundamentals of Investments: Valuation and Management, Fifth Edition by Bradford D. Jordan and Thomas W. Miller, Jr. Copyright © 2009, 2008, 2005, 2002, 2000 by The McGraw-Hill Companies, Inc.
Both are reprinted with permission of the publisher. Many custom published texts are modified versions or adaptations of our best-selling textbooks. Some adaptations are printed in black and white to keep prices at a minimum, while others are in color.

67890 KNG KNG 13 12 11

ISBN-13: 978-0-07-738894-2
ISBN-10: 0-07-738894-1

Learning Solutions Representative: Nikki Schmitt
Production Editor: Lynn Nagel
Printer/Binder: King Printing
Photo Credits: Forest © 2009 JupiterImages Corporation

To our families and friends with love and gratitude.

S.A.R. R.W.W. B.D.J.

STEPHEN A. ROSS

Sloan School of Management, Franco Modigliani Professor of Finance and Economics, Massachusetts Institute of Technology

Stephen A. Ross is the Franco Modigliani Professor of Finance and Economics at the Sloan School of Management, Massachusetts Institute of Technology. One of the most widely published authors in finance and economics, Professor Ross is recognized for his work in developing the Arbitrage Pricing Theory and his substantial contributions to the discipline through his research in signaling, agency theory, option pricing, and the theory of the term structure of interest rates, among other topics. A past president of the American Finance Association, he currently serves as an associate editor of several academic and practitioner journals. He is a trustee of CalTech.

RANDOLPH W. WESTERFIELD

Marshall School of Business, University of Southern California

Randolph W. Westerfield is Dean Emeritus of the University of Southern California's Marshall School of Business and is the Charles B. Thornton Professor of Finance.

He came to USC from the Wharton School, University of Pennsylvania, where he was the chairman of the finance department and a member of the finance faculty for 20 years. He is a member of several public company boards of directors including Health Management Associates, Inc., and the Nicholas Applegate growth fund. His areas of expertise include corporate financial policy, investment management, and stock market price behavior.

BRADFORD D. JORDAN

Gatton College of Business and Economics, University of Kentucky

Bradford D. Jordan is Professor of Finance and holder of the Richard W. and Janis H. Furst Endowed Chair in Finance at the University of Kentucky. He has a long-standing interest in both applied and theoretical issues in corporate finance and has extensive experience teaching all levels of corporate finance and financial management policy. Professor Jordan has published numerous articles on issues such as cost of capital, capital structure, and the behavior of security prices. He is a past president of the Southern Finance Association, and he is coauthor of *Fundamentals of Investments: Valuation and Management,* 5e, a leading investments text, also published by McGraw-Hill/Irwin.

Preface from the Authors

When the three of us decided to write a book, we were united by one strongly held principle: Corporate finance should be developed in terms of a few integrated, powerful ideas. We believed that the subject was all too often presented as a collection of loosely related topics, unified primarily by virtue of being bound together in one book, and we thought there must be a better way.

One thing we knew for certain was that we didn't want to write a "me-too" book. So, with a lot of help, we took a hard look at what was truly important and useful. In doing so, we were led to eliminate topics of dubious relevance, downplay purely theoretical issues, and minimize the use of extensive and elaborate calculations to illustrate points that are either intuitively obvious or of limited practical use.

As a result of this process, three basic themes became our central focus in writing *Fundamentals of Corporate Finance:*

AN EMPHASIS ON INTUITION

We always try to separate and explain the principles at work on a common sense, intuitive level before launching into any specifics. The underlying ideas are discussed first in very general terms and then by way of examples that illustrate in more concrete terms how a financial manager might proceed in a given situation.

A UNIFIED VALUATION APPROACH

We treat net present value (NPV) as the basic concept underlying corporate finance. Many texts stop well short of consistently integrating this important principle. The most basic and important notion, that NPV represents the excess of market value over cost, often is lost in an overly mechanical approach that emphasizes computation at the expense of comprehension. In contrast, every subject we cover is firmly rooted in valuation, and care is taken throughout to explain how particular decisions have valuation effects.

A MANAGERIAL FOCUS

Students shouldn't lose sight of the fact that financial management concerns management. We emphasize the role of the financial manager as decision maker, and we stress the need for managerial input and judgment. We consciously avoid "black box" approaches to finance, and, where appropriate, the approximate, pragmatic nature of financial analysis is made explicit, possible pitfalls are described, and limitations are discussed.

In retrospect, looking back to our 1991 first edition IPO, we had the same hopes and fears as any entrepreneurs. How would we be received in the market? At the time, we had no idea that just 18 years later, we would be working on a ninth edition. We certainly never dreamed that in those years we would work with friends and colleagues from around the world to create country-specific Australian, Canadian, and South African editions, an International edition, Chinese, French, Polish, Portuguese, Thai, Russian, Korean, and Spanish language editions, and an entirely separate book, *Essentials of Corporate Finance,* now in its sixth edition.

Today, as we prepare to once more enter the market, our goal is to stick with the basic principles that have brought us this far. However, based on the enormous amount of feedback we have received from you and your colleagues, we have made this edition and its package even *more flexible* than previous editions. We offer flexibility in coverage, by continuing to offer two editions, and flexibility in pedagogy, by providing a wide variety of features in the book to help students to learn about corporate finance. We also provide flexibility in package options by offering the most extensive collection of teaching, learning, and technology aids of any corporate finance text. Whether you use only the textbook, or the book in conjunction with our other products, we believe you will find a combination with this edition that will meet your current as well as your changing course needs.

Stephen A. Ross
Randolph W. Westerfield
Bradford D. Jordan

Coverage

This book was designed and developed explicitly for a first course in business or corporate finance, for both finance majors and non-majors alike. In terms of background or prerequisites, the book is nearly self-contained, assuming some familiarity with basic algebra and accounting concepts, while still reviewing important accounting principles very early on. The organization of this text has been developed to give instructors the flexibility they need. Two important changes have been made to the ninth edition chapter organization, one of which is the exciting addition of a behavioral finance chapter in the Alternate Edition. Also, the chapter on options and corporate finance, Chapter 14 in the eighth edition, has been moved to the Alternate Edition.

The following grid presents, for each chapter, some of the most significant features as well as a few selected chapter highlights of the ninth edition of *Fundamentals*. Of course, in every chapter, opening vignettes, boxed features, in-chapter illustrated examples using real companies, and end-of-chapter material have been thoroughly updated as well.

Chapters	Selected Topics of Interest	Benefits to You
PART 1 Overview of Corporate Finance		
Chapter 1 Introduction to Corporate Finance	Sarbanes–Oxley.	
	Goal of the firm and agency problems.	Stresses value creation as the most fundamental aspect of management and describes agency issues that can arise.
	Ethics, financial management, and executive compensation.	Brings in real-world issues concerning conflicts of interest and current controversies surrounding ethical conduct and management pay.
Chapter 2 Financial Statements, Taxes, and Cash Flow	*Minicase:* Cash Flows and Financial Statements at Sunset Boards, Inc.	Reinforces key cash flow concepts in a small-business setting.
	Cash flow vs. earnings.	Clearly defines cash flow and spells out the differences between cash flow and earnings.
	Market values vs. book values.	Emphasizes the relevance of market values over book values.
PART 2 Financial Statements and Long-Term Financial Planning		
Chapter 3 Working with Financial Statements	*Ratios:* PEG, price-to-sales, and Tobin's Q. Expanded Du Pont analysis.	Expands the basic Du Pont equation to better explore the interrelationships between operating and financial performance.
	Du Pont analysis for real companies using data from S&P *Market Insight*.	Analysis shows students how to get and use real-world data, thereby applying key chapter ideas.
	Ratio and financial statement analysis using smaller firm data.	Uses firm data from *RMA* to show students how to actually get and evaluate financial statements benchmarks.
	Understanding financial statements.	Thorough coverage of standardized financial statements and key ratios.

Chapters	Selected Topics of Interest	Benefits to You
Chapter 4 Long-Term Financial Planning and Growth	Expanded discussion on sustainable growth calculations. *Minicase:* Planning for Growth at S&S Air.	Illustrates the importance of financial planning in a small firm.
	Explanation of alternative formulas for sustainable and internal growth rates.	Explanation of growth rate formulas clears up a common misunderstanding about these formulas and the circumstances under which alternative formulas are correct.
	Thorough coverage of sustainable growth as a planning tool.	Provides a vehicle for examining the interrelationships between operations, financing, and growth.
	Long-range financial planning.	Covers percentage of sales approach to creating *pro forma* statements.

PART 3 Valuation of Future Cash Flows

Chapters	Selected Topics of Interest	Benefits to You
Chapter 5 Introduction to Valuation: The Time Value of Money	First of two chapters on time value of money.	Relatively short chapter introduces just the basic ideas on time value of money to get students started on this traditionally difficult topic.
Chapter 6 Discounted Cash Flow Valuation	Growing annuities and perpetuities. Second of two chapters on time value of money. *New minicase:* The MBA Decision.	Covers more advanced time value topics with numerous examples, calculator tips, and Excel spreadsheet exhibits. Contains many real-world examples.
Chapter 7 Interest Rates and Bond Valuation	Inflation and present values.	Clears up the pricing of bonds between coupon payment dates and also bond market quoting conventions.
	"Clean" vs. "dirty" bond prices and accrued interest.	
	NASD's new TRACE system and transparency in the corporate bond market.	Up-to-date discussion of new developments in fixed income with regard to price, volume, and transactions reporting.
	"Make-whole" call provisions. *Minicase:* Financing S&S Air's Expansion Plans with a Bond Issue.	Up-to-date discussion of a relatively new type of call provision that has become very common.
	Bond valuation.	Complete coverage of bond valuation and bond features.
	Interest rates.	Discusses real versus nominal rates and the determinants of the term structure.
Chapter 8 Stock Valuation	*Minicase:* Stock Valuation at Ragan, Inc.	Examines the debt issuance process for a small firm.
	Stock valuation.	Thorough coverage of constant and non-constant growth models.
	NYSE and NASDAQ Market Operations.	Up-to-date description of major stock market operations

Chapters	Selected Topics of Interest	Benefits to You
PART 4 Capital Budgeting		
Chapter 9 Net Present Value and Other Investment Criteria	Modified internal rate of return (MIRR) *New case:* Bullock Gold Mining. First of three chapters on capital budgeting.	Relatively short chapter introduces key ideas on an intuitive level to help students with this traditionally difficult topic.
	NPV, IRR, payback, discounted payback, and accounting rate of return.	Consistent, balanced examination of advantages and disadvantages of various criteria.
Chapter 10 Making Capital Investment Decisions	Project cash flow.	Thorough coverage of project cash flows and the relevant numbers for a project analysis.
	Alternative cash flow definitions.	Emphasizes the equivalence of various formulas, thereby removing common misunderstandings.
	Special cases of DCF analysis.	Considers important applications of chapter tools.
Chapter 11 Project Analysis and Evaluation	*Minicase:* Conch Republic Electronics.	Analyzes capital budgeting issues and complexities.
	Sources of value.	Stresses the need to understand the economic basis for value creation in a project.
	Scenario and sensitivity "what-if" analyses.	Illustrates how to actually apply and interpret these tools in a project analysis.
	Break-even analysis.	Covers cash, accounting, and financial break-even levels.
PART 5 Risk and Return		
Chapter 12 Some Lessons from Capital Market History	*Minicase:* A Job at S&S Air.	
	Expanded discussion of geometric vs. arithmetic returns.	Discusses calculation and interpretation of geometric returns. Clarifies common misconceptions regarding appropriate use of arithmetic vs. geometric average returns.
	Capital market history.	Extensive coverage of historical returns, volatilities, and risk premiums.
	Market efficiency.	Efficient markets hypothesis discussed along with common misconceptions.
	New! The equity risk premium.	New section discusses the equity premium puzzle and latest international evidence.
Chapter 13 Return, Risk, and the Security Market Line	*Minicase:* The Beta for Colgate-Palmolive.	
	Diversification, systematic and unsystematic risk.	Illustrates basics of risk and return in a straightforward fashion.
	Beta and the security market line.	Develops the security market line with an intuitive approach that bypasses much of the usual portfolio theory and statistics.

Chapters	Selected Topics of Interest	Benefits to You
PART 6 Cost of Capital and Long-Term Financial Policy		
Chapter 14 Cost of Capital	Internal equity and flotation costs.	
	Geometric vs. arithmetic growth rates.	Both approaches are used in practice. Clears up issues surrounding growth rate estimates.
	Cost of capital estimation.	Contains a complete, Web-based illustration of cost of capital for a real company.
Chapter 15 Raising Capital	*Minicase:* S&S Air Goes Public.	
	Dutch auction IPOs.	Explains uniform price auctions using recent Google IPO as an example.
	IPO "quiet periods."	Explains the SEC's quiet period rules.
	Rights vs. warrants.	Clarifies the option-like nature of rights prior to their expiration dates.
	IPO valuation.	Extensive, up-to-date discussion of IPOs, including the 1999–2000 period.
Chapter 16 Financial Leverage and Capital Structure Policy	The pecking-order theory of capital structure.	
	Minicase: Stephenson Real Estate Recapitalization.	
	Basics of financial leverage.	Illustrates effect of leverage on risk and return.
	Optimal capital structure.	Describes the basic trade-offs leading to an optimal capital structure.
	Financial distress and bankruptcy.	Briefly surveys the bankruptcy process.
Chapter 17 Dividends and Dividend Policy	*Minicase:* Electronic Timing, Inc.	Analyzes cost of capital estimation for a non-public firm.
	Very recent survey evidence on dividend policy.	New survey results show the most important (and least important) factors considered by financial managers in setting dividend policy.
	Effect of new tax laws.	Discusses implications of new, lower dividend, and capital gains rates.
	Dividends and dividend policy.	Describes dividend payments and the factors favoring higher and lower payout policies.
	New! Optimal payout policy.	Extensive discussion of the latest research and survey evidence on dividend policy, including life-cycle theory.
	Stock repurchases.	Thorough coverage of buybacks as an alternative to cash dividends.

Coverage *(continued)*

Chapters	Selected Topics of Interest	Benefits to You
PART 7 Short-Term Financial Planning and Management		
Chapter 18 Short-Term Finance and Planning	Operating and cash cycles.	Stresses the importance of cash flow timing.
	Short-term financial planning.	Illustrates creation of cash budgets and potential need for financing.
Chapter 19 Cash and Liquidity Management	Check Clearing Act of the 21st Century.	
	Minicase: Cash Management at Webb Corporation.	
	Float management.	Thorough coverage of float management and potential ethical issues.
	Cash collection and disbursement.	Examination of systems used by firms to handle cash inflows and outflows.
Chapter 20 Credit and Inventory Management	*Minicase:* Credit Policy at Howlett Industries.	Evaluates working capital issues for a small firm.
	Credit management	Analysis of credit policy and implementation.
	Inventory management	Brief overview of important inventory concepts.
PART 8 Topics in Corporate Finance		
Chapter 21 International Corporate Finance	*Minicase:* S&S Air Goes International.	
	Foreign exchange.	Covers essentials of exchange rates and their determination.
	International capital budgeting.	Shows how to adapt basic DCF approach to handle exchange rates.
	Exchange rate and political risk.	Discusses hedging and issues surrounding sovereign risk.
Chapter 22 Behavioral Finance: Implications for Financial Management	*New!* Behavioral finance.	Unique and innovative coverage of the effects of biases and heuristics on financial management decisions. New "In Their Own Words" box by Hersh Shefrin.
	New! Case against efficient markets.	Presents the behavioral case for market inefficiency and related evidence pro and con.
Chapter 23 Risk Management: An Introduction to Financial Engineering	*Minicase:* Chatman Mortgage, Inc.	
	Volatility and risk.	Illustrates need to manage risk and some of the most important types of risk.
	Hedging with forwards, options, and swaps.	Shows how many risks can be managed with financial derivatives.

In-Text Study Features

To meet the varied needs of its intended audience, *Fundamentals of Corporate Finance* is rich in valuable learning tools and support.

CHAPTER-OPENING VIGNETTES

Vignettes drawn from real-world events introduce students to the chapter concepts. For examples, see Chapter 4, page 87; Chapter 5, page 119.

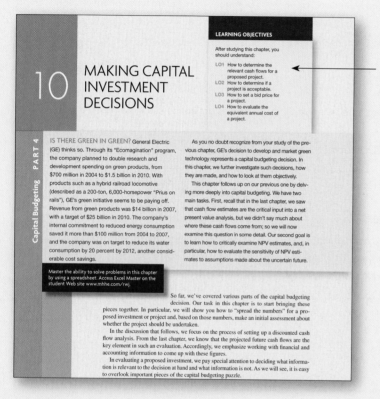

CHAPTER LEARNING OBJECTIVES

New to this edition, this feature maps out the topics and learning goals in every chapter. Each end-of-chapter problem and test bank question is linked to a learning objective, to help you organize your assessment of knowledge and comprehension.

PEDAGOGICAL USE OF COLOR

This learning tool continues to be an important feature of *Fundamentals of Corporate Finance*. In almost every chapter, color plays an extensive, nonschematic, and largely self-evident role. A guide to the functional use of color is on the endsheets of the text.

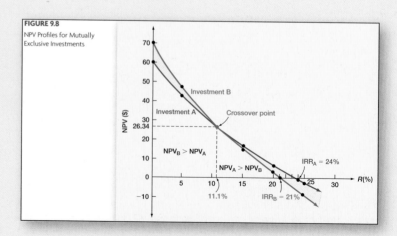

FIGURE 9.8

NPV Profiles for Mutually Exclusive Investments

IN THEIR OWN WORDS BOXES

This series of boxes are the popular articles updated from previous editions written by a distinguished scholar or practitioner on key topics in the text. Boxes include essays by Merton Miller on capital structure, Fischer Black on dividends, and Roger Ibbotson on capital market history. A complete list of "In Their Own Words" boxes appears on page xlii.

IN THEIR OWN WORDS ...

Jeremy J. Siegel on Stocks for the Long Run

The most fascinating characteristic about the data on real financial market returns that I collected is the stability of the long-run real equity returns. The compound annual (geometric) real return on U.S. stocks averaged 6.8% per year from 1802 through 2007 and this return had remained remarkably stable over long-term periods. From 1802 through 1871, the real return averaged 7.0%, from 1871, when the Cowles Foundation data became available, through 1925, the real return on stocks averaged 6.6% per year, and since 1925, which the well-known Ibbotson data cover, the real return has averaged 6.7%. Despite the fact that the price level has increased over ten times since the end of the Second World War, real stock returns have still averaged 6.8%.

The long run stability of real returns on stocks is strongly indicative of *mean reversion of equity return*. Mean reversion means that stock returns can be very volatile in the short run, but show a remarkable stability in the long run. When my research was first published, there was much skepticism of the mean reversion properties of equity market returns, but now this concept is widely accepted for stocks. If mean reversion prevails, portfolios geared for the long-term should have a greater share of equities than short-term portfolios. This conclusion has long been the "conventional" wisdom on investing, but it does not follow if stock returns follow a random walk, a concept widely accepted by academics in the 1970s and 1980s.

When my data first appeared, there was also much discussion of "survivorship bias," the fact that the U.S. stock returns are unusually good because the U.S. was the most successful capitalist country. But three British researchers, Elroy Dimson, Paul Marsh, and Michael Staunton, surveyed stock returns in 16 countries since the beginning of the 20th century and wrote up their results in a book entitled *Triumph of the Optimists*. The authors concluded that U.S. stock returns do not give a distorted picture of the superiority of stocks over bonds worldwide.

Jeremy J. Siegel is the Russell E. Palmer Professor of Finance at The Wharton School of the University of Pennsylvania and author of Stocks for the Long Run *and* The Future Investors. *His research covers macroeconomics and monetary policy, financial market returns, and long-term economic trends.*

WORK THE WEB

Bond quotes have become more available with the rise of the Internet. One site where you can find current bond prices is cxa.marketwatch.com/finra/MarketData/Default.aspx. We went to the Web site and searched for bonds issued by Chevron. Here is a look at part of what we found for one of the bonds:

CVX.GP / CUSIP: 881685BD2

Search for Bond Trade Activity   Add to Watchlist

Last: **$108.500**   Yield: **5.934%**

Security Category:	Corporate
Issue Description:	GTD DEB
Issuer Name:	TEXACO CAP INC
Coupon Rate:	7.500%
Coupon Type:	Fixed
Maturity Date:	03/01/2043

Price | Yield

Price ■   5/7/2008

$120
$115
$110
$105
$100
$95

Aug/07   Oct/07   Jan/08   May/08

5 day 3 mo 6 mo **1 year**

Composite Trade Information

Last Sale

Date	05/07/2008
Price	$108.500
Yield	5.934%

Daily Trade Summary

High Price / Equivalent Yield	$108.500 / 6.57100%
Low Price / Equivalent Yield	$105.750 / 5.93400%
Net Change (Price)	$1.000

The bond has a coupon rate of 7.50 percent and matures on March 1, 2043. The last sale on this bond was at a price of 108.50 percent of par, which gives a yield to maturity of about 5.93 percent. Not only does the site provide the most recent price and yield information, but it also provides more important information about the bond, such as the credit rating, coupon date, call date, and call price. We'll leave it up to you to have a look at the page and the rest of the information available there.

Questions

1. Go to this Web site and find the bond shown above. When was this bond issued? What was the size of the bond issue? What were the yield to maturity and price when the bond was issued?
2. When you search for Chevron bonds (CVX), you will find bonds for several companies listed. Why do you think Chevron has bonds issued with different corporate names?

ENHANCED! WORK THE WEB BOXES

These boxes show students how to research financial issues using the Web and then how to use the information they find to make business decisions. **New** to this edition, now all of the Work the Web boxes also include interactive follow-up questions and exercises.

REAL-WORLD EXAMPLES

Actual events are integrated throughout the text, tying chapter concepts to real life through illustration and reinforcing the relevance of the material. Some examples tie into the chapter opening vignette for added reinforcement. See Example 5.10 on page 133.

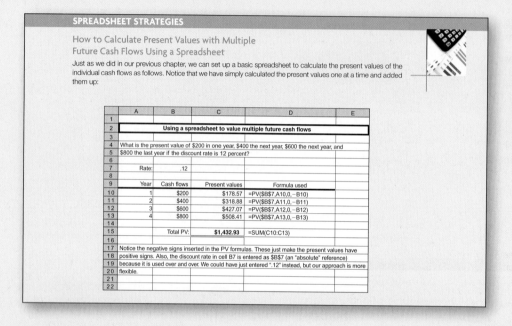

CALCULATOR HINTS

Brief calculator tutorials appear in selected chapters to help students learn or brush up on their financial calculator skills. These complement the Spreadsheet Strategies.

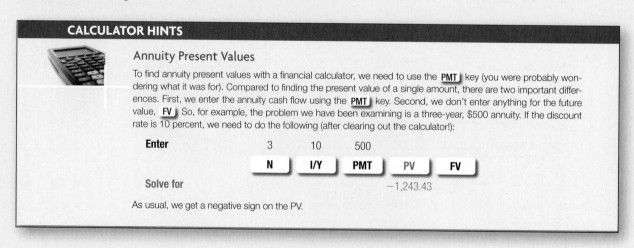

CONCEPT BUILDING

Chapter sections are intentionally kept short to promote a step-by-step, building block approach to learning. Each section is then followed by a series of short concept questions that highlight the key ideas just presented. Students use these questions to make sure they can identify and understand the most important concepts as they read.

Concept Questions

3.3a What are the five groups of ratios? Give two or three examples of each kind.

3.3b Given the total debt ratio, what other two ratios can be computed? Explain how.

3.3c Turnover ratios all have one of two figures as the numerator. What are these two figures? What do these ratios measure? How do you interpret the results?

3.3d Profitability ratios all have the same figure in the numerator. What is it? What do these ratios measure? How do you interpret the results?

SUMMARY TABLES

These tables succinctly restate key principles, results, and equations. They appear whenever it is useful to emphasize and summarize a group of related concepts. For examples, see Chapter 6, page 161.

EXAMPLE 9.4   Calculating the IRR

A project has a total up-front cost of $435.44. The cash flows are $100 in the first year, $200 in the second year, and $300 in the third year. What's the IRR? If we require an 18 percent return, should we take this investment?

We'll describe the NPV profile and find the IRR by calculating some NPVs at different discount rates. You should check our answers for practice. Beginning with 0 percent, we have:

Discount Rate	NPV
0%	$164.56
5%	100.36
10%	46.15
15%	.00
20%	− 39.61

The NPV is zero at 15 percent, so 15 percent is the IRR. If we require an 18 percent return, then we should not take the investment. The reason is that the NPV is negative at 18 percent (verify that it is −$24.47). The IRR rule tells us the same thing in this case. We shouldn't take this investment because its 15 percent return is below our required 18 percent return.

LABELED EXAMPLES

Separate numbered and titled examples are extensively integrated into the chapters. These examples provide detailed applications and illustrations of the text material in a step-by-step format. Each example is completely self-contained so students don't have to search for additional information. Based on our classroom testing, these examples are among the most useful learning aids because they provide both detail and explanation.

KEY TERMS

Key Terms are printed in bold type and defined within the text the first time they appear. They also appear in the margins with definitions for easy location and identification by the student. See Chapter 7, page 203 for an example.

EXPLANATORY WEB LINKS

These Web links are provided in the margins of the text. They are specifically selected to accompany text material and provide students and instructors with a quick way to check for additional information using the Internet.

If you go to the Web site and click on a particular bond, you will get a lot of information about the bond, including the credit rating, the call schedule, original issue information, and trade information.

As we mentioned before, the U.S. Treasury market is the largest securities market in the world. As with bond markets in general, it is an OTC market, so there is limited transparency. However, unlike the situation with bond markets in general, trading in Treasury issues, particularly recently issued ones, is very heavy. Each day, representative prices for outstanding Treasury issues are reported.

Figure 7.4 shows a portion of the daily Treasury note and bond listings from the Web site wsj.com. The entry that begins "2021 Nov 15" is highlighted. This information tells us that the bond will mature in November of 2021. The next column is the coupon rate, which is 8.000 percent for this bond. Treasury bonds all make semiannual payments and have a face value of $1,000, so this bond will pay $40 per six months until it matures.

The Federal Reserve Bank of St. Louis maintains dozens of online files containing macroeconomic data as well as rates on U.S. Treasury issues. Go to www.stls.frb.org/fred/files.

KEY EQUATIONS

Called out in the text, key equations are identified by an equation number. The list in Appendix B shows the key equations by chapter, providing students with a convenient reference.

Based on our examples, we can now write the general expression for the value of a bond. If a bond has (1) a face value of F paid at maturity, (2) a coupon of C paid per period, (3) t periods to maturity, and (4) a yield of r per period, its value is:

$$\text{Bond value} = C \times [1 - 1/(1 + r)^t]/r \; + \; F/(1 + r)^t$$

$$\text{Bond value} = \begin{array}{c} \text{Present value} \\ \text{of the coupons} \end{array} + \begin{array}{c} \text{Present value} \\ \text{of the face amount} \end{array}$$

[7.1]

HIGHLIGHTED CONCEPTS

Throughout the text, important ideas are pulled out and presented in a highlighted box—signaling to students that this material is particularly relevant and critical for their understanding. For examples, see Chapter 7, page 218; Chapter 9, page 265.

CHAPTER SUMMARY AND CONCLUSIONS

Every chapter ends with a concise, but thorough, summary of the important ideas—helping students review the key points and providing closure to the chapter.

5.1 Calculating Future Values Assume you deposit $10,000 today in an account that pays 6 percent interest. How much will you have in five years?

5.2 Calculating Present Values Suppose you have just celebrated your 19th birthday. A rich uncle has set up a trust fund for you that will pay you $150,000 when you turn 30. If the relevant discount rate is 9 percent, how much is this fund worth today?

5.3 Calculating Rates of Return You've been offered an investment that will double your money in 10 years. What rate of return are you being offered? Check your answer using the Rule of 72.

5.4 Calculating the Number of Periods You've been offered an investment that will pay you 9 percent per year. If you invest $15,000, how long until you have $30,000? How long until you have $45,000?

ANSWERS TO CHAPTER REVIEW AND SELF-TEST PROBLEMS

5.1 We need to calculate the future value of $10,000 at 6 percent for five years. The future value factor is:

$$1.06^5 = 1.3382$$

The future value is thus $10,000 \times 1.3382 = \$13,382.26$.

5.2 We need the present value of $150,000 to be paid in 11 years at 9 percent. The discount factor is:

$$1/1.09^{11} = 1/2.5804 = .3875$$

The present value is thus about $58,130.

CHAPTER REVIEW AND SELF-TEST PROBLEMS

Appearing after the Summary and Conclusion, each chapter includes a Chapter Review and Self-Test Problem section. These questions and answers allow students to test their abilities in solving key problems related to the chapter content and provide instant reinforcement.

CONCEPTS REVIEW AND CRITICAL THINKING QUESTIONS

This successful end-of-chapter section facilitates your students' knowledge of key principles, as well as intuitive understanding of the chapter concepts. A number of the questions relate to the chapter-opening vignette— reinforcing student critical-thinking skills and the learning of chapter material.

CONCEPTS REVIEW AND CRITICAL THINKING QUESTIONS

1. **Present Value** [LO2] The basic present value equation has four parts. What are they?
2. **Compounding** [LO1, 2] What is compounding? What is discounting?
3. **Compounding and Period** [LO1] As you increase the length of time involved, what happens to future values? What happens to present values?
4. **Compounding and Interest Rates** [LO1] What happens to a future value if you increase the rate r? What happens to a present value?
5. **Ethical Considerations** [LO2] Take a look back at Example 5.7. Is it deceptive advertising? Is it unethical to advertise a future value like this without a disclaimer?

   To answer the next five questions, refer to the TMCC security we discussed to open the chapter.

END-OF-CHAPTER QUESTIONS AND PROBLEMS

Students learn better when they have plenty of opportunity to practice; therefore, *FCF*, 9e provides extensive end-of-chapter questions and problems. The end-of-chapter support greatly exceeds typical introductory textbooks. The questions and problems are segregated into three learning levels: Basic, Intermediate, and Challenge. Answers to selected end-of-chapter material appear in Appendix C. Also, all problems are available in McGraw-Hill's Homework Manager—see page xxiii for details.

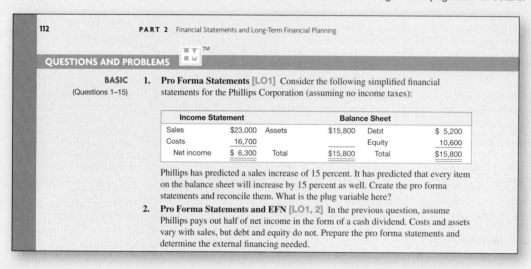

112   **PART 2** Financial Statements and Long-Term Financial Planning

QUESTIONS AND PROBLEMS ™

BASIC
(Questions 1–15)

1. **Pro Forma Statements** [LO1] Consider the following simplified financial statements for the Phillips Corporation (assuming no income taxes):

Income Statement			Balance Sheet			
Sales	$23,000	Assets	$15,800	Debt	$ 5,200
Costs	16,700			Equity	10,600
Net income	$ 6,300	Total	$15,800	Total	$15,800

Phillips has predicted a sales increase of 15 percent. It has predicted that every item on the balance sheet will increase by 15 percent as well. Create the pro forma statements and reconcile them. What is the plug variable here?

2. **Pro Forma Statements and EFN** [LO1, 2] In the previous question, assume Phillips pays out half of net income in the form of a cash dividend. Costs and assets vary with sales, but debt and equity do not. Prepare the pro forma statements and determine the external financing needed.

END-OF-CHAPTER CASES

Located at the end of the book's chapters, these minicases focus on real-life company situations that embody important corporate finance topics. Each case presents a new scenario, data, and a dilemma. Several questions at the end of each case require students to analyze and focus on all of the material they learned from each chapter.

MINICASE

Financing S&S Air's Expansion Plans with a Bond Issue

Mark Sexton and Todd Story, the owners of S&S Air, have decided to expand their operations. They instructed their newly hired financial analyst, Chris Guthrie, to enlist an underwriter to help sell $35 million in new 10-year bonds to finance construction. Chris has entered into discussions with Kim McKenzie, an underwriter from the firm of Raines and Warren, about which bond features S&S Air should consider and what coupon rate the issue will likely have.

Although Chris is aware of the bond features, he is uncertain about the costs and benefits of some features, so he isn't sure how each feature would affect the coupon rate of the bond issue. You are Kim's assistant, and she has asked you to prepare a memo to Chris describing the effect of each of the following bond features on the coupon rate of the bond. She would also like you to list any advantages or disadvantages of each feature:

QUESTIONS

1. The security of the bond—that is, whether the bond has collateral.

2. The seniority of the bond.

3. The presence of a sinking fund.

4. A call provision with specified call dates and call prices.

5. A deferred call accompanying the call provision.

6. A make-whole call provision.

7. Any positive covenants. Also, discuss several possible positive covenants S&S Air might consider.

8. Any negative covenants. Also, discuss several possible negative covenants S&S Air might consider.

9. A conversion feature (note that S&S Air is not a publicly traded company).

10. A floating-rate coupon.

WEB EXERCISES (ONLINE ONLY)

For instructors interested in integrating even more online resources and problems into their course, these Web activities show students how to learn from the vast amount of financial resources available on the Internet. In the 9th edition of *Fundamentals,* these Web exercises are available to students and instructors on the Online Learning Center.

Comprehensive Teaching and Learning Package

This edition of *Fundamentals* has several options in terms of the textbook, instructor supplements, student supplements, and multimedia products. Mix and match to create a package that is perfect for your course!

TEXTBOOK

As with the previous editions, we are offering two versions of this text. Choose the length and topics suitable for your course.

- Standard Edition (21 Chapters)
- Alternate Edition (27 Chapters)

Instructor's CD-ROM

Keep all the supplements in one place! This CD contains all the necessary supplements—Instructor's Manual, Solutions, Test Bank, Computerized Test Bank, and PowerPoint—all in one useful product in an electronic format.

- **Instructor's Manual (IM)**

  Prepared by Steve Dolvin, Butler University

  A great place to find new lecture ideas! The annotated outline for each chapter includes lecture tips, real-world tips, ethics notes, suggested PowerPoint slides, and, when appropriate, a video synopsis.

- **Solutions Manual (SM)**

  Prepared by Joseph Smolira, Belmont University

  The *Fundamentals* Solutions Manual provides detailed solutions to the extensive end-of-chapter material, including concept review questions, quantitative problems, and cases.

- **Test Bank**

  Prepared by Kay Johnson, Penn State University—Erie

  Over 100 questions and problems per chapter! Each chapter is divided into **FIVE** parts. *Part I* contains questions that test the understanding of the key terms in the book. *Part II* includes questions patterned after the learning objectives, concept questions, chapter-opening vignettes, boxes, and highlighted phrases. *Part III* contains multiple-choice problems patterned after the end-of-chapter questions, in basic, intermediate, and challenge levels. *Part IV* provides essay questions to test problem-solving skills and more advanced understanding of concepts. *Part V* is a **new** section that picks up questions directly from the end-of-chapter material and converts them into parallel test bank questions. For your reference, each TB question in this part is linked with its corresponding question in the EOC.

- **Computerized Test Bank (Windows)**

  Create your own tests in a snap! These additional questions are found in a computerized test bank utilizing McGraw-Hill's EZ Test testing software to quickly create customized exams. This user-friendly program allows instructors to sort questions by format; edit existing questions or add new ones; and scramble questions for multiple versions of the same test.

- **PowerPoint Presentations**

  Prepared by Steve Dolvin, Butler University

  The PowerPoint slides for the ninth edition have been revised to include a wealth of instructor material, including lecture tips, real-world examples, and international notes. Each presentation now also includes slides dedicated entirely to ethics notes that relate to the chapter topics. In addition, the PPTs provide exhibits and examples both from the book and from outside sources. Applicable slides have Web links that take you directly to specific Internet sites, or a spreadsheet link to show an example in Excel. Go to the Notes Page function for more tips and information while presenting the slides to your class.

Customize our content for your course! If you already have PowerPoint installed on your PC, you have the ability to add, delete, edit, print, or rearrange the complete presentation to focus on your course needs.

Videos (DVD Format)

Current set of videos on hot topics! McGraw-Hill/Irwin produced a series of finance videos that are 10-minute case studies on topics such as Financial Markets, Careers, Rightsizing, Capital Budgeting, EVA (Economic Value Added), Mergers and Acquisitions, and International Finance.

ONLINE SUPPORT

Online learning center at www.mhhe.com/rwj

The Online Learning Center (OLC) contains FREE access to additional Web-based study and teaching aids created for this text, such as:

Student Support

A great resource for those seeking additional practice, students can access self-grading quizzes, Excel template problems, electronic flashcards, and the brand new program, Excel Master, designed by Brad Jordan and Joe Smolira.

- **Premium Content Access**

  iPod Content—The library isn't the only place to study! Students lead active and mobile lives. Harness the power of one of the most popular technology tools today and study on the go. Our innovative approach allows you to download Narrated PowerPoints and quizzes right into your iPod or other MP3 player device.

  Narrated PowerPoint Slides—*Created by Kent Ragan, Missouri State University*. The narrated PowerPoints provide real-world examples accompanied by step by step instructions and explanations for solving problems presented in the chapter. The Concept Checks from the text are also integrated into the slides to reinforce the key topics in the chapter. Designed specifically to appeal to the different learning methods of students, the slides provide a visual and audio explanation of topics and problems. Click on the slide and listen to the accompanying narration! You can view this slides via computer or download them onto your video iPod.

Teaching Support

Along with having access to all of the same material your students can view on the book's OLC, you also have password protected access to the Instructor's Manual, solutions to end-of-chapter problems and cases, Instructor's PowerPoint, Excel Template Solutions, Video clips, and Video projects and questions.

WebCT and Blackboard course cartridges allow instructors to manage their course and administer examinations online. Increase ease, organization, and efficiency and ask your representative for more details about course cartridges today!

McGraw-Hill Investments Trader

Students receive free access to this Web-based portfolio simulation with a hypothetical $100,000 brokerage account to buy and sell stocks and mutual funds. Students can use the real data found at this site in conjunction with the chapters on investments. They can also compete against students around the United States. This site is powered by Stock-Trak, the leading provider of investment simulation services to the academic community.

McGraw-Hill's Homework Manager and Homework Manager Plus ™

Are you looking for a way to spend less time grading and to have more flexibility with the problems you assign as homework and tests? McGraw-Hill's Homework Manager is an exciting new package option developed for this text! Homework Manager is a Web-based tool for instructors and students for delivering, answering, and grading end-of-chapter problems and tests, and providing a limitless supply of self-graded practice for students.

All of the book's end-of-chapter Questions and Problems are loaded into Homework Manager, and instructors can choose to assign the exact problems as stated in the book, or algorithmic versions of them so each student has a unique set of variables for the problems. You create the assignments and control parameters such as do you want your students to receive hints, is this a graded assignment or practice, etc. The test bank is also available in Homework Manager, giving you the ability to use those questions for online tests. Both the problems and the tests are automatically graded and the results are stored in a private grade book, which is created when you set up your class. Detailed results let you see at a glance how each student does on an assignment or an individual problem—you can even see how many tries it took them to solve it. If you order this special package, students will receive a Homework Manager User's Guide and an access code packaged with their text.

There is also an enhanced version of McGraw-Hill's Homework Manager through the Homework Manager Plus package option. If you order the text packaged with Homework Manager Plus, your students will receive Homework Manager as described above, but with an integrated online text included. When students are in Homework Manager and need more help to solve a problem, there will be a link that takes them to the section of the text online that explains the concept they are struggling with. All of McGraw-Hill's media assets, such as videos, narrated lectures, and additional online quizzing, are also integrated at the appropriate places of the online text to provide students with a full learning experience. If you order this special package, students will receive the Homework Manager Plus card packaged with their text, which gives them access to all of these products.

McGraw-Hill's Homework Manager is powered by Brownstone.

AVAILABLE FOR PURCHASE & PACKAGING

Student Problem Manual ISBN 0077246225

Prepared by Thomas Eyssell, University of Missouri–St. Louis
Need additional reinforcement of the concepts? This valuable resource provides students with additional problems for practice. Each chapter begins with Concepts for Review, followed by Chapter Highlights. These re-emphasize the key terms and concepts in the chapter. A short Concept Test, averaging 10 questions and answers, appears next. Each chapter concludes with additional problems for the student to review. Answers to these problems appear at the end of the Student Problem Manual.

BusinessWeek

Your students can subscribe to 15 weeks of *BusinessWeek* for a special price of $8.25 in addition to the price of the text. Students will receive a pass-code card shrink-wrapped with their new text. The card directs students to a Web site where they enter the code and then gain access to *BusinessWeek's* registration page to enter address info and set up their print and online subscription.

FinGame Online 5.0
By LeRoy Brooks, John Carroll University
(ISBN 10: 0077219880/ISBN 13: 9780077219888)
Just $15.00 when packaged with this text. In this comprehensive simulation game, students control a hypothetical company over numerous periods of operation. The game is now tied to the text by exercises found on the Online Learning Center. As students make major financial and operating decisions for their company, they will develop and enhance their skills in financial management and financial accounting statement analysis.

Financial Analysis with an Electronic Calculator, Sixth Edition
By Mark A. White, University of Virginia, McIntire School of Commerce
(ISBN 10: 0073217093/ISBN 13: 9780073217093)
The information and procedures in this supplementary text enable students to master the use of financial calculators and develop a working knowledge of financial mathematics and problem solving. Complete instructions are included for solving all major problem types on three popular models: HP 10B and 12C, TI BA II Plus, and TI-84. Hands-on problems with detailed solutions allow students to practice the skills outlined in the text and obtain instant reinforcement. *Financial Analysis with an Electronic Calculator* is a self-contained supplement to the introductory financial management course.

Assurance of Learning Ready
Assurance of learning is an important element of many accreditation standards. *Fundamentals of Corporate Finance,* 9e, is designed specifically to support your assurance of learning initiatives.

Each chapter in the book begins with a list of numbered learning objectives that appear throughout the chapter, as well as in the end-of-chapter problems and exercises. Every test bank question is also linked to one of these objectives, in addition to level of difficulty, topic area, Bloom's Taxonomy level, and AACSB skill area. *EZ Test,* McGraw-Hill's easy-to-use test bank software, can search the test bank by these and other categories, providing an engine for targeted Assurance of Learning analysis and assessment.

AACSB Statement
The McGraw-Hill Companies is a proud corporate member of AACSB International. Understanding the importance and value of AACSB accreditation, the ninth edition of *Fundamentals of Corporate Finance* has sought to recognize the curricula guidelines detailed in the AACSB standards for business accreditation by connecting selected questions in the test bank to the general knowledge and skill guidelines found in the AACSB standards.

The statements contained in the test bank are provided only as a guide for the users of this text. The AACSB leaves content coverage and assessment within the purview of individual schools, the mission of the school, and the faculty. While *Fundamentals of Corporate Finance* and the teaching package make no claim of any specific AACSB qualification or evaluation, we have, within the test bank, labeled selected questions according to the six general knowledge and skills areas.

Acknowledgments

To borrow a phrase, writing an introductory finance textbook is easy—all you do is sit down at a word processor and open a vein. We never would have completed this book without the incredible amount of help and support we received from literally hundreds of our colleagues, students, editors, family members, and friends. We would like to thank, without implicating, all of you.

Clearly, our greatest debt is to our many colleagues (and their students) who, like us, wanted to try an alternative to what they were using and made the decision to change. Needless to say, without this support, we would not be publishing a ninth edition!

A great many of our colleagues read the drafts of our first and subsequent editions. The fact that this book has so little in common with our earliest drafts, along with the many changes and improvements we have made over the years, is a reflection of the value we placed on the many comments and suggestions that we received. To the following reviewers, then, we are grateful for their many contributions:

Ibrahim Affeneh
Sung C. Bae
Robert Benecke
Gary Benesh
Scott Besley
Sanjai Bhaghat
Elizabeth Booth
Denis Boudreaux
William Brent
Ray Brooks
Charles C. Brown
Mary Chaffin
Fan Chen
Raju Chenna
Barbara J. Childs
Charles M. Cox
Natalya Delcoure
Michael Dorigan
David A. Dumpe
Michael Dunn
Alan Eastman
Adrian C. Edwards
Steve Engel
Angelo V. Esposito
Cheri Etling
Thomas H. Eyssell
Michael Ferguson
Deborah Ann Ford
Jim Forjan

Micah Frankel
Jennifer R. Frazier
Deborah M. Giarusso
Devra Golbe
A. Steven Graham
Darryl E. J. Gurley
Wendy D. Habegger
David Harraway
John M. Harris, Jr.
R. Stevenson Hawkey
Delvin D. Hawley
Robert C. Higgins
Karen Hogan
Steve Isberg
James Jackson
Pankaj Jain
James M. Johnson
Randy Jorgensen
Jarl G. Kallberg
Terry Keasler
David N. Ketcher
Jim Keys
Kee Kim
Robert Kleinman
David Kuipers
Morris A. Lamberson
Qin Lan
Adam Y. C. Lei
George Lentz

John Lightstone
Jason Lin
Robert Lutz
Pawan Madhogarhia
Timothy Manuel
David G. Martin
Dubos J. Masson
John McDougald
Bob McElreath
Gordon Melms
Richard R. Mendenhall
Wayne Mikkelson
Lalatendu Misra
Karlyn Mitchell
Sunil Mohanty
Scott Moore
Frederick H. Mull
Michael J. Murray
Randy Nelson
Bulent Parker
Megan Partch
Samuel Penkar
Pamela P. Peterson
Robert Phillips
George A. Racette
Charu G. Raheja
Narendar V. Rao
Russ Ray
Ron Reiber

xxv

Thomas Rietz
Jay R. Ritter
Ricardo J. Rodriguez
Kenneth Roskelley
Gary Sanger
Travis Sapp
Martha A. Schary
Robert Schwebach
Roger Severns
Dilip K. Shome
Neil W. Sicherman
Timothy Smaby
Michael F. Spivey

Vic Stanton
Charlene Sullivan
George S. Swales, Jr.
Philip Swensen
Philip Swicegood
John G. Thatcher
Harry Thiewes
A. Frank Thompson
Joseph Trefzger
Michael R. Vetsuypens
Joe Walker
Jun Wang
James Washam

Alan Weatherford
Marsha Weber
Jill Wetmore
Mark White
Annie Wong
David J. Wright
Steve B. Wyatt
Tung-Hsiao Yang
Morris Yarmish
Michael Young
Mei Zhang
J. Kenton Zumwalt
Tom Zwirlein

Reviews from the following instructors helped us to shape our development plan for the ninth edition of *Fundamentals of Corporate Finance*.

Mike Anderson
University of Massachusetts, Dartmouth

Vigdis Boasson
Central Michigan University

Jim Boyd
Louisiana State University

Lawrence Byerly
Thomas More College

Steve Byers
Idaho State University

Steve Caples
McNeese State University

Asim Celik
University of Nevada, Reno

Christina Cella
Indiana University, Bloomington

Karen Hallows
George Mason University

Dina Layish
Binghamton University

Chun Lee
Loyola Marymount University

Scott Lowe
James Madison University

Bahlous Mejda
University of Alabama-Huntsville

Belinda Mucklow
University of Wisconsin, Madison

Barry Mulholland
University of Wisconsin, Oshkosh

Odom Oris
University of Texas, Tyler

Keith Osher
Boston University

Greg Pierce
Penn State University

Robert Puelz
Southern Methodist University

Stu Rosenstein
East Carolina University

Ivan Roten
Appalachian State University

Michael Sher
Metropolitan State University

Ahmad Sohrabian
California State Polytechnic University

Charlene Sullivan
Purdue University

Lee Swartz
University of Southern California

Brian Tarrant
Central Michigan University

Rhonda Tenkku
University of Missouri

George Turk
Florida State University

Elike Uchenna
Alabama A&M University

Gwendolyn Webb
Bernard M. Baruch College

Colbrin Wright
Central Michigan University

Several of our most respected colleagues contributed original essays for this edition, which are entitled "In Their Own Words," and appear in selected chapters. To these individuals we extend a special thanks:

Edward I. Altman
New York University

Fischer Black

Robert C. Higgins
University of Washington

Roger Ibbotson
Yale University, Ibbotson Associates

Erik Lie
University of Iowa

Robert C. Merton
Harvard University

Merton H. Miller

Jay R. Ritter
University of Florida

Richard Roll
University of California at Los Angeles

Jeremy Siegel
University of Pennsylvania

Hersh Shefrin
Santa Clara University

Bennett Stewart
Stern Stewart & Co.

Samuel C. Weaver
Lehigh University

We are lucky to have had skilled and experienced instructors developing the supplement material for this edition. Thank you to Steve Dolvin, Butler University, for his work thoroughly revising and updating the Instructor's Manual and the PowerPoint Presentations and for organizing and distributing the wealth of annotated instructor notes from the book into these teaching materials. We greatly appreciate the contributions of Joe Smolira, Belmont University, who worked closely with us to develop the Solutions Manual and to create Excel Templates for many of the end of chapter problems. Thank you also to Kay Johnson, Penn State University, Erie, for her thorough updating, revising, and tagging of every problem in the test bank. Thanks to Kent Ragan, Missouri State University, for expertly developing and extending the Student Narrated PowerPoint slides for the ninth edition. We owe a special thank you to Thomas Eyssell of the University of Missouri for his exceptional work on the Student Problem Manual.

The following University of Kentucky students did outstanding work on this edition of *Fundamentals*: Laura Coogan, Tony Cox, and Steve Hailey. To them fell the unenviable task of technical proofreading, and in particular, careful checking of each calculation throughout the text and Instructor's Manual.

Finally, in every phase of this project, we have been privileged to have had the complete and unwavering support of a great organization, McGraw-Hill/Irwin. We especially thank the McGraw-Hill/Irwin sales group. The suggestions they provide, their professionalism in assisting potential adopters, and the service they provide to current users have been a major factor in our success.

We are deeply grateful to the select group of professionals who served as our development team on this edition: Michele Janicek, Executive Editor; Elizabeth Hughes, Development Editor; Ashley Smith, Marketing Manager; Christine Vaughan, Lead Project Manager; Pam Verros, Designer; and Brian Nacik, Media Producer. Others at McGraw-Hill/Irwin, too numerous to list here, have improved the book in countless ways.

Throughout the development of this edition, we have taken great care to discover and eliminate errors. Our goal is to provide the best textbook available on the subject. To ensure that future editions are error-free, we gladly offer $10 per arithmetic error to the first individual reporting it as a modest token of our appreciation. More than this, we would like to hear from instructors and students alike. Please write and tell us how to make this a better text. Forward your comments to: Dr. Brad Jordan, c/o Editorial—Finance, McGraw-Hill/Irwin, 1333 Burr Ridge Parkway, Burr Ridge, IL 60527 or visit us online at www.mhhe.com/rwj.

Stephen A. Ross
Randolph W. Westerfield
Bradford D. Jordan

Brief Contents

Contents

PART 4   Capital Budgeting

CHAPTER 9

NET PRESENT VALUE AND OTHER INVESTMENT CRITERIA   260

CHAPTER 10

MAKING CAPITAL INVESTMENT DECISIONS   298

PART 5   Risk and Return

In Their Own Words Boxes

3

WORKING WITH FINANCIAL STATEMENTS

LEARNING OBJECTIVES

After studying this chapter, you should understand:

LO1 How to standardize financial statements for comparison purposes.

LO2 How to compute and, more importantly, interpret some common ratios.

LO3 The determinants of a firm's profitability.

LO4 Some of the problems and pitfalls in financial statement analysis.

THE PRICE OF A SHARE OF COMMON STOCK in hotel company Marriott International, Inc. closed at about $36 on April 3, 2008. At that price, Marriott had a price–earnings (PE) ratio of 21. That is, investors were willing to pay $21 for every dollar in income earned by Marriott. At the same time, investors were willing to pay $67, $32, and $12 for each dollar earned by Amazon.com, Apple, and Bank of America, respectively. At the other extreme were XM Satellite Radio and Sirius Satellite Radio, both relative newcomers to the stock market. Each had negative earnings for the previous year, yet XM was priced at about $12 per share and Sirius at about $3 per share.

Because they had negative earnings, their PE ratios would have been negative, so they were not reported. At the time, the typical stock in the S&P 500 Index of large company stocks was trading at a PE of about 19, or about 19 times earnings, as they say on Wall Street.

Price-to-earnings comparisons are examples of the use of financial ratios. As we will see in this chapter, there are a wide variety of financial ratios, all designed to summarize specific aspects of a firm's financial position. In addition to discussing how to analyze financial statements and compute financial ratios, we will have quite a bit to say about who uses this information and why.

Master the ability to solve problems in this chapter by using a spreadsheet. Access Excel Master on the student Web site www.mhhe.com/rwj.

In Chapter 2, we discussed some of the essential concepts of financial statements and cash flow. Part 2, this chapter and the next, continues where our earlier discussion left off. Our goal here is to expand your understanding of the uses (and abuses) of financial statement information.

Financial statement information will crop up in various places in the remainder of our book. Part 2 is not essential for understanding this material, but it will help give you an overall perspective on the role of financial statement information in corporate finance.

A good working knowledge of financial statements is desirable simply because such statements, and numbers derived from those statements, are the primary means of communicating financial information both within the firm and outside the firm. In short, much of the language of corporate finance is rooted in the ideas we discuss in this chapter.

Furthermore, as we will see, there are many different ways of using financial statement information and many different types of users. This diversity reflects the fact that financial statement information plays an important part in many types of decisions.

In the best of all worlds, the financial manager has full market value information about all of the firm's assets. This will rarely (if ever) happen. So, the reason we rely on accounting figures for much of our financial information is that we are almost always unable to obtain all (or even part) of the market information we want. The only meaningful yardstick for evaluating business decisions is whether they create economic value (see Chapter 1).

However, in many important situations, it will not be possible to make this judgment directly because we can't see the market value effects of decisions.

We recognize that accounting numbers are often just pale reflections of economic reality, but they are frequently the best available information. For privately held corporations, not-for-profit businesses, and smaller firms, for example, very little direct market value information exists at all. The accountant's reporting function is crucial in these circumstances.

Clearly, one important goal of the accountant is to report financial information to the user in a form useful for decision making. Ironically, the information frequently does not come to the user in such a form. In other words, financial statements don't come with a user's guide. This chapter and the next are first steps in filling this gap.

Cash Flow and Financial Statements: A Closer Look

3.1

At the most fundamental level, firms do two different things: They generate cash and they spend it. Cash is generated by selling a product, an asset, or a security. Selling a security involves either borrowing or selling an equity interest (shares of stock) in the firm. Cash is spent in paying for materials and labor to produce a product and in purchasing assets. Payments to creditors and owners also require the spending of cash.

In Chapter 2, we saw that the cash activities of a firm could be summarized by a simple identity:

Cash flow from assets = Cash flow to creditors + Cash flow to owners

This cash flow identity summarizes the total cash result of all transactions a firm engages in during the year. In this section, we return to the subject of cash flow by taking a closer look at the cash events during the year that lead to these total figures.

SOURCES AND USES OF CASH

Activities that bring in cash are called **sources of cash**. Activities that involve spending cash are called **uses** (or applications) **of cash**. What we need to do is to trace the changes in the firm's balance sheet to see how the firm obtained and spent its cash during some period.

To get started, consider the balance sheets for the Prufrock Corporation in Table 3.1. Notice that we have calculated the change in each of the items on the balance sheets.

Looking over the balance sheets for Prufrock, we see that quite a few things changed during the year. For example, Prufrock increased its net fixed assets by $149 and its inventory by $29. (Note that, throughout, all figures are in millions of dollars.) Where did the money come from? To answer this and related questions, we need to first identify those changes that used up cash (uses) and those that brought cash in (sources).

A little common sense is useful here. A firm uses cash by either buying assets or making payments. So, loosely speaking, an increase in an asset account means the firm, on a net basis, bought some assets—a use of cash. If an asset account went down, then on a net basis, the firm sold some assets. This would be a net source. Similarly, if a liability account goes down, then the firm has made a net payment—a use of cash.

Given this reasoning, there is a simple, albeit mechanical, definition you may find useful. An increase in a left-side (asset) account or a decrease in a right-side (liability or equity) account is a use of cash. Likewise, a decrease in an asset account or an increase in a liability (or equity) account is a source of cash.

sources of cash
A firm's activities that generate cash.

uses of cash
A firm's activities in which cash is spent. Also called *applications of cash.*

Company financial information can be found in many places on the Web, including www.financials.com, finance.yahoo.com, finance.google.com, and moneycentral.msn.com.

TABLE 3.1

PRUFROCK CORPORATION 2008 and 2009 Balance Sheets ($ in millions)			
	2008	**2009**	**Change**
Assets			
Current assets			
Cash	$ 84	$ 98	+$ 14
Accounts receivable	165	188	+ 23
Inventory	393	422	+ 29
Total	$ 642	$ 708	+$ 66
Fixed assets			
Net plant and equipment	$2,731	$2,880	+$149
Total assets	$3,373	$3,588	+$215
Liabilities and Owners' Equity			
Current liabilities			
Accounts payable	$ 312	$ 344	+$ 32
Notes payable	231	196	− 35
Total	$ 543	$ 540	−$ 3
Long-term debt	$ 531	$ 457	−$ 74
Owners' equity			
Common stock and paid-in surplus	$ 500	$ 550	+$ 50
Retained earnings	1,799	2,041	+ 242
Total	$2,299	$2,591	+$292
Total liabilities and owners' equity	$3,373	$3,588	+$215

Looking again at Prufrock, we see that inventory rose by $29. This is a net use because Prufrock effectively paid out $29 to increase inventories. Accounts payable rose by $32. This is a source of cash because Prufrock effectively has borrowed an additional $32 payable by the end of the year. Notes payable, on the other hand, went down by $35, so Prufrock effectively paid off $35 worth of short-term debt—a use of cash.

Based on our discussion, we can summarize the sources and uses of cash from the balance sheet as follows:

Sources of cash:	
Increase in accounts payable	$ 32
Increase in common stock	50
Increase in retained earnings	242
Total sources	$324
Uses of cash:	
Increase in accounts receivable	$ 23
Increase in inventory	29
Decrease in notes payable	35
Decrease in long-term debt	74
Net fixed asset acquisitions	149
Total uses	$310
Net addition to cash	$ 14

The net addition to cash is just the difference between sources and uses, and our $14 result here agrees with the $14 change shown on the balance sheet.

TABLE 3.2

PRUFROCK CORPORATION 2009 Income Statement ($ in millions)	
Sales	$2,311
Cost of goods sold	1,344
Depreciation	276
Earnings before interest and taxes	$ 691
Interest paid	141
Taxable income	$ 550
Taxes (34%)	187
Net income	$ 363
Dividends	$121
Addition to retained earnings	242

This simple statement tells us much of what happened during the year, but it doesn't tell the whole story. For example, the increase in retained earnings is net income (a source of funds) less dividends (a use of funds). It would be more enlightening to have these reported separately so we could see the breakdown. Also, we have considered only net fixed asset acquisitions. Total or gross spending would be more interesting to know.

To further trace the flow of cash through the firm during the year, we need an income statement. For Prufrock, the results for the year are shown in Table 3.2.

Notice here that the $242 addition to retained earnings we calculated from the balance sheet is just the difference between the net income of $363 and the dividends of $121.

THE STATEMENT OF CASH FLOWS

There is some flexibility in summarizing the sources and uses of cash in the form of a financial statement. However it is presented, the result is called the **statement of cash flows**.

We present a particular format for this statement in Table 3.3. The basic idea is to group all the changes into three categories: operating activities, financing activities, and investment activities. The exact form differs in detail from one preparer to the next.

Don't be surprised if you come across different arrangements. The types of information presented will be similar; the exact order can differ. The key thing to remember in this case is that we started out with $84 in cash and ended up with $98, for a net increase of $14. We're just trying to see what events led to this change.

Going back to Chapter 2, we note that there is a slight conceptual problem here. Interest paid should really go under financing activities, but unfortunately that's not the way the accounting is handled. The reason, you may recall, is that interest is deducted as an expense when net income is computed. Also, notice that the net purchase of fixed assets was $149. Because Prufrock wrote off $276 worth of assets (the depreciation), it must have actually spent a total of $149 + 276 = $425 on fixed assets.

Once we have this statement, it might seem appropriate to express the change in cash on a per-share basis, much as we did for net income. Ironically, despite the interest we might have in some measure of cash flow per share, standard accounting practice expressly prohibits reporting this information. The reason is that accountants feel that cash flow (or some component of cash flow) is not an alternative to accounting income, so only earnings per share are to be reported.

As shown in Table 3.4, it is sometimes useful to present the same information a bit differently. We will call this the "sources and uses of cash" statement. There is no such

statement of cash flows
A firm's financial statement that summarizes its sources and uses of cash over a specified period.

TABLE 3.3

PRUFROCK CORPORATION 2009 Statement of Cash Flows ($ in millions)	
Cash, beginning of year	$ 84
Operating activity	
Net income	$363
Plus:	
Depreciation	276
Increase in accounts payable	32
Less:	
Increase in accounts receivable	− 23
Increase in inventory	− 29
Net cash from operating activity	$619
Investment activity	
Fixed asset acquisitions	−$425
Net cash from investment activity	−$425
Financing activity	
Decrease in notes payable	−$ 35
Decrease in long-term debt	− 74
Dividends paid	− 121
Increase in common stock	50
Net cash from financing activity	−$180
Net increase in cash	$ 14
Cash, end of year	$ 98

TABLE 3.4

PRUFROCK CORPORATION 2009 Sources and Uses of Cash ($ in millions)	
Cash, beginning of year	$ 84
Sources of cash	
Operations:	
Net income	$363
Depreciation	276
	$639
Working capital:	
Increase in accounts payable	$ 32
Long-term financing:	
Increase in common stock	50
Total sources of cash	$721
Uses of cash	
Working capital:	
Increase in accounts receivable	$ 23
Increase in inventory	29
Decrease in notes payable	35
Long-term financing:	
Decrease in long-term debt	74
Fixed asset acquisitions	425
Dividends paid	121
Total uses of cash	$707
Net addition to cash	$ 14
Cash, end of year	$ 98

statement in financial accounting, but this arrangement resembles one used many years ago. As we will discuss, this form can come in handy, but we emphasize again that it is not the way this information is normally presented.

Now that we have the various cash pieces in place, we can get a good idea of what happened during the year. Prufrock's major cash outlays were fixed asset acquisitions and cash dividends. It paid for these activities primarily with cash generated from operations.

Prufrock also retired some long-term debt and increased current assets. Finally, current liabilities were not greatly changed, and a relatively small amount of new equity was sold. Altogether, this short sketch captures Prufrock's major sources and uses of cash for the year.

Concept Questions

3.1a What is a source of cash? Give three examples.

3.1b What is a use, or application, of cash? Give three examples.

Standardized Financial Statements   **3.2**

The next thing we might want to do with Prufrock's financial statements is compare them to those of other similar companies. We would immediately have a problem, however. It's almost impossible to directly compare the financial statements for two companies because of differences in size.

For example, Ford and GM are serious rivals in the auto market, but GM is much larger (in terms of market share), so it is difficult to compare them directly. For that matter, it's difficult even to compare financial statements from different points in time for the same company if the company's size has changed. The size problem is compounded if we try to compare GM and, say, Toyota. If Toyota's financial statements are denominated in yen, then we have size *and* currency differences.

To start making comparisons, one obvious thing we might try to do is to somehow standardize the financial statements. One common and useful way of doing this is to work with percentages instead of total dollars. In this section, we describe two different ways of standardizing financial statements along these lines.

COMMON-SIZE STATEMENTS

To get started, a useful way of standardizing financial statements is to express each item on the balance sheet as a percentage of assets and to express each item on the income statement as a percentage of sales. The resulting financial statements are called **common-size statements**. We consider these next.

Common-Size Balance Sheets   One way, though not the only way, to construct a common-size balance sheet is to express each item as a percentage of total assets. Prufrock's 2008 and 2009 common-size balance sheets are shown in Table 3.5.

Notice that some of the totals don't check exactly because of rounding. Also notice that the total change has to be zero because the beginning and ending numbers must add up to 100 percent.

In this form, financial statements are relatively easy to read and compare. For example, just looking at the two balance sheets for Prufrock, we see that current assets were 19.7 percent of total assets in 2009, up from 19.1 percent in 2008. Current liabilities declined

common-size statement
A standardized financial statement presenting all items in percentage terms. Balance sheet items are shown as a percentage of assets and income statement items as a percentage of sales.

TABLE 3.5

PRUFROCK CORPORATION Common-Size Balance Sheets 2008 and 2009			
	2008	**2009**	**Change**
Assets			
Current assets			
Cash	2.5%	2.7%	+ .2%
Accounts receivable	4.9	5.2	+ .3
Inventory	11.7	11.8	+ .1
Total	19.1	19.7	+ .6
Fixed assets			
Net plant and equipment	80.9	80.3	− .6
Total assets	100.0%	100.0%	.0
Liabilities and Owners' Equity			
Current liabilities			
Accounts payable	9.2%	9.6%	+ .4%
Notes payable	6.8	5.5	−1.3
Total	16.0	15.1	− .9
Long-term debt	15.7	12.7	−3.0
Owners' equity			
Common stock and paid-in surplus	14.8	15.3	+ .5
Retained earnings	53.3	56.9	+3.6
Total	68.1	72.2	+4.1
Total liabilities and owners' equity	100.0%	100.0%	.0

from 16.0 percent to 15.1 percent of total liabilities and equity over that same time. Similarly, total equity rose from 68.1 percent of total liabilities and equity to 72.2 percent.

Overall, Prufrock's liquidity, as measured by current assets compared to current liabilities, increased over the year. Simultaneously, Prufrock's indebtedness diminished as a percentage of total assets. We might be tempted to conclude that the balance sheet has grown "stronger." We will say more about this later.

Common-Size Income Statements   A useful way of standardizing the income statement is to express each item as a percentage of total sales, as illustrated for Prufrock in Table 3.6.

This income statement tells us what happens to each dollar in sales. For Prufrock, interest expense eats up $.061 out of every sales dollar and taxes take another $.081. When all is said and done, $.157 of each dollar flows through to the bottom line (net income), and that amount is split into $.105 retained in the business and $.052 paid out in dividends.

These percentages are useful in comparisons. For example, a relevant figure is the cost percentage. For Prufrock, $.582 of each $1 in sales goes to pay for goods sold. It would be interesting to compute the same percentage for Prufrock's main competitors to see how Prufrock stacks up in terms of cost control.

TABLE 3.6

PRUFROCK CORPORATION Common-Size Income Statement 2009	
Sales	100.0%
Cost of goods sold	58.2
Depreciation	11.9
Earnings before interest and taxes	29.9
Interest paid	6.1
Taxable income	23.8
Taxes (34%)	8.1
Net income	15.7%
Dividends	5.2%
Addition to retained earnings	10.5

Common-Size Statements of Cash Flows   Although we have not presented it here, it is also possible and useful to prepare a common-size statement of cash flows. Unfortunately, with the current statement of cash flows, there is no obvious denominator such as total assets or total sales. However, if the information is arranged in a way similar to that in Table 3.4, then each item can be expressed as a percentage of total sources (or total uses). The results can then be interpreted as the percentage of total sources of cash supplied or as the percentage of total uses of cash for a particular item.

COMMON–BASE YEAR FINANCIAL STATEMENTS: TREND ANALYSIS

Imagine we were given balance sheets for the last 10 years for some company and we were trying to investigate trends in the firm's pattern of operations. Does the firm use more or less debt? Has the firm grown more or less liquid? A useful way of standardizing financial statements in this case is to choose a base year and then express each item relative to the base amount. We will call the resulting statements **common–base year statements**.

For example, from 2008 to 2009, Prufrock's inventory rose from $393 to $422. If we pick 2008 as our base year, then we would set inventory equal to 1.00 for that year. For the next year, we would calculate inventory relative to the base year as $422/393 = 1.07$. In this case, we could say inventory grew by about 7 percent during the year. If we had multiple years, we would just divide the inventory figure for each one by $393. The resulting series is easy to plot, and it is then easy to compare companies. Table 3.7 summarizes these calculations for the asset side of the balance sheet.

common–base year statement
A standardized financial statement presenting all items relative to a certain base year amount.

COMBINED COMMON-SIZE AND BASE YEAR ANALYSIS

The trend analysis we have been discussing can be combined with the common-size analysis discussed earlier. The reason for doing this is that as total assets grow, most of the other accounts must grow as well. By first forming the common-size statements, we eliminate the effect of this overall growth.

For example, looking at Table 3.7, we see that Prufrock's accounts receivable were $165, or 4.9 percent of total assets, in 2008. In 2009, they had risen to $188, which was 5.2 percent of total assets. If we do our analysis in terms of dollars, then the 2009 figure would be $188/165 = 1.14$, representing a 14 percent increase in receivables. However, if we work with the common-size statements, then the 2009 figure would be $5.2\%/4.9\% = 1.06$. This tells us accounts receivable, as a percentage of total assets, grew by 6 percent. Roughly speaking, what we see is that of the 14 percent total increase, about 8 percent ($= 14\% - 6\%$) is attributable simply to growth in total assets.

TABLE 3.7

	Assets ($ in millions)		Common-Size Assets		Common–Base Year Assets	Combined Common-Size and Base Year Assets
PRUFROCK CORPORATION Summary of Standardized Balance Sheets (Asset Side Only)						
	2008	**2009**	**2008**	**2009**	**2009**	**2009**
Current assets						
Cash	$ 84	$ 98	2.5%	2.7%	1.17	1.08
Accounts receivable	165	188	4.9	5.2	1.14	1.06
Inventory	393	422	11.7	11.8	1.07	1.01
Total current assets	$ 642	$ 708	19.1	19.7	1.10	1.03
Fixed assets						
Net plant and equipment	$2,731	$2,880	80.9	80.3	1.05	.99
Total assets	$3,373	$3,588	100.0%	100.0%	1.06	1.00

NOTE: The common-size numbers are calculated by dividing each item by total assets for that year. For example, the 2008 common-size cash amount is $84/3,373 = 2.5%. The common–base year numbers are calculated by dividing each 2009 item by the base year (2008) dollar amount. The common-base cash is thus $98/84 = 1.17, representing a 17 percent increase. The combined common-size and base year figures are calculated by dividing each common-size amount by the base year (2008) common-size amount. The cash figure is therefore 2.7%/2.5% = 1.08, representing an 8 percent increase in cash holdings as a percentage of total assets. Columns may not total precisely due to rounding.

Concept Questions

3.2a Why is it often necessary to standardize financial statements?

3.2b Name two types of standardized statements and describe how each is formed.

3.3 Ratio Analysis

Another way of avoiding the problems involved in comparing companies of different sizes is to calculate and compare **financial ratios**. Such ratios are ways of comparing and investigating the relationships between different pieces of financial information. Using ratios eliminates the size problem because the size effectively divides out. We're then left with percentages, multiples, or time periods.

financial ratios
Relationships determined from a firm's financial information and used for comparison purposes.

There is a problem in discussing financial ratios. Because a ratio is simply one number divided by another, and because there are so many accounting numbers out there, we could examine a huge number of possible ratios. Everybody has a favorite. We will restrict ourselves to a representative sampling.

In this section, we only want to introduce you to some commonly used financial ratios. These are not necessarily the ones we think are the best. In fact, some of them may strike you as illogical or not as useful as some alternatives. If they do, don't be concerned. As a financial analyst, you can always decide how to compute your own ratios.

What you do need to worry about is the fact that different people and different sources seldom compute these ratios in exactly the same way, and this leads to much confusion. The specific definitions we use here may or may not be the same as ones you have seen or will see elsewhere. If you are ever using ratios as a tool for analysis, you should be careful to document how you calculate each one; and if you are comparing your numbers to numbers from another source, be sure you know how those numbers are computed.

We will defer much of our discussion of how ratios are used and some problems that come up with using them until later in the chapter. For now, for each of the ratios we discuss, we consider several questions:

1. How is it computed?
2. What is it intended to measure, and why might we be interested?
3. What is the unit of measurement?
4. What might a high or low value tell us? How might such values be misleading?
5. How could this measure be improved?

Financial ratios are traditionally grouped into the following categories:

1. Short-term solvency, or liquidity, ratios.
2. Long-term solvency, or financial leverage, ratios.
3. Asset management, or turnover, ratios.
4. Profitability ratios.
5. Market value ratios.

We will consider each of these in turn. In calculating these numbers for Prufrock, we will use the ending balance sheet (2009) figures unless we say otherwise. Also notice that the various ratios are color keyed to indicate which numbers come from the income statement and which come from the balance sheet.

SHORT-TERM SOLVENCY, OR LIQUIDITY, MEASURES

As the name suggests, short-term solvency ratios as a group are intended to provide information about a firm's liquidity, and these ratios are sometimes called *liquidity measures*. The primary concern is the firm's ability to pay its bills over the short run without undue stress. Consequently, these ratios focus on current assets and current liabilities.

For obvious reasons, liquidity ratios are particularly interesting to short-term creditors. Because financial managers work constantly with banks and other short-term lenders, an understanding of these ratios is essential.

One advantage of looking at current assets and liabilities is that their book values and market values are likely to be similar. Often (though not always), these assets and liabilities just don't live long enough for the two to get seriously out of step. On the other hand, like any type of near-cash, current assets and liabilities can and do change fairly rapidly, so today's amounts may not be a reliable guide to the future.

Go to www.reuters.com to examine comparative ratios for a huge number of companies.

Current Ratio   One of the best known and most widely used ratios is the *current ratio*. As you might guess, the current ratio is defined as follows:

$$\text{Current ratio} = \frac{\text{Current assets}}{\text{Current liabilities}} \qquad \text{[3.1]}$$

Here is Prufrock's 2009 current ratio:

$$\text{Current ratio} = \frac{\$708}{\$540} = 1.31 \text{ times}$$

Because current assets and liabilities are, in principle, converted to cash over the following 12 months, the current ratio is a measure of short-term liquidity. The unit of measurement is either dollars or times. So, we could say Prufrock has $1.31 in current assets for every $1 in current liabilities, or we could say Prufrock has its current liabilities covered 1.31 times over.

To a creditor—particularly a short-term creditor such as a supplier—the higher the current ratio, the better. To the firm, a high current ratio indicates liquidity, but it also may indicate an inefficient use of cash and other short-term assets. Absent some extraordinary circumstances, we would expect to see a current ratio of at least 1 because a current ratio of less than 1 would mean that net working capital (current assets less current liabilities) is negative. This would be unusual in a healthy firm, at least for most types of businesses.

The current ratio, like any ratio, is affected by various types of transactions. For example, suppose the firm borrows over the long term to raise money. The short-run effect would be an increase in cash from the issue proceeds and an increase in long-term debt. Current liabilities would not be affected, so the current ratio would rise.

Finally, note that an apparently low current ratio may not be a bad sign for a company with a large reserve of untapped borrowing power.

EXAMPLE 3.1 | **Current Events**

Suppose a firm pays off some of its suppliers and short-term creditors. What happens to the current ratio? Suppose a firm buys some inventory. What happens in this case? What happens if a firm sells some merchandise?

The first case is a trick question. What happens is that the current ratio moves away from 1. If it is greater than 1 (the usual case), it will get bigger; but if it is less than 1, it will get smaller. To see this, suppose the firm has $4 in current assets and $2 in current liabilities for a current ratio of 2. If we use $1 in cash to reduce current liabilities, then the new current ratio is ($4 − 1)/($2 − 1) = 3. If we reverse the original situation to $2 in current assets and $4 in current liabilities, then the change will cause the current ratio to fall to 1/3 from 1/2.

The second case is not quite as tricky. Nothing happens to the current ratio because cash goes down while inventory goes up—total current assets are unaffected.

In the third case, the current ratio will usually rise because inventory is normally shown at cost and the sale will normally be at something greater than cost (the difference is the markup). The increase in either cash or receivables is therefore greater than the decrease in inventory. This increases current assets, and the current ratio rises.

The Quick (or Acid-Test) Ratio Inventory is often the least liquid current asset. It's also the one for which the book values are least reliable as measures of market value because the quality of the inventory isn't considered. Some of the inventory may later turn out to be damaged, obsolete, or lost.

More to the point, relatively large inventories are often a sign of short-term trouble. The firm may have overestimated sales and overbought or overproduced as a result. In this case, the firm may have a substantial portion of its liquidity tied up in slow-moving inventory.

To further evaluate liquidity, the *quick,* or *acid-test, ratio* is computed just like the current ratio, except inventory is omitted:

$$\text{Quick ratio} = \frac{\text{Current assets} - \text{Inventory}}{\text{Current liabilities}} \qquad [3.2]$$

Notice that using cash to buy inventory does not affect the current ratio, but it reduces the quick ratio. Again, the idea is that inventory is relatively illiquid compared to cash.

For Prufrock, this ratio for 2009 was:

$$\text{Quick ratio} = \frac{\$708 - 422}{\$540} = .53 \text{ times}$$

The quick ratio here tells a somewhat different story than the current ratio because inventory accounts for more than half of Prufrock's current assets. To exaggerate the point, if this inventory consisted of, say, unsold nuclear power plants, then this would be a cause for concern.

To give an example of current versus quick ratios, based on recent financial statements, Wal-Mart and Manpower Inc. had current ratios of .81 and 1.60, respectively. However, Manpower carries no inventory to speak of, whereas Wal-Mart's current assets are virtually all inventory. As a result, Wal-Mart's quick ratio was only .21, whereas Manpower's was 1.60, the same as its current ratio.

Other Liquidity Ratios   We briefly mention three other measures of liquidity. A very short-term creditor might be interested in the *cash ratio:*

$$\text{Cash ratio} = \frac{\text{Cash}}{\text{Current liabilities}} \quad\quad\quad [3.3]$$

You can verify that for 2009 this works out to be .18 times for Prufrock.

Because net working capital, or NWC, is frequently viewed as the amount of short-term liquidity a firm has, we can consider the ratio of *NWC to total assets:*

$$\text{Net working capital to total assets} = \frac{\text{Net working capital}}{\text{Total assets}} \quad\quad\quad [3.4]$$

A relatively low value might indicate relatively low levels of liquidity. Here, this ratio works out to be ($708 − 540)/$3,588 = 4.7%.

Finally, imagine that Prufrock was facing a strike and cash inflows began to dry up. How long could the business keep running? One answer is given by the *interval measure:*

$$\text{Interval measure} = \frac{\text{Current assets}}{\text{Average daily operating costs}} \quad\quad\quad [3.5]$$

Total costs for the year, excluding depreciation and interest, were $1,344. The average daily cost was $1,344/365 = $3.68 per day.[1] The interval measure is thus $708/$3.68 = 192 days. Based on this, Prufrock could hang on for six months or so.[2]

The interval measure (or something similar) is also useful for newly founded or start-up companies that often have little in the way of revenues. For such companies, the interval measure indicates how long the company can operate until it needs another round of financing. The average daily operating cost for start-up companies is often called the burn rate, meaning the rate at which cash is burned in the race to become profitable.

LONG-TERM SOLVENCY MEASURES

Long-term solvency ratios are intended to address the firm's long-term ability to meet its obligations, or, more generally, its financial leverage. These are sometimes called *financial leverage ratios* or just *leverage ratios*. We consider three commonly used measures and some variations.

Total Debt Ratio   The *total debt ratio* takes into account all debts of all maturities to all creditors. It can be defined in several ways, the easiest of which is this:

$$\text{Total debt ratio} = \frac{\text{Total assets} - \text{Total equity}}{\text{Total assets}} \quad\quad\quad [3.6]$$

$$= \frac{\$3,588 - 2,591}{\$3,588} = .28 \text{ times}$$

The online Women's Business Center has more information about financial statements, ratios, and small business topics (www.onlinewbc.gov).

---

[1] For many of these ratios that involve average daily amounts, a 360-day year is often used in practice. This so-called banker's year has exactly four quarters of 90 days each and was computationally convenient in the days before pocket calculators. We'll use 365 days.

[2] Sometimes depreciation and/or interest is included in calculating average daily costs. Depreciation isn't a cash expense, so its inclusion doesn't make a lot of sense. Interest is a financing cost, so we excluded it by definition (we looked at only operating costs). We could, of course, define a different ratio that included interest expense.

In this case, an analyst might say that Prufrock uses 28 percent debt.[3] Whether this is high or low or whether it even makes any difference depends on whether capital structure matters, a subject we discuss in Part 6.

Prufrock has $.28 in debt for every $1 in assets. Therefore, there is $.72 in equity ($1 − .28) for every $.28 in debt. With this in mind, we can define two useful variations on the total debt ratio—the *debt–equity ratio* and the *equity multiplier:*

$$\text{Debt–equity ratio} = \text{Total debt/Total equity}$$
$$= \$.28/\$.72 = .39 \text{ times} \tag{3.7}$$

$$\text{Equity multiplier} = \text{Total assets/Total equity}$$
$$= \$1/\$.72 = 1.39 \text{ times} \tag{3.8}$$

The fact that the equity multiplier is 1 plus the debt–equity ratio is not a coincidence:

$$\text{Equity multiplier} = \text{Total assets/Total equity} = \$1/\$.72 = 1.39$$
$$= (\text{Total equity} + \text{Total debt})/\text{Total equity}$$
$$= 1 + \text{Debt–equity ratio} = 1.39 \text{ times}$$

The thing to notice here is that given any one of these three ratios, you can immediately calculate the other two; so, they all say exactly the same thing.

Ratios used to analyze technology firms can be found at www.chalfin.com under the "Publications" link.

A Brief Digression: Total Capitalization versus Total Assets   Frequently, financial analysts are more concerned with a firm's long-term debt than its short-term debt because the short-term debt will constantly be changing. Also, a firm's accounts payable may reflect trade practice more than debt management policy. For these reasons, the *long-term debt ratio* is often calculated as follows:

$$\text{Long-term debt ratio} = \frac{\text{Long-term debt}}{\text{Long-term debt} + \text{Total equity}}$$
$$= \frac{\$457}{\$457 + 2{,}591} = \frac{\$457}{\$3{,}048} = .15 \text{ times} \tag{3.9}$$

The $3,048 in total long-term debt and equity is sometimes called the firm's *total capitalization,* and the financial manager will frequently focus on this quantity rather than on total assets.

To complicate matters, different people (and different books) mean different things by the term *debt ratio.* Some mean a ratio of total debt, and some mean a ratio of long-term debt only, and, unfortunately, a substantial number are simply vague about which one they mean.

This is a source of confusion, so we choose to give two separate names to the two measures. The same problem comes up in discussing the debt–equity ratio. Financial analysts frequently calculate this ratio using only long-term debt.

Times Interest Earned   Another common measure of long-term solvency is the *times interest earned* (TIE) *ratio.* Once again, there are several possible (and common) definitions, but we'll stick with the most traditional:

$$\text{Times interest earned ratio} = \frac{\text{EBIT}}{\text{Interest}}$$
$$= \frac{\$691}{\$141} = 4.9 \text{ times} \tag{3.10}$$

---

[3]Total equity here includes preferred stock (discussed in Chapter 8 and elsewhere), if there is any. An equivalent numerator in this ratio would be Current liabilities + Long-term debt.

As the name suggests, this ratio measures how well a company has its interest obligations covered, and it is often called the *interest coverage ratio*. For Prufrock, the interest bill is covered 4.9 times over.

Cash Coverage   A problem with the TIE ratio is that it is based on EBIT, which is not really a measure of cash available to pay interest. The reason is that depreciation, a noncash expense, has been deducted out. Because interest is definitely a cash outflow (to creditors), one way to define the *cash coverage ratio* is this:

$$\text{Cash coverage ratio} = \frac{\text{EBIT} + \text{Depreciation}}{\text{Interest}}$$

$$= \frac{\$691 + 276}{\$141} = \frac{\$967}{\$141} = 6.9 \text{ times}$$

[3.11]

The numerator here, EBIT plus depreciation, is often abbreviated EBITD (earnings before interest, taxes, and depreciation—say "ebbit-dee"). It is a basic measure of the firm's ability to generate cash from operations, and it is frequently used as a measure of cash flow available to meet financial obligations.

A common variation on EBITD is earnings before interest, taxes, depreciation, and amortization (EBITDA—say "ebbit-dah"). Here *amortization* refers to a noncash deduction similar conceptually to depreciation, except it applies to an intangible asset (such as a patent) rather than a tangible asset (such as machine). Note that the word *amortization* here does not refer to the repayment of debt, a subject we discuss in a later chapter.

ASSET MANAGEMENT, OR TURNOVER, MEASURES

We next turn our attention to the efficiency with which Prufrock uses its assets. The measures in this section are sometimes called *asset utilization ratios*. The specific ratios we discuss can all be interpreted as measures of turnover. What they are intended to describe is how efficiently or intensively a firm uses its assets to generate sales. We first look at two important current assets: inventory and receivables.

Inventory Turnover and Days' Sales in Inventory   During the year, Prufrock had a cost of goods sold of $1,344. Inventory at the end of the year was $422. With these numbers, *inventory turnover* can be calculated as follows:

$$\text{Inventory turnover} = \frac{\text{Cost of goods sold}}{\text{Inventory}}$$

$$= \frac{\$1,344}{\$422} = 3.2 \text{ times}$$

[3.12]

In a sense, Prufrock sold off or turned over the entire inventory 3.2 times.[4] As long as we are not running out of stock and thereby forgoing sales, the higher this ratio is, the more efficiently we are managing inventory.

If we know we turned our inventory over 3.2 times during the year, we can immediately figure out how long it took us to turn it over on average. The result is the average *days' sales in inventory:*

$$\text{Days' sales in inventory} = \frac{365 \text{ days}}{\text{Inventory turnover}}$$

$$= \frac{365 \text{ days}}{3.2} = 114 \text{ days}$$

[3.13]

---

[4]Notice that we used cost of goods sold in the top of this ratio. For some purposes, it might be more useful to use sales instead of costs. For example, if we wanted to know the amount of sales generated per dollar of inventory, we could just replace the cost of goods sold with sales.

This tells us that, roughly speaking, inventory sits 114 days on average before it is sold. Alternatively, assuming we have used the most recent inventory and cost figures, it will take about 114 days to work off our current inventory.

For example, in February 2008, General Motors had a 153-day supply of its Chevrolet Silverado, more than the 60-day supply considered normal. This figure means that at the then-current rate of sales, it would have taken General Motors 153 days to deplete the available supply, or, equivalently, that General Motors had 153 days of Silverado sales in inventory. General Motors also had a 152-day supply of the GMC Sierra and a 164-day supply of the GMC Yukon. While these figures look very high (and they are), they also show why you should not look at any ratio in isolation. The reason that General Motors had such a large inventory was an expected strike at supplier American Axle & Manufacturing Holdings. General Motors wanted the excess inventory because it would be unable to produce any of these SUVs without the critical parts supplied by American Axle. By the end of March 2008, General Motors had temporarily closed two plants and had over 17,000 workers idled because of the strike at its supplier.

It might make more sense to use the average inventory in calculating turnover. Inventory turnover would then be $1,344/[($393 + 422)/2] = 3.3$ times.[5] It depends on the purpose of the calculation. If we are interested in how long it will take us to sell our current inventory, then using the ending figure (as we did initially) is probably better.

In many of the ratios we discuss in this chapter, average figures could just as well be used. Again, it depends on whether we are worried about the past, in which case averages are appropriate, or the future, in which case ending figures might be better. Also, using ending figures is common in reporting industry averages; so, for comparison purposes, ending figures should be used in such cases. In any event, using ending figures is definitely less work, so we'll continue to use them.

Receivables Turnover and Days' Sales in Receivables   Our inventory measures give some indication of how fast we can sell product. We now look at how fast we collect on those sales. The *receivables turnover* is defined much like inventory turnover:

$$\text{Receivables turnover} = \frac{\text{Sales}}{\text{Accounts receivable}}$$

$$= \frac{\$2,311}{\$188} = 12.3 \text{ times} \qquad \text{[3.14]}$$

Loosely speaking, Prufrock collected its outstanding credit accounts and reloaned the money 12.3 times during the year.[6]

This ratio makes more sense if we convert it to days, so here is the *days' sales in receivables:*

$$\text{Days' sales in receivables} = \frac{365 \text{ days}}{\text{Receivables turnover}}$$

$$= \frac{365}{12.3} = 30 \text{ days} \qquad \text{[3.15]}$$

Therefore, on average, Prufrock collects on its credit sales in 30 days. For obvious reasons, this ratio is frequently called the *average collection period* (ACP).

Note that if we are using the most recent figures, we could also say that we have 30 days' worth of sales currently uncollected. We will learn more about this subject when we study credit policy in a later chapter.

---

[5]Notice that we calculated the average as (Beginning value + Ending value)/2.

[6]Here we have implicitly assumed that all sales are credit sales. If they were not, we would simply use total credit sales in these calculations, not total sales.

EXAMPLE 3.2

Payables Turnover

Here is a variation on the receivables collection period. How long, on average, does it take for Prufrock Corporation to pay its bills? To answer, we need to calculate the accounts payable turnover rate using cost of goods sold. We will assume that Prufrock purchases everything on credit.

The cost of goods sold is $1,344, and accounts payable are $344. The turnover is therefore $1,344/$344 = 3.9 times. So, payables turned over about every 365/3.9 = 94 days. On average, then, Prufrock takes 94 days to pay. As a potential creditor, we might take note of this fact.

Asset Turnover Ratios   Moving away from specific accounts like inventory or receivables, we can consider several "big picture" ratios. For example, *NWC turnover* is:

$$\text{NWC turnover} = \frac{\text{Sales}}{\text{NWC}}$$

$$= \frac{\$2,311}{\$708 - 540} = 13.8 \text{ times} \qquad [3.16]$$

This ratio measures how much "work" we get out of our working capital. Once again, assuming we aren't missing out on sales, a high value is preferred. (Why?)

Similarly, *fixed asset turnover* is:

$$\text{Fixed asset turnover} = \frac{\text{Sales}}{\text{Net fixed assets}}$$

$$= \frac{\$2,311}{\$2,880} = .80 \text{ times} \qquad [3.17]$$

With this ratio, it probably makes more sense to say that for every dollar in fixed assets, Prufrock generated $.80 in sales.

Our final asset management ratio, the *total asset turnover,* comes up quite a bit. We will see it later in this chapter and in the next chapter. As the name suggests, the total asset turnover is:

$$\text{Total asset turnover} = \frac{\text{Sales}}{\text{Total assets}}$$

$$= \frac{\$2,311}{\$3,588} = .64 \text{ times} \qquad [3.18]$$

In other words, for every dollar in assets, Prufrock generated $.64 in sales.

To give an example of fixed and total asset turnover, based on recent financial statements, Southwest Airlines had a total asset turnover of .59, compared to .82 for IBM. However, the much higher investment in fixed assets in an airline is reflected in Southwest's fixed asset turnover of .80, compared to IBM's 1.46.

EXAMPLE 3.3

More Turnover

Suppose you find that a particular company generates $.40 in sales for every dollar in total assets. How often does this company turn over its total assets?

The total asset turnover here is .40 times per year. It takes 1/.40 = 2.5 years to turn total assets over completely.

PROFITABILITY MEASURES

The three measures we discuss in this section are probably the best known and most widely used of all financial ratios. In one form or another, they are intended to measure how efficiently a firm uses its assets and manages its operations. The focus in this group is on the bottom line, net income.

Profit Margin   Companies pay a great deal of attention to their *profit margins:*

$$\text{Profit margin} = \frac{\text{Net income}}{\text{Sales}}$$

$$= \frac{\$363}{\$2,311} = 15.7\%$$

[3.19]

This tells us that Prufrock, in an accounting sense, generates a little less than 16 cents in profit for every dollar in sales.

All other things being equal, a relatively high profit margin is obviously desirable. This situation corresponds to low expense ratios relative to sales. However, we hasten to add that other things are often not equal.

For example, lowering our sales price will usually increase unit volume but will normally cause profit margins to shrink. Total profit (or, more important, operating cash flow) may go up or down; so the fact that margins are smaller isn't necessarily bad. After all, isn't it possible that, as the saying goes, "Our prices are so low that we lose money on everything we sell, but we make it up in volume"?[7]

Return on Assets   *Return on assets* (ROA) is a measure of profit per dollar of assets. It can be defined several ways, but the most common is this:

$$\text{Return on assets} = \frac{\text{Net income}}{\text{Total assets}}$$

$$= \frac{\$363}{\$3,588} = 10.12\%$$

[3.20]

Return on Equity   *Return on equity* (ROE) is a measure of how the stockholders fared during the year. Because benefiting shareholders is our goal, ROE is, in an accounting sense, the true bottom-line measure of performance. ROE is usually measured as follows:

$$\text{Return on equity} = \frac{\text{Net income}}{\text{Total equity}}$$

$$= \frac{\$363}{\$2,591} = 14\%$$

[3.21]

For every dollar in equity, therefore, Prufrock generated 14 cents in profit; but again this is correct only in accounting terms.

Because ROA and ROE are such commonly cited numbers, we stress that it is important to remember they are accounting rates of return. For this reason, these measures should properly be called *return on book assets* and *return on book equity*. In fact, ROE is sometimes called *return on net worth*. Whatever it's called, it would be inappropriate to compare the result to, for example, an interest rate observed in the financial markets. We will have more to say about accounting rates of return in later chapters.

The fact that ROE exceeds ROA reflects Prufrock's use of financial leverage. We will examine the relationship between these two measures in more detail next.

EXAMPLE 3.4	ROE and ROA

Because ROE and ROA are usually intended to measure performance over a prior period, it makes a certain amount of sense to base them on average equity and average assets, respectively. For Prufrock, how would you calculate these?

continued

---

[7]No, it's not.

We first need to calculate average assets and average equity:

Average assets = ($3,373 + 3,588)/2 = $3,481
Average equity = ($2,299 + 2,591)/2 = $2,445

With these averages, we can recalculate ROA and ROE as follows:

$$ROA = \frac{\$363}{\$3,481} = 10.43\%$$

$$ROE = \frac{\$363}{\$2,445} = 14.85\%$$

These are slightly higher than our previous calculations because assets and equity grew during the year, with the result that the average is below the ending value.

MARKET VALUE MEASURES

Our final group of measures is based, in part, on information not necessarily contained in financial statements—the market price per share of stock. Obviously, these measures can be calculated directly only for publicly traded companies.

We assume that Prufrock has 33 million shares outstanding and the stock sold for $88 per share at the end of the year. If we recall that Prufrock's net income was $363 million, we can calculate its earnings per share:

$$EPS = \frac{\text{Net income}}{\text{Shares outstanding}} = \frac{\$363}{33} = \$11$$

Price–Earnings Ratio   The first of our market value measures, the *price–earnings* (PE) *ratio* (or multiple), is defined here:

$$PE\ ratio = \frac{\text{Price per share}}{\text{Earnings per share}}$$

$$= \frac{\$88}{\$11} = 8 \text{ times}$$

[3.22]

In the vernacular, we would say that Prufrock shares sell for eight times earnings, or we might say that Prufrock shares have or "carry" a PE multiple of 8.

PE ratios vary substantially across companies, but, in 2009, a typical large company in the United States had a PE in the 15–20 range. This is on the high side by historical standards, but not dramatically so. A low point for PEs was about 5 in 1974. PEs also vary across countries. For example, Japanese PEs have historically been much higher than those of their U.S. counterparts.

Because the PE ratio measures how much investors are willing to pay per dollar of current earnings, higher PEs are often taken to mean the firm has significant prospects for future growth. Of course, if a firm had no or almost no earnings, its PE would probably be quite large; so, as always, care is needed in interpreting this ratio.

Sometimes analysts divide PE ratios by expected future earnings growth rates (after multiplying the growth rate by 100). The result is the PEG ratio. Suppose Prufrock's anticipated growth rate in EPS was 6 percent. Its PEG ratio would then be 8/6 = 1.33. The idea behind the PEG ratio is that whether a PE ratio is high or low depends on expected future growth. High PEG ratios suggest that the PE is too high relative to growth, and vice versa.

Price–Sales Ratio   In some cases, companies will have negative earnings for extended periods, so their PE ratios are not very meaningful. A good example is a recent start-up. Such companies usually do have some revenues, so analysts will often look at the *price–sales ratio:*

Price–sales ratio = Price per share/Sales per share

In Prufrock's case, sales were $2,311, so here is the price–sales ratio:

Price–sales ratio = $88/($2,311/33) = $88/$70 = 1.26

As with PE ratios, whether a particular price–sales ratio is high or low depends on the industry involved.

Market-to-Book Ratio   A second commonly quoted market value measure is the *market-to-book ratio:*

$$\text{Market-to-book ratio} = \frac{\text{Market value per share}}{\text{Book value per share}}$$

$$= \frac{\$88}{(\$2{,}591/33)} = \frac{\$88}{\$78.5} = 1.12 \text{ times}$$

[3.23]

Notice that book value per share is total equity (not just common stock) divided by the number of shares outstanding.

Because book value per share is an accounting number, it reflects historical costs. In a loose sense, the market-to-book ratio therefore compares the market value of the firm's investments to their cost. A value less than 1 could mean that the firm has not been successful overall in creating value for its stockholders.

Market-to-book ratios in recent years appear high relative to past values. For example, for the 30 blue-chip companies that make up the widely followed Dow-Jones Industrial Average, the historical norm is about 1.7; however, the market-to-book ratio for this group has recently been twice this size.

Another ratio, called *Tobin's Q ratio,* is much like the market-to-book ratio. Tobin's Q is the market value of the firm's assets divided by their replacement cost:

Tobin's Q = Market value of firm's assets/Replacement cost of firm's assets
   = Market value of firm's debt and equity/Replacement cost of firm's assets

Notice that we used two equivalent numerators here: the market value of the firm's assets and the market value of its debt and equity.

Conceptually, the Q ratio is superior to the market-to-book ratio because it focuses on what the firm is worth today relative to what it would cost to replace it today. Firms with high Q ratios tend to be those with attractive investment opportunities or significant competitive advantages (or both). In contrast, the market-to-book ratio focuses on historical costs, which are less relevant.

As a practical matter, however, Q ratios are difficult to calculate with accuracy because estimating the replacement cost of a firm's assets is not an easy task. Also, market values for a firm's debt are often unobservable. Book values can be used instead in such cases, but accuracy may suffer.

CONCLUSION

This completes our definitions of some common ratios. We could tell you about more of them, but these are enough for now. We'll go on to discuss some ways of using these ratios instead of just how to calculate them. Table 3.8 summarizes the ratios we've discussed.

Concept Questions

3.3a What are the five groups of ratios? Give two or three examples of each kind.

3.3b Given the total debt ratio, what other two ratios can be computed? Explain how.

3.3c Turnover ratios all have one of two figures as the numerator. What are these two figures? What do these ratios measure? How do you interpret the results?

3.3d Profitability ratios all have the same figure in the numerator. What is it? What do these ratios measure? How do you interpret the results?

TABLE 3.8 Common Financial Ratios

I. Short-term solvency, or liquidity, ratios	II. Long-term solvency, or financial leverage, ratios
Current ratio $= \dfrac{\text{Current assets}}{\text{Current liabilities}}$	Total debt ratio $= \dfrac{\text{Total assets} - \text{Total equity}}{\text{Total assets}}$
Quick ratio $= \dfrac{\text{Current assets} - \text{Inventory}}{\text{Current liabilities}}$	Debt–equity ratio $=$ Total debt/Total equity
Cash ratio $= \dfrac{\text{Cash}}{\text{Current liabilities}}$	Equity multiplier $=$ Total assets/Total equity
Net working capital to total assets $= \dfrac{\text{Net working capital}}{\text{Total assets}}$	Long-term debt ratio $= \dfrac{\text{Long-term debt}}{\text{Long-term debt} + \text{Total equity}}$
Interval measure $= \dfrac{\text{Current assets}}{\text{Average daily operating costs}}$	Times interest earned ratio $= \dfrac{\text{EBIT}}{\text{Interest}}$
	Cash coverage ratio $= \dfrac{\text{EBIT} + \text{Depreciation}}{\text{Interest}}$

III. Asset management, or turnover, ratios	IV. Profitability ratios
Inventory turnover $= \dfrac{\text{Cost of goods sold}}{\text{Inventory}}$	Profit margin $= \dfrac{\text{Net income}}{\text{Sales}}$
Days' sales in inventory $= \dfrac{365 \text{ days}}{\text{Inventory turnover}}$	Return on assets (ROA) $= \dfrac{\text{Net income}}{\text{Total assets}}$
Receivables turnover $= \dfrac{\text{Sales}}{\text{Accounts receivable}}$	Return on equity (ROE) $= \dfrac{\text{Net income}}{\text{Total equity}}$
Days' sales in receivables $= \dfrac{365 \text{ days}}{\text{Receivables turnover}}$	ROE $= \dfrac{\text{Net income}}{\text{Sales}} \times \dfrac{\text{Sales}}{\text{Assets}} \times \dfrac{\text{Assets}}{\text{Equity}}$
NWC turnover $= \dfrac{\text{Sales}}{\text{NWC}}$	**V. Market value ratios**
Fixed asset turnover $= \dfrac{\text{Sales}}{\text{Net fixed assets}}$	Price–earnings ratio $= \dfrac{\text{Price per share}}{\text{Earnings per share}}$
Total asset turnover $= \dfrac{\text{Sales}}{\text{Total assets}}$	PEG ratio $= \dfrac{\text{Price–earnings ratio}}{\text{Earnings growth rate (\%)}}$
	Price–sales ratio $= \dfrac{\text{Price per share}}{\text{Sales per share}}$
	Market-to-book-ratio $= \dfrac{\text{Market value per share}}{\text{Book value per share}}$
	Tobin's Q Ratio $= \dfrac{\text{Market value of assets}}{\text{Replacement cost of assets}}$

The Du Pont Identity   3.4

As we mentioned in discussing ROA and ROE, the difference between these two profit-ability measures is a reflection of the use of debt financing, or financial leverage. We illustrate the relationship between these measures in this section by investigating a famous way of decomposing ROE into its component parts.

A CLOSER LOOK AT ROE

To begin, let's recall the definition of ROE:

$$\text{Return on equity} = \frac{\text{Net income}}{\text{Total equity}}$$

If we were so inclined, we could multiply this ratio by Assets/Assets without changing anything:

$$\text{Return on equity} = \frac{\text{Net income}}{\text{Total equity}} = \frac{\text{Net income}}{\text{Total equity}} \times \frac{\text{Assets}}{\text{Assets}}$$

$$= \frac{\text{Net income}}{\text{Assets}} \times \frac{\text{Assets}}{\text{Total equity}}$$

Notice that we have expressed the ROE as the product of two other ratios—ROA and the equity multiplier:

$$\text{ROE} = \text{ROA} \times \text{Equity multiplier} = \text{ROA} \times (1 + \text{Debt–equity ratio})$$

Looking back at Prufrock, for example, we see that the debt–equity ratio was .39 and ROA was 10.12 percent. Our work here implies that Prufrock's ROE, as we previously calculated, is this:

$$\text{ROE} = 10.12\% \times 1.39 = 14\%$$

The difference between ROE and ROA can be substantial, particularly for certain businesses. For example, in 2008, Bank of America has an ROA of only .53 percent, which is fairly typical for a large bank. However, banks tend to borrow a lot of money and, as a result, have relatively large equity multipliers. For Bank of America, ROE is about 5.75 percent, implying an equity multiplier of 10.85.

We can further decompose ROE by multiplying the top and bottom by total sales:

$$\text{ROE} = \frac{\text{Sales}}{\text{Sales}} \times \frac{\text{Net income}}{\text{Assets}} \times \frac{\text{Assets}}{\text{Total equity}}$$

If we rearrange things a bit, ROE looks like this:

$$\text{ROE} = \underbrace{\frac{\text{Net income}}{\text{Sales}} \times \frac{\text{Sales}}{\text{Assets}}}_{\text{Return on assets}} \times \frac{\text{Assets}}{\text{Total equity}}$$

[3.24]

$$= \text{Profit margin} \times \text{Total asset turnover} \times \text{Equity multiplier}$$

Du Pont identity
Popular expression breaking ROE into three parts: operating efficiency, asset use efficiency, and financial leverage.

What we have now done is to partition ROA into its two component parts, profit margin and total asset turnover. The last expression of the preceding equation is called the **Du Pont identity**, after the Du Pont Corporation, which popularized its use.

We can check this relationship for Prufrock by noting that the profit margin was 15.7 percent and the total asset turnover was .64:

$$\text{ROE} = \text{Profit margin} \times \text{Total asset turnover} \times \text{Equity multiplier}$$
$$= 15.7\% \qquad \times .64 \qquad\qquad \times 1.39$$
$$= 14\%$$

This 14 percent ROE is exactly what we had before.

The Du Pont identity tells us that ROE is affected by three things:

1. Operating efficiency (as measured by profit margin).
2. Asset use efficiency (as measured by total asset turnover).
3. Financial leverage (as measured by the equity multiplier).

Weakness in either operating or asset use efficiency (or both) will show up in a diminished return on assets, which will translate into a lower ROE.

Considering the Du Pont identity, it appears that the ROE could be leveraged up by increasing the amount of debt in the firm. However, notice that increasing debt also increases interest expense, which reduces profit margins, which acts to reduce ROE. So, ROE could go up or down, depending. More important, the use of debt financing has a number of other effects, and as we discuss at some length in Part 6, the amount of leverage a firm uses is governed by its capital structure policy.

The decomposition of ROE we've discussed in this section is a convenient way of systematically approaching financial statement analysis. If ROE is unsatisfactory by some measure, then the Du Pont identity tells you where to start looking for the reasons.

General Motors provides a good example of how Du Pont analysis can be very useful and also illustrates why care must be taken in interpreting ROE values. In 1989, GM had an ROE of 12.1 percent. By 1993, its ROE had improved to 44.1 percent, a dramatic improvement. On closer inspection, however, we find that over the same period GM's profit margin had declined from 3.4 to 1.8 percent, and ROA had declined from 2.4 to 1.3 percent. The decline in ROA was moderated only slightly by an increase in total asset turnover from .71 to .73 over the period.

Given this information, how is it possible for GM's ROE to have climbed so sharply? From our understanding of the Du Pont identity, it must be the case that GM's equity multiplier increased substantially. In fact, what happened was that GM's book equity value was almost wiped out overnight in 1992 by changes in the accounting treatment of pension liabilities. If a company's equity value declines sharply, its equity multiplier rises. In GM's case, the multiplier went from 4.95 in 1989 to 33.62 in 1993. In sum, the dramatic "improvement" in GM's ROE was almost entirely due to an accounting change that affected the equity multiplier and doesn't really represent an improvement in financial performance at all.

AN EXPANDED DU PONT ANALYSIS

So far, we've seen how the Du Pont equation lets us break down ROE into its basic three components: profit margin, total asset turnover, and financial leverage. We now extend this analysis to take a closer look at how key parts of a firm's operations feed into ROE. To get going, we went to the *S&P Market Insight* Web page (www.mhhe.com/edumarketinsight) and pulled abbreviated financial statements for science and technology giant Du Pont. What we found is summarized in Table 3.9.

Using the information in Table 3.9, Figure 3.1 shows how we can construct an expanded Du Pont analysis for Du Pont and present that analysis in chart form. The advantage of the extended Du Pont chart is that it lets us examine several ratios at once, thereby getting a better overall picture of a company's performance and also allowing us to determine possible items to improve.

Looking at the left side of our Du Pont chart in Figure 3.1, we see items related to profitability. As always, profit margin is calculated as net income divided by sales. But as our

TABLE 3.9

FINANCIAL STATEMENTS FOR DU PONT 12 months ending December 31, 2007 (All numbers are in millions)					
Income Statement		**Balance Sheet**			
Sales	$30,454	Current assets		Current liabilities	
CoGS	20,318	Cash	$ 1,436	Accounts payable	$ 2,723
Gross profit	$10,136	Accounts receivable	5,683	Notes payable	1,346
SG&A expense	4,547	Inventory	6,041	Other	4,472
Depreciation	1,371	Total	$13,160	Total	$ 8,541
EBIT	$ 4,218				
Interest	482	Fixed assets	$20,971	Total long-term debt	$14,454
EBT	$ 3,736				
Taxes	748			Total equity	$11,136
Net income	$ 2,988	Total assets	$34,131	Total liabilities and equity	$34,131

FIGURE 3.1 Extended Du Pont Chart for Du Pont

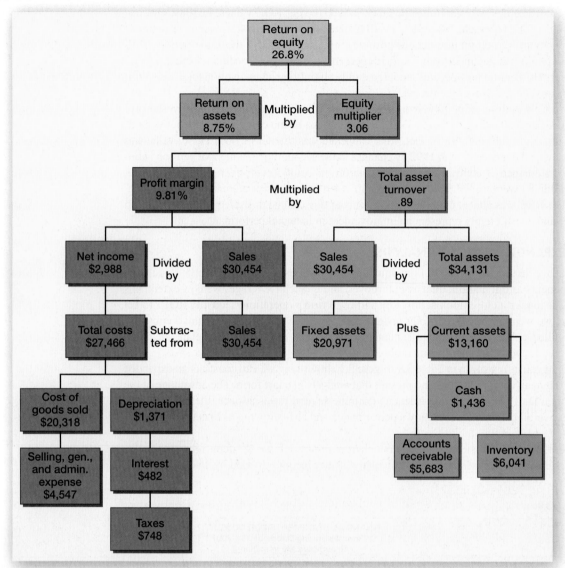

chart emphasizes, net income depends on sales and a variety of costs, such as cost of goods sold (CoGS) and selling, general, and administrative expenses (SG&A expense). Du Pont can increase its ROE by increasing sales and also by reducing one or more of these costs. In other words, if we want to improve profitability, our chart clearly shows us the areas on which we should focus.

Turning to the right side of Figure 3.1, we have an analysis of the key factors underlying total asset turnover. Thus, for example, we see that reducing inventory holdings through more efficient management reduces current assets, which reduces total assets, which then improves total asset turnover.

3.4a Return on assets, or ROA, can be expressed as the product of two ratios. Which two?

3.4b Return on equity, or ROE, can be expressed as the product of three ratios. Which three?

Using Financial Statement Information   3.5

Our last task in this chapter is to discuss in more detail some practical aspects of financial statement analysis. In particular, we will look at reasons for analyzing financial statements, how to get benchmark information, and some problems that come up in the process.

WHY EVALUATE FINANCIAL STATEMENTS?

As we have discussed, the primary reason for looking at accounting information is that we don't have, and can't reasonably expect to get, market value information. We stress that whenever we have market information, we will use it instead of accounting data. Also, if there is a conflict between accounting and market data, market data should be given precedence.

Financial statement analysis is essentially an application of "management by exception." In many cases, such analysis will boil down to comparing ratios for one business with average or representative ratios. Those ratios that seem to differ the most from the averages are tagged for further study.

Internal Uses Financial statement information has a variety of uses within a firm. Among the most important of these is performance evaluation. For example, managers are frequently evaluated and compensated on the basis of accounting measures of performance such as profit margin and return on equity. Also, firms with multiple divisions frequently compare the performance of those divisions using financial statement information.

Another important internal use we will explore in the next chapter is planning for the future. As we will see, historical financial statement information is useful for generating projections about the future and for checking the realism of assumptions made in those projections.

External Uses Financial statements are useful to parties outside the firm, including short-term and long-term creditors and potential investors. For example, we would find such information quite useful in deciding whether to grant credit to a new customer.

We would also use this information to evaluate suppliers, and suppliers would review our statements before deciding to extend credit to us. Large customers use this information to decide if we are likely to be around in the future. Credit-rating agencies rely on financial statements in assessing a firm's overall creditworthiness. The common theme here is that financial statements are a prime source of information about a firm's financial health.

We would also find such information useful in evaluating our main competitors. We might be thinking of launching a new product. A prime concern would be whether the competition would jump in shortly thereafter. In this case, we would be interested in learning about our competitors' financial strength to see if they could afford the necessary development.

Finally, we might be thinking of acquiring another firm. Financial statement information would be essential in identifying potential targets and deciding what to offer.

CHOOSING A BENCHMARK

Given that we want to evaluate a division or a firm based on its financial statements, a basic problem immediately comes up. How do we choose a benchmark, or a standard of comparison? We describe some ways of getting started in this section.

Time Trend Analysis   One standard we could use is history. Suppose we found that the current ratio for a particular firm is 2.4 based on the most recent financial statement information. Looking back over the last 10 years, we might find that this ratio had declined fairly steadily over that period.

Based on this, we might wonder if the liquidity position of the firm has deteriorated. It could be, of course, that the firm has made changes that allow it to more efficiently use its current assets, the nature of the firm's business has changed, or business practices have changed. If we investigate, we might find any of these possible explanations behind the decline. This is an example of what we mean by management by exception—a deteriorating time trend may not be bad, but it does merit investigation.

Peer Group Analysis   The second means of establishing a benchmark is to identify firms similar in the sense that they compete in the same markets, have similar assets, and operate in similar ways. In other words, we need to identify a *peer group*. There are obvious problems with doing this because no two companies are identical. Ultimately the choice of which companies to use as a basis for comparison is subjective.

One common way of identifying potential peers is based on **Standard Industrial Classification (SIC) codes**. These are four-digit codes established by the U.S. government for statistical reporting. Firms with the same SIC code are frequently assumed to be similar.

The first digit in a SIC code establishes the general type of business. For example, firms engaged in finance, insurance, and real estate have SIC codes beginning with 6. Each additional digit narrows down the industry. So, companies with SIC codes beginning with 60 are mostly banks and banklike businesses; those with codes beginning with 602 are mostly commercial banks; and SIC code 6025 is assigned to national banks that are members of the Federal Reserve system. Table 3.10 lists selected two-digit codes (the first two digits of the four-digit SIC codes) and the industries they represent.

SIC codes are far from perfect. For example, suppose you were examining financial statements for Wal-Mart, the largest retailer in the United States. The relevant two-digit SIC code is 53, General Merchandise Stores. In a quick scan of the nearest financial database, you would find about 20 large, publicly owned corporations with a similar SIC code, but you might not be comfortable with some of them. Target would seem to be a reasonable peer, but Neiman Marcus also carries the same industry code. Are Wal-Mart and Neiman Marcus really comparable?

As this example illustrates, it is probably not appropriate to blindly use SIC code–based averages. Instead, analysts often identify a set of primary competitors and then compute a set of averages based on just this group. Also, we may be more concerned with a group of the top firms in an industry, not the average firm. Such a group is called an *aspirant group* because we aspire to be like its members. In this case, a financial statement analysis reveals how far we have to go.

Beginning in 1997, a new industry classification system was initiated. Specifically, the North American Industry Classification System (NAICS, pronounced "nakes") is intended to replace the older SIC codes, and it will eventually. Currently, however, SIC codes are still widely used.

With these caveats about SIC codes in mind, we can now take a look at a specific industry. Suppose we are in the retail hardware business. Table 3.11 contains some condensed

Standard Industrial Classification (SIC) code
A U.S. government code used to classify a firm by its type of business operations.

Learn more about NAICS at www.naics.com.

Agriculture, Forestry, and Fishing	Wholesale Trade
01 Agriculture production—crops	50 Wholesale trade—durable goods
08 Forestry	51 Wholesale trade—nondurable goods
09 Fishing, hunting, and trapping	
Mining	**Retail Trade**
10 Metal mining	54 Food stores
12 Bituminous coal and lignite mining	55 Automobile dealers and gas stations
13 Oil and gas extraction	58 Eating and drinking places
Construction	**Finance, Insurance, and Real Estate**
15 Building construction	60 Banking
16 Construction other than building	63 Insurance
17 Construction—special trade contractors	65 Real estate
Manufacturing	**Services**
28 Chemicals and allied products	78 Motion pictures
29 Petroleum refining and related industries	80 Health services
35 Machinery, except electrical	82 Educational services
37 Transportation equipment	
Transportation, Communication, Electric, Gas, and Sanitary Service	
40 Railroad transportation	
45 Transportation by air	
49 Electric, gas, and sanitary services	

TABLE 3.10

Selected Two-Digit SIC Codes

common-size financial statements for this industry from the Risk Management Association (RMA, formerly known as Robert Morris Associates), one of many sources of such information. Table 3.12 contains selected ratios from the same source.

There is a large amount of information here, most of which is self-explanatory. On the right in Table 3.11, we have current information reported for different groups based on sales. Within each sales group, common-size information is reported. For example, firms with sales in the $10 million to $25 million range have cash and equivalents equal to 7 percent of total assets. There are 38 companies in this group, out of 326 in all.

On the left, we have three years' worth of summary historical information for the entire group. For example, operating profit fell from 3.0 percent of sales to 2.5 percent over that time.

Table 3.12 contains some selected ratios, again reported by sales groups on the right and time period on the left. To see how we might use this information, suppose our firm has a current ratio of 2. Based on these ratios, is this value unusual?

Looking at the current ratio for the overall group for the most recent year (third column from the left in Table 3.12), we see that three numbers are reported. The one in the middle, 2.5, is the median, meaning that half of the 326 firms had current ratios that were lower and half had bigger current ratios. The other two numbers are the upper and lower quartiles. So, 25 percent of the firms had a current ratio larger than 3.9 and 25 percent had a current ratio smaller than 1.6. Our value of 2 falls comfortably within these bounds, so it doesn't appear too unusual. This comparison illustrates how knowledge of the range of ratios is important

TABLE 3.11   Selected Financial Statement Information

			Retail—Hardware Stores SIC# 5072, 5251 (NAICS 444130)						
COMPARATIVE HISTORICAL DATA				**CURRENT DATA SORTED BY SALES**					
			Type of Statement						
21	12	10	Unqualified		4			2	4
51	51	50	Reviewed	1	10	8	13	13	5
94	81	94	Compiled	6	44	21	15	7	1
60	77	77	Tax Returns	17	33	15	7	3	2
81	86	95	Other	11	24	21	12	13	14
4/1/04–3/31/05 ALL 307	**4/1/05–3/31/06 ALL 307**	**4/1/06–3/31/07 ALL 326**	**NUMBER OF STATEMENTS**	**62 (4/1–9/30/06)**		**264 (10/1/06–3/31/07)**			
				0-1MM 35	**1-3MM 115**	**3-5MM 65**	**5-10MM 47**	**10-25MM 38**	**25MM & OVER 26**
			Assets						
6.1%	6.1%	6.0%	Cash & Equivalents	4.6%	6.5%	5.6%	6.7%	7.0%	4.7%
14.6	14.6	12.6	Trade Receivables (net)	7.4	9.9	14.0	15.2	17.6	16.7
50.0	51.3	52.2	Inventory	59.2	53.7	52.6	47.9	49.4	47.4
1.4	2.4	2.0	All Other Current	.9	2.7	1.8	2.3	1.1	1.9
72.2	74.4	72.9	Total Current	72.1	72.7	74.0	72.1	75.2	70.8
16.6	14.3	16.1	Fixed Assets (net)	14.9	16.4	14.0	15.7	16.4	22.6
2.3	2.6	2.0	Intangibles (net)	4.8	1.8	1.1	2.7	1.3	1.3
8.9	8.7	8.9	All Other Non-Current	8.2	9.1	10.9	9.6	7.2	5.4
100.0	100.0	100.0	Total	100.0	100.0	100.0	100.0	100.0	100.0
			Liabilities						
10.4	11.7	9.9	Notes Payable-Short Term	15.7	9.4	7.2	9.9	9.6	11.2
3.5	3.3	3.2	Cur. Mat.-L.T.D.	3.7	2.7	4.7	3.6	2.5	1.0
14.7	15.2	13.7	Trade Payables	14.7	11.2	14.4	15.1	14.6	17.4
.2	.2	.2	Income Taxes Payable	.0	.2	.2	.2	.1	.3
6.9	7.3	6.9	All Other Current	5.1	6.9	6.1	7.6	9.1	7.4
35.7	37.7	33.8	Total Current	39.2	30.3	32.7	36.4	35.9	37.4
21.3	19.5	20.3	Long-Term Debt	35.5	24.6	18.5	11.7	13.9	9.9
.2	.2	.1	Deferred Taxes	.0	.0	.1	.1	.2	.4
4.9	7.4	7.6	All Other Non-Current	11.4	8.3	10.1	4.8	2.6	5.3
37.9	35.3	38.2	Net Worth	13.8	36.7	38.6	47.0	47.4	47.0
100.0	100.0	100.0	Total Liabilities & Net Worth	100.0	100.0	100.0	100.0	100.0	100.0
			Income Data						
100.0	100.0	100.0	Net Sales	100.0	100.0	100.0	100.0	100.0	100.0
35.6	36.0	36.7	Gross Profit	38.3	37.9	37.3	35.5	33.9	34.4
32.6	34.1	34.2	Operating Expenses	38.9	35.1	34.4	32.9	30.2	31.7
3.0	2.0	2.5	Operating Profit	−.6	2.8	2.8	2.6	3.6	2.7
.2	−.1	.2	All Other Expenses (net)	1.2	.3	.1	−.2	.0	.2
2.7	2.1	2.3	Profit Before Taxes	−1.8	2.5	2.7	2.8	3.6	2.5

M = $ thousand; MM = $ million.

Interpretation of Statement Studies Figures: RMA cautions that the studies be regarded only as a general guideline and not as an absolute industry norm. This is due to limited samples within categories, the categorization of companies by their primary Standard Industrial Classification (SIC) number only, and different methods of operations by companies within the same industry. For these reasons, RMA recommends that the figures be used only as general guidelines in addition to other methods of financial analysis.

TABLE 3.12 Selected Ratios

Retail—Hardware Stores SIC# 5072, 5251 (NAICS 444130)									
COMPARATIVE HISTORICAL DATA				CURRENT DATA SORTED BY SALES					
			Type of Statement						
21	12	10	Unqualified		4			2	4
51	51	50	Reviewed	1	10	8	13	13	5
94	81	94	Compiled	6	44	21	15	7	1
60	77	77	Tax Returns	17	33	15	7	3	2
81	86	95	Other	11	24	21	12	13	14
4/1/04–3/31/05 ALL 307	4/1/05–3/31/06 ALL 307	4/1/06–3/31/07 ALL 326	**NUMBER OF STATEMENTS**	62 (4/1–9/30/06) 0-1MM 35	1-3MM 115	264 (10/1/06–3/31/07) 3-5MM 65	5-10MM 47	10-25MM 38	25MM & OVER 26
			Ratios						
3.5	3.5	3.9	Current	4.3	4.6	4.1	3.2	3.6	2.9
2.3	2.1	2.5		2.3	3.0	2.6	2.1	2.4	1.7
1.5	1.5	1.6		1.6	1.7	1.8	1.6	1.4	1.3
1.1	1.0	1.1	Quick	.6	1.4	1.4	1.0	1.3	1.2
.6	.5	.5		.3	.5	.5	.6	.7	.4
.3	.2	.2		.1	.2	.2	.3	.3	.2
6 58.1	7 55.3	7 50.5	Sales/Receivables	5 69.3	8 48.6	8 45.7	9 42.5	8 46.5	7 55.6
15 24.0	14 26.3	13 28.6		11 34.2	13 28.6	12 30.7	17 21.5	19 19.5	14 26.9
31 11.6	31 11.8	25 14.6		16 22.7	20 17.9	26 14.3	24 15.0	37 10.0	45 8.1
76 4.8	79 4.6	92 4.0	Cost of Sales/Inventory	154 2.4	115 3.2	94 3.9	75 4.9	59 6.2	77 4.8
116 3.1	121 3.0	136 2.7		209 1.7	152 2.4	125 2.9	98 3.7	108 3.4	97 3.8
161 2.3	178 2.0	187 2.0		323 1.1	191 1.9	168 2.2	167 2.2	180 2.0	147 2.5
18 20.7	17 21.6	15 24.5	Cost of Sales/Payables	11 31.8	13 27.2	17 21.1	19 19.0	15 24.9	21 17.6
28 13.0	27 13.3	27 13.7		28 13.2	25 14.7	27 13.5	27 13.4	24 15.3	33 11.0
42 8.8	45 8.1	43 8.6		56 6.6	38 9.7	47 7.8	39 9.3	39 9.4	64 6.8
4.4	4.1	3.9	Sales/Working Capital	2.7	3.6	4.1	4.2	4.8	5.1
6.8	6.6	5.5		4.4	5.0	6.2	6.8	6.1	8.7
12.6	12.1	9.7		10.5	7.1	10.1	12.2	11.6	19.1
9.1	8.5	7.2	EBIT/Interest	3.0	5.5	9.3	8.2	10.5	17.5
(285) 3.7	(282) 3.1	(304) 3.0		(33) 1.5	(104) 2.6	(62) 4.8	(45) 3.4	(34) 4.7	4.5
1.4		1.3		–.4	1.2	1.3	1.3	1.6	1.0
5.1	3.8	2.9	Net Profit + Depr., Dep., Amort./Cur. Mat. L/T/D		2.0	2.8	3.4	10.0	
(63) 2.0	(56) 1.6	(63) 1.5			(14) 1.3	(14) 1.5	(14) 2.0	(10) 1.7	
.7	.6	.8			.8	.5	.7	.8	
.1	.1	.1	Fixed/Worth	.1	.1	.1	.1	.1	.2
.4	.4	.3		1.4	.3	.3	.4	.3	.5
1.1	.9	1.0		–1.1	1.3	.8	.7	.7	.9
.7	.8	.7	Debt/Worth	1.8	.7	.7	.5	.4	.6
1.7	1.7	1.5		4.4	1.5	1.4	1.6	1.2	1.1
4.6	4.5	3.8		–5.9	4.9	3.8	2.9	2.3	1.8
30.2	29.7	32.3	% Profit Before Taxes/Tangible Net Worth	22.3	33.9	41.3	30.5	36.9	30.5
(274) 13.6	(269) 13.5	(287) 12.3		(21) 6.8	(98) 13.7	(59) 13.1	10.0	(36) 12.3	11.9
4.2	3.7	4.3		–2.2	5.6	4.5	2.5	4.7	3.5

(continued)

TABLE 3.12   (continued)

4/1/04–3/31/05 ALL 307	4/1/05–3/31/06 ALL 307	4/1/06–3/31/07 ALL 326	NUMBER OF STATEMENTS	62 (4/1–9/30/06)		264 (10/1/06–3/31/07)			
				0-1MM 35	1-3MM 115	3-5MM 65	5-10MM 47	10-25MM 38	25MM & OVER 26
11.2	10.5	11.1	% Profit Before Taxes/Total Assets	6.3	11.9	12.3	11.0	13.6	13.3
5.2	5.3	4.8		2.4	4.8	5.2	4.7	7.1	6.4
1.0	.7	1.0		−5.2	.9	1.2	1.4	3.1	.5
49.9	59.6	52.0	Sales/Net Fixed Assets	40.5	59.4	60.1	46.1	57.0	37.9
21.1	22.9	20.3		13.9	21.1	23.7	18.5	20.2	14.2
9.8	10.7	9.8		8.4	9.0	12.5	9.8	10.2	7.8
3.2	3.1	2.8	Sales/Total Assets	2.3	2.7	3.1	3.2	3.3	3.0
2.5	2.5	2.4		1.6	2.2	2.5	2.5	2.5	2.6
1.9	1.9	1.7		1.2	1.6	2.0	2.0	2.3	1.9
.7	.5	.7	% Depr., Dep., Amort./Sales	.6	.6	.7	.5	.7	.8
(249) 1.2	(262) 1.0	(274) 1.2		(26) 2.0	(94) 1.3	(63) 1.3	(43) 1.1	(33) 1.0	(25) 1.0
2.0	1.9	2.0		3.4	2.7	1.7	2.0	1.4	1.9
1.7	2.0	1.8	% Officers', Directors', Owners' Comp/Sales	3.0	2.2	2.1	1.3	1.3	
(164) 3.5	(187) 3.4	(193) 3.2		(23) 4.5	(69) 3.7	(44) 3.2	(31) 3.0	(19) 1.8	
6.2	5.7	5.3		8.2	5.7	5.1	4.8	2.7	
5346164M	5361226M	4969626M	Net Sales ($)	24032M	215140M	247741M	336160M	620293M	3526260M
2015818M	1926895M	1977145M	Total Assets ($)	16500M	109029M	106265M	157126M	251225M	1337000M

M = $ thousand; MM = $ million.

in addition to knowledge of the average. Notice how stable the current ratio has been for the last three years.

EXAMPLE 3.5   **More Ratios**

Take a look at the most recent numbers reported for Sales/Receivables and EBIT/Interest in Table 3.12. What are the overall median values? What are these ratios?

If you look back at our discussion, you will see that these are the receivables turnover and the times interest earned, or TIE, ratios. The median value for receivables turnover for the entire group is 28.6 times. So, the days in receivables would be 365/28.6 = 13, which is the bold-faced number reported. The median for the TIE is 3.0 times. The number in parentheses indicates that the calculation is meaningful for, and therefore based on, only 304 of the 326 companies. In this case, the reason is that only 304 companies paid any significant amount of interest.

There are many sources of ratio information in addition to the one we examine here. Our nearby *Work the Web* box shows how to get this information for just about any company, along with some useful benchmarking information. Be sure to look it over and then benchmark your favorite company.

PROBLEMS WITH FINANCIAL STATEMENT ANALYSIS

We close our chapter on financial statements by discussing some additional problems that can arise in using financial statements. In one way or another, the basic problem with financial statement analysis is that there is no underlying theory to help us identify which quantities to look at and to guide us in establishing benchmarks.

As we discuss in other chapters, there are many cases in which financial theory and economic logic provide guidance in making judgments about value and risk. Little such help exists with financial statements. This is why we can't say which ratios matter the most and what a high or low value might be.

One particularly severe problem is that many firms are conglomerates, owning more or less unrelated lines of business. The consolidated financial statements for such firms don't fit any neat industry category. Going back to department stores, for example, Sears has had an SIC code of 6710 (Holding Offices) because of its diverse financial and retailing operations. More generally, the kind of peer group analysis we have been describing works best when the firms are strictly in the same line of business, the industry is competitive, and there is only one way of operating.

Another problem that is becoming increasingly common is that major competitors and natural peer group members in an industry may be scattered around the globe. The automobile industry is an obvious example. The problem here is that financial statements from outside the

WORK THE WEB

As we discussed in this chapter, ratios are an important tool for examining a company's performance. Gathering the necessary financial statements to calculate ratios can be tedious and time-consuming. Fortunately many sites on the Web provide this information for free. One of the best is www.reuters.com. We went there, entered a ticker symbol ("AZO" for AutoZone), and selected the "Ratios" link. Here is an abbreviated look at the results:

AutoZone Inc AZO (NYSE)

Sector: Services **Industry:** Retail (Specialty) ▸ View **AZO** on other exchanges

As of 2:27 PM EST	Price Change	Percent Change
$117.07 USD	▾.71	▾.60%

FINANCIAL STRENGTH

	Company	Industry	Sector	S&P 500
Quick Ratio (MRQ)	.12	.89	.68	1.16
Current Ratio (MRQ)	1.01	1.76	1.07	1.64
LT Debt to Equity (MRQ)	7.42	.63	.93	.59
Total Debt to Equity (MRQ)	7.42	.68	1.13	.78
Interest Coverage (TTM)	8.84	20.88	8.80	14.00

Most of the information is self-explanatory. Interest Coverage ratio is the same as the Times Interest Earned ratio discussed in the text. The abbreviation MRQ refers to results from the most recent quarterly financial statements, and TTM refers to results covering the previous ("trailing") 12 months. This site also provides a comparison to the industry, business sector, and S&P 500 averages for the ratios. Other ratios available on the site have five-year averages calculated. Have a look!

Questions

1. Go to www.reuters.com and find the major ratio categories listed on this website. How do the categories differ from the categories listed in the textbook?
2. On www.reuters.com, the profitability ratios and management effectiveness ratios have the 5-year average ratios presented. How do these ratios for the current year for Microsoft compare to its 5-year average? How does Microsoft compare to the industry for these ratios?

United States do not necessarily conform at all to GAAP. The existence of different standards and procedures makes it difficult to compare financial statements across national borders.

Even companies that are clearly in the same line of business may not be comparable. For example, electric utilities engaged primarily in power generation are all classified in the same group (SIC 4911). This group is often thought to be relatively homogeneous. However, most utilities operate as regulated monopolies, so they don't compete much with each other, at least not historically. Many have stockholders, and many are organized as cooperatives with no stockholders. There are several different ways of generating power, ranging from hydroelectric to nuclear, so the operating activities of these utilities can differ quite a bit. Finally, profitability is strongly affected by regulatory environment, so utilities in different locations can be similar but show different profits.

Several other general problems frequently crop up. First, different firms use different accounting procedures—for inventory, for example. This makes it difficult to compare statements. Second, different firms end their fiscal years at different times. For firms in seasonal businesses (such as a retailer with a large Christmas season), this can lead to difficulties in comparing balance sheets because of fluctuations in accounts during the year. Finally, for any particular firm, unusual or transient events, such as a one-time profit from an asset sale, may affect financial performance. In comparing firms, such events can give misleading signals.

Concept Questions

3.5a What are some uses for financial statement analysis?

3.5b Why do we say that financial statement analysis is management by exception?

3.5c What are SIC codes and how might they be useful?

3.5d What are some problems that can come up with financial statement analysis?

3.6 Summary and Conclusions

This chapter has discussed aspects of financial statement analysis:

1. *Sources and uses of cash:* We discussed how to identify the ways in which businesses obtain and use cash, and we described how to trace the flow of cash through a business over the course of the year. We briefly looked at the statement of cash flows.

2. *Standardized financial statements:* We explained that differences in size make it difficult to compare financial statements, and we discussed how to form common-size and common–base period statements to make comparisons easier.

3. *Ratio analysis:* Evaluating ratios of accounting numbers is another way of comparing financial statement information. We therefore defined and discussed a number of the most commonly reported and used financial ratios. We also discussed the famous Du Pont identity as a way of analyzing financial performance.

4. *Using financial statements:* We described how to establish benchmarks for comparison and discussed some types of information that are available. We then examined potential problems that can arise.

After you have studied this chapter, we hope that you have some perspective on the uses and abuses of financial statements. You should also find that your vocabulary of business and financial terms has grown substantially.

3.1 Sources and Uses of Cash Consider the following balance sheets for the Philippe Corporation. Calculate the changes in the various accounts and, where applicable, identify the change as a source or use of cash. What were the major sources and uses of cash? Did the company become more or less liquid during the year? What happened to cash during the year?

PHILIPPE CORPORATION 2008 and 2009 Balance Sheets ($ in millions)		
	2008	2009
Assets		
Current assets		
Cash	$ 210	$ 215
Accounts receivable	355	310
Inventory	507	328
Total	$1,072	$ 853
Fixed assets		
Net plant and equipment	$6,085	$6,527
Total assets	$7,157	$7,380
Liabilities and Owners' Equity		
Current liabilities		
Accounts payable	$ 207	$ 298
Notes payable	1,715	1,427
Total	$1,922	$1,725
Long-term debt	$1,987	$2,308
Owners' equity		
Common stock and paid-in surplus	$1,000	$1,000
Retained earnings	2,248	2,347
Total	$3,248	$3,347
Total liabilities and owners' equity	$7,157	$7,380

3.2 Common-Size Statements Here is the most recent income statement for Philippe. Prepare a common-size income statement based on this information. How do you interpret the standardized net income? What percentage of sales goes to cost of goods sold?

PHILIPPE CORPORATION 2009 Income Statement ($ in millions)		
Sales		$4,053
Cost of goods sold		2,780
Depreciation		550
Earnings before interest and taxes		$ 723
Interest paid		502
Taxable income		$ 221
Taxes (34%)		75
Net income		$ 146
Dividends	$47	
Addition to retained earnings	99	

3.3 **Financial Ratios** Based on the balance sheets and income statement in the previous two problems, calculate the following ratios for 2009:

Current ratio _____

Quick ratio _____

Cash ratio _____

Inventory turnover _____

Receivables turnover _____

Days' sales in inventory _____

Days' sales in receivables _____

Total debt ratio _____

Long-term debt ratio _____

Times interest earned ratio _____

Cash coverage ratio _____

3.4 **ROE and the Du Pont Identity** Calculate the 2009 ROE for the Philippe Corporation and then break down your answer into its component parts using the Du Pont identity.

ANSWERS TO CHAPTER REVIEW AND SELF-TEST PROBLEMS

3.1 We've filled in the answers in the following table. Remember, increases in assets and decreases in liabilities indicate that we spent some cash. Decreases in assets and increases in liabilities are ways of getting cash.

Philippe used its cash primarily to purchase fixed assets and to pay off short-term debt. The major sources of cash to do this were additional long-term borrowing, reductions in current assets, and additions to retained earnings.

PHILIPPE CORPORATION 2008 and 2009 Balance Sheets ($ in millions)				
	2008	2009	Change	Source or Use of Cash
Assets				
Current assets				
Cash	$ 210	$ 215	+$ 5	
Accounts receivable	355	310	− 45	Source
Inventory	507	328	− 179	Source
Total	$1,072	$ 853	−$219	
Fixed assets				
Net plant and equipment	$6,085	$6,527	+$442	Use
Total assets	$7,157	$7,380	+$223	
Liabilities and Owners' Equity				
Current liabilities				
Accounts payable	$ 207	$ 298	+$ 91	Source
Notes payable	1,715	1,427	− 288	Use
Total	$1,922	$1,725	−$197	
Long-term debt	$1,987	$2,308	+$321	Source
Owners' equity				
Common stock and paid-in surplus	$1,000	$1,000	+$ 0	—
Retained earnings	2,248	2,347	+ 99	Source
Total	$3,248	$3,347	+$ 99	
Total liabilities and owners' equity	$7,157	$7,380	+$223	

The current ratio went from $1,072/1,922 = .56 to $853/1,725 = .49, so the firm's liquidity appears to have declined somewhat. Overall, however, the amount of cash on hand increased by $5.

3.2 We've calculated the common-size income statement here. Remember that we simply divide each item by total sales.

PHILIPPE CORPORATION 2009 Common-Size Income Statement	
Sales	100.0%
Cost of goods sold	68.6
Depreciation	13.6
Earnings before interest and taxes	17.8
Interest paid	12.3
Taxable income	5.5
Taxes (34%)	1.9
Net income	3.6%
Dividends	1.2%
Addition to retained earnings	2.4%

Net income is 3.6 percent of sales. Because this is the percentage of each sales dollar that makes its way to the bottom line, the standardized net income is the firm's profit margin. Cost of goods sold is 68.6 percent of sales.

3.3 We've calculated the following ratios based on the ending figures. If you don't remember a definition, refer back to Table 3.8.

Current ratio	$853/$1,725	= .49 times
Quick ratio	$525/$1,725	= .30 times
Cash ratio	$215/$1,725	= .12 times
Inventory turnover	$2,780/$328	= 8.48 times
Receivables turnover	$4,053/$310	= 13.07 times
Days' sales in inventory	365/8.48	= 43.06 days
Days' sales in receivables	365/13.07	= 27.92 days
Total debt ratio	$4,033/$7,380	= 54.6%
Long-term debt ratio	$2,308/$5,655	= 40.8%
Times interest earned ratio	$723/$502	= 1.44 times
Cash coverage ratio	$1,273/$502	= 2.54 times

3.4 The return on equity is the ratio of net income to total equity. For Philippe, this is $146/$3,347 = 4.4%, which is not outstanding.

Given the Du Pont identity, ROE can be written as follows:

ROE = Profit margin × Total asset turnover × Equity multiplier
= $146/$4,053 × $4,053/$7,380 × $7,380/$3,347
= 3.6% × .549 × 2.20
= 4.4%

Notice that return on assets, ROA, is 3.6% × .549 = 1.98%.

CONCEPTS REVIEW AND CRITICAL THINKING QUESTIONS

1. **Current Ratio [LO2]** What effect would the following actions have on a firm's current ratio? Assume that net working capital is positive.

   a. Inventory is purchased.

   b. A supplier is paid.

   c. A short-term bank loan is repaid.

   d. A long-term debt is paid off early.

   e. A customer pays off a credit account.

   f. Inventory is sold at cost.

   g. Inventory is sold for a profit.

2. **Current Ratio and Quick Ratio [LO2]** In recent years, Dixie Co. has greatly increased its current ratio. At the same time, the quick ratio has fallen. What has happened? Has the liquidity of the company improved?

3. **Current Ratio [LO2]** Explain what it means for a firm to have a current ratio equal to .50. Would the firm be better off if the current ratio were 1.50? What if it were 15.0? Explain your answers.

4. **Financial Ratios [LO2]** Fully explain the kind of information the following financial ratios provide about a firm:

   a. Quick ratio.

   b. Cash ratio.

   c. Total asset turnover.

   d. Equity multiplier.

   e. Long-term debt ratio.

   f. Times interest earned ratio.

   g. Profit margin.

   h. Return on assets.

   i. Return on equity.

   j. Price–earnings ratio.

5. **Standardized Financial Statements [LO1]** What types of information do common-size financial statements reveal about the firm? What is the best use for these common-size statements? What purpose do common–base year statements have? When would you use them?

6. **Peer Group Analysis [LO2]** Explain what peer group analysis is. As a financial manager, how could you use the results of peer group analysis to evaluate the performance of your firm? How is a peer group different from an aspirant group?

7. **Du Pont Identity [LO3]** Why is the Du Pont identity a valuable tool for analyzing the performance of a firm? Discuss the types of information it reveals compared to ROE considered by itself.

8. **Industry-Specific Ratios [LO2]** Specialized ratios are sometimes used in specific industries. For example, the so-called book-to-bill ratio is closely watched for semiconductor manufacturers. A ratio of .93 indicates that for every $100 worth of chips shipped over some period, only $93 worth of new orders were received. In January 2008, the semiconductor equipment industry's book-to-bill ratio was .89, compared to .85 during the month of December 2007. The book-to-bill ratio reached a recent low of .79 during September 2007. The three-month average of worldwide bookings in January 2008 was $1.12 billion, a decrease of 3 percent from December 2007, while the three-month average of billings was $1.27 billion, a 7 percent decrease from December 2007. What is this ratio intended to measure? Why do you think it is so closely followed?

9. **Industry-Specific Ratios [LO2]** So-called same-store sales are a very important measure for companies as diverse as McDonald's and Sears. As the name suggests, examining same-store sales means comparing revenues from the same stores or restaurants at two different points in time. Why might companies focus on same-store sales rather than total sales?

10. **Industry-Specific Ratios [LO2]** There are many ways of using standardized financial information beyond those discussed in this chapter. The usual goal is to put firms on an equal footing for comparison purposes. For example, for auto manufacturers, it is common to express sales, costs, and profits on a per-car basis. For each of the following industries, give an example of an actual company and discuss one or more potentially useful means of standardizing financial information:
    a. Public utilities.
    b. Large retailers.
    c. Airlines.
    d. Online services.
    e. Hospitals.
    f. College textbook publishers.

11. **Statement of Cash Flows [LO4]** In recent years, several manufacturing companies have reported the cash flow from the sale of Treasury securities in the cash from operations section of the statement of cash flows. What is the problem with this practice? Is there any situation in which this practice would be acceptable?

12. **Statement of Cash Flows [LO4]** Suppose a company lengthens the time it takes to pay suppliers. How would this affect the statement of cash flows? How sustainable is the change in cash flows from this practice?

HM™

QUESTIONS AND PROBLEMS

1. **Calculating Liquidity Ratios [LO2]** SDJ, Inc., has net working capital of $1,370, current liabilities of $3,720, and inventory of $1,950. What is the current ratio? What is the quick ratio?

    BASIC
    (Questions 1–17)

2. **Calculating Profitability Ratios [LO2]** Wakers, Inc., has sales of $29 million, total assets of $17.5 million, and total debt of $6.3 million. If the profit margin is 8 percent, what is net income? What is ROA? What is ROE?

3. **Calculating the Average Collection Period [LO2]** Ortiz Lumber Yard has a current accounts receivable balance of $431,287. Credit sales for the year just ended were $3,943,709. What is the receivables turnover? The days' sales in receivables? How long did it take on average for credit customers to pay off their accounts during the past year?

4. **Calculating Inventory Turnover [LO2]** The Blue Moon Corporation has ending inventory of $407,534, and cost of goods sold for the year just ended was $4,105,612. What is the inventory turnover? The days' sales in inventory? How long on average did a unit of inventory sit on the shelf before it was sold?

5. **Calculating Leverage Ratios [LO2]** Crystal Lake, Inc., has a total debt ratio of .63. What is its debt–equity ratio? What is its equity multiplier?

6. **Calculating Market Value Ratios [LO2]** Bach Corp. had additions to retained earnings for the year just ended of $430,000. The firm paid out $175,000 in cash dividends, and it has ending total equity of $5.3 million. If the company currently has 210,000 shares of common stock outstanding, what are earnings per share? Dividends per share? Book value per share? If the stock currently sells for $63 per share, what is the market-to-book ratio? The price–earnings ratio? If the company had sales of $4.5 million, what is the price–sales ratio?

7. **Du Pont Identity [LO4]** If Roten Rooters, Inc., has an equity multiplier of 2.80, total asset turnover of 1.15, and a profit margin of 5.5 percent, what is its ROE?

8. **Du Pont Identity [LO4]** Braam Fire Prevention Corp. has a profit margin of 6.80 percent, total asset turnover of 1.95, and ROE of 18.27 percent. What is this firm's debt–equity ratio?

9. **Sources and Uses of Cash [LO4]** Based only on the following information for Bennington Corp., did cash go up or down? By how much? Classify each event as a source or use of cash.

Decrease in inventory	$375
Decrease in accounts payable	190
Increase in notes payable	210
Increase in accounts receivable	105

10. **Calculating Average Payables Period [LO2]** Tortoise, Inc., had a cost of goods sold of $28,834. At the end of the year, the accounts payable balance was $6,105. How long on average did it take the company to pay off its suppliers during the year? What might a large value for this ratio imply?

11. **Cash Flow and Capital Spending [LO4]** For the year just ended, Ypsilanti Yak Yogurt shows an increase in its net fixed assets account of $835. The company took $148 in depreciation expense for the year. How much did the company spend on new fixed assets? Is this a source or use of cash?

12. **Equity Multiplier and Return on Equity [LO3]** Organic Chicken Company has a debt–equity ratio of .65. Return on assets is 8.5 percent, and total equity is $540,000. What is the equity multiplier? Return on equity? Net income?

Just Dew It Corporation reports the following balance sheet information for 2008 and 2009. Use this information to work Problems 13 through 17.

JUST DEW IT CORPORATION
2008 and 2009 Balance Sheets

Assets			Liabilities and Owners' Equity		
	2008	2009		2008	2009
Current assets			Current liabilities		
Cash	$ 8,436	$ 10,157	Accounts payable	$ 43,050	$ 46,821
Accounts receivable	21,530	23,406	Notes payable	18,384	17,382
Inventory	38,760	42,650	Total	$ 61,434	$ 64,203
Total	$ 68,726	$ 76,213			
			Long-term debt	$ 25,000	$ 32,000
			Owners' equity		
			Common stock and paid-in surplus	$ 40,000	$ 40,000
			Retained earnings	168,998	188,316
Net plant and equipment	$226,706	$248,306	Total	$208,998	$228,316
			Total liabilities and		
Total assets	$295,432	$324,519	owners' equity	$295,432	$324,519

13. **Preparing Standardized Financial Statements [LO1]** Prepare the 2008 and 2009 common-size balance sheets for Just Dew It.

14. **Preparing Standardized Financial Statements [LO1]** Prepare the 2009 common-base year balance sheet for Just Dew It.

15. **Preparing Standardized Financial Statements [LO1]** Prepare the 2009 combined common-size, common-base year balance sheet for Just Dew It.

16. **Sources and Uses of Cash** [LO4] For each account on this company's balance sheet, show the change in the account during 2009 and note whether this change was a source or use of cash. Do your numbers add up and make sense? Explain your answer for total assets as compared to your answer for total liabilities and owners' equity.

17. **Calculating Financial Ratios** [LO2] Based on the balance sheets given for Just Dew It, calculate the following financial ratios for each year:

   a. Current ratio.

   b. Quick ratio.

   c. Cash ratio.

   d. NWC to total assets ratio.

   e. Debt–equity ratio and equity multiplier.

   f. Total debt ratio and long-term debt ratio.

18. **Using the Du Pont Identity** [LO3] Y3K, Inc., has sales of $5,276, total assets of $3,105, and a debt–equity ratio of 1.40. If its return on equity is 15 percent, what is its net income?

19. **Days' Sales in Receivables** [LO2] A company has net income of $218,000, a profit margin of 8.70 percent, and an accounts receivable balance of $132,850. Assuming 70 percent of sales are on credit, what is the company's days' sales in receivables?

20. **Ratios and Fixed Assets** [LO2] The Ashwood Company has a long-term debt ratio of .45 and a current ratio of 1.25. Current liabilities are $875, sales are $5,780, profit margin is 9.5 percent, and ROE is 18.5 percent. What is the amount of the firm's net fixed assets?

21. **Profit Margin** [LO4] In response to complaints about high prices, a grocery chain runs the following advertising campaign: "If you pay your child $3 to go buy $50 worth of groceries, then your child makes twice as much on the trip as we do." You've collected the following information from the grocery chain's financial statements:

(millions)	
Sales	$750
Net income	22.5
Total assets	420
Total debt	280

   Evaluate the grocery chain's claim. What is the basis for the statement? Is this claim misleading? Why or why not?

22. **Return on Equity** [LO2] Firm A and firm B have debt–total asset ratios of 35% and 30% and returns on total assets of 12% and 11%, respectively. Which firm has a greater return on equity?

23. **Calculating the Cash Coverage Ratio** [LO2] Sherwood Inc.'s net income for the most recent year was $13,168. The tax rate was 34 percent. The firm paid $3,605 in total interest expense and deducted $2,382 in depreciation expense. What was the cash coverage ratio for the year?

24. **Cost of Goods Sold** [LO2] Holliman Corp. has current liabilities of $365,000, a quick ratio of .85, inventory turnover of 5.8, and a current ratio of 1.4. What is the cost of goods sold for the company?

25. **Ratios and Foreign Companies** [LO2] Prince Albert Canning PLC had a net loss of £13,482 on sales of £138,793 (both in thousands of pounds). What was the company's profit margin? Does the fact that these figures are quoted in a foreign currency make any difference? Why? In dollars, sales were $274,213,000. What was the net loss in dollars?

INTERMEDIATE
(Questions 18–30)

Visit us at www.mhhe.com/rwj

Some recent financial statements for Smolira Golf Corp. follow. Use this information to work Problems 26 through 30.

SMOLIRA GOLF 2008 and 2009 Balance Sheets					
Assets			**Liabilities and Owners' Equity**		
	2008	**2009**		**2008**	**2009**
Current assets			Current liabilities		
Cash	$21,860	$ 22,050	Accounts payable	$ 19,320	$ 22,850
Accounts receivable	11,316	13,850	Notes payable	10,000	9,000
Inventory	23,084	24,650	Other	9,643	11,385
Total	$56,260	$ 60,550	Total	$ 38,963	$ 43,235
			Long-term debt	$ 75,000	$ 85,000
			Owners' equity		
			Common stock and paid-in surplus	$ 25,000	$ 25,000
			Accumulated retained earnings	151,365	167,840
Fixed assets					
Net plant and equipment	234,068	260,525	Total	$176,365	$192,840
			Total liabilities and		
Total assets	$290,328	$321,075	owners' equity	$290,328	$321,075

SMOLIRA GOLF, Inc. 2009 Income Statement	
Sales	$305,830
Cost of goods sold	210,935
Depreciation	26,850
Earnings before interest and taxes	$ 68,045
Interest paid	11,930
Taxable income	$ 56,115
Taxes (35%)	19,640
Net income	$ 36,475
Dividends	$20,000
Retained earnings	16,475

26. **Calculating Financial Ratios [LO2]** Find the following financial ratios for Smolira Golf Corp. (use year-end figures rather than average values where appropriate):

Short-term solvency ratios:

a. Current ratio   _____

b. Quick ratio   _____

c. Cash ratio   _____

Asset utilization ratios:

d. Total asset turnover   _____

e. Inventory turnover   _____

f. Receivables turnover   _____

Long-term solvency ratios:

g. Total debt ratio   _____

h. Debt–equity ratio   _____

i. Equity multiplier   _____

j. Times interest earned ratio   _____

k. Cash coverage ratio   _____

Profitability ratios:

l. Profit margin   _____

m. Return on assets   _____

n. Return on equity   _____

27. **Du Pont Identity [LO3]** Construct the Du Pont identity for Smolira Golf Corp.

28. **Statement of Cash Flows [LO4]** Prepare the 2009 statement of cash flows for Smolira Golf Corp.

29. **Market Value Ratios [LO2]** Smolira Golf Corp. has 25,000 shares of common stock outstanding, and the market price for a share of stock at the end of 2009 was $43. What is the price–earnings ratio? What are the dividends per share? What is the market-to-book ratio at the end of 2009? If the company's growth rate is 9 percent, what is the PEG ratio?

30. **Tobin's Q [LO2]** What is Tobin's Q for Smolira Golf? What assumptions are you making about the book value of debt and the market value of debt? What about the book value of assets and the market value of assets? Are these assumptions realistic? Why or why not?

Ratio Analysis at S&S Air, Inc.

Chris Guthrie was recently hired by S&S Air, Inc., to assist the company with its financial planning and to evaluate the company's performance. Chris graduated from college five years ago with a finance degree. He has been employed in the finance department of a *Fortune* 500 company since then.

S&S Air was founded 10 years ago by friends Mark Sexton and Todd Story. The company has manufactured and sold light airplanes over this period, and the company's products have received high reviews for safety and reliability. The company has a niche market in that it sells primarily to individuals who own and fly their own airplanes. The company has two models; the Birdie, which sells for $53,000, and the Eagle, which sells for $78,000.

Although the company manufactures aircraft, its operations are different from commercial aircraft companies. S&S Air builds aircraft to order. By using prefabricated parts, the company can complete the manufacture of an airplane in only five weeks. The company also receives a deposit on each order, as well as another partial payment before the order is complete. In contrast, a commercial airplane may take one and one-half to two years to manufacture once the order is placed.

Mark and Todd have provided the following financial statements. Chris has gathered the industry ratios for the light airplane manufacturing industry.

S&S AIR, INC. 2009 Income Statement	
Sales	$30,499,420
Cost of goods sold	22,224,580
Other expenses	3,867,500
Depreciation	1,366,680
EBIT	$ 3,040,660
Interest	478,240
Taxable income	$ 2,562,420
Taxes (40%)	1,024,968
Net income	$ 1,537,452
Dividends	$560,000
Add to retained earnings	977,452

S&S AIR, INC. 2006 Balance Sheet			
Assets		**Liabilities and Equity**	
Current assets		Current liabilities	
Cash	$ 441,000	Accounts payable	$ 889,000
Accounts receivable	708,400	Notes payable	2,030,000
Inventory	1,037,120	Total current liabilities	$ 2,919,000
Total current assets	$ 2,186,520		
		Long-term debt	$ 5,320,000
Fixed assets			
		Shareholder equity	
Net plant and equipment	$16,122,400	Common stock	$ 350,000
		Retained earnings	9,719,920
		Total equity	$10,069,920
Total assets	$18,308,920	Total liabilities and equity	$18,308,920

Light Airplane Industry Ratios			
	Lower Quartile	Median	Upper Quartile
Current ratio	.50	1.43	1.89
Quick ratio	.21	.38	.62
Cash ratio	.08	.21	.39
Total asset turnover	.68	.85	1.38
Inventory turnover	4.89	6.15	10.89
Receivables turnover	6.27	9.82	14.11
Total debt ratio	.44	.52	.61
Debt–equity ratio	.79	1.08	1.56
Equity multiplier	1.79	2.08	2.56
Times interest earned	5.18	8.06	9.83
Cash coverage ratio	5.84	8.43	10.27
Profit margin	4.05%	6.98%	9.87%
Return on assets	6.05%	10.53%	13.21%
Return on equity	9.93%	16.54%	26.15%

QUESTIONS

1. Using the financial statements provided for S&S Air, calculate each of the ratios listed in the table for the light aircraft industry.

2. Mark and Todd agree that a ratio analysis can provide a measure of the company's performance. They have chosen Boeing as an aspirant company. Would you choose Boeing as an aspirant company? Why or why not? There are other aircraft manufacturers S&S Air could use as aspirant companies. Discuss whether it is appropriate to use any of the following companies: Bombardier, Embraer, Cirrus Design Corporation, and Cessna Aircraft Company.

3. Compare the performance of S&S Air to the industry. For each ratio, comment on why it might be viewed as positive or negative relative to the industry. Suppose you create an inventory ratio calculated as inventory divided by current liabilities. How do you think S&S Air's ratio would compare to the industry average?

LEARNING OBJECTIVES

After studying this chapter, you should understand:

LO1 How to apply the percentage of sales method.

LO2 How to compute the external financing needed to fund a firm's growth.

LO3 The determinants of a firm's growth.

LO4 Some of the problems in planning for growth.

LONG-TERM FINANCIAL PLANNING AND GROWTH

4

IN APRIL 2008, Pacific Ethanol, a California biofuel company, announced a larger-than-expected loss in the fourth quarter of the previous year. Pacific Ethanol is notable in that its CEO was California's secretary of state for eight years, and its investors include famous names such as Bill Gates. Of course, none of this guarantees good results. There were several factors that affected Pacific Ethanol's financial performance. Overexpansion in the relatively new ethanol industry caused a drop in the price. Meanwhile, farmers had planted less corn (from which ethanol is made), resulting in higher prices for raw materials. Finally,

Pacific Ethanol's relatively high debt required large interest payments, resulting in even worse performance. In fact, Pacific Ethanol was forced to look outside the company for a cash infusion. Of course, Pacific Ethanol was not alone. Both Cargill and Vera-Sun Energy scrapped plans for new ethanol plants, and Central Illinois Energy was forced to file for bankruptcy.

As these examples show, proper management of growth is vital. This chapter emphasizes the importance of planning for the future and discusses some tools firms use to think about, and manage, growth.

> Master the ability to solve problems in this chapter by using a spreadsheet. Access Excel Master on the student Web site www.mhhe.com/rwj.

A lack of effective long-range planning is a commonly cited reason for financial distress and failure. As we discuss in this chapter, long-range planning is a means of systematically thinking about the future and anticipating possible problems before they arrive. There are no magic mirrors, of course, so the best we can hope for is a logical and organized procedure for exploring the unknown. As one member of GM's board was heard to say, "Planning is a process that at best helps the firm avoid stumbling into the future backward."

Financial planning establishes guidelines for change and growth in a firm. It normally focuses on the big picture. This means it is concerned with the major elements of a firm's financial and investment policies without examining the individual components of those policies in detail.

Our primary goals in this chapter are to discuss financial planning and to illustrate the interrelatedness of the various investment and financing decisions a firm makes. In the chapters ahead, we will examine in much more detail how these decisions are made.

We first describe what is usually meant by *financial planning*. For the most part, we talk about long-term planning. Short-term financial planning is discussed in a later chapter. We examine what the firm can accomplish by developing a long-term financial plan. To do this, we develop a simple but useful long-range planning technique: the percentage of sales approach. We describe how to apply this approach in some simple cases, and we discuss some extensions.

To develop an explicit financial plan, managers must establish certain basic elements of the firm's financial policy:

1. *The firm's needed investment in new assets*: This will arise from the investment opportunities the firm chooses to undertake, and it is the result of the firm's capital budgeting decisions.

2. *The degree of financial leverage the firm chooses to employ*: This will determine the amount of borrowing the firm will use to finance its investments in real assets. This is the firm's capital structure policy.

3. *The amount of cash the firm thinks is necessary and appropriate to pay shareholders*: This is the firm's dividend policy.

4. *The amount of liquidity and working capital the firm needs on an ongoing basis*: This is the firm's net working capital decision.

As we will see, the decisions a firm makes in these four areas will directly affect its future profitability, need for external financing, and opportunities for growth.

A key lesson to be learned from this chapter is that a firm's investment and financing policies interact and thus cannot truly be considered in isolation from one another. The types and amounts of assets a firm plans on purchasing must be considered along with the firm's ability to raise the capital necessary to fund those investments. Many business students are aware of the classic three *P*s (or even four *P*s) of marketing. Not to be outdone, financial planners have no fewer than six *P*s: *Proper Prior Planning Prevents Poor Performance*.

Financial planning forces the corporation to think about goals. A goal frequently espoused by corporations is growth, and almost all firms use an explicit, companywide growth rate as a major component of their long-term financial planning. For example, in September 2007, Toyota Motor announced that it planned to sell about 9.8 million vehicles in 2008, and 10.4 million vehicles in 2009, becoming the first auto manufacturer to sell more than 10 million vehicles in a year. General Motors currently holds the auto sales record with 9.55 million vehicles sold in 1978.

There are direct connections between the growth a company can achieve and its financial policy. In the following sections, we show how financial planning models can be used to better understand how growth is achieved. We also show how such models can be used to establish the limits on possible growth.

4.1 What Is Financial Planning?

Financial planning formulates the way in which financial goals are to be achieved. A financial plan is thus a statement of what is to be done in the future. Many decisions have long lead times, which means they take a long time to implement. In an uncertain world, this requires that decisions be made far in advance of their implementation. If a firm wants to build a factory in 2012, for example, it might have to begin lining up contractors and financing in 2010 or even earlier.

GROWTH AS A FINANCIAL MANAGEMENT GOAL

Because the subject of growth will be discussed in various places in this chapter, we need to start out with an important warning: Growth, by itself, is not an appropriate goal for the financial manager. Clothing retailer J. Peterman Co., whose quirky catalogs were made famous on the TV show *Seinfeld*, learned this lesson the hard way. Despite its strong brand name and years of explosive revenue growth, the company was ultimately forced to file for bankruptcy—the victim of an overly ambitious, growth-oriented expansion plan.

Amazon.com, the big online retailer, is another example. At one time, Amazon's motto seemed to be "growth at any cost." Unfortunately, what really grew rapidly for the company were losses. Amazon refocused its business, explicitly sacrificing growth in the hope of achieving profitability. The plan seems to be working as Amazon.com turned a profit for the first time in the third quarter of 2003.

As we discussed in Chapter 1, the appropriate goal is increasing the market value of the owners' equity. Of course, if a firm is successful in doing this, then growth will usually result. Growth may thus be a desirable consequence of good decision making, but it is not an end unto itself. We discuss growth simply because growth rates are so commonly used in the planning process. As we will see, growth is a convenient means of summarizing various aspects of a firm's financial and investment policies. Also, if we think of growth as growth in the market value of the equity in the firm, then goals of growth and increasing the market value of the equity in the firm are not all that different.

You can find growth rates at www.reuters.com *and* finance.yahoo.com.

DIMENSIONS OF FINANCIAL PLANNING

It is often useful for planning purposes to think of the future as having a short run and a long run. The short run, in practice, is usually the coming 12 months. We focus our attention on financial planning over the long run, which is usually taken to be the coming two to five years. This time period is called the **planning horizon**, and it is the first dimension of the planning process that must be established.

In drawing up a financial plan, all of the individual projects and investments the firm will undertake are combined to determine the total needed investment. In effect, the smaller investment proposals of each operational unit are added up, and the sum is treated as one big project. This process is called **aggregation**. The level of aggregation is the second dimension of the planning process that needs to be determined.

Once the planning horizon and level of aggregation are established, a financial plan requires inputs in the form of alternative sets of assumptions about important variables. For example, suppose a company has two separate divisions: one for consumer products and one for gas turbine engines. The financial planning process might require each division to prepare three alternative business plans for the next three years:

planning horizon
The long-range time period on which the financial planning process focuses (usually the next two to five years).

aggregation
The process by which smaller investment proposals of each of a firm's operational units are added up and treated as one big project.

1. *A worst case*: This plan would require making relatively pessimistic assumptions about the company's products and the state of the economy. This kind of disaster planning would emphasize a division's ability to withstand significant economic adversity, and it would require details concerning cost cutting and even divestiture and liquidation. For example, sales of SUVs were sluggish in 2008 because of high gas prices. That left auto manufacturers like Ford and GM with large inventories and resulted in large price cuts and discounts.

2. *A normal case*: This plan would require making the most likely assumptions about the company and the economy.

3. *A best case*: Each division would be required to work out a case based on optimistic assumptions. It could involve new products and expansion and would then detail the financing needed to fund the expansion.

In this example, business activities are aggregated along divisional lines, and the planning horizon is three years. This type of planning, which considers all possible events, is particularly important for cyclical businesses (businesses with sales that are strongly affected by the overall state of the economy or business cycles).

WHAT CAN PLANNING ACCOMPLISH?

Because a company is likely to spend a lot of time examining the different scenarios that will become the basis for its financial plan, it seems reasonable to ask what the planning process will accomplish.

Examining Interactions   As we discuss in greater detail in the following pages, the financial plan must make explicit the linkages between investment proposals for the different operating activities of the firm and its available financing choices. In other words, if the firm is planning on expanding and undertaking new investments and projects, where will the financing be obtained to pay for this activity?

Exploring Options   The financial plan allows the firm to develop, analyze, and compare many different scenarios in a consistent way. Various investment and financing options can be explored, and their impact on the firm's shareholders can be evaluated. Questions concerning the firm's future lines of business and optimal financing arrangements are addressed. Options such as marketing new products or closing plants might be evaluated.

Avoiding Surprises   Financial planning should identify what may happen to the firm if different events take place. In particular, it should address what actions the firm will take if things go seriously wrong or, more generally, if assumptions made today about the future are seriously in error. As physicist Niels Bohr once observed, "Prediction is very difficult, particularly when it concerns the future." Thus, one purpose of financial planning is to avoid surprises and develop contingency plans.

For example, in April 2008, Boeing announced that the delivery of its new 787 Dreamliner was running 15 months behind schedule. Additionally, the company said that it would deliver no more than 25 airplanes in 2009, down from a previous estimate of 109. The reason for the delay was not lack of demand (Boeing had orders for more than 900 of the jets), but rather shortages of numerous parts and other bottlenecks. Thus, a lack of planning for sales growth can be a problem for even the biggest companies.

Ensuring Feasibility and Internal Consistency   Beyond a general goal of creating value, a firm will normally have many specific goals. Such goals might be couched in terms of market share, return on equity, financial leverage, and so on. At times, the linkages between different goals and different aspects of a firm's business are difficult to see. Not only does a financial plan make explicit these linkages, but it also imposes a unified structure for reconciling goals and objectives. In other words, financial planning is a way of verifying that the goals and plans made for specific areas of a firm's operations are feasible and internally consistent. Conflicting goals will often exist. To generate a coherent plan, goals and objectives will therefore have to be modified, and priorities will have to be established.

For example, one goal a firm might have is 12 percent growth in unit sales per year. Another goal might be to reduce the firm's total debt ratio from 40 to 20 percent. Are these two goals compatible? Can they be accomplished simultaneously? Maybe yes, maybe no. As we will discuss, financial planning is a way of finding out just what is possible—and, by implication, what is not possible.

Conclusion   Probably the most important result of the planning process is that it forces managers to think about goals and establish priorities. In fact, conventional business wisdom holds that financial plans don't work, but financial planning does. The future is inherently unknown. What we can do is establish the direction in which we want to travel and make some educated guesses about what we will find along the way. If we do a good job, we won't be caught off guard when the future rolls around.

Concept Questions

4.1a What are the two dimensions of the financial planning process?

4.1b Why should firms draw up financial plans?

Financial Planning Models: A First Look

4.2

Just as companies differ in size and products, the financial planning process will differ from firm to firm. In this section, we discuss some common elements in financial plans and develop a basic model to illustrate these elements. What follows is just a quick overview; later sections will take up the various topics in more detail.

A FINANCIAL PLANNING MODEL: THE INGREDIENTS

Most financial planning models require the user to specify some assumptions about the future. Based on those assumptions, the model generates predicted values for many other variables. Models can vary quite a bit in complexity, but almost all have the elements we discuss next.

Sales Forecast   Almost all financial plans require an externally supplied sales forecast. In our models that follow, for example, the sales forecast will be the "driver," meaning that the user of the planning model will supply this value, and most other values will be calculated based on it. This arrangement is common for many types of business; planning will focus on projected future sales and the assets and financing needed to support those sales.

Frequently, the sales forecast will be given as the growth rate in sales rather than as an explicit sales figure. These two approaches are essentially the same because we can calculate projected sales once we know the growth rate. Perfect sales forecasts are not possible, of course, because sales depend on the uncertain future state of the economy. To help a firm come up with its projections, some businesses specialize in macroeconomic and industry projections.

As we discussed previously, we frequently will be interested in evaluating alternative scenarios, so it isn't necessarily crucial that the sales forecast be accurate. In such cases, our goal is to examine the interplay between investment and financing needs at different possible sales levels, not to pinpoint what we expect to happen.

Pro Forma Statements   A financial plan will have a forecast balance sheet, income statement, and statement of cash flows. These are called *pro forma statements*, or *pro formas* for short. The phrase *pro forma* literally means "as a matter of form." In our case, this means the financial statements are the form we use to summarize the different events projected for the future. At a minimum, a financial planning model will generate these statements based on projections of key items such as sales.

Spreadsheets to use for pro forma statements can be obtained at www.jaxworks.com.

In the planning models we will describe, the pro formas are the output from the financial planning model. The user will supply a sales figure, and the model will generate the resulting income statement and balance sheet.

Asset Requirements   The plan will describe projected capital spending. At a minimum, the projected balance sheet will contain changes in total fixed assets and net working capital. These changes are effectively the firm's total capital budget. Proposed capital spending in different areas must thus be reconciled with the overall increases contained in the long-range plan.

Financial Requirements   The plan will include a section about the necessary financing arrangements. This part of the plan should discuss dividend policy and debt policy. Sometimes firms will expect to raise cash by selling new shares of stock or by borrowing. In this case, the plan will have to consider what kinds of securities have to be sold and what methods of issuance are most appropriate. These are subjects we consider in Part 6 of our book, where we discuss long-term financing, capital structure, and dividend policy.

The Plug   After the firm has a sales forecast and an estimate of the required spending on assets, some amount of new financing will often be necessary because projected total assets will exceed projected total liabilities and equity. In other words, the balance sheet will no longer balance.

Because new financing may be necessary to cover all of the projected capital spending, a financial "plug" variable must be selected. The plug is the designated source or sources of external financing needed to deal with any shortfall (or surplus) in financing and thereby bring the balance sheet into balance.

For example, a firm with a great number of investment opportunities and limited cash flow may have to raise new equity. Other firms with few growth opportunities and ample cash flow will have a surplus and thus might pay an extra dividend. In the first case, external equity is the plug variable. In the second, the dividend is used.

Economic Assumptions   The plan will have to state explicitly the economic environment in which the firm expects to reside over the life of the plan. Among the more important economic assumptions that will have to be made are the level of interest rates and the firm's tax rate.

A SIMPLE FINANCIAL PLANNING MODEL

We can begin our discussion of long-term planning models with a relatively simple example. The Computerfield Corporation's financial statements from the most recent year are as follows:

COMPUTERFIELD CORPORATION Financial Statements					
Income Statement			**Balance Sheet**		
Sales	$1,000	Assets	$500	Debt	$250
Costs	800			Equity	250
Net income	$ 200	Total	$500	Total	$500

Unless otherwise stated, the financial planners at Computerfield assume that all variables are tied directly to sales and current relationships are optimal. This means that all items will grow at exactly the same rate as sales. This is obviously oversimplified; we use this assumption only to make a point.

Suppose sales increase by 20 percent, rising from $1,000 to $1,200. Planners would then also forecast a 20 percent increase in costs, from $800 to $800 × 1.2 = $960. The pro forma income statement would thus be:

Pro Forma Income Statement	
Sales	$1,200
Costs	960
Net income	$ 240

The assumption that all variables will grow by 20 percent lets us easily construct the pro forma balance sheet as well:

Pro Forma Balance Sheet			
Assets	$600 (+100)	Debt	$ 300 (+ 50)
		Equity	300 (+ 50)
Total	$600 (+100)	Total	$600 (+100)

Notice that we have simply increased every item by 20 percent. The numbers in parentheses are the dollar changes for the different items.

Now we have to reconcile these two pro formas. How, for example, can net income be equal to $240 and equity increase by only $50? The answer is that Computerfield must have paid out the difference of $240 – 50 = $190, possibly as a cash dividend. In this case, dividends are the plug variable.

Suppose Computerfield does not pay out the $190. In this case, the addition to retained earnings is the full $240. Computerfield's equity will thus grow to $250 (the starting amount) plus $240 (net income), or $490, and debt must be retired to keep total assets equal to $600.

With $600 in total assets and $490 in equity, debt will have to be $600 – 490 = $110. Because we started with $250 in debt, Computerfield will have to retire $250 – 110 = $140 in debt. The resulting pro forma balance sheet would look like this:

Planware provides insight into cash flow forecasting (www.planware.org).

Pro Forma Balance Sheet			
Assets	$600 (+100)	Debt	$110 (−140)
		Equity	490 (+240)
Total	$600 (+100)	Total	$600 (+100)

In this case, debt is the plug variable used to balance projected total assets and liabilities.

This example shows the interaction between sales growth and financial policy. As sales increase, so do total assets. This occurs because the firm must invest in net working capital and fixed assets to support higher sales levels. Because assets are growing, total liabilities and equity (the right side of the balance sheet) will grow as well.

The thing to notice from our simple example is that the way the liabilities and owners' equity change depends on the firm's financing policy and its dividend policy. The growth in assets requires that the firm decide on how to finance that growth. This is strictly a managerial decision. Note that in our example, the firm needed no outside funds. This won't usually be the case, so we explore a more detailed situation in the next section.

Concept Questions

4.2a What are the basic components of a financial plan?

4.2b Why is it necessary to designate a plug in a financial planning model?

4.3 The Percentage of Sales Approach

In the previous section, we described a simple planning model in which every item increased at the same rate as sales. This may be a reasonable assumption for some elements. For others, such as long-term borrowing, it probably is not: The amount of long-term borrowing is something set by management, and it does not necessarily relate directly to the level of sales.

In this section, we describe an extended version of our simple model. The basic idea is to separate the income statement and balance sheet accounts into two groups—those that vary directly with sales and those that do not. Given a sales forecast, we will then be able to calculate how much financing the firm will need to support the predicted sales level.

percentage of sales approach
A financial planning method in which accounts are varied depending on a firm's predicted sales level.

The financial planning model we describe next is based on the **percentage of sales approach**. Our goal here is to develop a quick and practical way of generating pro forma statements. We defer discussion of some "bells and whistles" to a later section.

THE INCOME STATEMENT

We start out with the most recent income statement for the Rosengarten Corporation, as that shown in Table 4.1. Notice we have still simplified things by including costs, depreciation, and interest in a single cost figure.

Rosengarten has projected a 25 percent increase in sales for the coming year, so we are anticipating sales of $1,000 × 1.25 = $1,250. To generate a pro forma income statement, we assume that total costs will continue to run at $800/1,000 = 80% of sales. With this assumption, Rosengarten's pro forma income statement is shown in Table 4.2. The effect here of assuming that costs are a constant percentage of sales is to assume that the profit margin is constant. To check this, notice that the profit margin was $132/1,000 = 13.2%. In our pro forma, the profit margin is $165/1,250 = 13.2%; so it is unchanged.

dividend payout ratio
The amount of cash paid out to shareholders divided by net income.

Next, we need to project the dividend payment. This amount is up to Rosengarten's management. We will assume Rosengarten has a policy of paying out a constant fraction of net income in the form of a cash dividend. For the most recent year, the **dividend payout**

TABLE 4.1

ROSENGARTEN CORPORATION Income Statement	
Sales	$1,000
Costs	800
Taxable income	$ 200
Taxes (34%)	68
Net income	$ 132
Dividends	$44
Addition to retained earnings	88

TABLE 4.2

ROSENGARTEN CORPORATION Pro Forma Income Statement	
Sales (projected)	$1,250
Costs (80% of sales)	1,000
Taxable income	$ 250
Taxes (34%)	85
Net income	$ 165

ratio was this:

$$\text{Dividend payout ratio} = \text{Cash dividends/Net income} \qquad [4.1]$$
$$= \$44/132 = 33\ 1/3\%$$

We can also calculate the ratio of the addition to retained earnings to net income:

$$\text{Addition to retained earnings/Net income} = \$88/132 = 66\ 2/3\%$$

This ratio is called the **retention ratio** or **plowback ratio**, and it is equal to 1 minus the dividend payout ratio because everything not paid out is retained. Assuming that the payout ratio is constant, here are the projected dividends and addition to retained earnings:

Projected dividends paid to shareholders	$= \$165 \times 1/3 = \$\ 55$
Projected addition to retained earnings	$= \$165 \times 2/3 = \underline{\ \ 110}$
	$\underline{\$165}$

retention ratio
The addition to retained earnings divided by net income. Also called the *plowback ratio*.

THE BALANCE SHEET

To generate a pro forma balance sheet, we start with the most recent statement, as shown in Table 4.3.

On our balance sheet, we assume that some items vary directly with sales and others do not. For items that vary with sales, we express each as a percentage of sales for the year just completed. When an item does not vary directly with sales, we write "n/a" for "not applicable."

For example, on the asset side, inventory is equal to 60 percent of sales ($= \$600/1,000$) for the year just ended. We assume this percentage applies to the coming year, so for each $1 increase in sales, inventory will rise by $.60. More generally, the ratio of total assets to sales for the year just ended is $\$3,000/1,000 = 3$, or 300%.

This ratio of total assets to sales is sometimes called the **capital intensity ratio**. It tells us the amount of assets needed to generate $1 in sales; so the higher the ratio is, the more capital-intensive is the firm. Notice also that this ratio is just the reciprocal of the total asset turnover ratio we defined in the last chapter.

capital intensity ratio
A firm's total assets divided by its sales, or the amount of assets needed to generate $1 in sales.

TABLE 4.3

<table>
<tr><td colspan="6" align="center">ROSENGARTEN CORPORATION
Balance Sheet</td></tr>
<tr><td colspan="3" align="center">Assets</td><td colspan="3" align="center">Liabilities and Owners' Equity</td></tr>
<tr><td></td><td>$</td><td>Percentage of Sales</td><td></td><td>$</td><td>Percentage of Sales</td></tr>
<tr><td>Current assets</td><td></td><td></td><td>Current liabilities</td><td></td><td></td></tr>
<tr><td>Cash</td><td>$ 160</td><td>16%</td><td>Accounts payable</td><td>$ 300</td><td>30%</td></tr>
<tr><td>Accounts receivable</td><td>440</td><td>44</td><td>Notes payable</td><td>100</td><td>n/a</td></tr>
<tr><td>Inventory</td><td>600</td><td>60</td><td>Total</td><td>$ 400</td><td>n/a</td></tr>
<tr><td>Total</td><td>$1,200</td><td>120</td><td>Long-term debt</td><td>$ 800</td><td>n/a</td></tr>
<tr><td>Fixed assets</td><td></td><td></td><td>Owners' equity</td><td></td><td></td></tr>
<tr><td>Net plant and equipment</td><td>$1,800</td><td>180</td><td>Common stock and paid-in</td><td></td><td></td></tr>
<tr><td></td><td></td><td></td><td>surplus</td><td>$ 800</td><td>n/a</td></tr>
<tr><td></td><td></td><td></td><td>Retained earnings</td><td>1,000</td><td>n/a</td></tr>
<tr><td></td><td></td><td></td><td>Total</td><td>$1,800</td><td>n/a</td></tr>
<tr><td>Total assets</td><td>$3,000</td><td>300%</td><td>Total liabilities and owners' equity</td><td>$3,000</td><td>n/a</td></tr>
</table>

For Rosengarten, assuming that this ratio is constant, it takes $3 in total assets to generate $1 in sales (apparently Rosengarten is in a relatively capital-intensive business). Therefore, if sales are to increase by $100, Rosengarten will have to increase total assets by three times this amount, or $300.

On the liability side of the balance sheet, we show accounts payable varying with sales. The reason is that we expect to place more orders with our suppliers as sales volume increases, so payables will change "spontaneously" with sales. Notes payable, on the other hand, represent short-term debt such as bank borrowing. This item will not vary unless we take specific actions to change the amount, so we mark it as "n/a."

Similarly, we use "n/a" for long-term debt because it won't automatically change with sales. The same is true for common stock and paid-in surplus. The last item on the right side, retained earnings, will vary with sales, but it won't be a simple percentage of sales. Instead, we will explicitly calculate the change in retained earnings based on our projected net income and dividends.

We can now construct a partial pro forma balance sheet for Rosengarten. We do this by using the percentages we have just calculated wherever possible to calculate the projected amounts. For example, net fixed assets are 180 percent of sales; so, with a new sales level of $1,250, the net fixed asset amount will be $1.80 \times \$1,250 = \$2,250$, representing an increase of $2,250 - 1,800 = \$450$ in plant and equipment. It is important to note that for items that don't vary directly with sales, we initially assume no change and simply write in the original amounts. The result is shown in Table 4.4. Notice that the change in retained earnings is equal to the $110 addition to retained earnings we calculated earlier.

Inspecting our pro forma balance sheet, we notice that assets are projected to increase by $750. However, without additional financing, liabilities and equity will increase by only $185, leaving a shortfall of $750 - 185 = \$565$. We label this amount *external financing needed* (EFN).

TABLE 4.4

ROSENGARTEN CORPORATION Partial Pro Forma Balance Sheet					
Assets			**Liabilities and Owners' Equity**		
	Projected	**Change from Previous Year**		**Projected**	**Change from Previous Year**
Current assets			Current liabilities		
Cash	$ 200	$ 40	Accounts payable	$ 375	$ 75
Accounts receivable	550	110	Notes payable	100	0
Inventory	750	150	Total	$ 475	$ 75
Total	$1,500	$300	Long-term debt	$ 800	$ 0
Fixed assets					
Net plant and equipment	$2,250	$450	Owners' equity		
			Common stock and paid-in surplus	$ 800	$ 0
			Retained earnings	1,110	110
			Total	$1,910	$110
Total assets	$3,750	$750	Total liabilities and owners' equity	$3,185	$185
			External financing needed	$ 565	$565

A PARTICULAR SCENARIO

Our financial planning model now reminds us of one of those good news–bad news jokes. The good news is we're projecting a 25 percent increase in sales. The bad news is that this isn't going to happen unless Rosengarten can somehow raise $565 in new financing.

This is a good example of how the planning process can point out problems and potential conflicts. If, for example, Rosengarten has a goal of not borrowing any additional funds and not selling any new equity, then a 25 percent increase in sales is probably not feasible.

If we take the need for $565 in new financing as given, we know that Rosengarten has three possible sources: short-term borrowing, long-term borrowing, and new equity. The choice of some combination among these three is up to management; we will illustrate only one of the many possibilities.

Suppose Rosengarten decides to borrow the needed funds. In this case, the firm might choose to borrow some over the short term and some over the long term. For example, current assets increased by $300 whereas current liabilities rose by only $75. Rosengarten could borrow $300 − 75 = $225 in short-term notes payable and leave total net working capital unchanged. With $565 needed, the remaining $565 − 225 = $340 would have to come from long-term debt. Table 4.5 shows the completed pro forma balance sheet for Rosengarten.

We have used a combination of short- and long-term debt as the plug here, but we emphasize that this is just one possible strategy; it is not necessarily the best one by any means. There are many other scenarios we could (and should) investigate. The various ratios we discussed in Chapter 3 come in handy here. For example, with the scenario we have just examined, we would surely want to examine the current ratio and the total debt ratio to see if we were comfortable with the new projected debt levels.

Now that we have finished our balance sheet, we have all of the projected sources and uses of cash. We could finish off our pro formas by drawing up the projected statement of cash flows along the lines discussed in Chapter 3. We will leave this as an exercise and instead investigate an important alternative scenario.

TABLE 4.5

ROSENGARTEN CORPORATION Pro Forma Balance Sheet					
Assets			**Liabilities and Owners' Equity**		
	Projected	Change from Previous Year		Projected	Change from Previous Year
Current assets			Current liabilities		
Cash	$ 200	$ 40	Accounts payable	$ 375	$ 75
Accounts receivable	550	110	Notes payable	325	225
Inventory	750	150	Total	$ 700	$300
Total	$1,500	$300	Long-term debt	$1,140	$340
Fixed assets					
Net plant and equipment	$2,250	$450	Owners' equity		
			Common stock and paid-in surplus	$ 800	$ 0
			Retained earnings	1,110	110
			Total	$1,910	$110
Total assets	$3,750	$750	Total liabilities and owners' equity	$3,750	$750

AN ALTERNATIVE SCENARIO

The assumption that assets are a fixed percentage of sales is convenient, but it may not be suitable in many cases. In particular, note that we effectively assumed that Rosengarten was using its fixed assets at 100 percent of capacity because any increase in sales led to an increase in fixed assets. For most businesses, there would be some slack or excess capacity, and production could be increased by perhaps running an extra shift. According to the Federal Reserve, the overall capacity utilization for U.S. industrial companies in April 2007 was 81.6 percent, up from a low of 73.9 percent in 2001.

For example, in 2007, Toyota Motor announced it would build its seventh manufacturing plant in North America in Mississippi. At about the same time, Ford announced it would close up to 12 plants over the next five years, and General Motors announced that it would close up to 13 plants over the same period. Evidently, both Ford and General Motors had excess capacity, whereas Toyota did not.

In another example, in early 2004, Simmons announced it was closing its mattress factory in Ohio. The company stated it would increase mattress production at other plants to compensate for the closing. Apparently, Simmons had significant excess capacity in its production facilities.

If we assume that Rosengarten is operating at only 70 percent of capacity, then the need for external funds will be quite different. When we say "70 percent of capacity," we mean that the current sales level is 70 percent of the full-capacity sales level:

Current sales = $1,000 = .70 × Full-capacity sales

Full-capacity sales = $1,000/.70 = $1,429

This tells us that sales could increase by almost 43 percent—from $1,000 to $1,429—before any new fixed assets would be needed.

In our previous scenario, we assumed it would be necessary to add $450 in net fixed assets. In the current scenario, no spending on net fixed assets is needed because sales are projected to rise only to $1,250, which is substantially less than the $1,429 full-capacity level.

As a result, our original estimate of $565 in external funds needed is too high. We estimated that $450 in net new fixed assets would be needed. Instead, no spending on new net fixed assets is necessary. Thus, if we are currently operating at 70 percent capacity, we need only $565 − 450 = $115 in external funds. The excess capacity thus makes a considerable difference in our projections.

EXAMPLE 4.1	**EFN and Capacity Usage**

Suppose Rosengarten is operating at 90 percent capacity. What would sales be at full capacity? What is the capital intensity ratio at full capacity? What is EFN in this case?

Full-capacity sales would be $1,000/.90 = $1,111. From Table 4.3, we know that fixed assets are $1,800. At full capacity, the ratio of fixed assets to sales is this:

Fixed assets/Full-capacity sales = $1,800/1,111 = 1.62

So, Rosengarten needs $1.62 in fixed assets for every $1 in sales once it reaches full capacity. At the projected sales level of $1,250, then, it needs $1,250 × 1.62 = $2,025 in fixed assets. Compared to the $2,250 we originally projected, this is $225 less, so EFN is $565 − 225 = $340.

Current assets would still be $1,500, so total assets would be $1,500 + 2,025 = $3,525. The capital intensity ratio would thus be $3,525/1,250 = 2.82, which is less than our original value of 3 because of the excess capacity.

These alternative scenarios illustrate that it is inappropriate to blindly manipulate financial statement information in the planning process. The results depend critically on the assumptions made about the relationships between sales and asset needs. We return to this point a little later.

One thing should be clear by now. Projected growth rates play an important role in the planning process. They are also important to outside analysts and potential investors. Our nearby *Work the Web* box shows you how to obtain growth rate estimates for real companies.

Concept Questions

4.3a What is the basic idea behind the percentage of sales approach?

4.3b Unless it is modified, what does the percentage of sales approach assume about fixed asset capacity usage?

External Financing and Growth   4.4

External financing needed and growth are obviously related. All other things staying the same, the higher the rate of growth in sales or assets, the greater will be the need for external financing. In the previous section, we took a growth rate as given, and then we determined the amount of external financing needed to support that growth. In this section, we turn things around a bit. We will take the firm's financial policy as given and then examine the relationship between that financial policy and the firm's ability to finance new investments and thereby grow.

Once again, we emphasize that we are focusing on growth not because growth is an appropriate goal; instead, for our purposes, growth is simply a convenient means of examining the interactions between investment and financing decisions. In effect, we assume that the use of growth as a basis for planning is just a reflection of the very high level of aggregation used in the planning process.

EFN AND GROWTH

The first thing we need to do is establish the relationship between EFN and growth. To do this, we introduce the simplified income statement and balance sheet for the Hoffman Company in Table 4.6. Notice that we have simplified the balance sheet by combining short-term and long-term debt into a single total debt figure. Effectively, we are assuming that none of the current liabilities varies spontaneously with sales. This assumption isn't as restrictive as it sounds. If any current liabilities (such as accounts payable) vary with sales, we can assume that any such accounts have been netted out in current assets. Also, we continue to combine depreciation, interest, and costs on the income statement.

Suppose the Hoffman Company is forecasting next year's sales level at $600, a $100 increase. Notice that the percentage increase in sales is $100/500 = 20%. Using the percentage of sales approach and the figures in Table 4.6, we can prepare a pro forma income statement and balance sheet as in Table 4.7. As Table 4.7 illustrates, at a 20 percent growth rate, Hoffman needs $100 in new assets (assuming full capacity). The projected addition to retained earnings is $52.8, so the external financing needed (EFN) is $100 − 52.8 = $47.2.

Notice that the debt–equity ratio for Hoffman was originally (from Table 4.6) equal to $250/250 = 1.0. We will assume that the Hoffman Company does not wish to sell new

TABLE 4.6

HOFFMAN COMPANY Income Statement and Balance Sheet				
Income Statement				
Sales		$500		
Costs		400		
Taxable income		$100		
Taxes (34%)		34		
Net income		$ 66		
Dividends	$22			
Addition to retained earnings	44			
Balance Sheet				
Assets			**Liabilities and Owners' Equity**	
	$	Percentage of Sales	$	Percentage of Sales
Current assets	$200	40%	Total debt	$250	n/a
Net fixed assets	300	60	Owners' equity	250	n/a
Total assets	$500	100%	Total liabilities and owners' equity	$500	n/a

TABLE 4.7

HOFFMAN COMPANY Pro Forma Income Statement and Balance Sheet				
Income Statement				
Sales (projected)		$600.0		
Costs (80% of sales)		480.0		
Taxable income		$120.0		
Taxes (34%)		40.8		
Net income		$ 79.2		
Dividends	$26.4			
Addition to retained earnings	52.8			
Balance Sheet				
Assets			**Liabilities and Owners' Equity**	
	$	Percentage of Sales	$	Percentage of Sales
Current assets	$240.0	40%	Total debt	$250.0	n/a
Net fixed assets	360.0	60	Owners' equity	302.8	n/a
Total assets	$600.0	100%	Total liabilities and owners' equity	$552.8	n/a
			External financing needed	$ 47.2	n/a

equity. In this case, the $47.2 in EFN will have to be borrowed. What will the new debt–equity ratio be? From Table 4.7, we know that total owners' equity is projected at $302.8. The new total debt will be the original $250 plus $47.2 in new borrowing, or $297.2 total. The debt–equity ratio thus falls slightly from 1.0 to $297.2/302.8 = .98.

WORK THE WEB

Calculating company growth rates can involve detailed research, and a major part of a stock analyst's job is to estimate them. One place to find earnings and sales growth rates on the Web is Yahoo! Finance at finance.yahoo. com. We pulled up a quote for 3M Corporation and followed the "Analyst Estimates" link. Here is an abbreviated look at the results:

Revenue Est	Current Qtr Mar-08	Next Qtr Jun-08	Current Year Dec-08	Next Year Dec-09
Avg. Estimate	6.34B	6.63B	26.42B	28.05B
No. of Analysts	7	6	9	9
Low Estimate	6.10B	6.53B	26.01B	27.27B
High Estimate	6.52B	6.73B	26.86B	28.64B
Year Ago Sales	5.94B	6.14B	24.46B	26.42B
Sales Growth (year/est)	6.8%	8.0%	8.0%	6.2%

As shown, analysts expect, on average, revenue (sales) of $26.42 billion in 2008, growing to $28.05 billion in 2009, an increase of 6.2 percent. We also have the following table comparing MMM to some benchmarks:

Growth Est	MMM	Industry	Sector	S&P 500
Current Qtr.	5.5%	4.9%	8.9%	-4.7%
Next Qtr.	10.6%	10.6%	11.6%	15.8%
This Year	9.6%	4.1%	9.4%	10.7%
Next Year	9.9%	12.9%	14.7%	17.2%
Past 5 Years (per annum)	12.597%	N/A	N/A	N/A
Next 5 Years (per annum)	11.3%	12.31%	13.24%	N/A
Price/Earnings (avg. for comparison categories)	15.18	14.91	15.61	14.72
PEG Ratio (avg. for comparison categories)	1.34	1.21	1.18	N/A

As you can see, the estimated earnings growth rate for MMM is lower than the industry growth rate over the next five years. What does this mean for MMM stock? We'll get to that in a later chapter.

Questions

1. One of the things shown here is the projected sales growth for MMM during 2009 at the time this was captured from finance-yahoo.com. How does the current sales projection or the actual sales number differ from this projection? Can you think of any reasons for the difference?
2. On the same Web page, you can find the earnings history for MMM. How close have analysts been to estimating MMM earnings? In other words, what has the "surprise" been in MMM earnings?

TABLE 4.8

Growth and Projected EFN for the Hoffman Company

Projected Sales Growth	Increase in Assets Required	Addition to Retained Earnings	External Financing Needed, EFN	Projected Debt–Equity Ratio
0%	$ 0	$44.0	−$44.0	.70
5	25	46.2	−21.2	.77
10	50	48.4	1.6	.84
15	75	50.6	24.4	.91
20	100	52.8	47.2	.98
25	125	55.0	70.0	1.05

Table 4.8 shows EFN for several different growth rates. The projected addition to retained earnings and the projected debt–equity ratio for each scenario are also given (you should probably calculate a few of these for practice). In determining the debt–equity ratios, we assumed that any needed funds were borrowed, and we also assumed any surplus funds were used to pay off debt. Thus, for the zero growth case, debt falls by $44, from $250 to $206. In Table 4.8, notice that the increase in assets required is simply equal to the original assets of $500 multiplied by the growth rate. Similarly, the addition to retained earnings is equal to the original $44 plus $44 times the growth rate.

Table 4.8 shows that for relatively low growth rates, Hoffman will run a surplus, and its debt–equity ratio will decline. Once the growth rate increases to about 10 percent, however, the surplus becomes a deficit. Furthermore, as the growth rate exceeds approximately 20 percent, the debt–equity ratio passes its original value of 1.0.

Figure 4.1 illustrates the connection between growth in sales and external financing needed in more detail by plotting asset needs and additions to retained earnings from Table 4.8 against the growth rates. As shown, the need for new assets grows at a much faster rate than the addition to retained earnings, so the internal financing provided by the addition to retained earnings rapidly disappears.

FIGURE 4.1

Growth and Related Financing Needed for the Hoffman Company

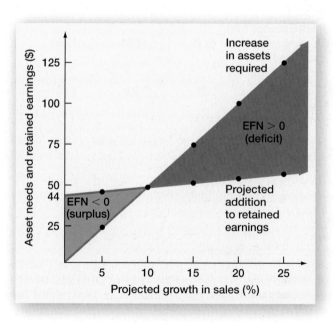

As this discussion shows, whether a firm runs a cash surplus or deficit depends on growth. Microsoft is a good example. Its revenue growth in the 1990s was amazing, averaging well over 30 percent per year for the decade. Growth slowed down noticeably over the 2000–2008 period; but nonetheless, Microsoft's combination of growth and substantial profit margins led to enormous cash surpluses. In part because Microsoft pays a relatively small dividend, the cash really piled up; in 2008, Microsoft's cash horde exceeded $22 billion.

FINANCIAL POLICY AND GROWTH

Based on our preceding discussion, we see that there is a direct link between growth and external financing. In this section, we discuss two growth rates that are particularly useful in long-range planning.

The Internal Growth Rate The first growth rate of interest is the maximum growth rate that can be achieved with no external financing of any kind. We will call this the **internal growth rate** because this is the rate the firm can maintain with internal financing only. In Figure 4.1, this internal growth rate is represented by the point where the two lines cross. At this point, the required increase in assets is exactly equal to the addition to retained earnings, and EFN is therefore zero. We have seen that this happens when the growth rate is slightly less than 10 percent. With a little algebra (see Problem 32 at the end of the chapter), we can define this growth rate more precisely:

internal growth rate
The maximum growth rate a firm can achieve without external financing of any kind.

$$\text{Internal growth rate} = \frac{\text{ROA} \times b}{1 - \text{ROA} \times b} \qquad [4.2]$$

Here, ROA is the return on assets we discussed in Chapter 3, and b is the plowback, or retention, ratio defined earlier in this chapter.

For the Hoffman Company, net income was $66 and total assets were $500. ROA is thus $66/500 = 13.2\%$. Of the $66 net income, $44 was retained, so the plowback ratio, b, is $44/66 = 2/3$. With these numbers, we can calculate the internal growth rate:

$$\begin{aligned}
\text{Internal growth rate} &= \frac{\text{ROA} \times b}{1 - \text{ROA} \times b} \\
&= \frac{.132 \times (2/3)}{1 - .132 \times (2/3)} \\
&= 9.65\%
\end{aligned}$$

Thus, the Hoffman Company can expand at a maximum rate of 9.65 percent per year without external financing.

The Sustainable Growth Rate We have seen that if the Hoffman Company wishes to grow more rapidly than at a rate of 9.65 percent per year, external financing must be arranged. The second growth rate of interest is the maximum growth rate a firm can achieve with no external *equity* financing while it maintains a constant debt–equity ratio. This rate is commonly called the **sustainable growth rate** because it is the maximum rate of growth a firm can maintain without increasing its financial leverage.

sustainable growth rate
The maximum growth rate a firm can achieve without external equity financing while maintaining a constant debt–equity ratio.

There are various reasons why a firm might wish to avoid equity sales. For example, as we discuss in Chapter 15, new equity sales can be expensive. Alternatively, the current owners may not wish to bring in new owners or contribute additional equity. Why a firm might view a particular debt–equity ratio as optimal is discussed in Chapters 14 and 16; for now, we will take it as given.

Based on Table 4.8, the sustainable growth rate for Hoffman is approximately 20 percent because the debt–equity ratio is near 1.0 at that growth rate. The precise value can be calculated (see Problem 32 at the end of the chapter):

$$\text{Sustainable growth rate} = \frac{\text{ROE} \times b}{1 - \text{ROE} \times b} \qquad [4.3]$$

This is identical to the internal growth rate except that ROE, return on equity, is used instead of ROA.

For the Hoffman Company, net income was $66 and total equity was $250; ROE is thus $66/250 = 26.4$ percent. The plowback ratio, b, is still 2/3, so we can calculate the sustainable growth rate as follows:

$$
\begin{aligned}
\text{Sustainable growth rate} &= \frac{\text{ROE} \times b}{1 - \text{ROE} \times b} \\
&= \frac{.264 \times (2/3)}{1 - .264 \times (2/3)} \\
&= 21.36\%
\end{aligned}
$$

Thus, the Hoffman Company can expand at a maximum rate of 21.36 percent per year without external equity financing.

EXAMPLE 4.2	Sustainable Growth

Suppose Hoffman grows at exactly the sustainable growth rate of 21.36 percent. What will the pro forma statements look like?

At a 21.36 percent growth rate, sales will rise from $500 to $606.8. The pro forma income statement will look like this:

HOFFMAN COMPANY Pro Forma Income Statement	
Sales (projected)	$606.8
Costs (80% of sales)	485.4
Taxable income	$121.4
Taxes (34%)	41.3
Net income	$ 80.1
Dividends	$26.7
Addition to retained earnings	53.4

We construct the balance sheet just as we did before. Notice, in this case, that owners' equity will rise from $250 to $303.4 because the addition to retained earnings is $53.4.

HOFFMAN COMPANY Pro Forma Balance Sheet					
Assets			**Liabilities and Owners' Equity**		
	$	**Percentage of Sales**		**$**	**Percentage of Sales**
Current assets	$242.7	40%	Total debt	$250.0	n/a
Net fixed assets	364.1	60	Owners' equity	303.4	n/a
Total assets	$606.8	100%	Total liabilities and owners' equity	$553.4	n/a
			External financing needed	$ 53.4	n/a

As illustrated, EFN is $53.4. If Hoffman borrows this amount, then total debt will rise to $303.4, and the debt–equity ratio will be exactly 1.0, which verifies our earlier calculation. At any other growth rate, something would have to change.

Determinants of Growth   In the last chapter, we saw that the return on equity, ROE, could be decomposed into its various components using the Du Pont identity. Because ROE appears so prominently in the determination of the sustainable growth rate, it is obvious that the factors important in determining ROE are also important determinants of growth.

From Chapter 3, we know that ROE can be written as the product of three factors:

ROE = Profit margin × Total asset turnover × Equity multiplier

If we examine our expression for the sustainable growth rate, we see that anything that increases ROE will increase the sustainable growth rate by making the top bigger and the bottom smaller. Increasing the plowback ratio will have the same effect.

Putting it all together, what we have is that a firm's ability to sustain growth depends explicitly on the following four factors:

1. *Profit margin*: An increase in profit margin will increase the firm's ability to generate funds internally and thereby increase its sustainable growth.
2. *Dividend policy*: A decrease in the percentage of net income paid out as dividends will increase the retention ratio. This increases internally generated equity and thus increases sustainable growth.
3. *Financial policy*: An increase in the debt–equity ratio increases the firm's financial leverage. Because this makes additional debt financing available, it increases the sustainable growth rate.
4. *Total asset turnover*: An increase in the firm's total asset turnover increases the sales generated for each dollar in assets. This decreases the firm's need for new assets as sales grow and thereby increases the sustainable growth rate. Notice that increasing total asset turnover is the same thing as decreasing capital intensity.

The sustainable growth rate is a very useful planning number. What it illustrates is the explicit relationship between the firm's four major areas of concern: its operating efficiency as measured by profit margin, its asset use efficiency as measured by total asset turnover, its dividend policy as measured by the retention ratio, and its financial policy as measured by the debt–equity ratio.

Given values for all four of these, there is only one growth rate that can be achieved. This is an important point, so it bears restating:

> **If a firm does not wish to sell new equity and its profit margin, dividend policy, financial policy, and total asset turnover (or capital intensity) are all fixed, then there is only one possible growth rate.**

As we described early in this chapter, one of the primary benefits of financial planning is that it ensures internal consistency among the firm's various goals. The concept of the sustainable growth rate captures this element nicely. Also, we now see how a financial planning model can be used to test the feasibility of a planned growth rate. If sales are to grow at a rate higher than the sustainable growth rate, the firm must increase profit margins, increase total asset turnover, increase financial leverage, increase earnings retention, or sell new shares.

The two growth rates, internal and sustainable, are summarized in Table 4.9.

TABLE 4.9

Summary of Internal and Sustainable Growth Rates

I.   Internal Growth Rate

$$\text{Internal growth rate} = \frac{\text{ROA} \times b}{1 - \text{ROA} \times b}$$

where

   ROA = Return on assets = Net income/Total assets

   b = Plowback (retention) ratio

   = Addition to retained earnings/Net income

The internal growth rate is the maximum growth rate that can be achieved with no external financing of any kind.

II.   Sustainable Growth Rate

$$\text{Sustainable growth rate} = \frac{\text{ROE} \times b}{1 - \text{ROE} \times b}$$

where

   ROE = Return on equity = Net income/Total equity

   b = Plowback (retention) ratio

   = Addition to retained earnings/Net income

The sustainable growth rate is the maximum growth rate that can be achieved with no external equity financing while maintaining a constant debt–equity ratio.

A NOTE ABOUT SUSTAINABLE GROWTH RATE CALCULATIONS

Very commonly, the sustainable growth rate is calculated using just the numerator in our expression, ROE $\times$ b. This causes some confusion, which we can clear up here. The issue has to do with how ROE is computed. Recall that ROE is calculated as net income divided by total equity. If total equity is taken from an ending balance sheet (as we have done consistently, and is commonly done in practice), then our formula is the right one. However, if total equity is from the beginning of the period, then the simpler formula is the correct one.

In principle, you'll get exactly the same sustainable growth rate regardless of which way you calculate it (as long as you match up the ROE calculation with the right formula). In reality, you may see some differences because of accounting-related complications. By the way, if you use the average of beginning and ending equity (as some advocate), yet another formula is needed. Also, all of our comments here apply to the internal growth rate as well.

A simple example is useful to illustrate these points. Suppose a firm has a net income of $20 and a retention ratio of .60. Beginning assets are $100. The debt–equity ratio is .25, so beginning equity is $80.

If we use beginning numbers, we get the following:

ROE = $20/80 = .25 = 25%

Sustainable growth = .60 $\times$ .25 = .15 = 15%

For the same firm, ending equity is $80 + .60 $\times$ $20 = $92. So, we can calculate this:

ROE = $20/92 = .2174 = 21.74%

Sustainable growth = .60 $\times$ .2174/(1 − .60 $\times$ .2174) = .15 = 15%

These growth rates are exactly the same (after accounting for a small rounding error in the second calculation). See if you don't agree that the internal growth rate is 12%.

Robert C. Higgins on Sustainable Growth

Most financial officers know intuitively that it takes money to make money. Rapid sales growth requires increased assets in the form of accounts receivable, inventory, and fixed plant, which, in turn, require money to pay for assets. They also know that if their company does not have the money when needed, it can literally "grow broke." The sustainable growth equation states these intuitive truths explicitly.

Sustainable growth is often used by bankers and other external analysts to assess a company's credit worthiness. They are aided in this exercise by several sophisticated computer software packages that provide detailed analyses of the company's past financial performance, including its annual sustainable growth rate.

Bankers use this information in several ways. Quick comparison of a company's actual growth rate to its sustainable rate tells the banker what issues will be at the top of management's financial agenda. If actual growth consistently exceeds sustainable growth, management's problem will be where to get the cash to finance growth. The banker thus can anticipate interest in loan products. Conversely, if sustainable growth consistently exceeds actual, the banker had best be prepared to talk about investment products, because management's problem will be what to do with all the cash that keeps piling up in the till.

Bankers also find the sustainable growth equation useful for explaining to financially inexperienced small business owners and overly optimistic entrepreneurs that, for the long-run viability of their business, it is necessary to keep growth and profitability in proper balance.

Finally, comparison of actual to sustainable growth rates helps a banker understand why a loan applicant needs money and for how long the need might continue. In one instance, a loan applicant requested $100,000 to pay off several insistent suppliers and promised to repay in a few months when he collected some accounts receivable that were coming due. A sustainable growth analysis revealed that the firm had been growing at four to six times its sustainable growth rate and that this pattern was likely to continue in the foreseeable future. This alerted the banker to the fact that impatient suppliers were only a symptom of the much more fundamental disease of overly rapid growth, and that a $100,000 loan would likely prove to be only the down payment on a much larger, multiyear commitment.

Robert C. Higgins is the Marguerite Reimers Professor of Finance at the Foster School of Business at the University of Washington. He pioneered the use of sustainable growth as a tool for financial analysis.

Profit Margins and Sustainable Growth	**EXAMPLE 4.3**

The Sandar Co. has a debt–equity ratio of .5, a profit margin of 3 percent, a dividend payout ratio of 40 percent, and a capital intensity ratio of 1. What is its sustainable growth rate? If Sandar desired a 10 percent sustainable growth rate and planned to achieve this goal by improving profit margins, what would you think?

ROE is $.03 \times 1 \times 1.5 = 4.5$ percent. The retention ratio is $1 - .40 = .60$. Sustainable growth is thus $.045(.60)/[1 - .045(.60)] = 2.77$ percent.

For the company to achieve a 10 percent growth rate, the profit margin will have to rise. To see this, assume that sustainable growth is equal to 10 percent and then solve for profit margin, PM:

$.10 = PM(1.5)(.6)/[1 - PM(1.5)(.6)]$

$PM = .1/.99 = 10.1\%$

For the plan to succeed, the necessary increase in profit margin is substantial, from 3 percent to about 10 percent. This may not be feasible.

Concept Questions

4.4a How is a firm's sustainable growth related to its accounting return on equity (ROE)?

4.4b What are the determinants of growth?

4.5 Some Caveats Regarding Financial Planning Models

Financial planning models do not always ask the right questions. A primary reason is that they tend to rely on accounting relationships and not financial relationships. In particular, the three basic elements of firm value tend to get left out—namely cash flow size, risk, and timing.

Because of this, financial planning models sometimes do not produce meaningful clues about what strategies will lead to increases in value. Instead, they divert the user's attention to questions concerning the association of, say, the debt–equity ratio and firm growth.

The financial model we used for the Hoffman Company was simple—in fact, too simple. Our model, like many in use today, is really an accounting statement generator at heart. Such models are useful for pointing out inconsistencies and reminding us of financial needs, but they offer little guidance concerning what to do about these problems.

In closing our discussion, we should add that financial planning is an iterative process. Plans are created, examined, and modified over and over. The final plan will be a result negotiated between all the different parties to the process. In fact, long-term financial planning in most corporations relies on what might be called the Procrustes approach.[1] Upper-level managers have a goal in mind, and it is up to the planning staff to rework and ultimately deliver a feasible plan that meets that goal.

The final plan will therefore implicitly contain different goals in different areas and also satisfy many constraints. For this reason, such a plan need not be a dispassionate assessment of what we think the future will bring; it may instead be a means of reconciling the planned activities of different groups and a way of setting common goals for the future.

Concept Questions

4.5a What are some important elements that are often missing in financial planning models?

4.5b Why do we say planning is an iterative process?

---

[1] In Greek mythology, Procrustes is a giant who seizes travelers and ties them to an iron bed. He stretches them or cuts off their legs as needed to make them fit the bed.

Summary and Conclusions   4.6

Financial planning forces the firm to think about the future. We have examined a number of features of the planning process. We described what financial planning can accomplish and the components of a financial model. We went on to develop the relationship between growth and financing needs, and we discussed how a financial planning model is useful in exploring that relationship.

Corporate financial planning should not become a purely mechanical activity. If it does, it will probably focus on the wrong things. In particular, plans all too often are formulated in terms of a growth target with no explicit linkage to value creation, and they frequently are overly concerned with accounting statements. Nevertheless, the alternative to financial planning is stumbling into the future. Perhaps the immortal Yogi Berra (the baseball catcher, not the cartoon character) put it best when he said, "Ya gotta watch out if you don't know where you're goin'. You just might not get there."[2]

CHAPTER REVIEW AND SELF-TEST PROBLEMS

4.1 **Calculating EFN** Based on the following information for the Skandia Mining Company, what is EFN if sales are predicted to grow by 10 percent? Use the percentage of sales approach and assume the company is operating at full capacity. The payout ratio is constant.

<table>
<tr><th colspan="6">SKANDIA MINING COMPANY
Financial Statements</th></tr>
<tr><th colspan="2">Income Statement</th><th colspan="4">Balance Sheet</th></tr>
<tr><th></th><th></th><th colspan="2">Assets</th><th colspan="2">Liabilities and Owners' Equity</th></tr>
<tr><td>Sales</td><td>$4,250.0</td><td>Current assets</td><td>$ 900.0</td><td>Current liabilities</td><td>$ 500.0</td></tr>
<tr><td>Costs</td><td>3,875.0</td><td>Net fixed assets</td><td>2,200.0</td><td>Long-term debt</td><td>1,800.0</td></tr>
<tr><td>Taxable income</td><td>$ 375.0</td><td></td><td></td><td>Owners' equity</td><td>800.0</td></tr>
<tr><td>Taxes (34%)</td><td>127.5</td><td></td><td></td><td>Total liabilities and owners'</td><td></td></tr>
<tr><td>Net income</td><td>$ 247.5</td><td>Total assets</td><td>$3,100.0</td><td>equity</td><td>$3,100.0</td></tr>
<tr><td> Dividends</td><td>$ 82.6</td><td></td><td></td><td></td><td></td></tr>
<tr><td> Addition to retained earnings</td><td>164.9</td><td></td><td></td><td></td><td></td></tr>
</table>

4.2 **EFN and Capacity Use** Based on the information in Problem 4.1, what is EFN, assuming 60 percent capacity usage for net fixed assets? Assuming 95 percent capacity?

4.3 **Sustainable Growth** Based on the information in Problem 4.1, what growth rate can Skandia maintain if no external financing is used? What is the sustainable growth rate?

---

[2]We're not *exactly* sure what this means either, but we like the sound of it.

4.1 We can calculate EFN by preparing the pro forma statements using the percentage of sales approach. Note that sales are forecast to be $4,250 \times 1.10 = \$4,675$.

SKANDIA MINING COMPANY
Pro Forma Financial Statements

Income Statement

Sales	$4,675.0	Forecast
Costs	4,262.7	91.18% of sales
Taxable income	$ 412.3	
Taxes (34%)	140.2	
Net income	$ 272.1	
Dividends	$ 90.8	33.37% of net income
Addition to retained earnings	181.3	

Balance Sheet

Assets			Liabilities and Owner's Equity		
Current assets	$ 990.0	21.18%	Current liabilities	$ 550.0	11.76%
Net fixed assets	2,420.0	51.76%	Long-term debt	1,800.0	n/a
			Owners' equity	981.3	n/a
Total assets	$3,410.0	72.94%	Total liabilities and owners' equity	$3,331.3	n/a
			EFN	$ 78.7	n/a

4.2 Full-capacity sales are equal to current sales divided by the capacity utilization. At 60 percent of capacity:

$$\$4,250 = .60 \times \text{Full-capacity sales}$$

$$\$7,083 = \text{Full-capacity sales}$$

With a sales level of $4,675, no net new fixed assets will be needed, so our earlier estimate is too high. We estimated an increase in fixed assets of $2,420 − 2,200 = $220. The new EFN will thus be $78.7 − 220 = −$141.3, a surplus. No external financing is needed in this case.

At 95 percent capacity, full-capacity sales are $4,474. The ratio of fixed assets to full-capacity sales is thus $2,200/4,474 = 49.17%. At a sales level of $4,675, we will thus need $4,675 \times .4917 = $2,298.7 in net fixed assets, an increase of $98.7. This is $220 − 98.7 = $121.3 less than we originally predicted, so the EFN is now $78.7 − 121.3 = −$42.6, a surplus. No additional financing is needed.

4.3 Skandia retains $b = 1 − .3337 = 66.63\%$ of net income. Return on assets is $247.5/3,100 = 7.98%. The internal growth rate is thus:

$$\frac{\text{ROA} \times b}{1 - \text{ROA} \times b} = \frac{.0798 \times .6663}{1 - .0798 \times .6663}$$

$$= 5.62\%$$

Return on equity for Skandia is $247.5/800 = 30.94%, so we can calculate the sustainable growth rate as follows:

$$\frac{\text{ROE} \times b}{1 - \text{ROE} \times b} = \frac{.3094 \times .6663}{1 - .3094 \times .6663}$$

$$= 25.97\%$$

1. **Sales Forecast** [LO1] Why do you think most long-term financial planning begins with sales forecasts? Put differently, why are future sales the key input?

2. **Sustainable Growth** [LO3] In the chapter, we used Rosengarten Corporation to demonstrate how to calculate EFN. The ROE for Rosengarten is about 7.3 percent, and the plowback ratio is about 67 percent. If you calculate the sustainable growth rate for Rosengarten, you will find it is only 5.14 percent. In our calculation for EFN, we used a growth rate of 25 percent. Is this possible? (*Hint:* Yes. How?)

3. **External Financing Needed** [LO2] Testaburger, Inc., uses no external financing and maintains a positive retention ratio. When sales grow by 15 percent, the firm has a negative projected EFN. What does this tell you about the firm's internal growth rate? How about the sustainable growth rate? At this same level of sales growth, what will happen to the projected EFN if the retention ratio is increased? What if the retention ratio is decreased? What happens to the projected EFN if the firm pays out all of its earnings in the form of dividends?

4. **EFN and Growth Rates** [LO2, 3] Broslofski Co. maintains a positive retention ratio and keeps its debt–equity ratio constant every year. When sales grow by 20 percent, the firm has a negative projected EFN. What does this tell you about the firm's sustainable growth rate? Do you know, with certainty, if the internal growth rate is greater than or less than 20 percent? Why? What happens to the projected EFN if the retention ratio is increased? What if the retention ratio is decreased? What if the retention ratio is zero?

   Use the following information to answer the next six questions: A small business called The Grandmother Calendar Company began selling personalized photo calendar kits. The kits were a hit, and sales soon sharply exceeded forecasts. The rush of orders created a huge backlog, so the company leased more space and expanded capacity; but it still could not keep up with demand. Equipment failed from overuse and quality suffered. Working capital was drained to expand production, and, at the same time, payments from customers were often delayed until the product was shipped. Unable to deliver on orders, the company became so strapped for cash that employee paychecks began to bounce. Finally, out of cash, the company ceased operations entirely three years later.

5. **Product Sales** [LO4] Do you think the company would have suffered the same fate if its product had been less popular? Why or why not?

6. **Cash Flow** [LO4] The Grandmother Calendar Company clearly had a cash flow problem. In the context of the cash flow analysis we developed in Chapter 2, what was the impact of customers not paying until orders were shipped?

7. **Product Pricing** [LO4] The firm actually priced its product to be about 20 percent less than that of competitors, even though the Grandmother calendar was more detailed. In retrospect, was this a wise choice?

8. **Corporate Borrowing** [LO4] If the firm was so successful at selling, why wouldn't a bank or some other lender step in and provide it with the cash it needed to continue?

9. **Cash Flow** [LO4] Which was the biggest culprit here: too many orders, too little cash, or too little production capacity?

10. **Cash Flow** [LO4] What are some of the actions that a small company like The Grandmother Calendar Company can take if it finds itself in a situation in which growth in sales outstrips production capacity and available financial resources? What other options (besides expansion of capacity) are available to a company when orders exceed capacity?

Visit us at www.mhhe.com/rwj

QUESTIONS AND PROBLEMS

BASIC
(Questions 1–15)

1. **Pro Forma Statements [LO1]** Consider the following simplified financial statements for the Phillips Corporation (assuming no income taxes):

Income Statement			Balance Sheet			
Sales	$23,000	Assets	$15,800	Debt		$ 5,200
Costs	16,700			Equity		10,600
Net income	$ 6,300	Total	$15,800	Total		$15,800

Phillips has predicted a sales increase of 15 percent. It has predicted that every item on the balance sheet will increase by 15 percent as well. Create the pro forma statements and reconcile them. What is the plug variable here?

2. **Pro Forma Statements and EFN [LO1, 2]** In the previous question, assume Phillips pays out half of net income in the form of a cash dividend. Costs and assets vary with sales, but debt and equity do not. Prepare the pro forma statements and determine the external financing needed.

3. **Calculating EFN [LO2]** The most recent financial statements for Zoso, Inc., are shown here (assuming no income taxes):

Income Statement			Balance Sheet			
Sales	$6,300	Assets	$18,300	Debt		$12,400
Costs	3,890			Equity		5,900
Net income	$2,410	Total	$18,300	Total		$18,300

Assets and costs are proportional to sales. Debt and equity are not. No dividends are paid. Next year's sales are projected to be $7,434. What is the external financing needed?

4. **EFN [LO2]** The most recent financial statements for GPS, Inc., are shown here:

Income Statement			Balance Sheet			
Sales	$19,500	Assets	$98,000	Debt		$52,500
Costs	15,000			Equity		45,500
Taxable income	$ 4,500	Total	$98,000	Total		$98,000
Taxes (40%)	1,800					
Net income	$ 2,700					

Assets and costs are proportional to sales. Debt and equity are not. A dividend of $1,400 was paid, and the company wishes to maintain a constant payout ratio. Next year's sales are projected to be $21,840. What is the external financing needed?

5. **EFN [LO2]** The most recent financial statements for Summer Tyme, Inc., are shown here:

Income Statement			Balance Sheet			
Sales	$4,200	Current assets	$ 3,600	Current liabilities		$ 2,100
Costs	3,300	Fixed assets	7,900	Long-term debt		3,650
Taxable income	$ 900			Equity		5,750
Taxes (34%)	306	Total	$11,500	Total		$11,500
Net income	$ 594					

Assets, costs, and current liabilities are proportional to sales. Long-term debt and equity are not. The company maintains a constant 40 percent dividend payout ratio. As with every other firm in its industry, next year's sales are projected to increase by exactly 15 percent. What is the external financing needed?

6. **Calculating Internal Growth [LO3]** The most recent financial statements for Live Co. are shown here:

Income Statement		Balance Sheet			
Sales	$13,250	Current assets	$10,400	Debt	$17,500
Costs	9,480	Fixed assets	28,750	Equity	21,650
Taxable income	$ 3,770	Total	$39,150	Total	$39,150
Taxes (40%)	1,508				
Net income	$ 2,262				

Assets and costs are proportional to sales. Debt and equity are not. The company maintains a constant 30 percent dividend payout ratio. No external equity financing is possible. What is the internal growth rate?

7. **Calculating Sustainable Growth [LO3]** For the company in the previous problem, what is the sustainable growth rate?

8. **Sales and Growth [LO2]** The most recent financial statements for Throwing Copper Co. are shown here:

Income Statement		Balance Sheet			
Sales	$42,000	Current assets	$ 21,000	Long-term debt	$ 51,000
Costs	28,500	Fixed assets	86,000	Equity	56,000
Taxable income	$13,500	Total	$107,000	Total	$107,000
Taxes (34%)	4,590				
Net income	$ 8,910				

Assets and costs are proportional to sales. The company maintains a constant 30 percent dividend payout ratio and a constant debt–equity ratio. What is the maximum increase in sales that can be sustained assuming no new equity is issued?

9. **Calculating Retained Earnings from Pro Forma Income [LO1]** Consider the following income statement for the Heir Jordan Corporation:

HEIR JORDAN CORPORATION	
Income Statement	
Sales	$38,000
Costs	18,400
Taxable income	$19,600
Taxes (34%)	6,664
Net income	$12,936
Dividends	$5,200
Addition to retained earnings	7,736

A 20 percent growth rate in sales is projected. Prepare a pro forma income statement assuming costs vary with sales and the dividend payout ratio is constant. What is the projected addition to retained earnings?

Visit us at www.mhhe.com/rwj

10. **Applying Percentage of Sales** [LO1] The balance sheet for the Heir Jordan Corporation follows. Based on this information and the income statement in the previous problem, supply the missing information using the percentage of sales approach. Assume that accounts payable vary with sales, whereas notes payable do not. Put "n/a" where needed.

HEIR JORDAN CORPORATION Balance Sheet					
Assets			**Liabilities and Owners' Equity**		
	$	Percentage of Sales		$	Percentage of Sales
Current assets			Current liabilities		
Cash	$ 3,050	—	Accounts payable	$ 1,300	—
Accounts receivable	6,900	—	Notes payable	6,800	—
Inventory	7,600	—	Total	$ 8,100	—
Total	$17,550	—	Long-term debt	$25,000	—
Fixed assets					
Net plant and equipment	$34,500	—	Owners' equity		—
			Common stock and paid-in surplus	$15,000	
			Retained earnings	3,950	—
			Total	$18,950	—
Total assets	$52,050	—	Total liabilities and owners' equity	$52,050	—

11. **EFN and Sales** [LO2] From the previous two questions, prepare a pro forma balance sheet showing EFN, assuming a 15 percent increase in sales, no new external debt or equity financing, and a constant payout ratio.

12. **Internal Growth** [LO3] If the Baseball Shoppe has an 8 percent ROA and a 20 percent payout ratio, what is its internal growth rate?

13. **Sustainable Growth** [LO3] If the Garnett Corp. has a 15 percent ROE and a 25 percent payout ratio, what is its sustainable growth rate?

14. **Sustainable Growth** [LO3] Based on the following information, calculate the sustainable growth rate for Kaleb's Kickboxing:

Profit margin   = 8.2%
Capital intensity ratio = .75
Debt–equity ratio   = .40
Net income   = $43,000
Dividends   = $12,000

15. **Sustainable Growth** [LO3] Assuming the following ratios are constant, what is the sustainable growth rate?

Total asset turnover = 2.50
Profit margin   = 7.8%
Equity multiplier   = 1.80
Payout ratio   = 60%

INTERMEDIATE
(Questions 16–27)

16. **Full-Capacity Sales** [LO1] Seaweed Mfg., Inc., is currently operating at only 95 percent of fixed asset capacity. Current sales are $550,000. How fast can sales grow before any new fixed assets are needed?

17. **Fixed Assets and Capacity Usage** [LO1] For the company in the previous problem, suppose fixed assets are $440,000 and sales are projected to grow to $630,000. How much in new fixed assets are required to support this growth in sales? Assume the company maintains its current operating capacity.

18. **Growth and Profit Margin** [LO3] McCormac Co. wishes to maintain a growth rate of 12 percent a year, a debt–equity ratio of 1.20, and a dividend payout ratio of 30 percent. The ratio of total assets to sales is constant at .75. What profit margin must the firm achieve?

19. **Growth and Debt–Equity Ratio** [LO3] A firm wishes to maintain a growth rate of 11.5 percent and a dividend payout ratio of 30 percent. The ratio of total assets to sales is constant at .60, and profit margin is 6.2 percent. If the firm also wishes to maintain a constant debt–equity ratio, what must it be?

20. **Growth and Assets** [LO3] A firm wishes to maintain an internal growth rate of 7 percent and a dividend payout ratio of 25 percent. The current profit margin is 5 percent, and the firm uses no external financing sources. What must total asset turnover be?

21. **Sustainable Growth** [LO3] Based on the following information, calculate the sustainable growth rate for Hendrix Guitars, Inc.:

    Profit margin   = 4.8%
    Total asset turnover = 1.25
    Total debt ratio   = .65
    Payout ratio   = 30%

22. **Sustainable Growth and Outside Financing** [LO3] You've collected the following information about St. Pierre, Inc.:

    Sales   = $195,000
    Net income = $17,500
    Dividends   = $9,300
    Total debt   = $86,000
    Total equity = $58,000

    What is the sustainable growth rate for St. Pierre, Inc.? If it does grow at this rate, how much new borrowing will take place in the coming year, assuming a constant debt–equity ratio? What growth rate could be supported with no outside financing at all?

23. **Sustainable Growth Rate** [LO3] Coheed, Inc., had equity of $135,000 at the beginning of the year. At the end of the year, the company had total assets of $250,000. During the year the company sold no new equity. Net income for the year was $19,000 and dividends were $2,500. What is the sustainable growth rate for the company? What is the sustainable growth rate if you use the formula $ROE \times b$ and beginning of period equity? What is the sustainable growth rate if you use end of period equity in this formula? Is this number too high or too low? Why?

24. **Internal Growth Rates** [LO3] Calculate the internal growth rate for the company in the previous problem. Now calculate the internal growth rate using $ROA \times b$ for both beginning of period and end of period total assets. What do you observe?

25. **Calculating EFN** [LO2] The most recent financial statements for Moose Tours, Inc., follow. Sales for 2009 are projected to grow by 20 percent. Interest expense will remain constant; the tax rate and the dividend payout rate will also remain constant. Costs, other expenses, current assets, and accounts payable increase

spontaneously with sales. If the firm is operating at full capacity and no new debt or equity is issued, what external financing is needed to support the 20 percent growth rate in sales?

MOOSE TOURS, INC. 2008 Income Statement	
Sales	$929,000
Costs	723,000
Other expenses	19,000
Earnings before interest and taxes	$187,000
Interest paid	14,000
Taxable income	$173,000
Taxes	60,550
Net income	$112,450
Dividends	$33,735
Addition to retained earnings	78,715

MOOSE TOURS, INC. Balance Sheet as of December 31, 2008			
Assets		**Liabilities and Owners' Equity**	
Current assets		Current liabilities	
Cash	$ 25,300	Accounts payable	$ 68,000
Accounts receivable	40,700	Notes payable	17,000
Inventory	86,900	Total	$ 85,000
Total	$152,900	Long-term debt	$158,000
Fixed assets		Owners' equity	
Net plant and equipment	413,000	Common stock and paid-in surplus	$140,000
		Retained earnings	182,900
		Total	$322,900
Total assets	$565,900	Total liabilities and owners' equity	$565,900

26. **Capacity Usage and Growth** [LO2] In the previous problem, suppose the firm was operating at only 80 percent capacity in 2008. What is EFN now?

27. **Calculating EFN** [LO2] In Problem 25, suppose the firm wishes to keep its debt–equity ratio constant. What is EFN now?

CHALLENGE (Questions 28–33)

28. **EFN and Internal Growth** [LO2, 3] Redo Problem 25 using sales growth rates of 15 and 25 percent in addition to 20 percent. Illustrate graphically the relationship between EFN and the growth rate, and use this graph to determine the relationship between them. At what growth rate is the EFN equal to zero? Why is this internal growth rate different from that found by using the equation in the text?

29. **EFN and Sustainable Growth** [LO2, 3] Redo Problem 27 using sales growth rates of 30 and 35 percent in addition to 20 percent. Illustrate graphically the relationship between EFN and the growth rate, and use this graph to determine the relationship between them. At what growth rate is the EFN equal to zero? Why is this sustainable growth rate different from that found by using the equation in the text?

30. **Constraints on Growth** [LO3] Nearside, Inc., wishes to maintain a growth rate of 12 percent per year and a debt–equity ratio of .30. Profit margin is 6.70 percent, and the ratio of total assets to sales is constant at 1.35. Is this growth rate possible? To

answer, determine what the dividend payout ratio must be. How do you interpret the result?

31. **EFN [LO2]** Define the following:

   S = Previous year's sales

   A = Total assets

   D = Total debt

   E = Total equity

   g = Projected growth in sales

   PM = Profit margin

   b = Retention (plowback) ratio

   Show that EFN can be written as follows:

   $$\text{EFN} = -\text{PM}(S)b + (A - \text{PM}(S)b) \times g$$

   Hint: Asset needs will equal A × g. The addition to retained earnings will equal PM(S)b × (1 + g).

32. **Growth Rates [LO3]** Based on the result in Problem 31, show that the internal and sustainable growth rates are as given in the chapter. *Hint:* For the internal growth rate, set EFN equal to zero and solve for g.

33. **Sustainable Growth Rate [LO3]** In the chapter, we discussed the two versions of the sustainable growth rate formula. Derive the formula ROE × b from the formula given in the chapter, where ROE is based on beginning of period equity. Also, derive the formula ROA × b from the internal growth rate formula.

MINICASE

Planning for Growth at S&S Air

After Chris completed the ratio analysis for S&S Air (see Chapter 3), Mark and Todd approached him about planning for next year's sales. The company had historically used little planning for investment needs. As a result, the company experienced some challenging times because of cash flow problems. The lack of planning resulted in missed sales, as well as periods when Mark and Todd were unable to draw salaries. To this end, they would like Chris to prepare a financial plan for the next year so the company can begin to address any outside investment requirements. The income statement and balance sheet are shown here:

S&S Air, Inc. 2008 Income Statement		
Sales		$30,499,420
Cost of goods sold		22,224,580
Other expenses		3,867,500
Depreciation		1,366,680
EBIT		$ 3,040,660
Interest		478,240
Taxable income		$ 2,562,420
Taxes (40%)		1,024,968
Net income		$ 1,537,452
Dividends	$560,000	
Add to retained earnings	977,452	

S&S Air, Inc. 2006 Balance Sheet			
Assets		**Liabilities and Equity**	
Current assets		Current liabilities	
Cash	$ 441,000	Accounts payable	$ 889,000
Accounts receivable	708,400	Notes payable	2,030,000
Inventory	1,037,120	Total current liabilities	$ 2,919,000
Total current assets	$ 2,186,520	Long-term debt	$ 5,320,000
Fixed assets			
Net plant and equipment	$16,122,400	Shareholder equity	
		Common stock	$ 350,000
		Retained earnings	9,719,920
		Total equity	$10,069,920
Total assets	$18,308,920	Total liabilities and equity	$18,308,920

QUESTIONS

1. Calculate the internal growth rate and sustainable growth rate for S&S Air. What do these numbers mean?

2. S&S Air is planning for a growth rate of 12 percent next year. Calculate the EFN for the company assuming the company is operating at full capacity. Can the company's sales increase at this growth rate?

3. Most assets can be increased as a percentage of sales. For instance, cash can be increased by any amount.

However, fixed assets must be increased in specific amounts because it is impossible, as a practical matter, to buy part of a new plant or machine. In this case, a company has a "staircase" or "lumpy" fixed cost structure. Assume S&S Air is currently producing at 100 percent capacity. As a result, to increase production, the company must set up an entirely new line at a cost of $5,000,000. Calculate the new EFN with this assumption. What does this imply about capacity utilization for the company next year?

INTRODUCTION TO VALUATION: THE TIME VALUE OF MONEY

5

TOYOTA MOTOR CREDIT CORPORATION (TMCC), a subsidiary of Toyota Motor, offered some securities for sale to the public on March 28, 2008. Under the terms of the deal, TMCC promised to repay the owner of one of these securities $100,000 on March 28, 2038, but investors would receive nothing until then. Investors paid TMCC $24,099 for each of these securities; so they gave up $24,099 on March 28, 2008, for the promise of a $100,000 payment 30 years later. Such a security, for which you pay some amount today in exchange for a promised lump sum to be received at a future date, is about the simplest possible type. Is giving up $24,099 in exchange for $100,000 in 30 years a good deal? On the plus side, you get back about $4 for every $1 you put up. That probably sounds good; but on the down side, you have to wait 30 years to get it. What you need to know is how to analyze this trade-off; this chapter gives you the tools you need.

Master the ability to solve problems in this chapter by using a spreadsheet. Access Excel Master on the student Web site www.mhhe.com/rwj.

One of the basic problems faced by the financial manager is how to determine the value today of cash flows expected in the future. For example, the jackpot in a PowerBall™ lottery drawing was $110 million. Does this mean the winning ticket was worth $110 million? The answer is no because the jackpot was actually going to pay out over a 20-year period at a rate of $5.5 million per year. How much was the ticket worth then? The answer depends on the time value of money, the subject of this chapter.

In the most general sense, the phrase *time value of money* refers to the fact that a dollar in hand today is worth more than a dollar promised at some time in the future. On a practical level, one reason for this is that you could earn interest while you waited; so a dollar today would grow to more than a dollar later. The trade-off between money now and money later thus depends on, among other things, the rate you can earn by investing. Our goal in this chapter is to explicitly evaluate this trade-off between dollars today and dollars at some future time.

A thorough understanding of the material in this chapter is critical to understanding material in subsequent chapters, so you should study it with particular care. We will present a number of examples in this chapter. In many problems, your answer may differ from ours slightly. This can happen because of rounding and is not a cause for concern.

5.1 # Future Value and Compounding

future value (FV)
The amount an investment
is worth after one or more
periods.

The first thing we will study is future value. **Future value (FV)** refers to the amount of money an investment will grow to over some period of time at some given interest rate. Put another way, future value is the cash value of an investment at some time in the future. We start out by considering the simplest case: a single-period investment.

INVESTING FOR A SINGLE PERIOD

Suppose you invest $100 in a savings account that pays 10 percent interest per year. How much will you have in one year? You will have $110. This $110 is equal to your original *principal* of $100 plus $10 in interest that you earn. We say that $110 is the future value of $100 invested for one year at 10 percent, and we simply mean that $100 today is worth $110 in one year, given that 10 percent is the interest rate.

In general, if you invest for one period at an interest rate of r, your investment will grow to $(1 + r)$ per dollar invested. In our example, r is 10 percent, so your investment grows to $1 + .10 = 1.1$ dollars per dollar invested. You invested $100 in this case, so you ended up with $100 \times 1.10 = \$110$.

INVESTING FOR MORE THAN ONE PERIOD

Going back to our $100 investment, what will you have after two years, assuming the interest rate doesn't change? If you leave the entire $110 in the bank, you will earn $110 \times .10 = \$11$ in interest during the second year, so you will have a total of $110 + 11 = \$121$. This $121 is the future value of $100 in two years at 10 percent. Another way of looking at it is that one year from now you are effectively investing $110 at 10 percent for a year. This is a single-period problem, so you'll end up with $1.10 for every dollar invested, or $110 \times 1.1 = \$121$ total.

This $121 has four parts. The first part is the $100 original principal. The second part is the $10 in interest you earned in the first year, and the third part is another $10 you earn in the second year, for a total of $120. The last $1 you end up with (the fourth part) is interest you earn in the second year on the interest paid in the first year: $10 \times .10 = \$1$.

This process of leaving your money and any accumulated interest in an investment for more than one period, thereby *reinvesting* the interest, is called **compounding**. Compounding the interest means earning **interest on interest**, so we call the result **compound interest**. With **simple interest**, the interest is not reinvested, so interest is earned each period only on the original principal.

compounding
The process of accumulat-
ing interest on an investment over time to earn
more interest.

interest on interest
Interest earned on the
reinvestment of previous
interest payments.

EXAMPLE 5.1	**Interest on Interest**

Suppose you locate a two-year investment that pays 14 percent per year. If you invest $325, how much will you have at the end of the two years? How much of this is simple interest? How much is compound interest?

At the end of the first year, you will have $325 \times (1 + .14) = \$370.50$. If you reinvest this entire amount and thereby compound the interest, you will have $370.50 \times 1.14 = \$422.37$ at the end of the second year. The total interest you earn is thus $422.37 - 325 = \$97.37$. Your $325 original principal earns $325 \times .14 = \$45.50$ in interest each year, for a two-year total of $91 in simple interest. The remaining $97.37 - 91 = \$6.37$ results from compounding. You can check this by noting that the interest earned in the first year is $45.50. The interest on interest earned in the second year thus amounts to $45.50 \times .14 = \$6.37$, as we calculated.

We now take a closer look at how we calculated the $121 future value. We multiplied $110 by 1.1 to get $121. The $110, however, was $100 also multiplied by 1.1. In other words:

$$\begin{aligned}\$121 &= \$110 \times 1.1 \\ &= (\$100 \times 1.1) \times 1.1 \\ &= \$100 \times (1.1 \times 1.1) \\ &= \$100 \times 1.1^2 \\ &= \$100 \times 1.21\end{aligned}$$

compound interest
Interest earned on both the initial principal and the interest reinvested from prior periods.

simple interest
Interest earned only on the original principal amount invested.

At the risk of belaboring the obvious, let's ask: How much would our $100 grow to after three years? Once again, in two years, we'll be investing $121 for one period at 10 percent. We'll end up with $1.10 for every dollar we invest, or $121 \times 1.1 = $133.10 total. This $133.10 is thus:

$$\begin{aligned}\$133.10 &= \$121 \times 1.1 \\ &= (\$110 \times 1.1) \times 1.1 \\ &= (\$100 \times 1.1) \times 1.1 \times 1.1 \\ &= \$100 \times (1.1 \times 1.1 \times 1.1) \\ &= \$100 \times 1.1^3 \\ &= \$100 \times 1.331\end{aligned}$$

For a discussion of time value concepts (and lots more) see www.financeprofessor.com.

You're probably noticing a pattern to these calculations, so we can now go ahead and state the general result. As our examples suggest, the future value of $1 invested for t periods at a rate of r per period is this:

$$\text{Future value} = \$1 \times (1 + r)^t \qquad [5.1]$$

The expression $(1 + r)^t$ is sometimes called the *future value interest factor* (or just *future value factor*) for $1 invested at r percent for t periods and can be abbreviated as FVIF(r, t).

In our example, what would your $100 be worth after five years? We can first compute the relevant future value factor as follows:

$$(1 + r)^t = (1 + .10)^5 = 1.1^5 = 1.6105$$

Your $100 will thus grow to:

$$\$100 \times 1.6105 = \$161.05$$

The growth of your $100 each year is illustrated in Table 5.1. As shown, the interest earned in each year is equal to the beginning amount multiplied by the interest rate of 10 percent.

Year	Beginning Amount	Simple Interest	Compound Interest	Total Interest Earned	Ending Amount
1	$100.00	$10	$ .00	$10.00	$110.00
2	110.00	10	1.00	11.00	121.00
3	121.00	10	2.10	12.10	133.10
4	133.10	10	3.31	13.31	146.41
5	146.41	10	4.64	14.64	161.05
		Total $50 simple interest	Total $11.05 compound interest	Total $61.05 interest	

TABLE 5.1

Future Value of $100 at 10 percent

FIGURE 5.1

Future Value, Simple
Interest, and Compound
Interest

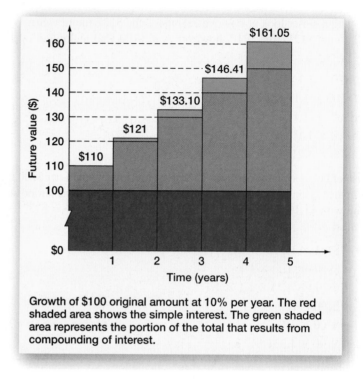

Growth of $100 original amount at 10% per year. The red
shaded area shows the simple interest. The green shaded
area represents the portion of the total that results from
compounding of interest.

In Table 5.1, notice the total interest you earn is $61.05. Over the five-year span of this
investment, the simple interest is $100 × .10 = $10 per year, so you accumulate $50 this
way. The other $11.05 is from compounding.

Figure 5.1 illustrates the growth of the compound interest in Table 5.1. Notice how the
simple interest is constant each year, but the amount of compound interest you earn gets
bigger every year. The amount of the compound interest keeps increasing because more
and more interest builds up and there is thus more to compound.

Future values depend critically on the assumed interest rate, particularly for long-lived
investments. Figure 5.2 illustrates this relationship by plotting the growth of $1 for differ-
ent rates and lengths of time. Notice the future value of $1 after 10 years is about $6.20 at
a 20 percent rate, but it is only about $2.60 at 10 percent. In this case, doubling the interest
rate more than doubles the future value.

To solve future value problems, we need to come up with the relevant future value factors. There are several different ways of doing this. In our example, we could have multiplied 1.1 by itself five times. This would work just fine, but it would get to be very tedious
for, say, a 30-year investment.

Fortunately, there are several easier ways to get future value factors. Most calculators
have a key labeled "y^x." You can usually just enter 1.1, press this key, enter 5, and press the
"=" key to get the answer. This is an easy way to calculate future value factors because it's
quick and accurate.

Alternatively, you can use a table that contains future value factors for some common
interest rates and time periods. Table 5.2 contains some of these factors. Table A.1 in the
appendix at the end of the book contains a much larger set. To use the table, find the column
that corresponds to 10 percent. Then look down the rows until you come to five periods.
You should find the factor that we calculated, 1.6105.

Tables such as 5.2 are not as common as they once were because they predate inexpensive calculators and are available only for a relatively small number of rates. Interest rates

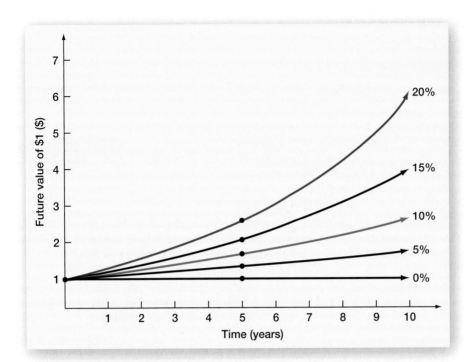

FIGURE 5.2

Future Value of $1 for Different Periods and Rates

TABLE 5.2

Future Value Interest Factors

| | Interest Rate | | | |
Number of Periods	5%	10%	15%	20%
1	1.0500	1.1000	1.1500	1.2000
2	1.1025	1.2100	1.3225	1.4400
3	1.1576	1.3310	1.5209	1.7280
4	1.2155	1.4641	1.7490	2.0736
5	1.2763	1.6105	2.0114	2.4883

are often quoted to three or four decimal places, so the tables needed to deal with these accurately would be quite large. As a result, the real world has moved away from using them. We will emphasize the use of a calculator in this chapter.

These tables still serve a useful purpose. To make sure you are doing the calculations correctly, pick a factor from the table and then calculate it yourself to see that you get the same answer. There are plenty of numbers to choose from.

Compound Interest

EXAMPLE 5.2

You've located an investment that pays 12 percent per year. That rate sounds good to you, so you invest $400. How much will you have in three years? How much will you have in seven years? At the end of seven years, how much interest will you have earned? How much of that interest results from compounding?

Based on our discussion, we can calculate the future value factor for 12 percent and three years as follows:

$(1 + r)^t = 1.12^3 = 1.4049$

(continued)

Your $400 thus grows to:

$400 × 1.4049 = $561.97

After seven years, you will have:

$400 × 1.12^7 = $400 × 2.2107 = $884.27

Thus, you will more than double your money over seven years.

Because you invested $400, the interest in the $884.27 future value is $884.27 − 400 = $484.27. At 12 percent, your $400 investment earns $400 × .12 = $48 in simple interest every year. Over seven years, the simple interest thus totals 7 × $48 = $336. The other $484.27 − 336 = $148.27 is from compounding.

The effect of compounding is not great over short time periods, but it really starts to add up as the horizon grows. To take an extreme case, suppose one of your more frugal ancestors had invested $5 for you at a 6 percent interest rate 200 years ago. How much would you have today? The future value factor is a substantial 1.06^{200} = 115,125.90 (you won't find this one in a table), so you would have $5 × 115,125.90 = $575,629.52 today. Notice that the simple interest is just $5 × .06 = $.30 per year. After 200 years, this amounts to $60. The rest is from reinvesting. Such is the power of compound interest!

EXAMPLE 5.3   How Much for That Island?

To further illustrate the effect of compounding for long horizons, consider the case of Peter Minuit and the American Indians. In 1626, Minuit bought all of Manhattan Island for about $24 in goods and trinkets. This sounds cheap, but the Indians may have gotten the better end of the deal. To see why, suppose the Indians had sold the goods and invested the $24 at 10 percent. How much would it be worth today?

About 383 years have passed since the transaction. At 10 percent, $24 will grow by quite a bit over that time. How much? The future value factor is roughly:

$(1 + r)^t = 1.1^{383} \approx 7,100,000,000,000,000$

That is, 7.1 followed by 14 zeroes. The future value is thus on the order of $24 × 7.1 = $170 *quadrillion* (give or take a few hundreds of trillions).

Well, $170 quadrillion is a lot of money. How much? If you had it, you could buy the United States. All of it. Cash. With money left over to buy Canada, Mexico, and the rest of the world, for that matter.

This example is something of an exaggeration, of course. In 1626, it would not have been easy to locate an investment that would pay 10 percent every year without fail for the next 383 years.

CALCULATOR HINTS

Using a Financial Calculator

Although there are the various ways of calculating future values we have described so far, many of you will decide that a financial calculator is the way to go. If you are planning on using one, you should read this extended hint; otherwise, skip it.

A financial calculator is simply an ordinary calculator with a few extra features. In particular, it knows some of the most commonly used financial formulas, so it can directly compute things like future values.

(continued)

Financial calculators have the advantage that they handle a lot of the computation, but that is really all. In other words, you still have to understand the problem; the calculator just does some of the arithmetic. In fact, there is an old joke (somewhat modified) that goes like this: Anyone can make a mistake on a time value of money problem, but to really screw one up takes a financial calculator! We therefore have two goals for this section. First, we'll discuss how to compute future values. After that, we'll show you how to avoid the most common mistakes people make when they start using financial calculators.

How to Calculate Future Values with a Financial Calculator

Examining a typical financial calculator, you will find five keys of particular interest. They usually look like this:

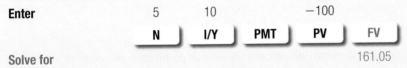

For now, we need to focus on four of these. The keys labeled **PV** and **FV** are just what you would guess: present value and future value. The key labeled **N** refers to the number of periods, which is what we have been calling *t*. Finally, **I/Y** stands for the interest rate, which we have called *r*.[1]

If we have the financial calculator set up right (see our next section), then calculating a future value is very simple. Take a look back at our question involving the future value of $100 at 10 percent for five years. We have seen that the answer is $161.05. The exact keystrokes will differ depending on what type of calculator you use, but here is basically all you do:

1. Enter −100. Press the **PV** key. (The negative sign is explained in the next section.)
2. Enter 10. Press the **I/Y** key. (Notice that we entered 10, not .10; see the next section.)
3. Enter 5. Press the **N** key.

Now we have entered all of the relevant information. To solve for the future value, we need to ask the calculator what the FV is. Depending on your calculator, either you press the button labeled "CPT" (for compute) and then press **FV**, or you just press **FV**. Either way, you should get 161.05. If you don't (and you probably won't if this is the first time you have used a financial calculator!), we will offer some help in our next section.

Before we explain the kinds of problems you are likely to run into, we want to establish a standard format for showing you how to use a financial calculator. Using the example we just looked at, in the future, we will illustrate such problems like this:

Enter	5	10		−100	
	N	**I/Y**	**PMT**	**PV**	**FV**
Solve for					161.05

Here is an important tip: Appendix D (which can be found on our Web site) contains more detailed instructions for the most common types of financial calculators. See if yours is included; if it is, follow the instructions there if you need help. Of course, if all else fails, you can read the manual that came with the calculator.

How to Get the Wrong Answer Using a Financial Calculator

There are a couple of common (and frustrating) problems that cause a lot of trouble with financial calculators. In this section, we provide some important *dos* and *don'ts*. If you just can't seem to get a problem to work out, you should refer back to this section.

There are two categories we examine: three things you need to do only once and three things you need to do every time you work a problem. The things you need to do just once deal with the following calculator settings:

1. *Make sure your calculator is set to display a large number of decimal places.* Most financial calculators display only two decimal places; this causes problems because we frequently work with numbers—like interest rates—that are very small.

(continued)

---

[1]The reason financial calculators use N and I/Y is that the most common use for these calculators is determining loan payments. In this context, N is the number of payments and I/Y is the interest rate on the loan. But as we will see, there are many other uses of financial calculators that don't involve loan payments and interest rates.

2. *Make sure your calculator is set to assume only one payment per period or per year*. Most financial calculators assume monthly payments (12 per year) unless you say otherwise.

3. *Make sure your calculator is in "end" mode*. This is usually the default, but you can accidently change to "begin" mode.

If you don't know how to set these three things, see Appendix D on our Web site or your calculator's operating manual. There are also three things you need to do *every time you work a problem*:

1. *Before you start, completely clear out the calculator*. This is very important. Failure to do this is the number one reason for wrong answers; you simply must get in the habit of clearing the calculator every time you start a problem. How you do this depends on the calculator (see Appendix D on our Web site), but you must do more than just clear the display. For example, on a Texas Instruments BA II Plus you must press `2nd` then `CLR TVM` for *clear time value of money*. There is a similar command on your calculator. Learn it!

   Note that turning the calculator off and back on won't do it. Most financial calculators remember everything you enter, even after you turn them off. In other words, they remember all your mistakes unless you explicitly clear them out. Also, if you are in the middle of a problem and make a mistake, *clear it out and start over*. Better to be safe than sorry.

2. *Put a negative sign on cash outflows*. Most financial calculators require you to put a negative sign on cash outflows and a positive sign on cash inflows. As a practical matter, this usually just means that you should enter the present value amount with a negative sign (because normally the present value represents the amount you give up today in exchange for cash inflows later). By the same token, when you solve for a present value, you shouldn't be surprised to see a negative sign.

3. *Enter the rate correctly*. Financial calculators assume that rates are quoted in percent, so if the rate is .08 (or 8 percent), you should enter 8, not .08.

If you follow these guidelines (especially the one about clearing out the calculator), you should have no problem using a financial calculator to work almost all of the problems in this and the next few chapters. We'll provide some additional examples and guidance where appropriate.

A NOTE ABOUT COMPOUND GROWTH

If you are considering depositing money in an interest-bearing account, then the interest rate on that account is just the rate at which your money grows, assuming you don't remove any of it. If that rate is 10 percent, then each year you simply have 10 percent more money than you had the year before. In this case, the interest rate is just an example of a compound growth rate.

The way we calculated future values is actually quite general and lets you answer some other types of questions related to growth. For example, your company currently has 10,000 employees. You've estimated that the number of employees grows by 3 percent per year. How many employees will there be in five years? Here, we start with 10,000 people instead of dollars, and we don't think of the growth rate as an interest rate, but the calculation is exactly the same:

$$10,000 \times 1.03^5 = 10,000 \times 1.1593 = 11,593 \text{ employees}$$

There will be about 1,593 net new hires over the coming five years.

To give another example, according to Value Line (a leading supplier of business information for investors), Wal-Mart's 2007 sales were about $374 billion. Suppose sales are projected to increase at a rate of 15 percent per year. What will Wal-Mart's sales be in the year 2012 if this is correct? Verify for yourself that the answer is about $752 billion—just over twice as large.

| **Dividend Growth** | **EXAMPLE 5.4** |

The TICO Corporation currently pays a cash dividend of $5 per share. You believe the dividend will be increased by 4 percent each year indefinitely. How big will the dividend be in eight years?

Here we have a cash dividend growing because it is being increased by management; but once again the calculation is the same:

Future value = $5 \times 1.04^8 = $5 \times 1.3686 = $6.84

The dividend will grow by $1.84 over that period. Dividend growth is a subject we will return to in a later chapter.

| **Concept Questions** |

5.1a What do we mean by the future value of an investment?

5.1b What does it mean to compound interest? How does compound interest differ from simple interest?

5.1c In general, what is the future value of $1 invested at r per period for t periods?

Present Value and Discounting   5.2

When we discuss future value, we are thinking of questions like: What will my $2,000 investment grow to if it earns a 6.5 percent return every year for the next six years? The answer to this question is what we call the future value of $2,000 invested at 6.5 percent for six years (verify that the answer is about $2,918).

Another type of question that comes up even more often in financial management is obviously related to future value. Suppose you need to have $10,000 in 10 years, and you can earn 6.5 percent on your money. How much do you have to invest today to reach your goal? You can verify that the answer is $5,327.26. How do we know this? Read on.

THE SINGLE-PERIOD CASE

We've seen that the future value of $1 invested for one year at 10 percent is $1.10. We now ask a slightly different question: How much do we have to invest today at 10 percent to get $1 in one year? In other words, we know the future value here is $1, but what is the **present value (PV)**? The answer isn't too hard to figure out. Whatever we invest today will be 1.1 times bigger at the end of the year. Because we need $1 at the end of the year:

Present value $\times$ 1.1 = $1

Or solving for the present value:

Present value = $1/1.1 = $.909

In this case, the present value is the answer to the following question: What amount, invested today, will grow to $1 in one year if the interest rate is 10 percent? Present value is thus just the reverse of future value. Instead of compounding the money forward into the future, we **discount** it back to the present.

present value (PV)
The current value of future cash flows discounted at the appropriate discount rate.

discount
Calculate the present value of some future amount.

EXAMPLE 5.5	Single-Period PV

Suppose you need $400 to buy textbooks next year. You can earn 7 percent on your money. How much do you have to put up today?

We need to know the PV of $400 in one year at 7 percent. Proceeding as in the previous example:

Present value $\times$ 1.07 = $400

We can now solve for the present value:

Present value = $400 $\times$ (1/1.07) = $373.83

Thus, $373.83 is the present value. Again, this just means that investing this amount for one year at 7 percent will give you a future value of $400.

From our examples, the present value of $1 to be received in one period is generally given as follows:

$$PV = \$1 \times [1/(1 + r)] = \$1/(1 + r)$$

We next examine how to get the present value of an amount to be paid in two or more periods into the future.

PRESENT VALUES FOR MULTIPLE PERIODS

Suppose you need to have $1,000 in two years. If you can earn 7 percent, how much do you have to invest to make sure you have the $1,000 when you need it? In other words, what is the present value of $1,000 in two years if the relevant rate is 7 percent?

Based on your knowledge of future values, you know the amount invested must grow to $1,000 over the two years. In other words, it must be the case that:

$$\begin{aligned} \$1,000 &= PV \times 1.07 \times 1.07 \\ &= PV \times 1.07^2 \\ &= PV \times 1.1449 \end{aligned}$$

Given this, we can solve for the present value:

Present value = $1,000/1.1449 = $873.44

Therefore, $873.44 is the amount you must invest to achieve your goal.

EXAMPLE 5.6	Saving Up

You would like to buy a new automobile. You have $50,000 or so, but the car costs $68,500. If you can earn 9 percent, how much do you have to invest today to buy the car in two years? Do you have enough? Assume the price will stay the same.

What we need to know is the present value of $68,500 to be paid in two years, assuming a 9 percent rate. Based on our discussion, this is:

$$PV = \$68,500/1.09^2 = \$68,500/1.1881 = \$57,655.08$$

You're still about $7,655 short, even if you're willing to wait two years.

	Interest Rate			
Number of Periods	5%	10%	15%	20%
1	.9524	.9091	.8696	.8333
2	.9070	.8264	.7561	.6944
3	.8638	.7513	.6575	.5787
4	.8227	.6830	.5718	.4823
5	.7835	.6209	.4972	.4019

TABLE 5.3

Present Value Interest Factors

As you have probably recognized by now, calculating present values is quite similar to calculating future values, and the general result looks much the same. The present value of $1 to be received t periods into the future at a discount rate of r is:

$$PV = \$1 \times [1/(1 + r)^t] = \$1/(1 + r)^t \qquad \text{[5.2]}$$

The quantity in brackets, $1/(1 + r)^t$, goes by several different names. Because it's used to discount a future cash flow, it is often called a *discount factor*. With this name, it is not surprising that the rate used in the calculation is often called the **discount rate**. We will tend to call it this in talking about present values. The quantity in brackets is also called the *present value interest factor* (or just *present value factor*) for $1 at r percent for t periods and is sometimes abbreviated as PVIF(r, t). Finally, calculating the present value of a future cash flow to determine its worth today is commonly called **discounted cash flow (DCF) valuation**.

To illustrate, suppose you need $1,000 in three years. You can earn 15 percent on your money. How much do you have to invest today? To find out, we have to determine the present value of $1,000 in three years at 15 percent. We do this by discounting $1,000 back three periods at 15 percent. With these numbers, the discount factor is:

$$1/(1 + .15)^3 = 1/1.5209 = .6575$$

The amount you must invest is thus:

$$\$1,000 \times .6575 = \$657.50$$

discount rate
The rate used to calculate the present value of future cash flows.

discounted cash flow (DCF) valuation
Calculating the present value of a future cash flow to determine its value today.

We say that $657.50 is the present or discounted value of $1,000 to be received in three years at 15 percent.

There are tables for present value factors just as there are tables for future value factors, and you use them in the same way (if you use them at all). Table 5.3 contains a small set. A much larger set can be found in Table A.2 in the book's appendix.

In Table 5.3, the discount factor we just calculated (.6575) can be found by looking down the column labeled "15%" until you come to the third row.

CALCULATOR HINTS

You solve present value problems on a financial calculator just as you do future value problems. For the example we just examined (the present value of $1,000 to be received in three years at 15 percent), you would do the following:

Enter	3	15			1,000
	N	**I/Y**	**PMT**	**PV**	**FV**
Solve for				−657.50	

Notice that the answer has a negative sign; as we discussed earlier, that's because it represents an outflow today in exchange for the $1,000 inflow later.

EXAMPLE 5.7 | **Deceptive Advertising?**

Businesses sometimes advertise that you should "Come try our product. If you do, we'll give you $100 just for coming by!" If you read the fine print, what you find out is that they will give you a savings certificate that will pay you $100 in 25 years or so. If the going interest rate on such certificates is 10 percent per year, how much are they really giving you today?

What you're actually getting is the present value of $100 to be paid in 25 years. If the discount rate is 10 percent per year, then the discount factor is:

$$1/1.1^{25} = 1/10.8347 = .0923$$

This tells you that a dollar in 25 years is worth a little more than nine cents today, assuming a 10 percent discount rate. Given this, the promotion is actually paying you about .0923 × $100 = $9.23. Maybe this is enough to draw customers, but it's not $100.

As the length of time until payment grows, present values decline. As Example 5.7 illustrates, present values tend to become small as the time horizon grows. If you look out far enough, they will always approach zero. Also, for a given length of time, the higher the discount rate is, the lower is the present value. Put another way, present values and discount rates are inversely related. Increasing the discount rate decreases the PV and vice versa.

The relationship between time, discount rates, and present values is illustrated in Figure 5.3. Notice that by the time we get to 10 years, the present values are all substantially smaller than the future amounts.

FIGURE 5.3

Present Value of $1 for Different Periods and Rates

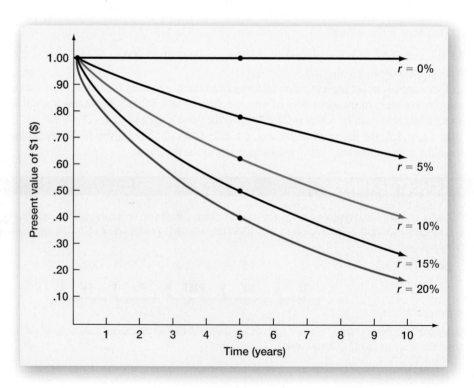

Concept Questions

5.2a What do we mean by the present value of an investment?

5.2b The process of discounting a future amount back to the present is the opposite of doing what?

5.2c What do we mean by discounted cash flow, or DCF, valuation?

5.2d In general, what is the present value of $1 to be received in t periods, assuming a discount rate of r per period?

More about Present and Future Values   5.3

If you look back at the expressions we came up with for present and future values, you will see a simple relationship between the two. We explore this relationship and some related issues in this section.

PRESENT VERSUS FUTURE VALUE

What we called the present value factor is just the reciprocal of (that is, 1 divided by) the future value factor:

Future value factor $= (1 + r)^t$

Present value factor $= 1/(1 + r)^t$

In fact, the easy way to calculate a present value factor on many calculators is to first calculate the future value factor and then press the "$1/x$" key to flip it over.

If we let FV_t stand for the future value after t periods, then the relationship between future value and present value can be written simply as one of the following:

$$PV \times (1 + r)^t = FV_t$$
$$PV = FV_t/(1 + r)^t = FV_t \times [1/(1 + r)^t]$$ [5.3]

This last result we will call the *basic present value equation*. We will use it throughout the text. A number of variations come up, but this simple equation underlies many of the most important ideas in corporate finance.

Evaluating Investments   **EXAMPLE 5.8**

To give you an idea of how we will be using present and future values, consider the following simple investment. Your company proposes to buy an asset for $335. This investment is very safe. You would sell off the asset in three years for $400. You know you could invest the $335 elsewhere at 10 percent with very little risk. What do you think of the proposed investment?

This is not a good investment. Why not? Because you can invest the $335 elsewhere at 10 percent. If you do, after three years it will grow to:

$335 $\times (1 + r)^t$ = $335 $\times 1.1^3$

            = $335 $\times 1.331$

            = $445.89

(continued)

Because the proposed investment pays out only $400, it is not as good as other alternatives we have. Another way of seeing the same thing is to notice that the present value of $400 in three years at 10 percent is:

$$\$400 \times [1/(1 + r)^t] = \$400/1.1^3 = \$400/1.331 = \$300.53$$

This tells us that we have to invest only about $300 to get $400 in three years, not $335. We will return to this type of analysis later on.

DETERMINING THE DISCOUNT RATE

For a downloadable, Windows-based financial calculator, go to www.calculator.org.

We frequently need to determine what discount rate is implicit in an investment. We can do this by looking at the basic present value equation:

$$PV = FV_t /(1 + r)^t$$

There are only four parts to this equation: the present value (PV), the future value (FV_t), the discount rate (r), and the life of the investment (t). Given any three of these, we can always find the fourth.

| EXAMPLE 5.9 | **Finding _r_ for a Single-Period Investment** |

You are considering a one-year investment. If you put up $1,250, you will get back $1,350. What rate is this investment paying?

First, in this single-period case, the answer is fairly obvious. You are getting a total of $100 in addition to your $1,250. The implicit rate on this investment is thus $100/1,250 = 8 percent.

More formally, from the basic present value equation, the present value (the amount you must put up today) is $1,250. The future value (what the present value grows to) is $1,350. The time involved is one period, so we have:

$$\$1,250 = \$1,350/(1 + r)^1$$
$$1 + r = \$1,350/1,250 = 1.08$$
$$r = 8\%$$

In this simple case, of course, there was no need to go through this calculation. But as we describe next, it gets a little harder with more than one period.

To illustrate what happens with multiple periods, let's say we are offered an investment that costs us $100 and will double our money in eight years. To compare this to other investments, we would like to know what discount rate is implicit in these numbers. This discount rate is called the *rate of return,* or sometimes just the *return,* on the investment. In this case, we have a present value of $100, a future value of $200 (double our money), and an eight-year life. To calculate the return, we can write the basic present value equation as:

$$PV = FV_t /(1 + r)^t$$
$$\$100 = \$200/(1 + r)^8$$

It could also be written as:

$$(1 + r)^8 = \$200/100 = 2$$

We now need to solve for r. There are three ways we could do it:

1. Use a financial calculator.
2. Solve the equation for $1 + r$ by taking the eighth root of both sides. Because this is the same thing as raising both sides to the power of $\frac{1}{8}$ or .125, this is actually easy to do with the "y^x" key on a calculator. Just enter 2, then press "y^x," enter .125, and press the "$=$" key. The eighth root should be about 1.09, which implies that r is 9 percent.
3. Use a future value table. The future value factor after eight years is equal to 2. If you look across the row corresponding to eight periods in Table A.1, you will see that a future value factor of 2 corresponds to the 9 percent column, again implying that the return here is 9 percent.

Actually, in this particular example, there is a useful "back of the envelope" means of solving for r—the Rule of 72. For reasonable rates of return, the time it takes to double your money is given approximately by $72/r\%$. In our example, this means that $72/r\% = 8$ years, implying that r is 9 percent, as we calculated. This rule is fairly accurate for discount rates in the 5 percent to 20 percent range.

Baseball Collectibles as Investments	**EXAMPLE 5.10**

In April 2008, the last baseball hit for a home run by Barry Bonds was auctioned off for about $376,000. The price of the ball was considered a bargain, in part because potential buyers were unsure if Bonds would play again. "Experts" on such collectibles often argue that collectibles such as this will double in value over a 10-year period.

So would the ball have been a good investment? By the Rule of 72, you already know the experts were predicting that the ball would double in value in 10 years; so the return predicted would be about $72/10 = 7.2$ percent per year, which is only so-so.

At one time at least, a rule of thumb in the rarefied world of fine art collecting was "your money back in 5 years, double your money in 10 years." Given this, let's see how an investment stacked up. In 1998, the Alberto Giacometti bronze statue *Homme Qui Marche III* sold for $2,972,500. Five years later, the statue was sold again, walking out the door at a price of $4,039,500. How did the seller do?

The rule of thumb has us doubling our money in 10 years; so, from the Rule of 72, we have that 7.2 percent per year was the norm. The statue was resold in almost exactly five years. The present value is $2,972,500, and the future value is $4,039,500. We need to solve for the unknown rate, r, as follows:

Why does the Rule of 72 work? See www.moneychimp.com.

$$\$2{,}972{,}500 = \$4{,}039{,}500/(1 + r)^5$$
$$(1 + r)^5 = 1.3590$$

Solving for r, we find the seller earned about 6.33 percent per year—less than the 7.2 percent rule of thumb. At least the seller made his money back.

What about other collectibles? To a philatelist (a stamp collector to you and us), one of the most prized stamps is the 1918 24-cent inverted Jenny C3a. The stamp is a collectible because it has a picture of an upside-down biplane. One of these stamps sold at auction for $825,000 in 2007. At what rate did its value grow? Verify for yourself that the answer is about 18.42 percent, assuming an 89-year period.

Of course not all collectibles perform as well. In 2008, an 1851 octagonal $50 gold coin minted in San Francisco sold for $189,750. Assuming that 157 years had passed, see if you agree that this collectible gained about 5.39 percent per year.

Perhaps the most desired coin for numismatists (coin collectors) is the 1933 $20 gold double eagle. Outside of the U.S. Mint and the Smithsonian, only one of these coins is in circulation. In 2002, the coin sold at auction for $7,590,020. See if you agree that this collectible gained about 20.5 percent per year.

A slightly more extreme example involves money bequeathed by Benjamin Franklin, who died on April 17, 1790. In his will, he gave 1,000 pounds sterling to Massachusetts and the city of Boston. He gave a like amount to Pennsylvania and the city of Philadelphia. The money had been paid to Franklin when he held political office, but he believed that politicians should not be paid for their service (it appears that this view is not widely shared by modern politicians).

Franklin originally specified that the money should be paid out 100 years after his death and used to train young people. Later, however, after some legal wrangling, it was agreed that the money would be paid out in 1990, 200 years after Franklin's death. By that time, the Pennsylvania bequest had grown to about $2 million; the Massachusetts bequest had grown to $4.5 million. The money was used to fund the Franklin Institutes in Boston and Philadelphia. Assuming that 1,000 pounds sterling was equivalent to $1,000, what rate of return did the two states earn? (The dollar did not become the official U.S. currency until 1792.)

For Pennsylvania, the future value is $2 million and the present value is $1,000. There are 200 years involved, so we need to solve for r in the following:

$$\$1,000 = \$2 \text{ million}/(1 + r)^{200}$$
$$(1 + r)^{200} = 2,000$$

Solving for r, we see that the Pennsylvania money grew at about 3.87 percent per year. The Massachusetts money did better; verify that the rate of return in this case was 4.3 percent. Small differences in returns can add up!

CALCULATOR HINTS

We can illustrate how to calculate unknown rates using a financial calculator with these numbers. For Pennsylvania, you would do the following:

Enter   200   −1,000   2,000,000

| N | I/Y | PMT | PV | FV |

Solve for   3.87

As in our previous examples, notice the minus sign on the present value, representing Franklin's outlay made many years ago. What do you change to work the problem for Massachusetts?

EXAMPLE 5.11 | **Saving for College**

You estimate that you will need about $80,000 to send your child to college in eight years. You have about $35,000 now. If you can earn 20 percent per year, will you make it? At what rate will you just reach your goal?

(continued)

If you can earn 20 percent, the future value of your $35,000 in eight years will be:

FV = $35,000 × 1.20⁸ = $35,000 × 4.2998 = $150,493.59

So, you will make it easily. The minimum rate is the unknown *r* in the following:

FV = $35,000 × (1 + *r*)⁸ = $80,000

(1 + *r*)⁸ = $80,000/35,000 = 2.2857

Therefore, the future value factor is 2.2857. Looking at the row in Table A.1 that corresponds to eight periods, we see that our future value factor is roughly halfway between the ones shown for 10 percent (2.1436) and 12 percent (2.4760), so you will just reach your goal if you earn approximately 11 percent. To get the exact answer, we could use a financial calculator or we could solve for *r*:

(1 + *r*)⁸ = $80,000/35,000 = 2.2857

1 + *r* = 2.2857^(1/8) = 2.2857^.125 = 1.1089

r = 10.89%

Only 18,262.5 Days to Retirement   **EXAMPLE 5.12**

You would like to retire in 50 years as a millionaire. If you have $10,000 today, what rate of return do you need to earn to achieve your goal?

The future value is $1,000,000. The present value is $10,000, and there are 50 years until payment. We need to calculate the unknown discount rate in the following:

$10,000 = $1,000,000/(1 + *r*)⁵⁰

(1 + *r*)⁵⁰ = 100

The future value factor is thus 100. You can verify that the implicit rate is about 9.65 percent.

Not taking the time value of money into account when computing growth rates or rates of return often leads to some misleading numbers in the real world. For example, the most loved (and hated) team in baseball, the New York Yankees, had the highest payroll during the 1988 season, about $19 million. In 2008, the Yankees again had the highest payroll, a staggering $210 million: an increase of 1,005 percent! If history is any guide, we can get a rough idea of the future growth in baseball payrolls. See if you don't agree that this represents an annual increase of 12.8 percent, a substantial growth rate, but much less than the gaudy 1,005 percent.

 How much do you need at retirement? Check out the "Money in Your 20s" link at www.about.com.

How about classic maps? A few years ago, the first map of America, printed in Rome in 1507, was valued at about $135,000, 69 percent more than the $80,000 it was worth 10 years earlier. Your return on investment if you were the proud owner of the map over those 10 years? Verify that it's about 5.4 percent per year—far worse than the 69 percent reported increase in price.

Whether with maps or baseball payrolls, it's easy to be misled when returns are quoted without considering the time value of money. However, it's not just the uninitiated who are guilty of this slight form of deception. The title of a feature article in a leading business magazine predicted the Dow Jones Industrial Average would soar to a 70 percent gain over the coming five years. Do you think it meant a 70 percent return per year on your money? Think again!

FINDING THE NUMBER OF PERIODS

Suppose we are interested in purchasing an asset that costs $50,000. We currently have $25,000. If we can earn 12 percent on this $25,000, how long until we have the $50,000? Finding the answer involves solving for the last variable in the basic present value equation, the number of periods. You already know how to get an approximate answer to this particular problem. Notice that we need to double our money. From the Rule of 72, this will take about $72/12 = 6$ years at 12 percent.

To come up with the exact answer, we can again manipulate the basic present value equation. The present value is $25,000, and the future value is $50,000. With a 12 percent discount rate, the basic equation takes one of the following forms:

$$\$25,000 = \$50,000/1.12^t$$
$$\$50,000/25,000 = 1.12^t = 2$$

We thus have a future value factor of 2 for a 12 percent rate. We now need to solve for t. If you look down the column in Table A.1 that corresponds to 12 percent, you will see that a future value factor of 1.9738 occurs at six periods. It will thus take about six years, as we calculated. To get the exact answer, we have to explicitly solve for t (or use a financial calculator). If you do this, you will see that the answer is 6.1163 years, so our approximation was quite close in this case.

CALCULATOR HINTS

If you use a financial calculator, here are the relevant entries:

Enter		12		−25,000	50,000
	N	I/Y	PMT	PV	FV
Solve for	6.1163				

| EXAMPLE 5.13 | **Waiting for Godot** |

You've been saving up to buy the Godot Company. The total cost will be $10 million. You currently have about $2.3 million. If you can earn 5 percent on your money, how long will you have to wait? At 16 percent, how long must you wait?

At 5 percent, you'll have to wait a long time. From the basic present value equation:

$$\$2.3 \text{ million} = \$10 \text{ million}/1.05^t$$
$$1.05^t = 4.35$$
$$t = 30 \text{ years}$$

At 16 percent, things are a little better. Verify for yourself that it will take about 10 years.

Learn more about using Excel for time value and other calculations at www.studyfinance.com.

U.S. EE Savings Bonds are a familiar investment for many. You purchase them for half of their $100 face value. In other words, you pay $50 today and get $100 at some point in the future when the bond "matures." You receive no interest in between, and the interest rate is adjusted every six months, so the length of time until your $50 grows to $100

SPREADSHEET STRATEGIES

Using a Spreadsheet for Time Value of Money Calculations

More and more, businesspeople from many different areas (not just finance and accounting) rely on spreadsheets to do all the different types of calculations that come up in the real world. As a result, in this section, we will show you how to use a spreadsheet to handle the various time value of money problems we presented in this chapter. We will use Microsoft Excel™, but the commands are similar for other types of software. We assume you are already familiar with basic spreadsheet operations.

As we have seen, you can solve for any one of the following four potential unknowns: future value, present value, the discount rate, or the number of periods. With a spreadsheet, there is a separate formula for each. In Excel, these are shown in a nearby box.

In these formulas, pv and fv are present and future value, nper is the number of periods, and rate is the discount, or interest, rate.

Two things are a little tricky here. First, unlike a financial calculator, the spreadsheet requires that the rate be entered as a decimal. Second, as with most financial calculators, you have to put a negative sign on either the present value or the future value to solve for the rate or the number of periods. For the same reason, if you solve for a present value, the answer will have a negative sign unless you input a negative future value. The same is true when you compute a future value.

To Find	Enter This Formula
Future value	= FV (rate,nper,pmt,pv)
Present value	= PV (rate,nper,pmt,fv)
Discount rate	= RATE (nper,pmt,pv,fv)
Number of periods	= NPER (rate,pmt,pv,fv)

To illustrate how you might use these formulas, we will go back to an example in the chapter. If you invest $25,000 at 12 percent per year, how long until you have $50,000? You might set up a spreadsheet like this:

	A	B	C	D	E	F	G	H
1								
2		Using a spreadsheet for time value of money calculations						
3								
4	If we invest $25,000 at 12 percent, how long until we have $50,000? We need to solve							
5	for the unknown number of periods, so we use the formula NPER(rate, pmt, pv, fv).							
6								
7	Present value (pv):	$25,000						
8	Future value (fv):	$50,000						
9	Rate (rate):	.12						
10								
11	Periods:	6.1162554						
12								
13	The formula entered in cell B11 is =NPER(B9,0,-B7,B8); notice that pmt is zero and that pv							
14	has a negative sign on it. Also notice that rate is entered as a decimal, not a percentage.							

depends on future interest rates. However, at worst, the bonds are guaranteed to be worth $100 at the end of 17 years, so this is the longest you would ever have to wait. If you do have to wait the full 17 years, what rate do you earn?

Because this investment is doubling in value in 17 years, the Rule of 72 tells you the answer right away: $72/17 = 4.24\%$. Remember, this is the minimum guaranteed return, so you might do better. This example finishes our introduction to basic time value concepts. Table 5.4 summarizes present and future value calculations for future reference. As our nearby *Work the Web* box shows, online calculators are widely available to handle these calculations; but it is still important to know what is really going on.

WORK THE WEB

How important is the time value of money? A recent search on one Web search engine returned over 259 million hits! Although you must understand the calculations behind the time value of money, the advent of financial calculators and spreadsheets has eliminated the need for tedious calculations. In fact, many Web sites offer time value of money calculators. The following is one example from www.investopedia.com. You have $10,000 today and will invest it at 11.5 percent for 35 years. How much will it be worth at that time? With the Investopedia calculator, you simply enter the values and hit Calculate. The results look like this:

Interest Rate Per Time Period:	11.5 %
Number of Time Periods:	35
Present Value:	10000
	Calculate
Future Value:	**$451,461.12**

Who said time value of money calculations are hard?

Questions

1. *Use the present value calculator on this Web site to answer the following: Suppose you want to have $140,000 in 25 years. If you can earn a 10 percent return, how much do you have to invest today?*
2. *Use the future value calculator on this Web site to answer the following question: Suppose you have $8,000 today that you plan to save for your retirement in 40 years. If you earn a return of 10.8 percent per year, how much will this account be worth when you are ready to retire?*

TABLE 5.4

Summary of Time Value Calculations

I. Symbols:

   PV = Present value, what future cash flows are worth today

   FV_t = Future value, what cash flows are worth in the future

     r = Interest rate, rate of return, or discount rate per period—typically, but not always, one year

     t = Number of periods—typically, but not always, the number of years

    C = Cash amount

II. Future Value of C Invested at r Percent for t Periods:

   $FV_t = C \times (1 + r)^t$

   The term $(1 + r)^t$ is called the *future value factor*.

III. Present Value of C to Be Received in t Periods at r Percent per Period:

   $PV = C/(1 + r)^t$

   The term $1/(1 + r)^t$ is called the *present value factor*.

IV. The Basic Present Value Equation Giving the Relationship between Present and Future Value:

   $PV = FV_t/(1 + r)^t$

Concept Questions

5.3a What is the basic present value equation?

5.3b What is the Rule of 72?

Summary and Conclusions   5.4

This chapter has introduced you to the basic principles of present value and discounted cash flow valuation. In it, we explained a number of things about the time value of money, including these:

1. For a given rate of return, we can determine the value at some point in the future of an investment made today by calculating the future value of that investment.
2. We can determine the current worth of a future cash flow or series of cash flows for a given rate of return by calculating the present value of the cash flow(s) involved.
3. The relationship between present value (PV) and future value (FV) for a given rate r and time t is given by the basic present value equation:

    $$PV = FV_t / (1 + r)^t$$

    As we have shown, it is possible to find any one of the four components (PV, FV_t, r, or t) given the other three.

  The principles developed in this chapter will figure prominently in the chapters to come. The reason for this is that most investments, whether they involve real assets or financial assets, can be analyzed using the discounted cash flow (DCF) approach. As a result, the DCF approach is broadly applicable and widely used in practice. Before going on, therefore, you might want to do some of the problems that follow.

CHAPTER REVIEW AND SELF-TEST PROBLEMS

5.1 Calculating Future Values Assume you deposit $10,000 today in an account that pays 6 percent interest. How much will you have in five years?

5.2 Calculating Present Values Suppose you have just celebrated your 19th birthday. A rich uncle has set up a trust fund for you that will pay you $150,000 when you turn 30. If the relevant discount rate is 9 percent, how much is this fund worth today?

5.3 Calculating Rates of Return You've been offered an investment that will double your money in 10 years. What rate of return are you being offered? Check your answer using the Rule of 72.

5.4 Calculating the Number of Periods You've been offered an investment that will pay you 9 percent per year. If you invest $15,000, how long until you have $30,000? How long until you have $45,000?

ANSWERS TO CHAPTER REVIEW AND SELF-TEST PROBLEMS

5.1 We need to calculate the future value of $10,000 at 6 percent for five years. The future value factor is:

  $$1.06^5 = 1.3382$$

  The future value is thus $10,000 \times 1.3382 = \$13,382.26$.

5.2 We need the present value of $150,000 to be paid in 11 years at 9 percent. The discount factor is:

  $$1/1.09^{11} = 1/2.5804 = .3875$$

  The present value is thus about $58,130.

5.3 Suppose you invest $1,000. You will have $2,000 in 10 years with this investment. So, $1,000 is the amount you have today, or the present value, and $2,000 is the amount you will have in 10 years, or the future value. From the basic present value equation, we have:

$$\$2,000 = \$1,000 \times (1 + r)^{10}$$
$$2 = (1 + r)^{10}$$

From here, we need to solve for r, the unknown rate. As shown in the chapter, there are several different ways to do this. We will take the 10th root of 2 (by raising 2 to the power of 1/10):

$$2^{(1/10)} = 1 + r$$
$$1.0718 = 1 + r$$
$$r = 7.18\%$$

Using the Rule of 72, we have $72/t = r\%$, or $72/10 = 7.2\%$, so, our answer looks good (remember that the Rule of 72 is only an approximation).

5.4 The basic equation is this:

$$\$30,000 = \$15,000 \times (1 + .09)^t$$
$$2 = (1 + .09)^t$$

If we solve for t, we find that $t = 8.04$ years. Using the Rule of 72, we get $72/9 = 8$ years, so once again our answer looks good. To get $45,000, verify for yourself that you will have to wait 12.75 years.

CONCEPTS REVIEW AND CRITICAL THINKING QUESTIONS

1. **Present Value** [LO2] The basic present value equation has four parts. What are they?
2. **Compounding** [LO1, 2] What is compounding? What is discounting?
3. **Compounding and Period** [LO1] As you increase the length of time involved, what happens to future values? What happens to present values?
4. **Compounding and Interest Rates** [LO1] What happens to a future value if you increase the rate r? What happens to a present value?
5. **Ethical Considerations** [LO2] Take a look back at Example 5.7. Is it deceptive advertising? Is it unethical to advertise a future value like this without a disclaimer?

    To answer the next five questions, refer to the TMCC security we discussed to open the chapter.

6. **Time Value of Money** [LO2] Why would TMCC be willing to accept such a small amount today ($24,099) in exchange for a promise to repay about four times that amount ($100,000) in the future?
7. **Call Provisions** [LO2] TMCC has the right to buy back the securities on the anniversary date at a price established when the securities were issued (this feature is a term of this particular deal). What impact does this feature have on the desirability of this security as an investment?
8. **Time Value of Money** [LO2] Would you be willing to pay $24,099 today in exchange for $100,000 in 30 years? What would be the key considerations in answering yes or no? Would your answer depend on who is making the promise to repay?
9. **Investment Comparison** [LO2] Suppose that when TMCC offered the security for $24,099 the U.S. Treasury had offered an essentially identical security. Do you think it would have had a higher or lower price? Why?

10. **Length of Investment [LO2]** The TMCC security is bought and sold on the New York Stock Exchange. If you looked at the price today, do you think the price would exceed the $24,099 original price? Why? If you looked in the year 2019, do you think the price would be higher or lower than today's price? Why?

QUESTIONS AND PROBLEMS

1. **Simple Interest versus Compound Interest [LO1]** First City Bank pays 8 percent simple interest on its savings account balances, whereas Second City Bank pays 8 percent interest compounded annually. If you made a $5,000 deposit in each bank, how much more money would you earn from your Second City Bank account at the end of 10 years?

BASIC
(Questions 1–15)

2. **Calculating Future Values [LO1]** For each of the following, compute the future value:

Present Value	Years	Interest Rate	Future Value
$ 2,250	11	10%	
8,752	7	8	
76,355	14	17	
183,796	8	7	

3. **Calculating Present Values [LO2]** For each of the following, compute the present value:

Present Value	Years	Interest Rate	Future Value
	6	7%	$ 15,451
	7	13	51,557
	23	14	886,073
	18	9	550,164

4. **Calculating Interest Rates [LO3]** Solve for the unknown interest rate in each of the following:

Present Value	Years	Interest Rate	Future Value
$ 240	2		$ 297
360	10		1,080
39,000	15		185,382
38,261	30		531,618

5. **Calculating the Number of Periods [LO4]** Solve for the unknown number of years in each of the following:

Present Value	Years	Interest Rate	Future Value
$ 560		9%	$ 1,284
810		10	4,341
18,400		17	364,518
21,500		15	173,439

6. **Calculating Interest Rates [LO3]** Assume the total cost of a college education will be $290,000 when your child enters college in 18 years. You presently have $55,000 to invest. What annual rate of interest must you earn on your investment to cover the cost of your child's college education?

Visit us at www.mhhe.com/rwj

7. **Calculating the Number of Periods** [LO4] At 7 percent interest, how long does it take to double your money? To quadruple it?

8. **Calculating Interest Rates** [LO3] In January 2007, the average house price in the United States was $314,600. In January 2000, the average price was $200,300. What was the annual increase in selling price?

9. **Calculating the Number of Periods** [LO4] You're trying to save to buy a new $170,000 Ferrari. You have $40,000 today that can be invested at your bank. The bank pays 5.3 percent annual interest on its accounts. How long will it be before you have enough to buy the car?

10. **Calculating Present Values** [LO2] Imprudential, Inc. has an unfunded pension liability of $650 million that must be paid in 20 years. To assess the value of the firm's stock, financial analysts want to discount this liability back to the present. If the relevant discount rate is 7.4 percent, what is the present value of this liability?

11. **Calculating Present Values** [LO2] You have just received notification that you have won the $1 million first prize in the Centennial Lottery. However, the prize will be awarded on your 100th birthday (assuming you're around to collect), 80 years from now. What is the present value of your windfall if the appropriate discount rate is 10 percent?

12. **Calculating Future Values** [LO1] Your coin collection contains fifty 1952 silver dollars. If your grandparents purchased them for their face value when they were new, how much will your collection be worth when you retire in 2057, assuming they appreciate at a 4.5 percent annual rate?

13. **Calculating Interest Rates and Future Values** [LO1, 3] In 1895, the first U.S. Open Golf Championship was held. The winner's prize money was $150. In 2007, the winner's check was $1,260,000. What was the percentage increase per year in the winner's check over this period? If the winner's prize increases at the same rate, what will it be in 2040?

14. **Calculating Interest Rates** [LO3] In 2008, a gold Morgan dollar minted in 1895 sold for $43,125. For this to have been true, what rate of return did this coin return for the lucky numismatist?

15. **Calculating Rates of Return** [LO3] Although appealing to more refined tastes, art as a collectible has not always performed so profitably. During 2003, Sotheby's sold the Edgar Degas bronze sculpture *Petite Danseuse de Quatorze Ans* at auction for a price of $10,311,500. Unfortunately for the previous owner, he had purchased it in 1999 at a price of $12,377,500. What was his annual rate of return on this sculpture?

INTERMEDIATE
(Questions 16–20)

16. **Calculating Rates of Return** [LO3] Referring to the TMCC security we discussed at the very beginning of the chapter:

    a. Based on the $24,099 price, what rate was TMCC paying to borrow money?

    b. Suppose that, on March 28, 2020, this security's price is $38,260. If an investor had purchased it for $24,099 at the offering and sold it on this day, what annual rate of return would she have earned?

    c. If an investor had purchased the security at market on March 28, 2020, and held it until it matured, what annual rate of return would she have earned?

17. **Calculating Present Values** [LO2] Suppose you are still committed to owning a $170,000 Ferrari (see Problem 9). If you believe your mutual fund can achieve a 12 percent annual rate of return and you want to buy the car in 9 years on the day you turn 30, how much must you invest today?

18. **Calculating Future Values [LO1]** You have just made your first $4,000 contribution to your retirement account. Assuming you earn an 11 percent rate of return and make no additional contributions, what will your account be worth when you retire in 45 years? What if you wait 10 years before contributing? (Does this suggest an investment strategy?)

19. **Calculating Future Values [LO1]** You are scheduled to receive $20,000 in two years. When you receive it, you will invest it for six more years at 8.4 percent per year. How much will you have in eight years?

20. **Calculating the Number of Periods [LO4]** You expect to receive $10,000 at graduation in two years. You plan on investing it at 11 percent until you have $75,000. How long will you wait from now?

Visit us at www.mhhe.com/rwj

6

DISCOUNTED CASH FLOW VALUATION

THE SIGNING OF BIG-NAME ATHLETES is often accompanied by great fanfare, but the numbers are often misleading. For example, in 2007, catcher Jorge Posada reached a deal with the New York Yankees, signing a contract with a reported value of $52.4 million. Not bad, especially for someone who makes a living using the "tools of ignorance" (jock jargon for a catcher's equipment). Another example is the contract signed by quarterback Tony Romo of the Dallas Cowboys, which had a stated value of about $67.5 million.

It looks like Jorge and Tony did pretty well, but then there was Jorge's teammate Alex Rodriguez, or A-Rod as he is known to fans, who signed for a stated value of $275 million. This amount was actually payable over several years and consisted of $2 million immediately, along with $28 million in the first year plus $245 million in future salary to be paid in the years 2009 through 2017. Jorge's and Tony's payments were similarly spread over time. Because all three contracts called for payments that are made at future dates, we must consider the time value of money, which means none of these players received the quoted amounts. How much did they really get? This chapter gives you the "tools of knowledge" to answer this question.

Master the ability to solve problems in this chapter by using a spreadsheet. Access Excel Master on the student Web site www.mhhe.com/rwj.

In our previous chapter, we covered the basics of discounted cash flow valuation. However, so far, we have dealt with only single cash flows. In reality, most investments have multiple cash flows. For example, if Target is thinking of opening a new department store, there will be a large cash outlay in the beginning and then cash inflows for many years. In this chapter, we begin to explore how to value such investments.

When you finish this chapter, you should have some very practical skills. For example, you will know how to calculate your own car payments or student loan payments. You will also be able to determine how long it will take to pay off a credit card if you make the minimum payment each month (a practice we do not recommend). We will show you how to compare interest rates to determine which are the highest and which are the lowest, and we will also show you how interest rates can be quoted in different—and at times deceptive—ways.

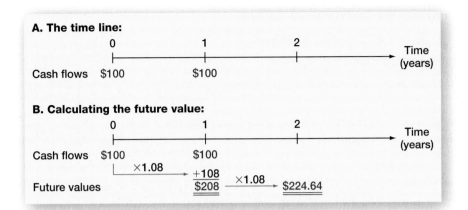

FIGURE 6.1

Drawing and Using a
Time Line

Future and Present Values of Multiple Cash Flows

6.1

Thus far, we have restricted our attention to either the future value of a lump sum present amount or the present value of some single future cash flow. In this section, we begin to study ways to value multiple cash flows. We start with future value.

FUTURE VALUE WITH MULTIPLE CASH FLOWS

Suppose you deposit $100 today in an account paying 8 percent. In one year, you will deposit another $100. How much will you have in two years? This particular problem is relatively easy. At the end of the first year, you will have $108 plus the second $100 you deposit, for a total of $208. You leave this $208 on deposit at 8 percent for another year. At the end of this second year, it is worth:

$208 × 1.08 = $224.64

Figure 6.1 is a *time line* that illustrates the process of calculating the future value of these two $100 deposits. Figures such as this are useful for solving complicated problems. Almost anytime you are having trouble with a present or future value problem, drawing a time line will help you see what is happening.

In the first part of Figure 6.1, we show the cash flows on the time line. The most important thing is that we write them down where they actually occur. Here, the first cash flow occurs today, which we label as time 0. We therefore put $100 at time 0 on the time line. The second $100 cash flow occurs one year from today, so we write it down at the point labeled as time 1. In the second part of Figure 6.1, we calculate the future values one period at a time to come up with the final $224.64.

| **Saving Up Revisited** | **EXAMPLE 6.1** |

You think you will be able to deposit $4,000 at the end of each of the next three years in a bank account paying 8 percent interest. You currently have $7,000 in the account. How much will you have in three years? In four years?

At the end of the first year, you will have:

$7,000 × 1.08 + 4,000 = $11,560

(continued)

At the end of the second year, you will have:

$$\$11,560 \times 1.08 + 4,000 = \$16,484.80$$

Repeating this for the third year gives:

$$\$16,484.80 \times 1.08 + 4,000 = \$21,803.58$$

Therefore, you will have $21,803.58 in three years. If you leave this on deposit for one more year (and don't add to it), at the end of the fourth year, you'll have:

$$\$21,803.58 \times 1.08 = \$23,547.87$$

When we calculated the future value of the two $100 deposits, we simply calculated the balance as of the beginning of each year and then rolled that amount forward to the next year. We could have done it another, quicker way. The first $100 is on deposit for two years at 8 percent, so its future value is:

$$\$100 \times 1.08^2 = \$100 \times 1.1664 = \$116.64$$

The second $100 is on deposit for one year at 8 percent, and its future value is thus:

$$\$100 \times 1.08 = \$108$$

The total future value, as we previously calculated, is equal to the sum of these two future values:

$$\$116.64 + 108 = \$224.64$$

Based on this example, there are two ways to calculate future values for multiple cash flows: (1) Compound the accumulated balance forward one year at a time or (2) calculate the future value of each cash flow first and then add them up. Both give the same answer, so you can do it either way.

To illustrate the two different ways of calculating future values, consider the future value of $2,000 invested at the end of each of the next five years. The current balance is zero, and the rate is 10 percent. We first draw a time line, as shown in Figure 6.2.

On the time line, notice that nothing happens until the end of the first year, when we make the first $2,000 investment. This first $2,000 earns interest for the next four (not five) years. Also notice that the last $2,000 is invested at the end of the fifth year, so it earns no interest at all.

Figure 6.3 illustrates the calculations involved if we compound the investment one period at a time. As illustrated, the future value is $12,210.20.

FIGURE 6.2

Time Line for $2,000 per Year for Five Years

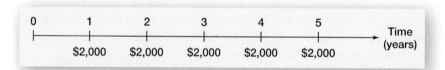

FIGURE 6.3 Future Value Calculated by Compounding Forward One Period at a Time

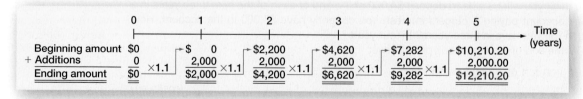

FIGURE 6.4   Future Value Calculated by Compounding Each Cash Flow Separately

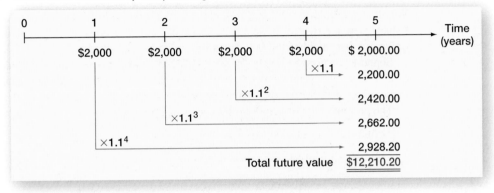

Figure 6.4 goes through the same calculations, but the second technique is used. Naturally, the answer is the same.

| **Saving Up Once Again** | **EXAMPLE 6.2** |

If you deposit $100 in one year, $200 in two years, and $300 in three years, how much will you have in three years? How much of this is interest? How much will you have in five years if you don't add additional amounts? Assume a 7 percent interest rate throughout.

We will calculate the future value of each amount in three years. Notice that the $100 earns interest for two years, and the $200 earns interest for one year. The final $300 earns no interest. The future values are thus:

$$
\begin{aligned}
\$100 \times 1.07^2 \quad &= \$114.49 \\
\$200 \times 1.07 \quad &= 214.00 \\
+\$300 \qquad\qquad &= \underline{300.00} \\
\text{Total future value} &= \$628.49
\end{aligned}
$$

The total future value is thus $628.49. The total interest is:

$628.49 − (100 + 200 + 300) = $28.49

How much will you have in five years? We know that you will have $628.49 in three years. If you leave that in for two more years, it will grow to:

$628.49 × 1.07² = $628.49 × 1.1449 = $719.56

Notice that we could have calculated the future value of each amount separately. Once again, be careful about the lengths of time. As we previously calculated, the first $100 earns interest for only four years, the second deposit earns three years' interest, and the last earns two years' interest:

$$
\begin{aligned}
\$100 \times 1.07^4 &= \$100 \times 1.3108 = \$131.08 \\
\$200 \times 1.07^3 &= \$200 \times 1.2250 = 245.01 \\
+\$300 \times 1.07^2 &= \$300 \times 1.1449 = \underline{343.47} \\
&\qquad\quad\text{Total future value} = \$719.56
\end{aligned}
$$

PRESENT VALUE WITH MULTIPLE CASH FLOWS

We often need to determine the present value of a series of future cash flows. As with future values, there are two ways we can do it. We can either discount back one period at a time, or we can just calculate the present values individually and add them up.

Suppose you need $1,000 in one year and $2,000 more in two years. If you can earn 9 percent on your money, how much do you have to put up today to exactly cover these amounts in the future? In other words, what is the present value of the two cash flows at 9 percent?

The present value of $2,000 in two years at 9 percent is:

$2,000/1.09^2 = $1,683.36

The present value of $1,000 in one year is:

$1,000/1.09 = $917.43

Therefore, the total present value is:

$1,683.36 + 917.43 = $2,600.79

To see why $2,600.79 is the right answer, we can check to see that after the $2,000 is paid out in two years, there is no money left. If we invest $2,600.79 for one year at 9 percent, we will have:

$2,600.79 × 1.09 = $2,834.86

We take out $1,000, leaving $1,834.86. This amount earns 9 percent for another year, leaving us with:

$1,834.86 × 1.09 = $2,000

This is just as we planned. As this example illustrates, the present value of a series of future cash flows is simply the amount you would need today to exactly duplicate those future cash flows (for a given discount rate).

An alternative way of calculating present values for multiple future cash flows is to discount back to the present, one period at a time. To illustrate, suppose we had an investment that was going to pay $1,000 at the end of every year for the next five years. To find the present value, we could discount each $1,000 back to the present separately and then add them up. Figure 6.5 illustrates this approach for a 6 percent discount rate; as shown, the answer is $4,212.37 (ignoring a small rounding error).

FIGURE 6.5

Present Value Calculated by Discounting Each Cash Flow Separately

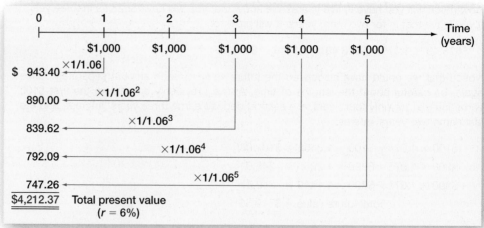

FIGURE 6.6   Present Value Calculated by Discounting Back One Period at a Time

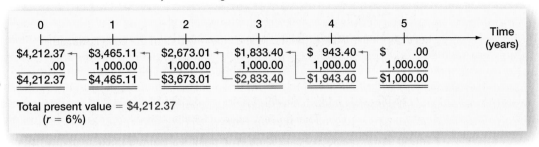

Total present value = $4,212.37
        (r = 6%)

Alternatively, we could discount the last cash flow back one period and add it to the next-to-the-last cash flow:

($1,000/1.06) + 1,000 = $943.40 + 1,000 = $1,943.40

We could then discount this amount back one period and add it to the year 3 cash flow:

($1,943.40/1.06) + 1,000 = $1,833.40 + 1,000 = $2,833.40

This process could be repeated as necessary. Figure 6.6 illustrates this appoach and the remaining calculations.

How Much Is It Worth?	**EXAMPLE 6.3**

You are offered an investment that will pay you $200 in one year, $400 the next year, $600 the next year, and $800 at the end of the fourth year. You can earn 12 percent on very similar investments. What is the most you should pay for this one?

We need to calculate the present value of these cash flows at 12 percent. Taking them one at a time gives:

$$\$200 \times 1/1.12^1 = \$200/1.1200 = \$\ \ 178.57$$
$$\$400 \times 1/1.12^2 = \$400/1.2544 = \ \ \ \ 318.88$$
$$\$600 \times 1/1.12^3 = \$600/1.4049 = \ \ \ \ 427.07$$
$$+\$800 \times 1/1.12^4 = \$800/1.5735 = \ \ \ \underline{\ \ \ 508.41}$$
$$\text{Total present value} = \underline{\underline{\$1,432.93}}$$

If you can earn 12 percent on your money, then you can duplicate this investment's cash flows for $1,432.93, so this is the most you should be willing to pay.

How Much Is It Worth? Part 2	**EXAMPLE 6.4**

You are offered an investment that will make three $5,000 payments. The first payment will occur four years from today. The second will occur in five years, and the third will follow in six years. If you can earn 11 percent, what is the most this investment is worth today? What is the future value of the cash flows?

We will answer the questions in reverse order to illustrate a point. The future value of the cash flows in six years is:

$$(\$5,000 \times 1.11^2) + (5,000 \times 1.11) + 5,000 = \$6,160.50 + 5,550 + 5,000$$
$$= \$16,710.50$$

(continued)

The present value must be:

$$\$16{,}710.50/1.11^6 = \$8{,}934.12$$

Let's check this. Taking them one at a time, the PVs of the cash flows are:

$$\$5{,}000 \times 1/1.11^6 = \$5{,}000/1.8704 = \$2{,}673.20$$
$$\$5{,}000 \times 1/1.11^5 = \$5{,}000/1.6851 = 2{,}967.26$$
$$+\$5{,}000 \times 1/1.11^4 = \$5{,}000/1.5181 = \underline{3{,}293.65}$$
$$\text{Total present value} = \underline{\underline{\$8{,}934.12}}$$

This is as we previously calculated. The point we want to make is that we can calculate present and future values in any order and convert between them using whatever way seems most convenient. The answers will always be the same as long as we stick with the same discount rate and are careful to keep track of the right number of periods.

CALCULATOR HINTS

How to Calculate Present Values with Multiple Future Cash Flows Using a Financial Calculator

To calculate the present value of multiple cash flows with a financial calculator, we will simply discount the individual cash flows one at a time using the same technique we used in our previous chapter, so this is not really new. However, we can show you a shortcut. We will use the numbers in Example 6.3 to illustrate.

To begin, of course we first remember to clear out the calculator! Next, from Example 6.3, the first cash flow is $200 to be received in one year and the discount rate is 12 percent, so we do the following:

Now, you can write down this answer to save it, but that's inefficient. All calculators have a memory where you can store numbers. Why not just save it there? Doing so cuts way down on mistakes because you don't have to write down and/or rekey numbers, and it's much faster.

Next we value the second cash flow. We need to change N to 2 and FV to 400. As long as we haven't changed anything else, we don't have to reenter I/Y or clear out the calculator, so we have:

You save this number by adding it to the one you saved in our first calculation, and so on for the remaining two calculations.

As we will see in a later chapter, some financial calculators will let you enter all of the future cash flows at once, but we'll discuss that subject when we get to it.

SPREADSHEET STRATEGIES

How to Calculate Present Values with Multiple Future Cash Flows Using a Spreadsheet

Just as we did in our previous chapter, we can set up a basic spreadsheet to calculate the present values of the individual cash flows as follows. Notice that we have simply calculated the present values one at a time and added them up:

	A	B	C	D	E
1					
2			Using a spreadsheet to value multiple future cash flows		
3					
4	What is the present value of $200 in one year, $400 the next year, $600 the next year, and				
5	$800 the last year if the discount rate is 12 percent?				
6					
7	Rate:	.12			
8					
9	Year	Cash flows	Present values	Formula used	
10	1	$200	$178.57	=PV($B$7,A10,0,−B10)	
11	2	$400	$318.88	=PV($B$7,A11,0,−B11)	
12	3	$600	$427.07	=PV($B$7,A12,0,−B12)	
13	4	$800	$508.41	=PV($B$7,A13,0,−B13)	
14					
15		Total PV:	$1,432.93	=SUM(C10:C13)	
16					
17	Notice the negative signs inserted in the PV formulas. These just make the present values have				
18	positive signs. Also, the discount rate in cell B7 is entered as $B$7 (an "absolute" reference)				
19	because it is used over and over. We could have just entered ".12" instead, but our approach is more				
20	flexible.				
21					
22					

A NOTE ABOUT CASH FLOW TIMING

In working present and future value problems, cash flow timing is critically important. In almost all such calculations, it is implicitly assumed that the cash flows occur at the *end* of each period. In fact, all the formulas we have discussed, all the numbers in a standard present value or future value table, and (very important) all the preset (or default) settings on a financial calculator assume that cash flows occur at the end of each period. Unless you are explicitly told otherwise, you should always assume that this is what is meant.

As a quick illustration of this point, suppose you are told that a three-year investment has a first-year cash flow of $100, a second-year cash flow of $200, and a third-year cash flow of $300. You are asked to draw a time line. Without further information, you should always assume that the time line looks like this:

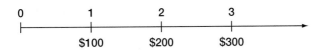

On our time line, notice how the first cash flow occurs at the end of the first period, the second at the end of the second period, and the third at the end of the third period.

We will close this section by answering the question we posed at the beginning of the chapter concerning baseball player Alex Rodriguez's contract. Recall that the contract called for $2 million immediately and $28 million in 2008. The remaining $245 million was to be paid as $33 million in 2009, $33 million in 2010, $32 million in 2011, $30 million in 2012, $32 million in 2013, $25 million in 2014, $21 million in 2015, and $20 million in 2016 and 2017. If 12 percent is the appropriate interest rate, what kind of deal did the Yankees' infielder field?

To answer, we can calculate the present value by discounting each year's salary back to the present as follows (notice we assume that all the payments are made at year-end):

Year 0 (2007): $ 2,000,000   = $ 2,000,000.00
Year 1 (2008): $28,000,000 $\times$ 1/1.12^1 = $25,000,000.00
Year 2 (2009): $33,000,000 $\times$ 1/1.12^2 = $26,307,397.96
Year 3 (2010): $33,000,000 $\times$ 1/1.12^3 = $23,488,748.18

.

.

Year 10 (2017): $20,000,000 $\times$ 1/1.12^{10} = $ 6,439,464.73

If you fill in the missing rows and then add (do it for practice), you will see that A-Rod's contract had a present value of about $163 million, or about 60 percent of the stated $275 million value.

Concept Questions

6.1a Describe how to calculate the future value of a series of cash flows.

6.1b Describe how to calculate the present value of a series of cash flows.

6.1c Unless we are explicitly told otherwise, what do we always assume about the timing of cash flows in present and future value problems?

6.2 Valuing Level Cash Flows: Annuities and Perpetuities

We will frequently encounter situations in which we have multiple cash flows that are all the same amount. For example, a common type of loan repayment plan calls for the borrower to repay the loan by making a series of equal payments over some length of time. Almost all consumer loans (such as car loans) and home mortgages feature equal payments, usually made each month.

More generally, a series of constant or level cash flows that occur at the end of each period for some fixed number of periods is called an ordinary **annuity**; more correctly, the cash flows are said to be in *ordinary annuity form*. Annuities appear frequently in financial arrangements, and there are some useful shortcuts for determining their values. We consider these next.

annuity
A level stream of cash flows for a fixed period of time.

PRESENT VALUE FOR ANNUITY CASH FLOWS

Suppose we were examining an asset that promised to pay $500 at the end of each of the next three years. The cash flows from this asset are in the form of a three-year, $500 annuity. If we wanted to earn 10 percent on our money, how much would we offer for this annuity?

From the previous section, we know that we can discount each of these $500 payments back to the present at 10 percent to determine the total present value:

$$\text{Present value} = (\$500/1.1^1) + (500/1.1^2) + (500/1.1^3)$$
$$= (\$500/1.1) + (500/1.21) + (500/1.331)$$
$$= \$454.55 + 413.22 + 375.66$$
$$= \$1{,}243.43$$

This approach works just fine. However, we will often encounter situations in which the number of cash flows is quite large. For example, a typical home mortgage calls for monthly payments over 30 years, for a total of 360 payments. If we were trying to determine the present value of those payments, it would be useful to have a shortcut.

Because the cash flows of an annuity are all the same, we can come up with a handy variation on the basic present value equation. The present value of an annuity of C dollars per period for t periods when the rate of return or interest rate is r is given by:

$$\text{Annuity present value} = C \times \left(\frac{1 - \text{Present value factor}}{r} \right)$$
$$= C \times \left\{ \frac{1 - [1/(1 + r)^t]}{r} \right\}$$

[6.1]

The term in parentheses on the first line is sometimes called the *present value interest factor for annuities* and abbreviated PVIFA(r, t).

The expression for the annuity present value may look a little complicated, but it isn't difficult to use. Notice that the term in square brackets on the second line, $1/(1 + r)^t$, is the same present value factor we've been calculating. In our example from the beginning of this section, the interest rate is 10 percent and there are three years involved. The usual present value factor is thus:

$$\text{Present value factor} = 1/1.1^3 = 1/1.331 = .751315$$

To calculate the annuity present value factor, we just plug this in:

$$\text{Annuity present value factor} = (1 - \text{Present value factor})/r$$
$$= (1 - .751315)/.10$$
$$= .248685/.10 = 2.48685$$

Just as we calculated before, the present value of our $500 annuity is then:

$$\text{Annuity present value} = \$500 \times 2.48685 = \$1{,}243.43$$

How Much Can You Afford?	**EXAMPLE 6.5**

After carefully going over your budget, you have determined you can afford to pay $632 per month toward a new sports car. You call up your local bank and find out that the going rate is 1 percent per month for 48 months. How much can you borrow?

To determine how much you can borrow, we need to calculate the present value of $632 per month for 48 months at 1 percent per month. The loan payments are in ordinary annuity

(continued)

form, so the annuity present value factor is:

$$\text{Annuity PV factor} = (1 - \text{Present value factor})/r$$
$$= [1 - (1/1.01^{48})]/.01$$
$$= (1 - .6203)/.01 = 37.9740$$

With this factor, we can calculate the present value of the 48 payments of $632 each as:

$$\text{Present value} = \$632 \times 37.9740 = \$24,000$$

Therefore, $24,000 is what you can afford to borrow and repay.

Annuity Tables   Just as there are tables for ordinary present value factors, there are tables for annuity factors as well. Table 6.1 contains a few such factors; Table A.3 in the appendix to the book contains a larger set. To find the annuity present value factor we calculated just before Example 6.5, look for the row corresponding to three periods and then find the column for 10 percent. The number you see at that intersection should be 2.4869 (rounded to four decimal places), as we calculated. Once again, try calculating a few of these factors yourself and compare your answers to the ones in the table to make sure you know how to do it. If you are using a financial calculator, just enter $1 as the payment and calculate the present value; the result should be the annuity present value factor.

TABLE 6.1

Annuity Present Value Interest Factors

| | Interest Rate | | | |
Number of Periods	5%	10%	15%	20%
1	.9524	.9091	.8696	.8333
2	1.8594	1.7355	1.6257	1.5278
3	2.7232	2.4869	2.2832	2.1065
4	3.5460	3.1699	2.8550	2.5887
5	4.3295	3.7908	3.3522	2.9906

CALCULATOR HINTS

Annuity Present Values

To find annuity present values with a financial calculator, we need to use the PMT key (you were probably wondering what it was for). Compared to finding the present value of a single amount, there are two important differences. First, we enter the annuity cash flow using the PMT key. Second, we don't enter anything for the future value, FV. So, for example, the problem we have been examining is a three-year, $500 annuity. If the discount rate is 10 percent, we need to do the following (after clearing out the calculator!):

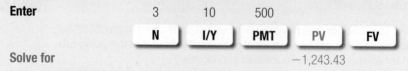

Enter	3	10	500		
	N	I/Y	PMT	PV	FV
Solve for				−1,243.43	

As usual, we get a negative sign on the PV.

SPREADSHEET STRATEGIES

Annuity Present Values

Using a spreadsheet to find annuity present values goes like this:

	A	B	C	D	E	F	G
1							
2	Using a spreadsheet to find annuity present values						
3							
4	What is the present value of $500 per year for 3 years if the discount rate is 10 percent?						
5	We need to solve for the unknown present value, so we use the formula PV(rate, nper, pmt, fv).						
6							
7	Payment amount per period:	$500					
8	Number of payments:	3					
9	Discount rate:	.1					
10							
11	Annuity present value:	**$1,243.43**					
12							
13	The formula entered in cell B11 is =PV(B9,B8,-B7,0); notice that fv is zero and that						
14	pmt has a negative sign on it. Also notice that rate is entered as a decimal, not a percentage.						
15							
16							
17							

Finding the Payment   Suppose you wish to start up a new business that specializes in the latest of health food trends, frozen yak milk. To produce and market your product, the Yak-kee Doodle Dandy, you need to borrow $100,000. Because it strikes you as unlikely that this particular fad will be long-lived, you propose to pay off the loan quickly by making five equal annual payments. If the interest rate is 18 percent, what will the payment be?

In this case, we know the present value is $100,000. The interest rate is 18 percent, and there are five years. The payments are all equal, so we need to find the relevant annuity factor and solve for the unknown cash flow:

$$\text{Annuity present value} = \$100{,}000 = C \times [(1 - \text{Present value factor})/r]$$
$$= C \times \{[1 - (1/1.18^5)]/.18\}$$
$$= C \times [(1 - .4371)/.18]$$
$$= C \times 3.1272$$
$$C = \$100{,}000/3.1272 = \$31{,}978$$

Therefore, you'll make five payments of just under $32,000 each.

CALCULATOR HINTS

Annuity Payments

Finding annuity payments is easy with a financial calculator. In our yak example, the PV is $100,000, the interest rate is 18 percent, and there are five years. We find the payment as follows:

Enter	5	18		100,000	
	N	I/Y	PMT	PV	FV
Solve for			−31,978		

Here, we get a negative sign on the payment because the payment is an outflow for us.

SPREADSHEET STRATEGIES

Annuity Payments

Using a spreadsheet to work the same problem goes like this:

	A	B	C	D	E	F	G
1							
2	**Using a spreadsheet to find annuity payments**						
3							
4	What is the annuity payment if the present value is $100,000, the interest rate is 18 percent, and						
5	there are 5 periods? We need to solve for the unknown payment in an annuity, so we use the						
6	formula PMT(rate, nper, pv, fv).						
7							
8	Annuity present value:	$100,000					
9	Number of payments:	5					
10	Discount rate:	.18					
11							
12	Annuity payment:	**$31,977.78**					
13							
14	The formula entered in cell B12 is =PMT(B10, B9, -B8,0); notice that fv is zero and that the payment						
15	has a negative sign because it is an outflow to us.						
16							

EXAMPLE 6.6   **Finding the Number of Payments**

You ran a little short on your spring break vacation, so you put $1,000 on your credit card. You can afford only the minimum payment of $20 per month. The interest rate on the credit card is 1.5 percent per month. How long will you need to pay off the $1,000?

What we have here is an annuity of $20 per month at 1.5 percent per month for some unknown length of time. The present value is $1,000 (the amount you owe today). We need to do a little algebra (or use a financial calculator):

$$\$1,000 = \$20 \times [(1 - \text{Present value factor})/.015]$$
$$(\$1,000/20) \times .015 = 1 - \text{Present value factor}$$
$$\text{Present value factor} = .25 = 1/(1 + r)^t$$
$$1.015^t = 1/.25 = 4$$

At this point, the problem boils down to asking, How long does it take for your money to quadruple at 1.5 percent per month? Based on our previous chapter, the answer is about 93 months:

$$1.015^{93} = 3.99 \approx 4$$

It will take you about 93/12 = 7.75 years to pay off the $1,000 at this rate. If you use a financial calculator for problems like this, you should be aware that some automatically round up to the next whole period.

CALCULATOR HINTS

Finding the Number of Payments

To solve this one on a financial calculator, do the following:

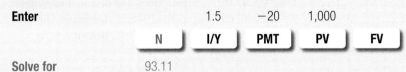

Enter	1.5		−20	1,000	
	N	I/Y	PMT	PV	FV

Solve for	93.11

Notice that we put a negative sign on the payment you must make, and we have solved for the number of months. You still have to divide by 12 to get our answer. Also, some financial calculators won't report a fractional value for N; they automatically (without telling you) round up to the next whole period (not to the nearest value). With a spreadsheet, use the function =NPER(rate,pmt,pv,fv); be sure to put in a zero for fv and to enter −20 as the payment.

Finding the Rate   The last question we might want to ask concerns the interest rate implicit in an annuity. For example, an insurance company offers to pay you $1,000 per year for 10 years if you will pay $6,710 up front. What rate is implicit in this 10-year annuity?

In this case, we know the present value ($6,710), we know the cash flows ($1,000 per year), and we know the life of the investment (10 years). What we don't know is the discount rate:

$$\$6,710 = \$1,000 \times [(1 - \text{Present value factor})/r]$$
$$\$6,710/1,000 = 6.71 = \{1 - [1/(1 + r)^{10}]\}/r$$

So, the annuity factor for 10 periods is equal to 6.71, and we need to solve this equation for the unknown value of r. Unfortunately, this is mathematically impossible to do directly. The only way to do it is to use a table or trial and error to find a value for r.

If you look across the row corresponding to 10 periods in Table A.3, you will see a factor of 6.7101 for 8 percent, so we see right away that the insurance company is offering just about 8 percent. Alternatively, we could just start trying different values until we got very close to the answer. Using this trial-and-error approach can be a little tedious, but fortunately machines are good at that sort of thing.[1]

To illustrate how to find the answer by trial and error, suppose a relative of yours wants to borrow $3,000. She offers to repay you $1,000 every year for four years. What interest rate are you being offered?

The cash flows here have the form of a four-year, $1,000 annuity. The present value is $3,000. We need to find the discount rate, r. Our goal in doing so is primarily to give you a feel for the relationship between annuity values and discount rates.

We need to start somewhere, and 10 percent is probably as good a place as any to begin. At 10 percent, the annuity factor is:

Annuity present value factor $= [1 - (1/1.10^4)]/.10 = 3.1699$

---

[1] Financial calculators rely on trial and error to find the answer. That's why they sometimes appear to be "thinking" before coming up with the answer. Actually, it is possible to directly solve for r if there are fewer than five periods, but it's usually not worth the trouble.

The present value of the cash flows at 10 percent is thus:

Present value = $1,000 × 3.1699 = $3,169.90

You can see that we're already in the right ballpark.

Is 10 percent too high or too low? Recall that present values and discount rates move in opposite directions: Increasing the discount rate lowers the PV and vice versa. Our present value here is too high, so the discount rate is too low. If we try 12 percent, we're almost there:

Present value = $1,000 × {[1 − (1/1.12^4)]/.12} = $3,037.35

We are still a little low on the discount rate (because the PV is a little high), so we'll try 13 percent:

Present value = $1,000 × {[1 − (1/1.13^4)]/.13} = $2,974.47

This is less than $3,000, so we now know that the answer is between 12 percent and 13 percent, and it looks to be about 12.5 percent. For practice, work at it for a while longer and see if you find that the answer is about 12.59 percent.

To illustrate a situation in which finding the unknown rate can be useful, let us consider that the Tri-State Megabucks lottery in Maine, Vermont, and New Hampshire offers you a choice of how to take your winnings (most lotteries do this). In a recent drawing, participants were offered the option of receiving a lump sum payment of $250,000 or an annuity of $500,000 to be received in equal installments over a 25-year period. (At the time, the lump sum payment was always half the annuity option.) Which option was better?

To answer, suppose you were to compare $250,000 today to an annuity of $500,000/25 = $20,000 per year for 25 years. At what rate do these have the same value? This is the same type of problem we've been looking at; we need to find the unknown rate, r, for a present value of $250,000, a $20,000 payment, and a 25-year period. If you grind through the calculations (or get a little machine assistance), you should find that the unknown rate is about 6.24 percent. You should take the annuity option if that rate is attractive relative to other investments available to you. Notice that we have ignored taxes in this example, and taxes can significantly affect our conclusion. Be sure to consult your tax adviser anytime you win the lottery.

CALCULATOR HINTS

Finding the Rate

Alternatively, you could use a financial calculator to do the following:

Enter	4		1,000	−3,000	
	N	**I/Y**	**PMT**	**PV**	**FV**
Solve for		12.59			

Notice that we put a negative sign on the present value (why?). With a spreadsheet, use the function =RATE(nper,pmt,pv,fv); be sure to put in a zero for fv and to enter 1,000 as the payment and −3,000 as the pv.

FUTURE VALUE FOR ANNUITIES

On occasion, it's also handy to know a shortcut for calculating the future value of an annuity. As you might guess, there are future value factors for annuities as well as present value factors. In general, here is the future value factor for an annuity:

Annuity FV factor = (Future value factor − 1)/r

$$= [(1 + r)^t − 1]/r \qquad \text{[6.2]}$$

To see how we use annuity future value factors, suppose you plan to contribute $2,000 every year to a retirement account paying 8 percent. If you retire in 30 years, how much will you have?

The number of years here, t, is 30, and the interest rate, r, is 8 percent; so we can calculate the annuity future value factor as:

Annuity FV factor = (Future value factor − 1)/r

$$= (1.08^{30} − 1)/.08$$
$$= (10.0627 − 1)/.08$$
$$= 113.2832$$

The future value of this 30-year, $2,000 annuity is thus:

Annuity future value = $2,000 × 113.28

$$= \$226,566$$

CALCULATOR HINTS

Future Values of Annuities

Of course, you could solve this problem using a financial calculator by doing the following:

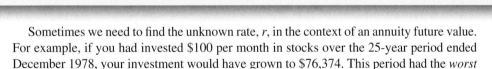

Enter	30	8	−2,000		
	N	**I/Y**	**PMT**	**PV**	**FV**
Solve for					226,566

Notice that we put a negative sign on the payment (why?). With a spreadsheet, use the function =FV(rate,nper, pmt,pv); be sure to put in a zero for pv and to enter −2,000 as the payment.

Sometimes we need to find the unknown rate, r, in the context of an annuity future value. For example, if you had invested $100 per month in stocks over the 25-year period ended December 1978, your investment would have grown to $76,374. This period had the *worst* stretch of stock returns of any 25-year period between 1925 and 2005. How bad was it?

Here we have the cash flows ($100 per month), the *future* value ($76,374), and the time period (25 years, or 300 months). We need to find the implicit rate, r:

$76,374 = $100 × [(Future value factor − 1)/r]

763.74 = [(1 + r)^{300} − 1]/r

Because this is the worst period, let's try 1 percent:

Annuity future value factor = (1.01^{300} − 1)/.01 = 1,878.85

We see that 1 percent is too high. From here, it's trial and error. See if you agree that r is about .55 percent per month. As you will see later in the chapter, this works out to be about 6.8 percent per year.

A NOTE ABOUT ANNUITIES DUE

So far we have only discussed ordinary annuities. These are the most important, but there is a fairly common variation. Remember that with an ordinary annuity, the cash flows occur at the end of each period. When you take out a loan with monthly payments, for example, the first loan payment normally occurs one month after you get the loan. However, when you lease an apartment, the first lease payment is usually due immediately. The second payment is due at the beginning of the second month, and so on. A lease is an example of an **annuity due**. An annuity due is an annuity for which the cash flows occur at the beginning of each period. Almost any type of arrangement in which we have to prepay the same amount each period is an annuity due.

annuity due
An annuity for which the cash flows occur at the beginning of the period.

There are several different ways to calculate the value of an annuity due. With a financial calculator, you simply switch it into "due" or "beginning" mode. Remember to switch it back when you are done! Another way to calculate the present value of an annuity due can be illustrated with a time line. Suppose an annuity due has five payments of $400 each, and the relevant discount rate is 10 percent. The time line looks like this:

0	1	2	3	4	5
$400	$400	$400	$400	$400	

Notice how the cash flows here are the same as those for a *four*-year ordinary annuity, except that there is an extra $400 at Time 0. For practice, check to see that the value of a four-year ordinary annuity at 10 percent is $1,267.95. If we add on the extra $400, we get $1,667.95, which is the present value of this annuity due.

Time value applications abound on the Web. See, for example, www.collegeboard.com, and personal.fidelity.com.

There is an even easier way to calculate the present or future value of an annuity due. If we assume cash flows occur at the end of each period when they really occur at the beginning, then we discount each one by one period too many. We could fix this by simply multiplying our answer by $(1 + r)$, where r is the discount rate. In fact, the relationship between the value of an annuity due and an ordinary annuity is just this:

$$\text{Annuity due value} = \text{Ordinary annuity value} \times (1 + r) \qquad [6.3]$$

This works for both present and future values, so calculating the value of an annuity due involves two steps: (1) Calculate the present or future value as though it were an ordinary annuity, and (2) multiply your answer by $(1 + r)$.

PERPETUITIES

We've seen that a series of level cash flows can be valued by treating those cash flows as an annuity. An important special case of an annuity arises when the level stream of cash flows continues forever. Such an asset is called a **perpetuity** because the cash flows are perpetual. Perpetuities are also called **consols**, particularly in Canada and the United Kingdom. See Example 6.7 for an important example of a perpetuity.

perpetuity
An annuity in which the cash flows continue forever.

consol
A type of perpetuity.

Because a perpetuity has an infinite number of cash flows, we obviously can't compute its value by discounting each one. Fortunately, valuing a perpetuity turns out to be the easiest possible case. The present value of a perpetuity is simply:

$$\text{PV for a perpetuity} = C/r \qquad [6.4]$$

For example, an investment offers a perpetual cash flow of $500 every year. The return you require on such an investment is 8 percent. What is the value of this investment? The value of this perpetuity is:

$$\text{Perpetuity PV} = C/r = \$500/.08 = \$6,250$$

TABLE 6.2

Summary of Annuity and
Perpetuity Calculations

I. Symbols:

PV = Present value, what future cash flows are worth today

FV_t = Future value, what cash flows are worth in the future

   r = Interest rate, rate of return, or discount rate per period—typically, but not always,
     one year

   t = Number of periods—typically, but not always, the number of years

   C = Cash amount

II. Future Value of C per Period for t Periods at r Percent per Period:

$FV_t = C \times \{[(1 + r)^t - 1]/r\}$

A series of identical cash flows is called an *annuity*, and the term $[(1 + r)^t - 1]/r$ is called
the *annuity future value factor*.

III. Present Value of C per Period for t Periods at r Percent per Period:

$PV = C \times \{1 - [1/(1 + r)^t]\}/r$

The term $\{1 - [1/(1 + r)^t]\}/r$ is called the *annuity present value factor*.

IV. Present Value of a Perpetuity of C per Period:

$PV = C/r$

A *perpetuity* has the same cash flow every year forever.

For future reference, Table 6.2 contains a summary of the annuity and perpetuity basic calculations we described. By now, you probably think that you'll just use online calculators to handle annuity problems. Before you do, see our nearby *Work the Web* box!

Preferred Stock   **EXAMPLE 6.7**

Preferred stock (or preference stock) is an important example of a perpetuity. When a corporation sells preferred stock, the buyer is promised a fixed cash dividend every period (usually every quarter) forever. This dividend must be paid before any dividend can be paid to regular stockholders—hence the term *preferred*.

Suppose the Fellini Co. wants to sell preferred stock at $100 per share. A similar issue of preferred stock already outstanding has a price of $40 per share and offers a dividend of $1 every quarter. What dividend will Fellini have to offer if the preferred stock is going to sell?

The issue that is already out has a present value of $40 and a cash flow of $1 every quarter forever. Because this is a perpetuity:

Present value = $40 = $1 × (1/r)

            r = 2.5%

To be competitive, the new Fellini issue will also have to offer 2.5 percent *per quarter;* so if the present value is to be $100, the dividend must be such that:

Present value = $100 = C × (1/.025)

            C = $2.50 (per quarter)

GROWING ANNUITIES AND PERPETUITIES

Annuities commonly have payments that grow over time. Suppose, for example, that we are looking at a lottery payout over a 20-year period. The first payment, made one year from now, will be $200,000. Every year thereafter, the payment will grow by 5 percent, so the payment in the second year will be $200,000 \times 1.05 = $210,000$. The payment in the third year will be $210,000 \times 1.05 = $220,500$, and so on. What's the present value if the appropriate discount rate is 11 percent?

If we use the symbol g to represent the growth rate, we can calculate the value of a growing annuity using a modified version of our regular annuity formula:

$$\text{Growing annuity present value} = C \times \left[\frac{1 - \left(\frac{1 + g}{1 + r}\right)^t}{r - g}\right] \qquad [6.5]$$

Plugging in the numbers from our lottery example (and letting $g = .05$), we get:

$$PV = \$200,000 \times \left[\frac{1 - \left(\frac{1 + .05}{1 + .11}\right)^{20}}{.11 - .05}\right] = \$200,000 \times 11.18169 = \$2,236,337.06$$

WORK THE WEB

As we discussed in the previous chapter, many Web sites have financial calculators. One of these sites is MoneyChimp, which is located at www.moneychimp.com. Suppose you are lucky enough to have $1,500,000. You think you will be able to earn a 10 percent return. How much can you withdraw each year for the next 30 years? Here is what MoneyChimp says:

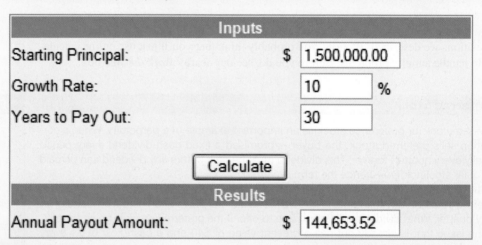

Inputs		
Starting Principal:	$	1,500,000.00
Growth Rate:		10 %
Years to Pay Out:		30
	Calculate	
Results		
Annual Payout Amount:	$	144,653.52

According to the MoneyChimp calculator, the answer is $144,653.52. How important is it to understand what you are doing? Calculate this one for yourself, and you should get $159,118.87. Which one is right? You are, of course! What's going on is that MoneyChimp assumes (but does not tell you) that the annuity is in the form of an annuity due, not an ordinary annuity. Recall that with an annuity due, the payments occur at the beginning of the period rather than the end of the period. The moral of the story is clear: *caveat calculator*.

Questions

1. Go to the calculator at www.moneychimp.com and find out how much the Web site says you could withdraw each year if you have $2,500,000, earn an 8 percent interest rate, and make annual withdrawals for 35 years. How much more are the withdrawals if they are in the form of an ordinary annuity?
2. Suppose you have $500,000 and want to make withdrawals each month for the next 10 years. The first withdrawal is today and the appropriate interest rate is 9 percent compounded monthly. Using this Web site, how much are your withdrawals?

There is also a formula for the present value of a growing perpetuity:

$$\text{Growing perpetuity present value} = C \times \left[\frac{1}{r - g}\right] = \frac{C}{r - g} \qquad \text{[6.6]}$$

In our lottery example, now suppose the payments continue forever. In this case, the present value is:

$$\text{PV} = \$200,000 \times \frac{1}{.11 - .05} = \$200,000 \times 16.6667 = \$3,333,333.33$$

The notion of a growing perpetuity may seem a little odd because the payments get bigger every period forever; but, as we will see in a later chapter, growing perpetuities play a key role in our analysis of stock prices.

Before we go on, there is one important note about our formulas for growing annuities and perpetuities. In both cases, the cash flow in the formula, C, is the cash flow that is going to occur exactly one period from today.

Concept Questions

6.2a In general, what is the present value of an annuity of C dollars per period at a discount rate of r per period? The future value?

6.2b In general, what is the present value of a perpetuity?

Comparing Rates: The Effect of Compounding

6.3

The next issue we need to discuss has to do with the way interest rates are quoted. This subject causes a fair amount of confusion because rates are quoted in many different ways. Sometimes the way a rate is quoted is the result of tradition, and sometimes it's the result of legislation. Unfortunately, at times, rates are quoted in deliberately deceptive ways to mislead borrowers and investors. We will discuss these topics in this section.

EFFECTIVE ANNUAL RATES AND COMPOUNDING

If a rate is quoted as 10 percent compounded semiannually, this means the investment actually pays 5 percent every six months. A natural question then arises: Is 5 percent every six months the same thing as 10 percent per year? It's easy to see that it is not. If you invest $1 at 10 percent per year, you will have $1.10 at the end of the year. If you invest at 5 percent every six months, then you'll have the future value of $1 at 5 percent for two periods:

$$\$1 \times 1.05^2 = \$1.1025$$

This is $.0025 more. The reason is simple: Your account was credited with $1 \times .05 = 5$ cents in interest after six months. In the following six months, you earned 5 percent on that nickel, for an extra $5 \times .05 = .25$ cents.

As our example illustrates, 10 percent compounded semiannually is actually equivalent to 10.25 percent per year. Put another way, we would be indifferent between

10 percent compounded semiannually and 10.25 percent compounded annually. Anytime we have compounding during the year, we need to be concerned about what the rate really is.

In our example, the 10 percent is called a **stated**, or **quoted, interest rate**. Other names are used as well. The 10.25 percent, which is actually the rate you will earn, is called the **effective annual rate (EAR)**. To compare different investments or interest rates, we will always need to convert to effective rates. Some general procedures for doing this are discussed next.

stated interest rate
The interest rate expressed in terms of the interest payment made each period. Also known as the *quoted interest rate*.

effective annual rate (EAR)
The interest rate expressed as if it were compounded once per year.

CALCULATING AND COMPARING EFFECTIVE ANNUAL RATES

To see why it is important to work only with effective rates, suppose you've shopped around and come up with the following three rates:

Bank A: 15 percent compounded daily

Bank B: 15.5 percent compounded quarterly

Bank C: 16 percent compounded annually

Which of these is the best if you are thinking of opening a savings account? Which of these is best if they represent loan rates?

To begin, Bank C is offering 16 percent per year. Because there is no compounding during the year, this is the effective rate. Bank B is actually paying $.155/4 = .03875$ or 3.875 percent per quarter. At this rate, an investment of $1 for four quarters would grow to:

$$\$1 \times 1.03875^4 = \$1.1642$$

The EAR, therefore, is 16.42 percent. For a saver, this is much better than the 16 percent rate Bank C is offering; for a borrower, it's worse.

Bank A is compounding every day. This may seem a little extreme, but it is common to calculate interest daily. In this case, the daily interest rate is actually:

$$.15/365 = .000411$$

This is .0411 percent per day. At this rate, an investment of $1 for 365 periods would grow to:

$$\$1 \times 1.000411^{365} = \$1.1618$$

The EAR is 16.18 percent. This is not as good as Bank B's 16.42 percent for a saver, and not as good as Bank C's 16 percent for a borrower.

This example illustrates two things. First, the highest quoted rate is not necessarily the best. Second, compounding during the year can lead to a significant difference between the quoted rate and the effective rate. Remember that the effective rate is what you actually get or what you pay.

If you look at our examples, you see that we computed the EARs in three steps. We first divided the quoted rate by the number of times that the interest is compounded. We then added 1 to the result and raised it to the power of the number of times the interest is compounded. Finally, we subtracted the 1. If we let m be the number of times the interest is compounded during the year, these steps can be summarized simply as:

$$EAR = [1 + (\text{Quoted rate}/m)]^m - 1 \qquad \text{[6.7]}$$

For example, suppose you are offered 12 percent compounded monthly. In this case, the interest is compounded 12 times a year; so m is 12. You can calculate the effective rate as:

$$
\begin{aligned}
\text{EAR} &= [1 + (\text{Quoted rate}/m)]^m - 1 \\
&= [1 + (.12/12)]^{12} - 1 \\
&= 1.01^{12} - 1 \\
&= 1.126825 - 1 \\
&= 12.6825\%
\end{aligned}
$$

What's the EAR?	**EXAMPLE 6.8**

A bank is offering 12 percent compounded quarterly. If you put $100 in an account, how much will you have at the end of one year? What's the EAR? How much will you have at the end of two years?

The bank is effectively offering $12\%/4 = 3\%$ every quarter. If you invest $100 for four periods at 3 percent per period, the future value is:

$$
\begin{aligned}
\text{Future value} &= \$100 \times 1.03^4 \\
&= \$100 \times 1.1255 \\
&= \$112.55
\end{aligned}
$$

The EAR is 12.55 percent: $\$100 \times (1 + .1255) = \$112.55$.

We can determine what you would have at the end of two years in two different ways. One way is to recognize that two years is the same as eight quarters. At 3 percent per quarter, after eight quarters, you would have:

$$\$100 \times 1.03^8 = \$100 \times 1.2668 = \$126.68$$

Alternatively, we could determine the value after two years by using an EAR of 12.55 percent; so after two years you would have:

$$\$100 \times 1.1255^2 = \$100 \times 1.2688 = \$126.68$$

Thus, the two calculations produce the same answer. This illustrates an important point. Anytime we do a present or future value calculation, the rate we use must be an actual or effective rate. In this case, the actual rate is 3 percent per quarter. The effective annual rate is 12.55 percent. It doesn't matter which one we use once we know the EAR.

Quoting a Rate	**EXAMPLE 6.9**

Now that you know how to convert a quoted rate to an EAR, consider going the other way. As a lender, you know you want to actually earn 18 percent on a particular loan. You want to quote a rate that features monthly compounding. What rate do you quote?

In this case, we know the EAR is 18 percent, and we know this is the result of monthly compounding. Let q stand for the quoted rate. We thus have:

$$
\begin{aligned}
\text{EAR} &= [1 + (\text{Quoted rate}/m)]^m - 1 \\
.18 &= [1 + (q/12)]^{12} - 1 \\
1.18 &= [1 + (q/12)]^{12}
\end{aligned}
$$

(continued)

We need to solve this equation for the quoted rate. This calculation is the same as the ones we did to find an unknown interest rate in Chapter 5:

$$1.18^{(1/12)} = 1 + (q/12)$$
$$1.18^{.08333} = 1 + (q/12)$$
$$1.0139 = 1 + (q/12)$$
$$q = .0139 \times 12$$
$$= 16.68\%$$

Therefore, the rate you would quote is 16.68 percent, compounded monthly.

EARs AND APRs

annual percentage rate (APR)
The interest rate charged per period multiplied by the number of periods per year.

Sometimes it's not altogether clear whether a rate is an effective annual rate. A case in point concerns what is called the **annual percentage rate (APR)** on a loan. Truth-in-lending laws in the United States require that lenders disclose an APR on virtually all consumer loans. This rate must be displayed on a loan document in a prominent and unambiguous way.

Given that an APR must be calculated and displayed, an obvious question arises: Is an APR an effective annual rate? Put another way, if a bank quotes a car loan at 12 percent APR, is the consumer actually paying 12 percent interest? Surprisingly, the answer is no. There is some confusion over this point, which we discuss next.

The confusion over APRs arises because lenders are required by law to compute the APR in a particular way. By law, the APR is simply equal to the interest rate per period multiplied by the number of periods in a year. For example, if a bank is charging 1.2 percent per month on car loans, then the APR that must be reported is 1.2% × 12 = 14.4%. So, an APR is in fact a quoted, or stated, rate in the sense we've been discussing. For example, an APR of 12 percent on a loan calling for monthly payments is really 1 percent per month. The EAR on such a loan is thus:

$$EAR = [1 + (APR/12)]^{12} - 1$$
$$= 1.01^{12} - 1 = 12.6825\%$$

EXAMPLE 6.10 | **What Rate Are You Paying?**

Depending on the issuer, a typical credit card agreement quotes an interest rate of 18 percent APR. Monthly payments are required. What is the actual interest rate you pay on such a credit card?

Based on our discussion, an APR of 18 percent with monthly payments is really .18/12 = .015 or 1.5 percent per month. The EAR is thus:

$$EAR = [1 + (.18/12)]^{12} - 1$$
$$= 1.015^{12} - 1$$
$$= 1.1956 - 1$$
$$= 19.56\%$$

This is the rate you actually pay.

It is somewhat ironic that truth-in-lending laws sometimes require lenders to be *un*truthful about the actual rate on a loan. There are also truth-in-saving laws that require banks and other borrowers to quote an "annual percentage yield," or APY, on things like savings accounts. To make things a little confusing, an APY is an EAR. As a result, by law, the rates quoted to borrowers (APRs) and those quoted to savers (APYs) are not computed the same way.

There can be a huge difference between the APR and EAR when interest rates are large. For example, consider "payday loans." Payday loans are short-term loans made to consumers, often for less than two weeks, and are offered by companies such as AmeriCash Advance and National Payday. The loans work like this: You write a check today that is postdated (the date on the check is in the future) and give it to the company. They give you some cash. When the check date arrives, you either go to the store and pay the cash amount of the check, or the company cashes it (or else automatically renews the loan).

For example, in one particular state, AmeriCash Advance allows you to write a check for $120 dated 15 days in the future, for which they give you $100 today. So what are the APR and EAR of this arrangement? First, we need to find the interest rate, which we can find by the FV equation as follows:

$$FV = PV \times (1 + r)^1$$
$$\$120 = \$100 \times (1 + r)^1$$
$$1.2 = (1 + r)$$
$$r = .20 \text{ or } 20\%$$

That doesn't seem too bad until you remember this is the interest rate for *15 days!* The APR of the loan is:

$$APR = .20 \times 365/15$$
$$APR = 4.8667 \text{ or } 486.67\%$$

And the EAR for this loan is:

$$EAR = (1 + \text{Quoted rate}/m)^m - 1$$
$$EAR = (1 + .20)^{365/15} - 1$$
$$EAR = 83.4780 \text{ or } 8,347.80\%$$

Now that's an interest rate! Just to see what a difference a day (or three) makes, AmeriCash will also allow you to write a postdated check for the same amount, but will give you 18 days to repay. Check for yourself that the APR of this arrangement is 405.56 percent and the EAR is 3,932.92 percent. Still not a loan we would like to take out!

TAKING IT TO THE LIMIT:
A NOTE ABOUT CONTINUOUS COMPOUNDING

If you made a deposit in a savings account, how often could your money be compounded during the year? If you think about it, there isn't really any upper limit. We've seen that daily compounding, for example, isn't a problem. There is no reason to stop here, however. We could compound every hour or minute or second. How high would the EAR get in this case? Table 6.3 illustrates the EARs that result as 10 percent is compounded at shorter and shorter intervals. Notice that the EARs do keep getting larger, but the differences get very small.

As the numbers in Table 6.3 seem to suggest, there is an upper limit to the EAR. If we let q stand for the quoted rate, then, as the number of times the interest is compounded gets extremely large, the EAR approaches:

$$EAR = e^q - 1 \qquad \text{[6.8]}$$

TABLE 6.3

Compounding Frequency and Effective Annual Rates

Compounding Period	Number of Times Compounded	Effective Annual Rate
Year	1	10.00000%
Quarter	4	10.38129
Month	12	10.47131
Week	52	10.50648
Day	365	10.51558
Hour	8,760	10.51703
Minute	525,600	10.51709

where e is the number 2.71828 (look for a key labeled "e^x" on your calculator). For example, with our 10 percent rate, the highest possible EAR is:

$$EAR = e^q - 1$$
$$= 2.71828^{.10} - 1$$
$$= 1.1051709 - 1$$
$$= 10.51709\%$$

In this case, we say that the money is continuously, or instantaneously, compounded. Interest is being credited the instant it is earned, so the amount of interest grows continuously.

EXAMPLE 6.11   **What's the Law?**

At one time, commercial banks and savings and loan associations (S&Ls) were restricted in the interest rates they could offer on savings accounts. Under what was known as Regulation Q, S&Ls were allowed to pay at most 5.5 percent, and banks were not allowed to pay more than 5.25 percent (the idea was to give the S&Ls a competitive advantage; it didn't work). The law did not say how often these rates could be compounded, however. Under Regulation Q, then, what were the maximum allowed interest rates?

The maximum allowed rates occurred with continuous, or instantaneous, compounding. For the commercial banks, 5.25 percent compounded continuously would be:

$$EAR = e^{.0525} - 1$$
$$= 2.71828^{.0525} - 1$$
$$= 1.0539026 - 1$$
$$= 5.39026\%$$

This is what banks could actually pay. Check for yourself to see that S&Ls could effectively pay 5.65406 percent.

Concept Questions

6.3a If an interest rate is given as 12 percent compounded daily, what do we call this rate?

6.3b What is an APR? What is an EAR? Are they the same thing?

6.3c In general, what is the relationship between a stated interest rate and an effective interest rate? Which is more relevant for financial decisions?

6.3d What does continuous compounding mean?

Loan Types and Loan Amortization   6.4

Whenever a lender extends a loan, some provision will be made for repayment of the principal (the original loan amount). A loan might be repaid in equal installments, for example, or it might be repaid in a single lump sum. Because the way that the principal and interest are paid is up to the parties involved, there are actually an unlimited number of possibilities.

In this section, we describe a few forms of repayment that come up quite often, and more complicated forms can usually be built up from these. The three basic types of loans are pure discount loans, interest-only loans, and amortized loans. Working with these loans is a very straightforward application of the present value principles that we have already developed.

PURE DISCOUNT LOANS

The *pure discount loan* is the simplest form of loan. With such a loan, the borrower receives money today and repays a single lump sum at some time in the future. A one-year, 10 percent pure discount loan, for example, would require the borrower to repay $1.10 in one year for every dollar borrowed today.

Because a pure discount loan is so simple, we already know how to value one. Suppose a borrower was able to repay $25,000 in five years. If we, acting as the lender, wanted a 12 percent interest rate on the loan, how much would we be willing to lend? Put another way, what value would we assign today to that $25,000 to be repaid in five years? Based on our work in Chapter 5, we know the answer is just the present value of $25,000 at 12 percent for five years:

$$\text{Present value} = \$25,000/1.12^5$$
$$= \$25,000/1.7623$$
$$= \$14,186$$

Pure discount loans are common when the loan term is short—say a year or less. In recent years, they have become increasingly common for much longer periods.

Treasury Bills   **EXAMPLE 6.12**

When the U.S. government borrows money on a short-term basis (a year or less), it does so by selling what are called *Treasury bills,* or *T-bills* for short. A T-bill is a promise by the government to repay a fixed amount at some time in the future—for example, 3 months or 12 months.

Treasury bills are pure discount loans. If a T-bill promises to repay $10,000 in 12 months, and the market interest rate is 7 percent, how much will the bill sell for in the market?

Because the going rate is 7 percent, the T-bill will sell for the present value of $10,000 to be repaid in one year at 7 percent:

$$\text{Present value} = \$10,000/1.07 = \$9,345.79$$

INTEREST-ONLY LOANS

A second type of loan repayment plan calls for the borrower to pay interest each period and to repay the entire principal (the original loan amount) at some point in the future. Loans with such a repayment plan are called *interest-only loans*. Notice that if there is just one period, a pure discount loan and an interest-only loan are the same thing.

For example, with a three-year, 10 percent, interest-only loan of $1,000, the borrower would pay $1,000 × .10 = $100 in interest at the end of the first and second years. At the end of the third year, the borrower would return the $1,000 along with another $100 in interest for that year. Similarly, a 50-year interest-only loan would call for the borrower to pay interest every year for the next 50 years and then repay the principal. In the extreme, the borrower pays the interest every period forever and never repays any principal. As we discussed earlier in the chapter, the result is a perpetuity.

Most corporate bonds have the general form of an interest-only loan. Because we will be considering bonds in some detail in the next chapter, we will defer further discussion of them for now.

AMORTIZED LOANS

With a pure discount or interest-only loan, the principal is repaid all at once. An alternative is an *amortized loan,* with which the lender may require the borrower to repay parts of the loan amount over time. The process of providing for a loan to be paid off by making regular principal reductions is called *amortizing* the loan.

A simple way of amortizing a loan is to have the borrower pay the interest each period plus some fixed amount. This approach is common with medium-term business loans. For example, suppose a business takes out a $5,000, five-year loan at 9 percent. The loan agreement calls for the borrower to pay the interest on the loan balance each year and to reduce the loan balance each year by $1,000. Because the loan amount declines by $1,000 each year, it is fully paid in five years.

In the case we are considering, notice that the total payment will decline each year. The reason is that the loan balance goes down, resulting in a lower interest charge each year, whereas the $1,000 principal reduction is constant. For example, the interest in the first year will be $5,000 × .09 = $450. The total payment will be $1,000 + 450 = $1,450. In the second year, the loan balance is $4,000, so the interest is $4,000 × .09 = $360, and the total payment is $1,360. We can calculate the total payment in each of the remaining years by preparing a simple *amortization schedule* as follows:

Year	Beginning Balance	Total Payment	Interest Paid	Principal Paid	Ending Balance
1	$5,000	$1,450	$ 450	$1,000	$4,000
2	4,000	1,360	360	1,000	3,000
3	3,000	1,270	270	1,000	2,000
4	2,000	1,180	180	1,000	1,000
5	1,000	1,090	90	1,000	0
Totals		$6,350	$1,350	$5,000	

Notice that in each year, the interest paid is given by the beginning balance multiplied by the interest rate. Also notice that the beginning balance is given by the ending balance from the previous year.

Probably the most common way of amortizing a loan is to have the borrower make a single, fixed payment every period. Almost all consumer loans (such as car loans) and mortgages work this way. For example, suppose our five-year, 9 percent, $5,000 loan was amortized this way. How would the amortization schedule look?

We first need to determine the payment. From our discussion earlier in the chapter, we know that this loan's cash flows are in the form of an ordinary annuity. In this case, we can solve for the payment as follows:

$$\$5,000 = C \times \{[1 - (1/1.09^5)]/.09\}$$
$$= C \times [(1 - .6499)/.09]$$

This gives us:

$$C = \$5,000/3.8897$$
$$= \$1,285.46$$

The borrower will therefore make five equal payments of $1,285.46. Will this pay off the loan? We will check by filling in an amortization schedule.

In our previous example, we knew the principal reduction each year. We then calculated the interest owed to get the total payment. In this example, we know the total payment. We will thus calculate the interest and then subtract it from the total payment to calculate the principal portion in each payment.

In the first year, the interest is $450, as we calculated before. Because the total payment is $1,285.46, the principal paid in the first year must be:

$$\text{Principal paid} = \$1,285.46 - 450 = \$835.46$$

The ending loan balance is thus:

$$\text{Ending balance} = \$5,000 - 835.46 = \$4,164.54$$

The interest in the second year is $4,164.54 \times .09 = \$374.81$, and the loan balance declines by $1,285.46 - 374.81 = \$910.65$. We can summarize all of the relevant calculations in the following schedule:

Year	Beginning Balance	Total Payment	Interest Paid	Principal Paid	Ending Balance
1	$5,000.00	$1,285.46	$ 450.00	$ 835.46	$4,164.54
2	4,164.54	1,285.46	374.81	910.65	3,253.88
3	3,253.88	1,285.46	292.85	992.61	2,261.27
4	2,261.27	1,285.46	203.51	1,081.95	1,179.32
5	1,179.32	1,285.46	106.14	1,179.32	0.00
Totals		$6,427.30	$1,427.31	$5,000.00	

Because the loan balance declines to zero, the five equal payments do pay off the loan. Notice that the interest paid declines each period. This isn't surprising because the loan balance is going down. Given that the total payment is fixed, the principal paid must be rising each period.

If you compare the two loan amortizations in this section, you will see that the total interest is greater for the equal total payment case: $1,427.31 versus $1,350. The reason for this is that the loan is repaid more slowly early on, so the interest is somewhat higher. This doesn't mean that one loan is better than the other; it simply means that one is effectively paid off faster than the other. For example, the principal reduction in the first year is $835.46 in the equal total payment case as compared to $1,000 in the first case. Many Web sites offer loan amortization schedules. See our nearby *Work the Web* box for an example.

WORK THE WEB

Preparing an amortization table is one of the more tedious time value of money applications. Using a spreadsheet makes it relatively easy, but there are also Web sites available that will prepare an amortization schedule very quickly and simply. One such site is www.bankrate.com. This site has a mortgage calculator for home loans, but the same calculations apply to most other types of loans such as car loans and student loans. Suppose you graduate with a student loan of $25,000 and will repay the loan over the next 10 years at 6.8 percent. What are your monthly payments? Using the calculator we get:

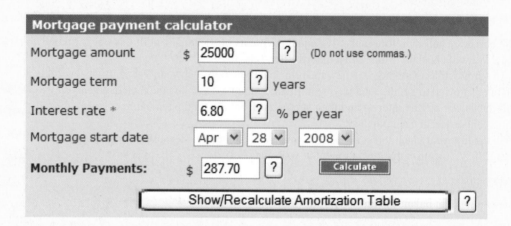

Try this example yourself and click the "Show/Recalculate Amortization Table" button. You will find that your first payment will consist of $146.03 in principal and $141.67 in interest. Over the life of the loan you will pay a total of $9,524.10 in interest.

Questions

1. *Suppose you take out a 30-year mortgage for $250,000 at an interest rate of 6.8 percent. Use this Web site to construct an amortization table for the loan. What are the interest payment and principal amounts in the 110th payment? How much in total interest will you pay over the life of the loan?*

2. *You take out a 30-year mortgage for $275,000 at an interest rate of 7.3 percent. How much will you pay in interest over the life of this loan? Now assume you pay an extra $100 per month on this loan. How much is your total interest now? How much sooner will the mortgage be paid off?*

We will close this chapter with an example that may be of particular relevance. Federal Stafford loans are an important source of financing for many college students, helping to cover the cost of tuition, books, new cars, condominiums, and many other things. Sometimes students do not seem to fully realize that Stafford loans have a serious drawback: They must be repaid in monthly installments, usually beginning six months after the student leaves school.

Some Stafford loans are subsidized, meaning that the interest does not begin to accrue until repayment begins (this is a good thing). If you are a dependent undergraduate student under this particular option, the total debt you can run up is, at most, $23,000. The maximum interest rate in 2008–2009 is 6.0 percent, or 6.0/12 = .50 percent per month. Under the "standard repayment plan," the loans are amortized over 10 years (subject to a minimum payment of $50).

Suppose you max out borrowing under this program and also get stuck paying the maximum interest rate. Beginning six months after you graduate (or otherwise depart the ivory tower), what will your monthly payment be? How much will you owe after making payments for four years?

Given our earlier discussions, see if you don't agree that your monthly payment assuming a $23,000 total loan is $255.35 per month. Also, as explained in Example 6.13, after making payments for four years, you still owe the present value of the remaining payments. There are 120 payments in all. After you make 48 of them (the first four years), you have 72 to go. By now, it should be easy for you to verify that the present value of $255.35 per month for 72 months at .50 percent per month is about $15,400, so you still have a long way to go.

Partial Amortization, or "Bite the Bullet"   **EXAMPLE 6.13**

A common arrangement in real estate lending might call for a 5-year loan with, say, a 15-year amortization. What this means is that the borrower makes a payment every month of a fixed amount based on a 15-year amortization. However, after 60 months, the borrower makes a single, much larger payment called a "balloon" or "bullet" to pay off the loan. Because the monthly payments don't fully pay off the loan, the loan is said to be partially amortized.

Suppose we have a $100,000 commercial mortgage with a 12 percent APR and a 20-year (240-month) amortization. Further suppose the mortgage has a five-year balloon. What will the monthly payment be? How big will the balloon payment be?

The monthly payment can be calculated based on an ordinary annuity with a present value of $100,000. There are 240 payments, and the interest rate is 1 percent per month. The payment is:

$$\$100,000 = C \times [(1 - 1/1.01^{240})/.01]$$
$$= C \times 90.8194$$
$$C = \$1,101.09$$

Now, there is an easy way and a hard way to determine the balloon payment. The hard way is to actually amortize the loan for 60 months to see what the balance is at that time. The easy way is to recognize that after 60 months, we have a 240 − 60 = 180-month loan. The payment is still $1,101.09 per month, and the interest rate is still 1 percent per month. The loan balance is thus the present value of the remaining payments:

$$\text{Loan balance} = \$1,101.09 \times [(1 - 1/1.01^{180})/.01]$$
$$= \$1,101.09 \times 83.3217$$
$$= \$91,744.69$$

The balloon payment is a substantial $91,744. Why is it so large? To get an idea, consider the first payment on the mortgage. The interest in the first month is $100,000 × .01 = $1,000. Your payment is $1,101.09, so the loan balance declines by only $101.09. Because the loan balance declines so slowly, the cumulative "pay down" over five years is not great.

SPREADSHEET STRATEGIES

Loan Amortization Using a Spreadsheet

Loan amortization is a common spreadsheet application. To illustrate, we will set up the problem that we examined earlier: a five-year, $5,000, 9 percent loan with constant payments. Our spreadsheet looks like this:

	A	B	C	D	E	F	G	H
1								
2			Using a spreadsheet to amortize a loan					
3								
4			Loan amount:	$5,000				
5			Interest rate:	.09				
6			Loan term:	5				
7			Loan payment:	**$1,285.46**				
8				Note: Payment is calculated using PMT(rate,nper,-pv,fv).				
9			Amortization table:					
10								
11		Year	Beginning	Total	Interest	Principal	Ending	
12			Balance	Payment	Paid	Paid	Balance	
13		1	$5,000.00	$1,285.46	$450.00	$835.46	$4,164.54	
14		2	4,164.54	1,285.46	374.81	910.65	3,253.88	
15		3	3,253.88	1,285.46	292.85	992.61	2,261.27	
16		4	2,261.27	1,285.46	203.51	1,081.95	1,179.32	
17		5	1,179.32	1,285.46	106.14	1,179.32	.00	
18		Totals		6,427.31	1,427.31	5,000.00		
19								
20			Formulas in the amortization table:					
21								
22		Year	Beginning	Total	Interest	Principal	Ending	
23			Balance	Payment	Paid	Paid	Balance	
24		1	=+D4	=$D$7	=+$D$5*C13	=+D13-E13	=+C13-F13	
25		2	=+G13	=$D$7	=+$D$5*C14	=+D14-E14	=+C14-F14	
26		3	=+G14	=$D$7	=+$D$5*C15	=+D15-E15	=+C15-F15	
27		4	=+G15	=$D$7	=+$D$5*C16	=+D16-E16	=+C16-F16	
28		5	=+G16	=$D$7	=+$D$5*C17	=+D17-E17	=+C17-F17	
29								
30			Note: Totals in the amortization table are calculated using the SUM formula.					
31								

Of course, it is possible to rack up much larger debts. According to the Association of American Medical Colleges, medical students who borrowed to attend medical school and graduated in 2007 had an average student loan balance of $140,000. Ouch! How long will it take the average student to pay off her medical school loans?

Let's say she makes a monthly payment of $1,000, and the loan has an interest rate of 7 percent per year, or .5833 percent per month. See if you agree that it will take 292 months, or just over 24 years, to pay off the loan. Maybe MD really stands for "mucho debt"!

Concept Questions

6.4a What is a pure discount loan? An interest-only loan?

6.4b What does it mean to amortize a loan?

6.4c What is a balloon payment? How do you determine its value?

Summary and Conclusions

6.5

This chapter rounded out your understanding of fundamental concepts related to the time value of money and discounted cash flow valuation. Several important topics were covered:

1. There are two ways of calculating present and future values when there are multiple cash flows. Both approaches are straightforward extensions of our earlier analysis of single cash flows.

2. A series of constant cash flows that arrive or are paid at the end of each period is called an ordinary annuity, and we described some useful shortcuts for determining the present and future values of annuities.

3. Interest rates can be quoted in a variety of ways. For financial decisions, it is important that any rates being compared be first converted to effective rates. The relationship between a quoted rate, such as an annual percentage rate (APR), and an effective annual rate (EAR) is given by:

$$EAR = [1 + (\text{Quoted rate}/m)]^m - 1$$

where m is the number of times during the year the money is compounded or, equivalently, the number of payments during the year.

4. Many loans are annuities. The process of providing for a loan to be paid off gradually is called amortizing the loan, and we discussed how amortization schedules are prepared and interpreted.

The principles developed in this chapter will figure prominently in the chapters to come. The reason for this is that most investments, whether they involve real assets or financial assets, can be analyzed using the discounted cash flow (DCF) approach. As a result, the DCF approach is broadly applicable and widely used in practice. For example, the next two chapters show how to value bonds and stocks using an extension of the techniques presented in this chapter. Before going on, therefore, you might want to do some of the problems that follow.

CHAPTER REVIEW AND SELF-TEST PROBLEMS

6.1 **Present Values with Multiple Cash Flows** A first-round draft choice quarterback has been signed to a three-year, $25 million contract. The details provide for an immediate cash bonus of $2 million. The player is to receive $5 million in salary at the end of the first year, $8 million the next, and $10 million at the end of the last year. Assuming a 15 percent discount rate, is this package worth $25 million? If not, how much is it worth?

6.2 **Future Value with Multiple Cash Flows** You plan to make a series of deposits in an individual retirement account. You will deposit $1,000 today, $2,000 in two years, and $2,000 in five years. If you withdraw $1,500 in three years and $1,000 in seven years, assuming no withdrawal penalties, how much will you have after eight years if the interest rate is 7 percent? What is the present value of these cash flows?

6.3 **Annuity Present Value** You are looking into an investment that will pay you $12,000 per year for the next 10 years. If you require a 15 percent return, what is the most you would pay for this investment?

6.4 **APR versus EAR** The going rate on student loans is quoted as 8 percent APR. The terms of the loans call for monthly payments. What is the effective annual rate (EAR) on such a student loan?

6.5 **It's the Principal That Matters** Suppose you borrow $10,000. You are going to repay the loan by making equal annual payments for five years. The interest rate on the loan is 14 percent per year. Prepare an amortization schedule for the loan. How much interest will you pay over the life of the loan?

6.6 **Just a Little Bit Each Month** You've recently finished your MBA at the Darnit School. Naturally, you must purchase a new BMW immediately. The car costs about $21,000. The bank quotes an interest rate of 15 percent APR for a 72-month loan with a 10 percent down payment. You plan on trading the car in for a new one in two years. What will your monthly payment be? What is the effective interest rate on the loan? What will the loan balance be when you trade the car in?

ANSWERS TO CHAPTER REVIEW AND SELF-TEST PROBLEMS

6.1 Obviously, the package is not worth $25 million because the payments are spread out over three years. The bonus is paid today, so it's worth $2 million. The present values for the three subsequent salary payments are:

$$(\$5/1.15) + (8/1.15^2) + (10/1.15^3) = (\$5/1.15) + (8/1.32) + (10/1.52)$$
$$= \$16.9721 \text{ million}$$

The package is worth a total of $18.9721 million.

6.2 We will calculate the future values for each of the cash flows separately and then add them up. Notice that we treat the withdrawals as negative cash flows:

$$\$1,000 \times 1.07^8 = \quad \$1,000 \times 1.7812 = \$ 1,718.19$$
$$\$2,000 \times 1.07^6 = \quad \$2,000 \times 1.5007 = \quad 3,001.46$$
$$-\$1,500 \times 1.07^5 = -\$1,500 \times 1.4026 = -2,103.83$$
$$\$2,000 \times 1.07^3 = \quad \$2,000 \times 1.2250 = \quad 2,450.09$$
$$-\$1,000 \times 1.07^1 = -\$1,000 \times 1.0700 = -1,070.00$$
$$\text{Total future value} \qquad\qquad\qquad = \$ 3,995.91$$

This value includes a small rounding error.

To calculate the present value, we could discount each cash flow back to the present or we could discount back a single year at a time. However, because we already know that the future value in eight years is $3,995.91, the easy way to get the PV is just to discount this amount back eight years:

$$\text{Present value} = \$3,995.91/1.07^8$$
$$= \$3,995.91/1.7182$$
$$= \$2,325.64$$

We again ignore a small rounding error. For practice, you can verify that this is what you get if you discount each cash flow back separately.

6.3 The most you would be willing to pay is the present value of $12,000 per year for 10 years at a 15 percent discount rate. The cash flows here are in ordinary annuity form, so the relevant present value factor is:

Annuity present value factor $= (1 - \text{Present value factor})/r$

$$= [1 - (1/1.15^{10})]/.15$$
$$= (1 - .2472)/.15$$
$$= 5.0188$$

The present value of the 10 cash flows is thus:

Present value $= \$12,000 \times 5.0188$
$$= \$60,225$$

This is the most you would pay.

6.4 A rate of 8 percent APR with monthly payments is actually $8\%/12 = .67\%$ per month. The EAR is thus:

$$\text{EAR} = [1 + (.08/12)]^{12} - 1 = 8.30\%$$

6.5 We first need to calculate the annual payment. With a present value of $10,000, an interest rate of 14 percent, and a term of five years, the payment can be determined from:

$$\$10,000 = \text{Payment} \times \{[1 - (1/1.14^5)]/.14\}$$
$$= \text{Payment} \times 3.4331$$

Therefore, the payment is $\$10,000/3.4331 = \$2,912.84$ (actually, it's $2,912.8355; this will create some small rounding errors in the following schedule). We can now prepare the amortization schedule as follows:

Year	Beginning Balance	Total Payment	Interest Paid	Principal Paid	Ending Balance
1	$10,000.00	$ 2,912.84	$1,400.00	$ 1,512.84	$8,487.16
2	8,487.16	2,912.84	1,188.20	1,724.63	6,762.53
3	6,762.53	2,912.84	946.75	1,966.08	4,796.45
4	4,796.45	2,912.84	671.50	2,241.33	2,555.12
5	2,555.12	2,912.84	357.72	2,555.12	0.00
Totals		$14,564.17	$4,564.17	$10,000.00	

6.6 The cash flows on the car loan are in annuity form, so we need to find only the payment. The interest rate is $15\%/12 = 1.25\%$ per month, and there are 72 months. The first thing we need is the annuity factor for 72 periods at 1.25 percent per period:

Annuity present value factor $= (1 - \text{Present value factor})/r$
$$= [1 - (1/1.0125^{72})]/.0125$$
$$= [1 - (1/2.4459)]/.0125$$
$$= (1 - .4088)/.0125$$
$$= 47.2925$$

The present value is the amount we finance. With a 10 percent down payment, we will be borrowing 90 percent of $21,000, or $18,900. To find the payment, we need to solve for C:

$$\$18,900 = C \times \text{Annuity present value factor}$$
$$= C \times 47.2925$$

Rearranging things a bit, we have:

$$C = \$18,900 \times (1/47.2925)$$
$$= \$18,900 \times .02115$$
$$= \$399.64$$

Your payment is just under $400 per month.

The actual interest rate on this loan is 1.25 percent per month. Based on our work in the chapter, we can calculate the effective annual rate as:

$$EAR = (1.0125)^{12} - 1 = 16.08\%$$

The effective rate is about one point higher than the quoted rate.

To determine the loan balance in two years, we could amortize the loan to see what the balance is at that time. This would be fairly tedious to do by hand. Using the information already determined in this problem, we can instead simply calculate the present value of the remaining payments. After two years, we have made 24 payments, so there are $72 - 24 = 48$ payments left. What is the present value of 48 monthly payments of $399.64 at 1.25 percent per month? The relevant annuity factor is:

$$\text{Annuity present value factor} = (1 - \text{Present value factor})/r$$
$$= [1 - (1/1.0125^{48})]/.0125$$
$$= [1 - (1/1.8154)]/.0125$$
$$= (1 - .5509)/.0125$$
$$= 35.9315$$

The present value is thus:

$$\text{Present value} = \$399.64 \times 35.9315 = \$14,359.66$$

You will owe about $14,360 on the loan in two years.

CONCEPTS REVIEW AND CRITICAL THINKING QUESTIONS

1. **Annuity Factors [LO1]** There are four pieces to an annuity present value. What are they?

2. **Annuity Period [LO1]** As you increase the length of time involved, what happens to the present value of an annuity? What happens to the future value?

3. **Interest Rates [LO1]** What happens to the future value of an annuity if you increase the rate r? What happens to the present value?

4. **Present Value [LO1]** What do you think about the Tri-State Megabucks lottery discussed in the chapter advertising a $500,000 prize when the lump sum option is $250,000? Is it deceptive advertising?

5. **Present Value [LO1]** If you were an athlete negotiating a contract, would you want a big signing bonus payable immediately and smaller payments in the future, or vice versa? How about looking at it from the team's perspective?

6. **Present Value [LO1]** Suppose two athletes sign 10-year contracts for $80 million. In one case, we're told that the $80 million will be paid in 10 equal installments. In the other case, we're told that the $80 million will be paid in 10 installments, but the installments will increase by 5 percent per year. Who got the better deal?

7. **APR and EAR [LO4]** Should lending laws be changed to require lenders to report EARs instead of APRs? Why or why not?

8. **Time Value [LO1]** On subsidized Stafford loans, a common source of financial aid for college students, interest does not begin to accrue until repayment begins. Who receives a bigger subsidy, a freshman or a senior? Explain. In words, how would you go about valuing the subsidy on a subsidized Stafford loan?

9. **Time Value [LO1]** Eligibility for a subsidized Stafford loan is based on current financial need. However, both subsidized and unsubsidized Stafford loans are repaid out of future income. Given this, do you see a possible objection to having two types?

10. **Time Value [LO1]** A viatical settlement is a lump sum of money given to a terminally ill individual in exchange for his life insurance policy. When the insured person dies, the purchaser receives the payout from the life insurance policy. What factors determine the value of the viatical settlement? Do you think such settlements are ethical? Why or why not?

HM™ **QUESTIONS AND PROBLEMS**

1. **Present Value and Multiple Cash Flows [LO1]** Seaborn Co. has identified an investment project with the following cash flows. If the discount rate is 10 percent, what is the present value of these cash flows? What is the present value at 18 percent? At 24 percent?

BASIC
(Questions 1–28)

Year	Cash Flow
1	$ 950
2	1,040
3	1,130
4	1,075

2. **Present Value and Multiple Cash Flows [LO1]** Investment X offers to pay you $6,000 per year for nine years, whereas Investment Y offers to pay you $8,000 per year for six years. Which of these cash flow streams has the higher present value if the discount rate is 5 percent? If the discount rate is 15 percent?

3. **Future Value and Multiple Cash Flows [LO1]** Paradise, Inc., has identified an investment project with the following cash flows. If the discount rate is 8 percent, what is the future value of these cash flows in year 4? What is the future value at a discount rate of 11 percent? At 24 percent?

Year	Cash Flow
1	$ 940
2	1,090
3	1,340
4	1,405

4. **Calculating Annuity Present Value [LO1]** An investment offers $5,300 per year for 15 years, with the first payment occurring one year from now. If the required return is 7 percent, what is the value of the investment? What would the value be if the payments occurred for 40 years? For 75 years? Forever?

5. **Calculating Annuity Cash Flows [LO1]** If you put up $34,000 today in exchange for a 7.65 percent, 15-year annuity, what will the annual cash flow be?

6. **Calculating Annuity Values [LO1]** Your company will generate $73,000 in annual revenue each year for the next eight years from a new information database. If the appropriate interest rate is 8.5 percent, what is the present value of the savings?

7. **Calculating Annuity Values [LO1]** If you deposit $4,000 at the end of each of the next 20 years into an account paying 11.2 percent interest, how much money will you have in the account in 20 years? How much will you have if you make deposits for 40 years?

8. **Calculating Annuity Values [LO1]** You want to have $90,000 in your savings account 10 years from now, and you're prepared to make equal annual deposits into the account at the end of each year. If the account pays 6.8 percent interest, what amount must you deposit each year?

9. **Calculating Annuity Values [LO2]** Dinero Bank offers you a $50,000, seven-year term loan at 7.5 percent annual interest. What will your annual loan payment be?

10. **Calculating Perpetuity Values [LO1]** The Maybe Pay Life Insurance Co. is trying to sell you an investment policy that will pay you and your heirs $25,000 per year forever. If the required return on this investment is 7.2 percent, how much will you pay for the policy?

11. **Calculating Perpetuity Values [LO1]** In the previous problem, suppose a sales associate told you the policy costs $375,000. At what interest rate would this be a fair deal?

12. **Calculating EAR [LO4]** Find the EAR in each of the following cases:

Stated Rate (APR)	Number of Times Compounded	Effective Rate (EAR)
8%	Quarterly	
16	Monthly	
12	Daily	
15	Infinite	

13. **Calculating APR [LO4]** Find the APR, or stated rate, in each of the following cases:

Stated Rate (APR)	Number of Times Compounded	Effective Rate (EAR)
	Semiannually	8.6%
	Monthly	19.8
	Weekly	9.4
	Infinite	16.5

14. **Calculating EAR [LO4]** First National Bank charges 14.2 percent compounded monthly on its business loans. First United Bank charges 14.5 percent compounded semiannually. As a potential borrower, which bank would you go to for a new loan?

15. **Calculating APR [LO4]** Barcain Credit Corp. wants to earn an effective annual return on its consumer loans of 16 percent per year. The bank uses daily compounding on its loans. What interest rate is the bank required by law to report to potential borrowers? Explain why this rate is misleading to an uninformed borrower.

16. **Calculating Future Values [LO1]** What is the future value of $2,100 in 17 years assuming an interest rate of 8.4 percent compounded semiannually?

17. **Calculating Future Values [LO1]** Gold Door Credit Bank is offering 9.3 percent   **Χ** compounded daily on its savings accounts. If you deposit $4,500 today, how much will you have in the account in 5 years? In 10 years? In 20 years?

18. **Calculating Present Values [LO1]** An investment will pay you $58,000 in seven years. If the appropriate discount rate is 10 percent compounded daily, what is the present value?

19. **EAR versus APR [LO4]** Big Dom's Pawn Shop charges an interest rate of 30 percent per month on loans to its customers. Like all lenders, Big Dom must report an APR to consumers. What rate should the shop report? What is the effective annual rate?

20. **Calculating Loan Payments [LO2, 4]** You want to buy a new sports coupe for $68,500, and the finance office at the dealership has quoted you a 6.9 percent APR loan for 60 months to buy the car. What will your monthly payments be? What is the effective annual rate on this loan?

21. **Calculating Number of Periods [LO3]** One of your customers is delinquent on his accounts payable balance. You've mutually agreed to a repayment schedule of $500 per month. You will charge 1.3 percent per month interest on the overdue balance. If the current balance is $18,000, how long will it take for the account to be paid off?

22. **Calculating EAR [LO4]** Friendly's Quick Loans, Inc., offers you "three for four or 1 knock on your door." This means you get $3 today and repay $4 when you get your paycheck in one week (or else). What's the effective annual return Friendly's earns on this lending business? If you were brave enough to ask, what APR would Friendly's say you were paying?

23. **Valuing Perpetuities [LO1]** Live Forever Life Insurance Co. is selling a perpetuity contract that pays $1,800 monthly. The contract currently sells for $95,000. What is the monthly return on this investment vehicle? What is the APR? The effective annual return?

24. **Calculating Annuity Future Values [LO1]** You are planning to make monthly deposits of $300 into a retirement account that pays 10 percent interest compounded monthly. If your first deposit will be made one month from now, how large will your retirement account be in 30 years?

25. **Calculating Annuity Future Values [LO1]** In the previous problem, suppose you make $3,600 annual deposits into the same retirement account. How large will your account balance be in 30 years?

26. **Calculating Annuity Present Values [LO1]** Beginning three months from now, you want to be able to withdraw $2,300 each quarter from your bank account to cover college expenses over the next four years. If the account pays .65 percent interest per quarter, how much do you need to have in your bank account today to meet your expense needs over the next four years?

27. **Discounted Cash Flow Analysis [LO1]** If the appropriate discount rate for the following cash flows is 11 percent compounded quarterly, what is the present value of the cash flows?

Year	Cash Flow
1	$ 725
2	980
3	0
4	1,360

28. **Discounted Cash Flow Analysis** [LO1] If the appropriate discount rate for the following cash flows is 8.45 percent per year, what is the present value of the cash flows?

Year	Cash Flow
1	$1,650
2	0
3	4,200
4	2,430

INTERMEDIATE
(Questions 29–56)

29. **Simple Interest versus Compound Interest** [LO4] First Simple Bank pays 7 percent simple interest on its investment accounts. If First Complex Bank pays interest on its accounts compounded annually, what rate should the bank set if it wants to match First Simple Bank over an investment horizon of 10 years?

30. **Calculating EAR** [LO4] You are looking at an investment that has an effective annual rate of 17 percent. What is the effective semiannual return? The effective quarterly return? The effective monthly return?

31. **Calculating Interest Expense** [LO2] You receive a credit card application from Shady Banks Savings and Loan offering an introductory rate of 1.5 percent per year, compounded monthly for the first six months, increasing thereafter to 18 percent compounded monthly. Assuming you transfer the $5,000 balance from your existing credit card and make no subsequent payments, how much interest will you owe at the end of the first year?

32. **Calculating Annuities** [LO1] You are planning to save for retirement over the next 30 years. To do this, you will invest $700 a month in a stock account and $300 a month in a bond account. The return of the stock account is expected to be 11 percent, and the bond account will pay 6 percent. When you retire, you will combine your money into an account with a 9 percent return. How much can you withdraw each month from your account assuming a 25-year withdrawal period?

33. **Calculating Future Values** [LO1] You have an investment that will pay you 1.17 percent per month. How much will you have per dollar invested in one year? In two years?

34. **Calculating Annuity Payments** [LO1] You want to be a millionaire when you retire in 40 years. How much do you have to save each month if you can earn a 12 percent annual return? How much do you have to save if you wait 10 years before you begin your deposits? 20 years?

35. **Calculating Rates of Return** [LO2] Suppose an investment offers to triple your money in 12 months (don't believe it). What rate of return per quarter are you being offered?

36. **Comparing Cash Flow Streams** [LO1] You've just joined the investment banking firm of Dewey, Cheatum, and Howe. They've offered you two different salary arrangements. You can have $95,000 per year for the next two years, or you can have $70,000 per year for the next two years, along with a $45,000 signing bonus today. The bonus is paid immediately, and the salary is paid at the end of each year. If the interest rate is 10 percent compounded monthly, which do you prefer?

37. **Growing Annuity [LO1]** You have just won the lottery and will receive $1,000,000 in one year. You will receive payments for 30 years, which will increase 5 percent per year. If the appropriate discount rate is 8 percent, what is the present value of your winnings?

38. **Growing Annuity [LO1]** Your job pays you only once a year for all the work you did over the previous 12 months. Today, December 31, you just received your salary of $50,000 and you plan to spend all of it. However, you want to start saving for retirement beginning next year. You have decided that one year from today you will begin depositing 5 percent of your annual salary in an account that will earn 11 percent per year. Your salary will increase at 4 percent per year throughout your career. How much money will you have on the date of your retirement 40 years from today?

39. **Present Value and Interest Rates [LO1]** What is the relationship between the value of an annuity and the level of interest rates? Suppose you just bought a 15-year annuity of $9,000 per year at the current interest rate of 10 percent per year. What happens to the value of your investment if interest rates suddenly drop to 5 percent? What if interest rates suddenly rise to 15 percent?

40. **Calculating the Number of Payments [LO2]** You're prepared to make monthly payments of $340, beginning at the end of this month, into an account that pays 6 percent interest compounded monthly. How many payments will you have made when your account balance reaches $20,000?

41. **Calculating Annuity Present Values [LO2]** You want to borrow $73,000 from your local bank to buy a new sailboat. You can afford to make monthly payments of $1,450, but no more. Assuming monthly compounding, what is the highest rate you can afford on a 60-month APR loan?

42. **Calculating Loan Payments [LO2]** You need a 30-year, fixed-rate mortgage to buy a new home for $240,000. Your mortgage bank will lend you the money at a 6.35 percent APR for this 360-month loan. However, you can afford monthly payments of only $1,150, so you offer to pay off any remaining loan balance at the end of the loan in the form of a single balloon payment. How large will this balloon payment have to be for you to keep your monthly payments at $1,150?

43. **Present and Future Values [LO1]** The present value of the following cash flow stream is $6,550 when discounted at 10 percent annually. What is the value of the missing cash flow?

Year	Cash Flow
1	$1,700
2	?
3	2,100
4	2,800

44. **Calculating Present Values [LO1]** You just won the TVM Lottery. You will receive $1 million today plus another 10 annual payments that increase by $500,000 per year. Thus, in one year, you receive $1.5 million. In two years you get $2 million, and so on. If the appropriate interest rate is 9 percent, what is the present value of your winnings?

45. **EAR versus APR [LO4]** You have just purchased a new warehouse. To finance the purchase, you've arranged for a 30-year mortgage loan for 80 percent of the $2,900,000 purchase price. The monthly payment on this loan will be $15,000. What is the APR on this loan? The EAR?

46. **Present Value and Break-Even Interest** [LO1] Consider a firm with a contract to sell an asset for $165,000 four years from now. The asset costs $94,000 to produce today. Given a relevant discount rate on this asset of 13 percent per year, will the firm make a profit on this asset? At what rate does the firm just break even?

47. **Present Value and Multiple Cash Flows** [LO1] What is the present value of $4,000 per year, at a discount rate of 10 percent, if the first payment is received 8 years from now and the last payment is received 25 years from now?

48. **Variable Interest Rates** [LO1] A 15-year annuity pays $1,500 per month, and payments are made at the end of each month. If the interest rate is 11 percent compounded monthly for the first seven years, and 7 percent compounded monthly thereafter, what is the present value of the annuity?

49. **Comparing Cash Flow Streams** [LO1] You have your choice of two investment accounts. Investment A is a 15-year annuity that features end-of-month $1,200 payments and has an interest rate of 8.5 percent compounded monthly. Investment B is an 8 percent continuously compounded lump sum investment, also good for 15 years. How much money would you need to invest in B today for it to be worth as much as investment A 15 years from now?

50. **Calculating Present Value of a Perpetuity** [LO1] Given an interest rate of 6.2 percent per year, what is the value at date $t = 7$ of a perpetual stream of $3,500 payments that begins at date $t = 15$?

51. **Calculating EAR** [LO4] A local finance company quotes a 16 percent interest rate on one-year loans. So, if you borrow $25,000, the interest for the year will be $4,000. Because you must repay a total of $29,000 in one year, the finance company requires you to pay $29,000/12, or $2,416.67, per month over the next 12 months. Is this a 16 percent loan? What rate would legally have to be quoted? What is the effective annual rate?

52. **Calculating Present Values** [LO1] A 5-year annuity of ten $7,000 semiannual payments will begin 8 years from now, with the first payment coming 8.5 years from now. If the discount rate is 10 percent compounded monthly, what is the value of this annuity five years from now? What is the value three years from now? What is the current value of the annuity?

53. **Calculating Annuities Due** [LO1] Suppose you are going to receive $10,000 per year for five years. The appropriate interest rate is 11 percent.

   a. What is the present value of the payments if they are in the form of an ordinary annuity? What is the present value if the payments are an annuity due?

   b. Suppose you plan to invest the payments for five years. What is the future value if the payments are an ordinary annuity? What if the payments are an annuity due?

   c. Which has the highest present value, the ordinary annuity or annuity due? Which has the highest future value? Will this always be true?

54. **Calculating Annuities Due** [LO1] You want to buy a new sports car from Muscle Motors for $68,000. The contract is in the form of a 60-month annuity due at an 7.85 percent APR. What will your monthly payment be?

55. **Amortization with Equal Payments** [LO3] Prepare an amortization schedule for a five-year loan of $42,000. The interest rate is 8 percent per year, and the loan calls for equal annual payments. How much interest is paid in the third year? How much total interest is paid over the life of the loan?

56. Amortization with Equal Principal Payments [LO3] Rework Problem 55 assuming that the loan agreement calls for a principal reduction of $8,400 every year instead of equal annual payments.

57. Calculating Annuity Values [LO1] Bilbo Baggins wants to save money to meet three objectives. First, he would like to be able to retire 30 years from now with retirement income of $20,000 per month for 25 years, with the first payment received 30 years and 1 month from now. Second, he would like to purchase a cabin in Rivendell in 10 years at an estimated cost of $380,000. Third, after he passes on at the end of the 25 years of withdrawals, he would like to leave an inheritance of $900,000 to his nephew Frodo. He can afford to save $2,500 per month for the next 10 years. If he can earn a 10 percent EAR before he retires and a 7 percent EAR after he retires, how much will he have to save each month in years 11 through 30?

CHALLENGE
(Questions 57–78)

58. Calculating Annuity Values [LO1] After deciding to buy a new car, you can either lease the car or purchase it on a three-year loan. The car you wish to buy costs $32,000. The dealer has a special leasing arrangement where you pay $99 today and $450 per month for the next three years. If you purchase the car, you will pay it off in monthly payments over the next three years at a 7 percent APR. You believe you will be able to sell the car for $23,000 in three years. Should you buy or lease the car? What break-even resale price in three years would make you indifferent between buying and leasing?

59. Calculating Annuity Values [LO1] An All-Pro defensive lineman is in contract negotiations. The team has offered the following salary structure:

Time	Salary
0	$7,000,000
1	$4,500,000
2	$5,000,000
3	$6,000,000
4	$6,800,000
5	$7,900,000
6	$8,800,000

All salaries are to be paid in lump sums. The player has asked you as his agent to renegotiate the terms. He wants a $9 million signing bonus payable today and a contract value increase of $1,400,000. He also wants an equal salary paid every three months, with the first paycheck three months from now. If the interest rate is 5.5 percent compounded daily, what is the amount of his quarterly check? Assume 365 days in a year.

60. Discount Interest Loans [LO4] This question illustrates what is known as *discount interest*. Imagine you are discussing a loan with a somewhat unscrupulous lender. You want to borrow $25,000 for one year. The interest rate is 15 percent. You and the lender agree that the interest on the loan will be .15 × $25,000 = $3,750. So the lender deducts this interest amount from the loan up front and gives you $21,250. In this case, we say that the discount is $3,750. What's wrong here?

61. Calculating Annuity Values [LO1] You are serving on a jury. A plaintiff is suing the city for injuries sustained after a freak street sweeper accident. In the trial, doctors testified that it will be five years before the plaintiff is able to return to work. The jury has already decided in favor of the plaintiff. You are the foreperson of the jury and propose that the jury give the plaintiff an award to cover the following: (a) The present value of two years' back pay. The plaintiff's annual salary for the last two years would have been $47,000 and $50,000, respectively. (b) The present value of five years' future salary. You assume the salary will be $55,000 per year. (c) $100,000 for pain and suffering. (d) $20,000 for court costs. Assume that the salary payments are equal amounts paid at the end of each month. If the interest rate you choose is an 8 percent EAR, what is the size of the settlement? If you were the plaintiff, would you like to see a higher or lower interest rate?

62. **Calculating EAR with Points [LO4]** You are looking at a one-year loan of $10,000. The interest rate is quoted as 8 percent plus three points. A *point* on a loan is simply 1 percent (one percentage point) of the loan amount. Quotes similar to this one are common with home mortgages. The interest rate quotation in this example requires the borrower to pay three points to the lender up front and repay the loan later with 8 percent interest. What rate would you actually be paying here?

63. **Calculating EAR with Points [LO4]** The interest rate on a one-year loan is quoted as 11 percent plus two points (see the previous problem). What is the EAR? Is your answer affected by the loan amount?

64. **EAR versus APR [LO4]** Two banks in the area offer 30-year, $240,000 mortgages at 6.8 percent and charge a $2,300 loan application fee. However, the application fee charged by Insecurity Bank and Trust is refundable if the loan application is denied, whereas that charged by I.M. Greedy and Sons Mortgage Bank is not. The current disclosure law requires that any fees that will be refunded if the applicant is rejected be included in calculating the APR, but this is not required with nonrefundable fees (presumably because refundable fees are part of the loan rather than a fee). What are the EARs on these two loans? What are the APRs?

65. **Calculating EAR with Add-On Interest [LO4]** This problem illustrates a deceptive way of quoting interest rates called *add-on interest*. Imagine that you see an advertisement for Crazy Judy's Stereo City that reads something like this: "$1,000 Instant Credit! 14% Simple Interest! Three Years to Pay! Low, Low Monthly Payments!" You're not exactly sure what all this means and somebody has spilled ink over the APR on the loan contract, so you ask the manager for clarification.

    Judy explains that if you borrow $1,000 for three years at 14 percent interest, in three years you will owe:

    $1,000 \times 1.14^3 = \$1,000 \times 1.41854 = \$1,481.54$

    Now, Judy recognizes that coming up with $1,481.54 all at once might be a strain, so she lets you make "low, low monthly payments" of $1,481.54/36 = $41.15 per month, even though this is extra bookkeeping work for her.

    Is this a 14 percent loan? Why or why not? What is the APR on this loan? What is the EAR? Why do you think this is called add-on interest?

66. **Calculating Annuity Payments [LO1]** This is a classic retirement problem. A time line will help in solving it. Your friend is celebrating her 35th birthday today and wants to start saving for her anticipated retirement at age 65. She wants to be able to withdraw $105,000 from her savings account on each birthday for 20 years following her retirement; the first withdrawal will be on her 66th birthday. Your

friend intends to invest her money in the local credit union, which offers 7 percent interest per year. She wants to make equal annual payments on each birthday into the account established at the credit union for her retirement fund.

a. If she starts making these deposits on her 36th birthday and continues to make deposits until she is 65 (the last deposit will be on her 65th birthday), what amount must she deposit annually to be able to make the desired withdrawals at retirement?

b. Suppose your friend has just inherited a large sum of money. Rather than making equal annual payments, she has decided to make one lump sum payment on her 35th birthday to cover her retirement needs. What amount does she have to deposit?

c. Suppose your friend's employer will contribute $1,500 to the account every year as part of the company's profit-sharing plan. In addition, your friend expects a $150,000 distribution from a family trust fund on her 55th birthday, which she will also put into the retirement account. What amount must she deposit annually now to be able to make the desired withdrawals at retirement?

67. **Calculating the Number of Periods** [LO2] Your Christmas ski vacation was great, but it unfortunately ran a bit over budget. All is not lost: You just received an offer in the mail to transfer your $10,000 balance from your current credit card, which charges an annual rate of 19.8 percent, to a new credit card charging a rate of 6.2 percent. How much faster could you pay the loan off by making your planned monthly payments of $200 with the new card? What if there was a 2 percent fee charged on any balances transferred?

68. **Future Value and Multiple Cash Flows** [LO1] An insurance company is offering a new policy to its customers. Typically, the policy is bought by a parent or grandparent for a child at the child's birth. The details of the policy are as follows: The purchaser (say, the parent) makes the following six payments to the insurance company:

First birthday:	$ 900
Second birthday:	$ 900
Third birthday:	$1,000
Fourth birthday:	$1,000
Fifth birthday:	$1,100
Sixth birthday:	$1,100

After the child's sixth birthday, no more payments are made. When the child reaches age 65, he or she receives $500,000. If the relevant interest rate is 12 percent for the first six years and 8 percent for all subsequent years, is the policy worth buying?

69. **Calculating a Balloon Payment** [LO2] You have just arranged for a $750,000 mortgage to finance the purchase of a large tract of land. The mortgage has an 8.1 percent APR, and it calls for monthly payments over the next 30 years. However, the loan has an eight-year balloon payment, meaning that the loan must be paid off then. How big will the balloon payment be?

70. **Calculating Interest Rates** [LO4] A financial planning service offers a college savings program. The plan calls for you to make six annual payments of $9,000 each, with the first payment occurring today, your child's 12th birthday. Beginning on your child's 18th birthday, the plan will provide $20,000 per year for four years. What return is this investment offering?

71. Break-Even Investment Returns [LO4] Your financial planner offers you two different investment plans. Plan X is a $20,000 annual perpetuity. Plan Y is a 20-year, $28,000 annual annuity. Both plans will make their first payment one year from today. At what discount rate would you be indifferent between these two plans?

72. Perpetual Cash Flows [LO1] What is the value of an investment that pays $15,000 every *other* year forever, if the first payment occurs one year from today and the discount rate is 10 percent compounded daily? What is the value today if the first payment occurs four years from today?

73. Ordinary Annuities and Annuities Due [LO1] As discussed in the text, an annuity due is identical to an ordinary annuity except that the periodic payments occur at the beginning of each period and not at the end of the period. Show that the relationship between the value of an ordinary annuity and the value of an otherwise equivalent annuity due is:

$$\text{Annuity due value} = \text{Ordinary annuity value} \times (1 + r)$$

Show this for both present and future values.

74. Calculating Growing Annuities [LO1] You have 40 years left until retirement and want to retire with $2 million. Your salary is paid annually, and you will receive $40,000 at the end of the current year. Your salary will increase at 3 percent per year, and you can earn an 11 percent return on the money you invest. If you save a constant percentage of your salary, what percentage of your salary must you save each year?

75. Calculating EAR [LO4] A check-cashing store is in the business of making personal loans to walk-up customers. The store makes only one-week loans at 7 percent interest per week.

   a. What APR must the store report to its customers? What EAR are customers actually paying?

   b. Now suppose the store makes one-week loans at 7 percent discount interest per week (see Problem 60). What's the APR now? The EAR?

   c. The check-cashing store also makes one-month add-on interest loans at 7 percent discount interest per week. Thus if you borrow $100 for one month (four weeks), the interest will be ($100 × 1.07^4) − 100 = $31.08. Because this is discount interest, your net loan proceeds today will be $68.92. You must then repay the store $100 at the end of the month. To help you out, though, the store lets you pay off this $100 in installments of $25 per week. What is the APR of this loan? What is the EAR?

76. Present Value of a Growing Perpetuity [LO1] What is the equation for the present value of a growing perpetuity with a payment of C one period from today if the payments grow by C each period?

77. Rule of 72 [LO4] Earlier, we discussed the Rule of 72, a useful approximation for many interest rates and periods for the time it takes a lump sum to double in value. For a 10 percent interest rate, show that the "Rule of 73" is slightly better. For what rate is the Rule of 72 exact? (*Hint:* Use the Solver function in Excel.)

78. Rule of 69.3 [LO4] A corollary to the Rule of 72 is the Rule of 69.3. The Rule of 69.3 is exactly correct except for rounding when interest rates are compounded continuously. Prove the Rule of 69.3 for continuously compounded interest.

The MBA Decision

Ben Bates graduated from college six years ago with a finance undergraduate degree. Although he is satisfied with his current job, his goal is to become an investment banker. He feels that an MBA degree would allow him to achieve this goal. After examining schools, he has narrowed his choice to either Wilton University or Mount Perry College. Although internships are encouraged by both schools, to get class credit for the internship, no salary can be paid. Other than internships, neither school will allow its students to work while enrolled in its MBA program.

Ben currently works at the money management firm of Dewey and Louis. His annual salary at the firm is $55,000 per year, and his salary is expected to increase at 3 percent per year until retirement. He is currently 28 years old and expects to work for 38 more years. His current job includes a fully paid health insurance plan, and his current average tax rate is 26 percent. Ben has a savings account with enough money to cover the entire cost of his MBA program.

The Ritter College of Business at Wilton University is one of the top MBA programs in the country. The MBA degree requires two years of full-time enrollment at the university. The annual tuition is $63,000, payable at the beginning of each school year. Books and other supplies are estimated to cost $2,500 per year. Ben expects that after graduation from Wilton, he will receive a job offer for about $98,000 per year, with a $15,000 signing bonus. The salary at this job will increase at 4 percent per year. Because of the higher salary, his average income tax rate will increase to 31 percent.

The Bradley School of Business at Mount Perry College began its MBA program 16 years ago. The Bradley School is smaller and less well known than the Ritter College. Bradley offers an accelerated one-year program, with a tuition cost of $80,000 to be paid upon matriculation. Books and other supplies for the program are expected to cost $3,500. Ben thinks that he will receive an offer of $81,000 per year upon graduation, with a $10,000 signing bonus. The salary at this job will increase at 3.5 percent per year. His average tax rate at this level of income will be 29 percent.

Both schools offer a health insurance plan that will cost $3,000 per year, payable at the beginning of the year. Ben also estimates that room and board expenses will cost $20,000 per year at both schools. The appropriate discount rate is 6.5 percent.

QUESTIONS

1. How does Ben's age affect his decision to get an MBA?

2. What other, perhaps nonquantifiable, factors affect Ben's decision to get an MBA?

3. Assuming all salaries are paid at the end of each year, what is the best option for Ben from a strictly financial standpoint?

4. Ben believes that the appropriate analysis is to calculate the future value of each option. How would you evaluate this statement?

5. What initial salary would Ben need to receive to make him indifferent between attending Wilton University and staying in his current position?

6. Suppose, instead of being able to pay cash for his MBA, Ben must borrow the money. The current borrowing rate is 5.4 percent. How would this affect his decision?

Visit us at www.mhhe.com/rwj

7

INTEREST RATES AND BOND VALUATION

After studying this chapter, you should understand:

LO1   Important bond features and types of bonds.

LO2   Bond values and yields and why they fluctuate.

LO3   Bond ratings and what they mean.

LO4   The impact of inflation on interest rates.

LO5   The term structure of interest rates and the determinants of bond yields.

IN ITS MOST BASIC FORM, a bond is a pretty simple thing. You lend a company some money, say $1,000. The company pays you interest regularly, and it repays the original loan amount of $1,000 at some point in the future. But bonds also can have complex features, and in 2008, a type of bond known as *a mortgage-backed security,* or *MBS,* was causing havoc in the global financial system.

An MBS, as the name suggests, is a bond that is backed by a pool of home mortgages. The bondholders receive payments derived from payments on the underlying mortgages, and these payments can be divided up in various ways to create different classes of bonds. Defaults on the underlying mortgages lead to losses to MBS bondholders, particularly those in the riskier classes, and as the U.S. housing crunch hit in 2007–2008, defaults increased sharply. Losses to investors were still piling up in mid-2008, so the total damage wasn't known, but estimates ranged from $250 billion to $500 billion or more, colossal sums by any measure.

Master the ability to solve problems in this chapter by using a spreadsheet. Access Excel Master on the student Web site www.mhhe.com/rwj.

Our goal in this chapter is to introduce you to bonds. We begin by showing how the techniques we developed in Chapters 5 and 6 can be applied to bond valuation. From there, we go on to discuss bond features and how bonds are bought and sold. One important thing we learn is that bond values depend, in large part, on interest rates. We therefore close the chapter with an examination of interest rates and their behavior.

Bonds and Bond Valuation   7.1

When a corporation or government wishes to borrow money from the public on a long-term basis, it usually does so by issuing or selling debt securities that are generically called *bonds*. In this section, we describe the various features of corporate bonds and some of the terminology associated with bonds. We then discuss the cash flows associated with a bond and how bonds can be valued using our discounted cash flow procedure.

BOND FEATURES AND PRICES

As we mentioned in our previous chapter, a bond is normally an interest-only loan, meaning that the borrower will pay the interest every period, but none of the principal will be repaid until the end of the loan. For example, suppose the Beck Corporation wants to borrow $1,000 for 30 years. The interest rate on similar debt issued by similar corporations is 12 percent. Beck will thus pay $.12 \times \$1,000 = \$120$ in interest every year for 30 years. At the end of 30 years, Beck will repay the $1,000. As this example suggests, a bond is a fairly simple financing arrangement. There is, however, a rich jargon associated with bonds, so we will use this example to define some of the more important terms.

In our example, the $120 regular interest payments that Beck promises to make are called the bond's **coupons**. Because the coupon is constant and paid every year, the type of bond we are describing is sometimes called a *level coupon bond*. The amount that will be repaid at the end of the loan is called the bond's **face value**, or **par value**. As in our example, this par value is usually $1,000 for corporate bonds, and a bond that sells for its par value is called a *par value bond*. Government bonds frequently have much larger face, or par, values. Finally, the annual coupon divided by the face value is called the **coupon rate** on the bond; in this case, because $120/1,000 = 12\%$, the bond has a 12 percent coupon rate.

The number of years until the face value is paid is called the bond's time to **maturity**. A corporate bond will frequently have a maturity of 30 years when it is originally issued, but this varies. Once the bond has been issued, the number of years to maturity declines as time goes by.

BOND VALUES AND YIELDS

As time passes, interest rates change in the marketplace. The cash flows from a bond, however, stay the same. As a result, the value of the bond will fluctuate. When interest rates rise, the present value of the bond's remaining cash flows declines, and the bond is worth less. When interest rates fall, the bond is worth more.

To determine the value of a bond at a particular point in time, we need to know the number of periods remaining until maturity, the face value, the coupon, and the market interest rate for bonds with similar features. This interest rate required in the market on a bond is called the bond's **yield to maturity (YTM)**. This rate is sometimes called the bond's *yield* for short. Given all this information, we can calculate the present value of the cash flows as an estimate of the bond's current market value.

For example, suppose the Xanth (pronounced "zanth") Co. were to issue a bond with 10 years to maturity. The Xanth bond has an annual coupon of $80. Similar bonds have a yield to maturity of 8 percent. Based on our preceding discussion, the Xanth bond will pay $80 per year for the next 10 years in coupon interest. In 10 years, Xanth will pay $1,000 to the owner of the bond. The cash flows from the bond are shown in Figure 7.1. What would this bond sell for?

As illustrated in Figure 7.1, the Xanth bond's cash flows have an annuity component (the coupons) and a lump sum (the face value paid at maturity). We thus estimate the

coupon
The stated interest payment made on a bond.

face value
The principal amount of a bond that is repaid at the end of the term. Also called *par value*.

coupon rate
The annual coupon divided by the face value of a bond.

maturity
The specified date on which the principal amount of a bond is paid.

yield to maturity (YTM)
The rate required in the market on a bond.

FIGURE 7.1   Cash Flows for Xanth Co. Bond

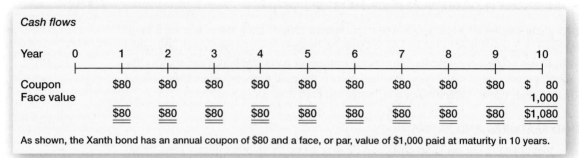

As shown, the Xanth bond has an annual coupon of $80 and a face, or par, value of $1,000 paid at maturity in 10 years.

market value of the bond by calculating the present value of these two components separately and adding the results together. First, at the going rate of 8 percent, the present value of the $1,000 paid in 10 years is:

$$\text{Present value} = \$1,000/1.08^{10} = \$1,000/2.1589 = \$463.19$$

Second, the bond offers $80 per year for 10 years; the present value of this annuity stream is:

$$
\begin{aligned}
\text{Annuity present value} &= \$80 \times (1 - 1/1.08^{10})/.08 \\
&= \$80 \times (1 - 1/2.1589)/.08 \\
&= \$80 \times 6.7101 \\
&= \$536.81
\end{aligned}
$$

We can now add the values for the two parts together to get the bond's value:

$$\text{Total bond value} = \$463.19 + 536.81 = \$1,000$$

This bond sells for exactly its face value. This is not a coincidence. The going interest rate in the market is 8 percent. Considered as an interest-only loan, what interest rate does this bond have? With an $80 coupon, this bond pays exactly 8 percent interest only when it sells for $1,000.

To illustrate what happens as interest rates change, suppose a year has gone by. The Xanth bond now has nine years to maturity. If the interest rate in the market has risen to 10 percent, what will the bond be worth? To find out, we repeat the present value calculations with 9 years instead of 10, and a 10 percent yield instead of an 8 percent yield. First, the present value of the $1,000 paid in nine years at 10 percent is:

$$\text{Present value} = \$1,000/1.10^{9} = \$1,000/2.3579 = \$424.10$$

Second, the bond now offers $80 per year for nine years; the present value of this annuity stream at 10 percent is:

$$
\begin{aligned}
\text{Annuity present value} &= \$80 \times (1 - 1/1.10^{9})/.10 \\
&= \$80 \times (1 - 1/2.3579)/.10 \\
&= \$80 \times 5.7590 \\
&= \$460.72
\end{aligned}
$$

We can now add the values for the two parts together to get the bond's value:

$$\text{Total bond value} = \$424.10 + 460.72 = \$884.82$$

Therefore, the bond should sell for about $885. In the vernacular, we say that this bond, with its 8 percent coupon, is priced to yield 10 percent at $885.

The Xanth Co. bond now sells for less than its $1,000 face value. Why? The market interest rate is 10 percent. Considered as an interest-only loan of $1,000, this bond pays only 8 percent, its coupon rate. Because this bond pays less than the going rate, investors are willing to lend only something less than the $1,000 promised repayment. Because the bond sells for less than face value, it is said to be a *discount bond.*

The only way to get the interest rate up to 10 percent is to lower the price to less than $1,000 so that the purchaser, in effect, has a built-in gain. For the Xanth bond, the price of $885 is $115 less than the face value, so an investor who purchased and kept the bond would get $80 per year and would have a $115 gain at maturity as well. This gain compensates the lender for the below-market coupon rate.

Another way to see why the bond is discounted by $115 is to note that the $80 coupon is $20 below the coupon on a newly issued par value bond, based on current market conditions. The bond would be worth $1,000 only if it had a coupon of $100 per year. In a sense, an investor who buys and keeps the bond gives up $20 per year for nine years. At 10 percent, this annuity stream is worth:

$$\text{Annuity present value} = \$20 \times (1 - 1/1.10^9)/.10$$
$$= \$20 \times 5.7590$$
$$= \$115.18$$

This is just the amount of the discount.

What would the Xanth bond sell for if interest rates had dropped by 2 percent instead of rising by 2 percent? As you might guess, the bond would sell for more than $1,000. Such a bond is said to sell at a *premium* and is called a *premium bond.*

This case is just the opposite of that of a discount bond. The Xanth bond now has a coupon rate of 8 percent when the market rate is only 6 percent. Investors are willing to pay a premium to get this extra coupon amount. In this case, the relevant discount rate is 6 percent, and there are nine years remaining. The present value of the $1,000 face amount is:

$$\text{Present value} = \$1,000/1.06^9 = \$1,000/1.6895 = \$591.89$$

The present value of the coupon stream is:

$$\text{Annuity present value} = \$80 \times (1 - 1/1.06^9)/.06$$
$$= \$80 \times (1 - 1/1.6895)/.06$$
$$= \$80 \times 6.8017$$
$$= \$544.14$$

We can now add the values for the two parts together to get the bond's value:

$$\text{Total bond value} = \$591.89 + 544.14 = \$1,136.03$$

Total bond value is therefore about $136 in excess of par value. Once again, we can verify this amount by noting that the coupon is now $20 too high, based on current market conditions. The present value of $20 per year for nine years at 6 percent is:

$$\text{Annuity present value} = \$20 \times (1 - 1/1.06^9)/.06$$
$$= \$20 \times 6.8017$$
$$= \$136.03$$

This is just as we calculated.

A good bond site to visit is bonds.yahoo.com, which has loads of useful information.

Online bond calculators are available at personal.fidelity.com; interest rate information is available at money.cnn.com/markets/bondcenter and www.bankrate.com.

Based on our examples, we can now write the general expression for the value of a bond. If a bond has (1) a face value of F paid at maturity, (2) a coupon of C paid per period, (3) t periods to maturity, and (4) a yield of r per period, its value is:

$$\text{Bond value} = C \times [1 - 1/(1 + r)^t]/r \;+\; F/(1 + r)^t$$

$$\text{Bond value} = \begin{array}{c}\text{Present value} \\ \text{of the coupons}\end{array} + \begin{array}{c}\text{Present value} \\ \text{of the face amount}\end{array}$$

[7.1]

EXAMPLE 7.1   Semiannual Coupons

In practice, bonds issued in the United States usually make coupon payments twice a year. So, if an ordinary bond has a coupon rate of 14 percent, then the owner will get a total of $140 per year, but this $140 will come in two payments of $70 each. Suppose we are examining such a bond. The yield to maturity is quoted at 16 percent.

Bond yields are quoted like APRs; the quoted rate is equal to the actual rate per period multiplied by the number of periods. In this case, with a 16 percent quoted yield and semiannual payments, the true yield is 8 percent per six months. The bond matures in seven years. What is the bond's price? What is the effective annual yield on this bond?

Based on our discussion, we know the bond will sell at a discount because it has a coupon rate of 7 percent every six months when the market requires 8 percent every six months. So, if our answer exceeds $1,000, we know we have made a mistake.

To get the exact price, we first calculate the present value of the bond's face value of $1,000 paid in seven years. This seven-year period has 14 periods of six months each. At 8 percent per period, the value is:

Present value = $1,000/1.08^{14} = $1,000/2.9372 = $340.46

The coupons can be viewed as a 14-period annuity of $70 per period. At an 8 percent discount rate, the present value of such an annuity is:

Annuity present value = $70 × (1 − 1/1.08^{14})/.08
 = $70 × (1 − .3405)/.08
 = $70 × 8.2442
 = $577.10

The total present value gives us what the bond should sell for:

Total present value = $340.46 + 577.10 = $917.56

To calculate the effective yield on this bond, note that 8 percent every six months is equivalent to:

Effective annual rate = (1 + .08)^2 − 1 = 16.64%

The effective yield, therefore, is 16.64 percent.

Visit investorguide.com *to learn more about bonds.*

As we have illustrated in this section, bond prices and interest rates always move in opposite directions. When interest rates rise, a bond's value, like any other present value, will decline. Similarly, when interest rates fall, bond values rise. Even if we are considering a bond that is riskless in the sense that the borrower is certain to make all the payments, there is still risk in owning a bond. We discuss this next.

INTEREST RATE RISK

The risk that arises for bond owners from fluctuating interest rates is called *interest rate risk*. How much interest rate risk a bond has depends on how sensitive its price is to interest rate changes. This sensitivity directly depends on two things: the time to maturity and the coupon rate. As we will see momentarily, you should keep the following in mind when looking at a bond:

1. All other things being equal, the longer the time to maturity, the greater the interest rate risk.

2. All other things being equal, the lower the coupon rate, the greater the interest rate risk.

We illustrate the first of these two points in Figure 7.2. As shown, we compute and plot prices under different interest rate scenarios for 10 percent coupon bonds with maturities of 1 year and 30 years. Notice how the slope of the line connecting the prices is much steeper for the 30-year maturity than it is for the 1-year maturity. This steepness tells us that a relatively small change in interest rates will lead to a substantial change in the bond's value. In comparison, the one-year bond's price is relatively insensitive to interest rate changes.

Intuitively, we can see that longer-term bonds have greater interest rate sensitivity because a large portion of a bond's value comes from the $1,000 face amount. The present value of this amount isn't greatly affected by a small change in interest rates if the amount is to be received in one year. Even a small change in the interest rate, however, once it is

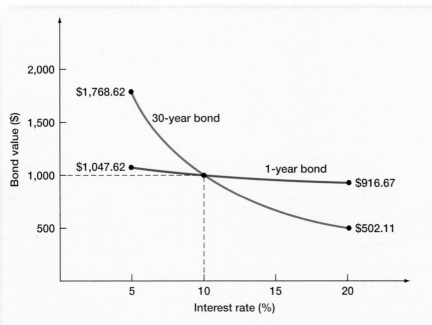

FIGURE 7.2

Interest Rate Risk and Time to Maturity

Value of a Bond with a 10 Percent Coupon Rate for Different Interest Rates and Maturities

	Time to Maturity	
Interest Rate	1 Year	30 Years
5%	$1,047.62	$1,768.62
10	1,000.00	1,000.00
15	956.52	671.70
20	916.67	502.11

compounded for 30 years, can have a significant effect on the present value. As a result, the present value of the face amount will be much more volatile with a longer-term bond.

The other thing to know about interest rate risk is that, like most things in finance and economics, it increases at a decreasing rate. In other words, if we compared a 10-year bond to a 1-year bond, we would see that the 10-year bond has much greater interest rate risk. However, if you were to compare a 20-year bond to a 30-year bond, you would find that the 30-year bond has somewhat greater interest rate risk because it has a longer maturity, but the difference in the risk would be fairly small.

The reason that bonds with lower coupons have greater interest rate risk is essentially the same. As we discussed earlier, the value of a bond depends on the present value of its coupons and the present value of the face amount. If two bonds with different coupon rates have the same maturity, then the value of the one with the lower coupon is proportionately more dependent on the face amount to be received at maturity. As a result, all other things being equal, its value will fluctuate more as interest rates change. Put another way, the bond with the higher coupon has a larger cash flow early in its life, so its value is less sensitive to changes in the discount rate.

Bonds are rarely issued with maturities longer than 30 years. However, low interest rates in recent years have led to the issuance of much longer-term issues. In the 1990s, Walt Disney issued "Sleeping Beauty" bonds with a 100-year maturity. Similarly, BellSouth (now known as AT&T), Coca-Cola, and Dutch banking giant ABN AMRO all issued bonds with 100-year maturities. These companies evidently wanted to lock in the historical low interest rates for a *long* time. The current record holder for corporations looks to be Republic National Bank, which sold bonds with 1,000 years to maturity. Before these fairly recent issues, it appears the last time 100-year bonds were issued was in May 1954, by the Chicago and Eastern Railroad. If you are wondering when the next 100-year bonds will be issued, you might have a long wait. The IRS has warned companies about such long-term issues and threatened to disallow the interest payment deduction on these bonds.

We can illustrate the effect of interest rate risk using the 100-year BellSouth issue. The following table provides some basic information about this issue, along with its prices on December 31, 1995, July 31, 1996, and May 6, 2008:

Maturity	Coupon Rate	Price on 12/31/95	Price on 7/31/96	Percentage Change in Price 1995–1996	Price on 5/6/08	Percentage Change in Price 1996–2008
2095	7.00%	$1,000.00	$800.00	−20.0%	$1,008.40	+26 %

Several things emerge from this table. First, interest rates apparently rose between December 31, 1995, and July 31, 1996 (why?). After that, however, they fell (why?). The bond's price first lost 20 percent and then gained 26 percent. These swings illustrate that longer-term bonds have significant interest rate risk.

FINDING THE YIELD TO MATURITY: MORE TRIAL AND ERROR

Frequently, we will know a bond's price, coupon rate, and maturity date, but not its yield to maturity. For example, suppose we are interested in a six-year, 8 percent coupon bond. A broker quotes a price of $955.14. What is the yield on this bond?

CHAPTER 7 Interest Rates and Bond Valuation   **197**

We've seen that the price of a bond can be written as the sum of its annuity and lump sum components. Knowing that there is an $80 coupon for six years and a $1,000 face value, we can say that the price is:

$$\$955.14 = \$80 \times [1 - 1/(1 + r)^6]/r + 1{,}000/(1 + r)^6$$

where r is the unknown discount rate, or yield to maturity. We have one equation here and one unknown, but we cannot solve it for r explicitly. The only way to find the answer is to use trial and error.

This problem is essentially identical to the one we examined in the last chapter when we tried to find the unknown interest rate on an annuity. However, finding the rate (or yield) on a bond is even more complicated because of the $1,000 face amount.

We can speed up the trial-and-error process by using what we know about bond prices and yields. In this case, the bond has an $80 coupon and is selling at a discount. We thus know that the yield is greater than 8 percent. If we compute the price at 10 percent:

$$
\begin{aligned}
\text{Bond value} &= \$80 \times (1 - 1/1.10^6)/.10 + 1{,}000/1.10^6 \\
&= \$80 \times 4.3553 + 1{,}000/1.7716 \\
&= \$912.89
\end{aligned}
$$

Current market rates are available at www.bankrate.com.

At 10 percent, the value we calculate is lower than the actual price, so 10 percent is too high. The true yield must be somewhere between 8 and 10 percent. At this point, it's "plug and chug" to find the answer. You would probably want to try 9 percent next. If you did, you would see that this is in fact the bond's yield to maturity.

A bond's yield to maturity should not be confused with its **current yield**, which is simply a bond's annual coupon divided by its price. In the example we just worked, the bond's annual coupon was $80, and its price was $955.14. Given these numbers, we see that the current yield is $80/955.14 = 8.38 percent, which is less than the yield to maturity of 9 percent. The reason the current yield is too low is that it considers only the coupon portion of your return; it doesn't consider the built-in gain from the price discount. For a premium bond, the reverse is true, meaning that current yield would be higher because it ignores the built-in loss.

current yield
A bond's annual coupon divided by its price.

Our discussion of bond valuation is summarized in Table 7.1.

I.	**Finding the Value of a Bond**

Bond value $= C \times [1 - 1/(1 + r)^t]/r + F/(1 + r)^t$

where

    C = Coupon paid each period

    r = Rate per period

    t = Number of periods

    F = Bond's face value

II.	**Finding the Yield on a Bond**

Given a bond value, coupon, time to maturity, and face value, it is possible to find the implicit discount rate, or yield to maturity, by trial and error only. To do this, try different discount rates until the calculated bond value equals the given value (or let a financial calculator do it for you). Remember that increasing the rate *decreases* the bond value.

TABLE 7.1

Summary of Bond Valuation

EXAMPLE 7.2   **Current Events**

A bond has a quoted price of $1,080.42. It has a face value of $1,000, a semiannual cou-pon of $30, and a maturity of five years. What is its current yield? What is its yield to matu-rity? Which is bigger? Why?

Notice that this bond makes semiannual payments of $30, so the annual payment is $60. The current yield is thus $60/1,080.42 = 5.55 percent. To calculate the yield to matu-rity, refer back to Example 7.1. In this case, the bond pays $30 every six months and has 10 six-month periods until maturity. So, we need to find r as follows:

$$\$1,080.42 = \$30 \times [1 - 1/(1 + r)^{10}]/r + 1,000/(1 + r)^{10}$$

After some trial and error, we find that r is equal to 2.1 percent. But, the tricky part is that this 2.1 percent is the yield *per six months*. We have to double it to get the yield to maturity, so the yield to maturity is 4.2 percent, which is less than the current yield. The reason is that the current yield ignores the built-in loss of the premium between now and maturity.

EXAMPLE 7.3   **Bond Yields**

You're looking at two bonds identical in every way except for their coupons and, of course, their prices. Both have 12 years to maturity. The first bond has a 10 percent annual coupon rate and sells for $935.08. The second has a 12 percent annual coupon rate. What do you think it would sell for?

Because the two bonds are similar, they will be priced to yield about the same rate. We first need to calculate the yield on the 10 percent coupon bond. Proceeding as before, we know that the yield must be greater than 10 percent because the bond is selling at a discount. The bond has a fairly long maturity of 12 years. We've seen that long-term bond prices are relatively sensitive to interest rate changes, so the yield is probably close to 10 percent. A little trial and error reveals that the yield is actually 11 percent:

$$\begin{aligned}
\text{Bond value} &= \$100 \times (1 - 1/1.11^{12})/.11 + 1,000/1.11^{12} \\
&= \$100 \times 6.4924 + 1,000/3.4985 \\
&= \$649.24 + 285.84 \\
&= \$935.08
\end{aligned}$$

With an 11 percent yield, the second bond will sell at a premium because of its $120 coupon. Its value is:

$$\begin{aligned}
\text{Bond value} &= \$120 \times (1 - 1/1.11^{12})/.11 + 1,000/1.11^{12} \\
&= \$120 \times 6.4924 + 1,000/3.4985 \\
&= \$779.08 + 285.84 \\
&= \$1,064.92
\end{aligned}$$

CALCULATOR HINTS

How to Calculate Bond Prices and Yields Using a Financial Calculator

Many financial calculators have fairly sophisticated built-in bond valuation routines. However, these vary quite a lot in implementation, and not all financial calculators have them. As a result, we will illustrate a simple way to han-dle bond problems that will work on just about any financial calculator.

(continued)

To begin, of course, we first remember to clear out the calculator! Next, for Example 7.3, we have two bonds to consider, both with 12 years to maturity. The first one sells for $935.08 and has a 10 percent annual coupon rate. To find its yield, we can do the following:

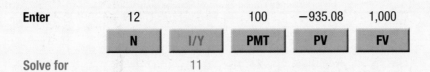

Enter	12		100	−935.08	1,000
	N	I/Y	PMT	PV	FV
Solve for		11			

Notice that here we have entered both a future value of $1,000, representing the bond's face value, and a payment of 10 percent of $1,000, or $100, per year, representing the bond's annual coupon. Also, notice that we have a negative sign on the bond's price, which we have entered as the present value.

For the second bond, we now know that the relevant yield is 11 percent. It has a 12 percent annual coupon and 12 years to maturity, so what's the price? To answer, we just enter the relevant values and solve for the present value of the bond's cash flows:

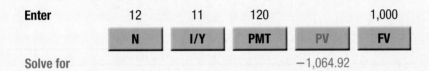

Enter	12	11	120		1,000
	N	I/Y	PMT	PV	FV
Solve for				−1,064.92	

There is an important detail that comes up here. Suppose we have a bond with a price of $902.29, 10 years to maturity, and a coupon rate of 6 percent. As we mentioned earlier, most bonds actually make semiannual payments. Assuming that this is the case for the bond here, what's the bond's yield? To answer, we need to enter the relevant numbers like this:

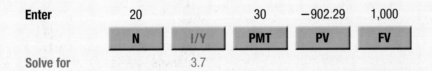

Enter	20		30	−902.29	1,000
	N	I/Y	PMT	PV	FV
Solve for		3.7			

Notice that we entered $30 as the payment because the bond actually makes payments of $30 every six months. Similarly, we entered 20 for N because there are actually 20 six-month periods. When we solve for the yield, we get 3.7 percent. The tricky thing to remember is that this is the yield *per six months,* so we have to double it to get the right answer: 2 × 3.7 = 7.4 percent, which would be the bond's reported yield.

SPREADSHEET STRATEGIES

How to Calculate Bond Prices and Yields Using a Spreadsheet

Most spreadsheets have fairly elaborate routines available for calculating bond values and yields; many of these routines involve details we have not discussed. However, setting up a simple spreadsheet to calculate prices or

(continued)

yields is straightforward, as our next two spreadsheets show:

	A	B	C	D	E	F	G	H
1								
2	**Using a spreadsheet to calculate bond values**							
3								
4	Suppose we have a bond with 22 years to maturity, a coupon rate of 8 percent, and a yield to							
5	maturity of 9 percent. If the bond makes semiannual payments, what is its price today?							
6								
7	Settlement date:	1/1/00						
8	Maturity date:	1/1/22						
9	Annual coupon rate:	.08						
10	Yield to maturity:	.09						
11	Face value (% of par):	100						
12	Coupons per year:	2						
13	Bond price (% of par):	**90.49**						
14								
15	The formula entered in cell B13 is =PRICE(B7,B8,B9,B10,B11,B12); notice that face value and bond							
16	price are given as a percentage of face value.							

	A	B	C	D	E	F	G	H
1								
2	**Using a spreadsheet to calculate bond yields**							
3								
4	Suppose we have a bond with 22 years to maturity, a coupon rate of 8 percent, and a price of							
5	$960.17. If the bond makes semiannual payments, what is its yield to maturity?							
6								
7	Settlement date:	1/1/00						
8	Maturity date:	1/1/22						
9	Annual coupon rate:	.08						
10	Bond price (% of par):	96.017						
11	Face value (% of par):	100						
12	Coupons per year:	2						
13	Yield to maturity:	**.084**						
14								
15	The formula entered in cell B13 is =YIELD(B7,B8,B9,B10,B11,B12); notice that face value and bond							
16	price are entered as a percentage of face value.							
17								

In our spreadsheets, notice that we had to enter two dates: a settlement date and a maturity date. The settlement date is just the date you actually pay for the bond, and the maturity date is the day the bond actually matures. In most of our problems, we don't explicitly have these dates, so we have to make them up. For example, because our bond has 22 years to maturity, we just picked 1/1/2000 (January 1, 2000) as the settlement date and 1/1/2022 (January 1, 2022) as the maturity date. Any two dates would do as long as they are exactly 22 years apart, but these are particularly easy to work with. Finally, notice that we had to enter the coupon rate and yield to maturity in annual terms and then explicitly provide the number of coupon payments per year.

Concept Questions

7.1a What are the cash flows associated with a bond?

7.1b What is the general expression for the value of a bond?

7.1c Is it true that the only risk associated with owning a bond is that the issuer will not make all the payments? Explain.

More about Bond Features   7.2

In this section, we continue our discussion of corporate debt by describing in some detail the basic terms and features that make up a typical long-term corporate bond. We discuss additional issues associated with long-term debt in subsequent sections.

Securities issued by corporations may be classified roughly as *equity securities* and *debt securities*. At the crudest level, a debt represents something that must be repaid; it is the result of borrowing money. When corporations borrow, they generally promise to make regularly scheduled interest payments and to repay the original amount borrowed (that is, the principal). The person or firm making the loan is called the *creditor* or *lender*. The corporation borrowing the money is called the *debtor* or *borrower*.

From a financial point of view, the main differences between debt and equity are the following:

1. Debt is not an ownership interest in the firm. Creditors generally do not have voting power.
2. The corporation's payment of interest on debt is considered a cost of doing business and is fully tax deductible. Dividends paid to stockholders are *not* tax deductible.
3. Unpaid debt is a liability of the firm. If it is not paid, the creditors can legally claim the assets of the firm. This action can result in liquidation or reorganization, two of the possible consequences of bankruptcy. Thus, one of the costs of issuing debt is the possibility of financial failure. This possibility does not arise when equity is issued.

Information for bond investors can be found at www.investinginbonds.com.

IS IT DEBT OR EQUITY?

Sometimes it is not clear if a particular security is debt or equity. For example, suppose a corporation issues a perpetual bond with interest payable solely from corporate income if and only if earned. Whether this is really a debt is hard to say and is primarily a legal and semantic issue. Courts and taxing authorities would have the final say.

Corporations are adept at creating exotic, hybrid securities that have many features of equity but are treated as debt. Obviously, the distinction between debt and equity is important for tax purposes. So, one reason that corporations try to create a debt security that is really equity is to obtain the tax benefits of debt and the bankruptcy benefits of equity.

As a general rule, equity represents an ownership interest, and it is a residual claim. This means that equity holders are paid after debt holders. As a result of this, the risks and benefits associated with owning debt and equity are different. To give just one example, note that the maximum reward for owning a debt security is ultimately fixed by the amount of the loan, whereas there is no upper limit to the potential reward from owning an equity interest.

LONG-TERM DEBT: THE BASICS

Ultimately, all long-term debt securities are promises made by the issuing firm to pay principal when due and to make timely interest payments on the unpaid balance. Beyond this, a number of features distinguish these securities from one another. We discuss some of these features next.

The maturity of a long-term debt instrument is the length of time the debt remains outstanding with some unpaid balance. Debt securities can be *short-term* (with maturities of one year or less) or *long-term* (with maturities of more than one year).[1] Short-term debt is sometimes referred to as *unfunded debt*.[2]

Debt securities are typically called *notes, debentures,* or *bonds.* Strictly speaking, a bond is a secured debt. However, in common usage, the word *bond* refers to all kinds of secured and unsecured debt. We will therefore continue to use the term generically to refer to long-term debt. Also, usually the only difference between a note and a bond is the original maturity. Issues with an original maturity of 10 years or less are often called notes. Longer-term issues are called bonds.

The two major forms of long-term debt are public issue and privately placed. We concentrate on public-issue bonds. Most of what we say about them holds true for private-issue, long-term debt as well. The main difference between public-issue and privately placed debt is that the latter is directly placed with a lender and not offered to the public. Because this is a private transaction, the specific terms are up to the parties involved.

There are many other dimensions to long-term debt, including such things as security, call features, sinking funds, ratings, and protective covenants. The following table illustrates these features for a bond issued by drug maker Bristol-Myers Squibb. If some of these terms are unfamiliar, have no fear. We will discuss them all presently.

Information about individual bonds can be found at www.finra.org/marketdata and www.bondresources.com.

Features of a Bristol-Myers Squibb Bond		
Term		**Explanation**
Amount of issue	$1 billion	The company issued $1 billion worth of bonds.
Date of issue	05/01/2008	The bonds were sold on 05/01/2008.
Maturity	05/01/2038	The bonds mature on 05/01/2038.
Face value	$1,000	The denomination of the bonds is $1,000.
Annual coupon	6.125	Each bondholder will receive $61.25 per bond per year (6.125% of face value).
Offer price	99.375	The offer price will be 99.375% of the $1,000 face value, or $993.75, per bond.
Coupon payment dates	5/01, 11/01	Coupons of $61.25/2 = $30.625 will be paid on these dates.
Security	None	The bonds are not secured by specific assets.
Sinking fund	None	The bonds have no sinking fund.
Call provision	At any time	The bonds do not have a deferred call.
Call price	Treasury rate plus .30%	The bonds have a "make whole" call price.
Rating	Moody's A2 S&P A	The bonds have a relatively high credit rating (but not the best possible rating).

Many of these features will be detailed in the bond indenture, so we discuss this first.

---

[1] There is no universally agreed-upon distinction between short-term and long-term debt. In addition, people often refer to *intermediate-term debt,* which has a maturity of more than 1 year and less than 3 to 5, or even 10, years.

[2] The word *funding* is part of the jargon of finance. It generally refers to the long term. Thus, a firm planning to "fund" its debt requirements may be replacing short-term debt with long-term debt.

THE INDENTURE

The **indenture** is the written agreement between the corporation (the borrower) and its creditors. It is sometimes referred to as the *deed of trust*.[3] Usually, a trustee (a bank, perhaps) is appointed by the corporation to represent the bondholders. The trust company must (1) make sure the terms of the indenture are obeyed, (2) manage the sinking fund (described in the following pages), and (3) represent the bondholders in default—that is, if the company defaults on its payments to them.

The bond indenture is a legal document. It can run several hundred pages and generally makes for tedious reading. It is an important document, however, because it generally includes the following provisions:

1. The basic terms of the bonds.
2. The total amount of bonds issued.
3. A description of property used as security.
4. The repayment arrangements.
5. The call provisions.
6. Details of the protective covenants.

We discuss these features next.

Terms of a Bond   Corporate bonds usually have a face value (that is, a denomination) of $1,000. This *principal value* is stated on the bond certificate. So, if a corporation wanted to borrow $1 million, 1,000 bonds would have to be sold. The par value (that is, initial accounting value) of a bond is almost always the same as the face value, and the terms are used interchangeably in practice.

Corporate bonds are usually in **registered form**. For example, the indenture might read as follows:

> **Interest is payable semiannually on July 1 and January 1 of each year to the person in whose name the bond is registered at the close of business on June 15 or December 15, respectively.**

This means that the company has a registrar who will record the ownership of each bond and record any changes in ownership. The company will pay the interest and principal by check mailed directly to the address of the owner of record. A corporate bond may be registered and have attached "coupons." To obtain an interest payment, the owner must separate a coupon from the bond certificate and send it to the company registrar (the paying agent).

Alternatively, the bond could be in **bearer form**. This means that the certificate is the basic evidence of ownership, and the corporation will "pay the bearer." Ownership is not otherwise recorded, and, as with a registered bond with attached coupons, the holder of the bond certificate detaches the coupons and sends them to the company to receive payment.

There are two drawbacks to bearer bonds. First, they are difficult to recover if they are lost or stolen. Second, because the company does not know who owns its bonds, it cannot notify bondholders of important events. Bearer bonds were once the dominant type, but they are now much less common (in the United States) than registered bonds.

indenture
The written agreement between the corporation and the lender detailing the terms of the debt issue.

registered form
The form of bond issue in which the registrar of the company records ownership of each bond; payment is made directly to the owner of record.

bearer form
The form of bond issue in which the bond is issued without record of the owner's name; payment is made to whomever holds the bond.

---

[3]The words *loan agreement* or *loan contract* are usually used for privately placed debt and term loans.

Security   Debt securities are classified according to the collateral and mortgages used to protect the bondholder.

Collateral is a general term that frequently means securities (for example, bonds and stocks) that are pledged as security for payment of debt. For example, collateral trust bonds often involve a pledge of common stock held by the corporation. However, the term *collateral* is commonly used to refer to any asset pledged on a debt.

Mortgage securities are secured by a mortgage on the real property of the borrower. The property involved is usually real estate—for example, land or buildings. The legal document that describes the mortgage is called a *mortgage trust indenture* or *trust deed*.

Sometimes mortgages are on specific property, such as a railroad car. More often, blanket mortgages are used. A *blanket mortgage* pledges all the real property owned by the company.[4]

Bonds frequently represent unsecured obligations of the company. A **debenture** is an unsecured bond, for which no specific pledge of property is made. The term **note** is generally used for such instruments if the maturity of the unsecured bond is less than 10 or so years when the bond is originally issued. Debenture holders have a claim only on property not otherwise pledged—in other words, the property that remains after mortgages and collateral trusts are taken into account. The Bristol-Myers Squibb bonds in the table are an example of such an issue.

The terminology that we use here and elsewhere in this chapter is standard in the United States. Outside the United States, these same terms can have different meanings. For example, bonds issued by the British government ("gilts") are called treasury "stock." Also, in the United Kingdom, a debenture is a *secured* obligation.

At the current time, public bonds issued in the United States by industrial and financial companies are typically debentures. However, most utility and railroad bonds are secured by a pledge of assets.

debenture
An unsecured debt, usually with a maturity of 10 years or more.

note
An unsecured debt, usually with a maturity under 10 years.

The Securities Industry and Financial Markets Association (SIFMA) Web site is www.sifma.org.

Seniority   In general terms, *seniority* indicates preference in position over other lenders, and debts are sometimes labeled as *senior* or *junior* to indicate seniority. Some debt is *subordinated,* as in, for example, a subordinated debenture.

In the event of default, holders of subordinated debt must give preference to other specified creditors. Usually, this means that the subordinated lenders will be paid off only after the specified creditors have been compensated. However, debt cannot be subordinated to equity.

Repayment   Bonds can be repaid at maturity, at which time the bondholder will receive the stated, or face, value of the bond; or they may be repaid in part or in entirety before maturity. Early repayment in some form is more typical and is often handled through a sinking fund.

A **sinking fund** is an account managed by the bond trustee for the purpose of repaying the bonds. The company makes annual payments to the trustee, who then uses the funds to retire a portion of the debt. The trustee does this by either buying up some of the bonds in the market or calling in a fraction of the outstanding bonds. This second option is discussed in the next section.

There are many different kinds of sinking fund arrangements, and the details would be spelled out in the indenture. For example:

1. Some sinking funds start about 10 years after the initial issuance.
2. Some sinking funds establish equal payments over the life of the bond.

sinking fund
An account managed by the bond trustee for early bond redemption.

---

[4]Real property includes land and things "affixed thereto." It does not include cash or inventories.

3. Some high-quality bond issues establish payments to the sinking fund that are not sufficient to redeem the entire issue. As a consequence, there is the possibility of a large "balloon payment" at maturity.

The Call Provision   A **call provision** allows the company to repurchase or "call" part or all of the bond issue at stated prices over a specific period. Corporate bonds are usually callable.

Generally, the call price is above the bond's stated value (that is, the par value). The difference between the call price and the stated value is the **call premium**. The amount of the call premium may become smaller over time. One arrangement is to initially set the call premium equal to the annual coupon payment and then make it decline to zero as the call date moves closer to the time of maturity.

Call provisions are often not operative during the first part of a bond's life. This makes the call provision less of a worry for bondholders in the bond's early years. For example, a company might be prohibited from calling its bonds for the first 10 years. This is a **deferred call provision**. During this period of prohibition, the bond is said to be **call protected**.

In recent few years, a new type of call provision, a "make-whole" call, has become widespread in the corporate bond market. With such a feature, bondholders receive approximately what the bonds are worth if they are called. Because bondholders don't suffer a loss in the event of a call, they are "made whole."

To determine the make-whole call price, we calculate the present value of the remaining interest and principal payments at a rate specified in the indenture. For example, looking at our Bristol-Myers Squibb issue, we see that the discount rate is "Treasury rate plus .30%." What this means is that we determine the discount rate by first finding a U.S. Treasury issue with the same maturity. We calculate the yield to maturity on the Treasury issue and then add on .30 percent to get the discount rate we use.

Notice that with a make-whole call provision, the call price is higher when interest rates are lower and vice versa (why?). Also notice that, as is common with a make-whole call, the Bristol-Myers Squibb issue does not have a deferred call feature. Why might investors not be too concerned about the absence of this feature?

Protective Covenants   A **protective covenant** is that part of the indenture or loan agreement that limits certain actions a company might otherwise wish to take during the term of the loan. Protective covenants can be classified into two types: negative covenants and positive (or affirmative) covenants.

A *negative covenant* is a "thou shalt not" type of covenant. It limits or prohibits actions the company might take. Here are some typical examples:

1. The firm must limit the amount of dividends it pays according to some formula.
2. The firm cannot pledge any assets to other lenders.
3. The firm cannot merge with another firm.
4. The firm cannot sell or lease any major assets without approval by the lender.
5. The firm cannot issue additional long-term debt.

A *positive covenant* is a "thou shalt" type of covenant. It specifies an action the company agrees to take or a condition the company must abide by. Here are some examples:

1. The company must maintain its working capital at or above some specified minimum level.
2. The company must periodically furnish audited financial statements to the lender.
3. The firm must maintain any collateral or security in good condition.

---

call provision
An agreement giving the corporation the option to repurchase a bond at a specified price prior to maturity.

call premium
The amount by which the call price exceeds the par value of a bond.

deferred call provision
A call provision prohibiting the company from redeeming a bond prior to a certain date.

call-protected bond
A bond that, during a certain period, cannot be redeemed by the issuer.

protective covenant
A part of the indenture limiting certain actions that might be taken during the term of the loan, usually to protect the lender's interest.

Want detailed information about the amount and terms of the debt issued by a particular firm? Check out its latest financial statements by searching SEC filings at www.sec.gov.

This is only a partial list of covenants; a particular indenture may feature many different ones.

Concept Questions

7.2a What are the distinguishing features of debt compared to equity?

7.2b What is the indenture? What are protective covenants? Give some examples.

7.2c What is a sinking fund?

7.3 Bond Ratings

Firms frequently pay to have their debt rated. The two leading bond-rating firms are Moody's and Standard & Poor's (S&P). The debt ratings are an assessment of the creditworthiness of the corporate issuer. The definitions of creditworthiness used by Moody's and S&P are based on how likely the firm is to default and the protection creditors have in the event of a default.

It is important to recognize that bond ratings are concerned *only* with the possibility of default. Earlier, we discussed interest rate risk, which we defined as the risk of a change in the value of a bond resulting from a change in interest rates. Bond ratings do not address this issue. As a result, the price of a highly rated bond can still be quite volatile.

Bond ratings are constructed from information supplied by the corporation. The rating classes and some information concerning them are shown in the following table:

	Investment-Quality Bond Ratings				Low-Quality, Speculative, and/or "Junk" Bond Ratings					
	High Grade		Medium Grade		Low Grade		Very Low Grade			
Standard & Poor's	AAA	AA	A	BBB	BB	B	CCC	CC	C	D
Moody's	Aaa	Aa	A	Baa	Ba	B	Caa	Ca	C	

Moody's	S&P	
Aaa	AAA	Debt rated Aaa and AAA has the highest rating. Capacity to pay interest and principal is extremely strong.
Aa	AA	Debt rated Aa and AA has a very strong capacity to pay interest and repay principal. Together with the highest rating, this group comprises the high-grade bond class.
A	A	Debt rated A has a strong capacity to pay interest and repay principal, although it is somewhat more susceptible to the adverse effects of changes in circumstances and economic conditions than debt in high-rated categories.
Baa	BBB	Debt rated Baa and BBB is regarded as having an adequate capacity to pay interest and repay principal. Whereas it normally exhibits adequate protection parameters, adverse economic conditions or changing circumstances are more likely to lead to a weakened capacity to pay interest and repay principal for debt in this category than in higher-rated categories. These bonds are medium-grade obligations.
Ba; B Caa Ca C	BB; B CCC CC C	Debt rated in these categories is regarded, on balance, as predominantly speculative with respect to capacity to pay interest and repay principal in accordance with the terms of the obligation. BB and Ba indicate the lowest degree of speculation, and Ca, CC, and C the highest degree of speculation. Although such debt is likely to have some quality and protective characteristics, these are outweighed by large uncertainties or major risk exposures to adverse conditions. Issues rated C by Moody's are typically in default.
	D	Debt rated D is in default, and payment of interest and/or repayment of principal is in arrears.

Note: At times, both Moody's and S&P use adjustments (called notches) to these ratings. S&P uses plus and minus signs: A+ is the strongest A rating and A− the weakest. Moody's uses a 1, 2, or 3 designation, with 1 being the highest.

The highest rating a firm's debt can have is AAA or Aaa, and such debt is judged to be the best quality and to have the lowest degree of risk. For example, the 100-year BellSouth issue we discussed earlier was rated AAA. This rating is not awarded very often: As of 2008, only six nonfinancial U.S. companies had AAA ratings. AA or Aa ratings indicate very good quality debt and are much more common.

A large part of corporate borrowing takes the form of low-grade, or "junk," bonds. If these low-grade corporate bonds are rated at all, they are rated below investment grade by the major rating agencies. Investment-grade bonds are bonds rated at least BBB by S&P or Baa by Moody's.

Rating agencies don't always agree. To illustrate, some bonds are known as "crossover" or "5B" bonds. The reason is that they are rated triple-B (or Baa) by one rating agency and double-B (or Ba) by another, a "split rating." For example, in April 2008, Centerpoint Energy sold an issue of 10-year notes rated BBB– by S&P and Ba1 by Moody's.

A bond's credit rating can change as the issuer's financial strength improves or deteriorates. For example, in May 2008, S&P downgraded cellular company Sprint Nextel's long-term debt from investment grade to junk bond status. Bonds that drop into junk territory like this are called *fallen angels*. Sprint Nextel was downgraded for a lot of reasons, but S&P was concerned about an increased use of financial leverage and increased costs.

Credit ratings are important because defaults really do occur, and when they do, investors can lose heavily. For example, in 2000, AmeriServe Food Distribution, Inc., which supplied restaurants such as Burger King with everything from burgers to giveaway toys, defaulted on $200 million in junk bonds. After the default, the bonds traded at just 18 cents on the dollar, leaving investors with a loss of more than $160 million.

Even worse in AmeriServe's case, the bonds had been issued only four months earlier, thereby making AmeriServe an NCAA champion. Although that might be a good thing for a college basketball team such as the University of Kentucky Wildcats, in the bond market it means "No Coupon At All," and it's not a good thing for investors.

Want to know what criteria are commonly used to rate corporate and municipal bonds? Go to www.standardandpoors. com, www.moodys.com, or www.fitchinv.com.

If you're nervous about the level of debt piled up by the U.S. government, don't go to www.publicdebt.treas.gov or to www.brillig.com/ debt_clock! Learn all about government bonds at www.ny.frb.org.

Concept Questions

7.3a What does a bond rating say about the risk of fluctuations in a bond's value resulting from interest rate changes?

7.3b What is a junk bond?

Some Different Types of Bonds 7.4

Thus far we have considered only "plain vanilla" corporate bonds. In this section, we briefly look at bonds issued by governments and also at bonds with unusual features.

GOVERNMENT BONDS

The biggest borrower in the world—by a wide margin—is everybody's favorite family member, Uncle Sam. In 2008, the total debt of the U.S. government was $9.4 *trillion,* or about $31,000 per citizen (and growing!). When the government wishes to borrow money for more than one year, it sells what are known as Treasury notes and bonds to the public (in fact, it does so every month). Currently, outstanding Treasury notes and bonds have original maturities ranging from 2 to 30 years.

Most U.S. Treasury issues are just ordinary coupon bonds. Some older issues are callable, and a few have some unusual features. There are two important things to keep in mind, however. First, U.S. Treasury issues, unlike essentially all other bonds, have no default risk because (we hope) the Treasury can always come up with the money to make the payments. Second, Treasury issues are exempt from state income taxes (though not federal income taxes). In other words, the coupons you receive on a Treasury note or bond are taxed only at the federal level.

State and local governments also borrow money by selling notes and bonds. Such issues are called *municipal* notes and bonds, or just "munis." Unlike Treasury issues, munis have varying degrees of default risk, and, in fact, they are rated much like corporate issues. Also, they are almost always callable. The most intriguing thing about munis is that their coupons are exempt from federal income taxes (though not necessarily state income taxes), which makes them very attractive to high-income, high–tax bracket investors.

Because of the enormous tax break they receive, the yields on municipal bonds are much lower than the yields on taxable bonds. For example, in May 2008, long-term Aa-rated corporate bonds were yielding about 5.74 percent. At the same time, long-term Aa munis were yielding about 4.59 percent. Suppose an investor was in a 30 percent tax bracket. All else being the same, would this investor prefer a Aa corporate bond or a Aa municipal bond?

Another good bond market site is money.cnn.com.

To answer, we need to compare the *aftertax* yields on the two bonds. Ignoring state and local taxes, the muni pays 4.59 percent on both a pretax and an aftertax basis. The corporate issue pays 5.74 percent before taxes, but it pays only $.0574 \times (1 - .30) = .040$, or 4.0 percent, once we account for the 30 percent tax bite. Given this, the muni has a better yield.

EXAMPLE 7.4   **Taxable versus Municipal Bonds**

Suppose taxable bonds are currently yielding 8 percent, while at the same time, munis of comparable risk and maturity are yielding 6 percent. Which is more attractive to an investor in a 40 percent bracket? What is the break-even tax rate? How do you interpret this rate?

For an investor in a 40 percent tax bracket, a taxable bond yields $8 \times (1 - .40) = 4.8$ percent after taxes, so the muni is much more attractive. The break-even tax rate is the tax rate at which an investor would be indifferent between a taxable and a nontaxable issue. If we let t^* stand for the break-even tax rate, then we can solve for it as follows:

$$.08 \times (1 - t^*) = .06$$
$$1 - t^* = .06/.08 = .75$$
$$t^* = .25$$

Thus, an investor in a 25 percent tax bracket would make 6 percent after taxes from either bond.

ZERO COUPON BONDS

zero coupon bond
A bond that makes no coupon payments and is thus initially priced at a deep discount.

A bond that pays no coupons at all must be offered at a price that is much lower than its stated value. Such bonds are called **zero coupon bonds**, or just *zeroes*.[5]

Suppose the Eight-Inch Nails (EIN) Company issues a $1,000 face value, five-year zero coupon bond. The initial price is set at $508.35. Even though no interest payments are made on the bond, zero coupon bond calculations use semiannual periods to be consistent with coupon bond calculations. Using semiannual periods, it is straightforward to verify

---

[5]A bond issued with a very low coupon rate (as opposed to a zero coupon rate) is an *original-issue discount (OID) bond.*

Year	Beginning Value	Ending Value	Implicit Interest Expense	Straight-line Interest Expense
1	$508.35	$ 582.01	$ 73.66	$ 98.33
2	582.01	666.34	84.33	98.33
3	666.34	762.90	96.56	98.33
4	762.90	873.44	110.54	98.33
5	873.44	1,000.00	126.56	98.33
Total			$491.65	$491.65

TABLE 7.2

Interest Expense for EIN's Zeroes

that, at this price, the bond yields 14 percent to maturity. The total interest paid over the life of the bond is $1,000 − 508.35 = $491.65.

For tax purposes, the issuer of a zero coupon bond deducts interest every year even though no interest is actually paid. Similarly, the owner must pay taxes on interest accrued every year, even though no interest is actually received.

The way in which the yearly interest on a zero coupon bond is calculated is governed by tax law. Before 1982, corporations could calculate the interest deduction on a straight-line basis. For EIN, the annual interest deduction would have been $491.65/5 = $98.33 per year.

Under current tax law, the implicit interest is determined by amortizing the loan. We do this by first calculating the bond's value at the beginning of each year. For example, after one year, the bond will have four years until maturity, so it will be worth $1,000/1.07^8 = $582.01; the value in two years will be $1,000/1.07^6 = $666.34; and so on. The implicit interest each year is simply the change in the bond's value for the year. The values and interest expenses for the EIN bond are listed in Table 7.2.

Notice that under the old rules, zero coupon bonds were more attractive because the deductions for interest expense were larger in the early years (compare the implicit interest expense with the straight-line expense).

Under current tax law, EIN could deduct $73.66 in interest paid the first year and the owner of the bond would pay taxes on $73.66 in taxable income (even though no interest was actually received). This second tax feature makes taxable zero coupon bonds less attractive to individuals. However, they are still a very attractive investment for tax-exempt investors with long-term dollar-denominated liabilities, such as pension funds, because the future dollar value is known with relative certainty.

Some bonds are zero coupon bonds for only part of their lives. For example, General Motors has a debenture outstanding that matures on March 15, 2036. For the first 20 years of its life, no coupon payments will be made; but, after 20 years, it will begin paying coupons semiannually at a rate of 7.75 percent per year.

FLOATING-RATE BONDS

The conventional bonds we have talked about in this chapter have fixed-dollar obligations because the coupon rates are set as fixed percentages of the par values. Similarly, the principal amounts are set equal to the par values. Under these circumstances, the coupon payments and principal are completely fixed.

With *floating-rate bonds (floaters),* the coupon payments are adjustable. The adjustments are tied to an interest rate index such as the Treasury bill interest rate or the 30-year Treasury bond rate. The EE Savings Bonds we mentioned in Chapter 5 are a good example of a floater. For EE bonds purchased after May 1, 1997, the interest rate is adjusted every six months. The rate that the bonds earn for a particular six-month period is determined by taking 90 percent of the average yield on ordinary five-year Treasury notes over the previous six months.

The value of a floating-rate bond depends on exactly how the coupon payment adjustments are defined. In most cases, the coupon adjusts with a lag to some base rate. For example, suppose a coupon rate adjustment is made on June 1. The adjustment might be based on the simple average of Treasury bond yields during the previous three months. In addition, the majority of floaters have the following features:

1. The holder has the right to redeem the note at par on the coupon payment date after some specified amount of time. This is called a *put* provision, and it is discussed in the following section.
2. The coupon rate has a floor and a ceiling, meaning that the coupon is subject to a minimum and a maximum. In this case, the coupon rate is said to be "capped," and the upper and lower rates are sometimes called the *collar*.

A particularly interesting type of floating-rate bond is an *inflation-linked* bond. Such bonds have coupons that are adjusted according to the rate of inflation (the principal amount may be adjusted as well). The U.S. Treasury began issuing such bonds in January of 1997. The issues are sometimes called "TIPS," or Treasury Inflation-Protected Securities. Other countries, including Canada, Israel, and Britain, have issued similar securities.

Official information about U.S. inflation-indexed bonds is at www.publicdebt.treas. gov.

OTHER TYPES OF BONDS

Many bonds have unusual or exotic features. So-called catastrophe, or cat, bonds provide an interesting example. In February 2008, the Caitlin Group Limited, a reinsurance company, issued $150 million in cat bonds (reinsurance companies sell insurance to insurance companies). These cat bonds were unique in that they were not based on a specific risk such as an earthquake or hurricane, but rather were triggered if the Caitlin Group lost more than an aggregate amount during any year.

The largest single cat bond issue to date is a series of six bonds sold by Merna Reinsurance in 2007. The six bond issues were to cover various catastrophes the company faced due to its reinsurance of State Farm. The six bonds totaled about $1.2 billion in par value, a large portion of the record $7 billion in cat bonds issued during 2007.

At this point, cat bonds probably seem pretty risky. It therefore might be surprising to learn that since cat bonds were first issued in 1997, only one has not been paid in full. Because of Hurricane Katrina, bondholders in that one issue lost $190 million.

Another possible bond feature is a *warrant*. A warrant gives the buyer of a bond the right to purchase shares of stock in the company at a fixed price. Such a right would be very valuable if the stock price climbed substantially (a later chapter discusses this subject in greater depth). Because of the value of this feature, bonds with warrants are often issued at a very low coupon rate.

As these examples illustrate, bond features are really limited only by the imaginations of the parties involved. Unfortunately, there are far too many variations for us to cover in detail here. We therefore close this discussion by mentioning a few of the more common types.

Income bonds are similar to conventional bonds, except that coupon payments depend on company income. Specifically, coupons are paid to bondholders only if the firm's income is sufficient. This would appear to be an attractive feature, but income bonds are not very common.

A *convertible bond* can be swapped for a fixed number of shares of stock anytime before maturity at the holder's option. Convertibles are relatively common, but the number has been decreasing in recent years.

A *put bond* allows the *holder* to force the issuer to buy back the bond at a stated price. For example, International Paper Co. has bonds outstanding that allow the holder to force International Paper to buy the bonds back at 100 percent of face value if certain "risk" events happen. One such event is a change in credit rating from investment grade to lower than investment grade by Moody's or S&P. The put feature is therefore just the reverse of the call provision.

Edward I. Altman on Junk Bonds and Leveraged Loans

One of the most important developments in corporate finance over the last 30 years has been the reemergence of publicly owned and traded low-rated corporate debt. Originally offered to the public in the early 1900s to help finance some of our emerging growth industries, these high-yield, high-risk bonds virtually disappeared after the rash of bond defaults during the Depression. Recently, however, the junk bond market has been catapulted from being an insignificant element in the corporate fixed-income market to being one of the fastest-growing and most controversial types of financing mechanisms. Technically, high-yield bonds are bonds issued by companies whose rating given by one or more of the major rating agencies, i.e., Fitch, Moody's or Standard & Poors, is below investment grade, e.g., below BBB– by S&P.

The term *junk* emanates from the dominant type of low-rated bond issues outstanding prior to 1977 when the "market" consisted almost exclusively of original-issue investment-grade bonds that fell from their lofty status to a higher-default risk, speculative-grade level. These so called fallen angels amounted to about $8.5 billion in 1977. At the end of 2008, fallen angels comprised about 25 percent of the $1 trillion publicly owned junk bond market. The high-yield bond market in Europe began to grow only recently and reached about €175 billion in 2008.

Beginning in 1977, issuers began to go directly to the public to raise debt capital for growth purposes. Early issuers of junk bonds were energy-related firms, cable TV companies, airlines, and assorted other industrial companies. The emerging growth company rationale coupled with relatively high returns to early investors helped legitimize this sector.

By far the most important and controversial aspect of junk bond financing was its role in the corporate restructuring movement from 1985 to 1989. High-leverage transactions and acquisitions, such as leveraged buyouts (LBOs), which occur when a firm is taken private, and leveraged recapitalizations (debt-for-equity swaps), transformed the face of corporate America, leading to a heated debate as to the economic and social consequences of firms' being transformed with debt-equity ratios of at least 6:1. Similar, but less emotional, comments accompanied a second LBO movement in 2004–2007.

These transactions involved increasingly large companies, and the multibillion dollar takeover became fairly common, finally capped by the huge $25+ billion RJR Nabisco LBO in 1989. LBOs were typically financed with about 60 percent senior bank and insurance company debt, about 25–30 percent subordinated public debt (junk bonds), and 10–15 percent equity. The junk bond segment is sometimes referred to as "mezzanine" financing because it lies between the "balcony" senior debt and the "basement" equity. In the most recent LBO binge, however, more than 30 percent of the financing was equity but the transactions were, on average, much larger than in the late 1980s, with only RJR Nabisco from the earlier vintage still in the "top-10 LBOs."

These restructurings resulted in huge fees to advisors and underwriters and huge premiums to the old shareholders who were bought out, and they continued as long as the market was willing to buy these new debt offerings at what appeared to be a favorable risk-return trade-off. The bottom fell out of the market in the last six months of 1989 due to a number of factors including a marked increase in defaults, government regulation against S&Ls' holding junk bonds, and at least one highly publicized bankruptcy of a highly leveraged financial restructuring—Federated Department Stores.

The default rate rose dramatically to 4 percent in 1989 and then skyrocketed in 1990 and 1991 to 10.1 percent and 10.3 percent, respectively, with about $19 billion of defaults in 1991. By the end of 1990, the pendulum of growth in new junk bond issues and returns to investors swung dramatically downward as prices plummeted and the new-issue market all but dried up. The year 1991 was a pivotal year in that, despite record defaults, bond prices and new issues rebounded strongly as the prospects for the future brightened.

In the early 1990s, the financial market was questioning the very survival of the junk bond market. The answer as to its survival was a resounding "yes," as the amount of new issues soared to record annual levels of $40 billion in 1992, almost $80 billion in 1993, and in 1997 reached an impressive $119 billion. Coupled with plummeting default rates (under 2.0 percent each year in the 1993–97 period) and attractive returns in these years, the risk-return characteristics have been extremely favorable.

The junk bond market in the late 1990s was a quieter one compared to that of the 1980s, but, in terms of growth and returns, it was healthier than ever before. While the low default rates in 1992–98 helped to fuel new investment funds and new issues, the market experienced its ups and downs in subsequent years. Indeed, default rates started to rise in 1999 and accelerated in 2000–2002. The latter year saw defaults reach record levels as the economy slipped into a recession and investors suffered from the excesses of lending in the late 1990s.

(continued)

Since the mid-1990s, a "sister" high-yield debt market has developed in the private leveraged loan market. This low-quality market grew enormously in the United States and Europe in the 2005–2007 period and was at least 30 percent larger than the high-yield bond market in 2008. One of the main reasons for the recent growth and popularity of leveraged loans issued by non-investment grade companies was that the issuing bank could easily sell these loans into structured finance vehicles called collateralized-loan-obligations (CLOs). Usually these private, leveraged loan debt securities have registered lower default rates than high-yield bonds but there were indications that this usual pattern was going to change due to its greater expansion and liberal terms in the years prior to 2008.

The market for leveraged financing rebounded quickly in 2003 and continued to prosper until the credit crisis of 2007–2008. With the "flight-to-quality" caused by the sub-prime mortgage market meltdown in the second-half of 2007 and 2008, returns to investors in high-yield bonds and leveraged loans fell considerably, new issues dried up and default rates increased from the unusually low-risk years that coincided with the leveraged excesses. Despite these highly volatile events and problems with liquidity, we are convinced that high-yield bonds, and its private debt companion, leveraged loans, will continue in the future to be a major source of corporate debt financing and a legitimate asset class for investors.

Edward I. Altman is Max L. Heine Professor of Finance and Director of Credit and Debt Markets Research at the NYU Salomon Center at the Stern School of Business. He is widely recognized as one of the world's leading experts on bankruptcy and credit analysis as well as the high-yield and distressed debt markets.

A given bond may have many unusual features. Two of the most recent exotic bonds are CoCo bonds, which have a coupon payment, and NoNo bonds, which are zero coupon bonds. CoCo and NoNo bonds are contingent convertible, putable, callable, subordinated bonds. The contingent convertible clause is similar to the normal conversion feature, except the contingent feature must be met. For example, a contingent feature may require that the company stock trade at 110 percent of the conversion price for 20 out of the most recent 30 days. Valuing a bond of this sort can be quite complex, and the yield to maturity calculation is often meaningless. For example, in 2008, a NoNo issued by Merrill Lynch was selling at a price of $2,090, with a yield to maturity of negative 122 percent. At the same time, a NoNo issued by Credit Suisse was selling for $1,373.75, which implied a yield to maturity of negative 198 percent!

Concept Questions

7.4a Why might an income bond be attractive to a corporation with volatile cash flows? Can you think of a reason why income bonds are not more popular?

7.4b What do you think would be the effect of a put feature on a bond's coupon? How about a convertibility feature? Why?

7.5 Bond Markets

Bonds are bought and sold in enormous quantities every day. You may be surprised to learn that the trading volume in bonds on a typical day is many, many times larger than the trading volume in stocks (by *trading volume* we simply mean the amount of money that changes hands). Here is a finance trivia question: What is the largest securities market in the world? Most people would guess the New York Stock Exchange. In fact, the largest securities market in the world in terms of trading volume is the U.S. Treasury market.

HOW BONDS ARE BOUGHT AND SOLD

As we mentioned all the way back in Chapter 1, most trading in bonds takes place over the counter, or OTC. Recall that this means there is no particular place where buying and

WORK THE WEB

Bond quotes have become more available with the rise of the Internet. One site where you can find current bond prices is cxa.marketwatch.com/finra/MarketData/Default.aspx. We went to the Web site and searched for bonds issued by Chevron. Here is a look at part of what we found for one of the bonds:

CVX.GP / CUSIP: 881685BD2   Search for Bond Trade Activity   Add to Watchlist

Last: **$108.500**   Yield: **5.934%**

Security Category:	Corporate
Issue Description:	GTD DEB
Issuer Name:	TEXACO CAP INC
Coupon Rate:	7.500%
Coupon Type:	Fixed
Maturity Date:	03/01/2043

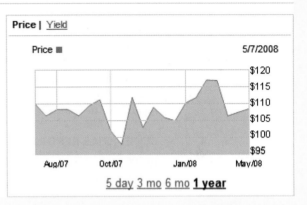

Price | Yield

Price ■   5/7/2008

5 day 3 mo 6 mo **1 year**

Composite Trade Information

Last Sale		Daily Trade Summary	
Date	05/07/2008	High Price / Equivalent Yield	$108.500 / 6.57100%
Price	$108.500	Low Price / Equivalent Yield	$105.750 / 5.93400%
Yield	5.934%	Net Change (Price)	$1.000

The bond has a coupon rate of 7.50 percent and matures on March 1, 2043. The last sale on this bond was at a price of 108.50 percent of par, which gives a yield to maturity of about 5.93 percent. Not only does the site provide the most recent price and yield information, but it also provides more important information about the bond, such as the credit rating, coupon date, call date, and call price. We'll leave it up to you to have a look at the page and the rest of the information available there.

Questions
1. Go to this Web site and find the bond shown above. When was this bond issued? What was the size of the bond issue? What were the yield to maturity and price when the bond was issued?
2. When you search for Chevron bonds (CVX), you will find bonds for several companies listed. Why do you think Chevron has bonds issued with different corporate names?

selling occur. Instead, dealers around the country (and around the world) stand ready to buy and sell. The various dealers are connected electronically.

One reason the bond markets are so big is that the number of bond issues far exceeds the number of stock issues. There are two reasons for this. First, a corporation would typically have only one common stock issue outstanding (there are exceptions to this that we discuss in our next chapter). However, a single large corporation could easily have a dozen or more note and bond issues outstanding. Beyond this, federal, state, and local borrowing is simply enormous. For example, even a small city would usually have a wide variety of notes and bonds outstanding, representing money borrowed to pay for things like roads, sewers, and schools. When you think about how many small cities there are in the United States, you begin to get the picture!

Because the bond market is almost entirely OTC, it has historically had little or no transparency. A financial market is *transparent* if it is possible to easily observe its prices and trading volume. On the New York Stock Exchange, for example, it is possible to see the price and quantity for every single transaction. In contrast, in the bond market, it is often not possible to observe either. Transactions are privately negotiated between parties, and there is little or no centralized reporting of transactions.

Although the total volume of trading in bonds far exceeds that in stocks, only a small fraction of the total bond issues that exist actually trade on a given day. This fact, combined with the lack of transparency in the bond market, means that getting up-to-date prices on individual bonds can be difficult or impossible, particularly for smaller corporate or municipal issues. Instead, a variety of sources of estimated prices exist and are commonly used.

BOND PRICE REPORTING

To learn more about TRACE, visit www.finra.org.

In 2002, transparency in the corporate bond market began to improve dramatically. Under new regulations, corporate bond dealers are now required to report trade information through what is known as the Trade Report and Compliance Engine (TRACE). Our nearby *Work the Web* box shows you how to get TRACE.

TRACE bond quotes are available at www.finra.org/marketdata. As shown in Figure 7.3, the Financial Industry Regulatory Authority (FINRA) provides a daily snapshot from TRACE by reporting the most active issues. The information shown is largely self-explanatory. Notice that the price of the iStar Financial bond dropped more than 1.6 percentage points on this day. What do you think happened to the yield to maturity for this bond? Figure 7.3 focuses on the most active bonds with investment grade ratings, but the most active high-yield and convertible bonds are also available on the Web site.

FIGURE 7.3

Sample TRACE Bond Quotations

Most Active Investment Grade Bonds

Issuer Name	Symbol	Coupon	Maturity	Rating Moody's/S&P/Fitch	High	Low	Last	Change	Yield%
J P MORGAN CHASE & CO	JPM.JPF	6.000%	Jan 2018	Aa2/AA-/AA-	104.361	102.730	103.501	-.023	5.526
MORGAN STANLEY	MS.GGO	6.625%	Apr 2018	Aa3/AA-/AA-	105.266	101.898	104.390	-.388	6.028
SPRINT NEXTEL CORP	S.HM	6.000%	Dec 2016	Baa3/BB/BB+	84.500	83.500	84.000	.000	8.690
ISTAR FINL INC	ISFI.GZ	5.950%	Oct 2013	Baa2/BBB/BBB	89.375	87.750	88.875	-1.625	8.556
WELLS FARGO & CO NEW	WFC.GDT	5.625%	Dec 2017	Aa1/AA+/AA	103.700	102.517	102.562	.294	5.280
NUCOR CORP	NUE.GE	6.400%	Dec 2037	A1/A+/NR	101.060	100.819	100.819	-.360	6.338
UNITED TECHNOLOGIES CORP	UTX.GJ	6.350%	Mar 2011	A2/A/A+	106.957	106.647	106.889	.229	3.730
AT&T INC	T.KG	5.500%	Feb 2018	A2/A/A	102.550	99.500	99.864	.029	5.517
AT&T INC	T.KE	4.950%	Jan 2013	A2/A/A	103.433	101.170	101.706	.294	4.538
GOLDMAN SACHS GROUP INC	GS.YW	6.150%	Apr 2018	Aa3/AA-/AA-	105.677	101.160	104.407	4.657	5.563

If you go to the Web site and click on a particular bond, you will get a lot of information about the bond, including the credit rating, the call schedule, original issue information, and trade information.

As we mentioned before, the U.S. Treasury market is the largest securities market in the world. As with bond markets in general, it is an OTC market, so there is limited transparency. However, unlike the situation with bond markets in general, trading in Treasury issues, particularly recently issued ones, is very heavy. Each day, representative prices for outstanding Treasury issues are reported.

Figure 7.4 shows a portion of the daily Treasury note and bond listings from the Web site wsj.com. The entry that begins "2021 Nov 15" is highlighted. This information tells us that the bond will mature in November of 2021. The next column is the coupon rate, which is 8.000 percent for this bond. Treasury bonds all make semiannual payments and have a face value of $1,000, so this bond will pay $40 per six months until it matures.

The next two pieces of information are the **bid** and **asked prices**. In general, in any OTC or dealer market, the bid price represents what a dealer is willing to pay for a security, and the asked price (or just "ask" price) is what a dealer is willing to take for it. The difference between the two prices is called the **bid–ask spread** (or just "spread"), and it represents the dealer's profit.

For historical reasons, Treasury prices are quoted in 32nds. Thus, the bid price on the 8 percent November 2021 bond, 136:29, actually translates into 136 29/32, or 136.90625 percent of face value. With a $1,000 face value, this price represents $1,369.0625. Because prices are quoted in 32nds, the smallest possible price change is 1/32. This change is called the "tick" size.

The next number quoted is the change in the asked price from the previous day, measured in ticks (in 32nds), so this issue's asked price rose by 5/32 of 1 percent, or .15625 percent, of face value from the previous day. Finally, the last number reported is the yield to maturity, based on the asked price. Notice that this is a premium bond because it sells for more than its face value. Not surprisingly, its yield to maturity (4.36 percent) is less than its coupon rate (8 percent).

The very last ordinary bond listed, the 2038 Feb 15, is often called the "bellwether" bond. This bond's yield is the one that is usually reported in the evening news. So, for example, when you hear that long-term interest rates rose, what is really being said is that the yield on this bond went up (and its price went down).

If you examine the yields on the various issues in Figure 7.4, you will clearly see that they vary by maturity. Why this occurs and what it might mean is one of the things we discuss in our next section.

A NOTE ABOUT BOND PRICE QUOTES

If you buy a bond between coupon payment dates, the price you pay is usually more than the price you are quoted. The reason is that standard convention in the bond market is to quote prices net of "accrued interest," meaning that accrued interest is deducted to arrive at the quoted price. This quoted price is called the **clean price**. The price you actually pay, however, includes the accrued interest. This price is the **dirty price**, also known as the "full" or "invoice" price.

An example is the easiest way to understand these issues. Suppose you buy a bond with a 12 percent annual coupon, payable semiannually. You actually pay $1,080 for this bond, so $1,080 is the dirty, or invoice, price. Further, on the day you buy it, the next coupon is due in four months, so you are between coupon dates. Notice that the next coupon will be $60.

The accrued interest on a bond is calculated by taking the fraction of the coupon period that has passed, in this case two months out of six, and multiplying this fraction by the next

The Federal Reserve Bank of St. Louis maintains dozens of online files containing macroeconomic data as well as rates on U.S. Treasury issues. Go to www.stls.frb.org/fred/files.

bid price
The price a dealer is willing to pay for a security.

asked price
The price a dealer is willing to take for a security.

bid–ask spread
The difference between the bid price and the asked price.

Current and historical Treasury yield information is available at www.publicdebt.treas.gov.

clean price
The price of a bond net of accrued interest; this is the price that is typically quoted.

dirty price
The price of a bond including accrued interest, also known as the *full* or *invoice price*. This is the price the buyer actually pays.

FIGURE 7.4

Sample *Wall Street Journal* U.S. Treasury Note and Bond Prices

Treasury Bonds

Maturity	Coupon	Bid	Asked	Chg	Asked yield
2013 Aug 15	12.000	103:00	103:01	−2	1.54
2014 May 15	13.250	111:16	111:17	+1	1.98
2014 Aug 15	12.500	113:02	113:03	+1	2 17
2014 Nov 15	11.750	114:10	114:11	unch.	2.21
2015 Feb 15	11.250	147:10	147:11	+1	3.38
2015 Aug 15	10.625	145:20	145:21	+2	3.48
2015 Nov 15	9.875	141:24	141:25	+1	3.52
2016 Feb 15	9.250	138:10	138:11	+1	3.57
2016 May 15	7.250	124:07	124:08	+2	3.73
2016 Nov 15	7.500	126:26	126:27	+2	3.79
2017 May 15	8.750	136:27	136:28	+2	3.87
2017 Aug 15	8.875	139:07	139:08	+2	3.81
2018 May 15	9.125	142:29	142:30	+4	3.91
2018 Nov 15	9.000	142:04	142:05	+4	4.04
2019 Feb 15	8.875	141:12	141:13	+4	4.09
2019 Aug 15	8.125	135:12	135:13	+4	4.16
2020 Feb 15	8.500	139:15	139:16	+4	4.21
2020 May 15	8.750	142:07	142:08	+4	4.23
2020 Aug 15	8.750	142:18	142:19	+4	4.26
2021 Feb 15	7.875	134:20	134:21	+4	4.32
2021 May 15	8.125	137:19	137:20	+5	4.32
2021 Aug 15	8.125	137:29	137:30	+5	4.34
2021 Nov 15	8.000	136:29	136:30	+5	4.36
2022 Aug 15	7.250	129:27	129:28	+4	4.41
2022 Nov 15	7.625	134:08	134:09	+5	4.40
2023 Feb 15	7.125	129:00	129:00	+4	4.43
2023 Aug 15	6.250	119:23	119:24	+3	4.45
2024 Nov 15	7.500	135:05	135:06	+5	4.47
2025 Feb 15	7.625	136:23	136:24	+4	4.48
2025 Aug 15	6.875	128:01	128:02	+5	4.52
2026 Feb 15	6.000	117:15	117:16	+4	4.55
2026 Aug 15	6.750	127:08	127:09	+4	4.54
2026 Nov 15	6.500	124:11	124:12	+4	4.54
2027 Feb 15	6.625	126:00	126:01	+4	4.55
2027 Aug 15	6.375	123:06	123:07	+4	4.55
2027 Nov 15	6.125	120.07	120:08	+5	4.55
2028 Aug 15	5.500	112:05	112:06	+5	4.57
2028 Nov 15	5.250	108.28	108:29	+4	4.57
2029 Feb 15	5.250	108:28	108:29	+5	4.58
2029 Aug 15	6.125	121:01	121:02	+5	4.56
2030 May 15	6.250	123:16	123:11	+5	4.55
2031 Feb 15	5.375	111:19	111:20	+6	4.55
2036 Feb 15	4.500	99:06	99:07	+5	4.55
2037 Feb 15	4.750	103:05	103:06	+5	4.55
2037 May 15	5.000	107:09	107:10	+5	4.54
2038 Feb 15	4.375	97:01	97:02	+5	4.55

coupon, $60. So, the accrued interest in this example is $2/6 \times \$60 = \$20$. The bond's quoted price (that is, its clean price) would be $\$1,080 - \$20 = \$1,060$.[6]

Concept Questions

7.5a Why do we say bond markets may have little or no transparency?

7.5b In general, what are bid and ask prices?

7.5c What is the difference between a bond's clean price and dirty price?

Inflation and Interest Rates

7.6

So far, we haven't considered the role of inflation in our various discussions of interest rates, yields, and returns. Because this is an important consideration, we consider the impact of inflation next.

REAL VERSUS NOMINAL RATES

In examining interest rates, or any other financial market rates such as discount rates, bond yields, rates of return, and required returns, it is often necessary to distinguish between **real rates** and **nominal rates**. Nominal rates are called "nominal" because they have not been adjusted for inflation. Real rates are rates that have been adjusted for inflation.

real rates
Interest rates or rates of return that have been adjusted for inflation.

nominal rates
Interest rates or rates of return that have not been adjusted for inflation.

To see the effect of inflation, suppose prices are currently rising by 5 percent per year. In other words, the rate of inflation is 5 percent. An investment is available that will be worth $115.50 in one year. It costs $100 today. Notice that with a present value of $100 and a future value in one year of $115.50, this investment has a 15.5 percent rate of return. In calculating this 15.5 percent return, we did not consider the effect of inflation, however, so this is the nominal return.

What is the impact of inflation here? To answer, suppose pizzas cost $5 apiece at the beginning of the year. With $100, we can buy 20 pizzas. Because the inflation rate is 5 percent, pizzas will cost 5 percent more, or $5.25, at the end of the year. If we take the investment, how many pizzas can we buy at the end of the year? Measured in pizzas, what is the rate of return on this investment?

Our $115.50 from the investment will buy us $\$115.50/5.25 = 22$ pizzas. This is up from 20 pizzas, so our pizza rate of return is 10 percent. What this illustrates is that even though the nominal return on our investment is 15.5 percent, our buying power goes up by only 10 percent because of inflation. Put another way, we are really only 10 percent richer. In this case, we say that the real return is 10 percent.

Alternatively, we can say that with 5 percent inflation, each of the $115.50 nominal dollars we get is worth 5 percent less in real terms, so the real dollar value of our investment in a year is:

$$\$115.50/1.05 = \$110$$

What we have done is to *deflate* the $115.50 by 5 percent. Because we give up $100 in current buying power to get the equivalent of $110, our real return is again 10 percent. Because

---

[6]The way accrued interest is calculated actually depends on the type of bond being quoted—for example, Treasury or corporate. The difference has to do with exactly how the fractional coupon period is calculated. In our example here, we implicitly treated the months as having exactly the same length (30 days each, 360 days in a year), which is consistent with the way corporate bonds are quoted. In contrast, for Treasury bonds, actual day counts are used.

we have removed the effect of future inflation here, this $110 is said to be measured in current dollars.

The difference between nominal and real rates is important and bears repeating:

> **The nominal rate on an investment is the percentage change in the number of dollars you have.**
>
> **The real rate on an investment is the percentage change in how much you can buy with your dollars—in other words, the percentage change in your buying power.**

THE FISHER EFFECT

Fisher effect
The relationship between nominal returns, real returns, and inflation.

Our discussion of real and nominal returns illustrates a relationship often called the **Fisher effect** (after the great economist Irving Fisher). Because investors are ultimately concerned with what they can buy with their money, they require compensation for inflation. Let R stand for the nominal rate and r stand for the real rate. The Fisher effect tells us that the relationship between nominal rates, real rates, and inflation can be written as:

$$1 + R = (1 + r) \times (1 + h) \tag{7.2}$$

where h is the inflation rate.

In the preceding example, the nominal rate was 15.50 percent and the inflation rate was 5 percent. What was the real rate? We can determine it by plugging in these numbers:

$$1 + .1550 = (1 + r) \times (1 + .05)$$
$$1 + r = 1.1550/1.05 = 1.10$$
$$r = 10\%$$

This real rate is the same as we found before. If we take another look at the Fisher effect, we can rearrange things a little as follows:

$$1 + R = (1 + r) \times (1 + h)$$
$$R = r + h + r \times h \tag{7.3}$$

What this tells us is that the nominal rate has three components. First, there is the real rate on the investment, r. Next, there is the compensation for the decrease in the value of the money originally invested because of inflation, h. The third component represents compensation for the fact that the dollars earned on the investment are also worth less because of the inflation.

This third component is usually small, so it is often dropped. The nominal rate is then approximately equal to the real rate plus the inflation rate:

$$R \approx r + h \tag{7.4}$$

EXAMPLE 7.5 | **The Fisher Effect**

If investors require a 10 percent real rate of return, and the inflation rate is 8 percent, what must be the approximate nominal rate? The exact nominal rate?

The nominal rate is approximately equal to the sum of the real rate and the inflation rate: 10% + 8% = 18%. From the Fisher effect, we have:

$$1 + R = (1 + r) \times (1 + h)$$
$$= 1.10 \times 1.08$$
$$= 1.1880$$

Therefore, the nominal rate will actually be closer to 19 percent.

It is important to note that financial rates, such as interest rates, discount rates, and rates of return, are almost always quoted in nominal terms. To remind you of this, we will henceforth use the symbol R instead of r in most of our discussions about such rates.

INFLATION AND PRESENT VALUES

One question that often comes up is the effect of inflation on present value calculations. The basic principle is simple: Either discount nominal cash flows at a nominal rate or discount real cash flows at a real rate. As long as you are consistent, you will get the same answer.

To illustrate, suppose you want to withdraw money each year for the next three years, and you want each withdrawal to have $25,000 worth of purchasing power as measured in current dollars. If the inflation rate is 4 percent per year, then the withdrawals will simply have to increase by 4 percent each year to compensate. The withdrawals each year will thus be:

$$C_1 = \$25,000(1.04) \ = \$26,000$$
$$C_2 = \$25,000(1.04)^2 = \$27,040$$
$$C_3 = \$25,000(1.04)^3 = \$28,121.60$$

What is the present value of these cash flows if the appropriate nominal discount rate is 10 percent? This is a standard calculation, and the answer is:

$$PV = \$26,000/1.10 + \$27,040/1.10^2 + \$28,121.60/1.10^3 = \$67,111.65$$

Notice that we discounted the nominal cash flows at a nominal rate.

To calculate the present value using real cash flows, we need the real discount rate. Using the Fisher equation, the real discount rate is:

$$1 + R = (1 + r)(1 + h)$$
$$1 + .10 = (1 + r)(1 + .04)$$
$$r = .0577$$

By design, the real cash flows are an annuity of $25,000 per year. So, the present value in real terms is:

$$PV = \$25,000[1 - (1/1.0577^3)]/.0577 = \$67,111.65$$

Thus, we get exactly the same answer (after allowing for a small rounding error in the real rate). Of course, you could also use the growing annuity equation we discussed in the previous chapter. The withdrawals are increasing at 4 percent per year; so using the growing annuity formula, the present value is:

$$PV = \$26,000 \left[\frac{1 - \left(\frac{1 + .04}{1 + .10}\right)^3}{.10 - .04} \right] = \$26,000(2.58122) = \$67,111.65$$

This is exactly the same present value we calculated before.

Concept Questions

7.6a What is the difference between a nominal and a real return? Which is more important to a typical investor?

7.6b What is the Fisher effect?

7.7 Determinants of Bond Yields

We are now in a position to discuss the determinants of a bond's yield. As we will see, the yield on any particular bond reflects a variety of factors, some common to all bonds and some specific to the issue under consideration.

THE TERM STRUCTURE OF INTEREST RATES

At any point in time, short-term and long-term interest rates will generally be different. Sometimes short-term rates are higher, sometimes lower. Figure 7.5 gives us a long-range perspective on this by showing over two centuries of short- and long-term interest rates. As shown, through time, the difference between short- and long-term rates has ranged from essentially zero to up to several percentage points, both positive and negative.

term structure of interest rates
The relationship between nominal interest rates on default-free, pure discount securities and time to maturity; that is, the pure time value of money.

The relationship between short- and long-term interest rates is known as the **term structure of interest rates**. To be a little more precise, the term structure of interest rates tells us what *nominal* interest rates are on *default-free, pure discount* bonds of all maturities. These rates are, in essence, "pure" interest rates because they involve no risk of default and a single, lump sum future payment. In other words, the term structure tells us the pure time value of money for different lengths of time.

When long-term rates are higher than short-term rates, we say that the term structure is upward sloping; when short-term rates are higher, we say it is downward sloping. The term structure can also be "humped." When this occurs, it is usually because rates increase at first, but then begin to decline as we look at longer- and longer-term rates. The most common shape of the term structure, particularly in modern times, is upward sloping; but the degree of steepness has varied quite a bit.

FIGURE 7.5   U.S. Interest Rates: 1800–2007

SOURCE: Jeremy J. Siegel, *Stocks for the Long Run,* 3rd edition, © McGraw-Hill, 2004, updated by the authors.

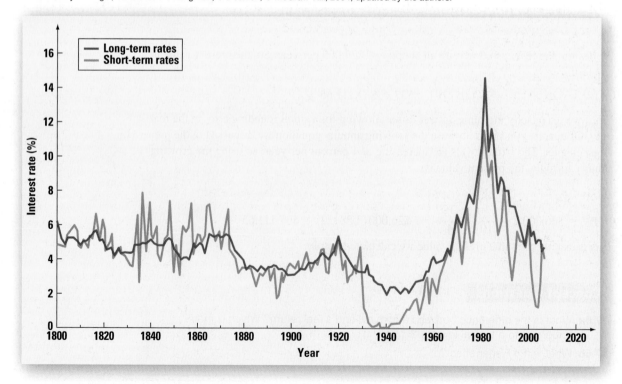

What determines the shape of the term structure? There are three basic components. The first two are the ones we discussed in our previous section: The real rate of interest and the rate of inflation. The real rate of interest is the compensation investors demand for forgoing the use of their money. You can think of it as the pure time value of money after adjusting for the effects of inflation.

The real rate of interest is the basic component underlying every interest rate, regardless of the time to maturity. When the real rate is high, all interest rates will tend to be higher, and vice versa. Thus, the real rate doesn't really determine the shape of the term structure; instead, it mostly influences the overall level of interest rates.

In contrast, the prospect of future inflation strongly influences the shape of the term structure. Investors thinking about lending money for various lengths of time recognize that future inflation erodes the value of the dollars that will be returned. As a result, investors demand compensation for this loss in the form of higher nominal rates. This extra compensation is called the **inflation premium**.

inflation premium
The portion of a nominal interest rate that represents compensation for expected future inflation.

If investors believe the rate of inflation will be higher in the future, then long-term nominal interest rates will tend to be higher than short-term rates. Thus, an upward-sloping term structure may reflect anticipated increases in inflation. Similarly, a downward-sloping term structure probably reflects the belief that inflation will be falling in the future.

The third, and last, component of the term structure has to do with interest rate risk. As we discussed earlier in the chapter, longer-term bonds have much greater risk of loss resulting from changes in interest rates than do shorter-term bonds. Investors recognize this risk, and they demand extra compensation in the form of higher rates for bearing it. This extra compensation is called the **interest rate risk premium**. The longer is the term to maturity, the greater is the interest rate risk, so the interest rate risk premium increases with maturity. However, as we discussed earlier, interest rate risk increases at a decreasing rate, so the interest rate risk premium does as well.[7]

interest rate risk premium
The compensation investors demand for bearing interest rate risk.

Putting the pieces together, we see that the term structure reflects the combined effect of the real rate of interest, the inflation premium, and the interest rate risk premium. Figure 7.6 shows how these can interact to produce an upward-sloping term structure (in the top part of Figure 7.6) or a downward-sloping term structure (in the bottom part).

In the top part of Figure 7.6, notice how the rate of inflation is expected to rise gradually. At the same time, the interest rate risk premium increases at a decreasing rate, so the combined effect is to produce a pronounced upward-sloping term structure. In the bottom part of Figure 7.6, the rate of inflation is expected to fall in the future, and the expected decline is enough to offset the interest rate risk premium and produce a downward-sloping term structure. Notice that if the rate of inflation was expected to decline by only a small amount, we could still get an upward-sloping term structure because of the interest rate risk premium.

We assumed in drawing Figure 7.6 that the real rate would remain the same. Actually, expected future real rates could be larger or smaller than the current real rate. Also, for simplicity, we used straight lines to show expected future inflation rates as rising or declining, but they do not necessarily have to look like this. They could, for example, rise and then fall, leading to a humped yield curve.

BOND YIELDS AND THE YIELD CURVE: PUTTING IT ALL TOGETHER

Going back to Figure 7.4, recall that we saw that the yields on Treasury notes and bonds of different maturities are not the same. Each day, in addition to the Treasury prices and yields

---

[7]In days of old, the interest rate risk premium was called a "liquidity" premium. Today, the term *liquidity premium* has an altogether different meaning, which we explore in our next section. Also, the interest rate risk premium is sometimes called a *maturity risk premium*. Our terminology is consistent with the modern view of the term structure.

FIGURE 7.6

The Term Structure of
Interest Rates

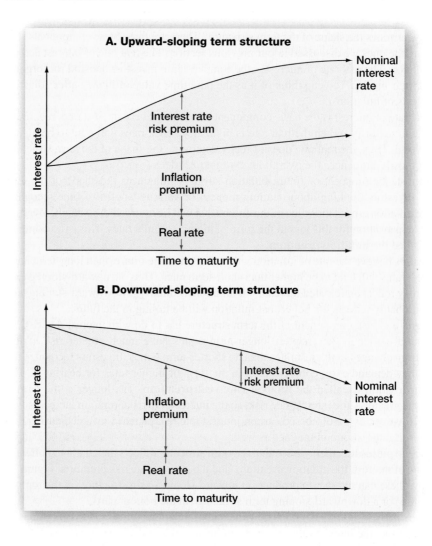

A. Upward-sloping term structure

Nominal
interest
rate

Interest rate
risk premium

Inflation
premium

Real rate

Interest rate

Time to maturity

B. Downward-sloping term structure

Interest rate
risk premium

Nominal
interest
rate

Inflation
premium

Real rate

Interest rate

Time to maturity

Treasury yield curve
A plot of the yields on
Treasury notes and bonds
relative to maturity.

*Online
yield curve information
is available at
www.bloomberg.com/
markets.*

default risk premium
The portion of a nominal
interest rate or bond yield
that represents
compensation for the
possibility of default.

shown in Figure 7.4, *The Wall Street Journal* provides a plot of Treasury yields relative to maturity. This plot is called the **Treasury yield curve** (or just the yield curve). Figure 7.7 shows the yield curve as of May 2008.

As you probably now suspect, the shape of the yield curve reflects the term structure of interest rates. In fact, the Treasury yield curve and the term structure of interest rates are almost the same thing. The only difference is that the term structure is based on pure discount bonds, whereas the yield curve is based on coupon bond yields. As a result, Treasury yields depend on the three components that underlie the term structure—the real rate, expected future inflation, and the interest rate risk premium.

Treasury notes and bonds have three important features that we need to remind you of: They are default-free, they are taxable, and they are highly liquid. This is not true of bonds in general, so we need to examine what additional factors come into play when we look at bonds issued by corporations or municipalities.

The first thing to consider is credit risk—that is, the possibility of default. Investors recognize that issuers other than the Treasury may or may not make all the promised payments on a bond, so they demand a higher yield as compensation for this risk. This extra compensation is called the **default risk premium**. Earlier in the chapter, we saw how bonds were

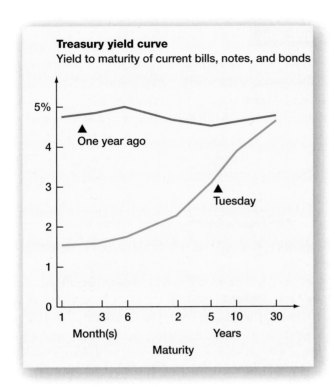

FIGURE 7.7

The Treasury Yield Curve: May, 2008

Source: Reprinted by permission of *The Wall Street Journal,* via Copyright Clearance Center © 2008 by Dow Jones & Company, Inc., 2008. All Rights Reserved Worldwide.

rated based on their credit risk. What you will find if you start looking at bonds of different ratings is that lower-rated bonds have higher yields.

An important thing to recognize about a bond's yield is that it is calculated assuming that all the promised payments will be made. As a result, it is really a promised yield, and it may or may not be what you will earn. In particular, if the issuer defaults, your actual yield will be lower—probably much lower. This fact is particularly important when it comes to junk bonds. Thanks to a clever bit of marketing, such bonds are now commonly called high-yield bonds, which has a much nicer ring to it; but now you recognize that these are really high *promised* yield bonds.

Next, recall that we discussed earlier how municipal bonds are free from most taxes and, as a result, have much lower yields than taxable bonds. Investors demand the extra yield on a taxable bond as compensation for the unfavorable tax treatment. This extra compensation is the **taxability premium**.

Finally, bonds have varying degrees of liquidity. As we discussed earlier, there are an enormous number of bond issues, most of which do not trade regularly. As a result, if you wanted to sell quickly, you would probably not get as good a price as you could otherwise. Investors prefer liquid assets to illiquid ones, so they demand a **liquidity premium** on top of all the other premiums we have discussed. As a result, all else being the same, less liquid bonds will have higher yields than more liquid bonds.

taxability premium
The portion of a nominal interest rate or bond yield that represents compensation for unfavorable tax status.

liquidity premium
The portion of a nominal interest rate or bond yield that represents compensation for lack of liquidity.

CONCLUSION

If we combine all of the things we have discussed regarding bond yields, we find that bond yields represent the combined effect of no fewer than six things. The first is the real rate of interest. On top of the real rate are five premiums representing compensation for (1) expected future inflation, (2) interest rate risk, (3) default risk, (4) taxability, and (5) lack of liquidity. As a result, determining the appropriate yield on a bond requires careful analysis of each of these effects.

Concept Questions

7.7a What is the term structure of interest rates? What determines its shape?
7.7b What is the Treasury yield curve?
7.7c What six components make up a bond's yield?

7.8 Summary and Conclusions

This chapter has explored bonds, bond yields, and interest rates:

1. Determining bond prices and yields is an application of basic discounted cash flow principles.

2. Bond values move in the direction opposite that of interest rates, leading to potential gains or losses for bond investors.

3. Bonds have a variety of features spelled out in a document called the indenture.

4. Bonds are rated based on their default risk. Some bonds, such as Treasury bonds, have no risk of default, whereas so-called junk bonds have substantial default risk.

5. A wide variety of bonds exist, many of which contain exotic or unusual features.

6. Almost all bond trading is OTC, with little or no market transparency in many cases. As a result, bond price and volume information can be difficult to find for some types of bonds.

7. Bond yields and interest rates reflect the effect of six different things: the real interest rate and five premiums that investors demand as compensation for inflation, interest rate risk, default risk, taxability, and lack of liquidity.

In closing, we note that bonds are a vital source of financing to governments and corporations of all types. Bond prices and yields are a rich subject, and our one chapter, necessarily, touches on only the most important concepts and ideas. There is a great deal more we could say, but, instead, we will move on to stocks in our next chapter.

CHAPTER REVIEW AND SELF-TEST PROBLEMS

7.1   **Bond Values**   A Microgates Industries bond has a 10 percent coupon rate and a $1,000 face value. Interest is paid semiannually, and the bond has 20 years to maturity. If investors require a 12 percent yield, what is the bond's value? What is the effective annual yield on the bond?

7.2   **Bond Yields**   A Macrohard Corp. bond carries an 8 percent coupon, paid semiannually. The par value is $1,000, and the bond matures in six years. If the bond currently sells for $911.37, what is its yield to maturity? What is the effective annual yield?

ANSWERS TO CHAPTER REVIEW AND SELF-TEST PROBLEMS

7.1   Because the bond has a 10 percent coupon yield and investors require a 12 percent return, we know that the bond must sell at a discount. Notice that, because the bond pays interest semiannually, the coupons amount to $100/2 = $50 every six months.

The required yield is 12%/2 = 6% every six months. Finally, the bond matures in 20 years, so there are a total of 40 six-month periods.

The bond's value is thus equal to the present value of $50 every six months for the next 40 six-month periods plus the present value of the $1,000 face amount:

Bond value = $50 × [(1 − 1/1.06^{40})/.06] + 1,000/1.06^{40}
= $50 × 15.04630 + 1,000/10.2857
= $849.54

Notice that we discounted the $1,000 back 40 periods at 6 percent per period, rather than 20 years at 12 percent. The reason is that the effective annual yield on the bond is 1.06^2 − 1 = 12.36%, not 12 percent. We thus could have used 12.36 percent per year for 20 years when we calculated the present value of the $1,000 face amount, and the answer would have been the same.

7.2 The present value of the bond's cash flows is its current price, $911.37. The coupon is $40 every six months for 12 periods. The face value is $1,000. So the bond's yield is the unknown discount rate in the following:

$911.37 = $40 × [1 − 1/(1 + r)^{12}]/r + 1,000/(1 + r)^{12}

The bond sells at a discount. Because the coupon rate is 8 percent, the yield must be something in excess of that.

If we were to solve this by trial and error, we might try 12 percent (or 6 percent per six months):

Bond value = $40 × (1 − 1/1.06^{12})/.06 + 1,000/1.06^{12}
= $832.32

This is less than the actual value, so our discount rate is too high. We now know that the yield is somewhere between 8 and 12 percent. With further trial and error (or a little machine assistance), the yield works out to be 10 percent, or 5 percent every six months.

By convention, the bond's yield to maturity would be quoted as 2 × 5% = 10%. The effective yield is thus 1.05^2 − 1 = 10.25%.

CONCEPTS REVIEW AND CRITICAL THINKING QUESTIONS

1. **Treasury Bonds [LO1]** Is it true that a U.S. Treasury security is risk-free?
2. **Interest Rate Risk [LO2]** Which has greater interest rate risk, a 30-year Treasury bond or a 30-year BB corporate bond?
3. **Treasury Pricing [LO1]** With regard to bid and ask prices on a Treasury bond, is it possible for the bid price to be higher? Why or why not?
4. **Yield to Maturity [LO2]** Treasury bid and ask quotes are sometimes given in terms of yields, so there would be a bid yield and an ask yield. Which do you think would be larger? Explain.
5. **Call Provisions [LO1]** A company is contemplating a long-term bond issue. It is debating whether to include a call provision. What are the benefits to the company from including a call provision? What are the costs? How do these answers change for a put provision?
6. **Coupon Rate [LO1]** How does a bond issuer decide on the appropriate coupon rate to set on its bonds? Explain the difference between the coupon rate and the required return on a bond.

7. **Real and Nominal Returns [LO4]** Are there any circumstances under which an investor might be more concerned about the nominal return on an investment than the real return?

8. **Bond Ratings [LO3]** Companies pay rating agencies such as Moody's and S&P to rate their bonds, and the costs can be substantial. However, companies are not required to have their bonds rated; doing so is strictly voluntary. Why do you think they do it?

9. **Bond Ratings [LO3]** U.S. Treasury bonds are not rated. Why? Often, junk bonds are not rated. Why?

10. **Term Structure [LO5]** What is the difference between the term structure of interest rates and the yield curve?

11. **Crossover Bonds [LO3]** Looking back at the crossover bonds we discussed in the chapter, why do you think split ratings such as these occur?

12. **Municipal Bonds [LO1]** Why is it that municipal bonds are not taxed at the federal level, but are taxable across state lines? Why are U.S. Treasury bonds not taxable at the state level? (You may need to dust off the history books for this one.)

13. **Bond Market [LO1]** What are the implications for bond investors of the lack of transparency in the bond market?

14. **Rating Agencies [LO3]** A controversy erupted regarding bond-rating agencies when some agencies began to provide unsolicited bond ratings. Why do you think this is controversial?

15. **Bonds as Equity [LO1]** The 100-year bonds we discussed in the chapter have something in common with junk bonds. Critics charge that, in both cases, the issuers are really selling equity in disguise. What are the issues here? Why would a company want to sell "equity in disguise"?

QUESTIONS AND PROBLEMS ^{TM}

BASIC
(Questions 1–14)

1. **Interpreting Bond Yields [LO1]** Is the yield to maturity on a bond the same thing as the required return? Is YTM the same thing as the coupon rate? Suppose today a 10 percent coupon bond sells at par. Two years from now, the required return on the same bond is 8 percent. What is the coupon rate on the bond then? The YTM?

2. **Interpreting Bond Yields [LO2]** Suppose you buy a 7 percent coupon, 20-year bond today when it's first issued. If interest rates suddenly rise to 15 percent, what happens to the value of your bond? Why?

3. **Bond Prices [LO2]** Staind, Inc., has 7.5 percent coupon bonds on the market that have 10 years left to maturity. The bonds make annual payments. If the YTM on these bonds is 8.75 percent, what is the current bond price?

4. **Bond Yields [LO2]** Ackerman Co. has 9 percent coupon bonds on the market with nine years left to maturity. The bonds make annual payments. If the bond currently sells for $934, what is its YTM?

5. **Coupon Rates [LO2]** Kiss the Sky Enterprises has bonds on the market making annual payments, with 13 years to maturity, and selling for $1,045. At this price, the bonds yield 7.5 percent. What must the coupon rate be on the bonds?

6. **Bond Prices [LO2]** Grohl Co. issued 11-year bonds a year ago at a coupon rate of 6.9 percent. The bonds make semiannual payments. If the YTM on these bonds is 7.4 percent, what is the current bond price?

7. **Bond Yields** [LO2] Ngata Corp. issued 12-year bonds 2 years ago at a coupon rate of 8.4 percent. The bonds make semiannual payments. If these bonds currently sell for 105 percent of par value, what is the YTM?

8. **Coupon Rates** [LO2] Ashes Divide Corporation has bonds on the market with 14.5 years to maturity, a YTM of 6.8 percent, and a current price of $924. The bonds make semiannual payments. What must the coupon rate be on these bonds?

9. **Calculating Real Rates of Return** [LO4] If Treasury bills are currently paying 7 percent and the inflation rate is 3.8 percent, what is the approximate real rate of interest? The exact real rate?

10. **Inflation and Nominal Returns** [LO4] Suppose the real rate is 3 percent and the inflation rate is 4.7 percent. What rate would you expect to see on a Treasury bill?

11. **Nominal and Real Returns** [LO4] An investment offers a 14 percent total return over the coming year. Bill Bernanke thinks the total real return on this investment will be only 9 percent. What does Bill believe the inflation rate will be over the next year?

12. **Nominal versus Real Returns** [LO4] Say you own an asset that had a total return last year of 11.4 percent. If the inflation rate last year was 4.8 percent, what was your real return?

13. **Using Treasury Quotes** [LO2] Locate the Treasury issue in Figure 7.4 maturing in November 2027. Is this a note or a bond? What is its coupon rate? What is its bid price? What was the *previous* day's asked price?

14. **Using Treasury Quotes** [LO2] Locate the Treasury bond in Figure 7.4 maturing in November 2024. Is this a premium or a discount bond? What is its current yield? What is its yield to maturity? What is the bid–ask spread?

15. **Bond Price Movements** [LO2] Bond X is a premium bond making annual payments. The bond pays an 8 percent coupon, has a YTM of 6 percent, and has 13 years to maturity. Bond Y is a discount bond making annual payments. This bond pays a 6 percent coupon, has a YTM of 8 percent, and also has 13 years to maturity. If interest rates remain unchanged, what do you expect the price of these bonds to be one year from now? In three years? In eight years? In 12 years? In 13 years? What's going on here? Illustrate your answers by graphing bond prices versus time to maturity.

INTERMEDIATE
(Questions 15–28)

16. **Interest Rate Risk** [LO2] Both Bond Sam and Bond Dave have 9 percent coupons, make semiannual payments, and are priced at par value. Bond Sam has 3 years to maturity, whereas Bond Dave has 20 years to maturity. If interest rates suddenly rise by 2 percent, what is the percentage change in the price of Bond Sam? Of Bond Dave? If rates were to suddenly fall by 2 percent instead, what would the percentage change in the price of Bond Sam be then? Of Bond Dave? Illustrate your answers by graphing bond prices versus YTM. What does this problem tell you about the interest rate risk of longer-term bonds?

17. **Interest Rate Risk** [LO2] Bond J is a 4 percent coupon bond. Bond K is a 12 percent coupon bond. Both bonds have nine years to maturity, make semiannual payments, and have a YTM of 8 percent. If interest rates suddenly rise by 2 percent, what is the percentage price change of these bonds? What if rates suddenly fall by 2 percent instead? What does this problem tell you about the interest rate risk of lower-coupon bonds?

18. **Bond Yields** [LO2] One More Time Software has 9.2 percent coupon bonds on the market with nine years to maturity. The bonds make semiannual payments and currently sell for 106.8 percent of par. What is the current yield on the bonds? The YTM? The effective annual yield?

19. **Bond Yields [LO2]** Seether Co. wants to issue new 20-year bonds for some much-needed expansion projects. The company currently has 8 percent coupon bonds on the market that sell for $930, make semiannual payments, and mature in 20 years. What coupon rate should the company set on its new bonds if it wants them to sell at par?

20. **Accrued Interest [LO2]** You purchase a bond with an invoice price of $968. The bond has a coupon rate of 7.4 percent, and there are four months to the next semiannual coupon date. What is the clean price of the bond?

21. **Accrued Interest [LO2]** You purchase a bond with a coupon rate of 6.8 percent and a clean price of $1,073. If the next semiannual coupon payment is due in two months, what is the invoice price?

22. **Finding the Bond Maturity [LO2]** River Corp. has 8 percent coupon bonds making annual payments with a YTM of 7.2 percent. The current yield on these bonds is 7.55 percent. How many years do these bonds have left until they mature?

23. **Using Bond Quotes [LO2]** Suppose the following bond quotes for IOU Corporation appear in the financial page of today's newspaper. Assume the bond has a face value of $1,000 and the current date is April 15, 2009. What is the yield to maturity of the bond? What is the current yield?

Company (Ticker)	Coupon	Maturity	Last Price	Last Yield	EST Vol (000s)
IOU (IOU)	7.2	Apr 15, 2023	108.96	??	1,827

24. **Bond Prices versus Yields [LO2]**
   a. What is the relationship between the price of a bond and its YTM?
   b. Explain why some bonds sell at a premium over par value while other bonds sell at a discount. What do you know about the relationship between the coupon rate and the YTM for premium bonds? What about for discount bonds? For bonds selling at par value?
   c. What is the relationship between the current yield and YTM for premium bonds? For discount bonds? For bonds selling at par value?

25. **Interest on Zeroes [LO2]** Tesla Corporation needs to raise funds to finance a plant expansion, and it has decided to issue 25-year zero coupon bonds to raise the money. The required return on the bonds will be 9 percent.
   a. What will these bonds sell for at issuance?
   b. Using the IRS amortization rule, what interest deduction can the company take on these bonds in the first year? In the last year?
   c. Repeat part (b) using the straight-line method for the interest deduction.
   d. Based on your answers in (b) and (c), which interest deduction method would Tesla Corporation prefer? Why?

26. **Zero Coupon Bonds [LO2]** Suppose your company needs to raise $30 million and you want to issue 30-year bonds for this purpose. Assume the required return on your bond issue will be 8 percent, and you're evaluating two issue alternatives: an 8 percent semiannual coupon bond and a zero coupon bond. Your company's tax rate is 35 percent.
   a. How many of the coupon bonds would you need to issue to raise the $30 million? How many of the zeroes would you need to issue?
   b. In 30 years, what will your company's repayment be if you issue the coupon bonds? What if you issue the zeroes?

c. Based on your answers in (a) and (b), why would you ever want to issue the zeroes? To answer, calculate the firm's aftertax cash outflows for the first year under the two different scenarios. Assume the IRS amortization rules apply for the zero coupon bonds.

27. Finding the Maturity [LO2] You've just found a 10 percent coupon bond on the market that sells for par value. What is the maturity on this bond?

28. Real Cash Flows [LO4] You want to have $1.5 million in real dollars in an account when you retire in 40 years. The nominal return on your investment is 11 percent and the inflation rate is 3.8 percent. What real amount must you deposit each year to achieve your goal?

29. Components of Bond Returns [LO2] Bond P is a premium bond with a 12 percent coupon. Bond D is a 6 percent coupon bond currently selling at a discount. Both bonds make annual payments, have a YTM of 9 percent, and have five years to maturity. What is the current yield for bond P? For bond D? If interest rates remain unchanged, what is the expected capital gains yield over the next year for bond P? For bond D? Explain your answers and the interrelationships among the various types of yields.

CHALLENGE
(Questions 29–35)

30. Holding Period Yield [LO2] The YTM on a bond is the interest rate you earn on your investment if interest rates don't change. If you actually sell the bond before it matures, your realized return is known as the *holding period yield* (HPY).

a. Suppose that today you buy a 7 percent annual coupon bond for $1,060. The bond has 10 years to maturity. What rate of return do you expect to earn on your investment?

b. Two years from now, the YTM on your bond has declined by 1 percent, and you decide to sell. What price will your bond sell for? What is the HPY on your investment? Compare this yield to the YTM when you first bought the bond. Why are they different?

31. Valuing Bonds [LO2] The McKeegan Corporation has two different bonds currently outstanding. Bond M has a face value of $20,000 and matures in 20 years. The bond makes no payments for the first six years, then pays $1,100 every six months over the subsequent eight years, and finally pays $1,400 every six months over the last six years. Bond N also has a face value of $20,000 and a maturity of 20 years; it makes no coupon payments over the life of the bond. If the required return on both these bonds is 7 percent compounded semiannually, what is the current price of bond M? Of bond N?

32. Valuing the Call Feature [LO2] Consider the prices in the following three Treasury issues as of May 15, 2007:

6.500	May 13n	106:10	106:12	−13	5.28
8.250	May 13	103:14	103:16	− 3	5.24
12.000	May 13	134:25	134:31	−15	5.32

The bond in the middle is callable in February 2008. What is the implied value of the call feature? (*Hint:* Is there a way to combine the two noncallable issues to create an issue that has the same coupon as the callable bond?)

33. Treasury Bonds [LO2] The following Treasury bond quote appeared in *The Wall Street Journal* on May 11, 2004:

9.125	May 09	100:03	100:04	. . .	−2.15

Why would anyone buy this Treasury bond with a negative yield to maturity? How is this possible?

34. **Real Cash Flows [LO4]** When Marilyn Monroe died, ex-husband Joe DiMaggio vowed to place fresh flowers on her grave every Sunday as long as he lived. The week after she died in 1962, a bunch of fresh flowers that the former baseball player thought appropriate for the star cost about $5. Based on actuarial tables, "Joltin' Joe" could expect to live for 30 years after the actress died. Assume that the EAR is 8.4 percent. Also, assume that the price of the flowers will increase at 3.7 percent per year, when expressed as an EAR. Assuming that each year has exactly 52 weeks, what is the present value of this commitment? Joe began purchasing flowers the week after Marilyn died.

35. **Real Cash Flows [LO4]** You are planning to save for retirement over the next 30 years. To save for retirement, you will invest $900 a month in a stock account in real dollars and $450 a month in a bond account in real dollars. The effective annual return of the stock account is expected to be 11 percent, and the bond account will earn 7 percent. When you retire, you will combine your money into an account with a 9 percent effective return. The inflation rate over this period is expected to be 4 percent. How much can you withdraw each month from your account in real terms assuming a 25-year withdrawal period? What is the nominal dollar amount of your last withdrawal?

Visit us at www.mhhe.com/rwj

MINICASE

Financing S&S Air's Expansion Plans with a Bond Issue

Mark Sexton and Todd Story, the owners of S&S Air, have decided to expand their operations. They instructed their newly hired financial analyst, Chris Guthrie, to enlist an underwriter to help sell $35 million in new 10-year bonds to finance construction. Chris has entered into discussions with Kim McKenzie, an underwriter from the firm of Raines and Warren, about which bond features S&S Air should consider and what coupon rate the issue will likely have.

Although Chris is aware of the bond features, he is uncertain about the costs and benefits of some features, so he isn't sure how each feature would affect the coupon rate of the bond issue. You are Kim's assistant, and she has asked you to prepare a memo to Chris describing the effect of each of the following bond features on the coupon rate of the bond. She would also like you to list any advantages or disadvantages of each feature:

QUESTIONS

1. The security of the bond—that is, whether the bond has collateral.
2. The seniority of the bond.
3. The presence of a sinking fund.
4. A call provision with specified call dates and call prices.
5. A deferred call accompanying the call provision.
6. A make-whole call provision.
7. Any positive covenants. Also, discuss several possible positive covenants S&S Air might consider.
8. Any negative covenants. Also, discuss several possible negative covenants S&S Air might consider.
9. A conversion feature (note that S&S Air is not a publicly traded company).
10. A floating-rate coupon.

STOCK VALUATION

8

WHEN THE STOCK MARKET CLOSED on May 8, 2008, the common stock of McGraw-Hill, publisher of fine quality college textbooks, was going for $40.80 per share. On that same day, stock in Carnival Corp., the cruise line company, closed at $40.46, while stock in Adobe Systems, the software developer, closed at $39.24. Because the stock prices of these three companies were so similar, you might expect that they would be offering similar dividends to their stockholders, but you would be wrong. In fact, Carnival's annual dividend was $2.90 per share, McGraw-Hill's was $.88 per share, and Adobe Systems was paying no dividends at all!

As we will see in this chapter, the dividends currently being paid are one of the primary factors we look at when attempting to value common stocks. However, it is obvious from looking at Adobe that current dividends are not the end of the story. This chapter explores dividends, stock values, and the connection between the two.

Master the ability to solve problems in this chapter by using a spreadsheet. Access Excel Master on the student Web site www.mhhe.com/rwj.

In our previous chapter, we introduced you to bonds and bond valuation. In this chapter, we turn to the other major source of financing for corporations: common and preferred stock. We first describe the cash flows associated with a share of stock and then go on to develop a famous result, the dividend growth model. From there, we move on to examine various important features of common and preferred stock, focusing on shareholder rights. We close the chapter with a discussion of how shares of stock are traded and how stock prices and other important information are reported in the financial press.

8.1 Common Stock Valuation

A share of common stock is more difficult to value in practice than a bond for at least three reasons. First, with common stock, not even the promised cash flows are known in advance. Second, the life of the investment is essentially forever because common stock has no maturity. Third, there is no way to easily observe the rate of return that the market requires. Nonetheless, as we will see, there are cases in which we can come up with the present value of the future cash flows for a share of stock and thus determine its value.

CASH FLOWS

Imagine that you are considering buying a share of stock today. You plan to sell the stock in one year. You somehow know that the stock will be worth $70 at that time. You predict that the stock will also pay a $10 per share dividend at the end of the year. If you require a 25 percent return on your investment, what is the most you would pay for the stock? In other words, what is the present value of the $10 dividend along with the $70 ending value at 25 percent?

If you buy the stock today and sell it at the end of the year, you will have a total of $80 in cash. At 25 percent:

Present value = ($10 + 70)/1.25 = $64

Therefore, $64 is the value you would assign to the stock today.

More generally, let P_0 be the current price of the stock, and assign P_1 to be the price in one period. If D_1 is the cash dividend paid at the end of the period, then:

$$P_0 = (D_1 + P_1)/(1 + R)$$ [8.1]

where R is the required return in the market on this investment.

Notice that we really haven't said much so far. If we wanted to determine the value of a share of stock today (P_0), we would first have to come up with the value in one year (P_1). This is even harder to do, so we've only made the problem more complicated.

What is the price in one period, P_1? We don't know in general. Instead, suppose we somehow knew the price in two periods, P_2. Given a predicted dividend in two periods, D_2, the stock price in one period would be:

$$P_1 = (D_2 + P_2)/(1 + R)$$

If we were to substitute this expression for P_1 into our expression for P_0, we would have:

$$P_0 = \frac{D_1 + P_1}{1 + R} = \frac{D_1 + \dfrac{D_2 + P_2}{1 + R}}{1 + R}$$

$$= \frac{D_1}{(1 + R)^1} + \frac{D_2}{(1 + R)^2} + \frac{P_2}{(1 + R)^2}$$

Now we need to get a price in two periods. We don't know this either, so we can procrastinate again and write:

$$P_2 = (D_3 + P_3)/(1 + R)$$

If we substitute this back in for P_2, we have:

$$P_0 = \frac{D_1}{(1+R)^1} + \frac{D_2}{(1+R)^2} + \frac{P_2}{(1+R)^2}$$

$$= \frac{D_1}{(1+R)^1} + \frac{D_2}{(1+R)^2} + \frac{\dfrac{D_3+P_3}{1+R}}{(1+R)^2}$$

$$= \frac{D_1}{(1+R)^1} + \frac{D_2}{(1+R)^2} + \frac{D_3}{(1+R)^3} + \frac{P_3}{(1+R)^3}$$

You should start to notice that we can push the problem of coming up with the stock price off into the future forever. Note that no matter what the stock price is, the present value is essentially zero if we push the sale of the stock far enough away.[1] What we are eventually left with is the result that the current price of the stock can be written as the present value of the dividends beginning in one period and extending out forever:

$$P_0 = \frac{D_1}{(1+R)^1} + \frac{D_2}{(1+R)^2} + \frac{D_3}{(1+R)^3} + \frac{D_4}{(1+R)^4} + \frac{D_5}{(1+R)^5} + \cdots$$

We have illustrated here that the price of the stock today is equal to the present value of all of the future dividends. How many future dividends are there? In principle, there can be an infinite number. This means that we still can't compute a value for the stock because we would have to forecast an infinite number of dividends and then discount them all. In the next section, we consider some special cases in which we can get around this problem.

Growth Stocks | EXAMPLE 8.1

You might be wondering about shares of stock in companies such as Yahoo! that currently pay no dividends. Small, growing companies frequently plow back everything and thus pay no dividends. Are such shares worth nothing? It depends. When we say that the value of the stock is equal to the present value of the future dividends, we don't rule out the possibility that some number of those dividends are zero. They just can't *all* be zero.

Imagine a company that has a provision in its corporate charter that prohibits the paying of dividends now or ever. The corporation never borrows any money, never pays out any money to stockholders in any form whatsoever, and never sells any assets. Such a corporation couldn't really exist because the IRS wouldn't like it, and the stockholders could always vote to amend the charter if they wanted to. If it did exist, however, what would the stock be worth?

The stock is worth absolutely nothing. Such a company is a financial "black hole." Money goes in, but nothing valuable ever comes out. Because nobody would ever get any return on this investment, the investment has no value. This example is a little absurd, but it illustrates that when we speak of companies that don't pay dividends, what we really mean is that they are not *currently* paying dividends.

[1]The only assumption we make about the stock price is that it is a finite number no matter how far away we push it. It can be extremely large, just not infinitely so. Because no one has ever observed an infinite stock price, this assumption is plausible.

SOME SPECIAL CASES

In a few useful special circumstances, we can come up with a value for the stock. What we have to do is make some simplifying assumptions about the pattern of future dividends. The three cases we consider are the following: (1) The dividend has a zero growth rate, (2) the dividend grows at a constant rate, and (3) the dividend grows at a constant rate after some length of time. We consider each of these separately.

Zero Growth   The case of zero growth is one we've already seen. A share of common stock in a company with a constant dividend is much like a share of preferred stock. From Chapter 6 (Example 6.7), we know that the dividend on a share of preferred stock has zero growth and thus is constant through time. For a zero-growth share of common stock, this implies that:

$$D_1 = D_2 = D_3 = D = \text{constant}$$

So, the value of the stock is:

$$P_0 = \frac{D}{(1 + R)^1} + \frac{D}{(1 + R)^2} + \frac{D}{(1 + R)^3} + \frac{D}{(1 + R)^4} + \frac{D}{(1 + R)^5} + \cdots$$

Because the dividend is always the same, the stock can be viewed as an ordinary perpetuity with a cash flow equal to D every period. The per-share value is thus given by:

$$P_0 = D/R \qquad\qquad\qquad [8.2]$$

where R is the required return.

For example, suppose the Paradise Prototyping Company has a policy of paying a $10 per share dividend every year. If this policy is to be continued indefinitely, what is the value of a share of stock if the required return is 20 percent? The stock in this case amounts to an ordinary perpetuity, so the stock is worth $10/.20 = $50 per share.

Constant Growth   Suppose we know that the dividend for some company always grows at a steady rate. Call this growth rate g. If we let D_0 be the dividend just paid, then the next dividend, D_1, is:

$$D_1 = D_0 \times (1 + g)$$

The dividend in two periods is:

$$\begin{aligned} D_2 &= D_1 \times (1 + g) \\ &= [D_0 \times (1 + g)] \times (1 + g) \\ &= D_0 \times (1 + g)^2 \end{aligned}$$

We could repeat this process to come up with the dividend at any point in the future. In general, from our discussion of compound growth in Chapter 6, we know that the dividend t periods into the future, D_t, is given by:

$$D_t = D_0 \times (1 + g)^t$$

As we have previously seen, an asset with cash flows that grow at a constant rate forever is called a *growing perpetuity*.

The assumption of steady dividend growth might strike you as peculiar. Why would the dividend grow at a constant rate? The reason is that, for many companies, steady growth in dividends is an explicit goal. For example, in 2008, Procter & Gamble, the Cincinnati-based maker of personal care and household products, increased its dividend by 14.3 percent to $1.60 per share; this increase was notable because it was the 52nd in a row. The subject of dividend growth falls under the general heading of dividend policy, so we will defer further discussion of it to a later chapter.

| Dividend Growth | EXAMPLE 8.2 |

The Hedless Corporation has just paid a dividend of $3 per share. The dividend of this company grows at a steady rate of 8 percent per year. Based on this information, what will the dividend be in five years?

Here we have a $3 current amount that grows at 8 percent per year for five years. The future amount is thus:

$3 \times 1.08^5 = \$3 \times 1.4693 = \$4.41$

The dividend will therefore increase by $1.41 over the coming five years.

If the dividend grows at a steady rate, then we have replaced the problem of forecasting an infinite number of future dividends with the problem of coming up with a single growth rate, a considerable simplification. In this case, if we take D_0 to be the dividend just paid and g to be the constant growth rate, the value of a share of stock can be written as:

$$P_0 = \frac{D_1}{(1 + R)^1} + \frac{D_2}{(1 + R)^2} + \frac{D_3}{(1 + R)^3} + \cdots$$

$$= \frac{D_0(1 + g)^1}{(1 + R)^1} + \frac{D_0(1 + g)^2}{(1 + R)^2} + \frac{D_0(1 + g)^3}{(1 + R)^3} + \cdots$$

As long as the growth rate, g, is less than the discount rate, r, the present value of this series of cash flows can be written simply as:

$$P_0 = \frac{D_0 \times (1 + g)}{R - g} = \frac{D_1}{R - g} \qquad [8.3]$$

This elegant result goes by a lot of different names. We will call it the **dividend growth model**. By any name, it is easy to use. To illustrate, suppose D_0 is $2.30, R is 13 percent, and g is 5 percent. The price per share in this case is:

$P_0 = D_0 \times (1 + g)/(R - g)$

$\quad = \$2.30 \times 1.05/(.13 - .05)$

$\quad = \$2.415/.08$

$\quad = \$30.19$

dividend growth model
A model that determines the current price of a stock as its dividend next period divided by the discount rate less the dividend growth rate.

We can actually use the dividend growth model to get the stock price at any point in time, not just today. In general, the price of the stock as of time t is:

$$P_t = \frac{D_t \times (1 + g)}{R - g} = \frac{D_{t+1}}{R - g} \qquad [8.4]$$

In our example, suppose we are interested in the price of the stock in five years, P_5. We first need the dividend at time 5, D_5. Because the dividend just paid is $2.30 and the growth rate is 5 percent per year, D_5 is:

$D_5 = \$2.30 \times 1.05^5 = \$2.30 \times 1.2763 = \$2.935$

From the dividend growth model, we get the price of the stock in five years:

$$P_5 = \frac{D_5 \times (1 + g)}{R - g} = \frac{\$2.935 \times 1.05}{.13 - .05} = \frac{\$3.0822}{.08} = \$38.53$$

| **EXAMPLE 8.3** | **Gordon Growth Company** |

The next dividend for the Gordon Growth Company will be $4 per share. Investors require a 16 percent return on companies such as Gordon. Gordon's dividend increases by 6 percent every year. Based on the dividend growth model, what is the value of Gordon's stock today? What is the value in four years?

The only tricky thing here is that the next dividend, D_1, is given as $4, so we won't multiply this by $(1 + g)$. With this in mind, the price per share is given by:

$P_0 = D_1/(R - g)$
$\quad = \$4/(.16 - .06)$
$\quad = \$4/.10$
$\quad = \$40$

Because we already have the dividend in one year, we know that the dividend in four years is equal to $D_1 \times (1 + g)^3 = \$4 \times 1.06^3 = \$4.764$. The price in four years is therefore:

$P_4 = D_4 \times (1 + g)/(R - g)$
$\quad = \$4.764 \times 1.06/(.16 - .06)$
$\quad = \$5.05/.10$
$\quad = \$50.50$

Notice in this example that P_4 is equal to $P_0 \times (1 + g)^4$.

$P_4 = \$50.50 = \$40 \times 1.06^4 = P_0 \times (1 + g)^4$

To see why this is so, notice first that:

$P_4 = D_5/(R - g)$

However, D_5 is just equal to $D_1 \times (1 + g)^4$, so we can write P_4 as:

$P_4 = D_1 \times (1 + g)^4/(R - g)$
$\quad = [D_1/(R - g)] \times (1 + g)^4$
$\quad = P_0 \times (1 + g)^4$

This last example illustrates that the dividend growth model makes the implicit assumption that the stock price will grow at the same constant rate as the dividend. This really isn't too surprising. What it tells us is that if the cash flows on an investment grow at a constant rate through time, so does the value of that investment.

You might wonder what would happen with the dividend growth model if the growth rate, g, were greater than the discount rate, R. It looks like we would get a negative stock price because $R - g$ would be less than zero. This is not what would happen.

Instead, if the constant growth rate exceeds the discount rate, then the stock price is infinitely large. Why? If the growth rate is bigger than the discount rate, the present value of the dividends keeps getting bigger. Essentially the same is true if the growth rate and the discount rate are equal. In both cases, the simplification that allows us to replace the infinite stream of dividends with the dividend growth model is "illegal," so the answers we get from the dividend growth model are nonsense unless the growth rate is less than the discount rate.

Finally, the expression we came up with for the constant growth case will work for any growing perpetuity, not just dividends on common stock. As we saw in Chapter 6, if C_1 is the next cash flow on a growing perpetuity, then the present value of the cash flows is given by:

Present value $= C_1/(R - g) = C_0(1 + g)/(R - g)$

Notice that this expression looks like the result for an ordinary perpetuity except that we have $R - g$ on the bottom instead of just R.

Nonconstant Growth   The next case we consider is nonconstant growth. The main reason to consider this case is to allow for "supernormal" growth rates over some finite length of time. As we discussed earlier, the growth rate cannot exceed the required return indefinitely, but it certainly could do so for some number of years. To avoid the problem of having to forecast and discount an infinite number of dividends, we will require that the dividends start growing at a constant rate sometime in the future.

For a simple example of nonconstant growth, consider the case of a company that is currently not paying dividends. You predict that, in five years, the company will pay a dividend for the first time. The dividend will be $.50 per share. You expect that this dividend will then grow at a rate of 10 percent per year indefinitely. The required return on companies such as this one is 20 percent. What is the price of the stock today?

To see what the stock is worth today, we first find out what it will be worth once dividends are paid. We can then calculate the present value of that future price to get today's price. The first dividend will be paid in five years, and the dividend will grow steadily from then on. Using the dividend growth model, we can say that the price in four years will be:

$$P_4 = D_4 \times (1 + g)/(R - g)$$
$$= D_5/(R - g)$$
$$= \$.50/(.20 - .10)$$
$$= \$5$$

If the stock will be worth $5 in four years, then we can get the current value by discounting this price back four years at 20 percent:

$$P_0 = \$5/1.20^4 = \$5/2.0736 = \$2.41$$

The stock is therefore worth $2.41 today.

The problem of nonconstant growth is only slightly more complicated if the dividends are not zero for the first several years. For example, suppose you have come up with the following dividend forecasts for the next three years:

Year	Expected Dividend
1	$1.00
2	$2.00
3	$2.50

After the third year, the dividend will grow at a constant rate of 5 percent per year. The required return is 10 percent. What is the value of the stock today?

In dealing with nonconstant growth, a time line can be helpful. Figure 8.1 illustrates one for this problem. The important thing to notice is when constant growth starts. As we've shown, for this problem, constant growth starts at time 3. This means we can use our constant growth model to determine the stock price at time 3, P_3. By far the most common mistake in this situation is to incorrectly identify the start of the constant growth phase and, as a result, calculate the future stock price at the wrong time.

As always, the value of the stock is the present value of all the future dividends. To calculate this present value, we first have to compute the present value of the stock price three years down the road, just as we did before. We then have to add in the present value of the

FIGURE 8.1

Nonconstant Growth

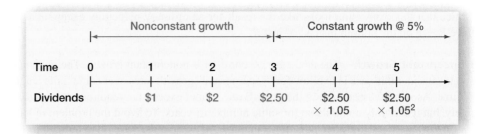

dividends that will be paid between now and then. So, the price in three years is:

$$P_3 = D_3 \times (1 + g)/(R - g)$$
$$= \$2.50 \times 1.05/(.10 - .05)$$
$$= \$52.50$$

We can now calculate the total value of the stock as the present value of the first three dividends plus the present value of the price at time 3, P_3:

$$P_0 = \frac{D_1}{(1 + R)^1} + \frac{D_2}{(1 + R)^2} + \frac{D_3}{(1 + R)^3} + \frac{P_3}{(1 + R)^3}$$
$$= \frac{\$1}{1.10} + \frac{2}{1.10^2} + \frac{2.50}{1.10^3} + \frac{52.50}{1.10^3}$$
$$= \$.91 + 1.65 + 1.88 + 39.44$$
$$= \$43.88$$

The value of the stock today is thus $43.88.

EXAMPLE 8.4   **Supernormal Growth**

Chain Reaction, Inc., has been growing at a phenomenal rate of 30 percent per year because of its rapid expansion and explosive sales. You believe this growth rate will last for three more years and will then drop to 10 percent per year. If the growth rate then remains at 10 percent indefinitely, what is the total value of the stock? Total dividends just paid were $5 million, and the required return is 20 percent.

Chain Reaction's situation is an example of supernormal growth. It is unlikely that a 30 percent growth rate can be sustained for any extended time. To value the equity in this company, we first need to calculate the total dividends over the supernormal growth period:

Year	Total Dividends (in millions)
1	$5.00 × 1.3 = $ 6.500
2	6.50 × 1.3 = 8.450
3	8.45 × 1.3 = 10.985

The price at time 3 can be calculated as:

$$P_3 = D_3 \times (1 + g)/(R - g)$$

where g is the long-run growth rate. So, we have:

$$P_3 = \$10.985 \times 1.10/(.20 - .10) = \$120.835$$

(continued)

To determine the value today, we need the present value of this amount plus the present value of the total dividends:

$$P_0 = \frac{D_1}{(1+R)^1} + \frac{D_2}{(1+R)^2} + \frac{D_3}{(1+R)^3} + \frac{P_3}{(1+R)^3}$$

$$= \frac{\$6.50}{1.20} + \frac{8.45}{1.20^2} + \frac{10.985}{1.20^3} + \frac{120.835}{1.20^3}$$

$$= \$5.42 + 5.87 + 6.36 + 69.93$$

$$= \$87.58$$

The total value of the stock today is thus $87.58 million. If there were, for example, 20 million shares, then the stock would be worth $87.58/20 = $4.38 per share.

Two-Stage Growth   The last case we consider is a special case of nonconstant growth: two-stage growth. Here, the idea is that the dividend will grow at a rate of g_1 for t years and then grow at a rate of g_2 thereafter forever. In this case, the value of the stock can be written as:

$$P_0 = \frac{D_1}{R - g_1} \times \left[1 - \left(\frac{1+g_1}{1+R}\right)^t\right] + \frac{P_t}{(1+R)^t} \qquad [8.5]$$

Notice that the first term in our expression is the present value of a growing annuity, which we discussed in Chapter 6. In this first stage, g_1 can be greater than R. The second part is the present value of the stock price once the second stage begins at time t.

We can calculate P_t as follows:

$$P_t = \frac{D_{t+1}}{R - g_2} = \frac{D_0 \times (1+g_1)^t \times (1+g_2)}{R - g_2} \qquad [8.6]$$

In this calculation, we need the dividend at time $t + 1$, D_{t+1}, to get the stock price at time t, P_t. Notice that to get it, we grew the current dividend, D_0, at rate g_1 for t periods and then grew it one period at rate g_2. Also, in this second stage, g_2 must be less than R.

Two-Stage Growth   **EXAMPLE 8.5**

The Highfield Company's dividend is expected to grow at 20 percent for the next five years. After that, the growth is expected to be 4 percent forever. If the required return is 10 percent, what's the value of the stock? The dividend just paid was $2.

There is a fair amount of computation here, but it is mostly just "plug and chug" with a calculator. We can start by calculating the stock price five years from now, P_5:

$$P_5 = \frac{D_6}{R - g_2} = \frac{D_0 \times (1+g_1)^5 \times (1+g_2)}{R - g_2}$$

$$= \frac{\$2 \times (1+.20)^5 \times (1+.04)}{.10 - .04} = \frac{\$5.18}{.06}$$

$$= \$86.26$$

We then plug into our two-stage growth formula to get the price today:

$$P_0 = \frac{D_1}{R - g_1} \times \left[1 - \left(\frac{1+g_1}{1+R}\right)^t\right] + \frac{P_t}{(1+R)^t}$$

$$= \frac{\$2 \times (1+.20)}{.10 - .20} \times \left[1 - \left(\frac{1+.20}{1+.10}\right)^5\right] + \frac{\$86.26}{(1+.10)^5}$$

$$= \$66.64$$

(continued)

Notice that we were given D_0 = \$2 here, so we had to grow it by 20 percent for one period to get D_1. Notice also that g_1 is bigger than R in this problem, but that fact does not cause a problem.

COMPONENTS OF THE REQUIRED RETURN

Thus far, we have taken the required return, or discount rate, R, as given. We will have quite a bit to say about this subject in Chapters 12 and 13. For now, we want to examine the implications of the dividend growth model for this required return. Earlier, we calculated P_0 as:

$$P_0 = D_1/(R - g)$$

If we rearrange this to solve for R, we get:

$$R - g = D_1/P_0$$
$$R = D_1/P_0 + g \qquad [8.7]$$

This tells us that the total return, R, has two components. The first of these, D_1/P_0, is called the **dividend yield**. Because this is calculated as the expected cash dividend divided by the current price, it is conceptually similar to the current yield on a bond.

The second part of the total return is the growth rate, g. We know that the dividend growth rate is also the rate at which the stock price grows (see Example 8.3). Thus, this growth rate can be interpreted as the **capital gains yield**—that is, the rate at which the value of the investment grows.[2]

To illustrate the components of the required return, suppose we observe a stock selling for \$20 per share. The next dividend will be \$1 per share. You think that the dividend will grow by 10 percent per year more or less indefinitely. What return does this stock offer if this is correct?

The dividend growth model calculates total return as:

$$R = \text{Dividend yield} + \text{Capital gains yield}$$
$$R = \quad D_1/P_0 \quad + \quad\quad g$$

In this case, total return works out to be:

$$R = \$1/20 + 10\%$$
$$= 5\% + 10\%$$
$$= 15\%$$

This stock, therefore, has an expected return of 15 percent.

We can verify this answer by calculating the price in one year, P_1, using 15 percent as the required return. Based on the dividend growth model, this price is:

$$P_1 = D_1 \times (1 + g)/(R - g)$$
$$= \$1 \times 1.10/(.15 - .10)$$
$$= \$1.10/.05$$
$$= \$22$$

dividend yield
A stock's expected cash dividend divided by its current price.

capital gains yield
The dividend growth rate, or the rate at which the value of an investment grows.

---

[2]Here and elsewhere, we use the term *capital gains* a little loosely. For the record, a capital gain (or loss) is, strictly speaking, something defined by the IRS. For our purposes, it would be more accurate (but less common) to use the term *price appreciation* instead of *capital gain*.

Notice that this $22 is $20 × 1.1, so the stock price has grown by 10 percent as it should. If you pay $20 for the stock today, you will get a $1 dividend at the end of the year, and you will have a $22 − 20 = $2 gain. Your dividend yield is thus $1/20 = 5%. Your capital gains yield is $2/20 = 10%, so your total return would be 5% + 10% = 15%.

To get a feel for actual numbers in this context, consider that, according to the 2008 Value Line *Investment Survey*, Procter & Gamble's dividends were expected to grow by 9 percent over the next 5 or so years, compared to a historical growth rate of 10.5 percent over the preceding 5 years and 11 percent over the preceding 10 years. In 2008, the projected dividend for the coming year was given as $1.67. The stock price at that time was about $66 per share. What is the return investors require on P&G? Here, the dividend yield is 2.5 percent and the capital gains yield is 9 percent, giving a total required return of 11.5 percent on P&G stock.

Our discussion of stock valuation is summarized in Table 8.1.

TABLE 8.1

Summary of Stock Valuation

I.   The General Case

In general, the price today of a share of stock, P_0, is the present value of all of its future dividends, $D_1, D_2, D_3, \ldots$:

$$P_0 = \frac{D_1}{(1+R)^1} + \frac{D_2}{(1+R)^2} + \frac{D_3}{(1+R)^3} + \cdots$$

where R is the required return.

II.   Constant Growth Case

If the dividend grows at a steady rate, g, then the price can be written as:

$$P_0 = \frac{D_1}{R-g}$$

This result is called the *dividend growth model.*

III.   Nonconstant Growth

If the dividend grows steadily after t periods, then the price can be written as:

$$P_0 = \frac{D_1}{(1+R)^1} + \frac{D_2}{(1+R)^2} + \cdots + \frac{D_t}{(1+R)^t} + \frac{P_t}{(1+R)^t}$$

where

$$P_t = \frac{D_t \times (1+g)}{(R-g)}$$

IV.   Two-Stage Growth

If the dividend grows at rate g_1 for t periods and then grows at rate g_2 thereafter, then the price can be written as:

$$P_0 = \frac{D_1}{R-g_1} \times \left[1 - \left(\frac{1+g_1}{1+R}\right)^t\right] + \frac{P_t}{(1+R)^t}$$

where

$$P_t = \frac{D_{t+1}}{R-g_2} = \frac{D_0 \times (1+g_1)^t \times (1+g_2)}{R-g_2}$$

V.   The Required Return

The required return, R, can be written as the sum of two things:

$$R = D_1/P_0 + g$$

where D_1/P_0 is the *dividend yield* and g is the *capital gains yield* (which is the same thing as the growth rate in dividends for the steady growth case).

8.2 Some Features of Common and Preferred Stocks

In discussing common stock features, we focus on shareholder rights and dividend payments. For preferred stock, we explain what *preferred* means, and we also debate whether preferred stock is really debt or equity.

COMMON STOCK FEATURES

common stock
Equity without priority for dividends or in bankruptcy.

The term **common stock** means different things to different people, but it is usually applied to stock that has no special preference either in receiving dividends or in bankruptcy.

Shareholder Rights   The conceptual structure of the corporation assumes that shareholders elect directors who, in turn, hire managers to carry out their directives. Shareholders, therefore, control the corporation through the right to elect the directors. Generally, only shareholders have this right.

Directors are elected each year at an annual meeting. Although there are exceptions (discussed next), the general idea is "one share, one vote" (*not* one share*holder*, one vote). Corporate democracy is thus very different from our political democracy. With corporate democracy, the "golden rule" prevails absolutely.[3]

Directors are elected at an annual shareholders' meeting by a vote of the holders of a majority of shares who are present and entitled to vote. However, the exact mechanism for electing directors differs across companies. The most important difference is whether shares must be voted cumulatively or voted straight.

To illustrate the two different voting procedures, imagine that a corporation has two shareholders: Smith with 20 shares and Jones with 80 shares. Both want to be a director. Jones does not want Smith, however. We assume there are a total of four directors to be elected.

cumulative voting
A procedure in which a shareholder may cast all votes for one member of the board of directors.

The effect of **cumulative voting** is to permit minority participation.[4] If cumulative voting is permitted, the total number of votes that each shareholder may cast is determined first. This is usually calculated as the number of shares (owned or controlled) multiplied by the number of directors to be elected.

With cumulative voting, the directors are elected all at once. In our example, this means that the top four vote getters will be the new directors. A shareholder can distribute votes however he or she wishes.

Will Smith get a seat on the board? If we ignore the possibility of a five-way tie, then the answer is yes. Smith will cast $20 \times 4 = 80$ votes, and Jones will cast $80 \times 4 = 320$ votes. If Smith gives all his votes to himself, he is assured of a directorship. The reason is

[3]The golden rule: Whosoever has the gold makes the rules.

[4]By *minority participation,* we mean participation by shareholders with relatively small amounts of stock.

that Jones can't divide 320 votes among four candidates in such a way as to give all of them more than 80 votes, so Smith will finish fourth at worst.

In general, if there are *N* directors up for election, then $1/(N + 1)$ percent of the stock plus one share will guarantee you a seat. In our current example, this is $1/(4 + 1) = 20\%$. So the more seats that are up for election at one time, the easier (and cheaper) it is to win one.

With **straight voting**, the directors are elected one at a time. Each time, Smith can cast 20 votes and Jones can cast 80. As a consequence, Jones will elect all of the candidates. The only way to guarantee a seat is to own 50 percent plus one share. This also guarantees that you will win every seat, so it's really all or nothing.

straight voting
A procedure in which a shareholder may cast all votes for each member of the board of directors.

Buying the Election   EXAMPLE 8.6

Stock in JRJ Corporation sells for $20 per share and features cumulative voting. There are 10,000 shares outstanding. If three directors are up for election, how much does it cost to ensure yourself a seat on the board?

The question here is how many shares of stock it will take to get a seat. The answer is 2,501, so the cost is $2,501 \times \$20 = \$50,020$. Why 2,501? Because there is no way the remaining 7,499 votes can be divided among three people to give all of them more than 2,501 votes. For example, suppose two people receive 2,502 votes and the first two seats. A third person can receive at most $10,000 - 2,502 - 2,502 - 2,501 = 2,495$, so the third seat is yours.

As we've illustrated, straight voting can "freeze out" minority shareholders; that is why many states have mandatory cumulative voting. In states where cumulative voting is mandatory, devices have been worked out to minimize its impact.

One such device is to stagger the voting for the board of directors. With staggered elections, only a fraction of the directorships are up for election at a particular time. Thus if only two directors are up for election at any one time, it will take $1/(2 + 1) = 33.33\%$ of the stock plus one share to guarantee a seat.

Overall, staggering has two basic effects:

1. Staggering makes it more difficult for a minority to elect a director when there is cumulative voting because there are fewer directors to be elected at one time.

2. Staggering makes takeover attempts less likely to be successful because it makes it more difficult to vote in a majority of new directors.

We should note that staggering may serve a beneficial purpose. It provides "institutional memory"—that is, continuity on the board of directors. This may be important for corporations with significant long-range plans and projects.

Proxy Voting A **proxy** is the grant of authority by a shareholder to someone else to vote his or her shares. For convenience, much of the voting in large public corporations is actually done by proxy.

proxy
A grant of authority by a shareholder allowing another individual to vote his or her shares.

As we have seen, with straight voting, each share of stock has one vote. The owner of 10,000 shares has 10,000 votes. Large companies have hundreds of thousands or even millions of shareholders. Shareholders can come to the annual meeting and vote in person, or they can transfer their right to vote to another party.

Obviously, management always tries to get as many proxies as possible transferred to it. However, if shareholders are not satisfied with management, an "outside" group of shareholders can try to obtain votes via proxy. They can vote by proxy in an attempt to replace management by electing enough directors. The resulting battle is called a *proxy fight*.

Classes of Stock   Some firms have more than one class of common stock. Often the classes are created with unequal voting rights. The Ford Motor Company, for example, has Class B common stock, which is not publicly traded (it is held by Ford family interests and trusts). This class has 40 percent of the voting power, even though it represents less than 10 percent of the total number of shares outstanding.

There are many other cases of corporations with different classes of stock. For example, at one time, General Motors had its "GM Classic" shares (the original) and two additional classes, Class E ("GME") and Class H ("GMH"). These classes were created to help pay for two large acquisitions, Electronic Data Systems and Hughes Aircraft. Another good example is Google, the Web search company, which only recently became publicly owned. Google has two classes of common stock, A and B. The Class A shares are held by the public, and each share has one vote. The Class B shares are held by company insiders, and each Class B share has 10 votes. As a result, Google's founders and managers control the company.

Historically, the New York Stock Exchange did not allow companies to create classes of publicly traded common stock with unequal voting rights. Exceptions (like Ford) appear to have been made. In addition, many non-NYSE companies have dual classes of common stock.

A primary reason for creating dual or multiple classes of stock has to do with control of the firm. If such stock exists, management of a firm can raise equity capital by issuing non-voting or limited-voting stock while maintaining control.

The subject of unequal voting rights is controversial in the United States, and the idea of one share, one vote has a strong following and a long history. Interestingly, however, shares with unequal voting rights are quite common in the United Kingdom and elsewhere around the world.

Other Rights   The value of a share of common stock in a corporation is directly related to the general rights of shareholders. In addition to the right to vote for directors, shareholders usually have the following rights:

1. The right to share proportionally in dividends paid.
2. The right to share proportionally in assets remaining after liabilities have been paid in a liquidation.
3. The right to vote on stockholder matters of great importance, such as a merger. Voting is usually done at the annual meeting or a special meeting.

In addition, stockholders sometimes have the right to share proportionally in any new stock sold. This is called the *preemptive right*.

Essentially, a preemptive right means that a company that wishes to sell stock must first offer it to the existing stockholders before offering it to the general public. The purpose is to give stockholders the opportunity to protect their proportionate ownership in the corporation.

dividends
Payments by a corporation to shareholders, made in either cash or stock.

Dividends   A distinctive feature of corporations is that they have shares of stock on which they are authorized by law to pay dividends to their shareholders. **Dividends** paid to shareholders represent a return on the capital directly or indirectly contributed to the corporation by the shareholders. The payment of dividends is at the discretion of the board of directors.

Some important characteristics of dividends include the following:

1. Unless a dividend is declared by the board of directors of a corporation, it is not a liability of the corporation. A corporation cannot default on an undeclared dividend.

As a consequence, corporations cannot become bankrupt because of nonpayment of dividends. The amount of the dividend and even whether it is paid are decisions based on the business judgment of the board of directors.

2. The payment of dividends by the corporation is not a business expense. Dividends are not deductible for corporate tax purposes. In short, dividends are paid out of the corporation's aftertax profits.

3. Dividends received by individual shareholders are taxable. In 2008, the tax rate was 15 percent, but this favorable rate may change. However, corporations that own stock in other corporations are permitted to exclude 70 percent of the dividend amounts they receive and are taxed on only the remaining 30 percent.[5]

PREFERRED STOCK FEATURES

Preferred stock differs from common stock because it has preference over common stock in the payment of dividends and in the distribution of corporation assets in the event of liquidation. *Preference* means only that the holders of the preferred shares must receive a dividend (in the case of an ongoing firm) before holders of common shares are entitled to anything.

Preferred stock is a form of equity from a legal and tax standpoint. It is important to note, however, that holders of preferred stock sometimes have no voting privileges.

preferred stock
Stock with dividend priority over common stock, normally with a fixed dividend rate, sometimes without voting rights.

Stated Value   Preferred shares have a stated liquidating value, usually $100 per share. The cash dividend is described in terms of dollars per share. For example, General Motors "$5 preferred" easily translates into a dividend yield of 5 percent of stated value.

Cumulative and Noncumulative Dividends   A preferred dividend is *not* like interest on a bond. The board of directors may decide not to pay the dividends on preferred shares, and their decision may have nothing to do with the current net income of the corporation.

Dividends payable on preferred stock are either *cumulative* or *noncumulative;* most are cumulative. If preferred dividends are cumulative and are not paid in a particular year, they will be carried forward as an *arrearage*. Usually, both the accumulated (past) preferred dividends and the current preferred dividends must be paid before the common shareholders can receive anything.

Unpaid preferred dividends are *not* debts of the firm. Directors elected by the common shareholders can defer preferred dividends indefinitely. However, in such cases, common shareholders must also forgo dividends. In addition, holders of preferred shares are often granted voting and other rights if preferred dividends have not been paid for some time. For example, as of summer 1996, USAir had failed to pay dividends on one of its preferred stock issues for six quarters. As a consequence, the holders of the shares were allowed to nominate two people to represent their interests on the airline's board. Because preferred stockholders receive no interest on the accumulated dividends, some have argued that firms have an incentive to delay paying preferred dividends; but, as we have seen, this may mean sharing control with preferred stockholders.

Is Preferred Stock Really Debt?   A good case can be made that preferred stock is really debt in disguise, a kind of equity bond. Preferred shareholders receive a stated dividend

[5]For the record, the 70 percent exclusion applies when the recipient owns less than 20 percent of the outstanding stock in a corporation. If a corporation owns more than 20 percent but less than 80 percent, the exclusion is 80 percent. If more than 80 percent is owned, the corporation can file a single "consolidated" return and the exclusion is effectively 100 percent.

only; and if the corporation is liquidated, preferred shareholders get a stated value. Often, preferred stocks carry credit ratings much like those of bonds. Furthermore, preferred stock is sometimes convertible into common stock, and preferred stocks are often callable.

In addition, many issues of preferred stock have obligatory sinking funds. The existence of such a sinking fund effectively creates a final maturity because it means that the entire issue will ultimately be retired. For these reasons, preferred stock seems to be a lot like debt. However, for tax purposes, preferred dividends are treated like common stock dividends.

In the 1990s, firms began to sell securities that looked a lot like preferred stocks but are treated as debt for tax purposes. The new securities were given interesting acronyms like TOPrS (trust-originated preferred securities, or toppers), MIPS (monthly income preferred securities), and QUIPS (quarterly income preferred securities), among others. Because of various specific features, these instruments can be counted as debt for tax purposes, making the interest payments tax deductible. Payments made to investors in these instruments are treated as interest for personal income taxes. Until 2003, interest payments and dividends were taxed at the same marginal tax rate. When the tax rate on dividend payments was reduced, these instruments were not included, so individuals must still pay their higher income tax rate on dividend payments received from these instruments.

Concept Questions

8.2a What is a proxy?

8.2b What rights do stockholders have?

8.2c Why is preferred stock called *preferred*?

8.3 The Stock Markets

primary market
The market in which new securities are originally sold to investors.

Back in Chapter 1, we briefly mentioned that shares of stock are bought and sold on various stock exchanges, the two most important of which are the New York Stock Exchange and the NASDAQ. From our earlier discussion, recall that the stock market consists of a **primary market** and a **secondary market**. In the primary, or new issue, market, shares of stock are first brought to the market and sold to investors. In the secondary market, existing shares are traded among investors.

secondary market
The market in which previously issued securities are traded among investors.

In the primary market, companies sell securities to raise money. We will discuss this process in detail in a later chapter. We therefore focus mainly on secondary market activity in this section. We conclude with a discussion of how stock prices are quoted in the financial press.

dealer
An agent who buys and sells securities from inventory.

DEALERS AND BROKERS

Because most securities transactions involve dealers and brokers, it is important to understand exactly what is meant by the terms *dealer* and *broker*. A **dealer** maintains an inventory and stands ready to buy and sell at any time. In contrast, a **broker** brings buyers and sellers together but does not maintain an inventory. Thus, when we speak of used car dealers and real estate brokers, we recognize that the used car dealer maintains an inventory, whereas the real estate broker does not.

broker
An agent who arranges security transactions among investors.

In the securities markets, a dealer stands ready to buy securities from investors wishing to sell them and sell securities to investors wishing to buy them. Recall from our previous chapter that the price the dealer is willing to pay is called the *bid price*. The price at which the dealer will sell is called the *ask price* (sometimes called the asked, offered, or offering price). The difference between the bid and ask prices is called the *spread,* and it is the basic source of dealer profits.

Dealers exist in all areas of the economy, not just the stock markets. For example, your local college bookstore is probably both a primary and a secondary market textbook dealer. If you buy a new book, this is a primary market transaction. If you buy a used book, this is a secondary market transaction, and you pay the store's ask price. If you sell the book back, you receive the store's bid price (often half of the ask price). The bookstore's spread is the difference between the two prices.

In contrast, a securities broker arranges transactions between investors, matching investors wishing to buy securities with investors wishing to sell securities. The distinctive characteristic of security brokers is that they do not buy or sell securities for their own accounts. Facilitating trades by others is their business.

How big is the bid–ask spread on your favorite stock? Check out the latest quotes at www.bloomberg.com.

ORGANIZATION OF THE NYSE

The New York Stock Exchange, or NYSE, popularly known as the Big Board, celebrated its bicentennial a few years ago. It has occupied its current location on Wall Street since the turn of the twentieth century. Measured in terms of dollar volume of activity and the total value of shares listed, it is the largest stock market in the world.

Members   The NYSE has 1,366 exchange **members**. Prior to 2006, the exchange members were said to own "seats" on the exchange, and collectively the members of the exchange were also the owners. For this and other reasons, seats were valuable and were bought and sold fairly regularly. Seat prices reached a record $4 million in 2005.

In 2006, all of this changed when the NYSE became a publicly owned corporation. Naturally, its stock is listed on the NYSE. Now, instead of purchasing seats, exchange members must purchase trading licenses, the number of which is still limited to 1,366. In 2008, a license would set you back a cool $40,000—per year. Having a license entitles you to buy and sell securities on the floor of the exchange. Different members play different roles in this regard.

The largest number of NYSE members are registered as **commission brokers**. The business of a commission broker is to execute customer orders to buy and sell stocks. A commission broker's primary responsibility to customers is to get the best possible prices for their orders. The exact number varies, but usually about 500 NYSE members are commission brokers. NYSE commission brokers typically are employees of brokerage companies such as Merrill Lynch.

Second in number of NYSE members are **specialists**, so named because each of them acts as an assigned dealer for a small set of securities. With a few exceptions, each security listed for trading on the NYSE is assigned to a single specialist. Specialists are also called *market makers* because they are obligated to maintain a fair, orderly market for the securities assigned to them.

Specialists post bid prices and ask prices for securities assigned to them. Specialists make a market by standing ready to buy at bid prices and sell at asked prices when there is a temporary disparity between the flow of buy orders and that of sell orders for a security. In this capacity, they act as dealers for their own accounts.

member
As of 2006, a member is the owner of a trading license on the NYSE.

commission brokers
NYSE members who execute customer orders to buy and sell stock transmitted to the exchange floor.

specialist
A NYSE member acting as a dealer in a small number of securities on the exchange floor; often called a *market maker*.

floor brokers
NYSE members who
execute orders for
commission brokers on a
fee basis; sometimes called
$2 brokers.

Third in number of exchange members are **floor brokers**. Floor brokers are used by commission brokers who are too busy to handle certain orders themselves. Such commission brokers will delegate some orders to floor brokers for execution. Floor brokers are sometimes called *$2 brokers,* a name earned when the standard fee for their service was only $2.

SuperDOT system
An electronic NYSE system
allowing orders to be
transmitted directly to the
specialist.

In recent years, floor brokers have become less important on the exchange floor because of the efficient **SuperDOT system** (the *DOT* stands for Designated Order Turnaround), which allows orders to be transmitted electronically directly to the specialist. SuperDOT trading now accounts for a substantial percentage of all trading on the NYSE, particularly on smaller orders.

floor traders
NYSE members who trade
for their own accounts,
trying to anticipate
temporary price
fluctuations.

Finally, a small number of NYSE members are **floor traders** who independently trade for their own accounts. Floor traders try to anticipate temporary price fluctuations and profit from them by buying low and selling high. In recent decades, the number of floor traders has declined substantially, suggesting that it has become increasingly difficult to profit from short-term trading on the exchange floor.

Operations   Now that we have a basic idea of how the NYSE is organized and who the major players are, we turn to the question of how trading actually takes place. Fundamentally, the business of the NYSE is to attract and process **order flow**. The term *order flow* means the flow of customer orders to buy and sell stocks. The customers of the NYSE are the millions of individual investors and tens of thousands of institutional investors who place their orders to buy and sell shares in NYSE-listed companies. The NYSE has been quite successful in attracting order flow. Currently, it is not unusual for well over a billion shares to change hands in a single day.

order flow
The flow of customer
orders to buy and sell
securities.

Floor Activity   It is quite likely that you have seen footage of the NYSE trading floor on television, or you may have visited the NYSE and viewed exchange floor activity from the visitors' gallery (it's worth the trip). Either way, you would have seen a big room, about the size of a basketball gym. This big room is called, technically, "the Big Room." There are a few other, smaller rooms that you normally don't see, one of which is called "the Garage" because that is what it was before it was taken over for trading.

On the floor of the exchange are a number of stations, each with a roughly figure-eight shape. These stations have multiple counters with numerous terminal screens above and on the sides. People operate behind and in front of the counters in relatively stationary positions.

*Take a virtual
field trip to the New York
Stock Exchange at
www.nyse.com.*

Other people move around on the exchange floor, frequently returning to the many telephones positioned along the exchange walls. In all, you may be reminded of worker ants moving around an ant colony. It is natural to wonder, "What are all those people doing down there (and why are so many wearing funny-looking coats)?"

As an overview of exchange floor activity, here is a quick look at what goes on. Each of the counters at a figure-eight–shaped station is a **specialist's post**. Specialists normally operate in front of their posts to monitor and manage trading in the stocks assigned to them. Clerical employees working for the specialists operate behind the counter. Moving from the many telephones lining the walls of the exchange out to the exchange floor and back again are swarms of commission brokers, receiving telephoned customer orders, walking out to specialists' posts where the orders can be executed, and returning to confirm order executions and receive new customer orders.

specialist's post
A fixed place on the
exchange floor where the
specialist operates.

To better understand activity on the NYSE trading floor, imagine yourself as a commission broker. Your phone clerk has just handed you an order to sell 20,000 shares of Wal-Mart for a customer of the brokerage company that employs you. The customer wants to sell the stock at the best possible price as soon as possible. You immediately walk (running violates exchange rules) to the specialist's post where Wal-Mart stock is traded.

As you approach the specialist's post where Wal-Mart is traded, you check the terminal screen for information on the current market price. The screen reveals that the last executed trade was at 60.10 and that the specialist is bidding 60 per share. You could immediately sell to the specialist at 60, but that would be too easy.

Instead, as the customer's representative, you are obligated to get the best possible price. It is your job to "work" the order, and your job depends on providing satisfactory order execution service. So, you look around for another broker who represents a customer who wants to buy Wal-Mart stock. Luckily, you quickly find another broker at the specialist's post with an order to buy 20,000 shares. Noticing that the specialist is asking 60.10 per share, you both agree to execute your orders with each other at a price of 60.05. This price is exactly halfway between the specialist's bid and ask prices, and it saves each of your customers .05 × 20,000 = $1,000 as compared to dealing at the posted prices.

For a very actively traded stock, there may be many buyers and sellers around the specialist's post, and most of the trading will be done directly between brokers. This is called trading in the "crowd." In such cases, the specialist's responsibility is to maintain order and to make sure that all buyers and sellers receive a fair price. In other words, the specialist essentially functions as a referee.

More often, however, there will be no crowd at the specialist's post. Going back to our Wal-Mart example, suppose you are unable to quickly find another broker with an order to buy 20,000 shares. Because you have an order to sell immediately, you may have no choice but to sell to the specialist at the bid price of 60. In this case, the need to execute an order quickly takes priority, and the specialist provides the liquidity necessary to allow immediate order execution.

Finally, note that colored coats are worn by many of the people on the floor of the exchange. The color of the coat indicates the person's job or position. Clerks, runners, visitors, exchange officials, and so on wear particular colors to identify themselves. Also, things can get a little hectic on a busy day, with the result that good clothing doesn't last long; the cheap coats offer some protection.

NASDAQ OPERATIONS

In terms of total dollar volume of trading, the second largest stock market in the United States is NASDAQ (say "Naz-dak"). The somewhat odd name originally was an acronym for the National Association of Securities Dealers Automated Quotations system, but NASDAQ is now a name in its own right.

Introduced in 1971, the NASDAQ market is a computer network of securities dealers and others that disseminates timely security price quotes to computer screens worldwide. NASDAQ dealers act as market makers for securities listed on NASDAQ. As market makers, NASDAQ dealers post bid and ask prices at which they accept sell and buy orders, respectively. With each price quote, they also post the number of stock shares that they obligate themselves to trade at their quoted prices.

Like NYSE specialists, NASDAQ market makers trade on an inventory basis—that is, using their inventory as a buffer to absorb buy and sell order imbalances. Unlike the NYSE specialist system, NASDAQ features multiple market makers for actively traded stocks. Thus, there are two key differences between the NYSE and NASDAQ:

1. NASDAQ is a computer network and has no physical location where trading takes place.
2. NASDAQ has a multiple market maker system rather than a specialist system.

over-the-counter (OTC) market
Securities market in which trading is almost exclusively done through dealers who buy and sell for their own inventories.

Traditionally, a securities market largely characterized by dealers who buy and sell securities for their own inventories is called an **over-the-counter (OTC) market**. Consequently, NASDAQ is often referred to as an OTC market. However, in their efforts to promote a distinct image, NASDAQ officials prefer that the term OTC not be used when referring to the NASDAQ market. Nevertheless, old habits die hard, and many people still refer to NASDAQ as an OTC market.

By 2008, the NASDAQ had grown to the point that it was, by some measures, bigger than the NYSE. For example, on May 7, 2008, 2.3 billion shares were traded on the NASDAQ versus 1.3 billion on the NYSE. In dollars, NASDAQ trading volume for the day was $68.6 billion compared to $48.8 billion for the NYSE.

NASDAQ
(www.nasdaq.com) *has a great Web site; check it out!*

The NASDAQ is actually made up of three separate markets: the NASDAQ Global Select Market, the NASDAQ Global Market, and the NASDAQ Capital Market. As the market for NASDAQ's larger and more actively traded securities, the Global Select Market lists about 1,200 companies (as of early 2008), including some of the best-known companies in the world, such as Microsoft and Intel. Global Market companies are somewhat smaller in size, and NASDAQ lists about 1,450 of these. Finally, the smallest companies listed on NASDAQ are in the NASDAQ Capital Market; about 550 are currently listed. Of course, as Capital Market companies become more established, they may move up to the Global Market or Global Select Market.

electronic communications network (ECN)
A Web site that allows investors to trade directly with each other.

ECNs In a very important development in the late 1990s, the NASDAQ system was opened to so-called **electronic communications networks (ECNs)**. ECNs are basically Web sites that allow investors to trade directly with one another. Investor buy and sell orders placed on ECNs are transmitted to the NASDAQ and displayed along with market maker bid and ask prices. As a result, the ECNs open up the NASDAQ by essentially allowing individual investors, not just market makers, to enter orders. As a result, the ECNs act to increase liquidity and competition.

Of course, the NYSE and NASDAQ are not the only places stocks are traded. See our nearby *Work the Web* box for a discussion of somewhat wilder markets.

You can get real-time stock quotes on the Web. See finance.yahoo.com *for details.*

STOCK MARKET REPORTING

In recent years, the reporting of stock prices and related information has increasingly moved from traditional print media, such as *The Wall Street Journal,* to various Web sites. Yahoo! Finance (finance.yahoo.com) is a good example. We went there and requested a

---

WORK THE WEB

Where do companies go when they can't (or don't want to) meet the listing requirements of the larger stock exchanges? Two options are the Over-the-Counter Bulletin Board (OTCBB) and the Pink Sheets. These two electronic markets are part of the Wild, Wild West of stock trading. The somewhat odd names have simple explanations. The OTCBB began as an electronic bulletin board that was created to facilitate OTC trading in nonlisted stocks. The name "Pink Sheets" just reflects the fact that, at one time, prices for such stocks were quoted on pink sheets of paper.

The well-known markets such as NASDAQ and the NYSE have relatively strict listing requirements. If a company fails to meet these requirements, it can be delisted. The OTCBB and the Pink Sheets, on the other hand, have no listing requirements. The OTCBB does require that companies file financial statements with the SEC (or other relevant agency), but the Pink Sheets does not.

(continued)

Stocks traded on these markets often have very low prices and are frequently referred to as *penny stocks, microcaps,* or even *nanocaps*. Relatively few brokers do any research on these companies, so information is often spread through word of mouth or the Internet, not the most reliable of sources. In fact, for many stocks, these markets often look like big electronic rumor mills and gossip factories. To get a feel for what trading looks like, we captured a typical screen from the OTCBB Web site (www.otcbb.com):

Market Statistics

Data delayed 15-20 minutes

OTCBB ▾   Vol Actives ▾   GO

Name	Symbol	Last	Tick	Chg	% Chg	Open	High	Low	Volume
Earth Biofuels Inc.	EBOF	.016	▲	.001	6.67%	.016	.02	.014	771.16 m
SmarTire Systems Inc.	SMTR	.0002	—	.00	.00%	.0001	.0002	.0001	211.87 m
Syndication Inc.	SYDI	.0002	▼	-.0001	-33.33%	.0002	.0003	.0002	118.12 m
iVoice Inc.	IVOI	.0002	—	.00	.00%	.0001	.0002	.0001	72.12 m
AmeriResource Technologies Inc.	ARRT	.0001	—	.00	.00%	.0001	.0001	.0001	36.97 m
Avitar Inc.	AVTI	.0006	▼	-.0002	-25.00%	.0008	.0009	.0006	21.8 m
Universal Detection Technology	UDTT	.0005	—	.00	.00%	.0004	.0005	.0004	20.9 m
Fonix Corp.	FNIX	.0002	▲	.0001	100.00%	.0002	.0002	.0001	18.85 m
Spongetech Delivery Systems Inc.	SPNG	.0468	▲	.0068	17.00%	.042	.048	.04	17.14 m
Gulf Coast Oil & Gas Inc.	GCOG	.0016	▲	.0002	14.29%	.0014	.0016	.0012	16.56 m

First, take a look at the returns. Fonix Corp. had a return at this point in the day of 100 percent! That's not something you see very often. Of course, the big return was generated with a whopping price increase of $.0001 per share. A stock listed on the OTCBB is often the most actively traded stock on any particular day. For example, by the end of this particular day, Microsoft was the most active stock on NASDAQ, trading about 69.5 million shares. Four stocks on the OTCBB traded even more shares. Earth Biofuels, Inc., led the way with slightly over 771 million shares traded. But, at an average price of, say $.015 per share, the total dollar volume in Earth Biofuels was all of $11,565,000. In contrast, trades in Microsoft amounted to about $2 billion.

The Pink Sheets (www.pinksheets.com) is operated by a privately owned company. To be listed on the Pink Sheets, a company just has to find a market maker willing to trade in the company's stock. Companies list on the Pink Sheets for various reasons. Small companies that do not wish to meet listing requirements are one type. Foreign companies often list on the Pink Sheets because they do not prepare their financial statements according to GAAP, a requirement for listing on U.S. stock exchanges. There are many companies that were formerly listed on bigger stock markets that were either delisted involuntarily or chose to "go dark" for various reasons, including, as we discussed in Chapter 1, the costs associated with Sarbox compliance.

All in all, the OTCBB and Pink Sheets can be pretty wild places to trade. Low stock prices allow for huge percentage returns on small stock price movements. Be advised, however, that attempts at manipulation and fraud are commonplace. Also, stocks on these markets are often thinly traded, meaning there is little volume. It is not unusual for a stock listed on either market to have no trades on a given day. Even two or three days in a row without a trade in a particular stock is not uncommon.

Questions

1. After the close of the markets (4 PM Eastern time), go to finance.yahoo.com and find the stocks on the major exchanges that were the most active during the day. Now go to www.otcbb.com and find the most active stocks traded on the OTCBB for the same day. How many stocks on the OTCBB were more active than the most active stock on the NYSE? The NASDAQ?

2. What were the biggest percentage winners and losers on the OTCBB during the current day? How much did the stock price increase or decrease to account for this change?

stock quote on wholesale club Costco, which is listed on the NASDAQ. Here is a portion of what we found:

Most of this information is self-explanatory. Two prices are reported, one in real time ($73.31) and one with a 15-minute delay ($73.28). Availability of real-time prices for free is a relatively new development. The reported change is from the previous day's closing price. The opening price is the first trade of the day. We see the bid and ask prices of $73.27 and $73.28, respectively, along with the market "depth," which is the number of shares sought at the bid price and offered at the ask price. The "1y Target Est" is the average estimated stock price one year ahead based on estimates from security analysts who follow the stock.

Moving to the second column, we have the range of prices for this day, followed by the range over the previous 52 weeks. Volume is the number of shares traded today, followed by average daily volume over the last three months. Market cap is number of shares outstanding (from the most recent quarterly financial statements) multiplied by the current price per share. P/E is the PE ratio we discussed in Chapter 3. The earnings per share (EPS) used in the calculation is "ttm," meaning "trailing twelve months." Finally, we have the dividend on the stock, which is actually the most recent quarterly dividend multiplied by 4, and the dividend yield. Notice that the yield is just the reported dividend divided by the stock price: $.64/$73.28 = .009 = .9%.

Concept Questions

8.3a What is the difference between a securities broker and a securities dealer?

8.3b Which is bigger, the bid price or the ask price? Why?

8.3c How does NASDAQ differ from the NYSE?

8.4 Summary and Conclusions

This chapter has covered the basics of stocks and stock valuation:

1. The cash flows from owning a share of stock come in the form of future dividends. We saw that in certain special cases it is possible to calculate the present value of all the future dividends and thus come up with a value for the stock.

2. As the owner of shares of common stock in a corporation, you have various rights, including the right to vote to elect corporate directors. Voting in corporate elections can be either cumulative or straight. Most voting is actually done by proxy, and a

proxy battle breaks out when competing sides try to gain enough votes to elect their candidates for the board.

3. In addition to common stock, some corporations have issued preferred stock. The name stems from the fact that preferred stockholders must be paid first, before common stockholders can receive anything. Preferred stock has a fixed dividend.

4. The two biggest stock markets in the United States are the NYSE and NASDAQ. We discussed the organization and operation of these two markets, and we saw how stock price information is reported in the financial press.

This chapter completes Part 3 of our book. By now, you should have a good grasp of what we mean by *present value*. You should also be familiar with how to calculate present values, loan payments, and so on. In Part 4, we cover capital budgeting decisions. As you will see, the techniques you learned in Chapters 5–8 form the basis for our approach to evaluating business investment decisions.

CHAPTER REVIEW AND SELF-TEST PROBLEMS

8.1 Dividend Growth and Stock Valuation The Brigapenski Co. has just paid a cash dividend of $2 per share. Investors require a 16 percent return from investments such as this. If the dividend is expected to grow at a steady 8 percent per year, what is the current value of the stock? What will the stock be worth in five years?

8.2 More Dividend Growth and Stock Valuation In Self-Test Problem 8.1, what would the stock sell for today if the dividend was expected to grow at 20 percent per year for the next three years and then settle down to 8 percent per year, indefinitely?

ANSWERS TO CHAPTER REVIEW AND SELF-TEST PROBLEMS

8.1 The last dividend, D_0, was $2. The dividend is expected to grow steadily at 8 percent. The required return is 16 percent. Based on the dividend growth model, we can say that the current price is:

$$P_0 = D_1/(R - g) = D_0 \times (1 + g)/(R - g)$$
$$= \$2 \times 1.08/(.16 - .08)$$
$$= \$2.16/.08$$
$$= \$27$$

We could calculate the price in five years by calculating the dividend in five years and then using the growth model again. Alternatively, we could recognize that the stock price will increase by 8 percent per year and calculate the future price directly. We'll do both. First, the dividend in five years will be:

$$D_5 = D_0 \times (1 + g)^5$$
$$= \$2 \times 1.08^5$$
$$= \$2.9387$$

The price in five years would therefore be:

$$P_5 = D_5 \times (1 + g)/(R - g)$$
$$= \$2.9387 \times 1.08/.08$$
$$= \$3.1738/.08$$
$$= \$39.67$$

Once we understand the dividend model, however, it's easier to notice that:

$$P_5 = P_0 \times (1 + g)^5$$
$$= \$27 \times 1.08^5$$
$$= \$27 \times 1.4693$$
$$= \$39.67$$

Notice that both approaches yield the same price in five years.

8.2   In this scenario, we have supernormal growth for the next three years. We'll need to calculate the dividends during the rapid growth period and the stock price in three years. The dividends are:

$$D_1 = \$2.00 \times 1.20 = \$2.400$$
$$D_2 = \$2.40 \times 1.20 = \$2.880$$
$$D_3 = \$2.88 \times 1.20 = \$3.456$$

After three years, the growth rate falls to 8 percent indefinitely. The price at that time, P_3, is thus:

$$P_3 = D_3 \times (1 + g)/(R - g)$$
$$= \$3.456 \times 1.08/(.16 - .08)$$
$$= \$3.7325/.08$$
$$= \$46.656$$

To complete the calculation of the stock's present value, we have to determine the present value of the three dividends and the future price:

$$P_0 = \frac{D_1}{(1 + R)^1} + \frac{D_2}{(1 + R)^2} + \frac{D_3}{(1 + R)^3} + \frac{P_3}{(1 + R)^3}$$
$$= \frac{\$2.40}{1.16} + \frac{2.88}{1.16^2} + \frac{3.456}{1.16^3} + \frac{46.656}{1.16^3}$$
$$= \$2.07 + 2.14 + 2.21 + 29.89$$
$$= \$36.31$$

CONCEPTS REVIEW AND CRITICAL THINKING QUESTIONS

1. **Stock Valuation [LO1]** Why does the value of a share of stock depend on dividends?

2. **Stock Valuation [LO1]** A substantial percentage of the companies listed on the NYSE and NASDAQ don't pay dividends, but investors are nonetheless willing to buy shares in them. How is this possible given your answer to the previous question?

3. **Dividend Policy [LO1]** Referring to the previous questions, under what circumstances might a company choose not to pay dividends?

4. **Dividend Growth Model [LO1]** Under what two assumptions can we use the dividend growth model presented in the chapter to determine the value of a share of stock? Comment on the reasonableness of these assumptions.

5. **Common versus Preferred Stock [LO1]** Suppose a company has a preferred stock issue and a common stock issue. Both have just paid a $2 dividend. Which do you think will have a higher price, a share of the preferred or a share of the common?

6. **Dividend Growth Model** [LO1] Based on the dividend growth model, what are the two components of the total return on a share of stock? Which do you think is typically larger?

7. **Growth Rate** [LO1] In the context of the dividend growth model, is it true that the growth rate in dividends and the growth rate in the price of the stock are identical?

8. **Voting Rights** [LO2] When it comes to voting in elections, what are the differences between U.S. political democracy and U.S. corporate democracy?

9. **Corporate Ethics** [LO2] Is it unfair or unethical for corporations to create classes of stock with unequal voting rights?

10. **Voting Rights** [LO2] Some companies, such as Reader's Digest, have created classes of stock with no voting rights at all. Why would investors buy such stock?

11. **Stock Valuation** [LO1] Evaluate the following statement: Managers should not focus on the current stock value because doing so will lead to an overemphasis on short-term profits at the expense of long-term profits.

12. **Two-Stage Dividend Growth Model** [LO1] One of the assumptions of the two-stage growth model is that the dividends drop immediately from the high growth rate to the perpetual growth rate. What do you think about this assumption? What happens if this assumption is violated?

HM™

QUESTIONS AND PROBLEMS

Visit us at www.mhhe.com/rwj

1. **Stock Values** [LO1] The Jackson–Timberlake Wardrobe Co. just paid a dividend of $1.95 per share on its stock. The dividends are expected to grow at a constant rate of 6 percent per year indefinitely. If investors require an 11 percent return on The Jackson–Timberlake Wardrobe Co. stock, what is the current price? What will the price be in three years? In 15 years?

BASIC
(Questions 1–9)

2. **Stock Values** [LO1] The next dividend payment by Hot Wings, Inc., will be $2.10 per share. The dividends are anticipated to maintain a 5 percent growth rate forever. If the stock currently sells for $48 per share, what is the required return?

3. **Stock Values** [LO1] For the company in the previous problem, what is the dividend yield? What is the expected capital gains yield?

4. **Stock Values** [LO1] Metroplex Corporation will pay a $3.04 per share dividend next year. The company pledges to increase its dividend by 3.8 percent per year indefinitely. If you require an 11 percent return on your investment, how much will you pay for the company's stock today?

5. **Stock Valuation** [LO1] Keenan Co. is expected to maintain a constant 5.2 percent growth rate in its dividends indefinitely. If the company has a dividend yield of 6.3 percent, what is the required return on the company's stock?

6. **Stock Valuation** [LO1] Suppose you know that a company's stock currently sells for $47 per share and the required return on the stock is 11 percent. You also know that the total return on the stock is evenly divided between a capital gains yield and a dividend yield. If it's the company's policy to always maintain a constant growth rate in its dividends, what is the current dividend per share?

7. **Stock Valuation** [LO1] Apocalyptica Corp. pays a constant $9.75 dividend on its stock. The company will maintain this dividend for the next 11 years and will then cease paying dividends forever. If the required return on this stock is 10 percent, what is the current share price?

8. **Valuing Preferred Stock [LO1]** Resnor, Inc., has an issue of preferred stock outstanding that pays a $5.50 dividend every year in perpetuity. If this issue currently sells for $108 per share, what is the required return?

9. **Stock Valuation and Required Return [LO1]** Red, Inc., Yellow Corp., and Blue Company each will pay a dividend of $2.35 next year. The growth rate in dividends for all three companies is 5 percent. The required return for each company's stock is 8 percent, 11 percent, and 14 percent, respectively. What is the stock price for each company? What do you conclude about the relationship between the required return and the stock price?

INTERMEDIATE
(Questions 10–21)

10. **Stock Valuation [LO1]** Great Pumpkin Farms just paid a dividend of $3.50 on its stock. The growth rate in dividends is expected to be a constant 5 percent per year indefinitely. Investors require a 14 percent return on the stock for the first three years, a 12 percent return for the next three years, and a 10 percent return thereafter. What is the current share price?

11. **Nonconstant Growth [LO1]** Metallica Bearings, Inc., is a young start-up company. No dividends will be paid on the stock over the next nine years because the firm needs to plow back its earnings to fuel growth. The company will pay a $10 per share dividend in 10 years and will increase the dividend by 5 percent per year thereafter. If the required return on this stock is 14 percent, what is the current share price?

12. **Nonconstant Dividends [LO1]** Bread, Inc., has an odd dividend policy. The company has just paid a dividend of $6 per share and has announced that it will increase the dividend by $4 per share for each of the next five years, and then never pay another dividend. If you require an 11 percent return on the company's stock, how much will you pay for a share today?

13. **Nonconstant Dividends [LO1]** Far Side Corporation is expected to pay the following dividends over the next four years: $11, $8, $5, and $2. Afterward, the company pledges to maintain a constant 5 percent growth rate in dividends forever. If the required return on the stock is 12 percent, what is the current share price?

14. **Supernormal Growth [LO1]** Marcel Co. is growing quickly. Dividends are expected to grow at a 30 percent rate for the next three years, with the growth rate falling off to a constant 6 percent thereafter. If the required return is 13 percent and the company just paid a $1.80 dividend, what is the current share price?

15. **Supernormal Growth [LO1]** Eva Corp. is experiencing rapid growth. Dividends are expected to grow at 25 percent per year during the next three years, 15 percent over the following year, and then 8 percent per year indefinitely. The required return on this stock is 13 percent, and the stock currently sells for $76 per share. What is the projected dividend for the coming year?

16. **Negative Growth [LO1]** Antiques R Us is a mature manufacturing firm. The company just paid a $10.46 dividend, but management expects to reduce the payout by 4 percent per year indefinitely. If you require an 11.5 percent return on this stock, what will you pay for a share today?

17. **Finding the Dividend [LO1]** Teder Corporation stock currently sells for $64 per share. The market requires a 10 percent return on the firm's stock. If the company maintains a constant 4.5 percent growth rate in dividends, what was the most recent dividend per share paid on the stock?

18. **Valuing Preferred Stock [LO1]** E-Eyes.com Bank just issued some new preferred stock. The issue will pay a $20 annual dividend in perpetuity, beginning 20 years

from now. If the market requires a 6.4 percent return on this investment, how much does a share of preferred stock cost today?

19. **Using Stock Quotes** [LO3] You have found the following stock quote for RJW Enterprises, Inc., in the financial pages of today's newspaper. What was the closing price for this stock that appeared in *yesterday's* paper? If the company currently has 25 million shares of stock outstanding, what was net income for the most recent four quarters?

52-WEEK		STOCK (DIV)	YLD %	PE	VOL 100s	CLOSE	NET CHG
HI	LO						
72.18	53.17	RJW 1.48	2.1	19	17652	??	−.23

20. **Two-Stage Dividend Growth Model** [LO1] Thirsty Cactus Corp. just paid a dividend of $1.25 per share. The dividends are expected to grow at 28 percent for the next eight years and then level off to a 6 percent growth rate indefinitely. If the required return is 13 percent, what is the price of the stock today?

21. **Two-Stage Dividend Growth Model** [LO1] Chartreuse County Choppers Inc. is experiencing rapid growth. The company expects dividends to grow at 25 percent per year for the next 11 years before leveling off at 6 percent into perpetuity. The required return on the company's stock is 12 percent. If the dividend per share just paid was $1.74, what is the stock price?

22. **Capital Gains versus Income** [LO1] Consider four different stocks, all of which have a required return of 19 percent and a most recent dividend of $4.50 per share. Stocks W, X, and Y are expected to maintain constant growth rates in dividends for the foreseeable future of 10 percent, 0 percent, and −5 percent per year, respectively. Stock Z is a growth stock that will increase its dividend by 20 percent for the next two years and then maintain a constant 12 percent growth rate thereafter. What is the dividend yield for each of these four stocks? What is the expected capital gains yield? Discuss the relationship among the various returns that you find for each of these stocks.

CHALLENGE
(Questions 22–28)

23. **Stock Valuation** [LO1] Most corporations pay quarterly dividends on their common stock rather than annual dividends. Barring any unusual circumstances during the year, the board raises, lowers, or maintains the current dividend once a year and then pays this dividend out in equal quarterly installments to its shareholders.

    a. Suppose a company currently pays a $3.20 annual dividend on its common stock in a single annual installment, and management plans on raising this dividend by 6 percent per year indefinitely. If the required return on this stock is 12 percent, what is the current share price?

    b. Now suppose the company in (a) actually pays its annual dividend in equal quarterly installments; thus, the company has just paid a $.80 dividend per share, as it has for the previous three quarters. What is your value for the current share price now? (*Hint:* Find the equivalent annual end-of-year dividend for each year.) Comment on whether you think this model of stock valuation is appropriate.

24. **Nonconstant Growth** [LO1] Storico Co. just paid a dividend of $2.45 per share. The company will increase its dividend by 20 percent next year and will then reduce its dividend growth rate by 5 percentage points per year until it reaches the industry average of 5 percent dividend growth, after which the company will keep a constant growth rate forever. If the required return on Storico stock is 11 percent, what will a share of stock sell for today?

25. **Nonconstant Growth [LO1]** This one's a little harder. Suppose the current share price for the firm in the previous problem is $63.82 and all the dividend information remains the same. What required return must investors be demanding on Storico stock? (*Hint:* Set up the valuation formula with all the relevant cash flows, and use trial and error to find the unknown rate of return.)

26. **Constant Dividend Growth Model [LO1]** Assume a stock has dividends that grow at a constant rate forever. If you value the stock using the constant dividend growth model, how many years worth of dividends constitute one-half of the stock's current price?

27. **Two-Stage Dividend Growth [LO1]** Regarding the two-stage dividend growth model in the chapter, show that the price of a share of stock today can be written as follows:

$$P_0 = \frac{D_0 \times (1 + g_1)}{R - g_1} \times \left[1 - \left(\frac{1 + g_1}{1 + R}\right)^t\right] + \left(\frac{1 + g_1}{1 + R}\right)^t \times \frac{D_0 \times (1 + g_2)}{R - g_2}$$

Can you provide an intuitive interpretation of this expression?

28. **Two-Stage Dividend Growth [LO1]** The chapter shows that in the two-stage dividend growth model, the growth rate in the first stage, g_1, can be greater than or less than the discount rate, R. Can they be exactly equal? (*Hint:* Yes, but what does the expression for the value of the stock look like?)

MINICASE

Stock Valuation at Ragan, Inc.

Ragan, Inc., was founded nine years ago by brother and sister Carrington and Genevieve Ragan. The company manufactures and installs commercial heating, ventilation, and cooling (HVAC) units. Ragan, Inc., has experienced rapid growth because of a proprietary technology that increases the energy efficiency of its units. The company is equally owned by Carrington and Genevieve. The original partnership agreement between the siblings gave each 50,000 shares of stock. In the event either wished to sell stock, the shares first had to be offered to the other at a discounted price.

Although neither sibling wants to sell, they have decided they should value their holdings in the company. To get started, they have gathered the following information about their main competitors:

Expert HVAC Corporation's negative earnings per share were the result of an accounting write-off last year. Without the write-off, earnings per share for the company would have been $1.06.

Last year, Ragan, Inc., had an EPS of $4.54 and paid a dividend to Carrington and Genevieve of $63,000 each. The company also had a return on equity of 25 percent. The siblings believe that 20 percent is an appropriate required return for the company.

QUESTIONS

1. Assuming the company continues its current growth rate, what is the value per share of the company's stock?

Ragan, Inc., Competitors					
	EPS	DPS	Stock Price	ROE	R
Arctic Cooling, Inc.	$ .79	$.20	$14.18	10.00%	10.00%
National Heating & Cooling	1.38	.62	11.87	13.00	13.00
Expert HVAC Corp.	−.48	.38	13.21	14.00	12.00
Industry Average	$ .56	$.40	$13.09	12.33%	11.67%

2. To verify their calculations, Carrington and Genevieve have hired Josh Schlessman as a consultant. Josh was previously an equity analyst and covered the HVAC industry. Josh has examined the company's financial statements, as well as examining its competitors. Although Ragan, Inc., currently has a technological advantage, his research indicates that other companies are investigating methods to improve efficiency. Given this, Josh believes that the company's technological advantage will last only for the next five years. After that period, the company's growth will likely slow to the industry growth average. Additionally, Josh believes that the required return used by the company is too high. He believes the industry average required return is more appropriate. Under this growth rate assumption, what is your estimate of the stock price?

3. What is the industry average price–earnings ratio? What is the price–earnings ratio for Ragan, Inc.? Is this the relationship you would expect between the two ratios? Why?

4. Carrington and Genevieve are unsure how to interpret the price–earnings ratio. After some head scratching, they've come up with the following expression for the price–earnings ratio:

$$\frac{P_0}{E_1} = \frac{1-b}{R - (ROE \times b)}$$

Beginning with the constant dividend growth model, verify this result. What does this expression imply about the relationship between the dividend payout ratio, the required return on the stock, and the company's ROE?

5. Assume the company's growth rate slows to the industry average in five years. What future return on equity does this imply, assuming a constant payout ratio?

6. After discussing the stock value with Josh, Carrington and Genevieve agree that they would like to increase the value of the company stock. Like many small business owners, they want to retain control of the company, but they do not want to sell stock to outside investors. They also feel that the company's debt is at a manageable level and do not want to borrow more money. How can they increase the price of the stock? Are there any conditions under which this strategy would not increase the stock price?

6.5 Price Ratio Analysis

Price ratios are widely used by financial analysts, more so even than dividend discount models. Of course, all valuation methods try to accomplish the same thing, which is to appraise the economic value of a company's stock. However, analysts readily agree that no single method can adequately handle this task on all occasions. In this section, we therefore examine several of the most popular price ratio methods and provide examples of their use in financial analysis.

PRICE-EARNINGS RATIOS

price-earnings (P/E) ratio
Current stock price divided by annual earnings per share (EPS).

earnings yield (E/P)
Inverse of the P/E ratio: earnings per share divided by price per share.

The most popular price ratio used to assess the value of common stock is a company's **price-earnings ratio**, abbreviated as **P/E ratio**. In fact, as we saw in Chapter 3, P/E ratios are reported in the financial press every day. As we discussed, a price-earnings ratio is calculated as the ratio of a firm's current stock price divided by its annual earnings per share (EPS).

The inverse of a P/E ratio is called an **earnings yield**, and it is measured as earnings per share divided by the current stock price (**E/P**). Clearly, an earnings yield and a price-earnings ratio are simply two ways to measure the same thing. In practice, earnings yields are less commonly stated and used than P/E ratios.

Because most companies report earnings each quarter, annual earnings per share can be calculated either as the most recent quarterly earnings per share times four or as the sum of the last four quarterly earnings per share figures. Most analysts prefer the first method of multiplying the latest quarterly earnings per share value times four. However, some published data sources, including *The Wall Street Journal,* report annual earnings per share as the sum of the last four quarters' figures. The difference is usually small, but it can sometimes be a source of confusion.

growth stocks
A term often used to describe high-P/E stocks.

Financial analysts often refer to high-P/E stocks as **growth stocks**. To see why, notice that a P/E ratio is measured as the *current* stock price over *current* earnings per share. Now, consider two companies with the same current earnings per share, where one company is a high-growth company and the other is a low-growth company. Which company do you think should have a higher stock price, the high-growth company or the low-growth company?

This question is a no-brainer. All else equal, we would be surprised if the high-growth company did not have a higher stock price, and therefore a higher P/E ratio. In general, companies with higher expected earnings growth will have higher P/E ratios, which is why high-P/E stocks are often referred to as growth stocks.

WWW

Visit the Starbucks and GM Web sites at
www.starbucks.com
and
www.gm.com

To give an example, Starbucks Corporation is a specialty coffee retailer with a history of aggressive sales growth. Its stock trades on NASDAQ under the ticker symbol SBUX. In mid-2007, SBUX stock traded at $26.88 with earnings per share (EPS) of $.87, and so had a P/E ratio of $26.88/$.87 = 30.90. This P/E ratio is well above the average P/E ratio of about 16.8 for the S&P 500 (of which SBUX is a member). SBUX has never paid a dividend. Instead, Starbucks reinvests all earnings. So far this strategy has been successful, as the firm has grown at an average rate of 26 percent over the preceding five years.

The reason high-P/E stocks are called growth stocks seems obvious enough; however, in a seeming defiance of logic, low-P/E stocks are often referred to as **value stocks**. The reason is that low-P/E stocks are often viewed as "cheap" relative to *current* earnings. (Notice again the emphasis on "current.") This suggests that these stocks may represent good investment values, and hence the term value stocks.

value stocks
A term often used to describe low-P/E stocks.

In mid-2007, shares of the well-known S&P 500 auto company General Motors (GM) were trading at a price of $31.08. With earnings per share of EPS = $3.75, the P/E ratio is $31.08/$3.75 = 8.29. This is well below the S&P 500 average, and so General Motors might be considered a value stock.

Having said all this, we want to emphasize that the terms "growth stock" and "value stock" are mostly just commonly used labels. Of course, only time will tell whether a high-P/E stock actually turns out to be a high-growth stock, or whether a low-P/E stock is really a good value. The nearby *Investment Updates* box contains additional discussion of P/E ratios.

PRICE-CASH FLOW RATIOS

Instead of price-earnings (P/E) ratios, many analysts prefer to look at price-cash flow (P/CF) ratios. A **price-cash flow (P/CF) ratio** is measured as a company's current stock price divided by its current annual cash flow per share. Like earnings, cash flow is normally reported quarterly and most analysts multiply the last quarterly cash flow figure by four to obtain annual cash flow. Again, like earnings, many published data sources report annual cash flow as a sum of the latest four quarterly cash flows.

price-cash flow (P/CF) ratio
Current stock price divided by current cash flow per share.

cash flow
In the context of the price-cash flow ratio, usually taken to be net income plus depreciation.

There are a variety of definitions of **cash flow**. In this context, the most common measure is simply calculated as net income plus depreciation, so this is the one we use here. In a later chapter, we examine in detail how cash flow is calculated in a firm's financial statements. Cash flow is usually reported in a firm's financial statements and labeled as cash flow from operations (or operating cash flow).

The difference between earnings and cash flow is often confusing, largely because of the way that standard accounting practice defines net income. Essentially, net income is measured as revenues minus expenses. Obviously, this is logical. However, not all expenses are actually cash expenses. The most important exception is depreciation.

ONCE A RUST BELT RELIC, U.S. STEEL IS NOW PROFITABLE, EFFICIENT . . . AND UNDERVALUED

Regardless of whether Pittsburgh-based U.S. Steel begins a major buyback program soon, its shares now look attractive, trading around $40. The current price is less than six times projected 2004 profits of $7.35 and six times the Wall Street consensus estimate for 2005 of $6.47 a share.

Bulls note that the 2005 consensus assumes a marked decline in domestic steel prices, which have more than doubled this year to about $650 a ton for benchmark hot-rolled products, up from $300 in late 2003. If steel prices hold around current levels, U.S. Steel could earn $10 or more a share in 2005. That may sound outlandish, but the company netted $2.56 a share from operations in the third quarter and could earn $3 in the current one.

"U.S. Steel is very undervalued," says Alan Fournier, a principal at Pennant Capital Management, a Chatham, N.J., investment firm. "The company is worth 50 percent more than where it's trading."

David Tepper, the head of Appaloosa Management, the company's second-largest shareholder, recently told management on its earnings conference call that U.S. Steel "has the lowest valuation" among the world's major steel makers. The latest publicly disclosed data shows that Tepper's Chatham, N.J.-based firm, a distressed-debt specialist that manages $3 billion, owns 5 percent of the company's 130 million outstanding shares.

Fournier and Tepper want U.S. Steel to buy back stock with its strong earnings and cash flow. Management has resisted those requests, preferring to use free cash to pay down debt, fund pension obligations, and make acquisitions.

Many investors still view U.S. Steel as a rusting relic of a bygone era when steel producers ruled American industry. But the company is now one of the globe's leading steel makers at a time when the industry may be on the brink of years of prosperity. U.S. Steel has world-class mills in the United States and central Europe. It also controls a vast supply of iron ore, a critical steel input in tight supply.

Indeed, U.S. Steel's integrated structure, which made it the industry leader in the early 20th century, is also a major advantage in the early 21st century. "Our position has never been better in my 20-plus years at the company," says John Surma, U.S. Steel's chief executive. "World appetite for steel is strong, and I don't see why that should change. Supply is constrained."

U.S. Steel is the biggest U.S.-based producer, with total expected 2004 production of 22 million tons, but it ranks sixth globally and accounts for just 2 percent of total world production. U.S. Steel generally is viewed as an asset acquirer—last year, it bought a steel outfit in Serbia—but it's conceivable the company could be taken over. One potential buyer is Arcelor, Europe's largest steel manufacturer.

The steel market's strength is being driven by rising demand from China, which now consumes 30 percent of the world's annual output of 1 billion tons. Chinese demand has doubled in the past four years. India, Eastern Europe, and the states of the former Soviet Union are sources of significant steel demand. Domestic steel consumption also has been high. U.S. Steel has a highly profitable steel plant in Slovakia, which is turning into a center of European auto production.

The Street worries that the sharp increase in steel prices will reverse, as it often has in the past. The cycle last turned down—in brutal fashion—in 2001, leading to bankruptcies of nearly half the U.S. steel industry. Given the importance of Chinese demand, steel stocks have been vulnerable to any sign of a slowdown in China's economy. U.S. Steel shares dipped last month when spot prices fell about $100 a ton from their peak summer level of $750.

U.S. Steel stock (with its famed ticker symbol X) rose over $3 last week amid some positive analyst comments. Goldman Sachs' Aldo Mazzaferro raised his rating to Outperform from In-Line, telling clients that the company "appears to be on the verge of a major breakout in earnings power." He lifted his 2005 profit projection to $8.25 a share from $7.90 and boosted his price target to $58 from $49.

Source: Andrew Bary, *Barron's*, November 8, 2004. Copyright © 2005 ProQuest Information and Learning Company. All rights reserved.

When a firm acquires a long-lived asset, such as a new factory, standard accounting practice does not deduct the cost of the factory all at once, even though it is actually paid for all at once. Instead, the cost is deducted over time. These deductions do not represent actual cash payments, however. The actual cash payment occurred when the factory was purchased. At this point you may be a little confused about why the difference is important, but hang in there for a few more paragraphs.

Most analysts agree that in examining a company's financial performance, cash flow can be more informative than net income. To see why, consider the hypothetical example of two identical companies: Twiddle-Dee Co. and Twiddle-Dum Co. Suppose that both companies have the same constant revenues and expenses in each year over a three-year period. These constant revenues and cash expenses (excluding depreciation) yield the same constant annual cash flows, and they are stated as follows:

	Twiddle-Dee	Twiddle-Dum
Revenues	$5,000	$5,000
Cash expenses	−3,000	−3,000
Cash flow	$2,000	$2,000

Thus, both companies have the same $2,000 cash flow in each of the three years of this hypothetical example.

Next, suppose that both companies incur total depreciation of $3,000 spread out over the three-year period. Standard accounting practices sometimes allow a manager to choose among several depreciation schedules. Twiddle-Dee Co. chooses straight-line depreciation, and Twiddle-Dum Co. chooses accelerated depreciation. These two depreciation schedules are tabulated below:

	Twiddle-Dee	Twiddle-Dum
Year 1	$1,000	$1,500
Year 2	1,000	1,000
Year 3	1,000	500
Total	$3,000	$3,000

Note that total depreciation over the three-year period is the same for both companies. However, Twiddle-Dee Co. has the same $1,000 depreciation in each year, while Twiddle-Dum Co. has accelerated depreciation of $1,500 in the first year, $1,000 in the second year, and $500 depreciation in the third year.

Now, let's look at the resulting annual cash flows and net income figures for the two companies, recalling that in each year, Cash flow = Net income + Depreciation:

	Twiddle-Dee		Twiddle-Dum	
	Cash Flow	Net Income	Cash Flow	Net Income
Year 1	$2,000	$1,000	$2,000	$ 500
Year 2	2,000	1,000	2,000	1,000
Year 3	2,000	1,000	2,000	1,500
Total	$6,000	$3,000	$6,000	$3,000

Note that Twiddle-Dum Co.'s net income is lower in the first year and higher in the third year than Twiddle-Dee Co.'s net income. This is purely a result of Twiddle-Dum Co.'s accelerated depreciation schedule, and has nothing to do with Twiddle-Dum Co.'s actual profitability. However, an inexperienced analyst observing Twiddle-Dum Co.'s rapidly rising annual earnings figures might incorrectly label Twiddle-Dum as a growth company. An experienced analyst would observe that there was no cash flow growth to support this naive conclusion.

Financial analysts typically use both price-earnings ratios and price-cash flow ratios. They point out that when a company's earnings per share is not significantly larger than its cash flow per share (CFPS), this is a signal, at least potentially, of good-quality earnings. The term "quality" means that the accounting earnings mostly reflect actual cash flow, not just accounting numbers. When earnings are bigger than cash flow, this may be a signal of poor quality earnings.

Going back to some of our earlier examples, Starbucks Corporation had cash flow per share of CFPS = $1.50, yielding a P/CF ratio of $26.88/$1.50 = 17.92. Notice that cash flow per share was roughly double earnings per share of $.87, suggesting high-quality earnings. GM had cash flow per share of CFPS = $22.75, yielding a P/CF ratio of $31.08/$22.75 = 1.37. GM cash flow per share is an unusually large 6.1 times its earnings per share, perhaps suggesting high-quality earnings.

PRICE-SALES RATIOS

An alternative view of a company's performance is provided by its **price-sales (P/S) ratio**. A price-sales ratio is calculated as the current price of a company's stock divided by its current annual sales revenue per share. A price-sales ratio focuses on a company's ability to generate sales growth. Essentially, a high P/S ratio would suggest high sales growth, while a low P/S ratio might indicate sluggish sales growth.

For example, Starbucks Corporation had sales per share of $12.65 to yield a price-sales ratio of P/S = $26.88/$12.65 = 2.12. GM had sales per share of $317.95 for a price-sales ratio of P/S = $31.08/$317.95 = .10. Notice the large variation in price-sales ratios for the two companies. The main reason for this difference is that the two companies are in very different kinds of businesses. Security analysts recognize that price-sales ratios cannot be compared in isolation from other important information.

PRICE-BOOK RATIOS

A very basic price ratio for a company is its **price-book (P/B) ratio**, sometimes called the market-book ratio. A price-book ratio is measured as the market value of a company's outstanding common stock divided by its book value of equity.

Price-book ratios are appealing because book values represent, in principle, historical cost. The stock price is an indicator of current value, so a price-book ratio simply measures what the equity is worth today relative to what it cost. A ratio bigger than 1.0 indicates that the firm has been successful in creating value for its stockholders. A ratio smaller than 1.0 indicates that the company is actually worth less than it cost.

This interpretation of the price-book ratio seems simple enough, but the truth is that because of varied and changing accounting standards, book values are difficult to interpret. For this and other reasons, price-book ratios may not have as much information value as they once did.

APPLICATIONS OF PRICE RATIO ANALYSIS

Price-earnings ratios, price-cash flow ratios, and price-sales ratios are commonly used to calculate estimates of expected future stock prices. This is done by multiplying a historical average price ratio by an expected future value for the price-ratio denominator variable. For example, Table 6.1 summarizes such a price ratio analysis for Intel Corporation (INTC) based on mid-2007 information.

In Table 6.1, the five-year average ratio row contains five-year average P/E, P/CF, and P/S ratios. The current value row contains values for earnings per share, cash flow per share, and sales per share; and the growth rate row contains five-year projected growth rates for EPS, CFPS, and SPS.

The expected price row contains expected stock prices one year hence. The basic idea is this. Because Intel had an average P/E ratio of 27.30, we will assume that Intel's stock price will be 27.30 times its earnings per share one year from now. To estimate Intel's earnings one year from now, we note that Intel's earnings are projected to grow at a rate of 8.5 percent per year. If earnings continue to grow at this rate, next year's earnings will be equal to this year's earnings times 1.085. Putting it all together, we have

$$\text{Expected price} = \text{Historical P/E ratio} \times \text{Projected EPS}$$
$$= \text{Historical P/E ratio} \times \text{Current EPS}$$
$$\times (1 + \text{Projected EPS growth rate})$$
$$= 27.30 \times \$.86 \times 1.085$$
$$= \$25.47$$

TABLE 6.1	Price Ratio Analysis for Intel Corporation (INTC) Mid-2007 Stock Price: $24.27		
	Earnings	**Cash Flow**	**Sales**
Five-year average price ratio	27.30 (P/E)	14.04 (P/CF)	4.51 (P/S)
Current value per share	$ .86 (EPS)	$ 1.68 (CFPS)	$ 6.14 (SPS)
Growth rate	8.5%	7.5%	7.0%
Expected stock price	$25.47	$25.36	$29.63

The same procedure is used to calculate an expected price based on cash flow per share:

$$\begin{aligned}
\text{Expected price} &= \text{Historical P/CF ratio} \times \text{Projected CFPS} \\
&= \text{Historical P/CF ratio} \times \text{Current CFPS} \\
&\quad \times (1 + \text{Projected CFPS growth rate}) \\
&= 14.04 \times \$1.68 \times 1.075 \\
&= \$25.36
\end{aligned}$$

Finally, an expected price based on sales per share is calculated as

$$\begin{aligned}
\text{Expected price} &= \text{Historical P/S ratio} \times \text{Projected SPS} \\
&= \text{Historical P/S ratio} \times \text{Current SPS} \\
&\quad \times (1 + \text{Projected SPS growth rate}) \\
&= 4.51 \times \$6.14 \times 1.07 \\
&= \$29.63
\end{aligned}$$

WWW

See Mickey's Web site at
www.disney.go.com

Notice that in the case of Intel, the price ratio methods yield prices ranging from about $25 to about $30. However, when this analysis was made in mid-2007 Intel's stock price was around $24.27. This difference may be explained by the fact that price ratios for Intel have fallen sharply in recent years. For example, Intel's P/E ratio fell from a high of 45.8 in 2002 to just 23.3 in 2006. With such a large price-ratio decline, a historical average price ratio may be inaccurate.

TABLE 6.2

Price Ratio Analysis for Disney Corporation (DIS) Mid-2007 Stock Price: $34.55

	Earnings	Cash Flow	Sales
Five-year average price ratio	24.90 (P/E)	14.70 (P/CF)	1.59 (P/S)
Current value per share	$ 1.61 (EPS)	$ 2.39 (CFPS)	$16.61 (SPS)
Growth rate	14.5%	13%	9%
Expected stock price	$45.90	$39.70	$28.79

EXAMPLE 6.15

Going to Disneyland

Table 6.2 contains information about Walt Disney Corporation. Calculate expected share prices using each of the three price ratio approaches we have discussed.

For example, using the P/E approach, we come up with the following estimates of the price of Walt Disney stock in one year:

$$\begin{aligned}
\text{Expected price} &= \text{Historical P/E ratio} \times \text{Current EPS} \\
&\quad \times (1 + \text{projected EPS growth}) \\
&= 24.90 \times \$1.61 \times 1.145 \\
&= \$45.90
\end{aligned}$$

CHECK THIS

6.5a   Why are high-P/E stocks sometimes called growth stocks?

6.5b   Why might an analyst prefer a price-cash flow ratio to a price-earnings ratio?

9

NET PRESENT VALUE AND OTHER INVESTMENT CRITERIA

After studying this chapter, you should understand:

LO1 The reasons why the net present value criterion is the best way to evaluate proposed investments.

LO2 The payback rule and some of its shortcomings.

LO3 The discounted payback rule and some of its shortcomings.

LO4 Accounting rates of return and some of the problems with them.

LO5 The internal rate of return criterion and its strengths and weaknesses.

LO6 The modified internal rate of return.

LO7 The profitability index and its relation to net present value.

IN 2008, THE AUTOMOBILE MANUFACTUR-ING INDUSTRY in North America was faced with chronic overcapacity. By some estimates, General Motors may have had as many as 12 factories more than it needed. But not all automobile manufacturers faced this problem. Toyota announced plans for its eighth North American assembly plant in Tupelo, Mississippi, a $1.3 billion (projected) investment. About the same time, Honda announced plans to build a new plant in southern Indiana at a cost of $550 million, and BMW announced an expansion of its Spartanburg, South Carolina, plant to build the new X6 model.

Toyota's new plant is an example of a capital budgeting decision. Decisions such as this one, with a

price tag of over $1 billion, are obviously major undertakings, and the risks and rewards must be carefully weighed. In this chapter, we discuss the basic tools used in making such decisions.

In Chapter 1, we saw that increasing the value of the stock in a company is the goal of financial management. Thus, what we need to know is how to tell whether a particular investment will achieve that or not. This chapter considers a variety of techniques that are used in practice for this purpose. More important, it shows how many of these techniques can be misleading, and it explains why the net present value approach is the right one.

Master the ability to solve problems in this chapter by using a spreadsheet. Access Excel Master on the student Web site www.mhhe.com/rwj.

In Chapter 1, we identified the three key areas of concern to the financial manager. The first of these involved the question: What fixed assets should we buy? We called this the *capital budgeting decision*. In this chapter, we begin to deal with the issues that arise in answering this question.

The process of allocating or budgeting capital is usually more involved than just deciding whether to buy a particular fixed asset. We frequently face broader issues like whether we should launch a new product or enter a new market. Decisions such as these determine the nature of a firm's operations and products for years to come, primarily because fixed asset investments are generally long-lived and not easily reversed once they are made.

The most fundamental decision a business must make concerns its product line. What services will we offer or what will we sell? In what markets will we compete? What new products will we introduce? The answer to any of these questions will require that the firm commit its scarce and valuable capital to certain types of assets. As a result, all of these strategic issues fall under the general heading of capital budgeting. The process of capital budgeting could thus be given a more descriptive (not to mention impressive) name: *strategic asset allocation.*

For the reasons we have discussed, the capital budgeting question is probably the most important issue in corporate finance. How a firm chooses to finance its operations (the capital structure question) and how a firm manages its short-term operating activities (the working capital question) are certainly issues of concern, but the fixed assets define the business of the firm. Airlines, for example, are airlines because they operate airplanes, regardless of how they finance them.

Any firm possesses a huge number of possible investments. Each possible investment is an option available to the firm. Some options are valuable and some are not. The essence of successful financial management, of course, is learning to identify which are which. With this in mind, our goal in this chapter is to introduce you to the techniques used to analyze potential business ventures to decide which are worth undertaking.

We present and compare a number of different procedures used in practice. Our primary goal is to acquaint you with the advantages and disadvantages of the various approaches. As we will see, the most important concept in this area is the idea of net present value. We consider this next.

Net Present Value   9.1

In Chapter 1, we argued that the goal of financial management is to create value for the stockholders. The financial manager must thus examine a potential investment in light of its likely effect on the price of the firm's shares. In this section, we describe a widely used procedure for doing this: The net present value approach.

THE BASIC IDEA

An investment is worth undertaking if it creates value for its owners. In the most general sense, we create value by identifying an investment worth more in the marketplace than it costs us to acquire. How can something be worth more than it costs? It's a case of the whole being worth more than the cost of the parts.

For example, suppose you buy a run-down house for $25,000 and spend another $25,000 on painters, plumbers, and so on to get it fixed up. Your total investment is $50,000. When the work is completed, you place the house back on the market and find that it's worth $60,000. The market value ($60,000) exceeds the cost ($50,000) by $10,000. What you have done here is to act as a manager and bring together some fixed assets (a house), some labor (plumbers, carpenters, and others), and some materials (carpeting, paint, and so on). The net result is that you have created $10,000 in value. Put another way, this $10,000 is the *value added* by management.

With our house example, it turned out *after the fact* that $10,000 in value had been created. Things thus worked out nicely. The real challenge, of course, would have been to somehow identify *ahead of time* whether investing the necessary $50,000 was a good idea in the first place. This is what capital budgeting is all about—namely, trying to determine whether a proposed investment or project will be worth more, once it is in place, than it costs.

For reasons that will be obvious in a moment, the difference between an investment's market value and its cost is called the **net present value** of the investment, abbreviated **NPV**. In other words, net present value is a measure of how much value is created or added today by undertaking an investment. Given our goal of creating value for the stockholders, the capital budgeting process can be viewed as a search for investments with positive net present values.

net present value (NPV)
The difference between an investment's market value and its cost.

With our run-down house, you can probably imagine how we would go about making the capital budgeting decision. We would first look at what comparable, fixed-up properties were selling for in the market. We would then get estimates of the cost of buying a particular property and bringing it to market. At this point, we would have an estimated total cost and an estimated market value. If the difference was positive, then this investment would be worth undertaking because it would have a positive estimated net present value. There is risk, of course, because there is no guarantee that our estimates will turn out to be correct.

As our example illustrates, investment decisions are greatly simplified when there is a market for assets similar to the investment we are considering. Capital budgeting becomes much more difficult when we cannot observe the market price for at least roughly comparable investments. The reason is that we then face the problem of estimating the value of an investment using only indirect market information. Unfortunately, this is precisely the situation the financial manager usually encounters. We examine this issue next.

ESTIMATING NET PRESENT VALUE

Imagine we are thinking of starting a business to produce and sell a new product—say organic fertilizer. We can estimate the start-up costs with reasonable accuracy because we know what we will need to buy to begin production. Would this be a good investment? Based on our discussion, you know that the answer depends on whether the value of the new business exceeds the cost of starting it. In other words, does this investment have a positive NPV?

This problem is much more difficult than our "fixer upper" house example because entire fertilizer companies are not routinely bought and sold in the marketplace, so it is essentially impossible to observe the market value of a similar investment. As a result, we must somehow estimate this value by other means.

Based on our work in Chapters 5 and 6, you may be able to guess how we will go about estimating the value of our fertilizer business. We will first try to estimate the future cash flows we expect the new business to produce. We will then apply our basic discounted cash flow procedure to estimate the present value of those cash flows. Once we have this estimate, we will then estimate NPV as the difference between the present value of the future cash flows and the cost of the investment. As we mentioned in Chapter 5, this procedure is

discounted cash flow (DCF) valuation
The process of valuing an investment by discounting its future cash flows.

often called **discounted cash flow (DCF) valuation**.

To see how we might go about estimating NPV, suppose we believe the cash revenues from our fertilizer business will be $20,000 per year, assuming everything goes as expected. Cash costs (including taxes) will be $14,000 per year. We will wind down the business in eight years. The plant, property, and equipment will be worth $2,000 as salvage at that time. The project costs $30,000 to launch. We use a 15 percent discount rate on new projects such as this one. Is this a good investment? If there are 1,000 shares of stock outstanding, what will be the effect on the price per share of taking this investment?

Find out more about capital budgeting for small businesses at www.smallbusinesslearning.net.

From a purely mechanical perspective, we need to calculate the present value of the future cash flows at 15 percent. The net cash inflow will be $20,000 cash income less $14,000 in costs per year for eight years. These cash flows are illustrated in Figure 9.1. As Figure 9.1 suggests, we effectively have an eight-year annuity of $20,000 − 14,000 = $6,000 per year, along with a single lump sum inflow of $2,000 in eight years. Calculating the present value of the future cash flows thus comes down to the same type of problem we considered in Chapter 6. The total present value is:

$$\text{Present value} = \$6,000 \times [1 - (1/1.15^8)]/.15 + (2,000/1.15^8)$$
$$= (\$6,000 \times 4.4873) + (2,000/3.0590)$$
$$= \$26,924 + 654$$
$$= \$27,578$$

FIGURE 9.1

Project Cash Flows ($000)

Time (years)	0	1	2	3	4	5	6	7	8
Initial cost	−$30								
Inflows		$ 20	$ 20	$ 20	$ 20	$ 20	$ 20	$ 20	$ 20
Outflows		−14	−14	−14	−14	−14	−14	−14	−14
Net inflow		$ 6	$ 6	$ 6	$ 6	$ 6	$ 6	$ 6	$ 6
Salvage									2
Net cash flow	−$30	$ 6	$ 6	$ 6	$ 6	$ 6	$ 6	$ 6	$ 8

When we compare this to the $30,000 estimated cost, we see that the NPV is:

$$\text{NPV} = -\$30,000 + 27,578 = -\$2,422$$

Therefore, this is *not* a good investment. Based on our estimates, taking it would *decrease* the total value of the stock by $2,422. With 1,000 shares outstanding, our best estimate of the impact of taking this project is a loss of value of $2,422/1,000 = $2.42 per share.

Our fertilizer example illustrates how NPV estimates can be used to determine whether an investment is desirable. From our example, notice that if the NPV is negative, the effect on share value will be unfavorable. If the NPV were positive, the effect would be favorable. As a consequence, all we need to know about a particular proposal for the purpose of making an accept–reject decision is whether the NPV is positive or negative.

Given that the goal of financial management is to increase share value, our discussion in this section leads us to the *net present value rule:*

> **An investment should be accepted if the net present value is positive and rejected if it is negative.**

In the unlikely event that the net present value turned out to be exactly zero, we would be indifferent between taking the investment and not taking it.

Two comments about our example are in order. First and foremost, it is not the rather mechanical process of discounting the cash flows that is important. Once we have the cash flows and the appropriate discount rate, the required calculations are fairly straightforward. The task of coming up with the cash flows and the discount rate is much more challenging. We will have much more to say about this in the next several chapters. For the remainder of this chapter, we take it as a given that we have estimates of the cash revenues and costs and, where needed, an appropriate discount rate.

The second thing to keep in mind about our example is that the −$2,422 NPV is an estimate. Like any estimate, it can be high or low. The only way to find out the true NPV would be to place the investment up for sale and see what we could get for it. We generally won't be doing this, so it is important that our estimates be reliable. Once again, we will say more about this later. For the rest of this chapter, we will assume the estimates are accurate.

Using the NPV Rule

EXAMPLE 9.1

Suppose we are asked to decide whether a new consumer product should be launched. Based on projected sales and costs, we expect that the cash flows over the five-year life of the project will be $2,000 in the first two years, $4,000 in the next two, and $5,000 in the last year. It will cost about $10,000 to begin production. We use a 10 percent discount rate to evaluate new products. What should we do here?

(continued)

Given the cash flows and discount rate, we can calculate the total value of the product by discounting the cash flows back to the present:

$$\text{Present value} = (\$2,000/1.1) + (2,000/1.1^2) + (4,000/1.1^3)$$
$$+ (4,000/1.1^4) + (5,000/1.1^5)$$
$$= \$1,818 + 1,653 + 3,005 + 2,732 + 3,105$$
$$= \$12,313$$

The present value of the expected cash flows is $12,313, but the cost of getting those cash flows is only $10,000, so the NPV is $12,313 − 10,000 = $2,313. This is positive; so, based on the net present value rule, we should take on the project.

As we have seen in this section, estimating NPV is one way of assessing the profitability of a proposed investment. It is certainly not the only way profitability is assessed, and we now turn to some alternatives. As we will see, when compared to NPV, each of the alternative ways of assessing profitability that we will examine is flawed in some key way; so NPV is the preferred approach in principle, if not always in practice.

SPREADSHEET STRATEGIES

Calculating NPVs with a Spreadsheet

Spreadsheets are commonly used to calculate NPVs. Examining the use of spreadsheets in this context also allows us to issue an important warning. Let's rework Example 9.1:

	A	B	C	D	E	F	G	H
1								
2			Using a spreadsheet to calculate net present values					
3								
4	From Example 9.1, the project's cost is $10,000. The cash flows are $2,000 per year for the first							
5	two years, $4,000 per year for the next two, and $5,000 in the last year. The discount rate is							
6	10 percent; what's the NPV?							
7								
8		Year	Cash Flow					
9		0	-$10,000		Discount rate =		10%	
10		1	2,000					
11		2	2,000		NPV =	$2,102.72	(wrong answer)	
12		3	4,000		NPV =	$2,312.99	(right answer)	
13		4	4,000					
14		5	5,000					
15								
16	The formula entered in cell F11 is =NPV(F9, C9:C14). This gives the wrong answer because the							
17	NPV function actually calculates present values, not *net* present values.							
18								
19	The formula entered in cell F12 is =NPV(F9, C10:C14) + C9. This gives the right answer because the							
20	NPV function is used to calculate the present value of the cash flows and then the initial cost is							
21	subtracted to calculate the answer. Notice that we added cell C9 because it is already negative.							

You can get a freeware NPV calculator at www.wheatworks.com.

In our spreadsheet example, notice that we have provided two answers. By comparing the answers to that found in Example 9.1, we see that the first answer is wrong even though we used the spreadsheet's NPV formula. What happened is that the "NPV" function in our spreadsheet is actually a PV function; unfortunately, one of the original spreadsheet programs many years ago got the definition wrong, and subsequent spreadsheets have copied it! Our second answer shows how to use the formula properly.

The example here illustrates the danger of blindly using calculators or computers without understanding what is going on; we shudder to think of how many capital budgeting decisions in the real world are based on incorrect use of this particular function. We will see another example of something that can go wrong with a spreadsheet later in the chapter.

The Payback Rule 9.2

It is common in practice to talk of the payback on a proposed investment. Loosely, the *payback* is the length of time it takes to recover our initial investment or "get our bait back." Because this idea is widely understood and used, we will examine it in some detail.

DEFINING THE RULE

We can illustrate how to calculate a payback with an example. Figure 9.2 shows the cash flows from a proposed investment. How many years do we have to wait until the accumulated cash flows from this investment equal or exceed the cost of the investment? As Figure 9.2 indicates, the initial investment is $50,000. After the first year, the firm has recovered $30,000, leaving $20,000. The cash flow in the second year is exactly $20,000, so this investment "pays for itself" in exactly two years. Put another way, the **payback period** is two years. If we require a payback of, say, three years or less, then this investment is acceptable. This illustrates the *payback period rule:*

payback period
The amount of time required for an investment to generate cash flows sufficient to recover its initial cost.

> **Based on the payback rule, an investment is acceptable if its calculated payback period is less than some prespecified number of years.**

In our example, the payback works out to be exactly two years. This won't usually happen, of course. When the numbers don't work out exactly, it is customary to work with fractional years. For example, suppose the initial investment is $60,000, and the cash flows are $20,000 in the first year and $90,000 in the second. The cash flows over the first two years are $110,000, so the project obviously pays back sometime in the second year. After the first year, the project has paid back $20,000, leaving $40,000 to be recovered. To figure

---

Calculating Payback EXAMPLE 9.2

Here are the projected cash flows from a proposed investment:

Year	Cash Flow
1	$100
2	200
3	500

This project costs $500. What is the payback period for this investment?

The initial cost is $500. After the first two years, the cash flows total $300. After the third year, the total cash flow is $800, so the project pays back sometime between the end of year 2 and the end of year 3. Because the accumulated cash flows for the first two years are $300, we need to recover $200 in the third year. The third-year cash flow is $500, so we will have to wait $200/500 = .4 year to do this. The payback period is thus 2.4 years, or about two years and five months.

FIGURE 9.2

Net Project Cash Flows

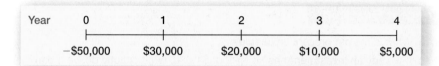

Year	0	1	2	3	4
	−$50,000	$30,000	$20,000	$10,000	$5,000

TABLE 9.1

Expected Cash Flows for Projects A through E

Year	A	B	C	D	E
0	−$100	−$200	−$200	−$200	−$ 50
1	30	40	40	100	100
2	40	20	20	100	−50,000,000
3	50	10	10	−200	
4	60		130	200	

out the fractional year, note that this $40,000 is $40,000/90,000 = 4/9 of the second year's cash flow. Assuming that the $90,000 cash flow is received uniformly throughout the year, the payback would be 1⅘ years.

Now that we know how to calculate the payback period on an investment, using the payback period rule for making decisions is straightforward. A particular cutoff time is selected—say, two years—and all investment projects that have payback periods of two years or less are accepted, whereas any that pay off in more than two years are rejected.

Table 9.1 illustrates cash flows for five different projects. The figures shown as the Year 0 cash flows are the costs of the investments. We examine these to indicate some peculiarities that can, in principle, arise with payback periods.

The payback for the first project, A, is easily calculated. The sum of the cash flows for the first two years is $70, leaving us with $100 − 70 = $30 to go. Because the cash flow in the third year is $50, the payback occurs sometime in that year. When we compare the $30 we need to the $50 that will be coming in, we get $30/50 = .6; so, payback will occur 60 percent of the way into the year. The payback period is thus 2.6 years.

Project B's payback is also easy to calculate: It *never* pays back because the cash flows never total up to the original investment. Project C has a payback of exactly four years because it supplies the $130 that B is missing in year 4. Project D is a little strange. Because of the negative cash flow in year 3, you can easily verify that it has two different payback periods, two years and four years. Which of these is correct? Both of them; the way the payback period is calculated doesn't guarantee a single answer. Finally, Project E is obviously unrealistic, but it does pay back in six months, thereby illustrating the point that a rapid payback does not guarantee a good investment.

ANALYZING THE RULE

When compared to the NPV rule, the payback period rule has some rather severe shortcomings. First, we calculate the payback period by simply adding up the future cash flows. There is no discounting involved, so the time value of money is completely ignored. The payback rule also fails to consider any risk differences. The payback would be calculated the same way for both very risky and very safe projects.

Perhaps the biggest problem with the payback period rule is coming up with the right cutoff period: We don't really have an objective basis for choosing a particular number. Put another way, there is no economic rationale for looking at payback in the first place, so we have no guide for how to pick the cutoff. As a result, we end up using a number that is arbitrarily chosen.

Year	Long	Short
0	−$250	−$250
1	100	100
2	100	200
3	100	0
4	100	0

TABLE 9.2

Investment Projected Cash Flows

Suppose we have somehow decided on an appropriate payback period of two years or less. As we have seen, the payback period rule ignores the time value of money for the first two years. More seriously, cash flows after the second year are ignored entirely. To see this, consider the two investments, Long and Short, in Table 9.2. Both projects cost $250. Based on our discussion, the payback on Long is $2 + (\$50/100) = 2.5$ years, and the payback on Short is $1 + (\$150/200) = 1.75$ years. With a cutoff of two years, Short is acceptable and Long is not.

Is the payback period rule guiding us to the right decisions? Maybe not. Suppose we require a 15 percent return on this type of investment. We can calculate the NPV for these two investments as:

$$\text{NPV(Short)} = -\$250 + (100/1.15) + (200/1.15^2) = -\$11.81$$

$$\text{NPV(Long)} = -\$250 + (100 \times \{[1 - (1/1.15^4)]/.15\}) = \$35.50$$

Now we have a problem. The NPV of the shorter-term investment is actually negative, meaning that taking it diminishes the value of the shareholders' equity. The opposite is true for the longer-term investment—it increases share value.

Our example illustrates two primary shortcomings of the payback period rule. First, by ignoring time value, we may be led to take investments (like Short) that actually are worth less than they cost. Second, by ignoring cash flows beyond the cutoff, we may be led to reject profitable long-term investments (like Long). More generally, using a payback period rule will tend to bias us toward shorter-term investments.

REDEEMING QUALITIES OF THE RULE

Despite its shortcomings, the payback period rule is often used by large and sophisticated companies when they are making relatively minor decisions. There are several reasons for this. The primary reason is that many decisions simply do not warrant detailed analysis because the cost of the analysis would exceed the possible loss from a mistake. As a practical matter, it can be said that an investment that pays back rapidly and has benefits extending beyond the cutoff period probably has a positive NPV.

Small investment decisions are made by the hundreds every day in large organizations. Moreover, they are made at all levels. As a result, it would not be uncommon for a corporation to require, for example, a two-year payback on all investments of less than $10,000. Investments larger than this would be subjected to greater scrutiny. The requirement of a two-year payback is not perfect for reasons we have seen, but it does exercise some control over expenditures and thus limits possible losses.

In addition to its simplicity, the payback rule has two other positive features. First, because it is biased toward short-term projects, it is biased toward liquidity. In other words, a payback rule tends to favor investments that free up cash for other uses quickly. This could be important for a small business; it would be less so for a large corporation. Second, the cash flows that are expected to occur later in a project's life are probably more uncertain. Arguably, a payback period rule adjusts for the extra riskiness of later cash flows, but it does so in a rather draconian fashion—by ignoring them altogether.

We should note here that some of the apparent simplicity of the payback rule is an illusion. The reason is that we still must come up with the cash flows first, and, as we discussed earlier, this is not at all easy to do. Thus, it would probably be more accurate to say that the *concept* of a payback period is both intuitive and easy to understand.

SUMMARY OF THE RULE

To summarize, the payback period is a kind of "break-even" measure. Because time value is ignored, you can think of the payback period as the length of time it takes to break even in an accounting sense, but not in an economic sense. The biggest drawback to the payback period rule is that it doesn't ask the right question. The relevant issue is the impact an investment will have on the value of the stock, not how long it takes to recover the initial investment.

Nevertheless, because it is so simple, companies often use it as a screen for dealing with the myriad minor investment decisions they have to make. There is certainly nothing wrong with this practice. As with any simple rule of thumb, there will be some errors in using it; but it wouldn't have survived all this time if it weren't useful. Now that you understand the rule, you can be on the alert for circumstances under which it might lead to problems. To help you remember, the following table lists the pros and cons of the payback period rule:

Advantages and Disadvantages of the Payback Period Rule	
Advantages	**Disadvantages**
1. Easy to understand.	1. Ignores the time value of money.
2. Adjusts for uncertainty of later cash flows.	2. Requires an arbitrary cutoff point.
3. Biased toward liquidity.	3. Ignores cash flows beyond the cutoff date.
	4. Biased against long-term projects, such as research and development, and new projects.

Concept Questions

9.2a In words, what is the payback period? The payback period rule?

9.2b Why do we say that the payback period is, in a sense, an accounting break-even measure?

9.3 The Discounted Payback

We saw that one shortcoming of the payback period rule was that it ignored time value. A variation of the payback period, the discounted payback period, fixes this particular problem. The **discounted payback period** is the length of time until the sum of the discounted cash flows is equal to the initial investment. The *discounted payback rule* would be:

discounted payback period
The length of time required for an investment's discounted cash flows to equal its initial cost.

> Based on the discounted payback rule, an investment is acceptable if its discounted payback is less than some prespecified number of years.

To see how we might calculate the discounted payback period, suppose we require a 12.5 percent return on new investments. We have an investment that costs $300 and has

Year	Cash Flow		Accumulated Cash Flow	
	Undiscounted	**Discounted**	**Undiscounted**	**Discounted**
1	$100	$89	$100	$ 89
2	100	79	200	168
3	100	70	300	238
4	100	62	400	300
5	100	55	500	355

TABLE 9.3

Ordinary and Discounted Payback

cash flows of $100 per year for five years. To get the discounted payback, we have to discount each cash flow at 12.5 percent and then start adding them. We do this in Table 9.3. In Table 9.3, we have both the discounted and the undiscounted cash flows. Looking at the accumulated cash flows, we see that the regular payback is exactly three years (look for the highlighted figure in year 3). The discounted cash flows total $300 only after four years, however, so the discounted payback is four years, as shown.[1]

How do we interpret the discounted payback? Recall that the ordinary payback is the time it takes to break even in an accounting sense. Because it includes the time value of money, the discounted payback is the time it takes to break even in an economic or financial sense. Loosely speaking, in our example, we get our money back, along with the interest we could have earned elsewhere, in four years.

Figure 9.3 illustrates this idea by comparing the *future* value at 12.5 percent of the $300 investment to the *future* value of the $100 annual cash flows at 12.5 percent. Notice that the two lines cross at exactly four years. This tells us that the value of the project's cash flows catches up and then passes the original investment in four years.

Table 9.3 and Figure 9.3 illustrate another interesting feature of the discounted payback period. If a project ever pays back on a discounted basis, then it must have a positive NPV.[2] This is true because, by definition, the NPV is zero when the sum of the discounted cash flows equals the initial investment. For example, the present value of all the cash flows in Table 9.3 is $355. The cost of the project was $300, so the NPV is obviously $55. This $55 is the value of the cash flow that occurs *after* the discounted payback (see the last line in Table 9.3). In general, if we use a discounted payback rule, we won't accidentally take any projects with a negative estimated NPV.

Based on our example, the discounted payback would seem to have much to recommend it. You may be surprised to find out that it is rarely used in practice. Why? Probably because it really isn't any simpler to use than NPV. To calculate a discounted payback, you have to discount cash flows, add them up, and compare them to the cost, just as you do with NPV. So, unlike an ordinary payback, the discounted payback is not especially simple to calculate.

A discounted payback period rule has a couple of other significant drawbacks. The biggest one is that the cutoff still has to be arbitrarily set, and cash flows beyond that point are ignored.[3] As a result, a project with a positive NPV may be found unacceptable because

---

[1]In this case, the discounted payback is an even number of years. This won't ordinarily happen, of course. However, calculating a fractional year for the discounted payback period is more involved than it is for the ordinary payback, and it is not commonly done.

[2]This argument assumes the cash flows, other than the first, are all positive. If they are not, then these statements are not necessarily correct. Also, there may be more than one discounted payback.

[3]If the cutoff were forever, then the discounted payback rule would be the same as the NPV rule. It would also be the same as the profitability index rule considered in a later section.

FIGURE 9.3

Future Value of Project
Cash Flows

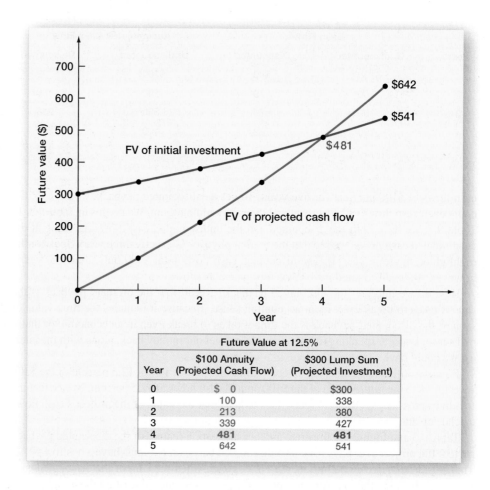

	Future Value at 12.5%	
Year	$100 Annuity (Projected Cash Flow)	$300 Lump Sum (Projected Investment)
0	$ 0	$300
1	100	338
2	213	380
3	339	427
4	**481**	**481**
5	642	541

the cutoff is too short. Also, just because one project has a shorter discounted payback than another does not mean it has a larger NPV.

All things considered, the discounted payback is a compromise between a regular payback and NPV that lacks the simplicity of the first and the conceptual rigor of the second. Nonetheless, if we need to assess the time it will take to recover the investment required by a project, then the discounted payback is better than the ordinary payback because it considers time value. In other words, the discounted payback recognizes that we could have invested the money elsewhere and earned a return on it. The ordinary payback does not take this into account. The advantages and disadvantages of the discounted payback rule are summarized in the following table:

Advantages and Disadvantages of the Discounted Payback Period Rule	
Advantages	**Disadvantages**
1. Includes time value of money.	1. May reject positive NPV investments.
2. Easy to understand.	2. Requires an arbitrary cutoff point.
3. Does not accept negative estimated NPV investments.	3. Ignores cash flows beyond the cutoff date.
4. Biased toward liquidity.	4. Biased against long-term projects, such as research and development, and new projects.

| **Calculating Discounted Payback** | **EXAMPLE 9.3** |

Consider an investment that costs $400 and pays $100 per year forever. We use a 20 percent discount rate on this type of investment. What is the ordinary payback? What is the discounted payback? What is the NPV?

The NPV and ordinary payback are easy to calculate in this case because the investment is a perpetuity. The present value of the cash flows is $100/.2 = $500, so the NPV is $500 − 400 = $100. The ordinary payback is obviously four years.

To get the discounted payback, we need to find the number of years such that a $100 annuity has a present value of $400 at 20 percent. In other words, the present value annuity factor is $400/100 = 4, and the interest rate is 20 percent per period; so what's the number of periods? If we solve for the number of periods, we find that the answer is a little less than nine years, so this is the discounted payback.

Concept Questions

9.3a In words, what is the discounted payback period? Why do we say it is, in a sense, a financial or economic break-even measure?

9.3b What advantage(s) does the discounted payback have over the ordinary payback?

The Average Accounting Return   9.4

Another attractive, but flawed, approach to making capital budgeting decisions involves the **average accounting return (AAR)**. There are many different definitions of the AAR. However, in one form or another, the AAR is always defined as:

$$\frac{\text{Some measure of average accounting profit}}{\text{Some measure of average accounting value}}$$

The specific definition we will use is:

$$\frac{\text{Average net income}}{\text{Average book value}}$$

To see how we might calculate this number, suppose we are deciding whether to open a store in a new shopping mall. The required investment in improvements is $500,000. The store would have a five-year life because everything reverts to the mall owners after that time. The required investment would be 100 percent depreciated (straight-line) over five years, so the depreciation would be $500,000/5 = $100,000 per year. The tax rate is 25 percent. Table 9.4 contains the projected revenues and expenses. Net income in each year, based on these figures, is also shown.

To calculate the average book value for this investment, we note that we started out with a book value of $500,000 (the initial cost) and ended up at $0. The average book value during the life of the investment is thus ($500,000 + 0)/2 = $250,000. As long as we use straight-line depreciation, the average investment will always be one-half of the initial investment.[4]

> **average accounting return (AAR)**
> An investment's average net income divided by its average book value.

---

[4]We could, of course, calculate the average of the six book values directly. In thousands, we would have ($500 + 400 + 300 + 200 + 100 + 0)/6 = $250.

TABLE 9.4

Projected Yearly Revenue and Costs for Average Accounting Return

	Year 1	Year 2	Year 3	Year 4	Year 5
Revenue	$433,333	$450,000	$266,667	$200,000	$133,333
Expenses	$200,000	$150,000	$100,000	$100,000	$100,000
Earnings before Depreciation	$233,333	$300,000	$166,667	$100,000	$ 33,333
Depreciation	$100,000	$100,000	$100,000	$100,000	$100,000
Earnings before Taxes	$133,333	$200,000	$ 66,667	$ 0	−$ 66,667
Taxes (25%)	33,333	50,000	16,667	0	− 16,667
Net Income	$100,000	$150,000	$ 50,000	$ 0	−$ 50,000

$$\text{Average net income} = \frac{\$100,000 + 150,000 + 50,000 + 0 - 50,000}{5} = \$50,000$$

$$\text{Average book value} = \frac{\$500,000 + 0}{2} = \$250,000$$

Looking at Table 9.4, we see that net income is $100,000 in the first year, $150,000 in the second year, $50,000 in the third year, $0 in Year 4, and −$50,000 in Year 5. The average net income, then, is:

$$[\$100,000 + 150,000 + 50,000 + 0 + (-50,000)]/5 = \$50,000$$

The average accounting return is:

$$AAR = \frac{\text{Average net income}}{\text{Average book value}} = \frac{\$50,000}{\$250,000} = 20\%$$

If the firm has a target AAR of less than 20 percent, then this investment is acceptable; otherwise it is not. The *average accounting return rule* is thus:

> **Based on the average accounting return rule, a project is acceptable if its average accounting return exceeds a target average accounting return.**

As we will now see, the use of this rule has a number of problems.

You should recognize the chief drawback to the AAR immediately. Above all else, the AAR is not a rate of return in any meaningful economic sense. Instead, it is the ratio of two accounting numbers, and it is not comparable to the returns offered, for example, in financial markets.[5]

One of the reasons the AAR is not a true rate of return is that it ignores time value. When we average figures that occur at different times, we are treating the near future and the more distant future in the same way. There was no discounting involved when we computed the average net income, for example.

The second problem with the AAR is similar to the problem we had with the payback period rule concerning the lack of an objective cutoff period. Because a calculated AAR is really not comparable to a market return, the target AAR must somehow be specified. There is no generally agreed-upon way to do this. One way of doing it is to calculate the AAR for the firm as a whole and use this as a benchmark, but there are lots of other ways as well.

---

[5]The AAR is closely related to the return on assets (ROA) discussed in Chapter 3. In practice, the AAR is sometimes computed by first calculating the ROA for each year and then averaging the results. This produces a number that is similar, but not identical, to the one we computed.

The third, and perhaps worst, flaw in the AAR is that it doesn't even look at the right things. Instead of cash flow and market value, it uses net income and book value. These are both poor substitutes. As a result, an AAR doesn't tell us what the effect on share price will be of taking an investment, so it doesn't tell us what we really want to know.

Does the AAR have any redeeming features? About the only one is that it almost always can be computed. The reason is that accounting information will almost always be available, both for the project under consideration and for the firm as a whole. We hasten to add that once the accounting information is available, we can always convert it to cash flows, so even this is not a particularly important fact. The AAR is summarized in the following table:

Advantages and Disadvantages of the Average Accounting Return	
Advantages	**Disadvantages**
1. Easy to calculate. 2. Needed information will usually be available.	1. Not a true rate of return; time value of money is ignored. 2. Uses an arbitrary benchmark cutoff rate. 3. Based on accounting (book) values, not cash flows and market values.

Concept Questions

9.4a What is an average accounting rate of return (AAR)?

9.4b What are the weaknesses of the AAR rule?

The Internal Rate of Return

9.5

We now come to the most important alternative to NPV, the **internal rate of return**, universally known as the **IRR**. As we will see, the IRR is closely related to NPV. With the IRR, we try to find a single rate of return that summarizes the merits of a project. Furthermore, we want this rate to be an "internal" rate in the sense that it depends only on the cash flows of a particular investment, not on rates offered elsewhere.

internal rate of return (IRR)
The discount rate that makes the NPV of an investment zero.

To illustrate the idea behind the IRR, consider a project that costs $100 today and pays $110 in one year. Suppose you were asked, "What is the return on this investment?" What would you say? It seems both natural and obvious to say that the return is 10 percent because, for every dollar we put in, we get $1.10 back. In fact, as we will see in a moment, 10 percent is the internal rate of return, or IRR, on this investment.

Is this project with its 10 percent IRR a good investment? Once again, it would seem apparent that this is a good investment only if our required return is less than 10 percent. This intuition is also correct and illustrates the *IRR rule:*

> **Based on the IRR rule, an investment is acceptable if the IRR exceeds the required return. It should be rejected otherwise.**

Imagine that we want to calculate the NPV for our simple investment. At a discount rate of R, the NPV is:

$$NPV = -\$100 + [110/(1 + R)]$$

Now, suppose we don't know the discount rate. This presents a problem, but we can still ask how high the discount rate would have to be before this project was deemed unacceptable. We know that we are indifferent between taking and not taking this investment when its NPV is just equal to zero. In other words, this investment is *economically* a break-even proposition when the NPV is zero because value is neither created nor destroyed. To find the break-even discount rate, we set NPV equal to zero and solve for R:

$$NPV = 0 = -\$100 + [110/(1 + R)]$$
$$\$100 = \$110/(1 + R)$$
$$1 + R = \$110/100 = 1.1$$
$$R = 10\%$$

This 10 percent is what we already have called the return on this investment. What we have now illustrated is that the internal rate of return on an investment (or just "return" for short) is the discount rate that makes the NPV equal to zero. This is an important observation, so it bears repeating:

> **The IRR on an investment is the required return that results in a zero NPV when it is used as the discount rate.**

The fact that the IRR is simply the discount rate that makes the NPV equal to zero is important because it tells us how to calculate the returns on more complicated investments. As we have seen, finding the IRR turns out to be relatively easy for a single-period investment. However, suppose you were now looking at an investment with the cash flows shown in Figure 9.4. As illustrated, this investment costs $100 and has a cash flow of $60 per year for two years, so it's only slightly more complicated than our single-period example. However, if you were asked for the return on this investment, what would you say? There doesn't seem to be any obvious answer (at least not to us). However, based on what we now know, we can set the NPV equal to zero and solve for the discount rate:

$$NPV = 0 = -\$100 + [60/(1 + IRR)] + [60/(1 + IRR)^2]$$

Unfortunately, the only way to find the IRR in general is by trial and error, either by hand or by calculator. This is precisely the same problem that came up in Chapter 5 when we found the unknown rate for an annuity and in Chapter 7 when we found the yield to maturity on a bond. In fact, we now see that in both of those cases, we were finding an IRR.

In this particular case, the cash flows form a two-period, $60 annuity. To find the unknown rate, we can try some different rates until we get the answer. If we were to start with a 0 percent rate, the NPV would obviously be $120 − 100 = $20. At a 10 percent discount rate, we would have:

$$NPV = -\$100 + (60/1.1) + (60/1.1^2) = \$4.13$$

FIGURE 9.4

Project Cash Flows

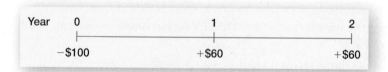

Year	0	1	2
	−$100	+$60	+$60

Discount Rate	NPV
0%	$20.00
5%	11.56
10%	4.13
15%	− 2.46
20%	− 8.33

TABLE 9.5

NPV at Different Discount Rates

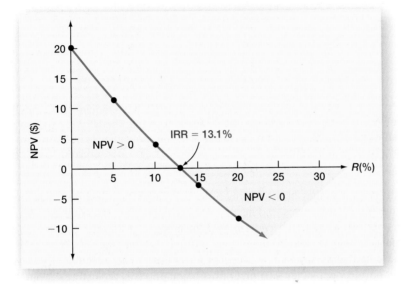

FIGURE 9.5

An NPV Profile

Now, we're getting close. We can summarize these and some other possibilities as shown in Table 9.5. From our calculations, the NPV appears to be zero with a discount rate between 10 percent and 15 percent, so the IRR is somewhere in that range. With a little more effort, we can find that the IRR is about 13.1 percent.[6] So, if our required return were less than 13.1 percent, we would take this investment. If our required return exceeded 13.1 percent, we would reject it.

By now, you have probably noticed that the IRR rule and the NPV rule appear to be quite similar. In fact, the IRR is sometimes simply called the *discounted cash flow,* or *DCF, return*. The easiest way to illustrate the relationship between NPV and IRR is to plot the numbers we calculated for Table 9.5. We put the different NPVs on the vertical axis, or *y*-axis, and the discount rates on the horizontal axis, or *x*-axis. If we had a very large number of points, the resulting picture would be a smooth curve called a **net present value profile**. Figure 9.5 illustrates the NPV profile for this project. Beginning with a 0 percent discount rate, we have $20 plotted directly on the *y*-axis. As the discount rate increases, the NPV declines smoothly. Where will the curve cut through the *x*-axis? This will occur where the NPV is just equal to zero, so it will happen right at the IRR of 13.1 percent.

In our example, the NPV rule and the IRR rule lead to identical accept–reject decisions. We will accept an investment using the IRR rule if the required return is less than 13.1 percent. As Figure 9.5 illustrates, however, the NPV is positive at any discount rate less than 13.1 percent, so we would accept the investment using the NPV rule as well. The two rules give equivalent results in this case.

net present value profile
A graphical representation of the relationship between an investment's NPVs and various discount rates.

---

[6]With a lot more effort (or a personal computer), we can find that the IRR is approximately (to 9 decimal places) 13.066238629 percent—not that anybody would ever want this many decimal places!

EXAMPLE 9.4	**Calculating the IRR**

A project has a total up-front cost of $435.44. The cash flows are $100 in the first year, $200 in the second year, and $300 in the third year. What's the IRR? If we require an 18 percent return, should we take this investment?

We'll describe the NPV profile and find the IRR by calculating some NPVs at different discount rates. You should check our answers for practice. Beginning with 0 percent, we have:

Discount Rate	NPV
0%	$164.56
5%	100.36
10%	46.15
15%	.00
20%	− 39.61

The NPV is zero at 15 percent, so 15 percent is the IRR. If we require an 18 percent return, then we should not take the investment. The reason is that the NPV is negative at 18 percent (verify that it is −$24.47). The IRR rule tells us the same thing in this case. We shouldn't take this investment because its 15 percent return is below our required 18 percent return.

At this point, you may be wondering if the IRR and NPV rules always lead to identical decisions. The answer is yes, as long as two very important conditions are met. First, the project's cash flows must be *conventional*, meaning that the first cash flow (the initial investment) is negative and all the rest are positive. Second, the project must be *independent*, meaning that the decision to accept or reject this project does not affect the decision to accept or reject any other. The first of these conditions is typically met, but the second often is not. In any case, when one or both of these conditions are not met, problems can arise. We discuss some of these next.

SPREADSHEET STRATEGIES

Calculating IRRs with a Spreadsheet

Because IRRs are so tedious to calculate by hand, financial calculators and especially spreadsheets are generally used. The procedures used by various financial calculators are too different for us to illustrate here, so we will focus on using a spreadsheet (financial calculators are covered in Appendix D). As the following example illustrates, using a spreadsheet is easy.

	A	B	C	D	E	F	G	H
1								
2			Using a spreadsheet to calculate internal rates of return					
3								
4	Suppose we have a four-year project that costs $500. The cash flows over the four-year life will be							
5	$100, $200, $300, and $400. What is the IRR?							
6								
7			Year	Cash Flow				
8			0	-$500				
9			1	100		IRR =	27.3%	
10			2	200				
11			3	300				
12			4	400				
13								
14								
15	The formula entered in cell F9 is =IRR(C8:C12). Notice that the year 0 cash flow has a negative							
16	sign representing the initial cost of the project.							
17								

PROBLEMS WITH THE IRR

The problems with the IRR come about when the cash flows are not conventional or when we are trying to compare two or more investments to see which is best. In the first case, surprisingly, the simple question: What's the return? can become difficult to answer. In the second case, the IRR can be a misleading guide.

Nonconventional Cash Flows   Suppose we have a strip-mining project that requires a $60 investment. Our cash flow in the first year will be $155. In the second year, the mine will be depleted, but we will have to spend $100 to restore the terrain. As Figure 9.6 illustrates, both the first and third cash flows are negative.

To find the IRR on this project, we can calculate the NPV at various rates:

Discount Rate	NPV
0%	−$5.00
10%	− 1.74
20%	− .28
30%	.06
40%	− .31

The NPV appears to be behaving in a peculiar fashion here. First, as the discount rate increases from 0 percent to 30 percent, the NPV starts out negative and becomes positive. This seems backward because the NPV is rising as the discount rate rises. It then starts getting smaller and becomes negative again. What's the IRR? To find out, we draw the NPV profile as shown in Figure 9.7.

In Figure 9.7, notice that the NPV is zero when the discount rate is 25 percent, so this is the IRR. Or is it? The NPV is also zero at $33\frac{1}{3}$ percent. Which of these is correct? The answer is both or neither; more precisely, there is no unambiguously correct answer. This is the **multiple rates of return** problem. Many financial computer packages (including a best-seller for personal computers) aren't aware of this problem and just report the first IRR that is found. Others report only the smallest positive IRR, even though this answer is no better than any other.

In our current example, the IRR rule breaks down completely. Suppose our required return is 10 percent. Should we take this investment? Both IRRs are greater than 10 percent, so, by the IRR rule, maybe we should. However, as Figure 9.7 shows, the NPV is negative at any discount rate less than 25 percent, so this is not a good investment. When should we take it? Looking at Figure 9.7 one last time, we see that the NPV is positive only if our required return is between 25 percent and $33\frac{1}{3}$ percent.

Nonconventional cash flows can occur in a variety of ways. For example, Northeast Utilities, owner of the Connecticut-located Millstone nuclear power plant, had to shut down the plant's three reactors in November 1995. The reactors were expected to be back online in January 1997. By some estimates, the cost of the shutdown would run about $334 million. In fact, all nuclear plants eventually have to be shut down forever, and the costs associated with decommissioning a plant are enormous, creating large negative cash flows at the end of the project's life.

multiple rates of return
The possibility that more than one discount rate will make the NPV of an investment zero.

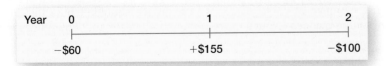

FIGURE 9.6

Project Cash Flows

FIGURE 9.7

NPV Profile

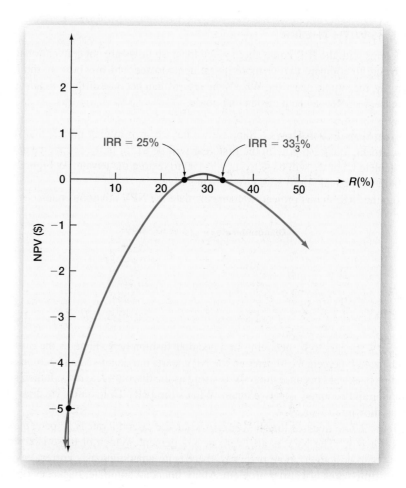

The moral of the story is that when the cash flows aren't conventional, strange things can start to happen to the IRR. This is not anything to get upset about, however, because the NPV rule, as always, works just fine. This illustrates the fact that, oddly enough, the obvious question—What's the rate of return?—may not always have a good answer.

EXAMPLE 9.5 | **What's the IRR?**

You are looking at an investment that requires you to invest $51 today. You'll get $100 in one year, but you must pay out $50 in two years. What is the IRR on this investment?

You're on the alert now for the nonconventional cash flow problem, so you probably wouldn't be surprised to see more than one IRR. However, if you start looking for an IRR by trial and error, it will take you a long time. The reason is that there is no IRR. The NPV is negative at every discount rate, so we shouldn't take this investment under any circumstances. What's the return on this investment? Your guess is as good as ours.

| **"I Think; Therefore, I Know How Many IRRs There Can Be."** | **EXAMPLE 9.6** |

We've seen that it's possible to get more than one IRR. If you wanted to make sure that you had found all of the possible IRRs, how could you do it? The answer comes from the great mathematician, philosopher, and financial analyst Descartes (of "I think; therefore I am" fame). Descartes' Rule of Sign says that the maximum number of IRRs that there can be is equal to the number of times that the cash flows change sign from positive to negative and/or negative to positive.[7]

In our example with the 25 percent and 33⅓ percent IRRs, could there be yet another IRR? The cash flows flip from negative to positive, then back to negative, for a total of two sign changes. Therefore, according to Descartes' rule, the maximum number of IRRs is two and we don't need to look for any more. Note that the actual number of IRRs can be less than the maximum (see Example 9.5).

Mutually Exclusive Investments Even if there is a single IRR, another problem can arise concerning **mutually exclusive investment decisions**. If two investments, X and Y, are mutually exclusive, then taking one of them means that we cannot take the other. Two projects that are not mutually exclusive are said to be independent. For example, if we own one corner lot, then we can build a gas station or an apartment building, but not both. These are mutually exclusive alternatives.

Thus far, we have asked whether a given investment is worth undertaking. However, a related question comes up often: Given two or more mutually exclusive investments, which one is the best? The answer is simple enough: The best one is the one with the largest NPV. Can we also say that the best one has the highest return? As we show, the answer is no.

To illustrate the problem with the IRR rule and mutually exclusive investments, consider the following cash flows from two mutually exclusive investments:

Year	Investment A	Investment B
0	−$100	−$100
1	50	20
2	40	40
3	40	50
4	30	60

mutually exclusive investment decisions
A situation in which taking one investment prevents the taking of another.

The IRR for A is 24 percent, and the IRR for B is 21 percent. Because these investments are mutually exclusive, we can take only one of them. Simple intuition suggests that investment A is better because of its higher return. Unfortunately, simple intuition is not always correct.

To see why investment A is not necessarily the better of the two investments, we've calculated the NPV of these investments for different required returns:

Discount Rate	NPV(A)	NPV(B)
0%	$60.00	$70.00
5	43.13	47.88
10	29.06	29.79
15	17.18	14.82
20	7.06	2.31
25	− 1.63	− 8.22

---

[7]To be more precise, the number of IRRs that are bigger than −100 percent is equal to the number of sign changes, or it differs from the number of sign changes by an even number. Thus, for example, if there are five sign changes, there are five IRRs, three IRRs, or one IRR. If there are two sign changes, there are either two IRRs or no IRRs.

FIGURE 9.8

NPV Profiles for Mutually
Exclusive Investments

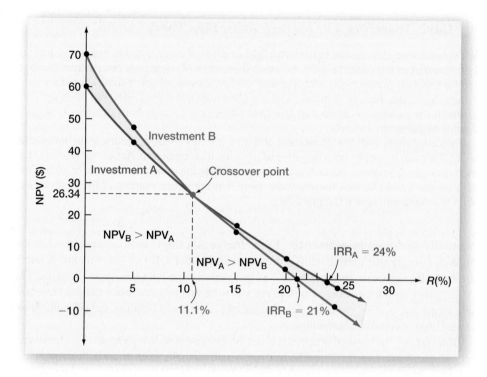

The IRR for A (24 percent) is larger than the IRR for B (21 percent). However, if you compare the NPVs, you'll see that which investment has the higher NPV depends on our required return. B has greater total cash flow, but it pays back more slowly than A. As a result, it has a higher NPV at lower discount rates.

In our example, the NPV and IRR rankings conflict for some discount rates. If our required return is 10 percent, for instance, then B has the higher NPV and is thus the better of the two even though A has the higher return. If our required return is 15 percent, then there is no ranking conflict: A is better.

The conflict between the IRR and NPV for mutually exclusive investments can be illustrated by plotting the investments' NPV profiles as we have done in Figure 9.8. In Figure 9.8, notice that the NPV profiles cross at about 11 percent. Notice also that at any discount rate less than 11 percent, the NPV for B is higher. In this range, taking B benefits us more than taking A, even though A's IRR is higher. At any rate greater than 11 percent, investment A has the greater NPV.

This example illustrates that when we have mutually exclusive projects, we shouldn't rank them based on their returns. More generally, anytime we are comparing investments to determine which is best, looking at IRRs can be misleading. Instead, we need to look at the relative NPVs to avoid the possibility of choosing incorrectly. Remember, we're ultimately interested in creating value for the shareholders, so the option with the higher NPV is preferred, regardless of the relative returns.

If this seems counterintuitive, think of it this way. Suppose you have two investments. One has a 10 percent return and makes you $100 richer immediately. The other has a 20 percent return and makes you $50 richer immediately. Which one do you like better? We would rather have $100 than $50, regardless of the returns, so we like the first one better.

EXAMPLE 9.7

Calculating the Crossover Rate

In Figure 9.8, the NPV profiles cross at about 11 percent. How can we determine just what this crossover point is? The *crossover rate,* by definition, is the discount rate that makes the NPVs of two projects equal. To illustrate, suppose we have the following two mutually exclusive investments:

Year	Investment A	Investment B
0	−$400	−$500
1	250	320
2	280	340

What's the crossover rate?

To find the crossover, first consider moving out of investment A and into investment B. If you make the move, you'll have to invest an extra $100 (= $500 − 400). For this $100 investment, you'll get an extra $70 (= $320 − 250) in the first year and an extra $60 (= $340 − 280) in the second year. Is this a good move? In other words, is it worth investing the extra $100?

Based on our discussion, the NPV of the switch, NPV(B − A), is:

$$\text{NPV(B − A)} = -\$100 + [70/(1 + R)] + [60/(1 + R)^2]$$

We can calculate the return on this investment by setting the NPV equal to zero and solving for the IRR:

$$\text{NPV(B − A)} = 0 = -\$100 + [70/(1 + R)] + [60/(1 + R)^2]$$

If you go through this calculation, you will find the IRR is exactly 20 percent. What this tells us is that at a 20 percent discount rate, we are indifferent between the two investments because the NPV of the difference in their cash flows is zero. As a consequence, the two investments have the same value, so this 20 percent is the crossover rate. Check to see that the NPV at 20 percent is $2.78 for both investments.

In general, you can find the crossover rate by taking the difference in the cash flows and calculating the IRR using the difference. It doesn't make any difference which one you subtract from which. To see this, find the IRR for (A − B); you'll see it's the same number. Also, for practice, you might want to find the exact crossover in Figure 9.8. (*Hint:* It's 11.0704 percent.)

Investing or Financing?   Consider the following two independent investments:

Year	Investment A	Investment B
0	−$100	$100
1	130	−130

The company initially pays out cash with investment A and initially receives cash for investment B. While most projects are more like investment A, projects like investment B also occur. For example, consider a corporation conducting a seminar where the participants pay in advance. Because large expenses are frequently incurred at the seminar date, cash inflows precede cash outflows.

For these two projects, suppose the required return for each investment project is 12 percent. According to the IRR decision rule, which, if either, project should we accept? If you calculate the IRRs, you will find that they are 30 percent for both projects.

According to the IRR decision rule, we should accept both projects. However, if we calculate the NPV of B at 12 percent, we get:

$$\$100 - \frac{\$130}{1.12} = -\$16.07$$

FIGURE 9.9   NPV Profile for Investing and Financing Investments

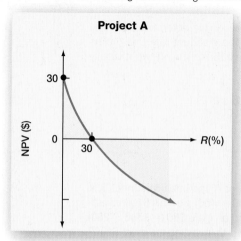

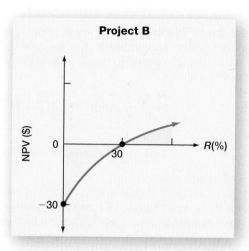

In this case, the NPV and IRR decision rules disagree. To see what's going on, Figure 9.9 shows the NPV profile for each project. As you can see, the NPV profile for B is upward sloping. Thus, the project should be accepted if the required return is *greater* than 30 percent.

When a project has cash flows like investment B's, the IRR is really a rate that you are paying, not receiving. For this reason, we say that the project has *financing type* cash flows, whereas investment A has *investing type* cash flows. You should take a project with financing-type cash flows only if it is an inexpensive source of financing, meaning that its IRR is *lower* than your required return.

REDEEMING QUALITIES OF THE IRR

Despite its flaws, the IRR is very popular in practice—more so than even the NPV. It probably survives because it fills a need that the NPV does not. In analyzing investments, people in general, and financial analysts in particular, seem to prefer talking about rates of return rather than dollar values.

In a similar vein, the IRR also appears to provide a simple way of communicating information about a proposal. One manager might say to another, "Remodeling the clerical wing has a 20 percent return." This may somehow seem simpler than saying, "At a 10 percent discount rate, the net present value is $4,000."

Finally, under certain circumstances, the IRR may have a practical advantage over the NPV. We can't estimate the NPV unless we know the appropriate discount rate, but we can still estimate the IRR. Suppose we didn't know the required return on an investment, but we found, for example, that it had a 40 percent return. We would probably be inclined to take it because it would be unlikely that the required return would be that high. The advantages and disadvantages of the IRR are summarized as follows:

Advantages and Disadvantages of the Internal Rate of Return	
Advantages	**Disadvantages**
1. Closely related to NPV, often leading to identical decisions.	1. May result in multiple answers or not deal with nonconventional cash flows.
2. Easy to understand and communicate.	2. May lead to incorrect decisions in comparisons of mutually exclusive investments.

THE MODIFIED INTERNAL RATE OF RETURN (MIRR)

To address some of the problems that can crop up with the standard IRR, it is often proposed that a modified version be used. As we will see, there are several different ways of calculating a modified IRR, or MIRR, but the basic idea is to modify the cash flows first and then calculate an IRR using the modified cash flows.

To illustrate, let's go back to the cash flows in Figure 9.6: $-\$60$, $+\$155$, and $-\$100$. As we saw, there are two IRRs, 25 percent and $33\frac{1}{3}$ percent. We next illustrate three different MIRRs, all of which have the property that only one answer will result, thereby eliminating the multiple IRR problem.

Method #1: The Discounting Approach   With the discounting approach, the idea is to discount all negative cash flows back to the present at the required return and add them to the initial cost. Then, calculate the IRR. Because only the first modified cash flow is negative, there will be only one IRR. The discount rate used might be the required return, or it might be some other externally supplied rate. We will use the project's required return.

If the required return on the project is 20 percent, then the modified cash flows look like this:

Time 0: $-\$60 + \dfrac{-\$100}{1.20^2} = -\$129.44$

Time 1: $+\$155$

Time 2: $+\$0$

If you calculate the MIRR now, you should get 19.74 percent.

Method #2: The Reinvestment Approach   With the reinvestment approach, we compound *all* cash flows (positive and negative) except the first out to the end of the project's life and then calculate the IRR. In a sense, we are "reinvesting" the cash flows and not taking them out of the project until the very end. The rate we use could be the required return on the project, or it could be a separately specified "reinvestment rate." We will use the project's required return. When we do, here are the modified cash flows:

Time 0: $-\$60$

Time 1: $+0$

Time 2: $-\$100 + (\$155 \times 1.2) = \$86$

The MIRR on this set of cash flows is 19.72 percent, or a little lower than we got using the discounting approach.

Method #3: The Combination Approach   As the name suggests, the combination approach blends our first two methods. Negative cash flows are discounted back to the present, and positive cash flows are compounded to the end of the project. In practice, different discount or compounding rates might be used, but we will again stick with the project's required return.

With the combination approach, the modified cash flows are as follows:

Time 0: $-\$60 + \dfrac{-\$100}{1.20^2} = -\$129.44$

Time 1: $+0$

Time 2: $\$155 \times 1.2 = \$186$

See if you don't agree that the MIRR is 19.87 percent, the highest of the three.

MIRR or IRR: Which Is Better?   MIRRs are controversial. At one extreme are those who claim that MIRRs are superior to IRRs, period. For example, by design, they clearly don't suffer from the multiple rate of return problem.

At the other end, detractors say that MIRR should stand for "meaningless internal rate of return." As our example makes clear, one problem with MIRRs is that there are different ways of calculating them, and there is no clear reason to say one of our three methods is better than any other. The differences are small with our simple cash flows, but they could be much larger for a more complex project. Further, it's not clear how to interpret an MIRR. It may look like a rate of return, but it's a rate of return on a modified set of cash flows, not the project's actual cash flows.

We're not going to take sides. However, notice that calculating an MIRR requires discounting, compounding, or both, which leads to two obvious observations. First, if we have the relevant discount rate, why not calculate the NPV and be done with it? Second, because an MIRR depends on an externally supplied discount (or compounding) rate, the answer you get is not truly an "internal" rate of return, which, by definition, depends on only the project's cash flows.

We *will* take a stand on one issue that frequently comes up in this context. The value of a project does not depend on what the firm does with the cash flows generated by that project. A firm might use a project's cash flows to fund other projects, to pay dividends, or to buy an executive jet. It doesn't matter: How the cash flows are spent in the future does not affect their value today. As a result, there is generally no need to consider reinvestment of interim cash flows.

Concept Questions

9.5a Under what circumstances will the IRR and NPV rules lead to the same accept–reject decisions? When might they conflict?

9.5b Is it generally true that an advantage of the IRR rule over the NPV rule is that we don't need to know the required return to use the IRR rule?

9.6 The Profitability Index

profitability index (PI)
The present value of an investment's future cash flows divided by its initial cost. Also called the *benefit–cost ratio*.

Another tool used to evaluate projects is called the **profitability index (PI)** or benefit–cost ratio. This index is defined as the present value of the future cash flows divided by the initial investment. So, if a project costs $200 and the present value of its future cash flows is $220, the profitability index value would be $220/200 = 1.1$. Notice that the NPV for this investment is $20, so it is a desirable investment.

More generally, if a project has a positive NPV, then the present value of the future cash flows must be bigger than the initial investment. The profitability index would thus be bigger than 1 for a positive NPV investment and less than 1 for a negative NPV investment.

How do we interpret the profitability index? In our example, the PI was 1.1. This tells us that, per dollar invested, $1.10 in value or $.10 in NPV results. The profitability index thus measures "bang for the buck"—that is, the value created per dollar invested. For this reason, it is often proposed as a measure of performance for government or other not-for-profit investments. Also, when capital is scarce, it may make sense to allocate it to projects with the highest PIs. We will return to this issue in a later chapter.

The PI is obviously similar to the NPV. However, consider an investment that costs $5 and has a $10 present value and an investment that costs $100 with a $150 present value.

The first of these investments has an NPV of $5 and a PI of 2. The second has an NPV of $50 and a PI of 1.5. If these are mutually exclusive investments, then the second one is preferred even though it has a lower PI. This ranking problem is similar to the IRR ranking problem we saw in the previous section. In all, there seems to be little reason to rely on the PI instead of the NPV. Our discussion of the PI is summarized as follows:

Advantages and Disadvantages of the Profitability Index	
Advantages	**Disadvantages**
1. Closely related to NPV, generally leading to identical decisions. 2. Easy to understand and communicate. 3. May be useful when available investment funds are limited.	1. May lead to incorrect decisions in comparisons of mutually exclusive investments.

Concept Questions

9.6a What does the profitability index measure?
9.6b How would you state the profitability index rule?

The Practice of Capital Budgeting   9.7

Given that NPV seems to be telling us directly what we want to know, you might be wondering why there are so many other procedures and why alternative procedures are commonly used. Recall that we are trying to make an investment decision and that we are frequently operating under considerable uncertainty about the future. We can only *estimate* the NPV of an investment in this case. The resulting estimate can be very "soft," meaning that the true NPV might be quite different.

Because the true NPV is unknown, the astute financial manager seeks clues to help in assessing whether the estimated NPV is reliable. For this reason, firms would typically use multiple criteria for evaluating a proposal. For example, suppose we have an investment with a positive estimated NPV. Based on our experience with other projects, this one appears to have a short payback and a very high AAR. In this case, the different indicators seem to agree that it's "all systems go." Put another way, the payback and the AAR are consistent with the conclusion that the NPV is positive.

On the other hand, suppose we had a positive estimated NPV, a long payback, and a low AAR. This could still be a good investment, but it looks like we need to be much more careful in making the decision because we are getting conflicting signals. If the estimated NPV is based on projections in which we have little confidence, then further analysis is probably in order. We will consider how to evaluate NPV estimates in more detail in the next two chapters.

Large firms often have huge capital budgets. For example, in 2008, ExxonMobil announced that it expected to have about $25 billion in capital outlays during the year, up from $20 billion in 2007. About the same time, competitor ChevronTexaco announced that it would increase its capital budgeting for 2008 to $22.9 billion, up from $20 billion in 2007. Other companies with large capital spending budgets were General Motors, which projected capital spending of about $15 billion for 2008 and 2009 combined, and semiconductor company Intel, which projected capital spending of about $5.2 billion for 2008.

TABLE 9.6   Capital Budgeting Techniques in Practice

A. Historical Comparison of the Primary Use of Various Capital Budgeting Techniques							
	1959	1964	1970	1975	1977	1979	1981
Payback period	34%	24%	12%	15%	9%	10%	5.0%
Average accounting return (AAR)	34	30	26	10	25	14	10.7
Internal rate of return (IRR)	19	38	57	37	54	60	65.3
Net present value (NPV)	—	—	—	26	10	14	16.5
IRR or NPV	19	38	57	63	64	74	81.8

B. Percentage of CFOs Who Always or Almost Always Used a Given Technique in 1999				
Capital Budgeting Technique	Percentage Always or Almost Always Using	Average Score [Scale is 4 (always) to 0 (never)]		
		Overall	Large Firms	Small Firms
Internal rate of return	76%	3.09	3.41	2.87
Net present value	75	3.08	3.42	2.83
Payback period	57	2.53	2.25	2.72
Discounted payback period	29	1.56	1.55	1.58
Accounting rate of return	20	1.34	1.25	1.41
Profitability index	12	.83	.75	.88

SOURCES: J.R. Graham and C.R. Harvey, "The Theory and Practice of Corporate Finance: Evidence from the Field," *Journal of Financial Economics,* May–June 2001, pp. 187–244; J.S. Moore and A.K. Reichert, "An Analysis of the Financial Management Techniques Currently Employed by Large U.S. Corporations," *Journal of Business Finance and Accounting,* Winter 1983, pp. 623–45; M.T. Stanley and S.R. Block, "A Survey of Multinational Capital Budgeting," *The Financial Review,* March 1984, pp. 36–51.

Large-scale capital spending is often an industrywide occurrence. For example, in 2008, capital spending in the semiconductor industry was expected to be $51 billion. This tidy sum represented a 9 percent decrease over the industry capital spending in 2007, which was $56.04 billion. This decrease was in sharp contrast to the 18 percent increase from 2005 to 2006.

According to information released by the Census Bureau in 2008, capital investment for the economy as a whole was $1.31 trillion in 2006, $1.22 trillion in 2005, and $1.05 trillion in 2004. The totals for the three years therefore exceeded $3 trillion! Given the sums at stake, it is not too surprising that careful analysis of capital expenditures is something at which successful businesses seek to become adept.

There have been a number of surveys conducted asking firms what types of investment criteria they actually use. Table 9.6 summarizes the results of several of these. Panel A of the table is a historical comparison looking at the primary capital budgeting techniques used by large firms through time. In 1959, only 19 percent of the firms surveyed used either IRR or NPV, and 68 percent used either payback periods or accounting returns. It is clear that by the 1980s, IRR and NPV had become the dominant criteria.

Panel B of Table 9.6 summarizes the results of a 1999 survey of chief financial officers (CFOs) at both large and small firms in the United States. A total of 392 CFOs responded. What is shown is the percentage of CFOs who always or almost always used the various capital budgeting techniques we described in this chapter. Not surprisingly, IRR and NPV were the two most widely used techniques, particularly at larger firms. However, over half of the respondents always, or almost always, used the payback criterion as well. In fact, among smaller firms, payback was used just about as much as NPV and IRR. Less commonly used were discounted payback, accounting rates of return, and the profitability index. For future reference, the various criteria we have discussed are summarized in Table 9.7.

TABLE 9.7

Summary of Investment Criteria

I. Discounted Cash Flow Criteria

    A. *Net present value (NPV):* The NPV of an investment is the difference between its market value and its cost. The NPV rule is to take a project if its NPV is positive. NPV is frequently estimated by calculating the present value of the future cash flows (to estimate market value) and then subtracting the cost. NPV has no serious flaws; it is the preferred decision criterion.

    B. *Internal rate of return (IRR):* The IRR is the discount rate that makes the estimated NPV of an investment equal to zero; it is sometimes called the *discounted cash flow (DCF) return*. The IRR rule is to take a project when its IRR exceeds the required return. IRR is closely related to NPV, and it leads to exactly the same decisions as NPV for conventional, independent projects. When project cash flows are not conventional, there may be no IRR or there may be more than one. More seriously, the IRR cannot be used to rank mutually exclusive projects; the project with the highest IRR is not necessarily the preferred investment.

    C. *Modified internal rate of return (MIRR):* The MIRR is a modification to the IRR. A project's cash flows are modified by (1) discounting the negative cash flows back to the present; (2) compounding cash flows to the end of the project's life; or (3) combining (1) and (2). An IRR is then computed on the modified cash flows. MIRRs are guaranteed to avoid the multiple rate of return problem, but it is unclear how to interpret them; and they are not truly "internal" because they depend on externally supplied discounting or compounding rates.

    D. *Profitability index (PI):* The PI, also called the *benefit–cost ratio,* is the ratio of present value to cost. The PI rule is to take an investment if the index exceeds 1. The PI measures the present value of an investment per dollar invested. It is quite similar to NPV; but, like IRR, it cannot be used to rank mutually exclusive projects. However, it is sometimes used to rank projects when a firm has more positive NPV investments than it can currently finance.

II. Payback Criteria

    A. *Payback period:* The payback period is the length of time until the sum of an investment's cash flows equals its cost. The payback period rule is to take a project if its payback is less than some cutoff. The payback period is a flawed criterion, primarily because it ignores risk, the time value of money, and cash flows beyond the cutoff point.

    B. *Discounted payback period:* The discounted payback period is the length of time until the sum of an investment's discounted cash flows equals its cost. The discounted payback period rule is to take an investment if the discounted payback is less than some cutoff. The discounted payback rule is flawed, primarily because it ignores cash flows after the cutoff.

III. Accounting Criterion

    A. *Average accounting return (AAR):* The AAR is a measure of accounting profit relative to book value. It is *not* related to the IRR, but it is similar to the accounting return on assets (ROA) measure in Chapter 3. The AAR rule is to take an investment if its AAR exceeds a benchmark AAR. The AAR is seriously flawed for a variety of reasons, and it has little to recommend it.

Concept Questions

9.7a What are the most commonly used capital budgeting procedures?

9.7b If NPV is conceptually the best procedure for capital budgeting, why do you think multiple measures are used in practice?

9.8 Summary and Conclusions

This chapter has covered the different criteria used to evaluate proposed investments. The seven criteria, in the order we discussed them, are these:

1. Net present value (NPV).
2. Payback period.
3. Discounted payback period.
4. Average accounting return (AAR).
5. Internal rate of return (IRR).
6. Modified internal rate of return (MIRR).
7. Profitability index (PI).

We illustrated how to calculate each of these and discussed the interpretation of the results. We also described the advantages and disadvantages of each of them. Ultimately a good capital budgeting criterion must tell us two things. First, is a particular project a good investment? Second, if we have more than one good project, but we can take only one of them, which one should we take? The main point of this chapter is that only the NPV criterion can always provide the correct answer to both questions.

For this reason, NPV is one of the two or three most important concepts in finance, and we will refer to it many times in the chapters ahead. When we do, keep two things in mind: (1) NPV is always just the difference between the market value of an asset or project and its cost, and (2) the financial manager acts in the shareholders' best interests by identifying and taking positive NPV projects.

Finally, we noted that NPVs can't normally be observed in the market; instead, they must be estimated. Because there is always the possibility of a poor estimate, financial managers use multiple criteria for examining projects. The other criteria provide additional information about whether a project truly has a positive NPV.

CHAPTER REVIEW AND SELF-TEST PROBLEMS

9.1   Investment Criteria   This problem will give you some practice calculating NPVs and paybacks. A proposed overseas expansion has the following cash flows:

Year	Cash Flow
0	−$200
1	50
2	60
3	70
4	200

Calculate the payback, the discounted payback, and the NPV at a required return of 10 percent.

9.2   Mutually Exclusive Investments   Consider the following two mutually exclusive investments. Calculate the IRR for each and the crossover rate. Under what circumstances will the IRR and NPV criteria rank the two projects differently?

Year	Investment A	Investment B
0	−$75	−$75
1	20	60
2	40	50
3	70	15

9.3 **Average Accounting Return** You are looking at a three-year project with a projected net income of $2,000 in year 1, $4,000 in year 2, and $6,000 in year 3. The cost is $12,000, which will be depreciated straight-line to zero over the three-year life of the project. What is the average accounting return (AAR)?

ANSWERS TO CHAPTER REVIEW AND SELF-TEST PROBLEMS

9.1 In the following table, we have listed the cash flow, cumulative cash flow, discounted cash flow (at 10 percent), and cumulative discounted cash flow for the proposed project.

	Cash Flow		Accumulated Cash Flow	
Year	Undiscounted	Discounted	Undiscounted	Discounted
1	$ 50	$ 45.45	$ 50	$ 45.45
2	60	49.59	110	95.04
3	70	52.59	180	147.63
4	200	136.60	380	284.23

Recall that the initial investment was $200. When we compare this to accumulated undiscounted cash flows, we see that payback occurs between years 3 and 4. The cash flows for the first three years are $180 total, so, going into the fourth year, we are short by $20. The total cash flow in year 4 is $200, so the payback is 3 + ($20/200) = 3.10 years.

Looking at the accumulated discounted cash flows, we see that the discounted payback occurs between years 3 and 4. The sum of the discounted cash flows is $284.23, so the NPV is $84.23. Notice that this is the present value of the cash flows that occur after the discounted payback.

9.2 To calculate the IRR, we might try some guesses, as in the following table:

Discount Rate	NPV(A)	NPV(B)
0%	$55.00	$50.00
10	28.83	32.14
20	9.95	18.40
30	− 4.09	7.57
40	−14.80	− 1.17

Several things are immediately apparent from our guesses. First, the IRR on A must be between 20 percent and 30 percent (why?). With some more effort, we find that it's 26.79 percent. For B, the IRR must be a little less than 40 percent (again, why?); it works out to be 38.54 percent. Also, notice that at rates between 0 percent and 10 percent, the NPVs are very close, indicating that the crossover is in that vicinity.

To find the crossover exactly, we can compute the IRR on the difference in the cash flows. If we take the cash flows from A minus the cash flows from B, the resulting cash flows are:

Year	A – B
0	$ 0
1	– 40
2	– 10
3	55

These cash flows look a little odd; but the sign changes only once, so we can find an IRR. With some trial and error, you'll see that the NPV is zero at a discount rate of 5.42 percent, so this is the crossover rate.

The IRR for B is higher. However, as we've seen, A has the larger NPV for any discount rate less than 5.42 percent, so the NPV and IRR rankings will conflict in that range. Remember, if there's a conflict, we will go with the higher NPV. Our decision rule is thus simple: Take A if the required return is less than 5.42 percent, take B if the required return is between 5.42 percent and 38.54 percent (the IRR on B), and take neither if the required return is more than 38.54 percent.

9.3   Here we need to calculate the ratio of average net income to average book value to get the AAR. Average net income is:

Average net income = ($2,000 + 4,000 + 6,000)/3 = $4,000

Average book value is:

Average book value = $12,000/2 = $6,000

So the average accounting return is:

AAR = $4,000/6,000 = 66.67%

This is an impressive return. Remember, however, that it isn't really a rate of return like an interest rate or an IRR, so the size doesn't tell us a lot. In particular, our money is probably not going to grow at a rate of 66.67 percent per year, sorry to say.

CONCEPTS REVIEW AND CRITICAL THINKING QUESTIONS

1. **Payback Period and Net Present Value [LO1, 2]** If a project with conventional cash flows has a payback period less than the project's life, can you definitively state the algebraic sign of the NPV? Why or why not? If you know that the discounted payback period is less than the project's life, what can you say about the NPV? Explain.

2. **Net Present Value [LO1]** Suppose a project has conventional cash flows and a positive NPV. What do you know about its payback? Its discounted payback? Its profitability index? Its IRR? Explain.

3. **Payback Period [LO2]** Concerning payback:
   a. Describe how the payback period is calculated, and describe the information this measure provides about a sequence of cash flows. What is the payback criterion decision rule?
   b. What are the problems associated with using the payback period to evaluate cash flows?

c. What are the advantages of using the payback period to evaluate cash flows? Are there any circumstances under which using payback might be appropriate? Explain.

4. **Discounted Payback** [LO3] Concerning discounted payback:

a. Describe how the discounted payback period is calculated, and describe the information this measure provides about a sequence of cash flows. What is the discounted payback criterion decision rule?

b. What are the problems associated with using the discounted payback period to evaluate cash flows?

c. What conceptual advantage does the discounted payback method have over the regular payback method? Can the discounted payback ever be longer than the regular payback? Explain.

5. **Average Accounting Return** [LO4] Concerning AAR:

a. Describe how the average accounting return is usually calculated, and describe the information this measure provides about a sequence of cash flows. What is the AAR criterion decision rule?

b. What are the problems associated with using the AAR to evaluate a project's cash flows? What underlying feature of AAR is most troubling to you from a financial perspective? Does the AAR have any redeeming qualities?

6. **Net Present Value** [LO1] Concerning NPV:

a. Describe how NPV is calculated, and describe the information this measure provides about a sequence of cash flows. What is the NPV criterion decision rule?

b. Why is NPV considered a superior method of evaluating the cash flows from a project? Suppose the NPV for a project's cash flows is computed to be $2,500. What does this number represent with respect to the firm's shareholders?

7. **Internal Rate of Return** [LO5] Concerning IRR:

a. Describe how the IRR is calculated, and describe the information this measure provides about a sequence of cash flows. What is the IRR criterion decision rule?

b. What is the relationship between IRR and NPV? Are there any situations in which you might prefer one method over the other? Explain.

c. Despite its shortcomings in some situations, why do most financial managers use IRR along with NPV when evaluating projects? Can you think of a situation in which IRR might be a more appropriate measure to use than NPV? Explain.

8. **Profitability Index** [LO7] Concerning the profitability index:

a. Describe how the profitability index is calculated, and describe the information this measure provides about a sequence of cash flows. What is the profitability index decision rule?

b. What is the relationship between the profitability index and NPV? Are there any situations in which you might prefer one method over the other? Explain.

9. **Payback and Internal Rate of Return** [LO2, 5] A project has perpetual cash flows of C per period, a cost of I, and a required return of R. What is the relationship between the project's payback and its IRR? What implications does your answer have for long-lived projects with relatively constant cash flows?

10. **International Investment Projects** [LO1] In January 2008, automobile manufacturer Volkswagen announced plans to build an automatic transmission and engine plant in South Carolina. Volkswagen apparently felt that it would be better able to compete and create value with U.S.-based facilities. Other companies such as Fuji

Film and Swiss chemical company Lonza have reached similar conclusions and taken similar actions. What are some of the reasons that foreign manufacturers of products as diverse as automobiles, film, and chemicals might arrive at this same conclusion?

11. **Capital Budgeting Problems** [LO1] What difficulties might come up in actual applications of the various criteria we discussed in this chapter? Which one would be the easiest to implement in actual applications? The most difficult?

12. **Capital Budgeting in Not-for-Profit Entities** [LO1] Are the capital budgeting criteria we discussed applicable to not-for-profit corporations? How should such entities make capital budgeting decisions? What about the U.S. government? Should it evaluate spending proposals using these techniques?

13. **Modified Internal Rate of Return** [LO6] One of the less flattering interpretations of the acronym MIRR is "meaningless internal rate of return." Why do you think this term is applied to MIRR?

14. **Net Present Value** [LO1] It is sometimes stated that "the net present value approach assumes reinvestment of the intermediate cash flows at the required return." Is this claim correct? To answer, suppose you calculate the NPV of a project in the usual way. Next, suppose you do the following:

   a. Calculate the future value (as of the end of the project) of all the cash flows other than the initial outlay assuming they are reinvested at the required return, producing a single future value figure for the project.

   b. Calculate the NPV of the project using the single future value calculated in the previous step and the initial outlay. It is easy to verify that you will get the same NPV as in your original calculation only if you use the required return as the reinvestment rate in the previous step.

15. **Internal Rate of Return** [LO5] It is sometimes stated that "the internal rate of return approach assumes reinvestment of the intermediate cash flows at the internal rate of return." Is this claim correct? To answer, suppose you calculate the IRR of a project in the usual way. Next, suppose you do the following:

   a. Calculate the future value (as of the end of the project) of all the cash flows other than the initial outlay assuming they are reinvested at the IRR, producing a single future value figure for the project.

   b. Calculate the IRR of the project using the single future value calculated in the previous step and the initial outlay. It is easy to verify that you will get the same IRR as in your original calculation only if you use the IRR as the reinvestment rate in the previous step.

QUESTIONS AND PROBLEMS   ™

BASIC
(Questions 1–19)

1. **Calculating Payback** [LO2] What is the payback period for the following set of cash flows?

Year	Cash Flow
0	−$6,400
1	1,600
2	1,900
3	2,300
4	1,400

2. **Calculating Payback [LO2]** An investment project provides cash inflows of $765 per year for eight years. What is the project payback period if the initial cost is $2,400? What if the initial cost is $3,600? What if it is $6,500?

3. **Calculating Payback [LO2]** Buy Coastal, Inc., imposes a payback cutoff of three years for its international investment projects. If the company has the following two projects available, should it accept either of them?

Year	Cash Flow (A)	Cash Flow (B)
0	−$40,000	−$ 60,000
1	19,000	14,000
2	25,000	17,000
3	18,000	24,000
4	6,000	270,000

4. **Calculating Discounted Payback [LO3]** An investment project has annual cash inflows of $4,200, $5,300, $6,100, and $7,400, and a discount rate of 14 percent. What is the discounted payback period for these cash flows if the initial cost is $7,000? What if the initial cost is $10,000? What if it is $13,000?

5. **Calculating Discounted Payback [LO3]** An investment project costs $15,000 and has annual cash flows of $4,300 for six years. What is the discounted payback period if the discount rate is zero percent? What if the discount rate is 5 percent? If it is 19 percent?

6. **Calculating AAR [LO4]** You're trying to determine whether to expand your business by building a new manufacturing plant. The plant has an installation cost of $15 million, which will be depreciated straight-line to zero over its four-year life. If the plant has projected net income of $1,938,200, $2,201,600, $1,876,000, and $1,329,500 over these four years, what is the project's average accounting return (AAR)?

7. **Calculating IRR [LO5]** A firm evaluates all of its projects by applying the IRR rule. If the required return is 16 percent, should the firm accept the following project?

Year	Cash Flow
0	−$34,000
1	16,000
2	18,000
3	15,000

8. **Calculating NPV [LO1]** For the cash flows in the previous problem, suppose the firm uses the NPV decision rule. At a required return of 11 percent, should the firm accept this project? What if the required return was 30 percent?

9. **Calculating NPV and IRR [LO1, 5]** A project that provides annual cash flows of $28,500 for nine years costs $138,000 today. Is this a good project if the required return is 8 percent? What if it's 20 percent? At what discount rate would you be indifferent between accepting the project and rejecting it?

10. **Calculating IRR [LO5]** What is the IRR of the following set of cash flows?

Year	Cash Flow
0	−$19,500
1	9,800
2	10,300
3	8,600

11. **Calculating NPV** [LO1] For the cash flows in the previous problem, what is the NPV at a discount rate of zero percent? What if the discount rate is 10 percent? If it is 20 percent? If it is 30 percent?

12. **NPV versus IRR** [LO1, 5] Mahjong, Inc., has identified the following two mutually exclusive projects:

Year	Cash Flow (A)	Cash Flow (B)
0	−$43,000	−$43,000
1	23,000	7,000
2	17,900	13,800
3	12,400	24,000
4	9,400	26,000

   a. What is the IRR for each of these projects? Using the IRR decision rule, which project should the company accept? Is this decision necessarily correct?

   b. If the required return is 11 percent, what is the NPV for each of these projects? Which project will the company choose if it applies the NPV decision rule?

   c. Over what range of discount rates would the company choose project A? Project B? At what discount rate would the company be indifferent between these two projects? Explain.

13. **NPV versus IRR** [LO1, 5] Consider the following two mutually exclusive projects:

Year	Cash Flow (X)	Cash Flow (Y)
0	−$15,000	−$15,000
1	8,150	7,700
2	5,050	5,150
3	6,800	7,250

   Sketch the NPV profiles for X and Y over a range of discount rates from zero to 25 percent. What is the crossover rate for these two projects?

14. **Problems with IRR** [LO5] Light Sweet Petroleum, Inc., is trying to evaluate a generation project with the following cash flows:

Year	Cash Flow
0	−$45,000,000
1	78,000,000
2	−14,000,000

   a. If the company requires a 12 percent return on its investments, should it accept this project? Why?

   b. Compute the IRR for this project. How many IRRs are there? Using the IRR decision rule, should the company accept the project? What's going on here?

15. **Calculating Profitability Index** [LO7] What is the profitability index for the following set of cash flows if the relevant discount rate is 10 percent? What if the discount rate is 15 percent? If it is 22 percent?

Year	Cash Flow
0	−$14,000
1	7,300
2	6,900
3	5,700

16. **Problems with Profitability Index [LO1, 7]** The Weiland Computer Corporation is trying to choose between the following two mutually exclusive design projects:

Year	Cash Flow (I)	Cash Flow (II)
0	−$53,000	−$16,000
1	27,000	9,100
2	27,000	9,100
3	27,000	9,100

  a. If the required return is 10 percent and the company applies the profitability index decision rule, which project should the firm accept?

  b. If the company applies the NPV decision rule, which project should it take?

  c. Explain why your answers in (a) and (b) are different.

17. **Comparing Investment Criteria [LO1, 2, 3, 5, 7]** Consider the following two mutually exclusive projects:

Year	Cash Flow (A)	Cash Flow (B)
0	−$300,000	−$40,000
1	20,000	19,000
2	50,000	12,000
3	50,000	18,000
4	390,000	10,500

Whichever project you choose, if any, you require a 15 percent return on your investment.

  a. If you apply the payback criterion, which investment will you choose? Why?

  b. If you apply the discounted payback criterion, which investment will you choose? Why?

  c. If you apply the NPV criterion, which investment will you choose? Why?

  d. If you apply the IRR criterion, which investment will you choose? Why?

  e. If you apply the profitability index criterion, which investment will you choose? Why?

  f. Based on your answers in (a) through (e), which project will you finally choose? Why?

18. **NPV and Discount Rates [LO1]** An investment has an installed cost of $684,680. The cash flows over the four-year life of the investment are projected to be $263,279, $294,060, $227,604, and $174,356. If the discount rate is zero, what is the NPV? If the discount rate is infinite, what is the NPV? At what discount rate is the NPV just equal to zero? Sketch the NPV profile for this investment based on these three points.

19. **MIRR [LO6]** Slow Ride Corp. is evaluating a project with the following cash flows:

Year	Cash Flow
0	−$16,000
1	6,100
2	7,800
3	8,400
4	6,500
5	−5,100

The company uses a 10 percent interest rate on all of its projects. Calculate the MIRR of the project using all three methods.

INTERMEDIATE
(Questions 20–22)

20. **MIRR [LO6]** Suppose the company in the previous problem uses an 11 percent discount rate and an 8 percent reinvestment rate on all of its projects. Calculate the MIRR of the project using all three methods using these interest rates.

21. **NPV and the Profitability Index [LO1, 7]** If we define the NPV index as the ratio of NPV to cost, what is the relationship between this index and the profitability index?

22. **Cash Flow Intuition [LO1, 2]** A project has an initial cost of I, has a required return of R, and pays C annually for N years.

    a. Find C in terms of I and N such that the project has a payback period just equal to its life.

    b. Find C in terms of I, N, and R such that this is a profitable project according to the NPV decision rule.

    c. Find C in terms of I, N, and R such that the project has a benefit-cost ratio of 2.

CHALLENGE
(Questions 23–28)

23. **Payback and NPV [LO1, 2]** An investment under consideration has a payback of seven years and a cost of $724,000. If the required return is 12 percent, what is the worst-case NPV? The best-case NPV? Explain. Assume the cash flows are conventional.

24. **Multiple IRRs [LO5]** This problem is useful for testing the ability of financial calculators and computer software. Consider the following cash flows. How many different IRRs are there? (*Hint:* Search between 20 percent and 70 percent.) When should we take this project?

Year	Cash Flow
0	−$1,512
1	8,586
2	−18,210
3	17,100
4	−6,000

25. **NPV Valuation [LO1]** The Yurdone Corporation wants to set up a private cemetery business. According to the CFO, Barry M. Deep, business is "looking up." As a result, the cemetery project will provide a net cash inflow of $85,000 for the firm during the first year, and the cash flows are projected to grow at a rate of 6 percent per year forever. The project requires an initial investment of $1,400,000.

    a. If Yurdone requires a 13 percent return on such undertakings, should the cemetery business be started?

    b. The company is somewhat unsure about the assumption of a 6 percent growth rate in its cash flows. At what constant growth rate would the company just break even if it still required a 13 percent return on investment?

26. **Problems with IRR [LO5]** A project has the following cash flows:

Year	Cash Flow
0	$58,000
1	−34,000
2	−45,000

What is the IRR for this project? If the required return is 12 percent, should the firm accept the project? What is the NPV of this project? What is the NPV of the project if the required return is 0 percent? 24 percent? What is going on here? Sketch the NPV profile to help you with your answer.

27. **Problems with IRR [LO5]** McKeekin Corp. has a project with the following cash flows:

Year	Cash Flow
0	$20,000
1	−26,000
2	13,000

What is the IRR of the project? What is happening here?

28. **NPV and IRR [LO1, 5]** Anderson International Limited is evaluating a project in Erewhon. The project will create the following cash flows:

Year	Cash Flow
0	−$750,000
1	205,000
2	265,000
3	346,000
4	220,000

All cash flows will occur in Erewhon and are expressed in dollars. In an attempt to improve its economy, the Erewhonian government has declared that all cash flows created by a foreign company are "blocked" and must be reinvested with the government for one year. The reinvestment rate for these funds is 4 percent. If Anderson uses an 11 percent required return on this project, what are the NPV and IRR of the project? Is the IRR you calculated the MIRR of the project? Why or why not?

MINICASE

Bullock Gold Mining

Seth Bullock, the owner of Bullock Gold Mining, is evaluating a new gold mine in South Dakota. Dan Dority, the company's geologist, has just finished his analysis of the mine site. He has estimated that the mine would be productive for eight years, after which the gold would be completely mined. Dan has taken an estimate of the gold deposits to Alma Garrett, the company's financial officer. Alma has been asked by Seth to perform an analysis of the new mine and present her recommendation on whether the company should open the new mine.

Alma has used the estimates provided by Dan to determine the revenues that could be expected from the mine. She has also projected the expense of opening the mine and the annual operating expenses. If the company opens the mine, it will cost $600 million today, and it will have a cash outflow of $95 million nine years from today in costs associated with closing the mine and reclaiming the area surrounding it. The expected cash flows each year from the mine are shown in the table. Bullock Mining has a 12 percent required return on all of its gold mines.

Year	Cash Flow
0	−$600,000,000
1	75,000,000
2	120,000,000
3	160,000,000
4	210,000,000
5	240,000,000
6	160,000,000
7	130,000,000
8	90,000,000
9	−95,000,000

QUESTIONS

1. Construct a spreadsheet to calculate the payback period, internal rate of return, modified internal rate of return, and net present value of the proposed mine.

2. Based on your analysis, should the company open the mine?

3. Bonus question: Most spreadsheets do not have a built-in formula to calculate the payback period. Write a VBA script that calculates the payback period for a project.

10

MAKING CAPITAL INVESTMENT DECISIONS

LEARNING OBJECTIVES

After studying this chapter, you should understand:

LO1 How to determine the relevant cash flows for a proposed project.

LO2 How to determine if a project is acceptable.

LO3 How to set a bid price for a project.

LO4 How to evaluate the equivalent annual cost of a project.

IS THERE GREEN IN GREEN? General Electric (GE) thinks so. Through its "Ecomagination" program, the company planned to double research and development spending on green products, from $700 million in 2004 to $1.5 billion in 2010. With products such as a hybrid railroad locomotive (described as a 200-ton, 6,000-horsepower "Prius on rails"), GE's green initiative seems to be paying off. Revenue from green products was $14 billion in 2007, with a target of $25 billion in 2010. The company's internal commitment to reduced energy consumption saved it more than $100 million from 2004 to 2007, and the company was on target to reduce its water consumption by 20 percent by 2012, another considerable cost savings.

As you no doubt recognize from your study of the previous chapter, GE's decision to develop and market green technology represents a capital budgeting decision. In this chapter, we further investigate such decisions, how they are made, and how to look at them objectively.

This chapter follows up on our previous one by delving more deeply into capital budgeting. We have two main tasks. First, recall that in the last chapter, we saw that cash flow estimates are the critical input into a net present value analysis, but we didn't say much about where these cash flows come from; so we will now examine this question in some detail. Our second goal is to learn how to critically examine NPV estimates, and, in particular, how to evaluate the sensitivity of NPV estimates to assumptions made about the uncertain future.

Master the ability to solve problems in this chapter by using a spreadsheet. Access Excel Master on the student Web site www.mhhe.com/rwj.

So far, we've covered various parts of the capital budgeting decision. Our task in this chapter is to start bringing these pieces together. In particular, we will show you how to "spread the numbers" for a proposed investment or project and, based on those numbers, make an initial assessment about whether the project should be undertaken.

In the discussion that follows, we focus on the process of setting up a discounted cash flow analysis. From the last chapter, we know that the projected future cash flows are the key element in such an evaluation. Accordingly, we emphasize working with financial and accounting information to come up with these figures.

In evaluating a proposed investment, we pay special attention to deciding what information is relevant to the decision at hand and what information is not. As we will see, it is easy to overlook important pieces of the capital budgeting puzzle.

We will wait until the next chapter to describe in detail how to go about evaluating the results of our discounted cash flow analysis. Also, where needed, we will assume that we know the relevant required return, or discount rate. We continue to defer in-depth discussion of this subject to Part 5.

Project Cash Flows: A First Look

The effect of taking a project is to change the firm's overall cash flows today and in the future. To evaluate a proposed investment, we must consider these changes in the firm's cash flows and then decide whether they add value to the firm. The first (and most important) step, therefore, is to decide which cash flows are relevant.

RELEVANT CASH FLOWS

What is a relevant cash flow for a project? The general principle is simple enough: A relevant cash flow for a project is a change in the firm's overall future cash flow that comes about as a direct consequence of the decision to take that project. Because the relevant cash flows are defined in terms of changes in, or increments to, the firm's existing cash flow, they are called the **incremental cash flows** associated with the project.

The concept of incremental cash flow is central to our analysis, so we will state a general definition and refer back to it as needed:

incremental cash flows
The difference between a firm's future cash flows with a project and those without the project.

> The incremental cash flows for project evaluation consist of *any and all* changes in the firm's future cash flows that are a direct consequence of taking the project.

This definition of incremental cash flows has an obvious and important corollary: Any cash flow that exists regardless of *whether or not* a project is undertaken is *not* relevant.

THE STAND-ALONE PRINCIPLE

In practice, it would be cumbersome to actually calculate the future total cash flows to the firm with and without a project, especially for a large firm. Fortunately, it is not really necessary to do so. Once we identify the effect of undertaking the proposed project on the firm's cash flows, we need focus only on the project's resulting incremental cash flows. This is called the **stand-alone principle**.

What the stand-alone principle says is that once we have determined the incremental cash flows from undertaking a project, we can view that project as a kind of "minifirm" with its own future revenues and costs, its own assets, and, of course, its own cash flows. We will then be primarily interested in comparing the cash flows from this minifirm to the cost of acquiring it. An important consequence of this approach is that we will be evaluating the proposed project purely on its own merits, in isolation from any other activities or projects.

stand-alone principle
The assumption that evaluation of a project may be based on the project's incremental cash flows.

10.1a What are the relevant incremental cash flows for project evaluation?
10.1b What is the stand-alone principle?

Incremental Cash Flows

We are concerned here with only cash flows that are incremental and that result from a project. Looking back at our general definition, we might think it would be easy enough to decide whether a cash flow is incremental. Even so, in a few situations it is easy to make mistakes. In this section, we describe some common pitfalls and how to avoid them.

SUNK COSTS

sunk cost
A cost that has already been incurred and cannot be removed and therefore should not be considered in an investment decision.

A **sunk cost**, by definition, is a cost we have already paid or have already incurred the liability to pay. Such a cost cannot be changed by the decision today to accept or reject a project. Put another way, the firm will have to pay this cost no matter what. Based on our general definition of incremental cash flow, such a cost is clearly not relevant to the decision at hand. So, we will always be careful to exclude sunk costs from our analysis.

That a sunk cost is not relevant seems obvious given our discussion. Nonetheless, it's easy to fall prey to the fallacy that a sunk cost should be associated with a project. For example, suppose General Milk Company hires a financial consultant to help evaluate whether a line of chocolate milk should be launched. When the consultant turns in the report, General Milk objects to the analysis because the consultant did not include the hefty consulting fee as a cost of the chocolate milk project.

Who is correct? By now, we know that the consulting fee is a sunk cost: It must be paid whether or not the chocolate milk line is actually launched (this is an attractive feature of the consulting business).

OPPORTUNITY COSTS

opportunity cost
The most valuable alternative that is given up if a particular investment is undertaken.

When we think of costs, we normally think of out-of-pocket costs—namely those that require us to actually spend some amount of cash. An **opportunity cost** is slightly different; it requires us to give up a benefit. A common situation arises in which a firm already owns some of the assets a proposed project will be using. For example, we might be thinking of converting an old rustic cotton mill we bought years ago for $100,000 into upmarket condominiums.

If we undertake this project, there will be no direct cash outflow associated with buying the old mill because we already own it. For purposes of evaluating the condo project, should we then treat the mill as "free"? The answer is no. The mill is a valuable resource used by the project. If we didn't use it here, we could do something else with it. Like what? The obvious answer is that, at a minimum, we could sell it. Using the mill for the condo complex thus has an opportunity cost: We give up the valuable opportunity to do something else with the mill.[1]

There is another issue here. Once we agree that the use of the mill has an opportunity cost, how much should we charge the condo project for this use? Given that we paid $100,000, it might seem that we should charge this amount to the condo project. Is this correct? The answer is no, and the reason is based on our discussion concerning sunk costs.

The fact that we paid $100,000 some years ago is irrelevant. That cost is sunk. At a minimum, the opportunity cost that we charge the project is what the mill would sell for today (net of any selling costs) because this is the amount we give up by using the mill instead of selling it.[2]

SIDE EFFECTS

Remember that the incremental cash flows for a project include all the resulting changes in the *firm's* future cash flows. It would not be unusual for a project to have side, or spillover, effects, both good and bad. For example, in 2008, the time between the theatrical release of

---

[1]Economists sometimes use the acronym TANSTAAFL, which is short for "There ain't no such thing as a free lunch," to describe the fact that only very rarely is something truly free.

[2]If the asset in question is unique, then the opportunity cost might be higher because there might be other valuable projects we could undertake that would use it. However, if the asset in question is of a type that is routinely bought and sold (a used car, perhaps), then the opportunity cost is always the going price in the market because that is the cost of buying another similar asset.

a feature film and the release of the DVD had shrunk to 98 days compared to 200 days in 1998. This shortened release time was blamed for at least part of the decline in movie theater box office receipts. Of course, retailers cheered the move because it was credited with increasing DVD sales. A negative impact on the cash flows of an existing product from the introduction of a new product is called **erosion**.[3] In this case, the cash flows from the new line should be adjusted downward to reflect lost profits on other lines.

In accounting for erosion, it is important to recognize that any sales lost as a result of launching a new product might be lost anyway because of future competition. Erosion is relevant only when the sales would not otherwise be lost.

Side effects show up in a lot of different ways. For example, one of Walt Disney Company's concerns when it built Euro Disney was that the new park would drain visitors from the Florida park, a popular vacation destination for Europeans.

There are beneficial spillover effects, of course. For example, you might think that Hewlett-Packard would have been concerned when the price of a printer that sold for $500 to $600 in 1994 declined to below $100 by 2009, but such was not the case. HP realized that the big money is in the consumables that printer owners buy to keep their printers going, such as ink-jet cartridges, laser toner cartridges, and special paper. The profit margins for these products are substantial.

erosion
The cash flows of a new project that come at the expense of a firm's existing projects.

NET WORKING CAPITAL

Normally a project will require that the firm invest in net working capital in addition to long-term assets. For example, a project will generally need some amount of cash on hand to pay any expenses that arise. In addition, a project will need an initial investment in inventories and accounts receivable (to cover credit sales). Some of the financing for this will be in the form of amounts owed to suppliers (accounts payable), but the firm will have to supply the balance. This balance represents the investment in net working capital.

It's easy to overlook an important feature of net working capital in capital budgeting. As a project winds down, inventories are sold, receivables are collected, bills are paid, and cash balances can be drawn down. These activities free up the net working capital originally invested. So the firm's investment in project net working capital closely resembles a loan. The firm supplies working capital at the beginning and recovers it toward the end.

FINANCING COSTS

In analyzing a proposed investment, we will *not* include interest paid or any other financing costs such as dividends or principal repaid because we are interested in the cash flow generated by the assets of the project. As we mentioned in Chapter 2, interest paid, for example, is a component of cash flow to creditors, not cash flow from assets.

More generally, our goal in project evaluation is to compare the cash flow from a project to the cost of acquiring that project in order to estimate NPV. The particular mixture of debt and equity a firm actually chooses to use in financing a project is a managerial variable and primarily determines how project cash flow is divided between owners and creditors. This is not to say that financing arrangements are unimportant. They are just something to be analyzed separately. We will cover this in later chapters.

OTHER ISSUES

There are some other things to watch out for. First, we are interested only in measuring cash flow. Moreover, we are interested in measuring it when it actually occurs, not when it

---

[3]More colorfully, erosion is sometimes called *piracy* or *cannibalism*.

accrues in an accounting sense. Second, we are always interested in *aftertax* cash flow because taxes are definitely a cash outflow. In fact, whenever we write *incremental cash flows,* we mean aftertax incremental cash flows. Remember, however, that aftertax cash flow and accounting profit, or net income, are entirely different things.

Concept Questions

10.2a What is a sunk cost? An opportunity cost?

10.2b Explain what erosion is and why it is relevant.

10.2c Explain why interest paid is not a relevant cash flow for project evaluation.

10.3 Pro Forma Financial Statements and Project Cash Flows

The first thing we need when we begin evaluating a proposed investment is a set of pro forma, or projected, financial statements. Given these, we can develop the projected cash flows from the project. Once we have the cash flows, we can estimate the value of the project using the techniques we described in the previous chapter.

GETTING STARTED: PRO FORMA FINANCIAL STATEMENTS

pro forma financial statements
Financial statements projecting future years' operations.

Pro forma financial statements are a convenient and easily understood means of summarizing much of the relevant information for a project. To prepare these statements, we will need estimates of quantities such as unit sales, the selling price per unit, the variable cost per unit, and total fixed costs. We will also need to know the total investment required, including any investment in net working capital.

To illustrate, suppose we think we can sell 50,000 cans of shark attractant per year at a price of $4 per can. It costs us about $2.50 per can to make the attractant, and a new product such as this one typically has only a three-year life (perhaps because the customer base dwindles rapidly). We require a 20 percent return on new products.

Fixed costs for the project, including such things as rent on the production facility, will run $12,000 per year.[4] Further, we will need to invest a total of $90,000 in manufacturing equipment. For simplicity, we will assume that this $90,000 will be 100 percent depreciated over the three-year life of the project.[5] Furthermore, the cost of removing the equipment will roughly equal its actual value in three years, so it will be essentially worthless on a market value basis as well. Finally, the project will require an initial $20,000 investment in net working capital, and the tax rate is 34 percent.

In Table 10.1, we organize these initial projections by first preparing the pro forma income statement. Once again, notice that we have *not* deducted any interest expense. This will always be so. As we described earlier, interest paid is a financing expense, not a component of operating cash flow.

We can also prepare a series of abbreviated balance sheets that show the capital requirements for the project as we've done in Table 10.2. Here we have net working capital of

---

[4]By *fixed cost,* we literally mean a cash outflow that will occur regardless of the level of sales. This should not be confused with some sort of accounting period charge.

[5]We will also assume that a full year's depreciation can be taken in the first year.

Sales (50,000 units at $4/unit)	$200,000
Variable costs ($2.50/unit)	125,000
	$ 75,000
Fixed costs	12,000
Depreciation ($90,000/3)	30,000
EBIT	$ 33,000
Taxes (34%)	11,220
Net income	$ 21,780

TABLE 10.1

Projected Income Statement, Shark Attractant Project

	Year			
	0	1	2	3
Net working capital	$ 20,000	$20,000	$20,000	$20,000
Net fixed assets	90,000	60,000	30,000	0
Total investment	$110,000	$80,000	$50,000	$20,000

TABLE 10.2

Projected Capital Requirements, Shark Attractant Project

$20,000 in each year. Fixed assets are $90,000 at the start of the project's life (year 0), and they decline by the $30,000 in depreciation each year, ending up at zero. Notice that the total investment given here for future years is the total book, or accounting, value, not market value.

At this point, we need to start converting this accounting information into cash flows. We consider how to do this next.

PROJECT CASH FLOWS

To develop the cash flows from a project, we need to recall (from Chapter 2) that cash flow from assets has three components: operating cash flow, capital spending, and changes in net working capital. To evaluate a project, or minifirm, we need to estimate each of these.

Once we have estimates of the components of cash flow, we will calculate cash flow for our minifirm just as we did in Chapter 2 for an entire firm:

Project cash flow = Project operating cash flow

 − Project change in net working capital

 − Project capital spending

We consider these components next.

Project Operating Cash Flow   To determine the operating cash flow associated with a project, we first need to recall the definition of operating cash flow:

Operating cash flow = Earnings before interest and taxes

 + Depreciation

 − Taxes

To illustrate the calculation of operating cash flow, we will use the projected information from the shark attractant project. For ease of reference, Table 10.3 repeats the income statement in more abbreviated form.

Given the income statement in Table 10.3, calculating the operating cash flow is straightforward. As we see in Table 10.4, projected operating cash flow for the shark attractant project is $51,780.

TABLE 10.3

Projected Income
Statement, Abbreviated,
Shark Attractant Project

Sales	$200,000
Variable costs	125,000
Fixed costs	12,000
Depreciation	30,000
EBIT	$ 33,000
Taxes (34%)	11,220
Net income	$ 21,780

TABLE 10.4

Projected Operating Cash
Flow, Shark Attractant
Project

EBIT	$ 33,000
Depreciation	+ 30,000
Taxes	− 11,220
Operating cash flow	$51,780

TABLE 10.5

Projected Total Cash
Flows, Shark Attractant
Project

	Year			
	0	1	2	3
Operating cash flow		$51,780	$51,780	$51,780
Changes in NWC	−$ 20,000			+ 20,000
Capital spending	− 90,000			
Total project cash flow	−$110,000	$51,780	$51,780	$71,780

Project Net Working Capital and Capital Spending   We next need to take care of the fixed asset and net working capital requirements. Based on our balance sheets, we know that the firm must spend $90,000 up front for fixed assets and invest an additional $20,000 in net working capital. The immediate outflow is thus $110,000. At the end of the project's life, the fixed assets will be worthless, but the firm will recover the $20,000 that was tied up in working capital.[6] This will lead to a $20,000 *inflow* in the last year.

On a purely mechanical level, notice that whenever we have an investment in net working capital, that same investment has to be recovered; in other words, the same number needs to appear at some time in the future with the opposite sign.

PROJECTED TOTAL CASH FLOW AND VALUE

Given the information we've accumulated, we can finish the preliminary cash flow analysis as illustrated in Table 10.5.

Now that we have cash flow projections, we are ready to apply the various criteria we discussed in the last chapter. First, the NPV at the 20 percent required return is:

$$\text{NPV} = -\$110,000 + 51,780/1.2 + 51,780/1.2^2 + 71,780/1.2^3$$
$$= \$10,648$$

---

[6]In reality, the firm would probably recover something less than 100 percent of this amount because of bad debts, inventory loss, and so on. If we wanted to, we could just assume that, for example, only 90 percent was recovered and proceed from there.

Based on these projections, the project creates over $10,000 in value and should be accepted. Also, the return on this investment obviously exceeds 20 percent (because the NPV is positive at 20 percent). After some trial and error, we find that the IRR works out to be about 25.8 percent.

In addition, if required, we could calculate the payback and the average accounting return, or AAR. Inspection of the cash flows shows that the payback on this project is just a little over two years (verify that it's about 2.1 years).[7]

From the last chapter, we know that the AAR is average net income divided by average book value. The net income each year is $21,780. The average (in thousands) of the four book values (from Table 10.2) for total investment is ($110 + 80 + 50 + 20)/4 = $65. So the AAR is $21,780/65,000 = 33.51 percent.[8] We've already seen that the return on this investment (the IRR) is about 26 percent. The fact that the AAR is larger illustrates again why the AAR cannot be meaningfully interpreted as the return on a project.

Concept Questions

10.3a What is the definition of project operating cash flow? How does this differ from net income?

10.3b For the shark attractant project, why did we add back the firm's net working capital investment in the final year?

More about Project Cash Flow

10.4

In this section, we take a closer look at some aspects of project cash flow. In particular, we discuss project net working capital in more detail. We then examine current tax laws regarding depreciation. Finally, we work through a more involved example of the capital investment decision.

A CLOSER LOOK AT NET WORKING CAPITAL

In calculating operating cash flow, we did not explicitly consider the fact that some of our sales might be on credit. Also, we may not have actually paid some of the costs shown. In either case, the cash flow in question would not yet have occurred. We show here that these possibilities are not a problem as long as we don't forget to include changes in net working capital in our analysis. This discussion thus emphasizes the importance and the effect of doing so.

Suppose that during a particular year of a project we have the following simplified income statement:

Sales	$500
Costs	310
Net income	$190

---

[7]We're guilty of a minor inconsistency here. When we calculated the NPV and the IRR, we assumed that all the cash flows occurred at end of year. When we calculated the payback, we assumed that the cash flows occurred uniformly throughout the year.

[8]Notice that the average total book value is not the initial total of $110,000 divided by 2. The reason is that the $20,000 in working capital doesn't "depreciate."

Depreciation and taxes are zero. No fixed assets are purchased during the year. Also, to illustrate a point, we assume that the only components of net working capital are accounts receivable and payable. The beginning and ending amounts for these accounts are as follows:

	Beginning of Year	End of Year	Change
Accounts receivable	$880	$910	+$30
Accounts payable	550	605	+ 55
Net working capital	$330	$305	−$25

Based on this information, what is total cash flow for the year? We can first just mechanically apply what we have been discussing to come up with the answer. Operating cash flow in this particular case is the same as EBIT because there are no taxes or depreciation; thus, it equals $190. Also, notice that net working capital actually *declined* by $25. This just means that $25 was freed up during the year. There was no capital spending, so the total cash flow for the year is:

$$\text{Total cash flow} = \text{Operating cash flow} - \text{Change in NWC} - \text{Capital spending}$$
$$= \$190 - (-25) - 0$$
$$= \$215$$

Now, we know that this $215 total cash flow has to be "dollars in" less "dollars out" for the year. We could therefore ask a different question: What were cash revenues for the year? Also, what were cash costs?

To determine cash revenues, we need to look more closely at net working capital. During the year, we had sales of $500. However, accounts receivable rose by $30 over the same time period. What does this mean? The $30 increase tells us that sales exceeded collections by $30. In other words, we haven't yet received the cash from $30 of the $500 in sales. As a result, our cash inflow is $500 − 30 = $470. In general, cash income is sales minus the increase in accounts receivable.

Cash outflows can be similarly determined. We show costs of $310 on the income statement, but accounts payable increased by $55 during the year. This means that we have not yet paid $55 of the $310, so cash costs for the period are just $310 − 55 = $255. In other words, in this case, cash costs equal costs less the increase in accounts payable.[9]

Putting this information together, we calculate that cash inflows less cash outflows are $470 − 255 = $215, just as we had before. Notice that:

$$\text{Cash flow} = \text{Cash inflow} - \text{Cash outflow}$$
$$= (\$500 - 30) - (310 - 55)$$
$$= (\$500 - 310) - (30 - 55)$$
$$= \text{Operating cash flow} - \text{Change in NWC}$$
$$= \$190 - (-25)$$
$$= \$215$$

More generally, this example illustrates that including net working capital changes in our calculations has the effect of adjusting for the discrepancy between accounting sales and costs and actual cash receipts and payments.

---

[9]If there were other accounts, we might have to make some further adjustments. For example, a net increase in inventory would be a cash outflow.

Samuel Weaver on Capital Budgeting at The Hershey Company

The capital program at The Hershey Company and most Fortune 500 or Fortune 1,000 companies involves a three-phase approach: planning or budgeting, evaluation, and postcompletion reviews.

The first phase involves identification of likely projects at strategic planning time. These are selected to support the strategic objectives of the corporation. This identification is generally broad in scope with minimal financial evaluation attached. Projects are classified as new product, cost savings, capacity expansion, etc. As the planning process focuses more closely on the short-term plans (or budgets), major capital expenditures are scrutinized more rigorously. Project costs are more closely honed, and specific projects may be reconsidered.

Each project is then individually reviewed and authorized. Planning, developing, and refining cash flows underlie capital analysis at Hershey. Once the cash flows have been determined, the application of capital evaluation techniques such as those using net present value, internal rate of return, and payback period is routine. Presentation of the results is enhanced using sensitivity analysis, which plays a major role for management in assessing the critical assumptions and resulting impact.

The final phase relates to postcompletion reviews in which the original forecasts of the project's performance are compared to actual results and/or revised expectations.

Capital expenditure analysis is only as good as the assumptions that underlie the project. The old cliché of GIGO (garbage in, garbage out) applies in this case. Incremental cash flows primarily result from incremental sales or margin improvements (cost savings). For the most part, a range of incremental cash flows can be identified from marketing research or engineering studies. However, for a number of projects, correctly discerning the implications and the relevant cash flows is analytically challenging. For example, when a new product is introduced and is expected to generate millions of dollars' worth of sales, the appropriate analysis focuses on the incremental sales after accounting for cannibalization of existing products.

One of the problems that we face at Hershey deals with the application of net present value, NPV, versus internal rate of return, IRR. NPV offers us the correct investment indication when dealing with mutually exclusive alternatives. However, decision makers at all levels sometimes find it difficult to comprehend the result. Specifically, an NPV of, say, $535,000 needs to be interpreted. It is not enough to know that the NPV is positive or even that it is more positive than an alternative. Decision makers seek to determine a level of "comfort" regarding how profitable the investment is by relating it to other standards.

Although the IRR may provide a misleading indication of which project to select, the result is provided in a way that can be interpreted by all parties. The resulting IRR can be mentally compared to expected inflation, current borrowing rates, the cost of capital, an equity portfolio's return, and so on. An IRR of, say, 18 percent is readily interpretable by management. Perhaps this ease of understanding is why surveys indicate that many Fortune 500 or Fortune 1,000 companies use the IRR method (in conjunction with NPV) as a primary evaluation technique.

In addition to the NPV versus IRR problem, there are a limited number of projects for which traditional capital expenditure analysis is difficult to apply because the cash flows can't be determined. When new computer equipment is purchased, an office building is renovated, or a parking lot is repaved, it is essentially impossible to identify the cash flows, so the use of traditional evaluation techniques is limited. These types of "capital expenditure" decisions are made using other techniques that hinge on management's judgment.

Samuel Weaver, Ph.D., is the former director, financial planning and analysis, for Hershey Chocolate North America. He is a certified management accountant and certified financial manager. His position combined the theoretical with the pragmatic and involved the analysis of many different facets of finance in addition to capital expenditure analysis.

Cash Collections and Costs	EXAMPLE 10.1

For the year just completed, the Combat Wombat Telestat Co. (CWT) reports sales of $998 and costs of $734. You have collected the following beginning and ending balance sheet information:

(continued)

	Beginning	Ending
Accounts receivable	$100	$110
Inventory	100	80
Accounts payable	100	70
Net working capital	$100	$120

Based on these figures, what are cash inflows? Cash outflows? What happened to each account? What is net cash flow?

Sales were $998, but receivables rose by $10. So cash collections were $10 less than sales, or $988. Costs were $734, but inventories fell by $20. This means that we didn't replace $20 worth of inventory, so costs are actually overstated by this amount. Also, payables fell by $30. This means that, on a net basis, we actually paid our suppliers $30 more than we received from them, resulting in a $30 understatement of costs. Adjusting for these events, we calculate that cash costs are $734 − 20 + 30 = $744. Net cash flow is $988 − 744 = $244.

Finally, notice that net working capital increased by $20 overall. We can check our answer by noting that the original accounting sales less costs (= $998 − 734) are $264. In addition, CWT spent $20 on net working capital, so the net result is a cash flow of $264 − 20 = $244, as we calculated.

DEPRECIATION

As we note elsewhere, accounting depreciation is a noncash deduction. As a result, depreciation has cash flow consequences only because it influences the tax bill. The way that depreciation is computed for tax purposes is thus the relevant method for capital investment decisions. Not surprisingly, the procedures are governed by tax law. We now discuss some specifics of the depreciation system enacted by the Tax Reform Act of 1986. This system is a modification of the **accelerated cost recovery system (ACRS)** instituted in 1981.

accelerated cost recovery system (ACRS)
A depreciation method under U.S. tax law allowing for the accelerated write-off of property under various classifications.

Modified ACRS Depreciation (MACRS)   Calculating depreciation is normally mechanical. Although there are a number of *ifs, ands,* and *buts* involved, the basic idea under MACRS is that every asset is assigned to a particular class. An asset's class establishes its life for tax purposes. Once an asset's tax life is determined, the depreciation for each year is computed by multiplying the cost of the asset by a fixed percentage.[10] The expected salvage value (what we think the asset will be worth when we dispose of it) and the expected economic life (how long we expect the asset to be in service) are not explicitly considered in the calculation of depreciation.

Some typical depreciation classes are given in Table 10.6, and associated percentages (as specified by the IRS) are shown in Table 10.7.[11]

A nonresidential real property, such as an office building, is depreciated over 31.5 years using straight-line depreciation. A residential real property, such as an apartment building, is depreciated straight-line over 27.5 years. Remember that land cannot be depreciated.[12]

[10]Under certain circumstances, the cost of the asset may be adjusted before computing depreciation. The result is called the *depreciable basis,* and depreciation is calculated using this number instead of the actual cost.

[11]For the curious, these depreciation percentages are derived from a double-declining balance scheme with a switch to straight-line when the latter becomes advantageous. Further, there is a half-year convention, meaning that all assets are assumed to be placed in service midway through the tax year. This convention is maintained unless more than 40 percent of an asset's cost is incurred in the final quarter. In this case, a midquarter convention is used. The odd-looking rounding is courtesy of the IRS.

[12]There are, however, depletion allowances for firms in extraction-type lines of business (such as mining). These are somewhat similar to depreciation allowances.

Class	Examples
Three-year	Equipment used in research
Five-year	Autos, computers
Seven-year	Most industrial equipment

TABLE 10.6

Modified ACRS Property Classes

	Property Class		
Year	Three-Year	Five-Year	Seven-Year
1	33.33%	20.00%	14.29%
2	44.45	32.00	24.49
3	14.81	19.20	17.49
4	7.41	11.52	12.49
5		11.52	8.93
6		5.76	8.92
7			8.93
8			4.46

TABLE 10.7

Modified ACRS Depreciation Allowances

To illustrate how depreciation is calculated, we consider an automobile costing $12,000. Autos are normally classified as five-year property. Looking at Table 10.7, we see that the relevant figure for the first year of a five-year asset is 20 percent.[13] The depreciation in the first year is thus $12,000 × .20 = $2,400. The relevant percentage in the second year is 32 percent, so the depreciation in the second year is $12,000 × .32 = $3,840, and so on. We can summarize these calculations as follows:

Year	MACRS Percentage	Depreciation		
1	20.00%	.2000 × $12,000 =	$	2,400.00
2	32.00%	.3200 × 12,000 =		3,840.00
3	19.20%	.1920 × 12,000 =		2,304.00
4	11.52%	.1152 × 12,000 =		1,382.40
5	11.52%	.1152 × 12,000 =		1,382.40
6	5.76%	.0576 × 12,000 =		691.20
	100.00%			$12,000.00

Notice that the MACRS percentages sum up to 100 percent. As a result, we write off 100 percent of the cost of the asset, or $12,000 in this case.

Book Value versus Market Value In calculating depreciation under current tax law, the economic life and future market value of the asset are not an issue. As a result, the book value of an asset can differ substantially from its actual market value. For example, with our $12,000 car, book value after the first year is $12,000 less the first year's depreciation of $2,400, or $9,600. The remaining book values are summarized in Table 10.8. After six years, the book value of the car is zero.

Suppose we wanted to sell the car after five years. Based on historical averages, it would be worth, say, 25 percent of the purchase price, or .25 × $12,000 = $3,000. If we actually

---

[13]It may appear odd that five-year property is depreciated over six years. The tax accounting reason is that it is assumed we have the asset for only six months in the first year and, consequently, six months in the last year. As a result, there are five 12-month periods, but we have some depreciation in each of six different tax years.

TABLE 10.8

MACRS Book Values

Year	Beginning Book Value	Depreciation	Ending Book Value
1	$12,000.00	$2,400.00	$9,600.00
2	9,600.00	3,840.00	5,760.00
3	5,760.00	2,304.00	3,456.00
4	3,456.00	1,382.40	2,073.60
5	2,073.60	1,382.40	691.20
6	691.20	691.20	.00

sold it for this, then we would have to pay taxes at the ordinary income tax rate on the difference between the sale price of $3,000 and the book value of $691.20. For a corporation in the 34 percent bracket, the tax liability would be .34 × $2,308.80 = $784.99.[14]

The reason taxes must be paid in this case is that the difference between market value and book value is "excess" depreciation, and it must be "recaptured" when the asset is sold. What this means is that, as it turns out, we overdepreciated the asset by $3,000 − 691.20 = $2,308.80. Because we deducted $2,308.80 too much in depreciation, we paid $784.99 too little in taxes, and we simply have to make up the difference.

Notice that this is *not* a tax on a capital gain. As a general (albeit rough) rule, a capital gain occurs only if the market price exceeds the original cost. However, what is and what is not a capital gain is ultimately up to taxing authorities, and the specific rules can be complex. We will ignore capital gains taxes for the most part.

Finally, if the book value exceeds the market value, then the difference is treated as a loss for tax purposes. For example, if we sell the car after two years for $4,000, then the book value exceeds the market value by $1,760. In this case, a tax saving of .34 × $1,760 = $598.40 occurs.

---

[14]The rules are different and more complicated with real property. Essentially, in this case, only the difference between the actual book value and the book value that would have existed if straight-line depreciation had been used is recaptured. Anything above the straight-line book value is considered a capital gain.

EXAMPLE 10.2   MACRS Depreciation

The Staple Supply Co. has just purchased a new computerized information system with an installed cost of $160,000. The computer is treated as five-year property. What are the yearly depreciation allowances? Based on historical experience, we think that the system will be worth only $10,000 when Staple gets rid of it in four years. What are the tax consequences of the sale? What is the total aftertax cash flow from the sale?

The yearly depreciation allowances are calculated by just multiplying $160,000 by the five-year percentages found in Table 10.7:

Year	MACRS Percentage	Depreciation		Ending Book Value
1	20.00%	.2000 × $160,000 =	$ 32,000	$128,000
2	32.00	.3200 × 160,000 =	51,200	76,800
3	19.20	.1920 × 160,000 =	30,720	46,080
4	11.52	.1152 × 160,000 =	18,432	27,648
5	11.52	.1152 × 160,000 =	18,432	9,216
6	5.76	.0576 × 160,000 =	9,216	0
	100.00%		$160,000	

(continued)

Notice that we have also computed the book value of the system as of the end of each year. The book value at the end of year 4 is $27,648. If Staple sells the system for $10,000 at that time, it will have a loss of $17,648 (the difference) for tax purposes. This loss, of course, is like depreciation because it isn't a cash expense.

What really happens? Two things. First, Staple gets $10,000 from the buyer. Second, it saves .34 × $17,648 = $6,000 in taxes. So, the total aftertax cash flow from the sale is a $16,000 cash inflow.

AN EXAMPLE: THE MAJESTIC MULCH AND COMPOST COMPANY (MMCC)

At this point, we want to go through a somewhat more involved capital budgeting analysis. Keep in mind as you read that the basic approach here is exactly the same as that in the shark attractant example used earlier. We have just added some real-world detail (and a lot more numbers).

MMCC is investigating the feasibility of a new line of power mulching tools aimed at the growing number of home composters. Based on exploratory conversations with buyers for large garden shops, MMCC projects unit sales as follows:

Year	Unit Sales
1	3,000
2	5,000
3	6,000
4	6,500
5	6,000
6	5,000
7	4,000
8	3,000

The new power mulcher will sell for $120 per unit to start. When the competition catches up after three years, however, MMCC anticipates that the price will drop to $110.

The power mulcher project will require $20,000 in net working capital at the start. Subsequently, total net working capital at the end of each year will be about 15 percent of sales for that year. The variable cost per unit is $60, and total fixed costs are $25,000 per year.

It will cost about $800,000 to buy the equipment necessary to begin production. This investment is primarily in industrial equipment, which qualifies as seven-year MACRS property. The equipment will actually be worth about 20 percent of its cost in eight years, or .20 × $800,000 = $160,000. The relevant tax rate is 34 percent, and the required return is 15 percent. Based on this information, should MMCC proceed?

Operating Cash Flows   There is a lot of information here that we need to organize. The first thing we can do is calculate projected sales. Sales in the first year are projected at 3,000 units at $120 apiece, or $360,000 total. The remaining figures are shown in Table 10.9.

Next, we compute the depreciation on the $800,000 investment in Table 10.10. With this information, we can prepare the pro forma income statements, as shown in Table 10.11. From here, computing the operating cash flows is straightforward. The results are illustrated in the first part of Table 10.13.

Change in NWC   Now that we have the operating cash flows, we need to determine the changes in NWC. By assumption, net working capital requirements change as sales change. In each year, MMCC will generally either add to or recover some of its project net working

TABLE 10.9

Projected Revenues,
Power Mulcher Project

Year	Unit Price	Unit Sales	Revenues
1	$120	3,000	$360,000
2	120	5,000	600,000
3	120	6,000	720,000
4	110	6,500	715,000
5	110	6,000	660,000
6	110	5,000	550,000
7	110	4,000	440,000
8	110	3,000	330,000

TABLE 10.10

Annual Depreciation,
Power Mulcher Project

Year	MACRS Percentage	Depreciation	Ending Book Value
1	14.29%	.1429 × $800,000 = $114,320	$685,680
2	24.49	.2449 × 800,000 = 195,920	489,760
3	17.49	.1749 × 800,000 = 139,920	349,840
4	12.49	.1249 × 800,000 = 99,920	249,920
5	8.93	.0893 × 800,000 = 71,440	178,480
6	8.92	.0892 × 800,000 = 71,360	107,120
7	8.93	.0893 × 800,000 = 71,440	35,680
8	4.46	.0446 × 800,000 = 35,680	0
	100.00%	$800,000	

TABLE 10.11   Projected Income Statements, Power Mulcher Project

	Year							
	1	2	3	4	5	6	7	8
Unit price	$ 120	$ 120	$ 120	$ 110	$ 110	$ 110	$ 110	$ 110
Unit sales	3,000	5,000	6,000	6,500	6,000	5,000	4,000	3,000
Revenues	$360,000	$600,000	$720,000	$715,000	$660,000	$550,000	$440,000	$330,000
Variable costs	180,000	300,000	360,000	390,000	360,000	300,000	240,000	180,000
Fixed costs	25,000	25,000	25,000	25,000	25,000	25,000	25,000	25,000
Depreciation	114,320	195,920	139,920	99,920	71,440	71,360	71,440	35,680
EBIT	$ 40,680	$ 79,080	$195,080	$200,080	$203,560	$153,640	$103,560	$ 89,320
Taxes (34%)	13,831	26,887	66,327	68,027	69,210	52,238	35,210	30,369
Net income	$ 26,849	$ 52,193	$128,753	$132,053	$134,350	$101,402	$ 68,350	$ 58,951

capital. Recalling that NWC starts out at $20,000 and then rises to 15 percent of sales, we can calculate the amount of NWC for each year as shown in Table 10.12.

As illustrated, during the first year, net working capital grows from $20,000 to .15 × $360,000 = $54,000. The increase in net working capital for the year is thus $54,000 − 20,000 = $34,000. The remaining figures are calculated in the same way.

Year	Revenues	Net Working Capital	Cash Flow
0		$ 20,000	−$20,000
1	$360,000	54,000	− 34,000
2	600,000	90,000	− 36,000
3	720,000	108,000	− 18,000
4	715,000	107,250	750
5	660,000	99,000	8,250
6	550,000	82,500	16,500
7	440,000	66,000	16,500
8	330,000	49,500	16,500

TABLE 10.12

Changes in Net Working Capital, Power Mulcher Project

TABLE 10.13 Projected Cash Flows, Power Mulcher Project

					Year				
	0	1	2	3	4	5	6	7	8
I. Operating Cash Flow									
EBIT		$ 40,680	$ 79,080	$195,080	$200,080	$203,560	$153,640	$103,560	$89,320
Depreciation		114,320	195,920	139,920	99,920	71,440	71,360	71,440	35,680
Taxes		− 13,831	− 26,887	− 66,327	− 68,027	− 69,210	− 52,238	− 35,210	− 30,369
Operating cash flow		$141,169	$248,113	$268,673	$231,973	$205,790	$172,762	$139,790	$94,631
II. Net Working Capital									
Initial NWC	−$ 20,000								
Change in NWC		−$34,000	−$ 36,000	−$18,000	$ 750	$ 8,250	$ 16,500	$ 16,500	$ 16,500
NWC recovery									49,500
Total change in NWC	−$ 20,000	−$34,000	−$ 36,000	−$18,000	$ 750	$ 8,250	$ 16,500	$ 16,500	$ 66,000
III. Capital Spending									
Initial outlay	−$800,000								
Aftertax salvage									$105,600
Capital spending	−$800,000								$105,600

Remember that an increase in net working capital is a cash outflow, so we use a negative sign in this table to indicate an additional investment that the firm makes in net working capital. A positive sign represents net working capital returning to the firm. Thus, for example, $16,500 in NWC flows back to the firm in year 6. Over the project's life, net working capital builds to a peak of $108,000 and declines from there as sales begin to drop off.

We show the result for changes in net working capital in the second part of Table 10.13. Notice that at the end of the project's life, there is $49,500 in net working capital still to be recovered. Therefore, in the last year, the project returns $16,500 of NWC during the year and then returns the remaining $49,500 at the end of the year for a total of $66,000.

TABLE 10.14   Projected Total Cash Flows, Power Mulcher Project

	Year								
	0	**1**	**2**	**3**	**4**	**5**	**6**	**7**	**8**
Operating cash flow		$141,169	$248,113	$268,673	$231,973	$205,790	$172,762	$139,790	$ 94,631
Change in NWC	−$ 20,000	− 34,000	− 36,000	− 18,000	750	8,250	16,500	16,500	66,000
Capital spending	− 800,000								105,600
Total project cash flow	−$820,000	$107,169	$212,113	$250,673	$232,723	$214,040	$189,262	$156,290	$266,231
Cumulative cash flow	−$820,000	−$712,831	−$500,718	−$250,045	−$ 17,322	$196,718	$385,980	$542,270	$808,501
Discounted cash flow @ 15%	− 820,000	93,190	160,388	164,822	133,060	106,416	81,823	58,755	87,031

Net present value (15%) = $65,485
Internal rate of return = 17.24%
Payback   = 4.08 years

Capital Spending   Finally, we have to account for the long-term capital invested in the project. In this case, MMCC invests $800,000 at year 0. By assumption, this equipment will be worth $160,000 at the end of the project. It will have a book value of zero at that time. As we discussed earlier, this $160,000 excess of market value over book value is taxable, so the aftertax proceeds will be $160,000 × (1 − .34) = $105,600. These figures are shown in the third part of Table 10.13.

Total Cash Flow and Value   We now have all the cash flow pieces, and we put them together in Table 10.14. In addition to the total project cash flows, we have calculated the cumulative cash flows and the discounted cash flows. At this point, it's essentially plug-and-chug to calculate the net present value, internal rate of return, and payback.

If we sum the discounted flows and the initial investment, the net present value (at 15 percent) works out to be $65,485. This is positive, so, based on these preliminary projections, the power mulcher project is acceptable. The internal, or DCF, rate of return is greater than 15 percent because the NPV is positive. It works out to be 17.24 percent, again indicating that the project is acceptable.

Looking at the cumulative cash flows, we can see that the project has almost paid back after four years because the table shows that the cumulative cash flow is almost zero at that time. As indicated, the fractional year works out to be $17,322/214,040 = .08, so the payback is 4.08 years. We can't say whether or not this is good because we don't have a benchmark for MMCC. This is the usual problem with payback periods.

Conclusion   This completes our preliminary DCF analysis. Where do we go from here? If we have a great deal of confidence in our projections, there is no further analysis to be done. MMCC should begin production and marketing immediately. It is unlikely that this will be the case. It is important to remember that the result of our analysis is an estimate of NPV, and we will usually have less than complete confidence in our projections. This means we have more work to do. In particular, we will almost surely want to spend some time evaluating the quality of our estimates. We will take up this subject in the next chapter. For now, we look at some alternative definitions of operating cash flow, and we illustrate some different cases that arise in capital budgeting.

Alternative Definitions of Operating Cash Flow

10.5

The analysis we went through in the previous section is quite general and can be adapted to just about any capital investment problem. In the next section, we illustrate some particularly useful variations. Before we do so, we need to discuss the fact that there are different definitions of project operating cash flow that are commonly used, both in practice and in finance texts.

As we will see, the different approaches to operating cash flow that exist all measure the same thing. If they are used correctly, they all produce the same answer, and one is not necessarily any better or more useful than another. Unfortunately, the fact that alternative definitions are used does sometimes lead to confusion. For this reason, we examine several of these variations next to see how they are related.

In the discussion that follows, keep in mind that when we speak of cash flow, we literally mean dollars in less dollars out. This is all we are concerned with. Different definitions of operating cash flow simply amount to different ways of manipulating basic information about sales, costs, depreciation, and taxes to get at cash flow.

For a particular project and year under consideration, suppose we have the following estimates:

Sales = $1,500

Costs = $700

Depreciation = $600

With these estimates, notice that EBIT is:

$$\text{EBIT} = \text{Sales} - \text{Costs} - \text{Depreciation}$$
$$= \$1,500 - 700 - 600$$
$$= \$200$$

Once again, we assume that no interest is paid, so the tax bill is:

$$\text{Taxes} = \text{EBIT} \times T$$
$$= \$200 \times .34 = \$68$$

where T, the corporate tax rate, is 34 percent.

When we put all of this together, we see that project operating cash flow, OCF, is:

$$\text{OCF} = \text{EBIT} + \text{Depreciation} - \text{Taxes}$$
$$= \$200 + 600 - 68 = \$732$$

There are some other ways to determine OCF that could be (and are) used. We consider these next.

THE BOTTOM-UP APPROACH

Because we are ignoring any financing expenses, such as interest, in our calculations of project OCF, we can write project net income as:

$$\begin{aligned}\text{Project net income} &= \text{EBIT} - \text{Taxes} \\ &= \$200 - 68 \\ &= \$132\end{aligned}$$

If we simply add the depreciation to both sides, we arrive at a slightly different and very common expression for OCF:

$$\begin{aligned}\text{OCF} &= \text{Net income} + \text{Depreciation} \\ &= \$132 + 600 \\ &= \$732\end{aligned} \qquad\qquad \text{[10.1]}$$

This is the *bottom-up* approach. Here, we start with the accountant's bottom line (net income) and add back any noncash deductions such as depreciation. It is crucial to remember that this definition of operating cash flow as net income plus depreciation is correct only if there is no interest expense subtracted in the calculation of net income.

For the shark attractant project, net income was $21,780 and depreciation was $30,000, so the bottom-up calculation is:

$$\text{OCF} = \$21,780 + 30,000 = \$51,780$$

This is exactly the same OCF we had previously.

THE TOP-DOWN APPROACH

Perhaps the most obvious way to calculate OCF is:

$$\begin{aligned}\text{OCF} &= \text{Sales} - \text{Costs} - \text{Taxes} \\ &= \$1,500 - 700 - 68 = \$732\end{aligned} \qquad\qquad \text{[10.2]}$$

This is the *top-down* approach, the second variation on the basic OCF definition. Here, we start at the top of the income statement with sales and work our way down to net cash flow by subtracting costs, taxes, and other expenses. Along the way, we simply leave out any strictly noncash items such as depreciation.

For the shark attractant project, the operating cash flow can be readily calculated using the top-down approach. With sales of $200,000, total costs (fixed plus variable) of $137,000, and a tax bill of $11,220, the OCF is:

$$\text{OCF} = \$200,000 - 137,000 - 11,220 = \$51,780$$

This is just as we had before.

THE TAX SHIELD APPROACH

The third variation on our basic definition of OCF is the *tax shield* approach. This approach will be useful for some problems we consider in the next section. The tax shield definition of OCF is:

$$\text{OCF} = (\text{Sales} - \text{Costs}) \times (1 - T) + \text{Depreciation} \times T \qquad\qquad \text{[10.3]}$$

where T is again the corporate tax rate. Assuming that $T = 34\%$, the OCF works out to be:

$$\begin{aligned}\text{OCF} &= (\$1,500 - 700) \times .66 + 600 \times .34 \\ &= \$528 + 204 \\ &= \$732\end{aligned}$$

This is just as we had before.

This approach views OCF as having two components. The first part is what the project's cash flow would be if there were no depreciation expense. In this case, this would-have-been cash flow is $528.

The second part of OCF in this approach is the depreciation deduction multiplied by the tax rate. This is called the **depreciation tax shield**. We know that depreciation is a noncash expense. The only cash flow effect of deducting depreciation is to reduce our taxes, a benefit to us. At the current 34 percent corporate tax rate, every dollar in depreciation expense saves us 34 cents in taxes. So, in our example, the $600 depreciation deduction saves us $600 \times .34 = $204 in taxes.

For the shark attractant project we considered earlier in the chapter, the depreciation tax-shield would be $30,000 \times .34 = $10,200. The aftertax value for sales less costs would be ($200,000 - 137,000) \times (1 - .34) = $41,580. Adding these together yields the value of OCF:

OCF = $41,580 + 10,200 = $51,780

This calculation verifies that the tax shield approach is completely equivalent to the approach we used before.

> **depreciation tax shield**
> The tax saving that results from the depreciation deduction, calculated as depreciation multiplied by the corporate tax rate.

CONCLUSION

Now that we've seen that all of these approaches are the same, you're probably wondering why everybody doesn't just agree on one of them. One reason, as we will see in the next section, is that different approaches are useful in different circumstances. The best one to use is whichever happens to be the most convenient for the problem at hand.

Concept Questions

10.5a What are the top-down and bottom-up definitions of operating cash flow?

10.5b What is meant by the term *depreciation tax shield*?

Some Special Cases of Discounted Cash Flow Analysis

10.6

To finish our chapter, we look at three common cases involving discounted cash flow analysis. The first case involves investments that are primarily aimed at improving efficiency and thereby cutting costs. The second case we consider comes up when a firm is involved in submitting competitive bids. The third and final case arises in choosing between equipment options with different economic lives.

We could consider many other special cases, but these three are particularly important because problems similar to these are so common. Also, they illustrate some diverse applications of cash flow analysis and DCF valuation.

EVALUATING COST-CUTTING PROPOSALS

One decision we frequently face is whether to upgrade existing facilities to make them more cost-effective. The issue is whether the cost savings are large enough to justify the necessary capital expenditure.

For example, suppose we are considering automating some part of an existing production process. The necessary equipment costs $80,000 to buy and install. The automation will save $22,000 per year (before taxes) by reducing labor and material costs. For simplicity, assume that the equipment has a five-year life and is depreciated to zero on a straight-line basis over that period. It will actually be worth $20,000 in five years. Should we automate? The tax rate is 34 percent, and the discount rate is 10 percent.

As always, the first step in making such a decision is to identify the relevant incremental cash flows. First, determining the relevant capital spending is easy enough. The initial cost is $80,000. The aftertax salvage value is $20,000 × (1 − .34) = $13,200 because the book value will be zero in five years. Second, there are no working capital consequences here, so we don't need to worry about changes in net working capital.

Operating cash flows are the third component to consider. Buying the new equipment affects our operating cash flows in two ways. First, we save $22,000 before taxes every year. In other words, the firm's operating income increases by $22,000, so this is the relevant incremental project operating income.

Second (and it's easy to overlook this), we have an additional depreciation deduction. In this case, the depreciation is $80,000/5 = $16,000 per year.

Because the project has an operating income of $22,000 (the annual pretax cost saving) and a depreciation deduction of $16,000, taking the project will increase the firm's EBIT by $22,000 − 16,000 = $6,000, so this is the project's EBIT.

Finally, because EBIT is rising for the firm, taxes will increase. This increase in taxes will be $6,000 × .34 = $2,040. With this information, we can compute operating cash flow in the usual way:

EBIT	$ 6,000
+ Depreciation	16,000
− Taxes	2,040
Operating cash flow	$19,960

So, our aftertax operating cash flow is $19,960.

It might be somewhat more enlightening to calculate operating cash flow using a different approach. What is actually going on here is very simple. First, the cost savings increase our pretax income by $22,000. We have to pay taxes on this amount, so our tax bill increases by .34 × $22,000 = $7,480. In other words, the $22,000 pretax saving amounts to $22,000 × (1 − .34) = $14,520 after taxes.

Second, the extra $16,000 in depreciation isn't really a cash outflow, but it does reduce our taxes by $16,000 × .34 = $5,440. The sum of these two components is $14,520 + 5,440 = $19,960, just as we had before. Notice that the $5,440 is the depreciation tax shield we discussed earlier, and we have effectively used the tax shield approach here.

We can now finish our analysis. Based on our discussion, here are the relevant cash flows:

	Year					
	0	1	2	3	4	5
Operating cash flow		$19,960	$19,960	$19,960	$19,960	$19,960
Capital spending	−$80,000					13,200
Total cash flow	−$80,000	$19,960	$19,960	$19,960	$19,960	$33,160

At 10 percent, it's straightforward to verify that the NPV here is $3,860, so we should go ahead and automate.

To Buy or Not to Buy

EXAMPLE 10.3

We are considering the purchase of a $200,000 computer-based inventory management system. It will be depreciated straight-line to zero over its four-year life. It will be worth $30,000 at the end of that time. The system will save us $60,000 before taxes in inventory-related costs. The relevant tax rate is 39 percent. Because the new setup is more efficient than our existing one, we will be able to carry less total inventory and thus free up $45,000 in net working capital. What is the NPV at 16 percent? What is the DCF return (the IRR) on this investment?

We can first calculate the operating cash flow. The aftertax cost savings are $60,000 × (1 − .39) = $36,600. The depreciation is $200,000/4 = $50,000 per year, so the depreciation tax shield is $50,000 × .39 = $19,500. Operating cash flow is thus $36,600 + 19,500 = $56,100 per year.

The capital spending involves $200,000 up front to buy the system. The aftertax salvage is $30,000 × (1 − .39) = $18,300. Finally, and this is the somewhat tricky part, the initial investment in net working capital is a $45,000 *inflow* because the system frees up working capital. Furthermore, we will have to put this back in at the end of the project's life. What this really means is simple: While the system is in operation, we have $45,000 to use elsewhere.

To finish our analysis, we can compute the total cash flows:

	Year				
	0	1	2	3	4
Operating cash flow		$56,100	$56,100	$56,100	$56,100
Change in NWC	$ 45,000				− 45,000
Capital spending	− 200,000				18,300
Total cash flow	−$155,000	$56,100	$56,100	$56,100	$29,400

At 16 percent, the NPV is −$12,768, so the investment is not attractive. After some trial and error, we find that the NPV is zero when the discount rate is 11.48 percent, so the IRR on this investment is about 11.5 percent.

SETTING THE BID PRICE

Early on, we used discounted cash flow analysis to evaluate a proposed new product. A somewhat different (and common) scenario arises when we must submit a competitive bid to win a job. Under such circumstances, the winner is whoever submits the lowest bid.

There is an old joke concerning this process: The low bidder is whoever makes the biggest mistake. This is called the winner's curse. In other words, if you win, there is a good chance you underbid. In this section, we look at how to go about setting the bid price to avoid the winner's curse. The procedure we describe is useful any time we have to set a price on a product or service.

As with any other capital budgeting project, we must be careful to account for all relevant cash flows. For example, industry analysts estimated that the materials in Microsoft's Xbox 360 cost $470 before assembly. Other items such as the power supply, cables, and controllers increased the materials cost by another $55. At a retail price of $399, Microsoft obviously loses a significant amount on each Xbox 360 it sells. Why would a manufacturer sell at a price well below breakeven? A Microsoft spokesperson stated that the company believed that sales of its game software would make the Xbox 360 a profitable project.

To illustrate how to go about setting a bid price, imagine we are in the business of buying stripped-down truck platforms and then modifying them to customer specifications for resale. A local distributor has requested bids for 5 specially modified trucks each year for the next four years, for a total of 20 trucks in all.

We need to decide what price per truck to bid. The goal of our analysis is to determine the lowest price we can profitably charge. This maximizes our chances of being awarded the contract while guarding against the winner's curse.

Suppose we can buy the truck platforms for $10,000 each. The facilities we need can be leased for $24,000 per year. The labor and material cost to do the modification works out to be about $4,000 per truck. Total cost per year will thus be $24,000 + 5 \times (10,000 + 4,000) = $94,000$.

We will need to invest $60,000 in new equipment. This equipment will be depreciated straight-line to a zero salvage value over the four years. It will be worth about $5,000 at the end of that time. We will also need to invest $40,000 in raw materials inventory and other working capital items. The relevant tax rate is 39 percent. What price per truck should we bid if we require a 20 percent return on our investment?

We start by looking at the capital spending and net working capital investment. We have to spend $60,000 today for new equipment. The aftertax salvage value is $5,000 \times (1 - .39) = $3,050$. Furthermore, we have to invest $40,000 today in working capital. We will get this back in four years.

We can't determine the operating cash flow just yet because we don't know the sales price. Thus, if we draw a time line, here is what we have so far:

	Year				
	0	**1**	**2**	**3**	**4**
Operating cash flow		+OCF	+OCF	+OCF	+OCF
Change in NWC	−$ 40,000				$40,000
Capital spending	− 60,000				3,050
Total cash flow	−$100,000	+OCF	+OCF	+OCF	+OCF + $43,050

With this in mind, note that the key observation is the following: The lowest possible price we can profitably charge will result in a zero NPV at 20 percent. At that price, we earn exactly 20 percent on our investment.

Given this observation, we first need to determine what the operating cash flow must be for the NPV to equal zero. To do this, we calculate the present value of the $43,050 nonoperating cash flow from the last year and subtract it from the $100,000 initial investment:

$100,000 − 43,050/1.20^4 = $100,000 − 20,761 = $79,239$

Once we have done this, our time line is as follows:

	Year				
	0	**1**	**2**	**3**	**4**
Total cash flow	−$79,239	+OCF	+OCF	+OCF	+OCF

As the time line suggests, the operating cash flow is now an unknown ordinary annuity amount. The four-year annuity factor for 20 percent is 2.58873, so we have:

$\text{NPV} = 0 = -$79,239 + \text{OCF} \times 2.58873$

This implies that:

$\text{OCF} = $79,239/2.58873 = $30,609$

So the operating cash flow needs to be $30,609 each year.

We're not quite finished. The final problem is to find out what sales price results in an operating cash flow of $30,609. The easiest way to do this is to recall that operating cash flow can be written as net income plus depreciation (the bottom-up definition). The depreciation here is $60,000/4 = $15,000. Given this, we can determine what net income must be:

Operating cash flow = Net income + Depreciation

$30,609 = Net income + $15,000

Net income = $15,609

From here, we work our way backward up the income statement. If net income is $15,609, then our income statement is as follows:

Sales	?
Costs	$94,000
Depreciation	15,000
Taxes (39%)	?
Net income	$15,609

We can solve for sales by noting that:

Net income = (Sales − Costs − Depreciation) × (1 − T)

$15,609 = (Sales − $94,000 − $15,000) × (1 − .39)

Sales = $15,609/.61 + 94,000 + 15,000

= $134,589

Sales per year must be $134,589. Because the contract calls for five trucks per year, the sales price has to be $134,589/5 = $26,918. If we round this up a bit, it looks as though we need to bid about $27,000 per truck. At this price, were we to get the contract, our return would be just over 20 percent.

EVALUATING EQUIPMENT OPTIONS WITH DIFFERENT LIVES

The final problem we consider involves choosing among different possible systems, equipment setups, or procedures. Our goal is to choose the most cost-effective. The approach we consider here is necessary only when two special circumstances exist. First, the possibilities under evaluation have different economic lives. Second, and just as important, we will need whatever we buy more or less indefinitely. As a result, when it wears out, we will buy another one.

We can illustrate this problem with a simple example. Imagine we are in the business of manufacturing stamped metal subassemblies. Whenever a stamping mechanism wears out, we have to replace it with a new one to stay in business. We are considering which of two stamping mechanisms to buy.

Machine A costs $100 to buy and $10 per year to operate. It wears out and must be replaced every two years. Machine B costs $140 to buy and $8 per year to operate. It lasts for three years and must then be replaced. Ignoring taxes, which one should we choose if we use a 10 percent discount rate?

In comparing the two machines, we notice that the first is cheaper to buy, but it costs more to operate and it wears out more quickly. How can we evaluate these trade-offs? We can start by computing the present value of the costs for each:

Machine A: PV = −$100 + −10/1.1 + −10/1.1² = −$117.36

Machine B: PV = −$140 + −8/1.1 + −8/1.1² + −8/1.1³ = −$159.89

Notice that *all* the numbers here are costs, so they all have negative signs. If we stopped here, it might appear that A is more attractive because the PV of the costs is less. However, all we have really discovered so far is that A effectively provides two years' worth of stamping service for $117.36, whereas B effectively provides three years' worth for $159.89. These costs are not directly comparable because of the difference in service periods.

We need to somehow work out a cost per year for these two alternatives. To do this, we ask: What amount, paid each year over the life of the machine, has the same PV of costs? This amount is called the **equivalent annual cost (EAC)**.

Calculating the EAC involves finding an unknown payment amount. For example, for machine A, we need to find a two-year ordinary annuity with a PV of −$117.36 at 10 percent. Going back to Chapter 6, we know that the two-year annuity factor is:

equivalent annual cost (EAC)

The present value of a project's costs calculated on an annual basis.

$$\text{Annuity factor} = (1 - 1/1.10^2)/.10 = 1.7355$$

For machine A, then, we have:

$$\text{PV of costs} = -\$117.36 = \text{EAC} \times 1.7355$$
$$\text{EAC} = -\$117.36/1.7355$$
$$= -\$67.62$$

For machine B, the life is three years, so we first need the three-year annuity factor:

$$\text{Annuity factor} = (1 - 1/1.10^3)/.10 = 2.4869$$

We calculate the EAC for B just as we did for A:

$$\text{PV of costs} = -\$159.89 = \text{EAC} \times 2.4869$$
$$\text{EAC} = -\$159.89/2.4869$$
$$= -\$64.29$$

Based on this analysis, we should purchase B because it effectively costs $64.29 per year versus $67.62 for A. In other words, all things considered, B is cheaper. In this case, the longer life and lower operating cost are more than enough to offset the higher initial purchase price.

EXAMPLE 10.4	**Equivalent Annual Costs**

This extended example illustrates what happens to the EAC when we consider taxes. You are evaluating two different pollution control options. A filtration system will cost $1.1 million to install and $60,000 annually, before taxes, to operate. It will have to be completely replaced every five years. A precipitation system will cost $1.9 million to install but only $10,000 per year to operate. The precipitation equipment has an effective operating life of eight years. Straight-line depreciation is used throughout, and neither system has any salvage value. Which option should we select if we use a 12 percent discount rate? The tax rate is 34 percent.

We need to consider the EACs for the two systems because they have different service lives and will be replaced as they wear out. The relevant information can be summarized as follows:

	Filtration System	Precipitation System
Aftertax operating cost	−$ 39,600	−$ 6,600
Depreciation tax shield	74,800	80,750
Operating cash flow	$ 35,200	$ 74,150
Economic life	5 years	8 years
Annuity factor (12%)	3.6048	4.9676
Present value of operating cash flow	$ 126,888	$ 368,350
Capital spending	− 1,100,000	− 1,900,000
Total PV of costs	−$ 973,112	−$1,531,650

Notice that the operating cash flow is actually positive in both cases because of the large depreciation tax shields. This can occur whenever the operating cost is small relative to the purchase price.

To decide which system to purchase, we compute the EACs for both using the appropriate annuity factors:

Filtration system: $-\$973{,}112 = \text{EAC} \times 3.6048$

$$\text{EAC} = -\$269{,}951$$

Precipitation system: $-\$1{,}531{,}650 = \text{EAC} \times 4.9676$

$$\text{EAC} = -\$308{,}328$$

The filtration system is the cheaper of the two, so we select it. In this case, the longer life and smaller operating cost of the precipitation system are not sufficient to offset its higher initial cost.

Concept Questions

10.6a In setting a bid price, we used a zero NPV as our benchmark. Explain why this is appropriate.

10.6b Under what circumstances do we have to worry about unequal economic lives? How do you interpret the EAC?

Summary and Conclusions   10.7

This chapter has described how to put together a discounted cash flow analysis. In it, we covered:

1. The identification of relevant project cash flows: We discussed project cash flows and described how to handle some issues that often come up, including sunk costs, opportunity costs, financing costs, net working capital, and erosion.

2. Preparing and using pro forma, or projected, financial statements: We showed how information from such financial statements is useful in coming up with projected cash flows, and we also looked at some alternative definitions of operating cash flow.

3. The role of net working capital and depreciation in determining project cash flows: We saw that including the change in net working capital was important in cash flow analysis because it adjusted for the discrepancy between accounting revenues and costs and cash revenues and costs. We also went over the calculation of depreciation expense under current tax law.

4. Some special cases encountered in using discounted cash flow analysis: Here we looked at three special issues: evaluating cost-cutting investments, how to go about setting a bid price, and the unequal lives problem.

The discounted cash flow analysis we've covered here is a standard tool in the business world. It is a very powerful tool, so care should be taken in its use. The most important thing is to identify the cash flows in a way that makes economic sense. This chapter gives you a good start in learning to do this.

Visit us at www.mhhe.com/rwj

CHAPTER REVIEW AND SELF-TEST PROBLEMS

10.1 Capital Budgeting for Project X Based on the following information for project X, should we undertake the venture? To answer, first prepare a pro forma income statement for each year. Next calculate operating cash flow. Finish the problem by determining total cash flow and then calculating NPV assuming a 28 percent required return. Use a 34 percent tax rate throughout. For help, look back at our shark attractant and power mulcher examples.

Project X involves a new type of graphite composite in-line skate wheel. We think we can sell 6,000 units per year at a price of $1,000 each. Variable costs will run about $400 per unit, and the product should have a four-year life.

Fixed costs for the project will run $450,000 per year. Further, we will need to invest a total of $1,250,000 in manufacturing equipment. This equipment is seven-year MACRS property for tax purposes. In four years, the equipment will be worth about half of what we paid for it. We will have to invest $1,150,000 in net working capital at the start. After that, net working capital requirements will be 25 percent of sales.

10.2 Calculating Operating Cash Flow Mont Blanc Livestock Pens, Inc., has projected a sales volume of $1,650 for the second year of a proposed expansion project. Costs normally run 60 percent of sales, or about $990 in this case. The depreciation expense will be $100, and the tax rate is 35 percent. What is the operating cash flow? Calculate your answer using all of the approaches (including the top-down, bottom-up, and tax shield approaches) described in the chapter.

10.3 Spending Money to Save Money? For help on this one, refer back to the computerized inventory management system in Example 10.3. Here, we're contemplating a new automatic surveillance system to replace our current contract security system. It will cost $450,000 to get the new system. The cost will be depreciated straight-line to zero over the system's four-year expected life. The system is expected to be worth $250,000 at the end of four years after removal costs.

We think the new system will save us $125,000, before taxes, per year in contract security costs. The tax rate is 34 percent. What are the NPV and IRR for buying the new system? The required return is 17 percent.

ANSWERS TO CHAPTER REVIEW AND SELF-TEST PROBLEMS

10.1 To develop the pro forma income statements, we need to calculate the depreciation for each of the four years. The relevant MACRS percentages, depreciation allowances, and book values for the first four years are shown here:

Year	MACRS Percentage	Depreciation	Ending Book Value
1	14.29%	.1429 × $1,250,000 = $178,625	$1,071,375
2	24.49	.2449 × 1,250,000 = 306,125	765,250
3	17.49	.1749 × 1,250,000 = 218,625	546,625
4	12.49	.1249 × 1,250,000 = 156,125	390,500

The projected income statements, therefore, are as follows:

	Year			
	1	2	3	4
Sales	$6,000,000	$6,000,000	$6,000,000	$6,000,000
Variable costs	2,400,000	2,400,000	2,400,000	2,400,000
Fixed costs	450,000	450,000	450,000	450,000
Depreciation	178,625	306,125	218,625	156,125
EBIT	$2,971,375	$2,843,875	$2,931,375	$2,993,875
Taxes (34%)	− 1,010,268	− 966,918	− 996,668	− 1,017,918
Net income	$1,961,108	$1,876,958	$1,934,708	$1,975,958

Based on this information, here are the operating cash flows:

	Year			
	1	2	3	4
EBIT	$2,971,375	$2,843,875	$2,931,375	$2,993,875
Depreciation	178,625	306,125	218,625	156,125
Taxes	− 1,010,268	− 966,918	− 996,668	− 1,017,918
Operating cash flow	$2,139,732	$2,183,082	$2,153,332	$2,132,082

We now have to worry about the nonoperating cash flows. Net working capital starts out at $1,150,000 and then rises to 25 percent of sales, or $1,500,000. This is a $350,000 change in net working capital.

Finally, we have to invest $1,250,000 to get started. In four years, the book value of this investment will be $390,500, compared to an estimated market value of $625,000 (half of the cost). The aftertax salvage is thus $625,000 − .34 × ($625,000 − 390,500) = $545,270.

When we combine all this information, the projected cash flows for project X are as follows:

	Year				
	0	1	2	3	4
Operating cash flow		$2,139,732	$2,183,082	$2,153,332	$2,132,082
Change in NWC	−$1,150,000	− 350,000			1,500,000
Capital spending	− 1,250,000				545,270
Total cash flow	−$2,400,000	$1,789,732	$2,183,082	$2,153,332	$4,177,352

With these cash flows, the NPV at 28 percent is:

$$\text{NPV} = -\$2,400,000 + 1,789,732/1.28 + 2,183,082/1.28^2$$
$$+ 2,153,332/1.28^3 + 4,177,352/1.28^4$$
$$= \$2,913,649$$

So, this project appears quite profitable.

10.2 First, we can calculate the project's EBIT, its tax bill, and its net income:

$$\text{EBIT} = \text{Sales} - \text{Costs} - \text{Depreciation}$$
$$= \$1,650 - 990 - 100 = \$560$$
$$\text{Taxes} = \$560 \times .35 = \$196$$
$$\text{Net income} = \$560 - 196 = \$364$$

With these numbers, operating cash flow is:

$$OCF = EBIT + Depreciation - Taxes$$
$$= \$560 + 100 - 196$$
$$= \$464$$

Using the other OCF definitions, we have:

$$Bottom\text{-}up\ OCF = Net\ income + Depreciation$$
$$= \$364 + 100$$
$$= \$464$$

$$Top\text{-}down\ OCF = Sales - Costs - Taxes$$
$$= \$1,650 - 990 - 196$$
$$= \$464$$

$$Tax\ shield\ OCF = (Sales - Costs) \times (1 - .35) + Depreciation \times .35$$
$$= (\$1,650 - 990) \times .65 + 100 \times .35$$
$$= \$464$$

As expected, all of these definitions produce exactly the same answer.

10.3 The $125,000 pretax saving amounts to $(1 - .34) \times \$125,000 = \$82,500$ after taxes. The annual depreciation of $\$450,000/4 = \$112,500$ generates a tax shield of $.34 \times \$112,500 = \$38,250$ each year. Putting these together, we calculate that the operating cash flow is $\$82,500 + 38,250 = \$120,750$. Because the book value is zero in four years, the aftertax salvage value is $(1 - .34) \times \$250,000 = \$165,000$. There are no working capital consequences, so here are the cash flows:

	Year				
	0	1	2	3	4
Operating cash flow		$120,750	$120,750	$120,750	$120,750
Capital spending	−$450,000				165,000
Total cash flow	−$450,000	$120,750	$120,750	$120,750	$285,750

You can verify that the NPV at 17 percent is −$30,702, and the return on the new surveillance system is only about 13.96 percent. The project does not appear to be profitable.

CONCEPTS REVIEW AND CRITICAL THINKING QUESTIONS

1. **Opportunity Cost [LO1]** In the context of capital budgeting, what is an opportunity cost?

2. **Depreciation [LO1]** Given the choice, would a firm prefer to use MACRS depreciation or straight-line depreciation? Why?

3. **Net Working Capital [LO1]** In our capital budgeting examples, we assumed that a firm would recover all of the working capital it invested in a project. Is this a reasonable assumption? When might it not be valid?

4. **Stand-Alone Principle [LO1]** Suppose a financial manager is quoted as saying, "Our firm uses the stand-alone principle. Because we treat projects like minifirms in our evaluation process, we include financing costs because they are relevant at the firm level." Critically evaluate this statement.

5. **Equivalent Annual Cost [LO4]** When is EAC analysis appropriate for comparing two or more projects? Why is this method used? Are there any implicit assumptions required by this method that you find troubling? Explain.

6. **Cash Flow and Depreciation [LO1]** "When evaluating projects, we're concerned with only the relevant incremental aftertax cash flows. Therefore, because depreciation is a noncash expense, we should ignore its effects when evaluating projects." Critically evaluate this statement.

7. **Capital Budgeting Considerations [LO1]** A major college textbook publisher has an existing finance textbook. The publisher is debating whether to produce an "essentialized" version, meaning a shorter (and lower-priced) book. What are some of the considerations that should come into play?

To answer the next three questions, refer to the following example. In 2003, Porsche unveiled its new sports utility vehicle (SUV), the Cayenne. With a price tag of over $40,000, the Cayenne went from zero to 62 mph in 9.7 seconds. Porsche's decision to enter the SUV market was a response to the runaway success of other high-priced SUVs such as the Mercedes-Benz M-class. Vehicles in this class had generated years of high profits. The Cayenne certainly spiced up the market, and Porsche subsequently introduced the Cayenne Turbo, which goes from zero to 60 mph in 4.9 seconds and has a top speed of 171 mph. The price tag for the Cayenne Turbo in 2008? About $100,000!

Some analysts questioned Porsche's entry into the luxury SUV market. The analysts were concerned not only that Porsche was a late entry into the market, but also that the introduction of the Cayenne would damage Porsche's reputation as a maker of high-performance automobiles.

8. **Erosion [LO1]** In evaluating the Cayenne, would you consider the possible damage to Porsche's reputation erosion?

9. **Capital Budgeting [LO1]** Porsche was one of the last manufacturers to enter the sports utility vehicle market. Why would one company decide to proceed with a product when other companies, at least initially, decide not to enter the market?

10. **Capital Budgeting [LO1]** In evaluating the Cayenne, what do you think Porsche needs to assume regarding the substantial profit margins that exist in this market? Is it likely they will be maintained as the market becomes more competitive, or will Porsche be able to maintain the profit margin because of its image and the performance of the Cayenne?

QUESTIONS AND PROBLEMS

1. **Relevant Cash Flows [LO1]** Parker & Stone, Inc., is looking at setting up a new manufacturing plant in South Park to produce garden tools. The company bought some land six years ago for $6 million in anticipation of using it as a warehouse and distribution site, but the company has since decided to rent these facilities from a competitor instead. If the land were sold today, the company would net $6.4 million. The company wants to build its new manufacturing plant on this land; the plant will cost $14.2 million to build, and the site requires $890,000 worth of grading before it is suitable for construction. What is the proper cash flow amount to use as the initial investment in fixed assets when evaluating this project? Why?

BASIC
(Questions 1–18)

2. **Relevant Cash Flows [LO1]** Winnebagel Corp. currently sells 30,000 motor homes per year at $53,000 each, and 12,000 luxury motor coaches per year at

$91,000 each. The company wants to introduce a new portable camper to fill out its product line; it hopes to sell 19,000 of these campers per year at $13,000 each. An independent consultant has determined that if Winnebagel introduces the new campers, it should boost the sales of its existing motor homes by 4,500 units per year, and reduce the sales of its motor coaches by 900 units per year. What is the amount to use as the annual sales figure when evaluating this project? Why?

3. **Calculating Projected Net Income [LO1]** A proposed new investment has projected sales of $830,000. Variable costs are 60 percent of sales, and fixed costs are $181,000; depreciation is $77,000. Prepare a pro forma income statement assuming a tax rate of 35 percent. What is the projected net income?

4. **Calculating OCF [LO1]** Consider the following income statement:

Sales	$824,500
Costs	538,900
Depreciation	126,500
EBIT	?
Taxes (34%)	?
Net income	?

Fill in the missing numbers and then calculate the OCF. What is the depreciation tax shield?

5. **OCF from Several Approaches [LO1]** A proposed new project has projected sales of $108,000, costs of $51,000, and depreciation of $6,800. The tax rate is 35 percent. Calculate operating cash flow using the four different approaches described in the chapter and verify that the answer is the same in each case.

6. **Calculating Depreciation [LO1]** A piece of newly purchased industrial equipment costs $1,080,000 and is classified as seven-year property under MACRS. Calculate the annual depreciation allowances and end-of-the-year book values for this equipment.

7. **Calculating Salvage Value [LO1]** Consider an asset that costs $548,000 and is depreciated straight-line to zero over its eight-year tax life. The asset is to be used in a five-year project; at the end of the project, the asset can be sold for $105,000. If the relevant tax rate is 35 percent, what is the aftertax cash flow from the sale of this asset?

8. **Calculating Salvage Value [LO1]** An asset used in a four-year project falls in the five-year MACRS class for tax purposes. The asset has an acquisition cost of $7,900,000 and will be sold for $1,400,000 at the end of the project. If the tax rate is 35 percent, what is the aftertax salvage value of the asset?

9. **Calculating Project OCF [LO1]** Summer Tyme, Inc., is considering a new three-year expansion project that requires an initial fixed asset investment of $3.9 million. The fixed asset will be depreciated straight-line to zero over its three-year tax life, after which time it will be worthless. The project is estimated to generate $2,650,000 in annual sales, with costs of $840,000. If the tax rate is 35 percent, what is the OCF for this project?

10. **Calculating Project NPV [LO1]** In the previous problem, suppose the required return on the project is 12 percent. What is the project's NPV?

11. **Calculating Project Cash Flow from Assets [LO1]** In the previous problem, suppose the project requires an initial investment in net working capital of $300,000, and the fixed asset will have a market value of $210,000 at the end of the project. What is the project's year 0 net cash flow? Year 1? Year 2? Year 3? What is the new NPV?

12. **NPV and Modified ACRS [LO1]** In the previous problem, suppose the fixed asset actually falls into the three-year MACRS class. All the other facts are the same. What is the project's year 1 net cash flow now? Year 2? Year 3? What is the new NPV?

13. **Project Evaluation [LO1]** Dog Up! Franks is looking at a new sausage system with an installed cost of $560,000. This cost will be depreciated straight-line to zero over the project's five-year life, at the end of which the sausage system can be scrapped for $85,000. The sausage system will save the firm $165,000 per year in pretax operating costs, and the system requires an initial investment in net working capital of $29,000. If the tax rate is 34 percent and the discount rate is 10 percent, what is the NPV of this project?

14. **Project Evaluation [LO1]** Your firm is contemplating the purchase of a new $720,000 computer-based order entry system. The system will be depreciated straight-line to zero over its five-year life. It will be worth $75,000 at the end of that time. You will save $260,000 before taxes per year in order processing costs, and you will be able to reduce working capital by $110,000 (this is a one-time reduction). If the tax rate is 35 percent, what is the IRR for this project?

15. **Project Evaluation [LO1]** In the previous problem, suppose your required return on the project is 20 percent and your pretax cost savings are $300,000 per year. Will you accept the project? What if the pretax cost savings are $240,000 per year? At what level of pretax cost savings would you be indifferent between accepting the project and not accepting it?

16. **Calculating EAC [LO4]** A five-year project has an initial fixed asset investment of $270,000, an initial NWC investment of $25,000, and an annual OCF of −$42,000. The fixed asset is fully depreciated over the life of the project and has no salvage value. If the required return is 11 percent, what is this project's equivalent annual cost, or EAC?

17. **Calculating EAC [LO4]** You are evaluating two different silicon wafer milling machines. The Techron I costs $290,000, has a three-year life, and has pretax operating costs of $67,000 per year. The Techron II costs $510,000, has a five-year life, and has pretax operating costs of $35,000 per year. For both milling machines, use straight-line depreciation to zero over the project's life and assume a salvage value of $40,000. If your tax rate is 35 percent and your discount rate is 10 percent, compute the EAC for both machines. Which do you prefer? Why?

18. **Calculating a Bid Price [LO3]** Alson Enterprises needs someone to supply it with 185,000 cartons of machine screws per year to support its manufacturing needs over the next five years, and you've decided to bid on the contract. It will cost you $940,000 to install the equipment necessary to start production; you'll depreciate this cost straight-line to zero over the project's life. You estimate that in five years, this equipment can be salvaged for $70,000. Your fixed production costs will be $305,000 per year, and your variable production costs should be $9.25 per carton. You also need an initial investment in net working capital of $75,000. If your tax rate is 35 percent and you require a 12 percent return on your investment, what bid price should you submit?

19. **Cost-Cutting Proposals [LO2]** Geary Machine Shop is considering a four-year project to improve its production efficiency. Buying a new machine press for $560,000 is estimated to result in $210,000 in annual pretax cost savings. The press falls in the MACRS five-year class, and it will have a salvage value at the end of the project of $80,000. The press also requires an initial investment in spare parts

INTERMEDIATE
(Questions 19–30)

Visit us at www.mhhe.com/rwj

inventory of $20,000, along with an additional $3,000 in inventory for each succeeding year of the project. If the shop's tax rate is 35 percent and its discount rate is 9 percent, should the company buy and install the machine press?

20. Comparing Mutually Exclusive Projects [LO1] Dangerfield Industrial Systems Company (DISC) is trying to decide between two different conveyor belt systems. System A costs $430,000, has a four-year life, and requires $110,000 in pretax annual operating costs. System B costs $570,000, has a six-year life, and requires $98,000 in pretax annual operating costs. Both systems are to be depreciated straight-line to zero over their lives and will have zero salvage value. Whichever project is chosen, it will *not* be replaced when it wears out. If the tax rate is 34 percent and the discount rate is 11 percent, which project should the firm choose?

21. Comparing Mutually Exclusive Projects [LO4] Suppose in the previous problem that DISC always needs a conveyor belt system; when one wears out, it must be replaced. Which project should the firm choose now?

22. Calculating a Bid Price [LO3] Consider a project to supply 100 million postage stamps per year to the U.S. Postal Service for the next five years. You have an idle parcel of land available that cost $2,400,000 five years ago; if the land were sold today, it would net you $2,700,000 aftertax. The land can be sold for $3,200,000 after taxes in five years. You will need to install $4.1 million in new manufacturing plant and equipment to actually produce the stamps; this plant and equipment will be depreciated straight-line to zero over the project's five-year life. The equipment can be sold for $540,000 at the end of the project. You will also need $600,000 in initial net working capital for the project, and an additional investment of $50,000 in every year thereafter. Your production costs are .5 cents per stamp, and you have fixed costs of $950,000 per year. If your tax rate is 34 percent and your required return on this project is 12 percent, what bid price should you submit on the contract?

23. Interpreting a Bid Price [LO3] In the previous problem, suppose you were going to use a three-year MACRS depreciation schedule for your manufacturing equipment, and you could keep working capital investments down to only $25,000 per year. How would this new information affect your calculated bid price?

24. Comparing Mutually Exclusive Projects [LO4] Vandalay Industries is considering the purchase of a new machine for the production of latex. Machine A costs $2,900,000 and will last for six years. Variable costs are 35 percent of sales, and fixed costs are $170,000 per year. Machine B costs $5,100,000 and will last for nine years. Variable costs for this machine are 30 percent of sales and fixed costs are $130,000 per year. The sales for each machine will be $10 million per year. The required return is 10 percent, and the tax rate is 35 percent. Both machines will be depreciated on a straight-line basis. If the company plans to replace the machine when it wears out on a perpetual basis, which machine should you choose?

25. Equivalent Annual Cost [LO4] Compact fluorescent lamps (CFLs) have become more popular in recent years, but do they make financial sense? Suppose a typical 60-watt incandescent light bulb costs $.50 and lasts 1,000 hours. A 15-watt CFL, which provides the same light, costs $3.50 and lasts for 12,000 hours. A kilowatt-hour of electricity costs $.101, which is about the national average. A kilowatt-hour is 1,000 watts for 1 hour. If you require a 10 percent return and use a light fixture 500 hours per year, what is the equivalent annual cost of each light bulb?

26. Break-Even Cost [LO2] The previous problem suggests that using CFLs instead of incandescent bulbs is a no-brainer. However, electricity costs actually vary quite a bit depending on location and user type (you can get information on your rates from your local power company). An industrial user in West Virginia might pay $.04 per kilowatt-hour whereas a residential user in Hawaii might pay $.25. What's the break-even cost per kilowatt-hour in Problem 25?

27. **Break-Even Replacement** [LO2] The previous two problems suggest that using CFLs is a good idea from a purely financial perspective unless you live in an area where power is relatively inexpensive, but there is another wrinkle. Suppose you have a residence with a lot of incandescent bulbs that are used on average 500 hours a year. The average bulb will be about halfway through its life, so it will have 500 hours remaining (and you can't tell which bulbs are older or newer). At what cost per kilowatt-hour does it make sense to replace your incandescent bulbs today?

28. **Issues in Capital Budgeting** [LO1] The debate regarding CFLs versus incandescent bulbs (see Problems 25–27) has even more wrinkles. In no particular order:

   1. Incandescent bulbs generate a lot more heat than CFLs.
   2. CFL prices will probably decline relative to incandescent bulbs.
   3. CFLs unavoidably contain small amounts of mercury, a significant environmental hazard, and special precautions must be taken in disposing of burned-out units (and also in cleaning up a broken lamp). Currently, there is no agreed-upon way to recycle a CFL. Incandescent bulbs pose no disposal/breakage hazards.
   4. Depending on a light's location (or the number of lights), there can be a nontrivial cost to change bulbs (i.e., labor cost in a business).
   5. Coal-fired power generation accounts for a substantial portion of the mercury emissions in the U.S., though the emissions will drop sharply in the relatively near future.
   6. Power generation accounts for a substantial portion of CO_2 emissions in the U.S.
   7. CFLs are more energy and material intensive to manufacture. On-site mercury contamination and worker safety are issues.
   8. If you install a CFL in a permanent lighting fixture in a building, you will probably move long before the CFL burns out.
   9. Another lighting technology based on light emitting diodes (LEDs) exists and is improving. LEDs are currently much more expensive than CFLs, but costs are coming down. LEDs last much longer than CFLs and use even less power. Plus, LEDs don't contain mercury.
   10. GE announced in 2007 a new technology: high efficiency incandescent (HEI) bulbs. These new bulbs dramatically cut energy use and will, according to GE, ultimately be comparable to CFLs. They are targeted for 2010 release, though the initial product will not be as efficient as a CFL.

   Qualitatively, how do these issues affect your position in the CFL versus incandescent light bulb debate? Australia recently proposed banning the sale of incandescent bulbs altogether, as has at least one state legislator (from California, of course). Does your analysis suggest such a move is wise? Are there other regulations short of an outright ban that make sense to you?

29. **Replacement Decisions** [LO2] Your small remodeling business has two work vehicles. One is a small passenger car used for job-site visits and for other general business purposes. The other is a heavy truck used to haul equipment. The car gets

25 miles per gallon (mpg). The truck gets 10 mpg. You want to improve gas mileage to save money, and you have enough money to upgrade one vehicle. The upgrade cost will be the same for both vehicles. An upgraded car will get 40 mpg; an upgraded truck will get 12.5 mpg. The cost of gasoline is $3.70 per gallon. Assuming an upgrade is a good idea in the first place, which one should you upgrade? Both vehicles are driven 12,000 miles per year.

30. **Replacement Decisions [LO2]** In the previous problem, suppose you drive the truck x miles per year. How many miles would you have to drive the car before upgrading the car would be the better choice? *Hint:* Look at the relative gas savings.

CHALLENGE
(Questions 31–36)

31. **Calculating Project NPV [LO1]** You have been hired as a consultant for Pristine Urban-Tech Zither, Inc. (PUTZ), manufacturers of fine zithers. The market for zithers is growing quickly. The company bought some land three years ago for $1.4 million in anticipation of using it as a toxic waste dump site but has recently hired another company to handle all toxic materials. Based on a recent appraisal, the company believes it could sell the land for $1.5 million on an aftertax basis. In four years, the land could be sold for $1.6 million after taxes. The company also hired a marketing firm to analyze the zither market, at a cost of $125,000. An excerpt of the marketing report is as follows:

> The zither industry will have a rapid expansion in the next four years. With the brand name recognition that PUTZ brings to bear, we feel that the company will be able to sell 3,200, 4,300, 3,900, and 2,800 units each year for the next four years, respectively. Again, capitalizing on the name recognition of PUTZ, we feel that a premium price of $780 can be charged for each zither. Because zithers appear to be a fad, we feel at the end of the four-year period, sales should be discontinued.

PUTZ believes that fixed costs for the project will be $425,000 per year, and variable costs are 15 percent of sales. The equipment necessary for production will cost $4.2 million and will be depreciated according to a three-year MACRS schedule. At the end of the project, the equipment can be scrapped for $400,000. Net working capital of $125,000 will be required immediately. PUTZ has a 38 percent tax rate, and the required return on the project is 13 percent. What is the NPV of the project? Assume the company has other profitable projects.

32. **Project Evaluation [LO1]** Aguilera Acoustics, Inc. (AAI), projects unit sales for a new seven-octave voice emulation implant as follows:

Year	Unit Sales
1	93,000
2	105,000
3	128,000
4	134,000
5	87,000

Production of the implants will require $1,800,000 in net working capital to start and additional net working capital investments each year equal to 15 percent of the projected sales increase for the following year. Total fixed costs are $1,200,000 per year, variable production costs are $265 per unit, and the units are priced at $380 each. The equipment needed to begin production has an installed cost of $24,000,000. Because the implants are intended for professional singers, this equipment is considered industrial machinery and thus qualifies as seven-year MACRS property. In five years, this equipment can be sold for about 20 percent of its acquisition cost. AAI is in the 35 percent marginal tax bracket and has a required return on all its projects of 18 percent. Based on these preliminary project estimates, what is the NPV of the project? What is the IRR?

33. **Calculating Required Savings [LO2]** A proposed cost-saving device has an installed cost of $610,000. The device will be used in a five-year project but is classified as three-year MACRS property for tax purposes. The required initial net working capital investment is $55,000, the marginal tax rate is 35 percent, and the project discount rate is 12 percent. The device has an estimated year 5 salvage value of $40,000. What level of pretax cost savings do we require for this project to be profitable?

34. **Financial Break-Even Analysis [LO2]** To solve the bid price problem presented in the text, we set the project NPV equal to zero and found the required price using the definition of OCF. Thus the bid price represents a financial break-even level for the project. This type of analysis can be extended to many other types of problems.

    a. In Problem 18, assume that the price per carton is $13 and find the project NPV. What does your answer tell you about your bid price? What do you know about the number of cartons you can sell and still break even? How about your level of costs?

    b. Solve Problem 18 again with the price still at $13, but find the quantity of cartons per year that you can supply and still break even. *Hint:* It's less than 185,000.

    c. Repeat (b) with a price of $13 and a quantity of 185,000 cartons per year, and find the highest level of fixed costs you could afford and still break even. *Hint:* It's more than $305,000.

35. **Calculating a Bid Price [LO3]** Your company has been approached to bid on a contract to sell 17,500 voice recognition (VR) computer keyboards a year for four years. Due to technological improvements, beyond that time they will be outdated and no sales will be possible. The equipment necessary for the production will cost $3.4 million and will be depreciated on a straight-line basis to a zero salvage value. Production will require an investment in net working capital of $95,000 to be returned at the end of the project, and the equipment can be sold for $275,000 at the end of production. Fixed costs are $600,000 per year, and variable costs are $175 per unit. In addition to the contract, you feel your company can sell 3,000, 6,000, 8,000, and 5,000 additional units to companies in other countries over the next four years, respectively, at a price of $285. This price is fixed. The tax rate is 40 percent, and the required return is 13 percent. Additionally, the president of the company will undertake the project only if it has an NPV of $100,000. What bid price should you set for the contract?

36. **Replacement Decisions [LO2]** Suppose we are thinking about replacing an old computer with a new one. The old one cost us $650,000; the new one will cost $780,000. The new machine will be depreciated straight-line to zero over its five-year life. It will probably be worth about $150,000 after five years.

    The old computer is being depreciated at a rate of $130,000 per year. It will be completely written off in three years. If we don't replace it now, we will have to replace it in two years. We can sell it now for $210,000; in two years, it will probably be worth $60,000. The new machine will save us $145,000 per year in operating costs. The tax rate is 38 percent, and the discount rate is 12 percent.

a. Suppose we recognize that if we don't replace the computer now, we will be replacing it in two years. Should we replace now or should we wait? *Hint:* What we effectively have here is a decision either to "invest" in the old computer (by not selling it) or to invest in the new one. Notice that the two investments have unequal lives.

b. Suppose we consider only whether we should replace the old computer now without worrying about what's going to happen in two years. What are the relevant cash flows? Should we replace it or not? *Hint:* Consider the net change in the firm's aftertax cash flows if we do the replacement.

Conch Republic Electronics, Part 1

Conch Republic Electronics is a midsized electronics manufacturer located in Key West, Florida. The company president is Shelley Couts, who inherited the company. When it was founded over 70 years ago, the company originally repaired radios and other household appliances. Over the years, the company expanded into manufacturing and is now a reputable manufacturer of various electronic items. Jay McCanless, a recent MBA graduate, has been hired by the company's finance department.

One of the major revenue-producing items manufactured by Conch Republic is a personal digital assistant (PDA). Conch Republic currently has one PDA model on the market, and sales have been excellent. The PDA is a unique item in that it comes in a variety of tropical colors and is preprogrammed to play Jimmy Buffett music. However, as with any electronic item, technology changes rapidly, and the current PDA has limited features in comparison with newer models. Conch Republic spent $750,000 to develop a prototype for a new PDA that has all the features of the existing PDA but adds new features such as cell phone capability. The company has spent a further $200,000 for a marketing study to determine the expected sales figures for the new PDA.

Conch Republic can manufacture the new PDA for $155 each in variable costs. Fixed costs for the operation are estimated to run $4.7 million per year. The estimated sales volume is 74,000, 95,000, 125,000, 105,000, and 80,000 per each year for the next five years, respectively. The unit price of the new PDA will be $360. The necessary equipment can be purchased for $21.5 million and will be depreciated on a seven-year MACRS schedule. It is believed the value of the equipment in five years will be $4.1 million.

As previously stated, Conch Republic currently manufactures a PDA. Production of the existing model is expected to be terminated in two years. If Conch Republic does not introduce the new PDA, sales will be 80,000 units and 60,000 units for the next two years, respectively. The price of the existing PDA is $290 per unit, with variable costs of $120 each and fixed costs of $1,800,000 per year. If Conch Republic does introduce the new PDA, sales of the existing PDA will fall by 15,000 units per year, and the price of the existing units will have to be lowered to $255 each. Net working capital for the PDAs will be 20 percent of sales and will occur with the timing of the cash flows for the year; for example, there is no initial outlay for NWC, but changes in NWC will first occur in year 1 with the first year's sales. Conch Republic has a 35 percent corporate tax rate and a 12 percent required return.

Shelly has asked Jay to prepare a report that answers the following questions.

QUESTIONS

1. What is the payback period of the project?
2. What is the profitability index of the project?
3. What is the IRR of the project?
4. What is the NPV of the project?

After studying this chapter, you should understand:

LO1 How to perform and interpret a sensitivity analysis for a proposed investment.

LO2 How to perform and interpret a scenario analysis for a proposed investment.

LO3 How to determine and interpret cash, accounting, and financial break-even points.

LO4 How the degree of operating leverage can affect the cash flows of a project.

LO5 How capital rationing affects the ability of a company to accept projects.

PROJECT ANALYSIS AND EVALUATION

11

Capital Budgeting PART 4

IN THE SUMMER OF 2008, the movie *Speed Racer,* starring Emile Hirsch and Christina Ricci, spun its wheels at the box office. The Speed Racer slogan is "Go Speed Racer, Go!" but critics said "Don't go (see) Speed Racer, Don't go!" One critic said "the races felt like a drag." Others were even more harsh, saying the movie was "like spending two hours caroming through a pinball machine" and a "long, dreary, migraine-inducing slog."

Looking at the numbers, Warner Brothers spent close to $150 million making the movie, plus millions more for marketing and distribution. Unfortunately for Warner Brothers, *Speed Racer* crashed and burned, pulling in only $90 million worldwide. In fact,

about 4 of 10 movies lose money at the box office, though DVD sales often help the final tally. Of course, there are movies that do quite well. Also in 2008, the Paramount movie *Indiana Jones and the Kingdom of the Crystal Skull* raked in about $780 million worldwide at a production cost of $185 million.

Obviously, Warner Brothers didn't *plan* to lose $60 or so million on *Speed Racer,* but it happened. As the box office spinout of *Speed Racer* shows, projects don't always go as companies think they will. This chapter explores how this can happen, and what companies can do to analyze and possibly avoid these situations.

Master the ability to solve problems in this chapter by using a spreadsheet. Access Excel Master on the student Web site www.mhhe.com/rwj.

In our previous chapter, we discussed how to identify and organize the relevant cash flows for capital investment decisions. Our primary interest there was in coming up with a preliminary estimate of the net present value for a proposed project. In this chapter, we focus on assessing the reliability of such an estimate and on some additional considerations in project analysis.

We begin by discussing the need for an evaluation of cash flow and NPV estimates. We go on to develop some useful tools for such an evaluation. We also examine additional complications and concerns that can arise in project evaluation.

11.1 Evaluating NPV Estimates

As we discussed in Chapter 9, an investment has a positive net present value if its market value exceeds its cost. Such an investment is desirable because it creates value for its owner. The primary problem in identifying such opportunities is that most of the time we can't actually observe the relevant market value. Instead, we estimate it. Having done so, it is only natural to wonder whether our estimates are at least close to the true values. We consider this question next.

THE BASIC PROBLEM

Suppose we are working on a preliminary discounted cash flow analysis along the lines we described in the previous chapter. We carefully identify the relevant cash flows, avoiding such things as sunk costs, and we remember to consider working capital requirements. We add back any depreciation; we account for possible erosion; and we pay attention to opportunity costs. Finally, we double-check our calculations; when all is said and done, the bottom line is that the estimated NPV is positive.

Now what? Do we stop here and move on to the next proposal? Probably not. The fact that the estimated NPV is positive is definitely a good sign; but, more than anything, this tells us that we need to take a closer look.

If you think about it, there are two circumstances under which a DCF analysis could lead us to conclude that a project has a positive NPV. The first possibility is that the project really does have a positive NPV. That's the good news. The bad news is the second possibility: A project may appear to have a positive NPV because our estimate is inaccurate.

Notice that we could also err in the opposite way. If we conclude that a project has a negative NPV when the true NPV is positive, we lose a valuable opportunity.

PROJECTED VERSUS ACTUAL CASH FLOWS

There is a somewhat subtle point we need to make here. When we say something like "The projected cash flow in year 4 is $700," what exactly do we mean? Does this mean that we think the cash flow will actually be $700? Not really. It could happen, of course, but we would be surprised to see it turn out exactly that way. The reason is that the $700 projection is based on only what we know today. Almost anything could happen between now and then to change that cash flow.

Loosely speaking, we really mean that if we took all the possible cash flows that could occur in four years and averaged them, the result would be $700. So, we don't really expect a projected cash flow to be exactly right in any one case. What we do expect is that if we evaluate a large number of projects, our projections will be right on average.

FORECASTING RISK

The key inputs into a DCF analysis are projected future cash flows. If the projections are seriously in error, then we have a classic GIGO (garbage in, garbage out) system. In such a case, no matter how carefully we arrange the numbers and manipulate them, the resulting answer can still be grossly misleading. This is the danger in using a relatively sophisticated technique like DCF. It is sometimes easy to get caught up in number crunching and forget the underlying nuts-and-bolts economic reality.

forecasting risk
The possibility that errors in projected cash flows will lead to incorrect decisions. Also, estimation risk.

The possibility that we will make a bad decision because of errors in the projected cash flows is called **forecasting risk** (or *estimation risk*). Because of forecasting risk, there is the danger that we will think a project has a positive NPV when it really does not. How is this possible? It happens if we are overly optimistic about the future, and, as a result, our projected cash flows don't realistically reflect the possible future cash flows.

Forecasting risk can take many forms. For example, Microsoft spent several billion dollars developing and bringing the Xbox game console to market. Technologically more sophisticated, the Xbox was the best way to play against competitors over the Internet. Unfortunately, Microsoft sold only 9 million Xboxes in the first 14 months of sales, at the low end of Microsoft's expected range. The Xbox was arguably the best available game console at the time, so why didn't it sell better? The reason given by analysts was that there were far fewer games made for the Xbox. For example, the Playstation enjoyed a 2-to-1 edge in the number of games made for it.

So far, we have not explicitly considered what to do about the possibility of errors in our forecasts; so one of our goals in this chapter is to develop some tools that are useful in identifying areas where potential errors exist and where they might be especially damaging. In one form or another, we will be trying to assess the economic "reasonableness" of our estimates. We will also be wondering how much damage will be done by errors in those estimates.

SOURCES OF VALUE

The first line of defense against forecasting risk is simply to ask, "What is it about this investment that leads to a positive NPV?" We should be able to point to something specific as the source of value. For example, if the proposal under consideration involved a new product, then we might ask questions such as the following: Are we certain that our new product is significantly better than that of the competition? Can we truly manufacture at lower cost, or distribute more effectively, or identify undeveloped market niches, or gain control of a market?

These are just a few of the potential sources of value. There are many others. For example, in 2004, Google announced a new, free e-mail service: gmail. Why? Free e-mail service is widely available from big hitters like Microsoft and Yahoo! and, obviously, it's free! The answer is that Google's mail service is integrated with its acclaimed search engine, thereby giving it an edge. Also, offering e-mail lets Google expand its lucrative keyword-based advertising delivery. So, Google's source of value is leveraging its proprietary Web search and ad delivery technologies.

A key factor to keep in mind is the degree of competition in the market. A basic principle of economics is that positive NPV investments will be rare in a highly competitive environment. Therefore, proposals that appear to show significant value in the face of stiff competition are particularly troublesome, and the likely reaction of the competition to any innovations must be closely examined.

To give an example, in 2008, demand for flat screen LCD televisions was high, prices were high, and profit margins were fat for retailers. But, also in 2008, manufacturers of the screens, such as Samsung and Sony, were projected to pour several billion dollars into new production facilities. Thus, anyone thinking of entering this highly profitable market would do well to reflect on what the supply (and profit margin) situation will look like in just a few years.

It is also necessary to think about *potential* competition. For example, suppose home improvement retailer Lowe's identifies an area that is underserved and is thinking about opening a store. If the store is successful, what will happen? The answer is that Home Depot (or another competitor) will likely also build a store, thereby driving down volume and profits. So, we always need to keep in mind that success attracts imitators and competitors.

The point to remember is that positive NPV investments are probably not all that common, and the number of positive NPV projects is almost certainly limited for any given firm. If we can't articulate some sound economic basis for thinking ahead of time that we have found something special, then the conclusion that our project has a positive NPV should be viewed with some suspicion.

11.1a What is forecasting risk? Why is it a concern for the financial manager?

11.1b What are some potential sources of value in a new project?

11.2 Scenario and Other What-If Analyses

Our basic approach to evaluating cash flow and NPV estimates involves asking what-if questions. Accordingly, we discuss some organized ways of going about a what-if analysis. Our goal in performing such an analysis is to assess the degree of forecasting risk and to identify the most critical components of the success or failure of an investment.

GETTING STARTED

We are investigating a new project. Naturally, the first thing we do is estimate NPV based on our projected cash flows. We will call this initial set of projections the *base case*. Now, however, we recognize the possibility of error in these cash flow projections. After completing the base case, we thus wish to investigate the impact of different assumptions about the future on our estimates.

One way to organize this investigation is to put upper and lower bounds on the various components of the project. For example, suppose we forecast sales at 100 units per year. We know this estimate may be high or low, but we are relatively certain it is not off by more than 10 units in either direction. We thus pick a lower bound of 90 and an upper bound of 110. We go on to assign such bounds to any other cash flow components we are unsure about.

When we pick these upper and lower bounds, we are not ruling out the possibility that the actual values could be outside this range. What we are saying, again loosely speaking, is that it is unlikely that the true average (as opposed to our estimated average) of the possible values is outside this range.

An example is useful to illustrate the idea here. The project under consideration costs $200,000, has a five-year life, and has no salvage value. Depreciation is straight-line to zero. The required return is 12 percent, and the tax rate is 34 percent. In addition, we have compiled the following information:

	Base Case	**Lower Bound**	**Upper Bound**
Unit sales	6,000	5,500	6,500
Price per unit	$80	$75	$85
Variable costs per unit	$60	$58	$62
Fixed costs per year	$50,000	$45,000	$55,000

With this information, we can calculate the base-case NPV by first calculating net income:

Sales	$480,000
Variable costs	360,000
Fixed costs	50,000
Depreciation	40,000
EBIT	$ 30,000
Taxes (34%)	10,200
Net income	$ 19,800

Operating cash flow is thus $30,000 + 40,000 - 10,200 = \$59,800$ per year. At 12 percent, the five-year annuity factor is 3.6048, so the base-case NPV is:

$$\text{Base-case NPV} = -\$200,000 + 59,800 \times 3.6048$$
$$= \$15,567$$

Thus, the project looks good so far.

SCENARIO ANALYSIS

The basic form of what-if analysis is called **scenario analysis**. What we do is investigate the changes in our NPV estimates that result from asking questions like: What if unit sales realistically should be projected at 5,500 units instead of 6,000?

Once we start looking at alternative scenarios, we might find that most of the plausible ones result in positive NPVs. In this case, we have some confidence in proceeding with the project. If a substantial percentage of the scenarios look bad, the degree of forecasting risk is high and further investigation is in order.

We can consider a number of possible scenarios. A good place to start is with the worst-case scenario. This will tell us the minimum NPV of the project. If this turns out to be positive, we will be in good shape. While we are at it, we will go ahead and determine the other extreme, the best case. This puts an upper bound on our NPV.

To get the worst case, we assign the least favorable value to each item. This means *low* values for items like units sold and price per unit and *high* values for costs. We do the reverse for the best case. For our project, these values would be the following:

scenario analysis
The determination of what happens to NPV estimates when we ask what-if questions.

	Worst Case	Best Case
Unit sales	5,500	6,500
Price per unit	$75	$85
Variable costs per unit	$62	$58
Fixed costs per year	$55,000	$45,000

With this information, we can calculate the net income and cash flows under each scenario (check these for yourself):

Scenario	Net Income	Cash Flow	Net Present Value	IRR
Base case	$19,800	$59,800	$ 15,567	15.1%
Worst case*	− 15,510	24,490	− 111,719	−14.4
Best case	59,730	99,730	159,504	40.9

*We assume a tax credit is created in our worst-case scenario.

What we learn is that under the worst scenario, the cash flow is still positive at $24,490. That's good news. The bad news is that the return is −14.4 percent in this case, and the NPV is −$111,719. Because the project costs $200,000, we stand to lose a little more than half of the original investment under the worst possible scenario. The best case offers an attractive 41 percent return.

The terms *best case* and *worst case* are commonly used, and we will stick with them; but they are somewhat misleading. The absolutely best thing that could happen would be something absurdly unlikely, such as launching a new diet soda and subsequently learning that our (patented) formulation also just happens to cure the common cold. Similarly, the true worst case would involve some incredibly remote possibility of total disaster. We're not claiming that these things don't happen; once in a while they do. Some products, such as personal computers, succeed beyond the wildest expectations; and some, such as asbestos, turn out to be absolute catastrophes. Our point is that in assessing the reasonableness of an NPV estimate, we need to stick to cases that are reasonably likely to occur.

Instead of *best* and *worst,* then, it is probably more accurate to use the words *optimistic* and *pessimistic*. In broad terms, if we were thinking about a reasonable range for, say, unit sales, then what we call the best case would correspond to something near the upper end of that range. The worst case would simply correspond to the lower end.

Depending on the project, the best- and worst-case estimates can vary greatly. For example, in 2008, Roche Carolina, a subsidiary of the Roche Group, a Swiss global health care company, announced plans for converting its Florence, S.C., site to a solar heating and cooling system. The initial cost was estimated at $480,000 including a government grant. The range used for this initial cost was $+/-15$ percent. The annual savings were estimated at $39,500, with a range of $+/-30$ percent. In the end, the NPV was estimated at $170,000, with a range of $57,000 to $282,000, and the IRR was 18 percent, with a range of 11 percent to 25 percent.

As we have mentioned, there are an unlimited number of different scenarios that we could examine. At a minimum, we might want to investigate two intermediate cases by going halfway between the base amounts and the extreme amounts. This would give us five scenarios in all, including the base case.

Beyond this point, it is hard to know when to stop. As we generate more and more possibilities, we run the risk of experiencing "paralysis of analysis." The difficulty is that no matter how many scenarios we run, all we can learn are possibilities—some good and some bad. Beyond that, we don't get any guidance as to what to do. Scenario analysis is thus useful in telling us what can happen and in helping us gauge the potential for disaster, but it does not tell us whether to take a project.

Unfortunately, in practice, even the worst-case scenarios may not be low enough. Two recent examples show what we mean. The Eurotunnel, or Chunnel, may be one of the new wonders of the world. The tunnel under the English Channel connects England to France and covers 24 miles. It took 8,000 workers eight years to remove 9.8 million cubic yards of rock. When the tunnel was finally built, it cost $17.9 billion, or slightly more than twice the original estimate of $8.8 billion. And things got worse. Forecasts called for 16.8 million passengers in the first year, but only 4 million actually used it. Revenue estimates for 2003 were $2.88 billion, but actual revenue was only about one-third of that. The major problems faced by the Eurotunnel were increased competition from ferry services, which dropped their prices, and the rise of low-cost airlines. In 2006, things got so bad that the company operating the Eurotunnel was forced into negotiations with creditors to chop its $11.1 billion debt in half to avoid bankruptcy. The debt reduction appeared to help. In 2007, the Eurotunnel reported its first profit of €1 million ($1.6 million). Of course, this profit paled in comparison to the €204 million in losses accumulated since the Chunnel first opened in 1994.

Another example is the human transporter, or Segway. Trumpeted by inventor Dean Kamen as the replacement for automobiles in cities, the Segway came to market with great expectations. At the end of September 2003, the company recalled all of the transporters due to a mandatory software upgrade. Worse, the company had projected sales of 50,000 to 100,000 units in the first five months of production; but, three years later, only about 23,500 had been sold.

SENSITIVITY ANALYSIS

Sensitivity analysis is a variation on scenario analysis that is useful in pinpointing the areas where forecasting risk is especially severe. The basic idea with a sensitivity analysis is to freeze all of the variables except one and then see how sensitive our estimate of NPV is to changes in that one variable. If our NPV estimate turns out to be very sensitive to relatively small changes in the projected value of some component of project cash flow, then the forecasting risk associated with that variable is high.

sensitivity analysis
Investigation of what happens to NPV when only one variable is changed.

To illustrate how sensitivity analysis works, we go back to our base case for every item except unit sales. We can then calculate cash flow and NPV using the largest and smallest unit sales figures.

Scenario	Unit Sales	Cash Flow	Net Present Value	IRR
Base case	6,000	$59,800	$15,567	15.1%
Worst case	5,500	53,200	−8,226	10.3
Best case	6,500	66,400	39,357	19.7

For comparison, we now freeze everything except fixed costs and repeat the analysis:

A cash flow sensitivity analysis spreadsheet is available at www.toolkit.com.

Scenario	Fixed Costs	Cash Flow	Net Present Value	IRR
Base case	$50,000	$59,800	$15,567	15.1%
Worst case	55,000	56,500	3,670	12.7
Best case	45,000	63,100	27,461	17.4

What we see here is that given our ranges, the estimated NPV of this project is more sensitive to changes in projected unit sales than it is to changes in projected fixed costs. In fact, under the worst case for fixed costs, the NPV is still positive.

The results of our sensitivity analysis for unit sales can be illustrated graphically as in Figure 11.1. Here we place NPV on the vertical axis and unit sales on the horizontal axis. When we plot the combinations of unit sales versus NPV, we see that all possible combinations fall on a straight line. The steeper the resulting line is, the greater the sensitivity of the estimated NPV to changes in the projected value of the variable being investigated.

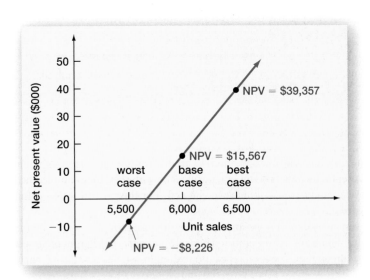

FIGURE 11.1

Sensitivity Analysis for Unit Sales

As we have illustrated, sensitivity analysis is useful in pinpointing which variables deserve the most attention. If we find that our estimated NPV is especially sensitive to changes in a variable that is difficult to forecast (such as unit sales), then the degree of forecasting risk is high. We might decide that further market research would be a good idea in this case.

Because sensitivity analysis is a form of scenario analysis, it suffers from the same drawbacks. Sensitivity analysis is useful for pointing out where forecasting errors will do the most damage, but it does not tell us what to do about possible errors.

SIMULATION ANALYSIS

simulation analysis
A combination of scenario and sensitivity analysis.

Scenario analysis and sensitivity analysis are widely used. With scenario analysis, we let all the different variables change, but we let them take on only a few values. With sensitivity analysis, we let only one variable change, but we let it take on many values. If we combine the two approaches, the result is a crude form of **simulation analysis**.

If we want to let all the items vary at the same time, we have to consider a very large number of scenarios, and computer assistance is almost certainly needed. In the simplest case, we start with unit sales and assume that any value in our 5,500 to 6,500 range is equally likely. We start by randomly picking one value (or by instructing a computer to do so). We then randomly pick a price, a variable cost, and so on.

Once we have values for all the relevant components, we calculate an NPV. We repeat this sequence as much as we desire, probably several thousand times. The result is many NPV estimates that we summarize by calculating the average value and some measure of how spread out the different possibilities are. For example, it would be of some interest to know what percentage of the possible scenarios result in negative estimated NPVs.

Because simulation analysis (or simulation) is an extended form of scenario analysis, it has the same problems. Once we have the results, no simple decision rule tells us what to do. Also, we have described a relatively simple form of simulation. To really do it right, we would have to consider the interrelationships between the different cash flow components. Furthermore, we assumed that the possible values were equally likely to occur. It is probably more realistic to assume that values near the base case are more likely than extreme values, but coming up with the probabilities is difficult, to say the least.

For these reasons, the use of simulation is somewhat limited in practice. However, recent advances in computer software and hardware (and user sophistication) lead us to believe it may become more common in the future, particularly for large-scale projects.

Concept Questions

11.2a What are scenario, sensitivity, and simulation analysis?

11.2b What are the drawbacks to the various types of what-if analysis?

11.3 Break-Even Analysis

It will frequently turn out that the crucial variable for a project is sales volume. If we are thinking of creating a new product or entering a new market, for example, the hardest thing to forecast accurately is how much we can sell. For this reason, sales volume is usually analyzed more closely than other variables.

Break-even analysis is a popular and commonly used tool for analyzing the relationship between sales volume and profitability. There are a variety of different break-even measures, and we have already seen several types. For example, we discussed (in Chapter 9) how the payback period can be interpreted as the length of time until a project breaks even, ignoring time value.

All break-even measures have a similar goal. Loosely speaking, we will always be asking, "How bad do sales have to get before we actually begin to lose money?" Implicitly, we will also be asking, "Is it likely that things will get that bad?" To get started on this subject, we first discuss fixed and variable costs.

FIXED AND VARIABLE COSTS

In discussing break-even, the difference between fixed and variable costs becomes very important. As a result, we need to be a little more explicit about the difference than we have been so far.

Variable Costs By definition, **variable costs** change as the quantity of output changes, and they are zero when production is zero. For example, direct labor costs and raw material costs are usually considered variable. This makes sense because if we shut down operations tomorrow, there will be no future costs for labor or raw materials.

variable costs
Costs that change when the quantity of output changes.

We will assume that variable costs are a constant amount per unit of output. This simply means that total variable cost is equal to the cost per unit multiplied by the number of units. In other words, the relationship between total variable cost (VC), cost per unit of output (v), and total quantity of output (Q) can be written simply as:

Total variable cost = Total quantity of output × Cost per unit of output

$$VC = Q \times v$$

For example, suppose variable costs (v) are $2 per unit. If total output (Q) is 1,000 units, what will total variable costs (VC) be?

$$
\begin{aligned}
VC &= Q \times v \\
&= 1{,}000 \times \$2 \\
&= \$2{,}000
\end{aligned}
$$

Similarly, if Q is 5,000 units, then VC will be $5{,}000 \times \$2 = \$10{,}000$. Figure 11.2 illustrates the relationship between output level and variable costs in this case. In Figure 11.2, notice that increasing output by one unit results in variable costs rising by $2, so "the rise over the run" (the slope of the line) is given by $\$2/1 = \$2$.

Variable Costs | EXAMPLE 11.1

The Blume Corporation is a manufacturer of pencils. It has received an order for 5,000 pencils, and the company has to decide whether to accept the order. From recent experience, the company knows that each pencil requires 5 cents in raw materials and 50 cents in direct labor costs. These variable costs are expected to continue to apply in the future. What will Blume's total variable costs be if it accepts the order?

In this case, the cost per unit is 50 cents in labor plus 5 cents in material for a total of 55 cents per unit. At 5,000 units of output, we have:

$$
\begin{aligned}
VC &= Q \times v \\
&= 5{,}000 \times \$.55 \\
&= \$2{,}750
\end{aligned}
$$

Therefore, total variable costs will be $2,750.

FIGURE 11.2

Output Level and Variable Costs

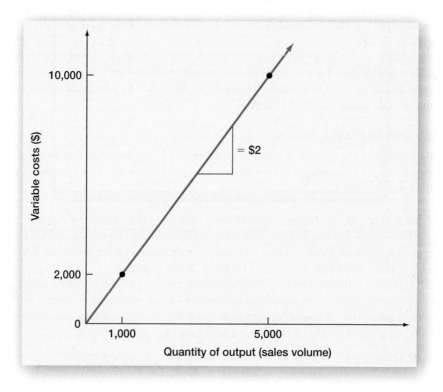

fixed costs

Costs that do not change when the quantity of output changes during a particular time period.

Fixed Costs **Fixed costs**, by definition, do not change during a specified time period. So, unlike variable costs, they do not depend on the amount of goods or services produced during a period (at least within some range of production). For example, the lease payment on a production facility and the company president's salary are fixed costs, at least over some period.

Naturally, fixed costs are not fixed forever. They are fixed only during some particular time, say, a quarter or a year. Beyond that time, leases can be terminated and executives "retired." More to the point, any fixed cost can be modified or eliminated given enough time; so, in the long run, all costs are variable.

Notice that when a cost is fixed, that cost is effectively a sunk cost because we are going to have to pay it no matter what.

Total Costs Total costs (TC) for a given level of output are the sum of variable costs (VC) and fixed costs (FC):

$$TC = VC + FC$$
$$= v \times Q + FC$$

So, for example, if we have variable costs of $3 per unit and fixed costs of $8,000 per year, our total cost is:

$$TC = \$3 \times Q + \$8,000$$

If we produce 6,000 units, our total production cost will be $3 × 6,000 + $8,000 = $26,000. At other production levels, we have the following:

Quantity Produced	Total Variable Costs	Fixed Costs	Total Costs
0	$ 0	$8,000	$ 8,000
1,000	3,000	8,000	11,000
5,000	15,000	8,000	23,000
10,000	30,000	8,000	38,000

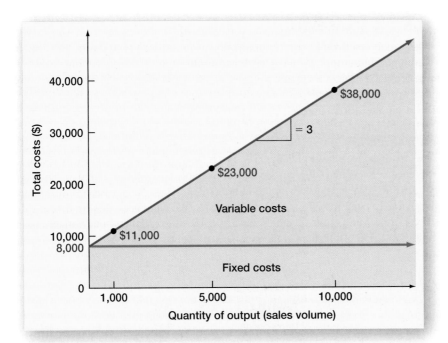

FIGURE 11.3

Output Level and Total Costs

By plotting these points in Figure 11.3, we see that the relationship between quantity produced and total costs is given by a straight line. In Figure 11.3, notice that total costs equal fixed costs when sales are zero. Beyond that point, every one-unit increase in production leads to a $3 increase in total costs, so the slope of the line is 3. In other words, the **marginal**, or **incremental, cost** of producing one more unit is $3.

marginal, or incremental, cost
The change in costs that occurs when there is a small change in output.

Average Cost versus Marginal Cost

EXAMPLE 11.2

Suppose the Blume Corporation has a variable cost per pencil of 55 cents. The lease payment on the production facility runs $5,000 per month. If Blume produces 100,000 pencils per year, what are the total costs of production? What is the average cost per pencil?

The fixed costs are $5,000 per month, or $60,000 per year. The variable cost is $.55 per pencil. So the total cost for the year, assuming that Blume produces 100,000 pencils, is:

$$\text{Total cost} = v \times Q + FC$$
$$= \$.55 \times 100,000 + \$60,000$$
$$= \$115,000$$

The average cost per pencil is $115,000/100,000 = $1.15.

Now suppose that Blume has received a special, one-shot order for 5,000 pencils. Blume has sufficient capacity to manufacture the 5,000 pencils on top of the 100,000 already produced, so no additional fixed costs will be incurred. Also, there will be no effect on existing orders. If Blume can get 75 cents per pencil for this order, should the order be accepted?

What this boils down to is a simple proposition. It costs 55 cents to make another pencil. Anything Blume can get for this pencil in excess of the 55-cent incremental cost contributes in a positive way toward covering fixed costs. The 75-cent **marginal**, or **incremental, revenue** exceeds the 55-cent marginal cost, so Blume should take the order.

The fixed cost of $60,000 is not relevant to this decision because it is effectively sunk, at least for the current period. In the same way, the fact that the average cost is $1.15 is irrelevant because this average reflects the fixed cost. As long as producing the extra 5,000 pencils truly does not cost anything beyond the 55 cents per pencil, then Blume should accept anything over that 55 cents.

marginal, or incremental, revenue
The change in revenue that occurs when there is a small change in output.

ACCOUNTING BREAK-EVEN

accounting break-even
The sales level that results in zero project net income.

The most widely used measure of break-even is **accounting break-even**. The accounting break-even point is simply the sales level that results in a zero project net income.

To determine a project's accounting break-even, we start off with some common sense. Suppose we retail one-petabyte computer disks for $5 apiece. We can buy disks from a wholesale supplier for $3 apiece. We have accounting expenses of $600 in fixed costs and $300 in depreciation. How many disks do we have to sell to break even—that is, for net income to be zero?

For every disk we sell, we pick up $5 − 3 = $2 toward covering our other expenses (this $2 difference between the selling price and the variable cost is often called the *contribution margin per unit*). We have to cover a total of $600 + 300 = $900 in accounting expenses, so we obviously need to sell $900/2 = 450 disks. We can check this by noting that at a sales level of 450 units, our revenues are $5 × 450 = $2,250 and our variable costs are $3 × 450 = $1,350. Thus, here is the income statement:

Sales	$2,250
Variable costs	1,350
Fixed costs	600
Depreciation	300
EBIT	$ 0
Taxes (34%)	0
Net income	$ 0

Remember, because we are discussing a proposed new project, we do not consider any interest expense in calculating net income or cash flow from the project. Also, notice that we include depreciation in calculating expenses here, even though depreciation is not a cash outflow. That is why we call it an accounting break-even. Finally, notice that when net income is zero, so are pretax income and, of course, taxes. In accounting terms, our revenues are equal to our costs, so there is no profit to tax.

Figure 11.4 presents another way to see what is happening. This figure looks a lot like Figure 11.3 except that we add a line for revenues. As indicated, total revenues are zero when output is zero. Beyond that, each unit sold brings in another $5, so the slope of the revenue line is 5.

From our preceding discussion, we know that we break even when revenues are equal to total costs. The line for revenues and the line for total costs cross right where output is at 450 units. As illustrated, at any level of output below 450, our accounting profit is negative, and at any level above 450, we have a positive net income.

ACCOUNTING BREAK-EVEN: A CLOSER LOOK

In our numerical example, notice that the break-even level is equal to the sum of fixed costs and depreciation, divided by price per unit less variable costs per unit. This is always true. To see why, we recall all of the following variables:

P = Selling price per unit
v = Variable cost per unit
Q = Total units sold
S = Total sales = $P \times Q$
VC = Total variable costs = $v \times Q$

FIGURE 11.4

Accounting Break-Even

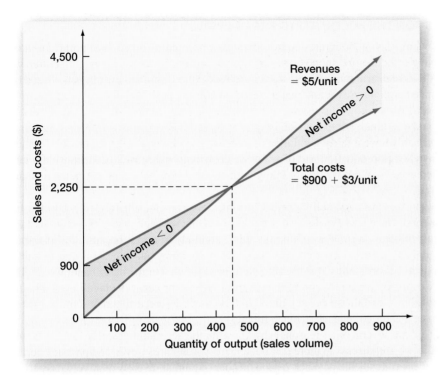

FC = Fixed costs

D = Depreciation

T = Tax rate

Project net income is given by:

Net income = (Sales − Variable costs − Fixed costs − Depreciation) × $(1 − T)$

$= (S − VC − FC − D) × (1 − T)$

From here, it is not difficult to calculate the break-even point. If we set this net income equal to zero, we get:

Net income $\overset{\text{SET}}{=} 0 = (S − VC − FC − D) × (1 − T)$

Divide both sides by $(1 − T)$ to get:

$S − VC − FC − D = 0$

As we have seen, this says that when net income is zero, so is pretax income. If we recall that $S = P × Q$ and $VC = v × Q$, then we can rearrange the equation to solve for the break-even level:

$$S − VC = FC + D$$
$$P × Q − v × Q = FC + D$$
$$(P − v) × Q = FC + D$$
$$Q = (FC + D)/(P − v) \qquad \text{[11.1]}$$

This is the same result we described earlier.

USES FOR THE ACCOUNTING BREAK-EVEN

Why would anyone be interested in knowing the accounting break-even point? To illustrate how it can be useful, suppose we are a small specialty ice cream manufacturer with a strictly local distribution. We are thinking about expanding into new markets. Based on the estimated cash flows, we find that the expansion has a positive NPV.

Going back to our discussion of forecasting risk, we know that it is likely that what will make or break our expansion is sales volume. The reason is that, in this case at least, we probably have a fairly good idea of what we can charge for the ice cream. Further, we know relevant production and distribution costs reasonably well because we are already in the business. What we do not know with any real precision is how much ice cream we can sell.

Given the costs and selling price, however, we can immediately calculate the break-even point. Once we have done so, we might find that we need to get 30 percent of the market just to break even. If we think that this is unlikely to occur, because, for example, we have only 10 percent of our current market, then we know our forecast is questionable and there is a real possibility that the true NPV is negative. On the other hand, we might find that we already have firm commitments from buyers for about the break-even amount, so we are almost certain we can sell more. In this case, the forecasting risk is much lower, and we have greater confidence in our estimates.

There are several other reasons why knowing the accounting break-even can be useful. First, as we will discuss in more detail later, accounting break-even and payback period are similar measures. Like payback period, accounting break-even is relatively easy to calculate and explain.

Second, managers are often concerned with the contribution a project will make to the firm's total accounting earnings. A project that does not break even in an accounting sense actually reduces total earnings.

Third, a project that just breaks even on an accounting basis loses money in a financial or opportunity cost sense. This is true because we could have earned more by investing elsewhere. Such a project does not lose money in an out-of-pocket sense. As described in the following pages, we get back exactly what we put in. For noneconomic reasons, opportunity losses may be easier to live with than out-of-pocket losses.

Concept Questions

11.3a How are fixed costs similar to sunk costs?

11.3b What is net income at the accounting break-even point? What about taxes?

11.3c Why might a financial manager be interested in the accounting break-even point?

11.4 Operating Cash Flow, Sales Volume, and Break-Even

Accounting break-even is one tool that is useful for project analysis. Ultimately, however, we are more interested in cash flow than accounting income. So, for example, if sales volume is the critical variable, then we need to know more about the relationship between sales volume and cash flow than just the accounting break-even.

Our goal in this section is to illustrate the relationship between operating cash flow and sales volume. We also discuss some other break-even measures. To simplify matters somewhat, we will ignore the effect of taxes. We start off by looking at the relationship between accounting break-even and cash flow.

ACCOUNTING BREAK-EVEN AND CASH FLOW

Now that we know how to find the accounting break-even, it is natural to wonder what happens with cash flow. To illustrate, suppose the Wettway Sailboat Corporation is considering whether to launch its new Margo-class sailboat. The selling price will be $40,000 per boat. The variable costs will be about half that, or $20,000 per boat, and fixed costs will be $500,000 per year.

The Base Case The total investment needed to undertake the project is $3,500,000. This amount will be depreciated straight-line to zero over the five-year life of the equipment. The salvage value is zero, and there are no working capital consequences. Wettway has a 20 percent required return on new projects.

Based on market surveys and historical experience, Wettway projects total sales for the five years at 425 boats, or about 85 boats per year. Ignoring taxes, should this project be launched?

To begin, ignoring taxes, the operating cash flow at 85 boats per year is:

$$\text{Operating cash flow} = \text{EBIT} + \text{Depreciation} - \text{Taxes}$$
$$= (S - \text{VC} - \text{FC} - D) + D - 0$$
$$= 85 \times (\$40,000 - 20,000) - 500,000$$
$$= \$1,200,000 \text{ per year}$$

At 20 percent, the five-year annuity factor is 2.9906, so the NPV is:

$$\text{NPV} = -\$3,500,000 + 1,200,000 \times 2.9906$$
$$= -\$3,500,000 + 3,588,720$$
$$= \$88,720$$

In the absence of additional information, the project should be launched.

Calculating the Break-Even Level To begin looking a little closer at this project, you might ask a series of questions. For example, how many new boats does Wettway need to sell for the project to break even on an accounting basis? If Wettway does break even, what will be the annual cash flow from the project? What will be the return on the investment in this case?

Before fixed costs and depreciation are considered, Wettway generates $40,000 − 20,000 = $20,000 per boat (this is revenue less variable cost). Depreciation is $3,500,000/5 = $700,000 per year. Fixed costs and depreciation together total $1.2 million, so Wettway needs to sell $(FC + D)/(P - v) = $1.2 million/20,000 = 60 boats per year to break even on an accounting basis. This is 25 boats less than projected sales; so, assuming that Wettway is confident its projection is accurate to within, say, 15 boats, it appears unlikely that the new investment will fail to at least break even on an accounting basis.

To calculate Wettway's cash flow in this case, we note that if 60 boats are sold, net income will be exactly zero. Recalling from the previous chapter that operating cash flow for a project can be written as net income plus depreciation (the bottom-up definition), we can see that the operating cash flow is equal to the depreciation, or $700,000 in this case. The internal rate of return is exactly zero (why?).

Payback and Break-Even   As our example illustrates, whenever a project breaks even on an accounting basis, the cash flow for that period will equal the depreciation. This result makes perfect accounting sense. For example, suppose we invest $100,000 in a five-year project. The depreciation is straight-line to a zero salvage, or $20,000 per year. If the project exactly breaks even every period, then the cash flow will be $20,000 per period.

The sum of the cash flows for the life of this project is 5 × $20,000 = $100,000, the original investment. What this shows is that a project's payback period is exactly equal to its life if the project breaks even every period. Similarly, a project that does better than break even has a payback that is shorter than the life of the project and has a positive rate of return.

The bad news is that a project that just breaks even on an accounting basis has a negative NPV and a zero return. For our sailboat project, the fact that Wettway will almost surely break even on an accounting basis is partially comforting because it means that the firm's "downside" risk (its potential loss) is limited, but we still don't know if the project is truly profitable. More work is needed.

SALES VOLUME AND OPERATING CASH FLOW

At this point, we can generalize our example and introduce some other break-even measures. From our discussion in the previous section, we know that, ignoring taxes, a project's operating cash flow, OCF, can be written simply as EBIT plus depreciation:

$$\begin{aligned} OCF &= [(P - v) \times Q - FC - D] + D \\ &= (P - v) \times Q - FC \end{aligned}$$ [11.2]

For the Wettway sailboat project, the general relationship (in thousands of dollars) between operating cash flow and sales volume is thus:

$$\begin{aligned} OCF &= (P - v) \times Q - FC \\ &= (\$40 - 20) \times Q - 500 \\ &= -\$500 + 20 \times Q \end{aligned}$$

What this tells us is that the relationship between operating cash flow and sales volume is given by a straight line with a slope of $20 and a y-intercept of −$500. If we calculate some different values, we get:

Quantity Sold	Operating Cash Flow
0	−$ 500
15	− 200
30	100
50	500
75	1,000

These points are plotted in Figure 11.5, where we have indicated three different break-even points. We discuss these next.

CASH FLOW, ACCOUNTING, AND FINANCIAL BREAK-EVEN POINTS

We know from the preceding discussion that the relationship between operating cash flow and sales volume (ignoring taxes) is:

$$OCF = (P - v) \times Q - FC$$

If we rearrange this and solve for Q, we get:

$$Q = (FC + OCF)/(P - v)$$ [11.3]

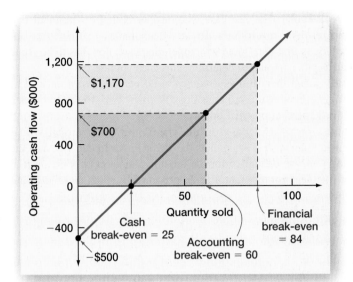

FIGURE 11.5

Operating Cash Flow and
Sales Volume

This tells us what sales volume (Q) is necessary to achieve any given OCF, so this result is more general than the accounting break-even. We use it to find the various break-even points in Figure 11.5.

Accounting Break-Even Revisited Looking at Figure 11.5, suppose operating cash flow is equal to depreciation (D). Recall that this situation corresponds to our break-even point on an accounting basis. To find the sales volume, we substitute the $700 depreciation amount for OCF in our general expression:

$Q = (FC + OCF)/(P - v)$
$ = (\$500 + 700)/20$
$ = 60$

This is the same quantity we had before.

Cash Break-Even We have seen that a project that breaks even on an accounting basis has a net income of zero, but it still has a positive cash flow. At some sales level below the accounting break-even, the operating cash flow actually goes negative. This is a particularly unpleasant occurrence. If it happens, we actually have to supply additional cash to the project just to keep it afloat.

To calculate the **cash break-even** (the point where operating cash flow is equal to zero), we put in a zero for OCF:

$Q = (FC + 0)/(P - v)$
$ = \$500/20$
$ = 25$

cash break-even
The sales level that results in a zero operating cash flow.

Wettway must therefore sell 25 boats to cover the $500 in fixed costs. As we show in Figure 11.5, this point occurs right where the operating cash flow line crosses the horizontal axis.

Notice that a project that just breaks even on a cash flow basis can cover its own fixed operating costs, but that is all. It never pays back anything, so the original investment is a complete loss (the IRR is -100 percent).

financial break-even
The sales level that results in a zero NPV.

Financial Break-Even   The last case we consider is that of **financial break-even**, the sales level that results in a zero NPV. To the financial manager, this is the most interesting case. What we do is first determine what operating cash flow has to be for the NPV to be zero. We then use this amount to determine the sales volume.

To illustrate, recall that Wettway requires a 20 percent return on its $3,500 (in thousands) investment. How many sailboats does Wettway have to sell to break even once we account for the 20 percent per year opportunity cost?

The sailboat project has a five-year life. The project has a zero NPV when the present value of the operating cash flows equals the $3,500 investment. Because the cash flow is the same each year, we can solve for the unknown amount by viewing it as an ordinary annuity. The five-year annuity factor at 20 percent is 2.9906, and the OCF can be determined as follows:

$$\$3,500 = OCF \times 2.9906$$
$$OCF = \$3,500/2.9906$$
$$= \$1,170$$

Wettway thus needs an operating cash flow of $1,170 each year to break even. We can now plug this OCF into the equation for sales volume:

$$Q = (\$500 + 1,170)/20$$
$$= 83.5$$

So, Wettway needs to sell about 84 boats per year. This is not good news.

As indicated in Figure 11.5, the financial break-even is substantially higher than the accounting break-even. This will often be the case. Moreover, what we have discovered is that the sailboat project has a substantial degree of forecasting risk. We project sales of 85 boats per year, but it takes 84 just to earn the required return.

Conclusion   Overall, it seems unlikely that the Wettway sailboat project would fail to break even on an accounting basis. However, there appears to be a very good chance that the true NPV is negative. This illustrates the danger in looking at just the accounting break-even.

What should Wettway do? Is the new project all wet? The decision at this point is essentially a managerial issue—a judgment call. The crucial questions are these:

1. How much confidence do we have in our projections?
2. How important is the project to the future of the company?
3. How badly will the company be hurt if sales turn out to be low? What options are available to the company in this case?

We will consider questions such as these in a later section. For future reference, our discussion of the different break-even measures is summarized in Table 11.1.

Concept Questions

11.4a If a project breaks even on an accounting basis, what is its operating cash flow?

11.4b If a project breaks even on a cash basis, what is its operating cash flow?

11.4c If a project breaks even on a financial basis, what do you know about its *discounted* payback?

I. The General Break-Even Expression

Ignoring taxes, the relation between operating cash flow (OCF) and quantity of output or sales volume (Q) is:

$$Q = \frac{FC + OCF}{P - v}$$

where

    FC = Total fixed costs

    P = Price per unit

    v = Variable cost per unit

As shown next, this relation can be used to determine the accounting, cash, and financial break-even points.

II. The Accounting Break-Even Point

Accounting break-even occurs when net income is zero. Operating cash flow is equal to depreciation when net income is zero, so the accounting break-even point is:

$$Q = \frac{FC + D}{P - v}$$

A project that always just breaks even on an accounting basis has a payback exactly equal to its life, a negative NPV, and an IRR of zero.

III. The Cash Break-Even Point

Cash break-even occurs when operating cash flow is zero. The cash break-even point is thus:

$$Q = \frac{FC}{P - v}$$

A project that always just breaks even on a cash basis never pays back, has an NPV that is negative and equal to the initial outlay, and has an IRR of −100 percent.

IV. The Financial Break-Even Point

Financial break-even occurs when the NPV of the project is zero. The financial break-even point is thus:

$$Q = \frac{FC + OCF^*}{P - v}$$

where OCF* is the level of OCF that results in a zero NPV. A project that breaks even on a financial basis has a discounted payback equal to its life, a zero NPV, and an IRR just equal to the required return.

TABLE 11.1

Summary of Break-Even Measures

Operating Leverage

11.5

We have discussed how to calculate and interpret various measures of break-even for a proposed project. What we have not explicitly discussed is what determines these points and how they might be changed. We now turn to this subject.

THE BASIC IDEA

Operating leverage is the degree to which a project or firm is committed to fixed production costs. A firm with low operating leverage will have low fixed costs compared to a firm with high operating leverage. Generally speaking, projects with a relatively heavy investment in plant and equipment will have a relatively high degree of operating leverage. Such projects are said to be *capital intensive*.

Anytime we are thinking about a new venture, there will normally be alternative ways of producing and delivering the product. For example, Wettway Corporation can purchase the necessary equipment and build all of the components for its sailboats in-house.

operating leverage
The degree to which a firm or project relies on fixed costs.

Alternatively, some of the work could be farmed out to other firms. The first option involves a greater investment in plant and equipment, greater fixed costs and depreciation, and, as a result, a higher degree of operating leverage.

IMPLICATIONS OF OPERATING LEVERAGE

Regardless of how it is measured, operating leverage has important implications for project evaluation. Fixed costs act like a lever in the sense that a small percentage change in operating revenue can be magnified into a large percentage change in operating cash flow and NPV. This explains why we call it operating "leverage."

The higher the degree of operating leverage, the greater is the potential danger from forecasting risk. The reason is that relatively small errors in forecasting sales volume can get magnified, or "levered up," into large errors in cash flow projections.

From a managerial perspective, one way of coping with highly uncertain projects is to keep the degree of operating leverage as low as possible. This will generally have the effect of keeping the break-even point (however measured) at its minimum level. We will illustrate this point in a bit, but first we need to discuss how to measure operating leverage.

MEASURING OPERATING LEVERAGE

One way of measuring operating leverage is to ask: If quantity sold rises by 5 percent, what will be the percentage change in operating cash flow? In other words, the **degree of operating leverage (DOL)** is defined such that:

Percentage change in OCF = DOL × Percentage change in Q

Based on the relationship between OCF and Q, DOL can be written as:[1]

$$DOL = 1 + FC/OCF \qquad [11.4]$$

The ratio FC/OCF simply measures fixed costs as a percentage of total operating cash flow. Notice that zero fixed costs would result in a DOL of 1, implying that percentage changes in quantity sold would show up one for one in operating cash flow. In other words, no magnification, or leverage, effect would exist.

To illustrate this measure of operating leverage, we go back to the Wettway sailboat project. Fixed costs were $500 and $(P - v)$ was $20, so OCF was:

$$OCF = -\$500 + 20 \times Q$$

Suppose Q is currently 50 boats. At this level of output, OCF is $-\$500 + 1{,}000 = \$500$.

If Q rises by 1 unit to 51, then the percentage change in Q is $(51 - 50)/50 = .02$, or 2%. OCF rises to $520, a change of $P - v = \$20$. The percentage change in OCF is $(\$520 - 500)/500 = .04$, or 4%. So a 2 percent increase in the number of boats sold

---

> **degree of operating leverage (DOL)**
> The percentage change in operating cash flow relative to the percentage change in quantity sold.

[1]To see this, note that if Q goes up by one unit, OCF will go up by $(P - v)$. In this case, the percentage change in Q is $1/Q$, and the percentage change in OCF is $(P - v)/OCF$. Given this, we have:

Percentage change in OCF = DOL × Percentage change in Q

$$(P - v)/OCF = DOL \times 1/Q$$

$$DOL = (P - v) \times Q/OCF$$

Also, based on our definitions of OCF:

$$OCF + FC = (P - v) \times Q$$

Thus, DOL can be written as:

$$DOL = (OCF + FC)/OCF$$

$$= 1 + FC/OCF$$

leads to a 4 percent increase in operating cash flow. The degree of operating leverage must be exactly 2.00. We can check this by noting that:

$$DOL = 1 + FC/OCF$$
$$= 1 + \$500/500$$
$$= 2$$

This verifies our previous calculations.

Our formulation of DOL depends on the current output level, Q. However, it can handle changes from the current level of any size, not just one unit. For example, suppose Q rises from 50 to 75, a 50 percent increase. With DOL equal to 2, operating cash flow should increase by 100 percent, or exactly double. Does it? The answer is yes, because, at a Q of 75, OCF is:

$$OCF = -\$500 + 20 \times 75 = \$1,000$$

Notice that operating leverage declines as output (Q) rises. For example, at an output level of 75, we have:

$$DOL = 1 + \$500/1,000$$
$$= 1.50$$

The reason DOL declines is that fixed costs, considered as a percentage of operating cash flow, get smaller and smaller, so the leverage effect diminishes.

Operating Leverage   **EXAMPLE 11.3**

The Sasha Corp. currently sells gourmet dog food for $1.20 per can. The variable cost is 80 cents per can, and the packaging and marketing operations have fixed costs of $360,000 per year. Depreciation is $60,000 per year. What is the accounting break-even? Ignoring taxes, what will be the increase in operating cash flow if the quantity sold rises to 10 percent above the break-even point?

The accounting break-even is $420,000/.40 = 1,050,000 cans. As we know, the operating cash flow is equal to the $60,000 depreciation at this level of production, so the degree of operating leverage is:

$$DOL = 1 + FC/OCF$$
$$= 1 + \$360,000/60,000$$
$$= 7$$

Given this, a 10 percent increase in the number of cans of dog food sold will increase operating cash flow by a substantial 70 percent.

To check this answer, we note that if sales rise by 10 percent, then the quantity sold will rise to 1,050,000 × 1.1 = 1,155,000. Ignoring taxes, the operating cash flow will be 1,155,000 × $.40 − 360,000 = $102,000. Compared to the $60,000 cash flow we had, this is exactly 70 percent more: $102,000/60,000 = 1.70.

OPERATING LEVERAGE AND BREAK-EVEN

We illustrate why operating leverage is an important consideration by examining the Wettway sailboat project under an alternative scenario. At a Q of 85 boats, the degree of operating leverage for the sailboat project under the original scenario is:

$$DOL = 1 + FC/OCF$$
$$= 1 + \$500/1,200$$
$$= 1.42$$

Also, recall that the NPV at a sales level of 85 boats was $88,720, and that the accounting break-even was 60 boats.

An option available to Wettway is to subcontract production of the boat hull assemblies. If the company does this, the necessary investment falls to $3,200,000 and the fixed operating costs fall to $180,000. However, variable costs will rise to $25,000 per boat because subcontracting is more expensive than producing in-house. Ignoring taxes, evaluate this option.

For practice, see if you don't agree with the following:

$$\text{NPV at 20\% (85 units)} = \$74,720$$
$$\text{Accounting break-even} = 55 \text{ boats}$$
$$\text{Degree of operating leverage} = 1.16$$

What has happened? This option results in a slightly lower estimated net present value, and the accounting break-even point falls to 55 boats from 60 boats.

Given that this alternative has the lower NPV, is there any reason to consider it further? Maybe there is. The degree of operating leverage is substantially lower in the second case. If Wettway is worried about the possibility of an overly optimistic projection, then it might prefer to subcontract.

There is another reason why Wettway might consider the second arrangement. If sales turned out to be better than expected, the company would always have the option of starting to produce in-house at a later date. As a practical matter, it is much easier to increase operating leverage (by purchasing equipment) than to decrease it (by selling off equipment). As we discuss in a later chapter, one of the drawbacks to discounted cash flow analysis is that it is difficult to explicitly include options of this sort in the analysis, even though they may be quite important.

Concept Questions

11.5a What is operating leverage?

11.5b How is operating leverage measured?

11.5c What are the implications of operating leverage for the financial manager?

11.6 Capital Rationing

capital rationing
The situation that exists if a firm has positive NPV projects but cannot find the necessary financing.

Capital rationing is said to exist when we have profitable (positive NPV) investments available but we can't get the funds needed to undertake them. For example, as division managers for a large corporation, we might identify $5 million in excellent projects, but find that, for whatever reason, we can spend only $2 million. Now what? Unfortunately, for reasons we will discuss, there may be no truly satisfactory answer.

SOFT RATIONING

soft rationing
The situation that occurs when units in a business are allocated a certain amount of financing for capital budgeting.

The situation we have just described is called **soft rationing**. This occurs when, for example, different units in a business are allocated some fixed amount of money each year for capital spending. Such an allocation is primarily a means of controlling and keeping track of overall spending. The important thing to note about soft rationing is that the corporation as a whole isn't short of capital; more can be raised on ordinary terms if management so desires.

If we face soft rationing, the first thing to do is to try to get a larger allocation. Failing that, one common suggestion is to generate as large a net present value as possible within the existing budget. This amounts to choosing projects with the largest benefit–cost ratio (profitability index).

Strictly speaking, this is the correct thing to do only if the soft rationing is a one-time event—that is, it won't exist next year. If the soft rationing is a chronic problem, then something is amiss. The reason goes all the way back to Chapter 1. Ongoing soft rationing means we are constantly bypassing positive NPV investments. This contradicts our goal of the firm. If we are not trying to maximize value, then the question of which projects to take becomes ambiguous because we no longer have an objective goal in the first place.

HARD RATIONING

With **hard rationing**, a business cannot raise capital for a project under any circumstances. For large, healthy corporations, this situation probably does not occur very often. This is fortunate because, with hard rationing, our DCF analysis breaks down, and the best course of action is ambiguous.

The reason DCF analysis breaks down has to do with the required return. Suppose we say our required return is 20 percent. Implicitly, we are saying we will take a project with a return that exceeds this. However, if we face hard rationing, then we are not going to take a new project no matter what the return on that project is, so the whole concept of a required return is ambiguous. About the only interpretation we can give this situation is that the required return is so large that no project has a positive NPV in the first place.

Hard rationing can occur when a company experiences financial distress, meaning that bankruptcy is a possibility. Also, a firm may not be able to raise capital without violating a preexisting contractual agreement. We discuss these situations in greater detail in a later chapter.

hard rationing
The situation that occurs when a business cannot raise financing for a project under any circumstances.

Concept Questions

11.6a What is capital rationing? What types are there?

11.6b What problems does capital rationing create for discounted cash flow analysis?

Summary and Conclusions   11.7

In this chapter, we looked at some ways of evaluating the results of a discounted cash flow analysis; we also touched on some of the problems that can come up in practice:

1. Net present value estimates depend on projected future cash flows. If there are errors in those projections, then our estimated NPVs can be misleading. We called this possibility *forecasting risk*.

2. Scenario and sensitivity analysis are useful tools for identifying which variables are critical to the success of a project and where forecasting problems can do the most damage.

3. Break-even analysis in its various forms is a particularly common type of scenario analysis that is useful for identifying critical levels of sales.

4. Operating leverage is a key determinant of break-even levels. It reflects the degree to which a project or a firm is committed to fixed costs. The degree of operating leverage tells us the sensitivity of operating cash flow to changes in sales volume.

5. Projects usually have future managerial options associated with them. These options may be important, but standard discounted cash flow analysis tends to ignore them.

6. Capital rationing occurs when apparently profitable projects cannot be funded. Standard discounted cash flow analysis is troublesome in this case because NPV is not necessarily the appropriate criterion.

The most important thing to carry away from reading this chapter is that estimated NPVs or returns should not be taken at face value. They depend critically on projected cash flows. If there is room for significant disagreement about those projected cash flows, the results from the analysis have to be taken with a grain of salt.

Despite the problems we have discussed, discounted cash flow analysis is still *the* way of attacking problems because it forces us to ask the right questions. What we have learned in this chapter is that knowing the questions to ask does not guarantee we will get all the answers.

CHAPTER REVIEW AND SELF-TEST PROBLEMS

Use the following base-case information to work the self-test problems:
A project under consideration costs $750,000, has a five-year life, and has no salvage value. Depreciation is straight-line to zero. The required return is 17 percent, and the tax rate is 34 percent. Sales are projected at 500 units per year. Price per unit is $2,500, variable cost per unit is $1,500, and fixed costs are $200,000 per year.

11.1 Scenario Analysis Suppose you think that the unit sales, price, variable cost, and fixed cost projections given here are accurate to within 5 percent. What are the upper and lower bounds for these projections? What is the base-case NPV? What are the best- and worst-case scenario NPVs?

11.2 Break-Even Analysis Given the base-case projections in the previous problem, what are the cash, accounting, and financial break-even sales levels for this project? Ignore taxes in answering.

ANSWERS TO CHAPTER REVIEW AND SELF-TEST PROBLEMS

11.1 We can summarize the relevant information as follows:

	Base Case	Lower Bound	Upper Bound
Unit sales	500	475	525
Price per unit	$ 2,500	$ 2,375	$ 2,625
Variable cost per unit	$ 1,500	$ 1,425	$ 1,575
Fixed cost per year	$200,000	$190,000	$210,000

Depreciation is $150,000 per year; knowing this, we can calculate the cash flows under each scenario. Remember that we assign high costs and low prices and volume for the worst case and just the opposite for the best case:

Scenario	Unit Sales	Unit Price	Unit Variable Cost	Fixed Costs	Cash Flow
Base case	500	$2,500	$1,500	$200,000	$249,000
Best case	525	2,625	1,425	190,000	341,400
Worst case	475	2,375	1,575	210,000	163,200

At 17 percent, the five-year annuity factor is 3.19935, so the NPVs are:

$$\text{Base-case NPV} = -\$750,000 + 3.19935 \times \$249,000$$
$$= \$46,638$$
$$\text{Best-case NPV} = -\$750,000 + 3.19935 \times \$341,400$$
$$= \$342,258$$
$$\text{Worst-case NPV} = -\$750,000 + 3.19935 \times \$163,200$$
$$= -\$227,866$$

11.2 In this case, we have $200,000 in cash fixed costs to cover. Each unit contributes $2,500 − 1,500 = $1,000 toward covering fixed costs. The cash break-even is thus $200,000/$1,000 = 200 units. We have another $150,000 in depreciation, so the accounting break-even is ($200,000 + 150,000)/$1,000 = 350 units.

To get the financial break-even, we need to find the OCF such that the project has a zero NPV. As we have seen, the five-year annuity factor is 3.19935 and the project costs $750,000, so the OCF must be such that:

$$\$750,000 = \text{OCF} \times 3.19935$$

So, for the project to break even on a financial basis, the project's cash flow must be $750,000/3.19935, or $234,423 per year. If we add this to the $200,000 in cash fixed costs, we get a total of $434,423 that we have to cover. At $1,000 per unit, we need to sell $434,423/$1,000 = 435 units.

CONCEPTS REVIEW AND CRITICAL THINKING QUESTIONS

1. **Forecasting Risk [LO1]** What is forecasting risk? In general, would the degree of forecasting risk be greater for a new product or a cost-cutting proposal? Why?

2. **Sensitivity Analysis and Scenario Analysis [LO1, 2]** What is the essential difference between sensitivity analysis and scenario analysis?

3. **Marginal Cash Flows [LO3]** A coworker claims that looking at all this marginal this and incremental that is just a bunch of nonsense, saying, "Listen, if our average revenue doesn't exceed our average cost, then we will have a negative cash flow, and we will go broke!" How do you respond?

4. **Operating Leverage [LO4]** At one time at least, many Japanese companies had a "no-layoff" policy (for that matter, so did IBM). What are the implications of such a policy for the degree of operating leverage a company faces?

5. **Operating Leverage [LO4]** Airlines offer an example of an industry in which the degree of operating leverage is fairly high. Why?

6. **Break-Even [LO3]** As a shareholder of a firm that is contemplating a new project, would you be more concerned with the accounting break-even point, the cash break-even point, or the financial break-even point? Why?

7. **Break-Even [LO3]** Assume a firm is considering a new project that requires an initial investment and has equal sales and costs over its life. Will the project reach the accounting, cash, or financial break-even point first? Which will it reach next? Last? Will this ordering always apply?

8. **Capital Rationing** [LO5] How are soft rationing and hard rationing different? What are the implications if a firm is experiencing soft rationing? Hard rationing?

9. **Capital Rationing** [LO5] Going all the way back to Chapter 1, recall that we saw that partnerships and proprietorships can face difficulties when it comes to raising capital. In the context of this chapter, the implication is that small businesses will generally face what problem?

QUESTIONS AND PROBLEMS   ™

BASIC
(Questions 1–15)

1. **Calculating Costs and Break-Even** [LO3] Night Shades Inc. (NSI) manufactures biotech sunglasses. The variable materials cost is $5.43 per unit, and the variable labor cost is $3.13 per unit.
   a. What is the variable cost per unit?
   b. Suppose NSI incurs fixed costs of $720,000 during a year in which total production is 280,000 units. What are the total costs for the year?
   c. If the selling price is $19.99 per unit, does NSI break even on a cash basis? If depreciation is $220,000 per year, what is the accounting break-even point?

2. **Computing Average Cost** [LO3] K-Too Everwear Corporation can manufacture mountain climbing shoes for $24.86 per pair in variable raw material costs and $14.08 per pair in variable labor expense. The shoes sell for $135 per pair. Last year, production was 120,000 pairs. Fixed costs were $1,550,000. What were total production costs? What is the marginal cost per pair? What is the average cost? If the company is considering a one-time order for an extra 5,000 pairs, what is the minimum acceptable total revenue from the order? Explain.

3. **Scenario Analysis** [LO2] Olin Transmissions, Inc., has the following estimates for its new gear assembly project: price = $1,900 per unit; variable costs = $240 per unit; fixed costs = $4.8 million; quantity = 95,000 units. Suppose the company believes all of its estimates are accurate only to within ±15 percent. What values should the company use for the four variables given here when it performs its best-case scenario analysis? What about the worst-case scenario?

4. **Sensitivity Analysis** [LO1] For the company in the previous problem, suppose management is most concerned about the impact of its price estimate on the project's profitability. How could you address this concern? Describe how you would calculate your answer. What values would you use for the other forecast variables?

5. **Sensitivity Analysis and Break-Even** [LO1, 3] We are evaluating a project that costs $724,000, has an eight-year life, and has no salvage value. Assume that depreciation is straight-line to zero over the life of the project. Sales are projected at 90,000 units per year. Price per unit is $43, variable cost per unit is $29, and fixed costs are $780,000 per year. The tax rate is 35 percent, and we require a 15 percent return on this project.
   a. Calculate the accounting break-even point. What is the degree of operating leverage at the accounting break-even point?
   b. Calculate the base-case cash flow and NPV. What is the sensitivity of NPV to changes in the sales figure? Explain what your answer tells you about a 500-unit decrease in projected sales.
   c. What is the sensitivity of OCF to changes in the variable cost figure? Explain what your answer tells you about a $1 decrease in estimated variable costs.

6. **Scenario Analysis [LO2]** In the previous problem, suppose the projections given for price, quantity, variable costs, and fixed costs are all accurate to within ±10 percent. Calculate the best-case and worst-case NPV figures.

7. **Calculating Break-Even [LO3]** In each of the following cases, calculate the accounting break-even and the cash break-even points. Ignore any tax effects in calculating the cash break-even.

Unit Price	Unit Variable Cost	Fixed Costs	Depreciation
$3,020	$2,275	$14,000,000	$6,500,000
38	27	73,000	150,000
11	4	1,200	840

8. **Calculating Break-Even [LO3]** In each of the following cases, find the unknown variable:

Accounting Break-Even	Unit Price	Unit Variable Cost	Fixed Costs	Depreciation
112,800	$41	$30	$ 820,000	?
165,000	?	43	3,200,000	$1,150,000
4,385	98	?	160,000	105,000

9. **Calculating Break-Even [LO3]** A project has the following estimated data: price = $57 per unit; variable costs = $32 per unit; fixed costs = $9,000; required return = 12 percent; initial investment = $18,000; life = four years. Ignoring the effect of taxes, what is the accounting break-even quantity? The cash break-even quantity? The financial break-even quantity? What is the degree of operating leverage at the financial break-even level of output?

10. **Using Break-Even Analysis [LO3]** Consider a project with the following data: accounting break-even quantity = 15,500 units; cash break-even quantity = 13,200 units; life = five years; fixed costs = $140,000; variable costs = $24 per unit; required return = 16 percent. Ignoring the effect of taxes, find the financial break-even quantity.

11. **Calculating Operating Leverage [LO4]** At an output level of 65,000 units, you calculate that the degree of operating leverage is 3.40. If output rises to 70,000 units, what will the percentage change in operating cash flow be? Will the new level of operating leverage be higher or lower? Explain.

12. **Leverage [LO4]** In the previous problem, suppose fixed costs are $130,000. What is the operating cash flow at 58,000 units? The degree of operating leverage?

13. **Operating Cash Flow and Leverage [LO4]** A proposed project has fixed costs of $73,000 per year. The operating cash flow at 8,000 units is $87,500. Ignoring the effect of taxes, what is the degree of operating leverage? If units sold rise from 8,000 to 8,500, what will be the increase in operating cash flow? What is the new degree of operating leverage?

14. **Cash Flow and Leverage [LO4]** At an output level of 10,000 units, you have calculated that the degree of operating leverage is 2.35. The operating cash flow is $43,000 in this case. Ignoring the effect of taxes, what are fixed costs? What will the operating cash flow be if output rises to 11,000 units? If output falls to 9,000 units?

15. **Leverage [LO4]** In the previous problem, what will be the new degree of operating leverage in each case?

INTERMEDIATE
(Questions 16–24)

16. **Break-Even Intuition** [LO3] Consider a project with a required return of $R\%$ that costs $\$I$ and will last for N years. The project uses straight-line depreciation to zero over the N-year life; there is no salvage value or net working capital requirements.

    a. At the accounting break-even level of output, what is the IRR of this project? The payback period? The NPV?

    b. At the cash break-even level of output, what is the IRR of this project? The payback period? The NPV?

    c. At the financial break-even level of output, what is the IRR of this project? The payback period? The NPV?

17. **Sensitivity Analysis** [LO1] Consider a four-year project with the following information: initial fixed asset investment = $\$490,000$; straight-line depreciation to zero over the four-year life; zero salvage value; price = $\$32$; variable costs = $\$19$; fixed costs = $\$210,000$; quantity sold = 110,000 units; tax rate = 34 percent. How sensitive is OCF to changes in quantity sold?

18. **Operating Leverage** [LO4] In the previous problem, what is the degree of operating leverage at the given level of output? What is the degree of operating leverage at the accounting break-even level of output?

19. **Project Analysis** [LO1, 2, 3, 4] You are considering a new product launch. The project will cost $\$1,700,000$, have a four-year life, and have no salvage value; depreciation is straight-line to zero. Sales are projected at 190 units per year; price per unit will be $\$18,000$, variable cost per unit will be $\$11,200$, and fixed costs will be $\$410,000$ per year. The required return on the project is 12 percent, and the relevant tax rate is 35 percent.

    a. Based on your experience, you think the unit sales, variable cost, and fixed cost projections given here are probably accurate to within ±10 percent. What are the upper and lower bounds for these projections? What is the base-case NPV? What are the best-case and worst-case scenarios?

    b. Evaluate the sensitivity of your base-case NPV to changes in fixed costs.

    c. What is the cash break-even level of output for this project (ignoring taxes)?

    d. What is the accounting break-even level of output for this project? What is the degree of operating leverage at the accounting break-even point? How do you interpret this number?

20. **Project Analysis** [LO1, 2] McGilla Golf has decided to sell a new line of golf clubs. The clubs will sell for $\$750$ per set and have a variable cost of $\$330$ per set. The company has spent $\$150,000$ for a marketing study that determined the company will sell 51,000 sets per year for seven years. The marketing study also determined that the company will lose sales of 11,000 sets of its high-priced clubs. The high-priced clubs sell at $\$1,200$ and have variable costs of $\$650$. The company will also increase sales of its cheap clubs by 9,500 sets. The cheap clubs sell for $\$420$ and have variable costs of $\$190$ per set. The fixed costs each year will be $\$8,100,000$. The company has also spent $\$1,000,000$ on research and development for the new clubs. The plant and equipment required will cost $\$22,400,000$ and will be depreciated on a straight-line basis. The new clubs will also require an increase in net working capital of $\$1,250,000$ that will be returned at the end of the project. The tax rate is 40 percent, and the cost of capital is 10 percent. Calculate the payback period, the NPV, and the IRR.

21. **Scenario Analysis** [LO2] In the previous problem, you feel that the values are accurate to within only ±10 percent. What are the best-case and worst-case NPVs? (*Hint:* The price and variable costs for the two existing sets of clubs are known with certainty; only the sales gained or lost are uncertain.)

22. **Sensitivity Analysis [LO1]** McGilla Golf would like to know the sensitivity of NPV to changes in the price of the new clubs and the quantity of new clubs sold. What is the sensitivity of the NPV to each of these variables?

23. **Break-Even Analysis [LO3]** Hybrid cars are touted as a "green" alternative; however, the financial aspects of hybrid ownership are not as clear. Consider the 2006 Honda Accord Hybrid, which had a list price of $5,450 (including tax consequences) more than a Honda Accord EX sedan. Additionally, the annual ownership costs (other than fuel) for the hybrid were expected to be $400 more than the traditional sedan. The EPA mileage estimate was 25 mpg for the hybrid and 23 mpg for the EX sedan.

    a. Assume that gasoline costs $3.60 per gallon and you plan to keep either car for six years. How many miles per year would you need to drive to make the decision to buy the hybrid worthwhile, ignoring the time value of money?

    b. If you drive 15,000 miles per year and keep either car for six years, what price per gallon would make the decision to buy the hybrid worthwhile, ignoring the time value of money?

    c. Rework parts (a) and (b) assuming the appropriate interest rate is 10 percent and all cash flows occur at the end of the year.

    d. What assumption did the analysis in the previous parts make about the resale value of each car?

24. **Break-Even Analysis [LO3]** In an effort to capture the large jet market, Airbus invested $13 billion developing its A380, which is capable of carrying 800 passengers. The plane has a list price of $280 million. In discussing the plane, Airbus stated that the company would break even when 249 A380s were sold.

    a. Assuming the break-even sales figure given is the cash flow break-even, what is the cash flow per plane?

    b. Airbus promised its shareholders a 20 percent rate of return on the investment. If sales of the plane continue in perpetuity, how many planes must the company sell per year to deliver on this promise?

    c. Suppose instead that the sales of the A380 last for only 10 years. How many planes must Airbus sell per year to deliver the same rate of return?

25. **Break-Even and Taxes [LO3]** This problem concerns the effect of taxes on the various break-even measures.

    CHALLENGE
    (Questions 25–30)

    a. Show that, when we consider taxes, the general relationship between operating cash flow, OCF, and sales volume, Q, can be written as:

    $$Q = \frac{FC + \dfrac{OCF - T \times D}{1 - T}}{P - v}$$

    b. Use the expression in part (a) to find the cash, accounting, and financial break-even points for the Wettway sailboat example in the chapter. Assume a 38 percent tax rate.

    c. In part (b), the accounting break-even should be the same as before. Why? Verify this algebraically.

26. **Operating Leverage and Taxes [LO4]** Show that if we consider the effect of taxes, the degree of operating leverage can be written as:

    $$DOL = 1 + [FC \times (1 - T) - T \times D]/OCF$$

    Notice that this reduces to our previous result if $T = 0$. Can you interpret this in words?

✗ 27. **Scenario Analysis [LO2]** Consider a project to supply Detroit with 35,000 tons of machine screws annually for automobile production. You will need an initial $3,200,000 investment in threading equipment to get the project started; the project will last for five years. The accounting department estimates that annual fixed costs will be $450,000 and that variable costs should be $185 per ton; accounting will depreciate the initial fixed asset investment straight-line to zero over the five-year project life. It also estimates a salvage value of $500,000 after dismantling costs. The marketing department estimates that the automakers will let the contract at a selling price of $230 per ton. The engineering department estimates you will need an initial net working capital investment of $360,000. You require a 13 percent return and face a marginal tax rate of 38 percent on this project.

    a. What is the estimated OCF for this project? The NPV? Should you pursue this project?

    b. Suppose you believe that the accounting department's initial cost and salvage value projections are accurate only to within ±15 percent; the marketing department's price estimate is accurate only to within ±10 percent; and the engineering department's net working capital estimate is accurate only to within ±5 percent. What is your worst-case scenario for this project? Your best-case scenario? Do you still want to pursue the project?

28. **Sensitivity Analysis [LO1]** In Problem 27, suppose you're confident about your own projections, but you're a little unsure about Detroit's actual machine screw requirement. What is the sensitivity of the project OCF to changes in the quantity supplied? What about the sensitivity of NPV to changes in quantity supplied? Given the sensitivity number you calculated, is there some minimum level of output below which you wouldn't want to operate? Why?

29. **Break-Even Analysis [LO3]** Use the results of Problem 25 to find the accounting, cash, and financial break-even quantities for the company in Problem 27.

30. **Operating Leverage [LO4]** Use the results of Problem 26 to find the degree of operating leverage for the company in Problem 27 at the base-case output level of 35,000 units. How does this number compare to the sensitivity figure you found in Problem 28? Verify that either approach will give you the same OCF figure at any new quantity level.

MINICASE

Conch Republic Electronics, Part 2

Shelley Couts, the owner of Conch Republic Electronics, had received the capital budgeting analysis from Jay McCanless for the new PDA the company is considering. Shelley was pleased with the results, but she still had concerns about the new PDA. Conch Republic had used a small market research firm for the past 20 years, but recently the founder of that firm retired. Because of this, she was not convinced the sales projections presented by the market research firm were entirely accurate. Additionally, because of rapid changes in technology, she was concerned that a competitor could enter the market. This would likely force Conch Republic to lower the sales price of its new PDA. For these reasons, she has asked Jay to analyze how changes in the price of the new PDA and changes in the quantity sold will affect the NPV of the project.

Shelley has asked Jay to prepare a memo answering the following questions.

QUESTIONS

1. How sensitive is the NPV to changes in the price of the new PDA?

2. How sensitive is the NPV to changes in the quantity sold of the new PDA?

SOME LESSONS FROM CAPITAL MARKET HISTORY

12

SOME LESSONS FROM CAPITAL MARKET HISTORY

LEARNING OBJECTIVES

After studying this chapter, you should understand:

LO1 How to calculate the return on an investment.

LO2 The historical returns on various important types of investments.

LO3 The historical risks on various important types of investments.

LO4 The implications of market efficiency.

LEARNING OBJECTIVES

After studying this chapter, you should understand:

LO1 How to calculate the return on an investment.

LO2 The historical returns on various important types of investments.

LO3 The historical risks on various important types of investments.

LO4 The implications of market efficiency.

WITH THE S&P 500 INDEX UP about 3.5 percent and the NASDAQ stock market index up about 9.8 percent in 2007, stock market performance overall was mixed. However, investors in First Solar, maker of solar panels, had to feel sunny about the 796 percent gain in that stock, and investors in Onyx Pharmaceuticals had to feel pretty good about Onyx's 426 percent gain. Of course, not all stocks increased in value during the year. Stock in Novastar Financial, a mortgage lender, fell 97 percent during the year, and stock in Atherogenics, a pharmaceutical company, dropped 96 percent. These examples show that there were tremendous potential profits to be made during 2007, but there was also the risk of losing money—lots of it. So what should you, as a stock market investor, expect when you invest your own money? In this chapter, we study more than eight decades of market history to find out.

Master the ability to solve problems in this chapter by using a spreadsheet. Access Excel Master on the student Web site www.mhhe.com/rwj.

Thus far, we haven't had much to say about what determines the required return on an investment. In one sense, the answer is simple: The required return depends on the risk of the investment. The greater the risk, the greater is the required return.

Having said this, we are left with a somewhat more difficult problem. How can we measure the amount of risk present in an investment? Put another way, what does it mean to say that one investment is riskier than another? Obviously, we need to define what we mean by *risk* if we are going to answer these questions. This is our task in the next two chapters.

From the last several chapters, we know that one of the responsibilities of the financial manager is to assess the value of proposed real asset investments. In doing this, it is important that we first look at what financial investments have to offer. At a minimum, the return we require from a proposed nonfinancial investment must be greater than what we can get by buying financial assets of similar risk.

Our goal in this chapter is to provide a perspective on what capital market history can tell us about risk and return. The most important thing to get out of this chapter is a feel for the numbers. What is a high return? What is a low one? More generally, what returns should we expect from financial assets, and what are the risks of such investments? This perspective is essential for understanding how to analyze and value risky investment projects.

We start our discussion of risk and return by describing the historical experience of investors in U.S. financial markets. In 1931, for example, the stock market lost 43 percent of its value. Just two years later, the stock market gained 54 percent. In more recent memory, the market lost about 25 percent of its value on October 19, 1987, alone. What lessons, if any, can financial managers learn from such shifts in the stock market? We will explore almost a century of market history to find out.

Not everyone agrees on the value of studying history. On the one hand, there is philosopher George Santayana's famous comment: "Those who do not remember the past are condemned to repeat it." On the other hand, there is industrialist Henry Ford's equally famous comment: "History is more or less bunk." Nonetheless, perhaps everyone would agree with Mark Twain's observation: "October. This is one of the peculiarly dangerous months to speculate in stocks in. The others are July, January, September, April, November, May, March, June, December, August, and February."

Two central lessons emerge from our study of market history. First, there is a reward for bearing risk. Second, the greater the potential reward is, the greater is the risk. To illustrate these facts about market returns, we devote much of this chapter to reporting the statistics and numbers that make up the modern capital market history of the United States. In the next chapter, these facts provide the foundation for our study of how financial markets put a price on risk.

The number of Web sites devoted to financial markets and instruments is astounding—and increasing daily. Be sure to check out the RWJ Web page for links to finance-related sites! (www.mhhe.com/rwj)

12.1 Returns

We wish to discuss historical returns on different types of financial assets. The first thing we need to do, then, is to briefly discuss how to calculate the return from investing.

DOLLAR RETURNS

How did the market do today? Find out at finance.yahoo.com.

If you buy an asset of any sort, your gain (or loss) from that investment is called the *return on your investment*. This return will usually have two components. First, you may receive some cash directly while you own the investment. This is called the *income component* of your return. Second, the value of the asset you purchase will often change. In this case, you have a capital gain or capital loss on your investment.[1]

To illustrate, suppose the Video Concept Company has several thousand shares of stock outstanding. You purchased some of these shares of stock in the company at the beginning of the year. It is now year-end, and you want to determine how well you have done on your investment.

First, over the year, a company may pay cash dividends to its shareholders. As a stockholder in Video Concept Company, you are a part owner of the company. If the company is profitable, it may choose to distribute some of its profits to shareholders (we discuss the details of dividend policy in a later chapter). So, as the owner of some stock, you will receive some cash. This cash is the income component from owning the stock.

In addition to the dividend, the other part of your return is the capital gain or capital loss on the stock. This part arises from changes in the value of your investment. For example, consider the cash flows illustrated in Figure 12.1. At the beginning of the year, the stock was selling for $37 per share. If you had bought 100 shares, you would have had a total outlay of $3,700. Suppose that, over the year, the stock paid a dividend of $1.85 per share. By the end of the year, then, you would have received income of:

$$\text{Dividend} = \$1.85 \times 100 = \$185$$

Also, the value of the stock has risen to $40.33 per share by the end of the year. Your 100 shares are now worth $4,033, so you have a capital gain of:

$$\text{Capital gain} = (\$40.33 - 37) \times 100 = \$333$$

---

[1]As we mentioned in an earlier chapter, strictly speaking, what is and what is not a capital gain (or loss) is determined by the IRS. We thus use the terms loosely.

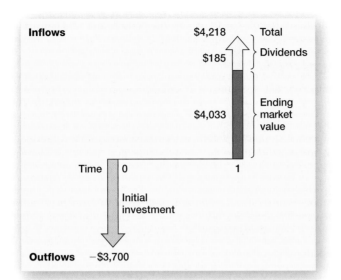

FIGURE 12.1

Dollar Returns

On the other hand, if the price had dropped to, say, $34.78, you would have a capital loss of:

Capital loss = ($34.78 − 37) × 100 = −$222

Notice that a capital loss is the same thing as a negative capital gain.

The total dollar return on your investment is the sum of the dividend and the capital gain:

Total dollar return = Dividend income + Capital gain (or loss)   [12.1]

In our first example, the total dollar return is thus given by:

Total dollar return = $185 + 333 = $518

Notice that if you sold the stock at the end of the year, the total amount of cash you would have would equal your initial investment plus the total return. In the preceding example, then:

Total cash if stock is sold = Initial investment + Total return   [12.2]
= $3,700 + 518
= $4,218

As a check, notice that this is the same as the proceeds from the sale of the stock plus the dividends:

Proceeds from stock sale + Dividends = $40.33 × 100 + 185
= $4,033 + 185
= $4,218

Suppose you hold on to your Video Concept stock and don't sell it at the end of the year. Should you still consider the capital gain as part of your return? Isn't this only a "paper" gain and not really a cash flow if you don't sell the stock?

The answer to the first question is a strong yes, and the answer to the second is an equally strong no. The capital gain is every bit as much a part of your return as the dividend, and you should certainly count it as part of your return. That you actually decided to keep the stock and not sell (you don't "realize" the gain) is irrelevant because you could have converted it to cash if you had wanted to. Whether you choose to do so or not is up to you.

After all, if you insisted on converting your gain to cash, you could always sell the stock at year-end and immediately reinvest by buying the stock back. There is no net difference between doing this and just not selling (assuming, of course, that there are no tax consequences from selling the stock). Again, the point is that whether you actually cash out and buy sodas (or whatever) or reinvest by not selling doesn't affect the return you earn.

PERCENTAGE RETURNS

It is usually more convenient to summarize information about returns in percentage terms, rather than dollar terms, because that way your return doesn't depend on how much you actually invest. The question we want to answer is this: How much do we get for each dollar we invest?

To answer this question, let P_t be the price of the stock at the beginning of the year and let D_{t+1} be the dividend paid on the stock during the year. Consider the cash flows in Figure 12.2. These are the same as those in Figure 12.1, except that we have now expressed everything on a per-share basis.

In our example, the price at the beginning of the year was $37 per share and the dividend paid during the year on each share was $1.85. As we discussed in Chapter 8, expressing the dividend as a percentage of the beginning stock price results in the dividend yield:

$$\text{Dividend yield} = D_{t+1}/P_t$$
$$= \$1.85/37 = .05 = 5\%$$

This says that for each dollar we invest, we get five cents in dividends.

The second component of our percentage return is the capital gains yield. Recall (from Chapter 8) that this is calculated as the change in the price during the year (the capital gain) divided by the beginning price:

$$\text{Capital gains yield} = (P_{t+1} - P_t)/P_t$$
$$= (\$40.33 - 37)/37$$
$$= \$3.33/37$$
$$= 9\%$$

 Go to www.smartmoney.com/marketmap *for a cool Java applet that shows today's returns by market sector.*

FIGURE 12.2

Percentage Returns

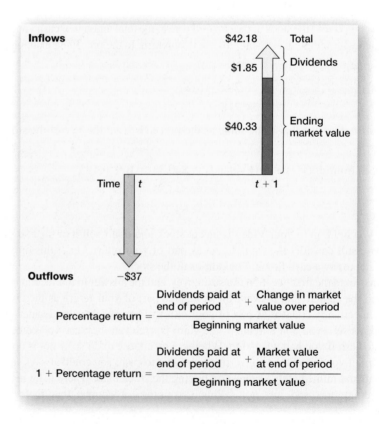

So, per dollar invested, we get nine cents in capital gains.

Putting it together, per dollar invested, we get 5 cents in dividends and 9 cents in capital gains; so we get a total of 14 cents. Our percentage return is 14 cents on the dollar, or 14 percent.

To check this, notice that we invested $3,700 and ended up with $4,218. By what percentage did our $3,700 increase? As we saw, we picked up $4,218 − 3,700 = $518. This is a $518/3,700 = 14% increase.

| **Calculating Returns** | **EXAMPLE 12.1** |

Suppose you bought some stock at the beginning of the year for $25 per share. At the end of the year, the price is $35 per share. During the year, you got a $2 dividend per share. This is the situation illustrated in Figure 12.3. What is the dividend yield? The capital gains yield? The percentage return? If your total investment was $1,000, how much do you have at the end of the year?

Your $2 dividend per share works out to a dividend yield of:

$$\text{Dividend yield} = D_{t+1}/P_t$$
$$= \$2/25 = .08 = 8\%$$

The per-share capital gain is $10, so the capital gains yield is:

$$\text{Capital gains yield} = (P_{t-1} - P_t)/P_t$$
$$= (\$35 - 25)/25$$
$$= \$10/25$$
$$= 40\%$$

The total percentage return is thus 48 percent.

If you had invested $1,000, you would have $1,480 at the end of the year, representing a 48 percent increase. To check this, note that your $1,000 would have bought you $1,000/25 = 40 shares. Your 40 shares would then have paid you a total of 40 × $2 = $80 in cash dividends. Your $10 per share gain would give you a total capital gain of $10 × 40 = $400. Add these together, and you get the $480 increase.

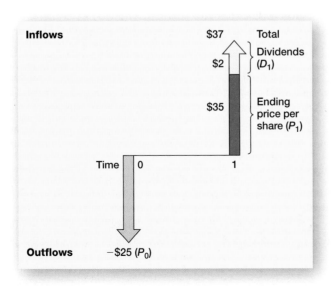

FIGURE 12.3

Cash Flow—An Investment Example

To give another example, stock in Goldman Sachs, the famous financial services company, began 2007 at $197.32 per share. Goldman paid dividends of $1.40 during 2007, and the stock price at the end of the year was $214.27. What was the return on Goldman for the year? For practice, see if you agree that the answer is 9.30 percent. Of course, negative returns occur as well. For example, again in 2007, JP Morgan Chase & Co.'s stock price at the beginning of the year was $46.09 per share, and dividends of $1.44 were paid. The stock ended the year at $42.92 per share. Verify that the loss was 3.75 percent for the year.

Concept Questions

12.1a What are the two parts of total return?

12.1b Why are unrealized capital gains or losses included in the calculation of returns?

12.1c What is the difference between a dollar return and a percentage return? Why are percentage returns more convenient?

12.2 The Historical Record

Roger Ibbotson and Rex Sinquefield conducted a famous set of studies dealing with rates of return in U.S. financial markets.[2] They presented year-to-year historical rates of return on five important types of financial investments. The returns can be interpreted as what you would have earned if you had held portfolios of the following:

1. *Large-company stocks:* This common stock portfolio is based on the Standard & Poor's (S&P) 500 index, which contains 500 of the largest companies (in terms of total market value of outstanding stock) in the United States.

For more about market history, visit www.globalfindata.com.

2. *Small-company stocks:* This is a portfolio composed of the stock corresponding to the smallest 20 percent of the companies listed on the New York Stock Exchange, again as measured by market value of outstanding stock.

3. *Long-term corporate bonds:* This is based on high-quality bonds with 20 years to maturity.

4. *Long-term U.S. government bonds:* This is based on U.S. government bonds with 20 years to maturity.

5. *U.S. Treasury bills:* This is based on Treasury bills (T-bills for short) with a one-month maturity.

These returns are not adjusted for inflation or taxes; thus, they are nominal, pretax returns.

In addition to the year-to-year returns on these financial instruments, the year-to-year percentage change in the consumer price index (CPI) is also computed. This is a commonly used measure of inflation, so we can calculate real returns using this as the inflation rate.

A FIRST LOOK

Before looking closely at the different portfolio returns, we take a look at the big picture. Figure 12.4 shows what happened to $1 invested in these different portfolios at the end of 1925. The growth in value for each of the different portfolios over the 82-year period ending in 2007 is given separately (the long-term corporate bonds are omitted). Notice that to get everything on a single graph, some modification in scaling is used. As is commonly

---

[2]R.G. Ibbotson and R.A. Sinquefield, *Stocks, Bonds, Bills, and Inflation* [SBBI] (Charlottesville, VA: Financial Analysis Research Foundation, 1982).

FIGURE 12.4 A $1 Investment in Different Types of Portfolios: 1925–2007 (Year-End 1925 = $1)

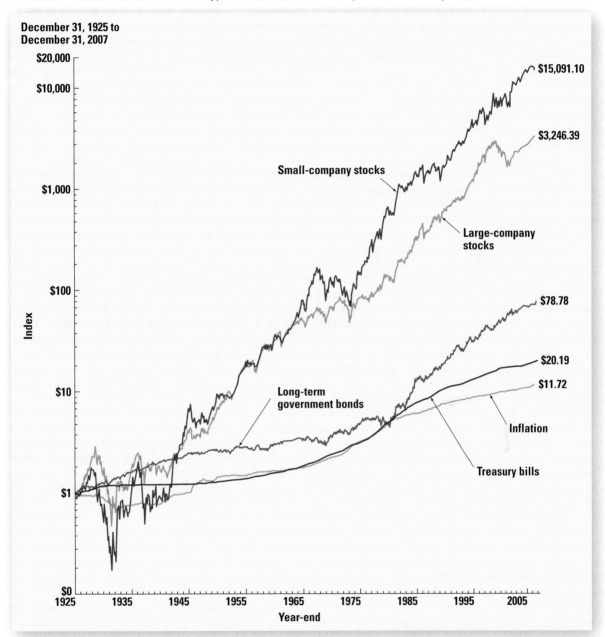

December 31, 1925 to
December 31, 2007

Small-company stocks — $15,091.10

Large-company stocks — $3,246.39

Long-term government bonds — $78.78

Treasury bills — $20.19

Inflation — $11.72

Index

Year-end

done with financial series, the vertical axis is scaled so that equal distances measure equal percentage (as opposed to dollar) changes in values.[3]

Looking at Figure 12.4, we see that the "small-cap" (short for small-capitalization) investment did the best overall. Every dollar invested grew to a remarkable $15,091.10 over the 82 years. The large-company common stock portfolio did less well; a dollar invested in it grew to $3,246.39.

Go to
bigcharts.marketwatch.com
to see both intraday and long-term charts.

---

[3]In other words, the scale is logarithmic.

At the other end, the T-bill portfolio grew to only $20.19. This is even less impressive when we consider the inflation over the period in question. As illustrated, the increase in the price level was such that $11.72 was needed at the end of the period just to replace the original $1.

Given the historical record, why would anybody buy anything other than small-cap stocks? If you look closely at Figure 12.4, you will probably see the answer. The T-bill portfolio and the long-term government bond portfolio grew more slowly than did the stock portfolios, but they also grew much more steadily. The small stocks ended up on top; but as you can see, they grew quite erratically at times. For example, the small stocks were the worst performers for about the first 10 years and had a smaller return than long-term government bonds for almost 15 years.

A CLOSER LOOK

To illustrate the variability of the different investments, Figures 12.5 through 12.8 plot the year-to-year percentage returns in the form of vertical bars drawn from the horizontal axis.

FIGURE 12.5

Year-by-Year Total Returns on Large-Company Common Stocks

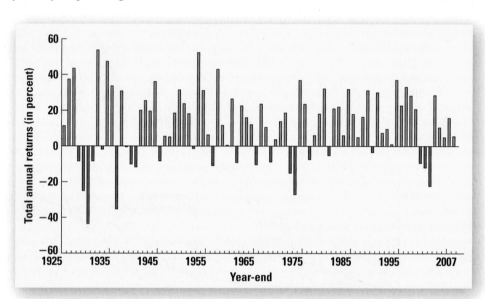

FIGURE 12.6

Year-by-Year Total Returns on Small-Company Stocks

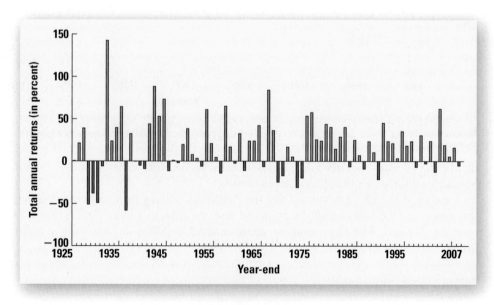

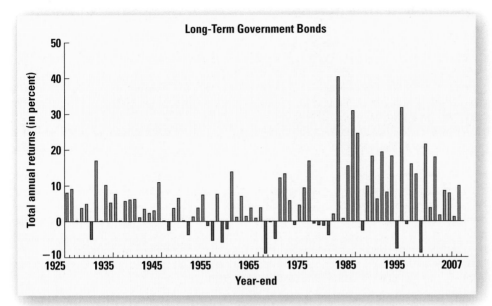

Long-Term Government Bonds

FIGURE 12.7

Year-by-Year Total Returns
on Bonds and Bills

Redrawn from *Stocks, Bonds,
Bills and Inflation: 2008
Yearbook,*™ annually updates
work by Roger G. Ibbotson
and Rex A. Sinquefield
(Chicago: Morningstar). All
rights reserved.

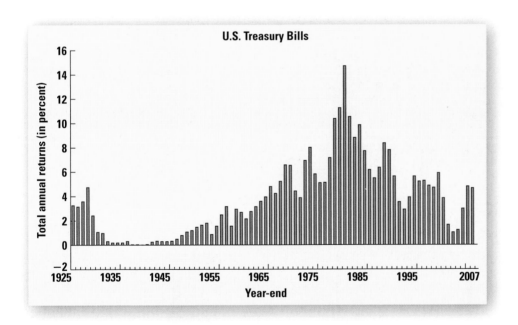

U.S. Treasury Bills

The height of the bar tells us the return for the particular year. For example, looking at the long-term government bonds (Figure 12.7), we see that the largest historical return (44.44 percent) occurred in 1982. This was a good year for bonds. In comparing these charts, notice the differences in the vertical axis scales. With these differences in mind, you can see how predictably the Treasury bills (Figure 12.7) behaved compared to the small stocks (Figure 12.6).

The returns shown in these bar graphs are sometimes very large. Looking at the graphs, for example, we see that the largest single-year return is a remarkable 142.87 percent for the small-cap stocks in 1933. In the same year, the large-company stocks returned "only" 52.94 percent. In contrast, the largest Treasury bill return was 15.21 percent in 1981. For future reference, the actual year-to-year returns for the S&P 500, long-term government bonds, Treasury bills, and the CPI are shown in Table 12.1.

Roger Ibbotson on Capital Market History

The financial markets are the most carefully documented human phenomena in history. Every day, over 2,000 NYSE stocks are traded, and at least 6,000 more stocks are traded on other exchanges and ECNs. Bonds, commodities, futures, and options also provide a wealth of data. These data daily fill much of *The Wall Street Journal* (and numerous other newspapers), and are available as they happen on numerous financial websites. A record actually exists of almost every transaction, providing not only a real-time database but also a historical record extending back, in many cases, more than a century.

The global market adds another dimension to this wealth of data. The Japanese stock market trades over a billion shares a day, and the London exchange reports trades on over 10,000 domestic and foreign issues a day.

The data generated by these transactions are quantifiable, quickly analyzed and disseminated, and made easily accessible by computer. Because of this, finance has increasingly come to resemble one of the exact sciences. The use of financial market data ranges from the simple, such as using the S&P 500 to measure the performance of a portfolio, to the incredibly complex. For example, only a few decades ago, the bond market was the most staid province on Wall Street. Today, it attracts swarms of traders seeking to exploit arbitrage opportunities—small temporary mispricings—using real-time data and computers to analyze them.

Financial market data are the foundation for the extensive empirical understanding we now have of the financial markets. The following is a list of some of the principal findings of such research:

- Risky securities, such as stocks, have higher average returns than riskless securities such as Treasury bills.

- Stocks of small companies have higher average returns than those of larger companies.

- Long-term bonds have higher average yields and returns than short-term bonds.

- The cost of capital for a company, project, or division can be predicted using data from the markets.

Because phenomena in the financial markets are so well measured, finance is the most readily quantifiable branch of economics. Researchers are able to do more extensive empirical research than in any other economic field, and the research can be quickly translated into action in the marketplace.

Roger Ibbotson is professor in the practice of management at the Yale School of Management. He is founder of Ibbotson Associates, now a Morningstar, Inc. company and a major supplier of financial data and analysis. He is also chairman of Zebra Capital, an equity hedge fund manager. An outstanding scholar, he is best known for his original estimates of the historical rates of return realized by investors in different markets and for his research on new issues.

FIGURE 12.8

Year-by-Year Inflation

Redrawn from *Stocks, Bonds, Bills and Inflation: 2008 Yearbook*,™ annually updates work by Roger G. Ibbotson and Rex A. Sinquefield (Chicago: Morningstar). All rights reserved.

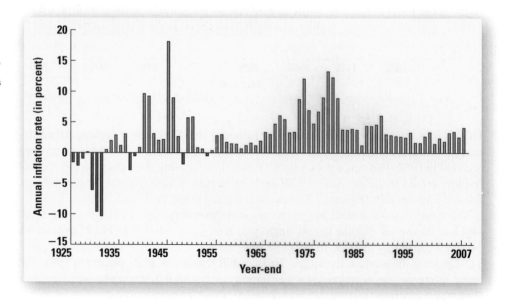

TABLE 12.1 Year-to-Year Total Returns: 1926–2007

Year	Large-Company Stocks	Long-Term Government Bonds	U.S. Treasury Bills	Consumer Price Index	Year	Large-Company Stocks	Long-Term Government Bonds	U.S. Treasury Bills	Consumer Price Index
1926	13.75%	5.69%	3.30%	−1.12%	1967	23.98	−2.86	4.39	3.04
1927	35.70	6.58	3.15	−2.26	1968	11.03	2.25	5.49	4.72
1928	45.08	1.15	4.05	−1.16	1969	−8.43	−5.63	6.90	6.20
1929	−8.80	4.39	4.47	.58	1970	3.94	18.92	6.50	5.57
1930	−25.13	4.47	2.27	−6.40	1971	14.30	11.24	4.36	3.27
1931	−43.60	−2.15	1.15	−9.32	1972	18.99	2.39	4.23	3.41
1932	−8.75	8.51	.88	−10.27	1973	−14.69	3.30	7.29	8.71
1933	52.95	1.92	.52	.76	1974	−26.47	4.00	7.99	12.34
1934	−2.31	7.59	.27	1.52	1975	37.23	5.52	5.87	6.94
1935	46.79	4.20	.17	2.99	1976	23.93	15.56	5.07	4.86
1936	32.49	5.13	.17	1.45	1977	−7.16	.38	5.45	6.70
1937	−35.45	1.44	.27	2.86	1978	6.57	−1.26	7.64	9.02
1938	31.63	4.21	.06	−2.78	1979	18.61	1.26	10.56	13.29
1939	−1.43	3.84	.04	.00	1980	32.50	−2.48	12.10	12.52
1940	−10.36	5.70	.04	.71	1981	−4.92	4.04	14.60	8.92
1941	−12.02	.47	.14	9.93	1982	21.55	44.28	10.94	3.83
1942	20.75	1.80	.34	9.03	1983	22.56	1.29	8.99	3.79
1943	25.38	2.01	.38	2.96	1984	6.27	15.29	9.90	3.95
1944	19.49	2.27	.38	2.30	1985	31.73	32.27	7.71	3.80
1945	36.21	5.29	.38	2.25	1986	18.67	22.39	6.09	1.10
1946	−8.42	.54	.38	18.13	1987	5.25	−3.03	5.88	4.43
1947	5.05	−1.02	.62	8.84	1988	16.61	6.84	6.94	4.42
1948	4.99	2.66	1.06	2.99	1989	31.69	18.54	8.44	4.65
1949	17.81	4.58	1.12	−2.07	1990	−3.10	7.74	7.69	6.11
1950	30.05	−.98	1.22	5.93	1991	30.46	19.36	5.43	3.06
1951	23.79	−.20	1.56	6.00	1992	7.62	7.34	3.48	2.90
1952	18.39	2.43	1.75	.75	1993	10.08	13.06	3.03	2.75
1953	−1.07	2.28	1.87	.75	1994	1.32	−7.32	4.39	2.67
1954	52.23	3.08	.93	−.74	1995	37.58	25.94	5.61	2.54
1955	31.62	−.73	1.80	.37	1996	22.96	.13	5.14	3.32
1956	6.91	−1.72	2.66	2.99	1997	33.36	12.02	5.19	1.70
1957	−10.50	6.82	3.28	2.90	1998	28.58	14.45	4.86	1.61
1958	43.57	−1.72	1.71	1.76	1999	21.04	−7.51	4.80	2.68
1959	12.01	−2.02	3.48	1.73	2000	−9.10	17.22	5.98	3.39
1960	.47	11.21	2.81	1.36	2001	−11.89	5.51	3.33	1.55
1961	26.84	2.20	2.40	.67	2002	−22.10	15.15	1.61	2.4
1962	−8.75	5.72	2.82	1.33	2003	28.89	2.01	.94	1.9
1963	22.70	1.79	3.23	1.64	2004	10.88	8.12	1.14	3.3
1964	16.43	3.71	3.62	.97	2005	4.91	6.89	2.79	3.4
1965	12.38	.93	4.06	1.92	2006	15.79	.28	4.97	2.54
1966	−10.06%	5.12%	4.94%	3.46%	2007	5.49	10.85	4.52	4.08

SOURCES: Authors' calculation based on data obtained from *Global Financial Data* and other sources.

12.3 Average Returns: The First Lesson

As you've probably begun to notice, the history of capital market returns is too complicated to be of much use in its undigested form. We need to begin summarizing all these numbers. Accordingly, we discuss how to go about condensing the detailed data. We start out by calculating average returns.

CALCULATING AVERAGE RETURNS

The obvious way to calculate the average returns on the different investments in Table 12.1 is simply to add up the yearly returns and divide by 82. The result is the historical average of the individual values.

For example, if you add up the returns for the large-company stocks in Figure 12.5 for the 82 years, you will get about 10.09. The average annual return is thus 10.09/82 = 12.3%. You interpret this 12.3 percent just like any other average. If you were to pick a year at random from the 82-year history and you had to guess what the return in that year was, the best guess would be 12.3 percent.

AVERAGE RETURNS: THE HISTORICAL RECORD

Table 12.2 shows the average returns for the investments we have discussed. As shown, in a typical year, the small-company stocks increased in value by 17.1 percent. Notice also how much larger the stock returns are than the bond returns.

These averages are, of course, nominal because we haven't worried about inflation. Notice that the average inflation rate was 3.1 percent per year over this 82-year span. The nominal return on U.S. Treasury bills was 3.8 percent per year. The average real return on Treasury bills was thus approximately .7 percent per year; so the real return on T-bills has been quite low historically.

At the other extreme, small stocks had an average real return of about 17.1% − 3.1% = 14%, which is relatively large. If you remember the Rule of 72 (Chapter 5), then you know that a quick back-of-the-envelope calculation tells us that 14 percent real growth doubles your buying power about every five years. Notice also that the real value of the large-company stock portfolio increased by over 9 percent in a typical year.

Investment	Average Return
Large-company stocks	12.3%
Small-company stocks	17.1
Long-term corporate bonds	6.2
Long-term government bonds	5.8
U.S. Treasury bills	3.8
Inflation	3.1

Investment	Average Return	Risk Premium
Large-company stocks	12.3%	8.5%
Small-company stocks	17.1	13.3
Long-term corporate bonds	6.2	2.4
Long-term government bonds	5.8	2.0
U.S. Treasury bills	3.8	.0

RISK PREMIUMS

Now that we have computed some average returns, it seems logical to see how they compare with each other. One such comparison involves government-issued securities. These are free of much of the variability we see in, for example, the stock market.

The government borrows money by issuing bonds in different forms. The ones we will focus on are the Treasury bills. These have the shortest time to maturity of the different government bonds. Because the government can always raise taxes to pay its bills, the debt represented by T-bills is virtually free of any default risk over its short life. Thus, we will call the rate of return on such debt the *risk-free return,* and we will use it as a kind of benchmark.

A particularly interesting comparison involves the virtually risk-free return on T-bills and the very risky return on common stocks. The difference between these two returns can be interpreted as a measure of the *excess return* on the average risky asset (assuming that the stock of a large U.S. corporation has about average risk compared to all risky assets).

We call this the "excess" return because it is the additional return we earn by moving from a relatively risk-free investment to a risky one. Because it can be interpreted as a reward for bearing risk, we will call it a **risk premium**.

Using Table 12.2, we can calculate the risk premiums for the different investments; these are shown in Table 12.3. We report only the nominal risk premiums because there is only a slight difference between the historical nominal and real risk premiums.

The risk premium on T-bills is shown as zero in the table because we have assumed that they are riskless.

risk premium
The excess return required from an investment in a risky asset over that required from a risk-free investment.

THE FIRST LESSON

Looking at Table 12.3, we see that the average risk premium earned by a typical large-company stock is $12.3\% - 3.8\% = 8.5\%$. This is a significant reward. The fact that it exists historically is an important observation, and it is the basis for our first lesson: Risky assets, on average, earn a risk premium. Put another way, there is a reward for bearing risk.

Why is this so? Why, for example, is the risk premium for small stocks so much larger than the risk premium for large stocks? More generally, what determines the relative sizes of the risk premiums for the different assets? The answers to these questions are at the heart of modern finance, and the next chapter is devoted to them. For now, we can find part of the answer by looking at the historical variability of the returns on these different investments. So, to get started, we now turn our attention to measuring variability in returns.

Concept Questions

12.3a What do we mean by *excess return* and *risk premium*?

12.3b What was the real (as opposed to nominal) risk premium on the common stock portfolio?

12.3c What was the nominal risk premium on corporate bonds? The real risk premium?

12.3d What is the first lesson from capital market history?

12.4 The Variability of Returns: The Second Lesson

We have already seen that the year-to-year returns on common stocks tend to be more volatile than the returns on, say, long-term government bonds. We now discuss measuring this variability of stock returns so we can begin examining the subject of risk.

FREQUENCY DISTRIBUTIONS AND VARIABILITY

To get started, we can draw a *frequency distribution* for the common stock returns like the one in Figure 12.9. What we have done here is to count up the number of times the annual return on the common stock portfolio falls within each 10 percent range. For example, in Figure 12.9, the height of 13 in the range of 10 to 20 percent means that 13 of the 82 annual returns were in that range.

FIGURE 12.9   Frequency Distribution of Returns on Large-Company Stocks: 1926–2007

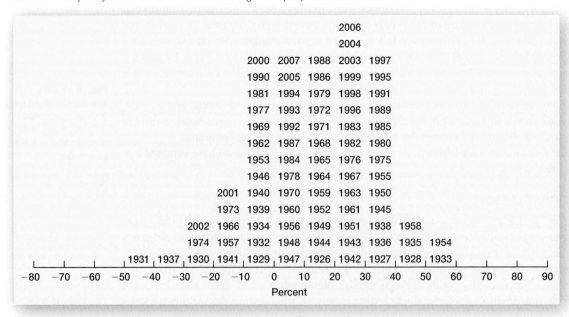

What we need to do now is to actually measure the spread in returns. We know, for example, that the return on small stocks in a typical year was 17.1 percent. We now want to know how much the actual return deviates from this average in a typical year. In other words, we need a measure of how volatile the return is. The **variance** and its square root, the **standard deviation**, are the most commonly used measures of volatility. We describe how to calculate them next.

variance
The average squared difference between the actual return and the average return.

THE HISTORICAL VARIANCE AND STANDARD DEVIATION

The variance essentially measures the average squared difference between the actual returns and the average return. The bigger this number is, the more the actual returns tend to differ from the average return. Also, the larger the variance or standard deviation is, the more spread out the returns will be.

standard deviation
The positive square root of the variance.

The way we will calculate the variance and standard deviation will depend on the specific situation. In this chapter, we are looking at historical returns; so the procedure we describe here is the correct one for calculating the *historical* variance and standard deviation. If we were examining projected future returns, then the procedure would be different. We describe this procedure in the next chapter.

To illustrate how we calculate the historical variance, suppose a particular investment had returns of 10 percent, 12 percent, 3 percent, and −9 percent over the last four years. The average return is $(.10 + .12 + .03 - .09)/4 = 4\%$. Notice that the return is never actually equal to 4 percent. Instead, the first return deviates from the average by $.10 - .04 = .06$, the second return deviates from the average by $.12 - .04 = .08$, and so on. To compute the variance, we square each of these deviations, add them up, and divide the result by the number of returns less 1, or 3 in this case. Most of this information is summarized in the following table:

For an easy-to-read review of basic stats, check out www.robertniles.com.

	(1) Actual Return	(2) Average Return	(3) Deviation (1) − (2)	(4) Squared Deviation
	.10	.04	.06	.0036
	.12	.04	.08	.0064
	.03	.04	−.01	.0001
	−.09	.04	−.13	.0169
Totals	.16		.00	.0270

In the first column, we write the four actual returns. In the third column, we calculate the difference between the actual returns and the average by subtracting out 4 percent. Finally, in the fourth column, we square the numbers in the third column to get the squared deviations from the average.

The variance can now be calculated by dividing .0270, the sum of the squared deviations, by the number of returns less 1. Let Var(R), or σ^2 (read this as "sigma squared"), stand for the variance of the return:

$$\text{Var}(R) = \sigma^2 = .027/(4 - 1) = .009$$

The standard deviation is the square root of the variance. So, if SD(R), or σ, stands for the standard deviation of return:

$$\text{SD}(R) = \sigma = \sqrt{.009} = .09487$$

The square root of the variance is used because the variance is measured in "squared" percentages and thus is hard to interpret. The standard deviation is an ordinary percentage, so the answer here could be written as 9.487 percent.

In the preceding table, notice that the sum of the deviations is equal to zero. This will always be the case, and it provides a good way to check your work. In general, if we have T historical returns, where T is some number, we can write the historical variance as:

$$\text{Var}(R) = \frac{1}{T-1}[(R_1 - \bar{R})^2 + \cdots + (R_T - \bar{R})^2] \qquad [12.3]$$

This formula tells us to do what we just did: Take each of the T individual returns $(R_1, R_2, \ldots)$ and subtract the average return, $\bar{R}$; square the results, and add them all up; and finally, divide this total by the number of returns less 1, $(T-1)$. The standard deviation is always the square root of $\text{Var}(R)$. Standard deviations are a widely used measure of volatility. Our nearby *Work the Web* box gives a real-world example.

EXAMPLE 12.2 | **Calculating the Variance and Standard Deviation**

Suppose the Supertech Company and the Hyperdrive Company have experienced the following returns in the last four years:

Year	Supertech Return	Hyperdrive Return
2005	−.20	.05
2006	.50	.09
2007	.30	−.12
2008	.10	.20

What are the average returns? The variances? The standard deviations? Which investment was more volatile?

To calculate the average returns, we add up the returns and divide by 4. The results are:

Supertech average return $= \bar{R} = .70/4 = .175$

Hyperdrive average return $= \bar{R} = .22/4 = .055$

To calculate the variance for Supertech, we can summarize the relevant calculations as follows:

Year	(1) Actual Return	(2) Average Return	(3) Deviation (1) − (2)	(4) Squared Deviation
2005	−.20	.175	−.375	.140625
2006	.50	.175	.325	.105625
2007	.30	.175	.125	.015625
2008	.10	.175	−.075	.005625
Totals	.70		.000	.267500

Because there are four years of returns, we calculate the variance by dividing .2675 by $(4 - 1) = 3$:

	Supertech	Hyperdrive
Variance (σ^2)	$.2675/3 = .0892$	$.0529/3 = .0176$
Standard deviation (σ)	$\sqrt{.0892} = .2987$	$\sqrt{.0176} = .1327$

For practice, verify that you get the same answer as we do for Hyperdrive. Notice that the standard deviation for Supertech, 29.87 percent, is a little more than twice Hyperdrive's 13.27 percent; Supertech is thus the more volatile investment.

THE HISTORICAL RECORD

Figure 12.10 summarizes much of our discussion of capital market history so far. It displays average returns, standard deviations, and frequency distributions of annual returns on a common scale. In Figure 12.10, for example, notice that the standard deviation for the small-stock portfolio (32.6 percent per year) is more than 10 times larger than the T-bill portfolio's standard deviation (3.1 percent per year). We will return to these figures momentarily.

NORMAL DISTRIBUTION

For many different random events in nature, a particular frequency distribution, the **normal distribution** (or *bell curve*), is useful for describing the probability of ending up in a given range. For example, the idea behind "grading on a curve" comes from the fact that exam score distributions often resemble a bell curve.

normal distribution
A symmetric, bell-shaped frequency distribution that is completely defined by its mean and standard deviation.

WORK THE WEB

Standard deviations are widely reported for mutual funds. For example, the Fidelity Magellan fund was one of the largest mutual funds in the United States at the time this was written. How volatile is it? To find out, we went to www.morningstar.com, entered the ticker symbol FMAGX, and clicked the "Risk Measures" link. Here is what we found:

Fidelity Magellan FMAGX

See Fund Family Data ▸▸

Volatility Measurements	Trailing 3-Yr through 04-30-08	*Trailing 5-Yr through 04-30-08	
Standard Deviation	11.48	Sharpe Ratio	.52
Mean	10.56	Bear Market Decile Rank*	5

Modern Portfolio Theory Statistics		Trailing 3-Yr through 04-30-08
	Standard Index S&P 500 TR	**Best Fit Index** Morningstar US Gr TR
R-Squared	79	92
Beta	1.15	.91
Alpha	1.19	.74

The standard deviation for the Fidelity Magellan Fund is 11.48 percent. When you consider that the average stock has a standard deviation of about 50 percent, this seems like a low number. The reason for the low standard deviation has to do with the power of diversification, a topic we discuss in the next chapter. The mean is the average return, so over the last three years, investors in the Magellan Fund gained 10.56 percent per year. Also, under the Volatility Measurements section, you will see the Sharpe ratio. The Sharpe ratio is calculated as the risk premium of the asset divided by the standard deviation. As such, it is a measure of return relative to the level of risk taken (as measured by standard deviation). The "beta" for the Fidelity Magellan Fund is 1.15. We will have more to say about this number—lots more—in the next chapter.

Questions

1. Go to the Morningstar Web site at www.morningstar.com. What does the Sharpe ratio measure? What does the Bear Market Decile Rank measure?
2. Get a quote for the Fidelity Magellan fund at Morningstar. What are the five sectors that have the highest percentage investment for this fund? What are the five stocks with the highest percentage investment?

FIGURE 12.10   Historical Returns, Standard Deviations, and Frequency Distributions: 1926–2007

SERIES	AVERAGE RETURN	STANDARD DEVIATION	DISTRIBUTION
Large-company stocks	12.3%	20.0%	
Small-company stocks	17.1	32.6	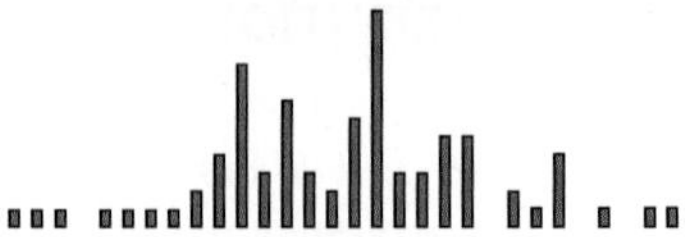 *
Long-term corporate bonds	6.2	8.4	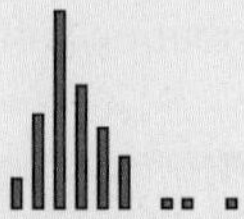
Long-term government bonds	5.8	9.2	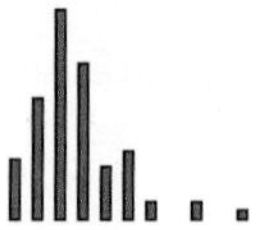
Intermediate-term government bonds	5.5	5.7	
U.S. Treasury bills	3.8	3.1	
Inflation	3.1	4.2	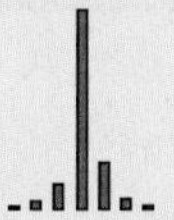

*The 1933 small-company stocks total return was 142.9 percent.

SOURCE: Modified from *Stocks, Bonds, Bills and Inflation 2008 Yearbook*,™ annually updates work by Roger G. Ibbotson and Rex A. Sinquefield (Chicago: Morningstar). All rights reserved.

Figure 12.11 illustrates a normal distribution and its distinctive bell shape. As you can see, this distribution has a much cleaner appearance than the actual return distributions illustrated in Figure 12.10. Even so, like the normal distribution, the actual distributions do appear to be at least roughly mound-shaped and symmetric. When this is true, the normal distribution is often a very good approximation.

Also, keep in mind that the distributions in Figure 12.10 are based on only 82 yearly observations, whereas Figure 12.11 is, in principle, based on an infinite number. So, if we had been able to observe returns for, say, 1,000 years, we might have filled in a lot of the irregularities and ended up with a much smoother picture in Figure 12.10. For our purposes, it is enough to observe that the returns are at least roughly normally distributed.

The usefulness of the normal distribution stems from the fact that it is completely described by the average and the standard deviation. If you have these two numbers, then there is nothing else to know. For example, with a normal distribution, the probability that we will end up within one standard deviation of the average is about 2/3. The probability

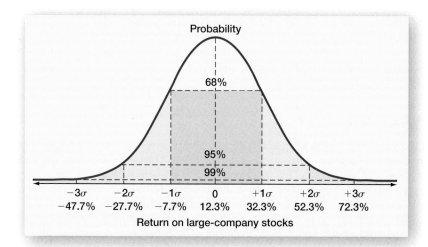

FIGURE 12.11

The Normal Distribution

NOTE: Illustrated returns are based on the historical return and standard deviation for a portfolio of large-firm common stocks.

that we will end up within two standard deviations is about 95 percent. Finally, the probability of being more than three standard deviations away from the average is less than 1 percent. These ranges and the probabilities are illustrated in Figure 12.11.

To see why this is useful, recall from Figure 12.10 that the standard deviation of returns on the large-company stocks is 20 percent. The average return is 12.3 percent. So, assuming that the frequency distribution is at least approximately normal, the probability that the return in a given year is in the range of −7.7 to 32.3 percent (12.3 percent plus or minus one standard deviation, 20 percent) is about 2/3. This range is illustrated in Figure 12.11. In other words, there is about one chance in three that the return will be *outside* this range. This literally tells you that, if you buy stocks in large companies, you should expect to be outside this range in one year out of every three. This reinforces our earlier observations about stock market volatility. However, there is only a 5 percent chance (approximately) that we would end up outside the range of −27.7 to 52.3 percent (12.3 percent plus or minus 2 × 20%). These points are also illustrated in Figure 12.11.

THE SECOND LESSON

Our observations concerning the year-to-year variability in returns are the basis for our second lesson from capital market history. On average, bearing risk is handsomely rewarded; but in a given year, there is a significant chance of a dramatic change in value. Thus our second lesson is this: The greater the potential reward, the greater is the risk.

USING CAPITAL MARKET HISTORY

Based on the discussion in this section, you should begin to have an idea of the risks and rewards from investing. For example, in mid-2008, Treasury bills were paying about 1.8 percent. Suppose we had an investment that we thought had about the same risk as a portfolio of large-firm common stocks. At a minimum, what return would this investment have to offer for us to be interested?

From Table 12.3, we see that the risk premium on large-company stocks has been 8.5 percent historically, so a reasonable estimate of our required return would be this premium plus the T-bill rate, 1.8% + 8.5% = 10.3%. This may strike you as being high; but if we were thinking of starting a new business, then the risks of doing so might resemble those of investing in small-company stocks. In this case, the historical risk premium is 13.3 percent, so we might require as much as 15.1 percent from such an investment at a minimum.

We will discuss the relationship between risk and required return in more detail in the next chapter. For now, you should notice that a projected internal rate of return, or IRR, on a risky investment in the 10 to 20 percent range isn't particularly outstanding. It depends on how much risk there is. This, too, is an important lesson from capital market history.

EXAMPLE 12.3   **Investing in Growth Stocks**

The term *growth stock* is frequently used as a euphemism for small-company stock. Are such investments suitable for "widows and orphans"? Before answering, you should consider the historical volatility. For example, from the historical record, what is the approximate probability that you will actually lose more than 16 percent of your money in a single year if you buy a portfolio of stocks of such companies?

Looking back at Figure 12.10, we see that the average return on small-company stocks is 17.1 percent and the standard deviation is 32.6 percent. Assuming the returns are approximately normal, there is about a 1/3 probability that you will experience a return outside the range of −15.5 to 49.7 percent (17.1% ± 32.6%).

Because the normal distribution is symmetric, the odds of being above or below this range are equal. There is thus a 1/6 chance (half of 1/3) that you will lose more than 15.5 percent. So you should expect this to happen once in every six years, on average. Such investments can thus be *very* volatile, and they are not well suited for those who cannot afford the risk.

MORE ON THE STOCK MARKET RISK PREMIUM

As we have discussed, the historical stock market risk premium has been substantial. In fact, based on standard economic models, it has been argued that the historical risk premium is *too* big and is thus an overestimate of what is likely to happen in the future.

Of course, any time we use the past to predict the future, there is the danger that the past period we observe isn't representative of what the future will hold. For example, in this chapter, we studied the period 1925–2007. Perhaps investors got lucky over this period and earned particularly high returns. Data from earlier years is available, though it is not of the same quality. With that caveat in mind, researchers have traced returns back to 1802, and the risk premiums seen in the pre-1925 era are perhaps a little smaller, but not dramatically so.

Another possibility is that the U.S. stock market experience was unusually good. Investors in at least some other major countries did not do as well because their financial markets were nearly or completely wiped out because of revolution, war, and/or hyperinflation. A recent study addresses this issue by examining data from 1900–2005 for 17 countries.

Figure 12.12 shows the historical average stock market risk premium for all 17 countries over the 106-year period. Looking at the numbers, the U.S. risk premium is the 10th highest at 7.4 percent (which differs from our earlier estimate because of the differing time periods examined). The overall average risk premium is 7.1 percent. These numbers make it clear that U.S. investors did well, but not exceptionally so relative to investors in many other countries.

So, is the U.S. stock market risk premium estimated from 1925–2007 too high? The evidence seems to suggest that the answer is "maybe a little." One thing we haven't stressed so far is that even with 106 years of data, the average risk premium is still not measured with great precision. From a statistical standpoint, the standard error associated with the U.S. estimated risk premium of 7.4 percent is about 2 percent. So, even one standard error range covers 5.4 to 9.4 percent.

FIGURE 12.12

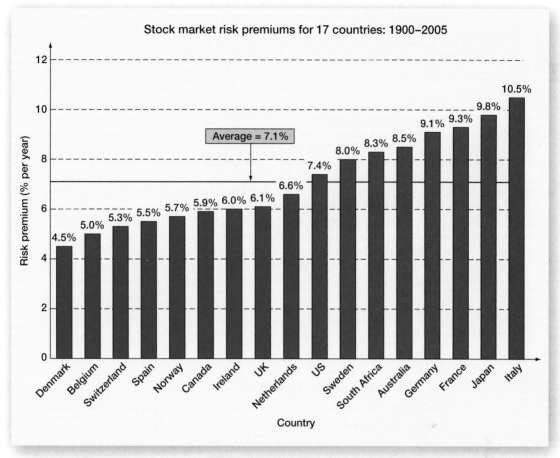

Stock market risk premiums for 17 countries: 1900–2005

SOURCE: Based on information in Elroy Dimson, Paul Marsh, and Michael Staunton, "The Worldwide Equity Premium: A Smaller Puzzle," in *Handbook of the Equity Risk Premium*, Rajnish Mehra, ed. (Elsevier: 2007).

Concept Questions

12.4a In words, how do we calculate a variance? A standard deviation?

12.4b With a normal distribution, what is the probability of ending up more than one standard deviation below the average?

12.4c Assuming that long-term corporate bonds have an approximately normal distribution, what is the approximate probability of earning 14.6 percent or more in a given year? With T-bills, roughly what is this probability?

12.4d What is the second lesson from capital market history?

More about Average Returns   **12.5**

Thus far in this chapter, we have looked closely at simple average returns. But there is another way of computing an average return. The fact that average returns are calculated two different ways leads to some confusion, so our goal in this section is to explain the two approaches and also the circumstances under which each is appropriate.

Jeremy J. Siegel on Stocks for the Long Run

The most fascinating characteristic about the data on real financial market returns that I collected is the stability of the long-run real equity returns. The compound annual (geometric) real return on U.S. stocks averaged 6.8% per year from 1802 through 2007 and this return had remained remarkably stable over long-term periods. From 1802 through 1871, the real return averaged 7.0%, from 1871, when the Cowles Foundation data became available, through 1925, the real return on stocks averaged 6.6% per year, and since 1925, which the well-known Ibbotson data cover, the real return has averaged 6.7%. Despite the fact that the price level has increased over ten times since the end of the Second World War, real stock returns have still averaged 6.8%.

The long run stability of real returns on stocks is strongly indicative of *mean reversion of equity return*. Mean reversion means that stock returns can be very volatile in the short run, but show a remarkable stability in the long run. When my research was first published, there was much skepticism of the mean reversion properties of equity market returns, but now this concept is widely accepted for stocks. If mean reversion prevails, portfolios geared for the long-term should have a greater share of equities than short-term portfolios. This conclusion has long been the "conventional" wisdom on investing, but it does not follow if stock returns follow a random walk, a concept widely accepted by academics in the 1970s and 1980s.

When my data first appeared, there was also much discussion of "survivorship bias," the fact that the U.S. stock returns are unusually good because the U.S. was the most successful capitalist country. But three British researchers, Elroy Dimson, Paul Marsh, and Michael Staunton, surveyed stock returns in 16 countries since the beginning of the 20th century and wrote up their results in a book entitled *Triumph of the Optimists*. The authors concluded that U.S. stock returns do not give a distorted picture of the superiority of stocks over bonds worldwide.

Jeremy J. Siegel is the Russell E. Palmer Professor of Finance at The Wharton School of the University of Pennsylvania and author of Stocks for the Long Run *and* The Future Investors. *His research covers macroeconomics and monetary policy, financial market returns, and long-term economic trends.*

ARITHMETIC VERSUS GEOMETRIC AVERAGES

Let's start with a simple example. Suppose you buy a particular stock for $100. Unfortunately, the first year you own it, it falls to $50. The second year you own it, it rises back to $100, leaving you where you started (no dividends were paid).

What was your average return on this investment? Common sense seems to say that your average return must be exactly zero because you started with $100 and ended with $100. But if we calculate the returns year-by-year, we see that you lost 50 percent the first year (you lost half of your money). The second year, you made 100 percent (you doubled your money). Your average return over the two years was thus $(-50\% + 100\%)/2 = 25\%$!

So which is correct, 0 percent or 25 percent? Both are correct: They just answer different questions. The 0 percent is called the **geometric average return**. The 25 percent is called the **arithmetic average return**. The geometric average return answers the question "What was your average compound return per year over a particular period?" The arithmetic average return answers the question "What was your return in an average year over a particular period?"

Notice that, in previous sections, the average returns we calculated were all arithmetic averages, so we already know how to calculate them. What we need to do now is (1) learn how to calculate geometric averages and (2) learn the circumstances under which one average is more meaningful than the other.

geometric average return
The average compound return earned per year over a multiyear period.

arithmetic average return
The return earned in an average year over a multiyear period.

CALCULATING GEOMETRIC AVERAGE RETURNS

First, to illustrate how we calculate a geometric average return, suppose a particular investment had annual returns of 10 percent, 12 percent, 3 percent, and −9 percent over the last four years. The geometric average return over this four-year period is calculated as $(1.10 \times 1.12 \times 1.03 \times .91)^{1/4} - 1 = 3.66\%$. In contrast, the average arithmetic return we have been calculating is $(.10 + .12 + .03 - .09)/4 = 4.0\%$.

In general, if we have T years of returns, the geometric average return over these T years is calculated using this formula:

$$\text{Geometric average return} = [(1 + R_1) \times (1 + R_2) \times \cdots \times (1 + R_T)]^{1/T} - 1 \qquad \textbf{[12.4]}$$

This formula tells us that four steps are required:

1. Take each of the T annual returns $R_1, R_2, \ldots, R_T$ and add 1 to each (after converting them to decimals!).
2. Multiply all the numbers from step 1 together.
3. Take the result from step 2 and raise it to the power of $1/T$.
4. Finally, subtract 1 from the result of step 3. The result is the geometric average return.

Calculating the Geometric Average Return   EXAMPLE 12.4

Calculate the geometric average return for S&P 500 large-cap stocks for the first five years in Table 12.1, 1926–193

First, convert percentages to decimal returns, add 1, and then calculate their product:

S&P 500 Returns	Product
13.75	1.1375
35.70	×1.3570
45.08	×1.4508
−8.80	×.9120
−25.13	×.7487
	1.5291

Notice that the number 1.5291 is what our investment is worth after five years if we started with a $1 investment. The geometric average return is then calculated as follows:

Geometric average return = $1.5291^{1/5} - 1 = .0887$, or 8.87%

Thus, the geometric average return is about 8.87 percent in this example. Here is a tip: If you are using a financial calculator, you can put $1 in as the present value, $1.5291 as the future value, and 5 as the number of periods. Then, solve for the unknown rate. You should get the same answer we did.

One thing you may have noticed in our examples thus far is that the geometric average returns seem to be smaller. This will always be true (as long as the returns are not all identical, in which case the two "averages" would be the same). To illustrate, Table 12.4 shows the arithmetic averages and standard deviations from Figure 12.10, along with the geometric average returns.

As shown in Table 12.4, the geometric averages are all smaller, but the magnitude of the difference varies quite a bit. The reason is that the difference is greater for more volatile investments. In fact, there is a useful approximation. Assuming all the numbers are expressed in decimals (as opposed to percentages), the geometric average return is approximately equal to the arithmetic average return minus half the variance. For example, looking at the large-company stocks, the arithmetic average is .123 and the standard deviation is .20, implying that the variance is .04. The approximate geometric average is thus .123 − .04/2 = .103, which is quite close to the actual value.

TABLE 12.4

Geometric versus
Arithmetic Average
Returns: 1926–2007

Series	Average Return		Standard Deviation
	Geometric	Arithmetic	
Large-company stocks	10.4%	12.3%	20.0%
Small-company stocks	12.5	17.1	32.6
Long-term corporate bonds	5.9	6.2	8.4
Long-term government bonds	5.5	5.8	9.2
Intermediate-term government bonds	5.3	5.5	5.7
U.S. Treasury bills	3.7	3.8	3.1
Inflation	3.0	3.1	4.2

EXAMPLE 12.5   **More Geometric Averages**

Take a look back at Figure 12.4. There, we showed the value of a $1 investment after 82 years. Use the value for the large-company stock investment to check the geometric average in Table 12.4.

In Figure 12.4, the large-company investment grew to $3,246.39 over 82 years. The geometric average return is thus

Geometric average return = $3,246.39^{1/82} - 1 = .1036$, or 10.4%

This 10.4% is the value shown in Table 12.4. For practice, check some of the other numbers in Table 12.4 the same way.

ARITHMETIC AVERAGE RETURN OR GEOMETRIC AVERAGE RETURN?

When we look at historical returns, the difference between the geometric and arithmetic average returns isn't too hard to understand. To put it slightly differently, the geometric average tells you what you actually earned per year on average, compounded annually. The arithmetic average tells you what you earned in a typical year. You should use whichever one answers the question you want answered.

A somewhat trickier question concerns which average return to use when forecasting future wealth levels, and there's a lot of confusion on this point among analysts and financial planners. First, let's get one thing straight: If you *know* the true arithmetic average return, then this is what you should use in your forecast. For example, if you know the arithmetic return is 10 percent, then your best guess of the value of a $1,000 investment in 10 years is the future value of $1,000 at 10 percent for 10 years, or $2,593.74.

The problem we face, however, is that we usually have only *estimates* of the arithmetic and geometric returns, and estimates have errors. In this case, the arithmetic average return is probably too high for longer periods and the geometric average is probably too low for shorter periods. So, you should regard long-run projected wealth levels calculated using arithmetic averages as optimistic. Short-run projected wealth levels calculated using geometric averages are probably pessimistic.

The good news is that there is a simple way of combining the two averages, which we will call *Blume's formula.*[4] Suppose we have calculated geometric and arithmetic return averages from N years of data, and we wish to use these averages to form a T-year average return forecast, R(T), where T is less than N. Here's how we do it:

$$R(T) = \frac{T-1}{N-1} \times \text{Geometric average} + \frac{N-T}{N-1} \times \text{Arithmetic average} \qquad [12.5]$$

[4]This elegant result is due to Marshal Blume ("Unbiased Estimates of Long-Run Expected Rates of Return," *Journal of the American Statistical Association,* September 1974, pp. 634–638).

For example, suppose that, from 25 years of annual returns data, we calculate an arithmetic average return of 12 percent and a geometric average return of 9 percent. From these averages, we wish to make 1-year, 5-year, and 10-year average return forecasts. These three average return forecasts are calculated as follows:

$$R(1) = \frac{1-1}{24} \times 9\% + \frac{25-1}{24} \times 12\% = 12\%$$

$$R(5) = \frac{5-1}{24} \times 9\% + \frac{25-5}{24} \times 12\% = 11.5\%$$

$$R(10) = \frac{10-1}{24} \times 9\% + \frac{25-10}{24} \times 12\% = 10.875\%$$

Thus, we see that 1-year, 5-year, and 10-year forecasts are 12 percent, 11.5 percent, and 10.875 percent, respectively.

As a practical matter, Blume's formula says that if you are using averages calculated over a long period (such as the 82 years we use) to forecast up to a decade or so into the future, then you should use the arithmetic average. If you are forecasting a few decades into the future (as you might do for retirement planning), then you should just split the difference between the arithmetic and geometric average returns. Finally, if for some reason you are doing very long forecasts covering many decades, use the geometric average.

This concludes our discussion of geometric versus arithmetic averages. One last note: In the future, when we say "average return," we mean arithmetic unless we explicitly say otherwise.

Concept Questions

12.5a If you wanted to forecast what the stock market is going to do over the next year, should you use an arithmetic or geometric average?

12.5b If you wanted to forecast what the stock market is going to do over the next century, should you use an arithmetic or geometric average?

Capital Market Efficiency

12.6

Capital market history suggests that the market values of stocks and bonds can fluctuate widely from year to year. Why does this occur? At least part of the answer is that prices change because new information arrives, and investors reassess asset values based on that information.

The behavior of market prices has been extensively studied. A question that has received particular attention is whether prices adjust quickly and correctly when new information arrives. A market is said to be "efficient" if this is the case. To be more precise, in an **efficient capital market**, current market prices fully reflect available information. By this we simply mean that, based on available information, there is no reason to believe that the current price is too low or too high.

efficient capital market
A market in which security prices reflect available information.

The concept of market efficiency is a rich one, and much has been written about it. A full discussion of the subject goes beyond the scope of our study of corporate finance. However, because the concept figures so prominently in studies of market history, we briefly describe the key points here.

PRICE BEHAVIOR IN AN EFFICIENT MARKET

To illustrate how prices behave in an efficient market, suppose the F-Stop Camera Corporation (FCC) has, through years of secret research and development, developed a camera with an autofocusing system whose speed will double that of the autofocusing systems now available. FCC's capital budgeting analysis suggests that launching the new camera will be

FIGURE 12.13

Reaction of Stock Price to New Information in Efficient and Inefficient Markets

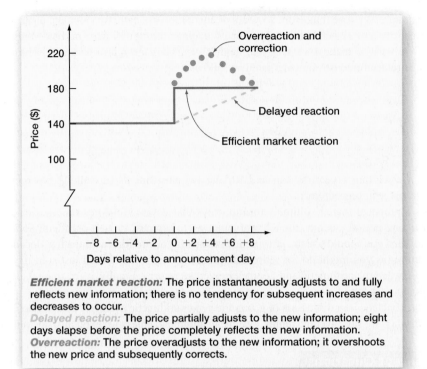

Efficient market reaction: The price instantaneously adjusts to and fully reflects new information; there is no tendency for subsequent increases and decreases to occur.
Delayed reaction: The price partially adjusts to the new information; eight days elapse before the price completely reflects the new information.
Overreaction: The price overadjusts to the new information; it overshoots the new price and subsequently corrects.

a highly profitable move; in other words, the NPV appears to be positive and substantial. The key assumption thus far is that FCC has not released any information about the new system; so, the fact of its existence is "inside" information only.

Now consider a share of stock in FCC. In an efficient market, its price reflects what is known about FCC's current operations and profitability, and it reflects market opinion about FCC's potential for future growth and profits. The value of the new autofocusing system is not reflected, however, because the market is unaware of the system's existence.

If the market agrees with FCC's assessment of the value of the new project, FCC's stock price will rise when the decision to launch is made public. For example, assume the announcement is made in a press release on Wednesday morning. In an efficient market, the price of shares in FCC will adjust quickly to this new information. Investors should not be able to buy the stock on Wednesday afternoon and make a profit on Thursday. This would imply that it took the stock market a full day to realize the implication of the FCC press release. If the market is efficient, the price of shares of FCC stock on Wednesday afternoon will already reflect the information contained in the Wednesday morning press release.

Figure 12.13 presents three possible stock price adjustments for FCC. In Figure 12.13, day 0 represents the announcement day. As illustrated, before the announcement, FCC's stock sells for $140 per share. The NPV per share of the new system is, say, $40, so the new price will be $180 once the value of the new project is fully reflected.

The solid line in Figure 12.13 represents the path taken by the stock price in an efficient market. In this case, the price adjusts immediately to the new information and no further changes in the price of the stock take place. The broken line in Figure 12.13 depicts a delayed reaction. Here it takes the market eight days or so to fully absorb the information. Finally, the dotted line illustrates an overreaction and subsequent adjustment to the correct price.

The broken line and the dotted line in Figure 12.13 illustrate paths that the stock price might take in an inefficient market. If, for example, stock prices don't adjust immediately to new information (the broken line), then buying stock immediately following the release of new information and then selling it several days later would be a positive NPV activity because the price is too low for several days after the announcement.

THE EFFICIENT MARKETS HYPOTHESIS

The **efficient markets hypothesis (EMH)** asserts that well-organized capital markets, such as the NYSE, are efficient markets, at least as a practical matter. In other words, an advocate of the EMH might argue that although inefficiencies may exist, they are relatively small and not common.

efficient markets hypothesis (EMH)
The hypothesis that actual capital markets, such as the NYSE, are efficient.

If a market is efficient, then there is a very important implication for market participants: All investments in that market are *zero* NPV investments. The reason is not complicated. If prices are neither too low nor too high, then the difference between the market value of an investment and its cost is zero; hence, the NPV is zero. As a result, in an efficient market, investors get exactly what they pay for when they buy securities, and firms receive exactly what their stocks and bonds are worth when they sell them.

What makes a market efficient is competition among investors. Many individuals spend their entire lives trying to find mispriced stocks. For any given stock, they study what has happened in the past to the stock price and the stock's dividends. They learn, to the extent possible, what a company's earnings have been, how much the company owes to creditors, what taxes it pays, what businesses it is in, what new investments are planned, how sensitive it is to changes in the economy, and so on.

Look under the "Contents" link at www.investorhome.com for more info on the EMH.

Not only is there a great deal to know about any particular company, but there is also a powerful incentive for knowing it—namely, the profit motive. If you know more about some company than other investors in the marketplace, you can profit from that knowledge by investing in the company's stock if you have good news and by selling it if you have bad news.

The logical consequence of all this information gathering and analysis is that mispriced stocks will become fewer and fewer. In other words, because of competition among investors, the market will become increasingly efficient. A kind of equilibrium comes into being with which there is just enough mispricing around for those who are best at identifying it to make a living at it. For most other investors, the activity of information gathering and analysis will not pay.[5]

SOME COMMON MISCONCEPTIONS ABOUT THE EMH

No other idea in finance has attracted as much attention as that of efficient markets, and not all of the attention has been flattering. Rather than rehash the arguments here, we will be content to observe that some markets are more efficient than others. For example, financial markets on the whole are probably much more efficient than real asset markets.

Having said this, however, we can also say that much of the criticism of the EMH is misguided because it is based on a misunderstanding of what the hypothesis says and what it doesn't say. For example, when the notion of market efficiency was first publicized and debated in the popular financial press, it was often characterized by words to the effect that

---

[5]The idea behind the EMH can be illustrated by the following short story: A student was walking down the hall with her finance professor when they both saw a $20 bill on the ground. As the student bent down to pick it up, the professor shook his head slowly and, with a look of disappointment on his face, said patiently to the student, "Don't bother. If it were really there, someone else would have picked it up already." The moral of the story reflects the logic of the efficient markets hypothesis: If you think you have found a pattern in stock prices or a simple device for picking winners, you probably have not.

The concept of an efficient market is a special application of the "no free lunch" principle. In an efficient financial market, costless trading policies will not generate "excess" returns. After adjusting for the riskiness of the policy, the trader's return will be no larger than the return of a randomly selected portfolio, at least on average.

This is often thought to imply something about the amount of "information" reflected in asset prices. However, it really doesn't mean that prices reflect all information nor even that they reflect publicly available information. Instead it means that the connection between unreflected information and prices is too subtle and tenuous to be easily or costlessly detected.

Relevant information is difficult and expensive to uncover and evaluate. Thus, if costless trading policies are ineffective, there must exist some traders who make a living by "beating the market." They cover their costs (including the opportunity cost of their time) by trading. The existence of such traders is actually a necessary precondition for markets to become efficient. Without such professional traders, prices would fail to reflect everything that is cheap and easy to evaluate.

Efficient market prices should approximate a random walk, meaning that they will appear to fluctuate more or less randomly. Prices can fluctuate nonrandomly to the extent that their departure from randomness is expensive to discern. Also, observed price series can depart from apparent randomness due to changes in preferences and expectations, but this is really a technicality and does not imply a free lunch relative to current investor sentiments.

Richard Roll is Allstate Professor of Finance at UCLA. He is a preeminent financial researcher, and he has written extensively in almost every area of modern finance. He is particularly well known for his insightful analyses and great creativity in understanding empirical phenomena.

"throwing darts at the financial page will produce a portfolio that can be expected to do as well as any managed by professional security analysts."[6]

Confusion over statements of this sort has often led to a failure to understand the implications of market efficiency. For example, sometimes it is wrongly argued that market efficiency means that it doesn't matter how you invest your money because the efficiency of the market will protect you from making a mistake. However, a random dart thrower might wind up with all of the darts sticking into one or two high-risk stocks that deal in genetic engineering. Would you really want all of your money in two such stocks?

A contest run by *The Wall Street Journal* provides a good example of the controversy surrounding market efficiency. Each month, the *Journal* asked four professional money managers to pick one stock each. At the same time, it threw four darts at the stock page to select a comparison group. In the 147 five-and one-half month contests from July 1990 to September 2002, the pros won 90 times.

The fact that the pros are ahead of the darts by 90 to 57 suggests that markets are not efficient. Or does it? One problem is that the darts naturally tend to select stocks of average risk. The pros, however, are playing to win and naturally select riskier stocks, or so it is argued. If this is true, then, on average, we *expect* the pros to win. Furthermore, the pros' picks are announced to the public at the start. This publicity may boost the prices of the shares involved somewhat, leading to a partially self-fulfilling prophecy. Unfortunately, the *Journal* discontinued the contest in 2002, so this test of market efficiency is no longer ongoing.

More than anything else, what efficiency implies is that the price a firm will obtain when it sells a share of its stock is a "fair" price in the sense that it reflects the value of that stock given the information available about the firm. Shareholders do not have to worry that they are paying too much for a stock with a low dividend or some other sort of characteristic

---

[6]B. G. Malkiel, *A Random Walk Down Wall Street,* (revised and updated ed.) (New York: Norton, 2003).

because the market has already incorporated that characteristic into the price. We sometimes say that the information has been "priced out."

The concept of efficient markets can be explained further by replying to a frequent objection. It is sometimes argued that the market cannot be efficient because stock prices fluctuate from day to day. If the prices are right, the argument goes, then why do they change so much and so often? From our discussion of the market, we can see that these price movements are in no way inconsistent with efficiency. Investors are bombarded with information every day. The fact that prices fluctuate is, at least in part, a reflection of that information flow. In fact, the absence of price movements in a world that changes as rapidly as ours would suggest inefficiency.

THE FORMS OF MARKET EFFICIENCY

It is common to distinguish between three forms of market efficiency. Depending on the degree of efficiency, we say that markets are either *weak form efficient, semistrong form efficient,* or *strong form efficient.* The difference between these forms relates to what information is reflected in prices.

We start with the extreme case. If the market is strong form efficient, then *all* information of *every* kind is reflected in stock prices. In such a market, there is no such thing as inside information. Therefore, in our FCC example, we apparently were assuming that the market was not strong form efficient.

Casual observation, particularly in recent years, suggests that inside information does exist, and it can be valuable to possess. Whether it is lawful or ethical to use that information is another issue. In any event, we conclude that private information about a particular stock may exist that is not currently reflected in the price of the stock. For example, prior knowledge of a takeover attempt could be very valuable.

The second form of efficiency, semistrong form efficiency, is the most controversial. If a market is semistrong form efficient, then all *public* information is reflected in the stock price. The reason this form is controversial is that it implies that a security analyst who tries to identify mispriced stocks using, for example, financial statement information, is wasting time because that information is already reflected in the current price.

The third form of efficiency, weak form efficiency, suggests that, at a minimum, the current price of a stock reflects the stock's own past prices. In other words, studying past prices in an attempt to identify mispriced securities is futile if the market is weak form efficient. Although this form of efficiency might seem rather mild, it implies that searching for patterns in historical prices that will be useful in identifying mispriced stocks will not work (this practice is quite common).

What does capital market history say about market efficiency? Here again, there is great controversy. At the risk of going out on a limb, we can say that the evidence seems to tell us three things. First, prices appear to respond rapidly to new information, and the response is at least not grossly different from what we would expect in an efficient market. Second, the future of market prices, particularly in the short run, is difficult to predict based on publicly available information. Third, if mispriced stocks exist, then there is no obvious means of identifying them. Put another way, simpleminded schemes based on public information will probably not be successful.

Concept Questions

12.6a What is an efficient market?

12.6b What are the forms of market efficiency?

12.7 Summary and Conclusions

This chapter has explored the subject of capital market history. Such history is useful because it tells us what to expect in the way of returns from risky assets. We summed up our study of market history with two key lessons:

1. Risky assets, on average, earn a risk premium. There is a reward for bearing risk.
2. The greater the potential reward from a risky investment, the greater is the risk.

These lessons have significant implications for the financial manager. We will consider these implications in the chapters ahead.

We also discussed the concept of market efficiency. In an efficient market, prices adjust quickly and correctly to new information. Consequently, asset prices in efficient markets are rarely too high or too low. How efficient capital markets (such as the NYSE) are is a matter of debate; but, at a minimum, they are probably much more efficient than most real asset markets.

Visit us at www.mhhe.com/rwj

CHAPTER REVIEW AND SELF-TEST PROBLEMS

12.1 Recent Return History Use Table 12.1 to calculate the average return over the years 1996 through 2000 for large-company stocks, long-term government bonds, and Treasury bills.

12.2 More Recent Return History Calculate the standard deviation for each security type using information from Problem 12.1. Which of the investments was the most volatile over this period?

ANSWERS TO CHAPTER REVIEW AND SELF-TEST PROBLEMS

12.1 We calculate the averages as follows:

	Actual Returns		
Year	Large-Company Stocks	Long-Term Government Bonds	Treasury Bills
1996	.2296	.0013	.0514
1997	.3336	.1202	.0519
1998	.2858	.1445	.0486
1999	.2104	−.0751	.0480
2000	−.0901	.1722	.0598
Average	.19386	.0726	.0519

12.2 We first need to calculate the deviations from the average returns. Using the averages from Problem 12.1, we get the following values:

Deviations from Average Returns			
Year	Large-Company Stocks	Long-Term Government Bonds	Treasury Bills
1996	.0357	−.0713	−.0005
1997	.1397	.0476	.0000
1998	.0919	.0719	−.0033
1999	.0165	−.1477	−.0039
2000	−.2840	.0996	.0079
Total	.0000	.0000	.0000

We square these deviations and calculate the variances and standard deviations:

Squared Deviations from Average Returns			
Year	Large-Company Stocks	Long-Term Government Bonds	Treasury Bills
1996	.0012773	.0050865	.0000003
1997	.0195273	.0022639	.0000000
1998	.0084530	.0051667	.0000112
1999	.0002736	.0218212	.0000155
2000	.0806333	.0099162	.0000618
Variance	.0275411	.0110636	.0000222
Std dev	.1659551	.1051838	.0047104

To calculate the variances, we added up the squared deviations and divided by 4, the number of returns less 1. Notice that the stocks had much more volatility than the bonds with a much larger average return. For large-company stocks, this was a particularly good period: The average return was 19.39 percent.

CONCEPTS REVIEW AND CRITICAL THINKING QUESTIONS

1. **Investment Selection [LO4]** Given that First Solar was up by over 796 percent for 2007, why didn't all investors hold this stock?

2. **Investment Selection [LO4]** Given that Novastar Financial was down by almost 97 percent for 2007, why did some investors hold the stock? Why didn't they sell out before the price declined so sharply?

3. **Risk and Return [LO2, 3]** We have seen that over long periods, stock investments have tended to substantially outperform bond investments. However, it is common to observe investors with long horizons holding entirely bonds. Are such investors irrational?

4. **Market Efficiency Implications [LO4]** Explain why a characteristic of an efficient market is that investments in that market have zero NPVs.

5. **Efficient Markets Hypothesis [LO4]** A stock market analyst is able to identify mispriced stocks by comparing the average price for the last 10 days to the average price for the last 60 days. If this is true, what do you know about the market?

6. **Semistrong Efficiency** [LO4] If a market is semistrong form efficient, is it also weak form efficient? Explain.

7. **Efficient Markets Hypothesis** [LO4] What are the implications of the efficient markets hypothesis for investors who buy and sell stocks in an attempt to "beat the market"?

8. **Stocks versus Gambling** [LO4] Critically evaluate the following statement: Playing the stock market is like gambling. Such speculative investing has no social value other than the pleasure people get from this form of gambling.

9. **Efficient Markets Hypothesis** [LO4] Several celebrated investors and stock pickers frequently mentioned in the financial press have recorded huge returns on their investments over the past two decades. Is the success of these particular investors an invalidation of the EMH? Explain.

10. **Efficient Markets Hypothesis** [LO4] For each of the following scenarios, discuss whether profit opportunities exist from trading in the stock of the firm under the conditions that (1) the market is not weak form efficient, (2) the market is weak form but not semistrong form efficient, (3) the market is semistrong form but not strong form efficient, and (4) the market is strong form efficient.

    a. The stock price has risen steadily each day for the past 30 days.

    b. The financial statements for a company were released three days ago, and you believe you've uncovered some anomalies in the company's inventory and cost control reporting techniques that are causing the firm's true liquidity strength to be understated.

    c. You observe that the senior managers of a company have been buying a lot of the company's stock on the open market over the past week.

QUESTIONS AND PROBLEMS

BASIC
(Questions 1–12)

1. **Calculating Returns** [LO1] Suppose a stock had an initial price of $91 per share, paid a dividend of $2.40 per share during the year, and had an ending share price of $102. Compute the percentage total return.

2. **Calculating Yields** [LO1] In Problem 1, what was the dividend yield? The capital gains yield?

3. **Return Calculations** [LO1] Rework Problems 1 and 2 assuming the ending share price is $83.

4. **Calculating Returns** [LO1] Suppose you bought a 7 percent coupon bond one year ago for $1,040. The bond sells for $1,070 today.

    a. Assuming a $1,000 face value, what was your total dollar return on this investment over the past year?

    b. What was your total nominal rate of return on this investment over the past year?

    c. If the inflation rate last year was 4 percent, what was your total real rate of return on this investment?

5. **Nominal versus Real Returns** [LO2] What was the average annual return on large-company stock from 1926 through 2007:

    a. In nominal terms?

    b. In real terms?

6. **Bond Returns [LO2]** What is the historical real return on long-term government bonds? On long-term corporate bonds?

7. **Calculating Returns and Variability [LO1]** Using the following returns, calculate the arithmetic average returns, the variances, and the standard deviations for X and Y.

	Returns	
Year	X	Y
1	8%	16%
2	21	38
3	17	14
4	−16	−21
5	9	26

8. **Risk Premiums [LO2, 3]** Refer to Table 12.1 in the text and look at the period from 1970 through 1975.
   a. Calculate the arithmetic average returns for large-company stocks and T-bills over this period.
   b. Calculate the standard deviation of the returns for large-company stocks and T-bills over this period.
   c. Calculate the observed risk premium in each year for the large-company stocks versus the T-bills. What was the average risk premium over this period? What was the standard deviation of the risk premium over this period?
   d. Is it possible for the risk premium to be negative before an investment is undertaken? Can the risk premium be negative after the fact? Explain.

9. **Calculating Returns and Variability [LO1]** You've observed the following returns on Crash-n-Burn Computer's stock over the past five years: 7 percent, −12 percent, 11 percent, 38 percent, and 14 percent.
   a. What was the arithmetic average return on Crash-n-Burn's stock over this five-year period?
   b. What was the variance of Crash-n-Burn's returns over this period? The standard deviation?

10. **Calculating Real Returns and Risk Premiums [LO1]** For Problem 9, suppose the average inflation rate over this period was 3.5 percent and the average T-bill rate over the period was 4.2 percent.
   a. What was the average real return on Crash-n-Burn's stock?
   b. What was the average nominal risk premium on Crash-n-Burn's stock?

11. **Calculating Real Rates [LO1]** Given the information in Problem 10, what was the average real risk-free rate over this time period? What was the average real risk premium?

12. **Effects of Inflation [LO2]** Look at Table 12.1 and Figure 12.7 in the text. When were T-bill rates at their highest over the period from 1926 through 2007? Why do you think they were so high during this period? What relationship underlies your answer?

13. **Calculating Investment Returns [LO1]** You bought one of Great White Shark Repellant Co.'s 8 percent coupon bonds one year ago for $1,030. These bonds make annual payments and mature six years from now. Suppose you decide to sell your

INTERMEDIATE
(Questions 13–22)

bonds today, when the required return on the bonds is 7 percent. If the inflation rate was 4.2 percent over the past year, what was your total real return on investment?

14. **Calculating Returns and Variability** [LO1] You find a certain stock that had returns of 7 percent, −12 percent, 18 percent, and 19 percent for four of the last five years. If the average return of the stock over this period was 10.5 percent, what was the stock's return for the missing year? What is the standard deviation of the stock's return?

15. **Arithmetic and Geometric Returns** [LO1] A stock has had returns of 3 percent, 38 percent, 21 percent, −15 percent, 29 percent, and −13 percent over the last six years. What are the arithmetic and geometric returns for the stock?

16. **Arithmetic and Geometric Returns** [LO1] A stock has had the following year-end prices and dividends:

Year	Price	Dividend
1	$60.18	–
2	73.66	$ .60
3	94.18	.64
4	89.35	.72
5	78.49	.80
6	95.05	1.20

What are the arithmetic and geometric returns for the stock?

17. **Using Return Distributions** [LO3] Suppose the returns on long-term corporate bonds are normally distributed. Based on the historical record, what is the approximate probability that your return on these bonds will be less than −2.2 percent in a given year? What range of returns would you expect to see 95 percent of the time? What range would you expect to see 99 percent of the time?

18. **Using Return Distributions** [LO3] Assuming that the returns from holding small-company stocks are normally distributed, what is the approximate probability that your money will double in value in a single year? What about triple in value?

19. **Distributions** [LO3] In Problem 18, what is the probability that the return is less than −100 percent (think)? What are the implications for the distribution of returns?

20. **Blume's Formula** [LO1] Over a 40-year period an asset had an arithmetic return of 15.3 percent and a geometric return of 11.9 percent. Using Blume's formula, what is your best estimate of the future annual returns over 5 years? 10 years? 20 years?

21. **Blume's Formula** [LO1, 2] Assume that the historical return on large-company stocks is a predictor of the future returns. What return would you estimate for large-company stocks over the next year? The next 5 years? 20 years? 30 years?

22. **Calculating Returns** [LO2, 3] Refer to Table 12.1 in the text and look at the period from 1973 through 1980:

   a. Calculate the average return for Treasury bills and the average annual inflation rate (consumer price index) for this period.

   b. Calculate the standard deviation of Treasury bill returns and inflation over this period.

   c. Calculate the real return for each year. What is the average real return for Treasury bills?

   d. Many people consider Treasury bills risk-free. What do these calculations tell you about the potential risks of Treasury bills?

23. **Using Probability Distributions** [LO3] Suppose the returns on large-company stocks are normally distributed. Based on the historical record, use the cumulative normal probability table (rounded to the nearest table value) in the appendix of the text to determine the probability that in any given year you will lose money by investing in common stock.

CHALLENGE
(Questions 23–24)

24. **Using Probability Distributions** [LO3] Suppose the returns on long-term corporate bonds and T-bills are normally distributed. Based on the historical record, use the cumulative normal probability table (rounded to the nearest table value) in the appendix of the text to answer the following questions:

    a. What is the probability that in any given year, the return on long-term corporate bonds will be greater than 10 percent? Less than 0 percent?

    b. What is the probability that in any given year, the return on T-bills will be greater than 10 percent? Less than 0 percent?

    c. In 1979, the return on long-term corporate bonds was −4.18 percent. How likely is it that such a low return will recur at some point in the future? T-bills had a return of 10.56 percent in this same year. How likely is it that such a high return on T-bills will recur at some point in the future?

MINICASE

A Job at S&S Air

You recently graduated from college, and your job search led you to S&S Air. Because you felt the company's business was taking off, you accepted a job offer. The first day on the job, while you are finishing your employment paperwork, Chris Guthrie, who works in Finance, stops by to inform you about the company's 401(k) plan.

A 401(k) plan is a retirement plan offered by many companies. Such plans are tax-deferred savings vehicles, meaning that any deposits you make into the plan are deducted from your current pretax income, so no current taxes are paid on the money. For example, assume your salary will be $50,000 per year. If you contribute $3,000 to the 401(k) plan, you will pay taxes on only $47,000 in income. There are also no taxes paid on any capital gains or income while you are invested in the plan, but you do pay taxes when you withdraw money at retirement. As is fairly common, the company also has a 5 percent match. This means that the company will match your contribution up to 5 percent of your salary, but you must contribute to get the match.

The 401(k) plan has several options for investments, most of which are mutual funds. A mutual fund is a portfolio of assets. When you purchase shares in a mutual fund, you are actually purchasing partial ownership of the fund's assets. The return of the fund is the weighted average of the return of the assets owned by the fund, minus any expenses. The largest expense is typically the management fee, paid to the fund manager. The management fee is compensation for the manager, who makes all of the investment decisions for the fund.

S&S Air uses Bledsoe Financial Services as its 401(k) plan administrator. Here are the investment options offered for employees:

Company Stock One option in the 401(k) plan is stock in S&S Air. The company is currently privately held. However, when you interviewed with the owners, Mark Sexton and Todd Story, they informed you the company stock was expected to go public in the next three to four years. Until then, a company stock price is simply set each year by the board of directors.

Bledsoe S&P 500 Index Fund This mutual fund tracks the S&P 500. Stocks in the fund are weighted exactly the same as the S&P 500. This means the fund return is approximately the return on the S&P 500, minus expenses. Because an index fund purchases assets based on the composition of the index it is following, the fund manager is not required to research stocks and make investment decisions. The result is that the fund expenses are usually low. The Bledsoe S&P 500 Index Fund charges expenses of .15 percent of assets per year.

Bledsoe Small-Cap Fund This fund primarily invests in small-capitalization stocks. As such, the returns of the fund are more volatile. The fund can also invest 10 percent of its assets in companies based outside the United States. This fund charges 1.70 percent in expenses.

Bledsoe Large-Company Stock Fund This fund invests primarily in large-capitalization stocks of companies based in the United States. The fund is managed by Evan Bledsoe and has outperformed the market in six of the last eight years. The fund charges 1.50 percent in expenses.

Bledsoe Bond Fund This fund invests in long-term corporate bonds issued by U.S-domiciled companies. The fund is restricted to investments in bonds with an investment-grade credit rating. This fund charges 1.40 percent in expenses.

Bledsoe Money Market Fund This fund invests in short-term, high credit-quality debt instruments, which include Treasury bills. As such, the return on the money market fund is only slightly higher than the return on Treasury bills. Because of the credit quality and short-term nature of the investments, there is only a very slight risk of negative return. The fund charges .60 percent in expenses.

QUESTIONS

1. What advantages do the mutual funds offer compared to the company stock?

2. Assume that you invest 5 percent of your salary and receive the full 5 percent match from S&S Air. What EAR do you earn from the match? What conclusions do you draw about matching plans?

3. Assume you decide you should invest at least part of your money in large-capitalization stocks of companies based in the United States. What are the advantages and disadvantages of choosing the Bledsoe Large-Company Stock Fund compared to the Bledsoe S&P 500 Index Fund?

4. The returns on the Bledsoe Small-Cap Fund are the most volatile of all the mutual funds offered in the 401(k) plan. Why would you ever want to invest in this fund? When you examine the expenses of the mutual funds, you will notice that this fund also has the highest expenses. Does this affect your decision to invest in this fund?

5. A measure of risk-adjusted performance that is often used is the Sharpe ratio. The Sharpe ratio is calculated as the risk premium of an asset divided by its standard deviation. The standard deviation and return of the funds over the past 10 years are listed in the following table. Calculate the Sharpe ratio for each of these funds. Assume that the expected return and standard deviation of the company stock will be 18 percent and 70 percent, respectively. Calculate the Sharpe ratio for the company stock. How appropriate is the Sharpe ratio for these assets? When would you use the Sharpe ratio?

	10-Year Annual Return	Standard Deviation
Bledsoe S&P 500 Index Fund	11.48%	15.82%
Bledsoe Small-Cap Fund	16.68	19.64
Bledsoe Large-Company Stock Fund	11.85	15.41
Bledsoe Bond Fund	9.67	10.83

6. What portfolio allocation would you choose? Why? Explain your thinking carefully.

After studying this chapter, you should understand:

LO1 How to calculate expected returns.

LO2 The impact of diversification.

LO3 The systematic risk principle.

LO4 The security market line and the risk-return trade-off.

RETURN, RISK, AND THE SECURITY MARKET LINE

13

IN MAY OF 2008, ExxonMobil, Hormel Foods (maker of authentic Spam), and BJ's Wholesale Club joined a host of other companies in announcing earnings. ExxonMobil announced a record first quarter profit of $10.9 billion, while Hormel and BJ's announced earnings increases of 14 percent and 26 percent, respectively. You would expect earnings increases to be good news, and they usually are. Even so, ExxonMobil's stock price dropped 3.6 percent. A similar fate awaited Hormel and BJ's. Their stock prices fell by 3.9 percent and 2.1 percent, respectively.

The news for these companies seems positive, but the stock prices fell for all three. So when is good news really good news? The answer is fundamental to understanding risk and return, and—the good news is—this chapter explores it in some detail.

Master the ability to solve problems in this chapter by using a spreadsheet. Access Excel Master on the student Web site www.mhhe.com/rwj.

In our last chapter, we learned some important lessons from capital market history. Most important, we learned that there is a reward, on average, for bearing risk. We called this reward a *risk premium*. The second lesson is that this risk premium is larger for riskier investments. This chapter explores the economic and managerial implications of this basic idea.

Thus far, we have concentrated mainly on the return behavior of a few large portfolios. We need to expand our consideration to include individual assets. Specifically, we have two tasks to accomplish. First, we have to define risk and discuss how to measure it. We then must quantify the relationship between an asset's risk and its required return.

When we examine the risks associated with individual assets, we find there are two types of risk: systematic and unsystematic. This distinction is crucial because, as we will see, systematic risk affects almost all assets in the economy, at least to some degree, whereas unsystematic risk affects at most a small number of assets. We then develop the principle of diversification, which shows that highly diversified portfolios will tend to have almost no unsystematic risk.

The principle of diversification has an important implication: To a diversified investor, only systematic risk matters. It follows that in deciding whether to buy a particular individual asset, a diversified investor will only be concerned with that asset's systematic risk. This is a key observation, and it allows us to say a great deal about the risks and returns on individual assets. In particular, it is the basis for a famous relationship between risk and return called the *security market line*, or SML. To develop the SML, we introduce the equally famous "beta" coefficient, one of the centerpieces of modern finance. Beta and the

SML are key concepts because they supply us with at least part of the answer to the question of how to determine the required return on an investment.

13.1   Expected Returns and Variances

In our previous chapter, we discussed how to calculate average returns and variances using historical data. We now begin to discuss how to analyze returns and variances when the information we have concerns future possible returns and their probabilities.

EXPECTED RETURN

We start with a straightforward case. Consider a single period of time—say a year. We have two stocks, L and U, which have the following characteristics: Stock L is expected to have a return of 25 percent in the coming year. Stock U is expected to have a return of 20 percent for the same period.

In a situation like this, if all investors agreed on the expected returns, why would anyone want to hold Stock U? After all, why invest in one stock when the expectation is that another will do better? Clearly, the answer must depend on the risk of the two investments. The return on Stock L, although it is *expected* to be 25 percent, could actually turn out to be higher or lower.

For example, suppose the economy booms. In this case, we think Stock L will have a 70 percent return. If the economy enters a recession, we think the return will be −20 percent. In this case, we say that there are two *states of the economy,* which means that these are the only two possible situations. This setup is oversimplified, of course, but it allows us to illustrate some key ideas without a lot of computation.

Suppose we think a boom and a recession are equally likely to happen, for a 50–50 chance of each. Table 13.1 illustrates the basic information we have described and some additional information about Stock U. Notice that Stock U earns 30 percent if there is a recession and 10 percent if there is a boom.

Obviously, if you buy one of these stocks, say Stock U, what you earn in any particular year depends on what the economy does during that year. However, suppose the probabilities stay the same through time. If you hold Stock U for a number of years, you'll earn 30 percent about half the time and 10 percent the other half. In this case, we say that your **expected return** on Stock U, $E(R_U)$, is 20 percent:

$$E(R_U) = .50 \times 30\% + .50 \times 10\% = 20\%$$

In other words, you should expect to earn 20 percent from this stock, on average.

For Stock L, the probabilities are the same, but the possible returns are different. Here, we lose 20 percent half the time, and we gain 70 percent the other half. The expected return on L, $E(R_L)$, is thus 25 percent:

$$E(R_L) = .50 \times -20\% + .50 \times 70\% = 25\%$$

Table 13.2 illustrates these calculations.

expected return
The return on a risky asset expected in the future.

TABLE 13.1

States of the Economy and Stock Returns

State of Economy	Probability of State of Economy	Rate of Return if State Occurs	
		Stock L	Stock U
Recession	.50	−20%	30%
Boom	.50	70	10
	1.00		

(1) State of Economy	(2) Probability of State of Economy	Stock L		Stock U	
		(3) Rate of Return if State Occurs	(4) Product (2) × (3)	(5) Rate of Return if State Occurs	(6) Product (2) × (5)
Recession	.50	−.20	−.10	.30	.15
Boom	.50	.70	.35	.10	.05
	1.00		$E(R_L) = .25 = 25\%$		$E(R_U) = .20 = 20\%$

TABLE 13.2

Calculation of Expected Return

In our previous chapter, we defined the risk premium as the difference between the return on a risky investment and that on a risk-free investment, and we calculated the historical risk premiums on some different investments. Using our projected returns, we can calculate the *projected*, or *expected, risk premium* as the difference between the expected return on a risky investment and the certain return on a risk-free investment.

For example, suppose risk-free investments are currently offering 8 percent. We will say that the risk-free rate, which we label as R_f, is 8 percent. Given this, what is the projected risk premium on Stock U? On Stock L? Because the expected return on Stock U, $E(R_U)$, is 20 percent, the projected risk premium is:

$$\text{Risk premium} = \text{Expected return} - \text{Risk-free rate} \qquad [13.1]$$
$$= E(R_U) - R_f$$
$$= 20\% - 8\%$$
$$= 12\%$$

Similarly, the risk premium on Stock L is $25\% - 8\% = 17\%$.

In general, the expected return on a security or other asset is simply equal to the sum of the possible returns multiplied by their probabilities. So, if we had 100 possible returns, we would multiply each one by its probability and add up the results. The result would be the expected return. The risk premium would then be the difference between this expected return and the risk-free rate.

Unequal Probabilities

EXAMPLE 13.1

Look again at Tables 13.1 and 13.2. Suppose you think a boom will occur only 20 percent of the time instead of 50 percent. What are the expected returns on Stocks U and L in this case? If the risk-free rate is 10 percent, what are the risk premiums?

The first thing to notice is that a recession must occur 80 percent of the time (1 − .20 = .80) because there are only two possibilities. With this in mind, we see that Stock U has a 30 percent return in 80 percent of the years and a 10 percent return in 20 percent of the years. To calculate the expected return, we again just multiply the possibilities by the probabilities and add up the results:

$$E(R_U) = .80 \times 30\% + .20 \times 10\% = 26\%$$

Table 13.3 summarizes the calculations for both stocks. Notice that the expected return on L is −2 percent.

The risk premium for Stock U is $26\% - 10\% = 16\%$ in this case. The risk premium for Stock L is negative: $-2\% - 10\% = -12\%$. This is a little odd; but, for reasons we discuss later, it is not impossible.

(continued)

TABLE 13.3

Calculation of Expected
Return

(1) State of Economy	(2) Probability of State of Economy	Stock L		Stock U	
		(3) Rate of Return if State Occurs	(4) Product (2) × (3)	(5) Rate of Return if State Occurs	(6) Product (2) × (5)
Recession	.80	−.20	−.16	.30	.24
Boom	.20	.70	.14	.10	.02
			$E(R_L) = -.2\%$		$E(R_U) = .26\%$

CALCULATING THE VARIANCE

To calculate the variances of the returns on our two stocks, we first determine the squared deviations from the expected return. We then multiply each possible squared deviation by its probability. We add these up, and the result is the variance. The standard deviation, as always, is the square root of the variance.

To illustrate, let us return to the Stock U we originally discussed, which has an expected return of $E(R_U) = 20\%$. In a given year, it will actually return either 30 percent or 10 percent. The possible deviations are thus $30\% - 20\% = 10\%$ and $10\% - 20\% = -10\%$. In this case, the variance is:

$$\text{Variance} = \sigma^2 = .50 \times (10\%)^2 + .50 \times(-10\%)^2 = .01$$

The standard deviation is the square root of this:

$$\text{Standard deviation} = \sigma = \sqrt{.01} = .10 = 10\%$$

Table 13.4 summarizes these calculations for both stocks. Notice that Stock L has a much larger variance.

When we put the expected return and variability information for our two stocks together, we have the following:

	Stock L	Stock U
Expected return, $E(R)$	25%	20%
Variance, σ^2	.2025	.0100
Standard deviation, σ	45%	10%

Stock L has a higher expected return, but U has less risk. You could get a 70 percent return on your investment in L, but you could also lose 20 percent. Notice that an investment in U will always pay at least 10 percent.

Which of these two stocks should you buy? We can't really say; it depends on your personal preferences. We can be reasonably sure that some investors would prefer L to U and some would prefer U to L.

You've probably noticed that the way we have calculated expected returns and variances here is somewhat different from the way we did it in the last chapter. The reason is that in Chapter 12, we were examining actual historical returns, so we estimated the average return and the variance based on some actual events. Here, we have projected *future* returns and their associated probabilities, so this is the information with which we must work.

TABLE 13.4

Calculation of Variance

(1) State of Economy	(2) Probability of State of Economy	(3) Return Deviation from Expected Return	(4) Squared Return Deviation from Expected Return	(5) Product (2) × (4)
Stock L				
Recession	.50	$-.20 - .25 = -.45$	$-.45^2 = .2025$	.10125
Boom	.50	$.70 - .25 = .45$	$.45^2 = .2025$	.10125
				$\sigma_L^2 = .20250$
Stock U				
Recession	.50	$.30 - .20 = .10$	$.10^2 = .01$	.005
Boom	.50	$.10 - .20 = -.10$	$-.10^2 = .01$	.005
				$\sigma_U^2 = .010$

More Unequal Probabilities   **EXAMPLE 13.2**

Going back to Example 13.1, what are the variances on the two stocks once we have unequal probabilities? The standard deviations?

We can summarize the needed calculations as follows:

(1) State of Economy	(2) Probability of State of Economy	(3) Return Deviation from Expected Return	(4) Squared Return Deviation from Expected Return	(5) Product (2) × (4)
Stock L				
Recession	.80	$-.20 - (-.02) = -.18$	.0324	.02592
Boom	.20	$.70 - (-.02) = .72$	.5184	.10368
				$\sigma_L^2 = .12960$
Stock U				
Recession	.80	$.30 - .26 = .04$	.0016	.00128
Boom	.20	$.10 - .26 = -.16$	.0256	.00512
				$\sigma_U^2 = .00640$

Based on these calculations, the standard deviation for L is $\sigma_L = \sqrt{.1296} = .36 = 36\%$. The standard deviation for U is much smaller: $\sigma_U = \sqrt{.0064} = .08$ or 8%.

Concept Questions

13.1a How do we calculate the expected return on a security?

13.1b In words, how do we calculate the variance of the expected return?

Portfolios   **13.2**

Thus far in this chapter, we have concentrated on individual assets considered separately. However, most investors actually hold a **portfolio** of assets. All we mean by this is that investors tend to own more than just a single stock, bond, or other asset. Given that this is so, portfolio return and portfolio risk are of obvious relevance. Accordingly, we now discuss portfolio expected returns and variances.

portfolio
A group of assets such as stocks and bonds held by an investor.

TABLE 13.5

Expected Return on an
Equally Weighted
Portfolio of Stock L and
Stock U

(1) State of Economy	(2) Probability of State of Economy	(3) Portfolio Return if State Occurs	(4) Product (2) × (3)
Recession	.50	$.50 \times -20\% + .50 \times 30\% = 5\%$	.025
Boom	.50	$.50 \times 70\% + .50 \times 10\% = 40\%$	.200
			$E(R_P) = 22.5\%$

PORTFOLIO WEIGHTS

There are many equivalent ways of describing a portfolio. The most convenient approach is to list the percentage of the total portfolio's value that is invested in each portfolio asset. We call these percentages the **portfolio weights**.

portfolio weight
The percentage of a portfolio's total value that is in a particular asset.

For example, if we have $50 in one asset and $150 in another, our total portfolio is worth $200. The percentage of our portfolio in the first asset is $50/$200 = .25. The percentage of our portfolio in the second asset is $150/$200, or .75. Our portfolio weights are thus .25 and .75. Notice that the weights have to add up to 1.00 because all of our money is invested somewhere.[1]

PORTFOLIO EXPECTED RETURNS

Let's go back to Stocks L and U. You put half your money in each. The portfolio weights are obviously .50 and .50. What is the pattern of returns on this portfolio? The expected return?

To answer these questions, suppose the economy actually enters a recession. In this case, half your money (the half in L) loses 20 percent. The other half (the half in U) gains 30 percent. Your portfolio return, R_P, in a recession is thus:

$$R_P = .50 \times -20\% + .50 \times 30\% = 5\%$$

Table 13.5 summarizes the remaining calculations. Notice that when a boom occurs, your portfolio will return 40 percent:

$$R_P = .50 \times 70\% + .50 \times 10\% = 40\%$$

As indicated in Table 13.5, the expected return on your portfolio, $E(R_P)$, is 22.5 percent.

We can save ourselves some work by calculating the expected return more directly. Given these portfolio weights, we could have reasoned that we expect half of our money to earn 25 percent (the half in L) and half of our money to earn 20 percent (the half in U). Our portfolio expected return is thus:

$$E(R_P) = .50 \times E(R_L) + .50 \times E(R_U)$$
$$= .50 \times 25\% + .50 \times 20\%$$
$$= 22.5\%$$

Want more information about investing? Visit www.thestreet.com.

This is the same portfolio expected return we calculated previously.

This method of calculating the expected return on a portfolio works no matter how many assets there are in the portfolio. Suppose we had n assets in our portfolio, where n is any number. If we let x_i stand for the percentage of our money in Asset i, then the expected return would be:

$$E(R_P) = x_1 \times E(R_1) + x_2 \times E(R_2) + \cdots + x_n \times E(R_n) \qquad [13.2]$$

---

[1] Some of it could be in cash, of course, but we would then just consider the cash to be one of the portfolio assets.

This says that the expected return on a portfolio is a straightforward combination of the expected returns on the assets in that portfolio. This seems somewhat obvious; but, as we will examine next, the obvious approach is not always the right one.

Portfolio Expected Return

EXAMPLE 13.3

Suppose we have the following projections for three stocks:

State of Economy	Probability of State of Economy	Returns if State Occurs		
		Stock A	Stock B	Stock C
Boom	.40	10%	15%	20%
Bust	.60	8	4	0

We want to calculate portfolio expected returns in two cases. First, what would be the expected return on a portfolio with equal amounts invested in each of the three stocks? Second, what would be the expected return if half of the portfolio were in A, with the remainder equally divided between B and C?

Based on what we've learned from our earlier discussions, we can determine that the expected returns on the individual stocks are (check these for practice):

$E(R_A) = 8.8\%$

$E(R_B) = 8.4\%$

$E(R_C) = 8.0\%$

If a portfolio has equal investments in each asset, the portfolio weights are all the same. Such a portfolio is said to be *equally weighted*. Because there are three stocks in this case, the weights are all equal to ⅓. The portfolio expected return is thus:

$E(R_P) = (1/3) \times 8.8\% + (1/3) \times 8.4\% + (1/3) \times 8\% = 8.4\%$

In the second case, verify that the portfolio expected return is 8.5 percent.

PORTFOLIO VARIANCE

From our earlier discussion, the expected return on a portfolio that contains equal investments in Stocks U and L is 22.5 percent. What is the standard deviation of return on this portfolio? Simple intuition might suggest that because half of the money has a standard deviation of 45 percent and the other half has a standard deviation of 10 percent, the portfolio's standard deviation might be calculated as:

$\sigma_P = .50 \times 45\% + .50 \times 10\% = 27.5\%$

Unfortunately, this approach is completely incorrect!

Let's see what the standard deviation really is. Table 13.6 summarizes the relevant calculations. As we see, the portfolio's variance is about .031, and its standard deviation is less than we thought—it's only 17.5 percent. What is illustrated here is that the variance on a portfolio is not generally a simple combination of the variances of the assets in the portfolio.

We can illustrate this point a little more dramatically by considering a slightly different set of portfolio weights. Suppose we put 2/11 (about 18 percent) in L and the other 9/11 (about 82 percent) in U. If a recession occurs, this portfolio will have a return of:

$R_P = (2/11) \times -20\% + (9/11) \times 30\% = 20.91\%$

TABLE 13.6

Variance on an Equally Weighted Portfolio of Stock L and Stock U

(1) State of Economy	(2) Probability of State of Economy	(3) Portfolio Return if State Occurs	(4) Squared Deviation from Expected Return	(5) Product (2) × (4)
Recession	.50	5%	$(.05 - .225)^2 = .030625$	.0153125
Boom	.50	40	$(.40 - .225)^2 = .030625$	.0153125
			$\sigma_P^2 = .030625$	
			$\sigma_P = \sqrt{.030625} = 17.5\%$	

If a boom occurs, this portfolio will have a return of:

$$R_P = (2/11) \times 70\% + (9/11) \times 10\% = 20.91\%$$

Notice that the return is the same no matter what happens. No further calculations are needed: This portfolio has a zero variance. Apparently, combining assets into portfolios can substantially alter the risks faced by the investor. This is a crucial observation, and we will begin to explore its implications in the next section.

EXAMPLE 13.4   **Portfolio Variance and Standard Deviation**

In Example 13.3, what are the standard deviations on the two portfolios? To answer, we first have to calculate the portfolio returns in the two states. We will work with the second portfolio, which has 50 percent in Stock A and 25 percent in each of Stocks B and C. The relevant calculations can be summarized as follows:

State of Economy	Probability of State of Economy	Rate of Return if State Occurs			
		Stock A	Stock B	Stock C	Portfolio
Boom	.40	10%	15%	20%	13.75%
Bust	.60	8	4	0	5.00

The portfolio return when the economy booms is calculated as:

$$E(R_P) = .50 \times 10\% + .25 \times 15\% + .25 \times 20\% = 13.75\%$$

The return when the economy goes bust is calculated the same way. The expected return on the portfolio is 8.5 percent. The variance is thus:

$$\sigma_P^2 = .40 \times (.1375 - .085)^2 + .60 \times (.05 - .085)^2$$
$$= .0018375$$

The standard deviation is thus about 4.3 percent. For our equally weighted portfolio, check to see that the standard deviation is about 5.4 percent.

Concept Questions

13.2a What is a portfolio weight?

13.2b How do we calculate the expected return on a portfolio?

13.2c Is there a simple relationship between the standard deviation on a portfolio and the standard deviations of the assets in the portfolio?

Announcements, Surprises, and Expected Returns

13.3

Now that we know how to construct portfolios and evaluate their returns, we begin to describe more carefully the risks and returns associated with individual securities. Thus far, we have measured volatility by looking at the difference between the actual return on an asset or portfolio, R, and the expected return, $E(R)$. We now look at why those deviations exist.

EXPECTED AND UNEXPECTED RETURNS

To begin, for concreteness, we consider the return on the stock of a company called Flyers. What will determine this stock's return in, say, the coming year?

The return on any stock traded in a financial market is composed of two parts. First, the normal, or expected, return from the stock is the part of the return that shareholders in the market predict or expect. This return depends on the information shareholders have that bears on the stock, and it is based on the market's understanding today of the important factors that will influence the stock in the coming year.

The second part of the return on the stock is the uncertain, or risky, part. This is the portion that comes from unexpected information revealed within the year. A list of all possible sources of such information would be endless, but here are a few examples:

News about Flyers research

Government figures released on gross domestic product (GDP)

The results from the latest arms control talks

The news that Flyers sales figures are higher than expected

A sudden, unexpected drop in interest rates

Based on this discussion, one way to express the return on Flyers stock in the coming year would be:

Total return = Expected return + Unexpected return

$$R = E(R) + U$$

[13.3]

where R stands for the actual total return in the year, $E(R)$ stands for the expected part of the return, and U stands for the unexpected part of the return. What this says is that the actual return, R, differs from the expected return, $E(R)$, because of surprises that occur during the year. In any given year, the unexpected return will be positive or negative; but, through time, the average value of U will be zero. This simply means that on average, the actual return equals the expected return.

ANNOUNCEMENTS AND NEWS

We need to be careful when we talk about the effect of news items on the return. For example, suppose Flyers's business is such that the company prospers when GDP grows at a relatively high rate and suffers when GDP is relatively stagnant. In this case, in deciding what return to expect this year from owning stock in Flyers, shareholders either implicitly or explicitly must think about what GDP is likely to be for the year.

When the government actually announces GDP figures for the year, what will happen to the value of Flyers's stock? Obviously, the answer depends on what figure is released. More to the point, however, the impact depends on how much of that figure is *new* information.

At the beginning of the year, market participants will have some idea or forecast of what the yearly GDP will be. To the extent that shareholders have predicted GDP, that prediction will already be factored into the expected part of the return on the stock, E(R). On the other hand, if the announced GDP is a surprise, the effect will be part of U, the unanticipated portion of the return. As an example, suppose shareholders in the market had forecast that the GDP increase this year would be .5 percent. If the actual announcement this year is exactly .5 percent, the same as the forecast, then the shareholders don't really learn anything, and the announcement isn't news. There will be no impact on the stock price as a result. This is like receiving confirmation of something you suspected all along; it doesn't reveal anything new.

A common way of saying that an announcement isn't news is to say that the market has already "discounted" the announcement. The use of the word *discount* here is different from the use of the term in computing present values, but the spirit is the same. When we discount a dollar in the future, we say it is worth less to us because of the time value of money. When we discount an announcement or a news item, we say that it has less of an impact on the price because the market already knew much of it.

Going back to Flyers, suppose the government announces that the actual GDP increase during the year has been 1.5 percent. Now shareholders have learned something—namely, that the increase is one percentage point higher than they had forecast. This difference between the actual result and the forecast, one percentage point in this example, is sometimes called the *innovation* or the *surprise*.

This distinction explains why what seems to be good news can actually be bad news (and vice versa). Going back to the companies we discussed in our chapter opener, even though ExxonMobil's earnings were a quarterly record, the company was facing increased refinery costs, which it was not passing along to consumers. As a result, profits from the refinery division fell by about 50 percent. Additionally, the company's production of crude oil had fallen.

A key idea to keep in mind about news and price changes is that news about the future is what matters. For Hormel, analysts welcomed the good news about earnings, but also noted that those numbers were, in a very real sense, yesterday's news. Looking to the future, the company's CEO announced that he expected grain and energy prices to rise for the rest of the year, dampening future profitability. For BJ's Wholesale Club, the earnings announcement came on a day when the market turned sour in general. Keep this in mind as you read our next section.

To summarize, an announcement can be broken into two parts: the anticipated, or expected, part and the surprise, or innovation:

$$\text{Announcement} = \text{Expected part} + \text{Surprise} \qquad [13.4]$$

The expected part of any announcement is the part of the information that the market uses to form the expectation, E(R), of the return on the stock. The surprise is the news that influences the unanticipated return on the stock, U.

Our discussion of market efficiency in the previous chapter bears on this discussion. We are assuming that relevant information known today is already reflected in the expected return. This is identical to saying that the current price reflects relevant publicly available information. We are thus implicitly assuming that markets are at least reasonably efficient in the semistrong form.

Henceforth, when we speak of news, we will mean the surprise part of an announcement and not the portion that the market has expected and therefore already discounted.

Concept Questions

13.3a What are the two basic parts of a return?

13.3b Under what conditions will a company's announcement have no effect on common stock prices?

Risk: Systematic and Unsystematic

13.4

The unanticipated part of the return, that portion resulting from surprises, is the true risk of any investment. After all, if we always receive exactly what we expect, then the investment is perfectly predictable and, by definition, risk-free. In other words, the risk of owning an asset comes from surprises—unanticipated events.

There are important differences, though, among various sources of risk. Look back at our previous list of news stories. Some of these stories are directed specifically at Flyers, and some are more general. Which of the news items are of specific importance to Flyers?

Announcements about interest rates or GDP are clearly important for nearly all companies, whereas news about Flyers's president, its research, or its sales is of specific interest to Flyers. We will distinguish between these two types of events because, as we will see, they have different implications.

SYSTEMATIC AND UNSYSTEMATIC RISK

The first type of surprise—the one that affects many assets—we will label **systematic risk**. A systematic risk is one that influences a large number of assets, each to a greater or lesser extent. Because systematic risks have marketwide effects, they are sometimes called *market risks*.

systematic risk
A risk that influences a large number of assets. Also, market risk.

The second type of surprise we will call **unsystematic risk**. An unsystematic risk is one that affects a single asset or a small group of assets. Because these risks are unique to individual companies or assets, they are sometimes called *unique* or *asset-specific risks*. We will use these terms interchangeably.

unsystematic risk
A risk that affects at most a small number of assets. Also, unique or asset-specific risk.

As we have seen, uncertainties about general economic conditions (such as GDP, interest rates, or inflation) are examples of systematic risks. These conditions affect nearly all companies to some degree. An unanticipated increase, or surprise, in inflation, for example, affects wages and the costs of the supplies that companies buy; it affects the value of the assets that companies own; and it affects the prices at which companies sell their products. Forces such as these, to which all companies are susceptible, are the essence of systematic risk.

In contrast, the announcement of an oil strike by a company will primarily affect that company and, perhaps, a few others (such as primary competitors and suppliers). It is unlikely to have much of an effect on the world oil market, however, or on the affairs of companies not in the oil business, so this is an unsystematic event.

SYSTEMATIC AND UNSYSTEMATIC COMPONENTS OF RETURN

The distinction between a systematic risk and an unsystematic risk is never really as exact as we make it out to be. Even the most narrow and peculiar bit of news about a company ripples through the economy. This is true because every enterprise, no matter how tiny, is a part of the economy. It's like the tale of a kingdom that was lost because one horse lost a shoe. This is mostly hairsplitting, however. Some risks are clearly much more general than others. We'll see some evidence on this point in just a moment.

The distinction between the types of risk allows us to break down the surprise portion, U, of the return on the Flyers stock into two parts. Earlier, we had the actual return broken down into its expected and surprise components:

$$R = E(R) + U$$

We now recognize that the total surprise component for Flyers, U, has a systematic and an unsystematic component, so:

$$R = E(R) + \text{Systematic portion} + \text{Unsystematic portion} \qquad [13.5]$$

Because it is traditional, we will use the Greek letter epsilon, ϵ, to stand for the unsystematic portion. Because systematic risks are often called market risks, we will use the letter m to stand for the systematic part of the surprise. With these symbols, we can rewrite the formula for the total return:

$$R = E(R) + U$$
$$= E(R) + m + \epsilon$$

The important thing about the way we have broken down the total surprise, U, is that the unsystematic portion, ϵ, is more or less unique to Flyers. For this reason, it is unrelated to the unsystematic portion of return on most other assets. To see why this is important, we need to return to the subject of portfolio risk.

Concept Questions

13.4a What are the two basic types of risk?
13.4b What is the distinction between the two types of risk?

13.5 Diversification and Portfolio Risk

For more about risk and diversification, visit www.investopedia.com/university.

We've seen earlier that portfolio risks can, in principle, be quite different from the risks of the assets that make up the portfolio. We now look more closely at the riskiness of an individual asset versus the risk of a portfolio of many different assets. We will once again examine some market history to get an idea of what happens with actual investments in U.S. capital markets.

THE EFFECT OF DIVERSIFICATION: ANOTHER LESSON FROM MARKET HISTORY

In our previous chapter, we saw that the standard deviation of the annual return on a portfolio of 500 large common stocks has historically been about 20 percent per year. Does this mean that the standard deviation of the annual return on a typical stock in that group of 500 is about 20 percent? As you might suspect by now, the answer is *no*. This is an extremely important observation.

To illustrate the relationship between portfolio size and portfolio risk, Table 13.7 illustrates typical average annual standard deviations for equally weighted portfolios that contain different numbers of randomly selected NYSE securities.

In Column 2 of Table 13.7, we see that the standard deviation for a "portfolio" of one security is about 49 percent. What this means is that if you randomly selected a single NYSE

TABLE 13.7

Standard Deviations of
Annual Portfolio Returns

(1) Number of Stocks in Portfolio	(2) Average Standard Deviation of Annual Portfolio Returns	(3) Ratio of Portfolio Standard Deviation to Standard Deviation of a Single Stock
1	49.24%	1.00
2	37.36	.76
4	29.69	.60
6	26.64	.54
8	24.98	.51
10	23.93	.49
20	21.68	.44
30	20.87	.42
40	20.46	.42
50	20.20	.41
100	19.69	.40
200	19.42	.39
300	19.34	.39
400	19.29	.39
500	19.27	.39
1,000	19.21	.39

These figures are from Table 1 in M. Statman, "How Many Stocks Make a Diversified Portfolio?" *Journal of Financial and Quantitative Analysis* 22 (September 1987), pp. 353–64. They were derived from E.J. Elton and M.J. Gruber, "Risk Reduction and Portfolio Size: An Analytic Solution," *Journal of Business* 50 (October 1977), pp. 415–37.

stock and put all your money into it, your standard deviation of return would typically be a substantial 49 percent per year. If you were to randomly select two stocks and invest half your money in each, your standard deviation would be about 37 percent on average, and so on.

The important thing to notice in Table 13.7 is that the standard deviation declines as the number of securities is increased. By the time we have 100 randomly chosen stocks, the portfolio's standard deviation has declined by about 60 percent, from 49 percent to about 20 percent. With 500 securities, the standard deviation is 19.27 percent, similar to the 20 percent we saw in our previous chapter for the large common stock portfolio. The small difference exists because the portfolio securities and time periods examined are not identical.

THE PRINCIPLE OF DIVERSIFICATION

Figure 13.1 illustrates the point we've been discussing. What we have plotted is the standard deviation of return versus the number of stocks in the portfolio. Notice in Figure 13.1 that the benefit in terms of risk reduction from adding securities drops off as we add more and more. By the time we have 10 securities, most of the effect is already realized; and by the time we get to 30 or so, there is little remaining benefit.

Figure 13.1 illustrates two key points. First, some of the riskiness associated with individual assets can be eliminated by forming portfolios. The process of spreading an investment across assets (and thereby forming a portfolio) is called *diversification*. The **principle of diversification** tells us that spreading an investment across many assets will eliminate some of the risk. The blue shaded area in Figure 13.1, labeled "diversifiable risk," is the part that can be eliminated by diversification.

principle of diversification
Spreading an investment across a number of assets will eliminate some, but not all, of the risk.

FIGURE 13.1

Portfolio Diversification

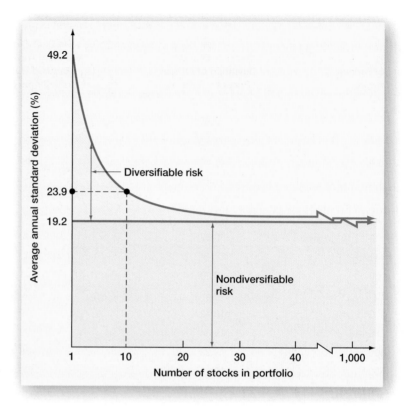

The second point is equally important. There is a minimum level of risk that cannot be eliminated simply by diversifying. This minimum level is labeled "nondiversifiable risk" in Figure 13.1. Taken together, these two points are another important lesson from capital market history: Diversification reduces risk, but only up to a point. Put another way, some risk is diversifiable and some is not.

To give a recent example of the impact of diversification, the Dow Jones Industrial Average (DJIA), which is a widely followed stock market index of 30 large, well-known U.S. stocks, was up about 9 percent in 2007. As we saw in our previous chapter, this gain represents a slightly below-average year for a portfolio of large-cap stocks. The biggest individual winners for the year were Honeywell (up 36 percent), Merck (up 33 percent), and McDonald's (up 33 percent). But not all 30 stocks were up: The losers included Citigroup (down a whopping 47 percent), Home Depot (down 33 percent), and General Motors (down 19 percent). Again, the lesson is clear: Diversification reduces exposure to extreme outcomes, both good and bad.

DIVERSIFICATION AND UNSYSTEMATIC RISK

From our discussion of portfolio risk, we know that some of the risk associated with individual assets can be diversified away and some cannot. We are left with an obvious question: Why is this so? It turns out that the answer hinges on the distinction we made earlier between systematic and unsystematic risk.

By definition, an unsystematic risk is one that is particular to a single asset or, at most, a small group. For example, if the asset under consideration is stock in a single company, the discovery of positive NPV projects such as successful new products and innovative cost savings will tend to increase the value of the stock. Unanticipated lawsuits, industrial accidents, strikes, and similar events will tend to decrease future cash flows and thereby reduce share values.

Here is the important observation: If we held only a single stock, the value of our investment would fluctuate because of company-specific events. If we hold a large portfolio, on the other hand, some of the stocks in the portfolio will go up in value because of positive company-specific events and some will go down in value because of negative events. The net effect on the overall value of the portfolio will be relatively small, however, because these effects will tend to cancel each other out.

Now we see why some of the variability associated with individual assets is eliminated by diversification. When we combine assets into portfolios, the unique, or unsystematic, events—both positive and negative—tend to "wash out" once we have more than just a few assets.

This is an important point that bears repeating:

> **Unsystematic risk is essentially eliminated by diversification, so a portfolio with many assets has almost no unsystematic risk.**

In fact, the terms *diversifiable risk* and *unsystematic risk* are often used interchangeably.

DIVERSIFICATION AND SYSTEMATIC RISK

We've seen that unsystematic risk can be eliminated by diversifying. What about systematic risk? Can it also be eliminated by diversification? The answer is no because, by definition, a systematic risk affects almost all assets to some degree. As a result, no matter how many assets we put into a portfolio, the systematic risk doesn't go away. Thus, for obvious reasons, the terms *systematic risk* and *nondiversifiable risk* are used interchangeably.

Because we have introduced so many different terms, it is useful to summarize our discussion before moving on. What we have seen is that the total risk of an investment, as measured by the standard deviation of its return, can be written as:

$$\text{Total risk} = \text{Systematic risk} + \text{Unsystematic risk} \qquad \text{[13.6]}$$

Systematic risk is also called *nondiversifiable risk* or *market risk.* Unsystematic risk is also called *diversifiable risk, unique risk,* or *asset-specific risk.* For a well-diversified portfolio, the unsystematic risk is negligible. For such a portfolio, essentially all of the risk is systematic.

Concept Questions

13.5a What happens to the standard deviation of return for a portfolio if we increase the number of securities in the portfolio?

13.5b What is the principle of diversification?

13.5c Why is some risk diversifiable? Why is some risk not diversifiable?

13.5d Why can't systematic risk be diversified away?

Systematic Risk and Beta   13.6

The question that we now begin to address is this: What determines the size of the risk premium on a risky asset? Put another way, why do some assets have a larger risk premium than other assets? The answer to these questions, as we discuss next, is also based on the distinction between systematic and unsystematic risk.

THE SYSTEMATIC RISK PRINCIPLE

Thus far, we've seen that the total risk associated with an asset can be decomposed into two components: systematic and unsystematic risk. We have also seen that unsystematic risk can be essentially eliminated by diversification. The systematic risk present in an asset, on the other hand, cannot be eliminated by diversification.

Based on our study of capital market history, we know that there is a reward, on average, for bearing risk. However, we now need to be more precise about what we mean by risk. The **systematic risk principle** states that the reward for bearing risk depends only on the systematic risk of an investment. The underlying rationale for this principle is straightforward: Because unsystematic risk can be eliminated at virtually no cost (by diversifying), there is no reward for bearing it. Put another way, the market does not reward risks that are borne unnecessarily.

The systematic risk principle has a remarkable and very important implication:

systematic risk principle
The expected return on a risky asset depends only on that asset's systematic risk.

> **The expected return on an asset depends only on that asset's systematic risk.**

For more about beta, see www.investools.com *and* moneycentral.msn.com.

There is an obvious corollary to this principle: No matter how much total risk an asset has, only the systematic portion is relevant in determining the expected return (and the risk premium) on that asset.

MEASURING SYSTEMATIC RISK

Because systematic risk is the crucial determinant of an asset's expected return, we need some way of measuring the level of systematic risk for different investments. The specific measure we will use is called the **beta coefficient**, for which we will use the Greek symbol β. A beta coefficient, or beta for short, tells us how much systematic risk a particular asset has relative to an average asset. By definition, an average asset has a beta of 1.0 relative to itself. An asset with a beta of .50, therefore, has half as much systematic risk as an average asset; an asset with a beta of 2.0 has twice as much.

beta coefficient
The amount of systematic risk present in a particular risky asset relative to that in an average risky asset.

Table 13.8 contains the estimated beta coefficients for the stocks of some well-known companies. The range of betas in Table 13.8 is typical for stocks of large U.S. corporations. Betas outside this range occur, but they are less common.

The important thing to remember is that the expected return, and thus the risk premium, of an asset depends only on its systematic risk. Because assets with larger betas have greater systematic risks, they will have greater expected returns. Thus, from Table 13.8, an investor who buys stock in ExxonMobil, with a beta of 1.14, should expect to earn less, on average, than an investor who buys stock in eBay, with a beta of about 2.13.

TABLE 13.8

Beta Coefficients for Selected Companies

SOURCE: Yahoo! Finance 2008 (*finance.yahoo.com*).

	Beta Coefficient (β_j)
The Gap	.48
Coca-Cola	.52
3M	.64
ExxonMobil	1.14
Abercrombie & Fitch	1.28
eBay	2.13
Google	2.60

One cautionary note is in order: Not all betas are created equal. Different providers use somewhat different methods for estimating betas, and significant differences sometimes occur. As a result, it is a good idea to look at several sources. See our nearby *Work the Web* box for more about beta.

Total Risk versus Beta
EXAMPLE 13.5

Consider the following information about two securities. Which has greater total risk? Which has greater systematic risk? Greater unsystematic risk? Which asset will have a higher risk premium?

	Standard Deviation	Beta
Security A	40%	.50
Security B	20	1.50

From our discussion in this section, Security A has greater total risk, but it has substantially less systematic risk. Because total risk is the sum of systematic and unsystematic risk, Security A must have greater unsystematic risk. Finally, from the systematic risk principle, Security B will have a higher risk premium and a greater expected return, despite the fact that it has less total risk.

PORTFOLIO BETAS

Earlier, we saw that the riskiness of a portfolio has no simple relationship to the risks of the assets in the portfolio. A portfolio beta, however, can be calculated, just like a portfolio expected return. For example, looking again at Table 13.8, suppose you put half of your money in ExxonMobil and half in Coca-Cola. What would the beta of this combination be? Because ExxonMobil has a beta of 1.14 and Coca-Cola has a beta of .52, the portfolio's beta, β_p, would be:

$$\beta_p = .50 \times \beta_{ExxonMobil} + .50 \times \beta_{Coca\text{-}Cola}$$
$$= .50 \times 1.14 + .50 \times .52$$
$$= .83$$

WORK THE WEB

You can find beta estimates at many sites on the Web. One of the best is finance.yahoo.com. Here is a snapshot of the "Key Statistics" screen for Amazon.com (AMZN):

Stock Price History	
Beta:	3.18
52-Week Change[3]:	14.30%
S&P500 52-Week Change[3]:	-9.22%
52-Week High (23-Oct-07)[3]:	101.09
52-Week Low (03-Mar-08)[3]:	61.20
50-Day Moving Average[3]:	76.84
200-Day Moving Average[3]:	78.69

(continued)

Management Effectiveness	
Return on Assets (ttm):	9.27%
Return on Equity (ttm):	55.73%

Income Statement	
Revenue (ttm):	15.96B
Revenue Per Share (ttm):	38.515
Qtrly Revenue Growth (yoy):	37.10%
Gross Profit (ttm):	3.35B
EBITDA (ttm):	957.00M
Net Income Avl to Common (ttm):	508.00M
Diluted EPS (ttm):	1.19
Qtrly Earnings Growth (yoy):	28.80%

The reported beta for Amazon.com is 3.18, which means that Amazon has about three times the systematic risk of a typical stock. You would expect that the company is very risky; and, looking at the other numbers, we agree. Amazon's ROA is 9.27 percent, a relatively good number. The reported ROE is about 55.73 percent, an amazing number! Why is Amazon's ROE so high? Until recently, the company had consistently lost money, and its accumulated losses over the years had entirely wiped out its book equity. As the result of recent profits, the shareholders equity account has become positive; but it is small, which leads to the large ROE. Given this, Amazon appears to be a good candidate for a high beta.

Questions

1. As we mentioned, the book value per share of stock for Amazon.com is relatively low. What is the current book value per share reported on this Web site?
2. What growth rate are analysts projecting for Amazon.com? How does this growth rate compare to the industry?

In general, if we had many assets in a portfolio, we would multiply each asset's beta by its portfolio weight and then add the results to get the portfolio's beta.

EXAMPLE 13.6   Portfolio Betas

Suppose we had the following investments:

Security	Amount Invested	Expected Return	Beta
Stock A	$1,000	8%	.80
Stock B	2,000	12	.95
Stock C	3,000	15	1.10
Stock D	4,000	18	1.40

What is the expected return on this portfolio? What is the beta of this portfolio? Does this portfolio have more or less systematic risk than an average asset?

(continued)

To answer, we first have to calculate the portfolio weights. Notice that the total amount invested is $10,000. Of this, $1,000/10,000 = 10\%$ is invested in Stock A. Similarly, 20 percent is invested in Stock B, 30 percent is invested in Stock C, and 40 percent is invested in Stock D. The expected return, $E(R_p)$, is thus:

$$E(R_p) = .10 \times E(R_A) + .20 \times E(R_B) + .30 \times E(R_C) + .40 \times E(R_D)$$
$$= .10 \times 8\% + .20 \times 12\% + .30 \times 15\% + .40 \times 18\%$$
$$= 14.9\%$$

Similarly, the portfolio beta, β_p, is:

$$\beta_p = .10 \times \beta_A + .20 \times \beta_B + .30 \times \beta_C + .40 \times \beta_D$$
$$= .10 \times .80 + .20 \times .95 + .30 \times 1.10 + .40 \times 1.40$$
$$= 1.16$$

This portfolio thus has an expected return of 14.9 percent and a beta of 1.16. Because the beta is larger than 1, this portfolio has greater systematic risk than an average asset.

Concept Questions

13.6a What is the systematic risk principle?

13.6b What does a beta coefficient measure?

13.6c True or false: The expected return on a risky asset depends on that asset's total risk. Explain.

13.6d How do you calculate a portfolio beta?

Betas are easy to find on the Web. Try finance.yahoo.com *and* money.cnn.com.

The Security Market Line   13.7

We're now in a position to see how risk is rewarded in the marketplace. To begin, suppose that Asset A has an expected return of $E(R_A) = 20\%$ and a beta of $\beta_A = 1.6$. Furthermore, suppose that the risk-free rate is $R_f = 8\%$. Notice that a risk-free asset, by definition, has no systematic risk (or unsystematic risk), so a risk-free asset has a beta of zero.

BETA AND THE RISK PREMIUM

Consider a portfolio made up of Asset A and a risk-free asset. We can calculate some different possible portfolio expected returns and betas by varying the percentages invested in these two assets. For example, if 25 percent of the portfolio is invested in Asset A, then the expected return is:

$$E(R_p) = .25 \times E(R_A) + (1 - .25) \times R_f$$
$$= .25 \times 20\% + .75 \times 8\%$$
$$= 11\%$$

Similarly, the beta on the portfolio, β_p, would be:

$$\beta_p = .25 \times \beta_A + (1 - .25) \times 0$$
$$= .25 \times 1.6$$
$$= .40$$

Notice that because the weights have to add up to 1, the percentage invested in the risk-free asset is equal to 1 minus the percentage invested in Asset A.

One thing that you might wonder about is whether it is possible for the percentage invested in Asset A to exceed 100 percent. The answer is yes. This can happen if the investor borrows at the risk-free rate. For example, suppose an investor has $100 and borrows an additional $50 at 8 percent, the risk-free rate. The total investment in Asset A would be $150, or 150 percent of the investor's wealth. The expected return in this case would be:

$$\begin{aligned}
E(R_p) &= 1.50 \times E(R_A) + (1 - 1.50) \times R_f \\
&= 1.50 \times 20\% - .50 \times 8\% \\
&= 26\%
\end{aligned}$$

The beta on the portfolio would be:

$$\begin{aligned}
\beta_P &= 1.50 \times \beta_A + (1 - 1.50) \times 0 \\
&= 1.50 \times 1.6 \\
&= 2.4
\end{aligned}$$

We can calculate some other possibilities, as follows:

Percentage of Portfolio in Asset A	Portfolio Expected Return	Portfolio Beta
0%	8%	.0
25	11	.4
50	14	.8
75	17	1.2
100	20	1.6
125	23	2.0
150	26	2.4

In Figure 13.2A, these portfolio expected returns are plotted against the portfolio betas. Notice that all the combinations fall on a straight line.

The Reward-to-Risk Ratio   What is the slope of the straight line in Figure 13.2A? As always, the slope of a straight line is equal to "the rise over the run." In this case, as we move out of the risk-free asset into Asset A, the beta increases from zero to 1.6 (a "run" of 1.6). At

FIGURE 13.2A

Portfolio Expected
Returns and Betas for
Asset A

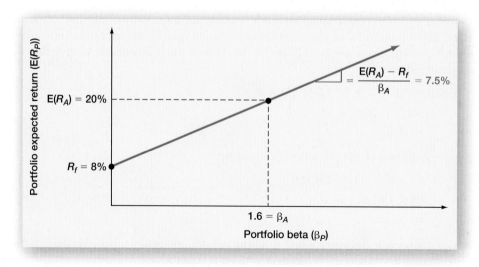

the same time, the expected return goes from 8 percent to 20 percent, a "rise" of 12 percent. The slope of the line is thus $12\%/1.6 = 7.5\%$.

Notice that the slope of our line is just the risk premium on Asset A, $E(R_A) - R_f$, divided by Asset A's beta, β_A:

$$\text{Slope} = \frac{E(R_A) - R_f}{\beta_A}$$

$$= \frac{20\% - 8\%}{1.6} = 7.5\%$$

What this tells us is that Asset A offers a *reward-to-risk* ratio of 7.5 percent.[2] In other words, Asset A has a risk premium of 7.50 percent per "unit" of systematic risk.

The Basic Argument   Now suppose we consider a second asset, Asset B. This asset has a beta of 1.2 and an expected return of 16 percent. Which investment is better, Asset A or Asset B? You might think that, once again, we really cannot say—some investors might prefer A; some investors might prefer B. Actually, however, we can say: A is better because, as we will demonstrate, B offers inadequate compensation for its level of systematic risk, at least, relative to A.

To begin, we calculate different combinations of expected returns and betas for portfolios of Asset B and a risk-free asset, just as we did for Asset A. For example, if we put 25 percent in Asset B and the remaining 75 percent in the risk-free asset, the portfolio's expected return will be:

$$E(R_P) = .25 \times E(R_B) + (1 - .25) \times R_f$$
$$= .25 \times 16\% + .75 \times 8\%$$
$$= 10\%$$

Similarly, the beta on the portfolio, β_P, would be:

$$\beta_P = .25 \times \beta_B + (1 - .25) \times 0$$
$$= .25 \times 1.2$$
$$= .30$$

Some other possibilities are as follows:

Percentage of Portfolio in Asset B	Portfolio Expected Return	Portfolio Beta
0%	8%	.0
25	10	.3
50	12	.6
75	14	.9
100	16	1.2
125	18	1.5
150	20	1.8

When we plot these combinations of portfolio expected returns and portfolio betas in Figure 13.2B, we get a straight line just as we did for Asset A.

---

[2] This ratio is sometimes called the *Treynor index*, after one of its originators.

FIGURE 13.2B

Portfolio Expected
Returns and Betas for
Asset B

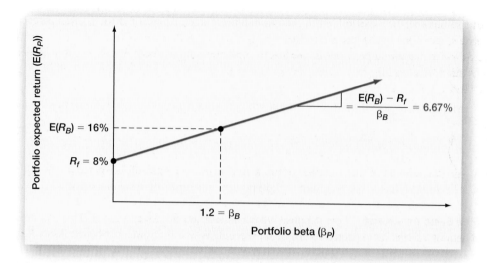

FIGURE 13.2C

Portfolio Expected
Returns and Betas for
Both Assets

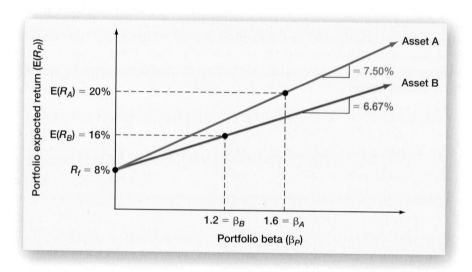

The key thing to notice is that when we compare the results for Assets A and B, as in Figure 13.2C, the line describing the combinations of expected returns and betas for Asset A is higher than the one for Asset B. This tells us that for any given level of systematic risk (as measured by β), some combination of Asset A and the risk-free asset always offers a larger return. This is why we were able to state that Asset A is a better investment than Asset B.

Another way of seeing that A offers a superior return for its level of risk is to note that the slope of our line for Asset B is:

$$\text{Slope} = \frac{E(R_B) - R_f}{\beta_B}$$

$$= \frac{16\% - 8\%}{1.2} = 6.67\%$$

Thus, Asset B has a reward-to-risk ratio of 6.67 percent, which is less than the 7.5 percent offered by Asset A.

The Fundamental Result   The situation we have described for Assets A and B could not persist in a well-organized, active market, because investors would be attracted to Asset A and away from Asset B. As a result, Asset A's price would rise and Asset B's price would fall. Because prices and returns move in opposite directions, A's expected return would decline and B's would rise.

This buying and selling would continue until the two assets plotted on exactly the same line, which means they would offer the same reward for bearing risk. In other words, in an active, competitive market, we must have the situation that:

$$\frac{E(R_A) - R_f}{\beta_A} = \frac{E(R_B) - R_f}{\beta_B}$$

This is the fundamental relationship between risk and return.

Our basic argument can be extended to more than just two assets. In fact, no matter how many assets we had, we would always reach the same conclusion:

> **The reward-to-risk ratio must be the same for all the assets in the market.**

This result is really not so surprising. What it says is that, for example, if one asset has twice as much systematic risk as another asset, its risk premium will simply be twice as large.

Because all of the assets in the market must have the same reward-to-risk ratio, they all must plot on the same line. This argument is illustrated in Figure 13.3. As shown, Assets A and B plot directly on the line and thus have the same reward-to-risk ratio. If an asset plotted above the line, such as C in Figure 13.3, its price would rise and its expected return would fall until it plotted exactly on the line. Similarly, if an asset plotted below the line, such as D in Figure 13.3, its expected return would rise until it too plotted directly on the line.

The arguments we have presented apply to active, competitive, well-functioning markets. The financial markets, such as the NYSE, best meet these criteria. Other markets,

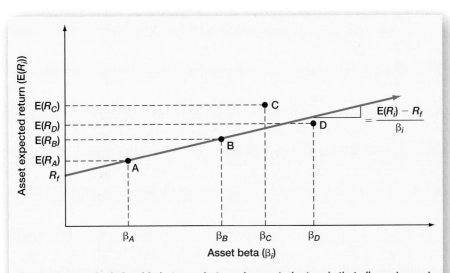

FIGURE 13.3

Expected Returns and Systematic Risk

The fundamental relationship between beta and expected return is that all assets must have the same reward-to-risk ratio, $[E(R_i) - R_f]/\beta_i$. This means that they would all plot on the same straight line. Assets A and B are examples of this behavior. Asset C's expected return is too high; asset D's is too low.

such as real asset markets, may or may not. For this reason, these concepts are most useful in examining financial markets. We will thus focus on such markets here. However, as we discuss in a later section, the information about risk and return gleaned from financial markets is crucial in evaluating the investments that a corporation makes in real assets.

| EXAMPLE 13.7 | Buy Low, Sell High |

An asset is said to be *overvalued* if its price is too high given its expected return and risk. Suppose you observe the following situation:

Security	Beta	Expected Return
SWMS Co.	1.3	14%
Insec Co.	.8	10

The risk-free rate is currently 6 percent. Is one of the two securities overvalued relative to the other?

To answer, we compute the reward-to-risk ratio for both. For SWMS, this ratio is $(14\% - 6\%)/1.3 = 6.15\%$. For Insec, this ratio is 5 percent. What we conclude is that Insec offers an insufficient expected return for its level of risk, at least relative to SWMS. Because its expected return is too low, its price is too high. In other words, Insec is overvalued relative to SWMS, and we would expect to see its price fall relative to SWMS's. Notice that we could also say SWMS is undervalued relative to Insec.

THE SECURITY MARKET LINE

The line that results when we plot expected returns and beta coefficients is obviously of some importance, so it's time we gave it a name. This line, which we use to describe the relationship between systematic risk and expected return in financial markets, is usually called the **security market line (SML)**. After NPV, the SML is arguably the most important concept in modern finance.

security market line (SML)
A positively sloped straight line displaying the relationship between expected return and beta.

Market Portfolios   It will be very useful to know the equation of the SML. There are many different ways we could write it, but one way is particularly common. Suppose we consider a portfolio made up of all of the assets in the market. Such a portfolio is called a market portfolio, and we will express the expected return on this market portfolio as $E(R_M)$.

Because all the assets in the market must plot on the SML, so must a market portfolio made up of those assets. To determine where it plots on the SML, we need to know the beta of the market portfolio, β_M. Because this portfolio is representative of all of the assets in the market, it must have average systematic risk. In other words, it has a beta of 1. We could therefore express the slope of the SML as:

$$\text{SML slope} = \frac{E(R_M) - R_f}{\beta_M} = \frac{E(R_M) - R_f}{1} = E(R_M) - R_f$$

market risk premium
The slope of the SML—the difference between the expected return on a market portfolio and the risk-free rate.

The term $E(R_M) - R_f$ is often called the **market risk premium** because it is the risk premium on a market portfolio.

The Capital Asset Pricing Model   To finish up, if we let $E(R_i)$ and β_i stand for the expected return and beta, respectively, on any asset in the market, then we know that asset must plot on the SML. As a result, we know that its reward-to-risk ratio is the same as the overall market's:

$$\frac{E(R_i) - R_f}{\beta_i} = E(R_M) - R_f$$

If we rearrange this, then we can write the equation for the SML as:

$$E(R_i) = R_f + [E(R_M) - R_f] \times \beta_i \qquad \text{[13.7]}$$

This result is the famous **capital asset pricing model (CAPM)**.

The CAPM shows that the expected return for a particular asset depends on three things:

1. *The pure time value of money:* As measured by the risk-free rate, R_f, this is the reward for merely waiting for your money, without taking any risk.
2. *The reward for bearing systematic risk:* As measured by the market risk premium, $E(R_M) - R_f$, this component is the reward the market offers for bearing an average amount of systematic risk in addition to waiting.
3. *The amount of systematic risk:* As measured by β_i, this is the amount of systematic risk present in a particular asset or portfolio, relative to that in an average asset.

By the way, the CAPM works for portfolios of assets just as it does for individual assets. In an earlier section, we saw how to calculate a portfolio's β. To find the expected return on a portfolio, we simply use this β in the CAPM equation.

Figure 13.4 summarizes our discussion of the SML and the CAPM. As before, we plot expected return against beta. Now we recognize that, based on the CAPM, the slope of the SML is equal to the market risk premium, $E(R_M) - R_f$.

This concludes our presentation of concepts related to the risk–return trade-off. For future reference, Table 13.9 summarizes the various concepts in the order in which we discussed them.

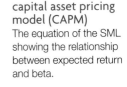

capital asset pricing model (CAPM)
The equation of the SML showing the relationship between expected return and beta.

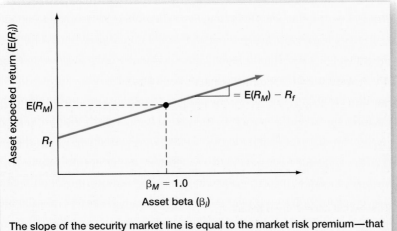

FIGURE 13.4

The Security Market Line (SML)

The slope of the security market line is equal to the market risk premium—that is, the reward for bearing an average amount of systematic risk. The equation describing the SML can be written:

$$E(R_i) = R_f + [E(R_M) - R_f] \times \beta_i$$

which is the capital asset pricing model (CAPM).

| EXAMPLE 13.8 | **Risk and Return** |

Suppose the risk-free rate is 4 percent, the market risk premium is 8.6 percent, and a particular stock has a beta of 1.3. Based on the CAPM, what is the expected return on this stock? What would the expected return be if the beta were to double?

With a beta of 1.3, the risk premium for the stock is $1.3 \times 8.6\%$, or 11.18 percent. The risk-free rate is 4 percent, so the expected return is 15.18 percent. If the beta were to double to 2.6, the risk premium would double to 22.36 percent, so the expected return would be 26.36 percent.

TABLE 13.9

Summary of Risk and Return

I.   Total Risk

The *total risk* of an investment is measured by the variance or, more commonly, the standard deviation of its return.

II.   Total Return

The *total return* on an investment has two components: the expected return and the unexpected return. The unexpected return comes about because of unanticipated events. The risk from investing stems from the possibility of an unanticipated event.

III. Systematic and Unsystematic Risks

Systematic risks (also called *market risks*) are unanticipated events that affect almost all assets to some degree because the effects are economywide. *Unsystematic risks* are unanticipated events that affect single assets or small groups of assets. Unsystematic risks are also called *unique* or *asset-specific risks*.

IV. The Effect of Diversification

Some, but not all, of the risk associated with a risky investment can be eliminated by diversification. The reason is that unsystematic risks, which are unique to individual assets, tend to wash out in a large portfolio, but systematic risks, which affect all of the assets in a portfolio to some extent, do not.

V.   The Systematic Risk Principle and Beta

Because unsystematic risk can be freely eliminated by diversification, the *systematic risk principle* states that the reward for bearing risk depends only on the level of systematic risk. The level of systematic risk in a particular asset, relative to the average, is given by the beta of that asset.

VI. The Reward-to-Risk Ratio and the Security Market Line

The *reward-to-risk ratio* for Asset i is the ratio of its risk premium, $E(R_i) - R_f$, to its beta, β_i:

$$\frac{E(R_i) - R_f}{\beta_i}$$

In a well-functioning market, this ratio is the same for every asset. As a result, when asset expected returns are plotted against asset betas, all assets plot on the same straight line, called the *security market line* (SML).

VII. The Capital Asset Pricing Model

From the SML, the expected return on Asset i can be written:

$$E(R_i) = R_f + [E(R_M) - R_f] \times \beta_i$$

This is the *capital asset pricing model* (CAPM). The expected return on a risky asset thus has three components. The first is the pure time value of money (R_f), the second is the market risk premium $[E(R_M) - R_f]$, and the third is the beta for that asset, (β_i).

The SML and the Cost of Capital: A Preview   13.8

Our goal in studying risk and return is twofold. First, risk is an extremely important consideration in almost all business decisions, so we want to discuss just what risk is and how it is rewarded in the market. Our second purpose is to learn what determines the appropriate discount rate for future cash flows. We briefly discuss this second subject now; we will discuss it in more detail in a subsequent chapter.

THE BASIC IDEA

The security market line tells us the reward for bearing risk in financial markets. At an absolute minimum, any new investment our firm undertakes must offer an expected return that is no worse than what the financial markets offer for the same risk. The reason for this is simply that our shareholders can always invest for themselves in the financial markets.

The only way we benefit our shareholders is by finding investments with expected returns that are superior to what the financial markets offer for the same risk. Such an investment will have a positive NPV. So, if we ask, "What is the appropriate discount rate?" the answer is that we should use the expected return offered in financial markets on investments with the same systematic risk.

In other words, to determine whether an investment has a positive NPV, we essentially compare the expected return on that new investment to what the financial market offers on an investment with the same beta. This is why the SML is so important: It tells us the "going rate" for bearing risk in the economy.

THE COST OF CAPITAL

The appropriate discount rate on a new project is the minimum expected rate of return an investment must offer to be attractive. This minimum required return is often called the **cost of capital** associated with the investment. It is called this because the required return is what the firm must earn on its capital investment in a project just to break even. It can thus be interpreted as the opportunity cost associated with the firm's capital investment.

cost of capital
The minimum required return on a new investment.

Notice that when we say an investment is attractive if its expected return exceeds what is offered in financial markets for investments of the same risk, we are effectively using the internal rate of return (IRR) criterion that we developed and discussed in Chapter 9. The only difference is that now we have a much better idea of what determines the required return on an investment. This understanding will be critical when we discuss cost of capital and capital structure in Part 6 of our book.

13.9　Summary and Conclusions

This chapter has covered the essentials of risk. Along the way, we have introduced a number of definitions and concepts. The most important of these is the security market line, or SML. The SML is important because it tells us the reward offered in financial markets for bearing risk. Once we know this, we have a benchmark against which we can compare the returns expected from real asset investments to determine if they are desirable.

Because we have covered quite a bit of ground, it's useful to summarize the basic economic logic underlying the SML as follows:

1. Based on capital market history, there is a reward for bearing risk. This reward is the risk premium on an asset.

2. The total risk associated with an asset has two parts: systematic risk and unsystematic risk. Unsystematic risk can be freely eliminated by diversification (this is the principle of diversification), so only systematic risk is rewarded. As a result, the risk premium on an asset is determined by its systematic risk. This is the systematic risk principle.

3. An asset's systematic risk, relative to the average, can be measured by its beta coefficient, β_i. The risk premium on an asset is then given by its beta coefficient multiplied by the market risk premium, $[E(R_M) - R_f] \times \beta_i$.

4. The expected return on an asset, $E(R_i)$, is equal to the risk-free rate, R_f, plus the risk premium:

$$E(R_i) = R_f + [E(R_M) - R_f] \times \beta_i$$

   This is the equation of the SML, and it is often called the capital asset pricing model (CAPM).

This chapter completes our discussion of risk and return. Now that we have a better understanding of what determines a firm's cost of capital for an investment, the next several chapters will examine more closely how firms raise the long-term capital needed for investment.

CHAPTER REVIEW AND SELF-TEST PROBLEMS

13.1　Expected Return and Standard Deviation　This problem will give you some practice calculating measures of prospective portfolio performance. There are two assets and three states of the economy:

State of Economy	Probability of State of Economy	Rate of Return if State Occurs	
		Stock A	**Stock B**
Recession	.20	−.15	.20
Normal	.50	.20	.30
Boom	.30	.60	.40

What are the expected returns and standard deviations for these two stocks?

13.2　Portfolio Risk and Return　Using the information in the previous problem, suppose you have $20,000 total. If you put $15,000 in Stock A and the remainder in Stock B, what will be the expected return and standard deviation of your portfolio?

13.3 Risk and Return Suppose you observe the following situation:

Security	Beta	Expected Return
Cooley, Inc.	1.8	22.00%
Moyer Co.	1.6	20.44%

If the risk-free rate is 7 percent, are these securities correctly priced? What would the risk-free rate have to be if they are correctly priced?

13.4 CAPM Suppose the risk-free rate is 8 percent. The expected return on the market is 16 percent. If a particular stock has a beta of .7, what is its expected return based on the CAPM? If another stock has an expected return of 24 percent, what must its beta be?

13.1 The expected returns are just the possible returns multiplied by the associated probabilities:

$$E(R_A) = (.20 \times -.15) + (.50 \times .20) + (.30 \times .60) = 25\%$$
$$E(R_B) = (.20 \times .20) + (.50 \times .30) + (.30 \times .40) = 31\%$$

The variances are given by the sums of the squared deviations from the expected returns multiplied by their probabilities:

$$\begin{aligned}
\sigma_A^2 &= .20 \times (-.15 - .25)^2 + .50 \times (.20 - .25)^2 + .30 \times (.60 - .25)^2 \\
&= (.20 \times -.40^2) + (.50 \times -.05^2) + (.30 \times .35^2) \\
&= (.20 \times .16) + (.50 \times .0025) + (.30 \times .1225) \\
&= .0700
\end{aligned}$$

$$\begin{aligned}
\sigma_B^2 &= .20 \times (.20 - .31)^2 + .50 \times (.30 - .31)^2 + .30 \times (.40 - .31)^2 \\
&= (.20 \times -.11^2) + (.50 \times -.01^2) + (.30 \times .09^2) \\
&= (.20 \times .0121) + (.50 \times .0001) + (.30 \times .0081) \\
&= .0049
\end{aligned}$$

The standard deviations are thus:

$$\sigma_A = \sqrt{.0700} = 26.46\%$$
$$\sigma_B = \sqrt{.0049} = 7\%$$

13.2 The portfolio weights are $15,000/20,000 = .75$ and $5,000/20,000 = .25$. The expected return is thus:

$$\begin{aligned}
E(R_P) &= .75 \times E(R_A) + .25 \times E(R_B) \\
&= (.75 \times 25\%) + (.25 \times 31\%) \\
&= 26.5\%
\end{aligned}$$

Alternatively, we could calculate the portfolio's return in each of the states:

State of Economy	Probability of State of Economy	Portfolio Return if State Occurs	
Recession	.20	$(.75 \times -.15) + (.25 \times .20) =$	−.0625
Normal	.50	$(.75 \times .20) + (.25 \times .30) =$	.2250
Boom	.30	$(.75 \times .60) + (.25 \times .40) =$	.5500

The portfolio's expected return is:

$$E(R_P) = (.20 \times -.0625) + (.50 \times .2250) + (.30 \times .5500) = 26.5\%$$

This is the same as we had before.

The portfolio's variance is:

$$\sigma_P^2 = .20 \times (-.0625 - .265)^2 + .50 \times (.225 - .265)^2$$
$$+ .30 \times (.55 - .265)^2$$
$$= .0466$$

So the standard deviation is $\sqrt{.0466} = 21.59\%$.

13.3 If we compute the reward-to-risk ratios, we get $(22\% - 7\%)/1.8 = 8.33\%$ for Cooley versus 8.4% for Moyer. Relative to that of Cooley, Moyer's expected return is too high, so its price is too low.

If they are correctly priced, then they must offer the same reward-to-risk ratio. The risk-free rate would have to be such that:

$$(22\% - R_f)/1.8 = (20.44\% - R_f)/1.6$$

With a little algebra, we find that the risk-free rate must be 8 percent:

$$22\% - R_f = (20.44\% - R_f)(1.8/1.6)$$
$$22\% - 20.44\% \times 1.125 = R_f - R_f \times 1.125$$
$$R_f = 8\%$$

13.4 Because the expected return on the market is 16 percent, the market risk premium is $16\% - 8\% = 8\%$. The first stock has a beta of .7, so its expected return is $8\% + .7 \times 8\% = 13.6\%$.

For the second stock, notice that the risk premium is $24\% - 8\% = 16\%$. Because this is twice as large as the market risk premium, the beta must be exactly equal to 2. We can verify this using the CAPM:

$$E(R_i) = R_f + [E(R_M) - R_f] \times \beta_i$$
$$24\% = 8\% + (16\% - 8\%) \times \beta_i$$
$$\beta_i = 16\%/8\%$$
$$= 2.0$$

CONCEPTS REVIEW AND CRITICAL THINKING QUESTIONS

1. **Diversifiable and Nondiversifiable Risks [LO3]** In broad terms, why is some risk diversifiable? Why are some risks nondiversifiable? Does it follow that an investor can control the level of unsystematic risk in a portfolio, but not the level of systematic risk?

2. **Information and Market Returns [LO3]** Suppose the government announces that, based on a just-completed survey, the growth rate in the economy is likely to be 2 percent in the coming year, as compared to 5 percent for the past year. Will security prices increase, decrease, or stay the same following this announcement? Does it make any difference whether the 2 percent figure was anticipated by the market? Explain.

3. **Systematic versus Unsystematic Risk [LO3]** Classify the following events as mostly systematic or mostly unsystematic. Is the distinction clear in every case?

   a. Short-term interest rates increase unexpectedly.

   b. The interest rate a company pays on its short-term debt borrowing is increased by its bank.

c. Oil prices unexpectedly decline.

d. An oil tanker ruptures, creating a large oil spill.

e. A manufacturer loses a multimillion-dollar product liability suit.

f. A Supreme Court decision substantially broadens producer liability for injuries suffered by product users.

4. **Systematic versus Unsystematic Risk** [LO3] Indicate whether the following events might cause stocks in general to change price, and whether they might cause Big Widget Corp.'s stock to change price:

a. The government announces that inflation unexpectedly jumped by 2 percent last month.

b. Big Widget's quarterly earnings report, just issued, generally fell in line with analysts' expectations.

c. The government reports that economic growth last year was at 3 percent, which generally agreed with most economists' forecasts.

d. The directors of Big Widget die in a plane crash.

e. Congress approves changes to the tax code that will increase the top marginal corporate tax rate. The legislation had been debated for the previous six months.

5. **Expected Portfolio Returns** [LO1] If a portfolio has a positive investment in every asset, can the expected return on the portfolio be greater than that on every asset in the portfolio? Can it be less than that on every asset in the portfolio? If you answer yes to one or both of these questions, give an example to support your answer.

6. **Diversification** [LO2] True or false: The most important characteristic in determining the expected return of a well-diversified portfolio is the variance of the individual assets in the portfolio. Explain.

7. **Portfolio Risk** [LO2] If a portfolio has a positive investment in every asset, can the standard deviation on the portfolio be less than that on every asset in the portfolio? What about the portfolio beta?

8. **Beta and CAPM** [LO4] Is it possible that a risky asset could have a beta of zero? Explain. Based on the CAPM, what is the expected return on such an asset? Is it possible that a risky asset could have a negative beta? What does the CAPM predict about the expected return on such an asset? Can you give an explanation for your answer?

9. **Corporate Downsizing** [LO1] In recent years, it has been common for companies to experience significant stock price changes in reaction to announcements of massive layoffs. Critics charge that such events encourage companies to fire longtime employees and that Wall Street is cheering them on. Do you agree or disagree?

10. **Earnings and Stock Returns** [LO1] As indicated by a number of examples in this chapter, earnings announcements by companies are closely followed by, and frequently result in, share price revisions. Two issues should come to mind. First, earnings announcements concern past periods. If the market values stocks based on expectations of the future, why are numbers summarizing past performance relevant? Second, these announcements concern accounting earnings. Going back to Chapter 2, such earnings may have little to do with cash flow—so, again, why are they relevant?

BASIC
(Questions 1–20)

1. **Determining Portfolio Weights [LO1]** What are the portfolio weights for a portfolio that has 180 shares of Stock A that sell for $45 per share and 140 shares of Stock B that sell for $27 per share?

2. **Portfolio Expected Return [LO1]** You own a portfolio that has $2,950 invested in Stock A and $3,700 invested in Stock B. If the expected returns on these stocks are 11 percent and 15 percent, respectively, what is the expected return on the portfolio?

3. **Portfolio Expected Return [LO1]** You own a portfolio that is 60 percent invested in Stock X, 25 percent in Stock Y, and 15 percent in Stock Z. The expected returns on these three stocks are 9 percent, 17 percent, and 13 percent, respectively. What is the expected return on the portfolio?

4. **Portfolio Expected Return [LO1]** You have $10,000 to invest in a stock portfolio. Your choices are Stock X with an expected return of 14 percent and Stock Y with an expected return of 10.5 percent. If your goal is to create a portfolio with an expected return of 12.4 percent, how much money will you invest in Stock X? In Stock Y?

5. **Calculating Expected Return [LO1]** Based on the following information, calculate the expected return:

State of Economy	Probability of State of Economy	Portfolio Return if State Occurs
Recession	.25	−.08
Boom	.75	.21

6. **Calculating Expected Return [LO1]** Based on the following information, calculate the expected return:

State of Economy	Probability of State of Economy	Portfolio Return if State Occurs
Recession	.20	−.05
Normal	.50	.12
Boom	.30	.25

7. **Calculating Returns and Standard Deviations [LO1]** Based on the following information, calculate the expected return and standard deviation for the two stocks:

State of Economy	Probability of State of Economy	Rate of Return if State Occurs	
		Stock A	Stock B
Recession	.15	.05	−.17
Normal	.65	.08	.12
Boom	.20	.13	.29

8. **Calculating Expected Returns [LO1]** A portfolio is invested 25 percent in Stock G, 55 percent in Stock J, and 20 percent in Stock K. The expected returns on these stocks are 8 percent, 15 percent, and 24 percent, respectively. What is the portfolio's expected return? How do you interpret your answer?

9. **Returns and Variances** [LO1] Consider the following information:

State of Economy	Probability of State of Economy	Rate of Return if State Occurs		
		Stock A	Stock B	Stock C
Boom	.35	.07	.15	.33
Bust	.65	.13	.03	−.06

    a. What is the expected return on an equally weighted portfolio of these three stocks?

    b. What is the variance of a portfolio invested 20 percent each in A and B and 60 percent in C?

10. **Returns and Standard Deviations** [LO1] Consider the following information:

State of Economy	Probability of State of Economy	Rate of Return if State Occurs		
		Stock A	Stock B	Stock C
Boom	.15	.30	.45	.33
Good	.45	.12	.10	.15
Poor	.35	.01	−.15	−.05
Bust	.05	−.06	−.30	−.09

    a. Your portfolio is invested 30 percent each in A and C, and 40 percent in B. What is the expected return of the portfolio?

    b. What is the variance of this portfolio? The standard deviation?

11. **Calculating Portfolio Betas** [LO4] You own a stock portfolio invested 25 percent in Stock Q, 20 percent in Stock R, 15 percent in Stock S, and 40 percent in Stock T. The betas for these four stocks are .84, 1.17, 1.11, and 1.36, respectively. What is the portfolio beta?

12. **Calculating Portfolio Betas** [LO4] You own a portfolio equally invested in a risk-free asset and two stocks. If one of the stocks has a beta of 1.38 and the total portfolio is equally as risky as the market, what must the beta be for the other stock in your portfolio?

13. **Using CAPM** [LO4] A stock has a beta of 1.05, the expected return on the market is 11 percent, and the risk-free rate is 5.2 percent. What must the expected return on this stock be?

14. **Using CAPM** [LO4] A stock has an expected return of 10.2 percent, the risk-free rate is 4.5 percent, and the market risk premium is 8.5 percent. What must the beta of this stock be?

15. **Using CAPM** [LO4] A stock has an expected return of 13.5 percent, its beta is 1.17, and the risk-free rate is 5.5 percent. What must the expected return on the market be?

16. **Using CAPM** [LO4] A stock has an expected return of 14 percent, its beta is 1.45, and the expected return on the market is 11.5 percent. What must the risk-free rate be?

17. **Using CAPM** [LO4] A stock has a beta of 1.35 and an expected return of 16 percent. A risk-free asset currently earns 4.8 percent.

    a. What is the expected return on a portfolio that is equally invested in the two assets?

    b. If a portfolio of the two assets has a beta of .95, what are the portfolio weights?

c. If a portfolio of the two assets has an expected return of 8 percent, what is its beta?

d. If a portfolio of the two assets has a beta of 2.70, what are the portfolio weights? How do you interpret the weights for the two assets in this case? Explain.

18.   **Using the SML [LO4]**   Asset W has an expected return of 15.2 percent and a beta of 1.25. If the risk-free rate is 5.3 percent, complete the following table for portfolios of Asset W and a risk-free asset. Illustrate the relationship between portfolio expected return and portfolio beta by plotting the expected returns against the betas. What is the slope of the line that results?

Percentage of Portfolio in Asset W	Portfolio Expected Return	Portfolio Beta
0%		
25		
50		
75		
100		
125		
150		

19.   **Reward-to-Risk Ratios [LO4]**   Stock Y has a beta of 1.3 and an expected return of 18.5 percent. Stock Z has a beta of .70 and an expected return of 12.1 percent. If the risk-free rate is 8 percent and the market risk premium is 7.5 percent, are these stocks correctly priced?

20.   **Reward-to-Risk Ratios [LO4]**   In the previous problem, what would the risk-free rate have to be for the two stocks to be correctly priced?

INTERMEDIATE
(Questions 21–24)

21.   **Portfolio Returns [LO2]**   Using information from the previous chapter on capital market history, determine the return on a portfolio that is equally invested in large-company stocks and long-term government bonds. What is the return on a portfolio that is equally invested in small-company stocks and Treasury bills?

22.   **CAPM [LO4]**   Using the CAPM, show that the ratio of the risk premiums on two assets is equal to the ratio of their betas.

23.   **Portfolio Returns and Deviations [LO2]**   Consider the following information about three stocks:

State of Economy	Probability of State of Economy	Rate of Return if State Occurs		
		Stock A	Stock B	Stock C
Boom	.35	.24	.36	.55
Normal	.50	.17	.13	.09
Bust	.15	.00	−.28	−.45

a. If your portfolio is invested 40 percent each in A and B and 20 percent in C, what is the portfolio expected return? The variance? The standard deviation?

b. If the expected T-bill rate is 3.80 percent, what is the expected risk premium on the portfolio?

c. If the expected inflation rate is 3.50 percent, what are the approximate and exact expected real returns on the portfolio? What are the approximate and exact expected real risk premiums on the portfolio?

24. **Analyzing a Portfolio [LO2]** You want to create a portfolio equally as risky as the 𝕏 market, and you have $1,000,000 to invest. Given this information, fill in the rest of the following table:

Asset	Investment	Beta
Stock A	$210,000	.85
Stock B	$320,000	1.20
Stock C		1.35
Risk-free asset		

25. **Analyzing a Portfolio [LO2, 4]** You have $100,000 to invest in a portfolio containing Stock X and Stock Y. Your goal is to create a portfolio that has an expected return of 18.5 percent. If Stock X has an expected return of 17.2 percent and a beta of 1.4, and Stock Y has an expected return of 13.6 percent and a beta of .95, how much money will you invest in stock Y? How do you interpret your answer? What is the beta of your portfolio?

CHALLENGE
(Questions 25–28)

26. **Systematic versus Unsystematic Risk [LO3]** Consider the following information about Stocks I and II:

State of Economy	Probability of State of Economy	Rate of Return if State Occurs	
		Stock I	Stock II
Recession	.25	.11	−.40
Normal	.50	.29	.10
Irrational exuberance	.25	.13	.56

The market risk premium is 8 percent, and the risk-free rate is 4 percent. Which stock has the most systematic risk? Which one has the most unsystematic risk? Which stock is "riskier"? Explain.

27. **SML [LO4]** Suppose you observe the following situation: 𝕏

Security	Beta	Expected Return
Pete Corp.	1.35	.132
Repete Co.	.80	.101

Assume these securities are correctly priced. Based on the CAPM, what is the expected return on the market? What is the risk-free rate?

28. **SML [LO4]** Suppose you observe the following situation:

State of Economy	Probability of State	Return if State Occurs	
		Stock A	Stock B
Bust	.15	−.08	−.05
Normal	.70	.13	.14
Boom	.15	.48	.29

a. Calculate the expected return on each stock.
b. Assuming the capital asset pricing model holds and stock A's beta is greater than stock B's beta by .25, what is the expected market risk premium?

The Beta for Colgate-Palmolive

Joey Moss, a recent finance graduate, has just begun his job with the investment firm of Covili and Wyatt. Paul Covili, one of the firm's founders, has been talking to Joey about the firm's investment portfolio.

As with any investment, Paul is concerned about the risk of the investment as well as the potential return. More specifically, because the company holds a diversified portfolio, Paul is concerned about the systematic risk of current and potential investments. One such position the company currently holds is stock in Colgate-Palmolive (CL). Colgate-Palmolive is the well-known manufacturer of consumer products under brand names such as Colgate, Palmolive, Softsoap, Irish Spring, Ajax, and others.

Covili and Wyatt currently uses a commercial data vendor for information about its positions. Because of this, Paul is unsure exactly how the numbers provided are calculated. The data provider considers its methods proprietary, and it will not disclose how stock betas and other information are calculated. Paul is uncomfortable with not knowing exactly how these numbers are being computed and also believes that it could be less expensive to calculate the necessary statistics in-house. To explore this question, Paul has asked Joey to do the following assignments.

QUESTIONS

1. Go to finance.yahoo.com and download the ending monthly stock prices for Colgate-Palmolive for the last 60 months. Use the adjusted closing price, which adjusts for dividend payments and stock splits. Next, download the ending value of the S&P 500 index over the same period. For the historical risk-free rate, go to the St. Louis Federal Reserve Web site (www.stlouisfed.org) and find the three-month Treasury bill secondary market rate. Download this file. What are the monthly returns, average monthly returns, and standard deviations for Colgate-Palmolive stock, the three-month Treasury bill, and the S&P 500 for this period?

2. Beta is often estimated by linear regression. A model often used is called the *market model*, which is:

$$R_t - R_{ft} = \alpha_i + \beta_i [R_{Mt} - R_{ft}] + \varepsilon_t$$

In this regression, R_t is the return on the stock and R_{ft} is the risk-free rate for the same period. R_{Mt} is the return on a stock market index such as the S&P 500 index. α_i is the regression intercept, and β_i is the slope (and the stock's estimated beta). ε_t represents the residuals for the regression. What do you think is the motivation for this particular regression? The intercept, α_i, is often called *Jensen's alpha*. What does it measure? If an asset has a positive Jensen's alpha, where would it plot with respect to the SML? What is the financial interpretation of the residuals in the regression?

3. Use the market model to estimate the beta for Colgate-Palmolive using the last 36 months of returns (the regression procedure in Excel is one easy way to do this). Plot the monthly returns on Colgate-Palmolive against the index and also show the fitted line.

4. When the beta of a stock is calculated using monthly returns, there is a debate over the number of months that should be used in the calculation. Rework the previous questions using the last 60 months of returns. How does this answer compare to what you calculated previously? What are some arguments for and against using shorter versus longer periods? Also, you've used monthly data, which are a common choice. You could have used daily, weekly, quarterly, or even annual data. What do you think are the issues here?

5. Compare your beta for Colgate-Palmolive to the beta you find on finance.yahoo.com. How similar are they? Why might they be different?

LEARNING OBJECTIVES

After studying this chapter, you should understand:

LO1 How to determine a firm's cost of equity capital.

LO2 How to determine a firm's cost of debt.

LO3 How to determine a firm's overall cost of capital.

LO4 How to correctly include flotation costs in capital budgeting projects.

LO5 Some of the pitfalls associated with a firm's overall cost of capital and what to do about them.

COST OF CAPITAL

14

WITH OVER 95,000 EMPLOYEES ON FIVE CONTINENTS, Germany-based BASF is a major international company. The company operates in a variety of industries, including agriculture, oil and gas, chemicals, and plastics. In an attempt to increase value, BASF launched BASF 2015, a comprehensive plan that included all functions within the company and challenged and encouraged all employees to act in an entrepreneurial manner. The major financial component of the strategy was that the company expected to earn its weighted average cost of capital, or WACC, plus a premium. So, what exactly is the WACC?

The WACC is the minimum return a company needs to earn to satisfy all of its investors, including stockholders, bondholders, and preferred stockholders. In 2007, for example, BASF pegged its WACC at 9 percent, and it increased this figure to 10 percent in 2008. In this chapter, we learn how to compute a firm's cost of capital and find out what it means to the firm and its investors. We will also learn when to use the firm's cost of capital, and, perhaps more important, when not to use it.

> Master the ability to solve problems in this chapter by using a spreadsheet. Access Excel Master on the student Web site www.mhhe.com/rwj.

Suppose you have just become the president of a large company, and the first decision you face is whether to go ahead with a plan to renovate the company's warehouse distribution system. The plan will cost the company $50 million, and it is expected to save $12 million per year after taxes over the next six years.

This is a familiar problem in capital budgeting. To address it, you would determine the relevant cash flows, discount them, and, if the net present value is positive, take on the project; if the NPV is negative, you would scrap it. So far, so good; but what should you use as the discount rate?

From our discussion of risk and return, you know that the correct discount rate depends on the riskiness of the project to renovate the warehouse distribution system. In particular, the new project will have a positive NPV only if its return exceeds what the financial markets offer on investments of similar risk. We called this minimum required return the *cost of capital* associated with the project.[1]

Thus, to make the right decision as president, you must examine what the capital markets have to offer and use this information to arrive at an estimate of the project's cost of capital. Our primary purpose in this chapter is to describe how to go about doing this. There are a variety of approaches to this task, and a number of conceptual and practical issues arise.

---

[1] The term *cost of money* is also used.

One of the most important concepts we develop is that of the *weighted average cost of capital* (WACC). This is the cost of capital for the firm as a whole, and it can be interpreted as the required return on the overall firm. In discussing the WACC, we will recognize the fact that a firm will normally raise capital in a variety of forms and that these different forms of capital may have different costs associated with them.

We also recognize in this chapter that taxes are an important consideration in determining the required return on an investment: We are always interested in valuing the aftertax cash flows from a project. We will therefore discuss how to incorporate taxes explicitly into our estimates of the cost of capital.

14.1 The Cost of Capital: Some Preliminaries

In Chapter 13, we developed the security market line, or SML, and used it to explore the relationship between the expected return on a security and its systematic risk. We concentrated on how the risky returns from buying securities looked from the viewpoint of, for example, a shareholder in the firm. This helped us understand more about the alternatives available to an investor in the capital markets.

In this chapter, we turn things around a bit and look more closely at the other side of the problem, which is how these returns and securities look from the viewpoint of the companies that issue them. The important fact to note is that the return an investor in a security receives is the cost of that security to the company that issued it.

REQUIRED RETURN VERSUS COST OF CAPITAL

When we say that the required return on an investment is, say, 10 percent, we usually mean that the investment will have a positive NPV only if its return exceeds 10 percent. Another way of interpreting the required return is to observe that the firm must earn 10 percent on the investment just to compensate its investors for the use of the capital needed to finance the project. This is why we could also say that 10 percent is the cost of capital associated with the investment.

To illustrate the point further, imagine that we are evaluating a risk-free project. In this case, how to determine the required return is obvious: We look at the capital markets and observe the current rate offered by risk-free investments, and we use this rate to discount the project's cash flows. Thus, the cost of capital for a risk-free investment is the risk-free rate.

If a project is risky, then, assuming that all the other information is unchanged, the required return is obviously higher. In other words, the cost of capital for this project, if it is risky, is greater than the risk-free rate, and the appropriate discount rate would exceed the risk-free rate.

We will henceforth use the terms *required return, appropriate discount rate*, and *cost of capital* more or less interchangeably because, as the discussion in this section suggests, they all mean essentially the same thing. The key fact to grasp is that the cost of capital associated with an investment depends on the risk of that investment. This is one of the most important lessons in corporate finance, so it bears repeating:

> **The cost of capital depends primarily on the use of the funds, not the source.**

It is a common error to forget this crucial point and fall into the trap of thinking that the cost of capital for an investment depends primarily on how and where the capital is raised.

FINANCIAL POLICY AND COST OF CAPITAL

We know that the particular mixture of debt and equity a firm chooses to employ—its capital structure—is a managerial variable. In this chapter, we will take the firm's financial policy as given. In particular, we will assume that the firm has a fixed debt–equity ratio that it maintains. This ratio reflects the firm's *target* capital structure. How a firm might choose that ratio is the subject of a later chapter.

From the preceding discussion, we know that a firm's overall cost of capital will reflect the required return on the firm's assets as a whole. Given that a firm uses both debt and equity capital, this overall cost of capital will be a mixture of the returns needed to compensate its creditors and those needed to compensate its stockholders. In other words, a firm's cost of capital will reflect both its cost of debt capital and its cost of equity capital. We discuss these costs separately in the sections that follow.

Concept Questions

14.1a What is the primary determinant of the cost of capital for an investment?

14.1b What is the relationship between the required return on an investment and the cost of capital associated with that investment?

The Cost of Equity

14.2

We begin with the most difficult question on the subject of cost of capital: What is the firm's overall **cost of equity**? The reason this is a difficult question is that there is no way of directly observing the return that the firm's equity investors require on their investment. Instead, we must somehow estimate it. This section discusses two approaches to determining the cost of equity: the dividend growth model approach and the security market line (SML) approach.

cost of equity
The return that equity investors require on their investment in the firm.

THE DIVIDEND GROWTH MODEL APPROACH

The easiest way to estimate the cost of equity capital is to use the dividend growth model we developed in Chapter 8. Recall that, under the assumption that the firm's dividend will grow at a constant rate g, the price per share of the stock, P_0, can be written as:

$$P_0 = \frac{D_0 \times (1 + g)}{R_E - g} = \frac{D_1}{R_E - g}$$

where D_0 is the dividend just paid and D_1 is the next period's projected dividend. Notice that we have used the symbol R_E (the E stands for equity) for the required return on the stock.

As we discussed in Chapter 8, we can rearrange this to solve for R_E as follows:

$$R_E = D_1/P_0 + g \qquad\qquad [14.1]$$

Because R_E is the return that the shareholders require on the stock, it can be interpreted as the firm's cost of equity capital.

Implementing the Approach   To estimate R_E using the dividend growth model approach, we obviously need three pieces of information: P_0, D_0 and g.[2] Of these, for a publicly traded, dividend-paying company, the first two can be observed directly, so they are easily obtained. Only the third component, the expected growth rate for dividends, must be estimated.

---

[2] Notice that if we have D_0 and g, we can simply calculate D_1 by multiplying D_0 by $(1 + g)$.

To illustrate how we estimate R_E, suppose Greater States Public Service, a large public utility, paid a dividend of $4 per share last year. The stock currently sells for $60 per share. You estimate that the dividend will grow steadily at a rate of 6 percent per year into the indefinite future. What is the cost of equity capital for Greater States?

Using the dividend growth model, we can calculate that the expected dividend for the coming year, D_1, is:

$$D_1 = D_0 \times (1 + g)$$
$$= \$4 \times 1.06$$
$$= \$4.24$$

Given this, the cost of equity, R_E, is:

$$R_E = D_1/P_0 + g$$
$$= \$4.24/60 + .06$$
$$= 13.07\%$$

The cost of equity is thus 13.07 percent.

Estimating g   To use the dividend growth model, we must come up with an estimate for g, the growth rate. There are essentially two ways of doing this: (1) Use historical growth rates, or (2) use analysts' forecasts of future growth rates. Analysts' forecasts are available from a variety of sources. Naturally, different sources will have different estimates, so one approach might be to obtain multiple estimates and then average them.

Alternatively, we might observe dividends for the previous, say, five years, calculate the year-to-year growth rates, and average them. For example, suppose we observe the following for some company:

Year	Dividend
2005	$1.10
2006	1.20
2007	1.35
2008	1.40
2009	1.55

Growth estimates can be found at www.zacks.com.

We can calculate the percentage change in the dividend for each year as follows:

Year	Dividend	Dollar Change	Percentage Change
2005	$1.10	—	—
2006	1.20	$.10	9.09%
2007	1.35	.15	12.50
2008	1.40	.05	3.70
2009	1.55	.15	10.71

Notice that we calculated the change in the dividend on a year-to-year basis and then expressed the change as a percentage. Thus, in 2006 for example, the dividend rose from $1.10 to $1.20, an increase of $.10. This represents a $.10/1.10 = 9.09\% increase.

If we average the four growth rates, the result is $(9.09 + 12.50 + 3.70 + 10.71)/4 = 9\%$, so we could use this as an estimate for the expected growth rate, g. Notice that this 9 percent growth rate we have calculated is a simple, or arithmetic average. Going back to Chapter 12, we also could calculate a geometric growth rate. Here, the dividend grows from $1.10 to $1.55 over a four-year period. What's the compound, or geometric growth rate? See if you don't agree that it's 8.95 percent; you can view this as a simple time value of money problem where $1.10 is the present value and $1.55 is the future value.

As usual, the geometric average (8.95 percent) is lower than the arithmetic average (9 percent), but the difference here is not likely to be of any practical significance. In general, if the dividend has grown at a relatively steady rate, as we assume when we use this approach, then it can't make much difference which way we calculate the average dividend growth rate.

Advantages and Disadvantages of the Approach The primary advantage of the dividend growth model approach is its simplicity. It is both easy to understand and easy to use. There are a number of associated practical problems and disadvantages.

First and foremost, the dividend growth model is obviously applicable only to companies that pay dividends. This means that the approach is useless in many cases. Furthermore, even for companies that pay dividends, the key underlying assumption is that the dividend grows at a constant rate. As our previous example illustrates, this will never be *exactly* the case. More generally, the model is really applicable only to cases in which reasonably steady growth is likely to occur.

A second problem is that the estimated cost of equity is very sensitive to the estimated growth rate. For a given stock price, an upward revision of g by just one percentage point, for example, increases the estimated cost of equity by at least a full percentage point. Because D_1 will probably be revised upward as well, the increase will actually be somewhat larger than that.

Finally, this approach really does not explicitly consider risk. Unlike the SML approach (which we consider next), there is no direct adjustment for the riskiness of the investment. For example, there is no allowance for the degree of certainty or uncertainty surrounding the estimated growth rate for dividends. As a result, it is difficult to say whether or not the estimated return is commensurate with the level of risk.[3]

THE SML APPROACH

In Chapter 13, we discussed the security market line, or SML. Our primary conclusion was that the required or expected return on a risky investment depends on three things:

1. The risk-free rate, R_f.
2. The market risk premium, $E(R_M) - R_f$.
3. The systematic risk of the asset relative to average, which we called its beta coefficient, β.

Using the SML, we can write the expected return on the company's equity, $E(R_E)$, as:

$$E(R_E) = R_f + \beta_E \times [E(R_M) - R_f]$$

where β_E is the estimated beta. To make the SML approach consistent with the dividend growth model, we will drop the Es denoting expectations and henceforth write the required return from the SML, R_E as:

$$R_E = R_f + \beta_E \times (R_M - R_f) \tag{14.2}$$

---

[3] There is an implicit adjustment for risk because the current stock price is used. All other things being equal, the higher the risk, the lower is the stock price. Further, the lower the stock price, the greater is the cost of equity, again assuming all the other information is the same.

Betas and T-bill rates can both be found at www.bloomberg.com.

Implementing the Approach   To use the SML approach, we need a risk-free rate, R_f, an estimate of the market risk premium, $R_M - R_f$, and an estimate of the relevant beta, β_E. In Chapter 12, we saw that one estimate of the market risk premium (based on large common stocks) is about 7 percent. U.S. Treasury bills are paying about 1.83 percent as this chapter is being written, so we will use this as our risk-free rate. Beta coefficients for publicly traded companies are widely available.[4]

To illustrate, in Chapter 13, we saw that eBay had an estimated beta of 2.13 (Table 13.8). We could thus estimate eBay's cost of equity as:

$$R_{eBay} = R_f + \beta_{eBay} \times (R_M - R_f)$$
$$= 1.83\% + 2.13 \times 7\%$$
$$= 16.74\%$$

Thus, using the SML approach, we calculate that eBay's cost of equity is about 16.74 percent.

Advantages and Disadvantages of the Approach   The SML approach has two primary advantages. First, it explicitly adjusts for risk. Second, it is applicable to companies other than just those with steady dividend growth. Thus, it may be useful in a wider variety of circumstances.

There are drawbacks, of course. The SML approach requires that two things be estimated: the market risk premium and the beta coefficient. To the extent that our estimates are poor, the resulting cost of equity will be inaccurate. For example, our estimate of the market risk premium, 7 percent, is based on about 100 years of returns on particular stock portfolios and markets. Using different time periods or different stocks and markets could result in very different estimates.

Finally, as with the dividend growth model, we essentially rely on the past to predict the future when we use the SML approach. Economic conditions can change quickly; so as always, the past may not be a good guide to the future. In the best of all worlds, both approaches (the dividend growth model and the SML) are applicable and the two result in similar answers. If this happens, we might have some confidence in our estimates. We might also wish to compare the results to those for other similar companies as a reality check.

EXAMPLE 14.1	**The Cost of Equity**

Suppose stock in Alpha Air Freight has a beta of 1.2. The market risk premium is 7 percent, and the risk-free rate is 6 percent. Alpha's last dividend was $2 per share, and the dividend is expected to grow at 8 percent indefinitely. The stock currently sells for $30. What is Alpha's cost of equity capital?

We can start off by using the SML. Doing this, we find that the expected return on the common stock of Alpha Air Freight is:

$$R_E = R_f + \beta_E \times (R_M - R_f)$$
$$= 6\% + 1.2 \times 7\%$$
$$= 14.4\%$$

(continued)

---

[4] We can also estimate beta coefficients directly by using historical data. For a discussion of how to do this, see Chapters 9, 10, and 12 in S.A. Ross, R.W. Westerfield, and J.J. Jaffe, *Corporate Finance*, 8th ed. (New York: McGraw-Hill, 2008).

This suggests that 14.4 percent is Alpha's cost of equity. We next use the dividend growth model. The projected dividend is $D_0 \times (1 + g) = \$2 \times 1.08 = \$2.16$ so the expected return using this approach is:

$$R_E = D_1/P_0 + g$$
$$= \$2.16/30 + .08$$
$$= 15.2\%$$

Our two estimates are reasonably close, so we might just average them to find that Alpha's cost of equity is approximately 14.8 percent.

Concept Questions

14.2a What do we mean when we say that a corporation's cost of equity capital is 16 percent?

14.2b What are two approaches to estimating the cost of equity capital?

The Costs of Debt and Preferred Stock

14.3

In addition to ordinary equity, firms use debt and, to a lesser extent, preferred stock to finance their investments. As we discuss next, determining the costs of capital associated with these sources of financing is much easier than determining the cost of equity.

THE COST OF DEBT

The **cost of debt** is the return the firm's creditors demand on new borrowing. In principle, we could determine the beta for the firm's debt and then use the SML to estimate the required return on debt just as we estimated the required return on equity. This isn't really necessary, however.

cost of debt
The return that lenders require on the firm's debt.

Unlike a firm's cost of equity, its cost of debt can normally be observed either directly or indirectly: The cost of debt is simply the interest rate the firm must pay on new borrowing, and we can observe interest rates in the financial markets. For example, if the firm already has bonds outstanding, then the yield to maturity on those bonds is the market-required rate on the firm's debt.

Alternatively, if we know that the firm's bonds are rated, say, AA, then we can simply find the interest rate on newly issued AA-rated bonds. Either way, there is no need to estimate a beta for the debt because we can directly observe the rate we want to know.

There is one thing to be careful about, though. The coupon rate on the firm's outstanding debt is irrelevant here. That rate just tells us roughly what the firm's cost of debt was back when the bonds were issued, not what the cost of debt is today.[5] This is why we have to look at the yield on the debt in today's marketplace. For consistency with our other notation, we will use the symbol R_D for the cost of debt.

---

[5] The firm's cost of debt based on its historic borrowing is sometimes called the *embedded debt cost*.

EXAMPLE 14.2 | **The Cost of Debt**

Suppose the General Tool Company issued a 30-year, 7 percent bond 8 years ago. The bond is currently selling for 96 percent of its face value, or $960. What is General Tool's cost of debt?

Going back to Chapter 7, we need to calculate the yield to maturity on this bond. Because the bond is selling at a discount, the yield is apparently greater than 7 percent, but not much greater because the discount is fairly small. You can check to see that the yield to maturity is about 7.37 percent, assuming annual coupons. General Tool's cost of debt, R_D, is thus 7.37 percent.

THE COST OF PREFERRED STOCK

Determining the *cost of preferred stock* is quite straightforward. As we discussed in Chapters 6 and 8, preferred stock has a fixed dividend paid every period forever, so a share of preferred stock is essentially a perpetuity. The cost of preferred stock, R_P, is thus:

$$R_P = D/P_0 \qquad\qquad [14.3]$$

where D is the fixed dividend and P_0 is the current price per share of the preferred stock. Notice that the cost of preferred stock is simply equal to the dividend yield on the preferred stock. Alternatively, because preferred stocks are rated in much the same way as bonds, the cost of preferred stock can be estimated by observing the required returns on other, similarly rated shares of preferred stock.

EXAMPLE 14.3 | **Alabama Power Co.'s Cost of Preferred Stock**

On May 30, 2008, Alabama Power Co. had two issues of ordinary preferred stock with a $25 par value that traded on the NYSE. One issue paid $1.30 annually per share and sold for $21.05 per share. The other paid $1.46 per share annually and sold for $24.35 per share. What is Alabama Power's cost of preferred stock?

Using the first issue, we calculate that the cost of preferred stock is:

$$R_P = D/P_0$$
$$= \$1.30/21.05$$
$$= 6.2\%$$

Using the second issue, we calculate that the cost is:

$$R_P = D/P_0$$
$$= \$1.46/24.35$$
$$= 6\%$$

So, Alabama Power's cost of preferred stock appears to be about 6.1 percent.

Concept Questions

14.3a Why is the coupon rate a bad estimate of a firm's cost of debt?

14.3b How can the cost of debt be calculated?

14.3c How can the cost of preferred stock be calculated?

The Weighted Average Cost of Capital

14.4

Now that we have the costs associated with the main sources of capital the firm employs, we need to worry about the specific mix. As we mentioned earlier, we will take this mix, which is the firm's capital structure, as given for now. Also, we will focus mostly on debt and ordinary equity in this discussion.

In Chapter 3, we mentioned that financial analysts frequently focus on a firm's total capitalization, which is the sum of its long-term debt and equity. This is particularly true in determining cost of capital; short-term liabilities are often ignored in the process. We will not explicitly distinguish between total value and total capitalization in the following discussion; the general approach is applicable with either.

THE CAPITAL STRUCTURE WEIGHTS

We will use the symbol E (for equity) to stand for the *market* value of the firm's equity. We calculate this by taking the number of shares outstanding and multiplying it by the price per share. Similarly, we will use the symbol D (for debt) to stand for the *market* value of the firm's debt. For long-term debt, we calculate this by multiplying the market price of a single bond by the number of bonds outstanding.

If there are multiple bond issues (as there normally would be), we repeat this calculation of D for each and then add up the results. If there is debt that is not publicly traded (because it is held by a life insurance company, for example), we must observe the yield on similar publicly traded debt and then estimate the market value of the privately held debt using this yield as the discount rate. For short-term debt, the book (accounting) values and market values should be somewhat similar, so we might use the book values as estimates of the market values.

Finally, we will use the symbol V (for value) to stand for the combined market value of the debt and equity:

$$V = E + D \qquad\qquad\qquad \text{[14.4]}$$

If we divide both sides by V, we can calculate the percentages of the total capital represented by the debt and equity:

$$100\% = E/V + D/V \qquad\qquad\qquad \text{[14.5]}$$

These percentages can be interpreted just like portfolio weights, and they are often called the *capital structure weights*.

For example, if the total market value of a company's stock were calculated as $200 million and the total market value of the company's debt were calculated as $50 million, then the combined value would be $250 million. Of this total, $E/V = $200 million/250 million = 80\%$, so 80 percent of the firm's financing would be equity and the remaining 20 percent would be debt.

We emphasize here that the correct way to proceed is to use the *market* values of the debt and equity. Under certain circumstances, such as when calculating figures for a privately owned company, it may not be possible to get reliable estimates of these quantities. In this case, we might go ahead and use the accounting values for debt and equity. Although this would probably be better than nothing, we would have to take the answer with a grain of salt.

TAXES AND THE WEIGHTED AVERAGE COST OF CAPITAL

There is one final issue we need to discuss. Recall that we are always concerned with after-tax cash flows. If we are determining the discount rate appropriate to those cash flows, then the discount rate also needs to be expressed on an aftertax basis.

As we discussed previously in various places in this book (and as we will discuss later), the interest paid by a corporation is deductible for tax purposes. Payments to stockholders, such as dividends, are not. What this means, effectively, is that the government pays some of the interest. Thus, in determining an aftertax discount rate, we need to distinguish between the pretax and the aftertax cost of debt.

To illustrate, suppose a firm borrows $1 million at 9 percent interest. The corporate tax rate is 34 percent. What is the aftertax interest rate on this loan? The total interest bill will be $90,000 per year. This amount is tax deductible, however, so the $90,000 interest reduces the firm's tax bill by $.34 \times \$90,000 = \$30,600$. The aftertax interest bill is thus $\$90,000 - 30,600 = \$59,400$. The aftertax interest rate is thus $\$59,400/1$ million $= 5.94\%$.

Notice that, in general, the aftertax interest rate is simply equal to the pretax rate multiplied by 1 minus the tax rate. If we use the symbol T_C to stand for the corporate tax rate, then the aftertax rate can be written as $R_D \times (1 - T_C)$. For example, using the numbers from the preceding paragraph, we find that the aftertax interest rate is $9\% \times (1 - .34) = 5.94\%$.

Bringing together the various topics we have discussed in this chapter, we now have the capital structure weights along with the cost of equity and the aftertax cost of debt. To calculate the firm's overall cost of capital, we multiply the capital structure weights by the associated costs and add them up. The total is the **weighted average cost of capital** (**WACC**):

$$\text{WACC} = (E/V) \times R_E + (D/V) \times R_D \times (1 - T_C)$$ [14.6]

This WACC has a straightforward interpretation. It is the overall return the firm must earn on its existing assets to maintain the value of its stock. It is also the required return on any investments by the firm that have essentially the same risks as existing operations. So, if we were evaluating the cash flows from a proposed expansion of our existing operations, this is the discount rate we would use.

If a firm uses preferred stock in its capital structure, then our expression for the WACC needs a simple extension. If we define P/V as the percentage of the firm's financing that comes from preferred stock, then the WACC is simply:

$$\text{WACC} = (E/V) \times R_E + (P/V) \times R_P + (D/V) \times R_D \times (1 - T_C)$$ [14.7]

where R_P is the cost of preferred stock.

To get a feel for actual, industry-level WACCs, visit www.ibbotson.com.

weighted average cost of capital (WACC)
The weighted average of the cost of equity and the aftertax cost of debt.

EXAMPLE 14.4　**Calculating the WACC**

The B.B. Lean Co. has 1.4 million shares of stock outstanding. The stock currently sells for $20 per share. The firm's debt is publicly traded and was recently quoted at 93 percent of face value. It has a total face value of $5 million, and it is currently priced to yield 11 percent. The risk-free rate is 8 percent, and the market risk premium is 7 percent. You've estimated that Lean has a beta of .74. If the corporate tax rate is 34 percent, what is the WACC of Lean Co.?

We can first determine the cost of equity and the cost of debt. Using the SML, we find that the cost of equity is $8\% + .74 \times 7\% = 13.18\%$. The total value of the equity is 1.4 million $\times \$20 = \$28$ million. The pretax cost of debt is the current yield to maturity on the

(continued)

outstanding debt, 11 percent. The debt sells for 93 percent of its face value, so its current market value is .93 × $5 million = $4.65 million. The total market value of the equity and debt together is $28 million + 4.65 million = $32.65 million.

From here, we can calculate the WACC easily enough. The percentage of equity used by Lean to finance its operations is $28 million/$32.65 million = 85.76%. Because the weights have to add up to 1, the percentage of debt is 1 − .8576 = 14.24%. The WACC is thus:

$$WACC = (E/V) \times R_E + (D/V) \times R_D \times (1 - T_C)$$
$$= .8576 \times 13.18\% + .1424 \times 11\% \times (1 - .34)$$
$$= 12.34\%$$

B.B. Lean thus has an overall weighted average cost of capital of 12.34 percent.

CALCULATING THE WACC FOR EASTMAN CHEMICAL

In this section, we illustrate how to calculate the WACC for Eastman Chemical Co., a leading international chemical company and maker of plastics such as those used in soft drink containers. It was created in 1993, when its former parent company, Eastman Kodak, split off the division as a separate company. Our goal is to take you through, on a step-by-step basis, the process of finding and using the information needed using online sources. As you will see, there is a fair amount of detail involved, but the necessary information is, for the most part, readily available.

Eastman's Cost of Equity   Our first stop is the main screen for Eastman available at finance.yahoo.com (ticker: EMN). As of mid-2008, here's what it looked like:

EASTMAN CHEM CO (NYSE: EMN)
After Hours: 76.5576 ↓-.05 (-.07%) 5:21pm ET

Last Trade:	**76.61**	Day's Range:	75.85 - 78.29
Trade Time:	**May 30**	52wk Range:	56.31 - 78.29
Change:	↓.28 (.36%)	Volume:	852,688
Prev Close:	76.89	Avg Vol (3m):	978,780
Open:	76.68	Market Cap:	5.83B
Bid:	N/A	P/E (ttm):	17.74
Ask:	N/A	EPS (ttm):	4.32
1y Target Est:	82.75	Div & Yield:	1.76 (2.30%)

Next, we went to the "Key Statistics" screen. According to this screen, Eastman has 76.15 million shares of stock outstanding. The book value per share is $24.898, but the stock sells for $76.61. Total equity is therefore about $1.896 billion on a book value basis, but it is closer to $5.834 billion on a market value basis.

Balance Sheet	
Total Cash (mrq):	793.00M
Total Cash Per Share (mrq):	10.413
Total Debt (mrq):	1.69B
Total Debt/Equity (mrq):	.89
Current Ratio (mrq):	2.014
Book Value Per Share (mrq):	24.898001

Stock Price History	
Beta:	.49
52-Week Change[3]:	15.48%
S&P500 52-Week Change[3]:	-8.85%
52-Week High (30-May-08)[3]:	78.29
52-Week Low (23-Jan-08)[3]:	56.31
50-Day Moving Average[3]:	73.47
200-Day Moving Average[3]:	66.21
Share Statistics	
Average Volume (3 month)[3]:	978,780
Average Volume (10 day)[3]:	640,912
Shares Outstanding[5]:	76.15M
Float:	70.72M
% Held by Insiders[1]:	14.13%
% Held by Institutions[1]:	76.70%
Shares Short (as of 12-May-08)[3]:	7.70M
Short Ratio (as of 12-May-08)[3]:	9
Short % of Float (as of 12-May-08)[3]:	10.20%
Shares Short (prior month)[3]:	6.98M

To estimate Eastman's cost of equity, we will assume a market risk premium of 7 percent, similar to what we calculated in Chapter 12. Eastman's beta on Yahoo! is .49, which is much lower than the beta of the average stock. To check this number, we went to finance.google.com and www.reuters.com. The beta estimates we found there were .85 and .96. These estimates are more realistic, and some financial judgment is required here. Because the beta estimate from Yahoo! is so much lower, we will ignore it and use an average of the other two betas. Thus, the beta estimate we will use is .905. According to the bond section of finance.yahoo.com, T-bills were paying about 1.83 percent. Using the CAPM to estimate the cost of equity, we find:

$$R_E = .0183 + .905(.07) = .0817 \text{ or } 8.17\%$$

Eastman has paid dividends for only a few years, so calculating the growth rate for the dividend discount model is problematic. However, under the analysts' estimates link at finance.yahoo.com, we found the following:

Growth Est	EMN	Industry	Sector	S&P 500
Current Qtr.	16.4%	18.9%	11.4%	-7.7%
Next Qtr.	7.1%	-4.9%	30.5%	18.7%
This Year	10.3%	24.0%	24.4%	8.1%
Next Year	.5%	19.9%	25.1%	19.1%
Past 5 Years (per annum)	36.097%	N/A	N/A	N/A
Next 5 Years (per annum)	6.5%	10.29%	10.34%	N/A
Price/Earnings (avg. for comparison categories)	13.78	17.1	16.67	15.19
PEG Ratio (avg. for comparison categories)	2.12	1.66	1.61	N/A

Analysts estimate the growth in earnings per share for the company will be 6.5 percent for the next five years. For now, we will use this growth rate in the dividend discount model to estimate the cost of equity; the link between earnings growth and dividends is discussed in a later chapter. The estimated cost of equity using the dividend discount model is:

$$R_E = \left[\frac{\$1.76\,(1 + .065)}{\$76.61} \right] + .065 = .0895 \text{ or } 8.95\%$$

Notice that the estimates for the cost of equity are different. This is often the case. Remember that each method of estimating the cost of equity relies on different assumptions, so different estimates of the cost of equity should not surprise us. If the estimates are different, there are two simple solutions. First, we could ignore one of the estimates. We would look at each estimate to see if one of them seemed too high or too low to be reasonable. Second, we could average the two estimates. Averaging the two estimates for Eastman's cost of equity gives us a cost of equity of 8.56 percent. This seems like a reasonable number, so we will use it in calculating the cost of capital in this example.

Eastman's Cost of Debt Eastman has six relatively long-term bond issues that account for essentially all of its long-term debt. To calculate the cost of debt, we will have to combine these six issues. What we will do is compute a weighted average. We went to www.finra.org/marketdata to find quotes on the bonds. We should note here that finding the yield to maturity for all of a company's outstanding bond issues on a single day is unusual. If you remember our previous discussion of bonds, the bond market is not as liquid as the stock market; on many days, individual bond issues may not trade. To find the book value of the bonds, we went to www.sec.gov and found the 10Q report dated March 31, 2008, and filed with the SEC on April 29, 2008. The basic information is as follows:

Coupon Rate	Maturity	Book Value (Face Value, in Millions)	Price (% of Par)	Yield to Maturity
3.25%	2008	$ 72	99.989	3.526%
7.00	2012	153	106.504	5.184
6.30	2018	195	98.750	6.465
7.25	2024	497	104.300	6.797
7.625	2024	200	105.840	7.013
7.60	2027	298	103.500	7.253

To calculate the weighted average cost of debt, we take the percentage of the total debt represented by each issue and multiply by the yield on the issue. We then add to get the overall weighted average debt cost. We use both book values and market values here for comparison. The results of the calculations are as follows:

Coupon Rate	Book Value (Face Value, in Millions)	Percentage of Total	Market Value (in Millions)	Percentage of Total	Yield to Maturity	Book Values	Market Values
3.25%	$ 72	.05	$ 71.99	.05	3.53%	.18%	.17%
7.00	153	.11	162.95	.11	5.18	.56	.58
6.30	195	.14	192.56	.13	6.47	.89	.85
7.25	497	.35	518.37	.35	6.80	2.39	2.40
7.625	200	.14	211.68	.14	7.01	.99	1.01
7.60	298	.21	308.43	.21	7.25	1.53	1.53
	$1,415	1.00	$1,465.99	1.00		6.54%	6.54%

As these calculations show, Eastman's cost of debt is 6.54 percent on a book value basis and 6.54 percent on a market value basis. Thus, for Eastman, whether market values or book values are used makes no difference. The reason is simply that the market values and book values are similar. This will often be the case and explains why companies frequently use book values for debt in WACC calculations. Also, Eastman has no preferred stock, so we don't need to consider its cost.

Eastman's WACC   We now have the various pieces necessary to calculate Eastman's WACC. First, we need to calculate the capital structure weights. On a book value basis, Eastman's equity and debt are worth $1.896 billion and $1.415 billion, respectively. The total value is $3.311 billion, so the equity and debt weights are $1.896 billion/3.311 billion = .57 and $1.415 billion/3.311 billion = .43, respectively. Assuming a tax rate of 35 percent, Eastman's WACC is:

$$\text{WACC} = .57 \times 8.56\% + .43 \times 6.54\% \times (1 - .35) = 6.72\%$$

Thus, using book value capital structure weights, we get about 6.72 percent for Eastman's WACC.

If we use market value weights, however, the WACC will be higher. To see why, notice that on a market value basis, Eastman's equity and debt are worth $5.834 billion and $1.466 billion, respectively. The capital structure weights are therefore $5.834 billion/7.300 billion = .80 and $1.466 billion/7.300 billion = .20, so the equity percentage is much higher. With these weights, Eastman's WACC is:

$$\text{WACC} = .80 \times 8.56\% + .20 \times 6.54\% \times (1 - .35) = 7.69\%$$

Thus, using market value weights, we get about 7.69 percent for Eastman's WACC, which is about 1 percent higher than the 6.72 percent WACC we got using book value weights.

As this example illustrates, using book values can lead to trouble, particularly if equity book values are used. Going back to Chapter 3, recall that we discussed the market-to-book ratio (the ratio of market value per share to book value per share). This ratio is usually substantially bigger than 1. For Eastman, for example, verify that it's about 3.08; so book values significantly overstate the percentage of Eastman's financing that comes from debt. In addition, if we were computing a WACC for a company that did not have publicly traded stock, we would try to come up with a suitable market-to-book ratio by looking at publicly traded companies, and we would then use this ratio to adjust the book value of the company under consideration. As we have seen, failure to do so can lead to significant underestimation of the WACC.

Our nearby *Work the Web* box explains more about the WACC and related topics.

SOLVING THE WAREHOUSE PROBLEM AND SIMILAR CAPITAL BUDGETING PROBLEMS

Now we can use the WACC to solve the warehouse problem we posed at the beginning of the chapter. However, before we rush to discount the cash flows at the WACC to estimate NPV, we need to make sure we are doing the right thing.

Going back to first principles, we need to find an alternative in the financial markets that is comparable to the warehouse renovation. To be comparable, an alternative must be of the same level of risk as the warehouse project. Projects that have the same risk are said to be in the same risk class.

The WACC for a firm reflects the risk and the target capital structure of the firm's existing assets as a whole. As a result, strictly speaking, the firm's WACC is the appropriate discount rate only if the proposed investment is a replica of the firm's existing operating activities.

WORK THE WEB

So how does our estimate of the WACC for Eastman Chemical compare to others? One place to find estimates for WACC is www.valuepro.net. We went there and found the following information for Eastman:

Online Valuation for EMN - 6 / 1 / 2008

Intrinsic Stock Value [88.06]   [Recalculate]   [Value Another Stock]

Excess Return Period (yrs)	10	Depreciation Rate (% of Rev)	4.13
Revenues ($mil)	6920.0	Investment Rate (% of Rev)	5.22
Growth Rate (%)	7.5	Working Capital (% of Rev)	10.51
Net Oper. Profit Margin (%)	8.31	Short-Term Assets ($mil)	2297.0
Tax Rate (%)	32.795	Short-Term Liab. ($mil)	1081
Stock Price ($)	73.9100	Equity Risk Premium (%)	3
Shares Outstanding (mil)	80.9	Company Beta	1.2075
10-Yr Treasury Yield (%)	5	Value Debt Out. ($mil)	1522
Bond Spread Treasury (%)	1.5	Value Pref. Stock Out. ($mil)	0
Preferred Stock Yield (%)	7.5	Company WACC (%)	7.76

As you can see, ValuePro estimates the WACC (Cost of Capital) for Eastman as 7.76 percent, which is about the same as our estimate of 7.69 percent. However, different inputs were used in the computations. For example, ValuePro uses an equity risk premium of only 3 percent. Calculating WACC requires the estimation of various inputs, and you must use your best judgment in these estimates.

Questions

1. Go to www.valuepro.net and look up the current WACC for Eastman Chemical on this Web site. How has the WACC changed? What are the possible reasons for the change?
2. Human Genome Sciences, Inc. (HGSI) is a biopharmaceutical company. Would you expect the WACC for this company to be higher or lower than the WACC for Eastman Chemical? Why? Go to www.valuepro.net and find the estimated WACC for HGSI. Was your assumption correct?

In broader terms, whether or not we can use the firm's WACC to value the warehouse project depends on whether the warehouse project is in the same risk class as the firm. We will assume that this project is an integral part of the overall business of the firm. In such cases, it is natural to think that the cost savings will be as risky as the general cash flows of the firm, and the project will thus be in the same risk class as the overall firm. More generally, projects like the warehouse renovation that are intimately related to the firm's existing operations are often viewed as being in the same risk class as the overall firm.

We can now see what the president should do. Suppose the firm has a target debt–equity ratio of $1/3$. From Chapter 3, we know that a debt–equity ratio of $D/E = 1/3$ implies that E/V is .75 and D/V is .25. The cost of debt is 10 percent, and the cost of equity is 20 percent. Assuming a 34 percent tax rate, the WACC will be:

$$\text{WACC} = (E/V) \times R_E + (D/V) \times R_D \times (1 - T_C)$$
$$= .75 \times 20\% + .25 \times 10\% \times (1 - .34)$$
$$= 16.65\%$$

Recall that the warehouse project had a cost of $50 million and expected aftertax cash flows (the cost savings) of $12 million per year for six years. The NPV (in millions) is thus:

$$\text{NPV} = -\$50 + \frac{12}{(1 + \text{WACC})^1} + \cdots + \frac{12}{(1+\text{WACC})^6}$$

Because the cash flows are in the form of an ordinary annuity, we can calculate this NPV using 16.65 percent (the WACC) as the discount rate as follows:

$$\text{NPV} = -\$50 + 12 \times \frac{1 - [1/(1 + .1665)^6]}{.1665}$$
$$= -\$50 + 12 \times 3.6222$$
$$= -\$6.53$$

Should the firm take on the warehouse renovation? The project has a negative NPV using the firm's WACC. This means that the financial markets offer superior projects in the same risk class (namely, the firm itself). The answer is clear: The project should be rejected. For future reference, our discussion of the WACC is summarized in Table 14.1.

EXAMPLE 14.5 | **Using the WACC**

A firm is considering a project that will result in initial aftertax cash savings of $5 million at the end of the first year. These savings will grow at the rate of 5 percent per year. The firm has a debt–equity ratio of .5, a cost of equity of 29.2 percent, and a cost of debt of 10 percent. The cost-saving proposal is closely related to the firm's core business, so it is viewed as having the same risk as the overall firm. Should the firm take on the project?

Assuming a 34 percent tax rate, the firm should take on this project if it costs less than $30 million. To see this, first note that the PV is:

$$\text{PV} = \frac{\$5 \text{ million}}{\text{WACC} - .05}$$

This is an example of a growing perpetuity as discussed in Chapter 6. The WACC is:

$$\text{WACC} = (E/V) \times R_E + (D/V) \times R_D \times (1 - T_C)$$
$$= 2/3 \times 29.2\% + 1/3 \times 10\% \times (1 - .34)$$
$$= 21.67\%$$

The PV is thus:

$$\text{PV} = \frac{\$5 \text{ million}}{.2167 - .05} = \$30 \text{ million}$$

The NPV will be positive only if the cost is less than $30 million.

TABLE 14.1

Summary of Capital Cost Calculations

I. The Cost of Equity, R_E

    A. Dividend growth model approach (from Chapter 8):

        $R_E = D_1/P_0 + g$

        where D_1 is the expected dividend in one period, g is the dividend growth rate, and P_0 is the current stock price.

    B. SML approach (from Chapter 13):

        $R_E = R_f + \beta_E \times (R_M - R_f)$

        where R_f is the risk-free rate, R_M is the expected return on the overall market, and β_E is the systematic risk of the equity.

II. The Cost of Debt, R_D

    A. For a firm with publicly held debt, the cost of debt can be measured as the yield to maturity on the outstanding debt. The coupon rate is irrelevant. Yield to maturity is covered in Chapter 7.

    B. If the firm has no publicly traded debt, then the cost of debt can be measured as the yield to maturity on similarly rated bonds (bond ratings are discussed in Chapter 7).

III. The Weighted Average Cost of Capital, WACC

    A. The firm's WACC is the overall required return on the firm as a whole. It is the appropriate discount rate to use for cash flows similar in risk to those of the overall firm.

    B. The WACC is calculated as:

        $WACC = (E/V) \times R_E + (D/V) \times R_D \times (1 - T_C)$

        where T_C is the corporate tax rate, E is the *market* value of the firm's equity, D is the *market* value of the firm's debt, and $V = E + D$. Note that E/V is the percentage of the firm's financing (in market value terms) that is equity, and D/V is the percentage that is debt.

PERFORMANCE EVALUATION: ANOTHER USE OF THE WACC

Performance evaluation is another use of the WACC. Probably the best-known approach in this area is the economic value added (EVA) method developed by Stern Stewart and Co. Companies such as AT&T, Coca-Cola, Quaker Oats, and Briggs and Stratton are among the firms that have been using EVA as a means of evaluating corporate performance. Similar approaches include market value added (MVA) and shareholder value added (SVA).

Visit www.sternstewart.com *for more about EVA.*

Although the details differ, the basic idea behind EVA and similar strategies is straightforward. Suppose we have $100 million in capital (debt and equity) tied up in our firm, and our overall WACC is 12 percent. If we multiply these together, we get $12 million. Referring back to Chapter 2, if our cash flow from assets is less than this, we are, on an overall basis, destroying value; if cash flow from assets exceeds $12 million, we are creating value.

In practice, evaluation strategies such as these suffer to a certain extent from problems with implementation. For example, it appears that many companies make extensive use of book values for debt and equity in computing cost of capital. Even so, by focusing on value creation, WACC-based evaluation procedures force employees and management to pay attention to the real bottom line: increasing share prices.

A firm's weighted average cost of capital has important applications other than the discount rate in capital project evaluations. For instance, it is a key ingredient to measure a firm's true economic profit, or what I like to call EVA, standing for economic value added. Accounting rules dictate that the interest expense a company incurs on its debt financing be deducted from its reported profit, but those same rules ironically forbid deducting a charge for the shareholders' funds a firm uses. In economic terms, equity capital is in fact a very costly financing source, because shareholders bear the risk of being paid last, after all other stakeholders and investors are paid first. But according to accountants, shareholders' equity is free.

This egregious oversight has dire practical consequences. For one thing, it means that the profit figure accountants certify to be correct is inherently at odds with the net present value decision rule. For instance, it is a simple matter for management to inflate its reported earnings and earnings-per-share in ways that actually harm the shareholders by investing capital in projects that earn less than the overall cost of capital but more than the aftertax cost of borrowing money, which amounts to a trivial hurdle in most cases, a couple percentage points at most. In effect, EPS requires management to vault a mere three foot hurdle when to satisfy shareholders managers must jump a ten foot hurdle that includes the cost of equity. A prime example of the way accounting profit leads smart managers to do dumb things was Enron, where former top executives Ken Lay and Jeff Skilling boldly declared in the firm's 2000 annual report that they were "laser-focused on earnings per share," and so they were. Bonuses were funded out of book profit, and project developers were paid for signing up new deals and not generating a decent return on investment. Consequently, Enron's EPS was on the rise while its true economic profit—its EVA—measured after deducting the full cost of capital, was plummeting in the years leading up to the firm's demise—the result of massive misallocations of capital to ill-advised energy and new economy projects. The point is, EVA measures economic profit, the profit that actually discounts to net present value, and the maximization of which is every company's most important financial goal; yet for all its popularity EPS is just an accounting contrivance that is wholly unrelated to the maximization of shareholder wealth or sending the right decision signals to management.

Starting in the early 1990s firms around the world—ranging from Coca-Cola, to Briggs & Stratton, Herman Miller, and Eli Lilly in America, Siemens in Germany, Tata Consulting and the Godrej Group out of India, Brahma Beer in Brazil, and many, many more—began to turn to EVA as a new and better way to measure performance and set goals, make decisions and determine bonuses, and to communicate with investors and to teach business and finance basics to managers and employees. Properly tailored and implemented, EVA is a natural way to bring the cost of capital to life, and to turn everyone in a company into a capital conscientious, owner-entrepreneur.

Bennett Stewart is a co-founder of Stern Stewart & Co. and also the CEO of EVA Dimensions, a firm providing EVA data, valuation modeling, and hedge fund management. Stewart pioneered the practical development of EVA as chronicled in his book, The Quest for Value.

Concept Questions

14.4a How is the WACC calculated?

14.4b Why do we multiply the cost of debt by $(1 - T_C)$ when we compute the WACC?

14.4c Under what conditions is it correct to use the WACC to determine NPV?

14.5 Divisional and Project Costs of Capital

As we have seen, using the WACC as the discount rate for future cash flows is appropriate only when the proposed investment is similar to the firm's existing activities. This is not as restrictive as it sounds. If we are in the pizza business, for example, and we are thinking of opening a new location, then the WACC is the discount rate to use. The same is true of a retailer thinking of a new store, a manufacturer thinking of expanding production, or a consumer products company thinking of expanding its markets.

Nonetheless, despite the usefulness of the WACC as a benchmark, there will clearly be situations in which the cash flows under consideration have risks distinctly different from those of the overall firm. We consider how to cope with this problem next.

THE SML AND THE WACC

When we are evaluating investments with risks that are substantially different from those of the overall firm, use of the WACC will potentially lead to poor decisions. Figure 14.1 illustrates why.

In Figure 14.1, we have plotted an SML corresponding to a risk-free rate of 7 percent and a market risk premium of 8 percent. To keep things simple, we consider an all-equity company with a beta of 1. As we have indicated, the WACC and the cost of equity are exactly equal to 15 percent for this company because there is no debt.

Suppose our firm uses its WACC to evaluate all investments. This means that any investment with a return of greater than 15 percent will be accepted and any investment with a return of less than 15 percent will be rejected. We know from our study of risk and return, however, that a desirable investment is one that plots above the SML. As Figure 14.1 illustrates, using the WACC for all types of projects can result in the firm's incorrectly accepting relatively risky projects and incorrectly rejecting relatively safe ones.

FIGURE 14.1   The Security Market Line (SML) and the Weighted Average Cost of Capital (WACC)

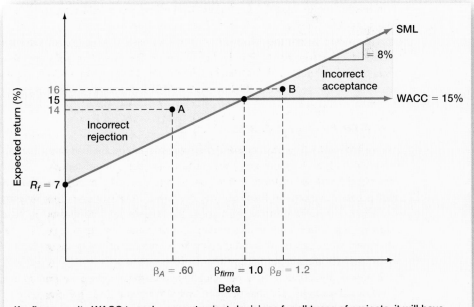

If a firm uses its WACC to make accept–reject decisions for all types of projects, it will have a tendency toward incorrectly accepting risky projects and incorrectly rejecting less risky projects.

For example, consider point A. This project has a beta of $\beta_A = .60$, as compared to the firm's beta of 1.0. It has an expected return of 14 percent. Is this a desirable investment? The answer is yes because its required return is only:

$$\text{Required return} = R_f + \beta_A \times (R_M - R_f)$$
$$= 7\% + .60 \times 8\%$$
$$= 11.8\%$$

However, if we use the WACC as a cutoff, then this project will be rejected because its return is less than 15 percent. This example illustrates that a firm that uses its WACC as a cutoff will tend to reject profitable projects with risks less than those of the overall firm.

At the other extreme, consider point B. This project has a beta of $\beta_B = 1.2$. It offers a 16 percent return, which exceeds the firm's cost of capital. This is not a good investment, however, because, given its level of systematic risk, its return is inadequate. Nonetheless, if we use the WACC to evaluate it, it will appear to be attractive. So the second error that will arise if we use the WACC as a cutoff is that we will tend to make unprofitable investments with risks greater than those of the overall firm. As a consequence, through time, a firm that uses its WACC to evaluate all projects will have a tendency to both accept unprofitable investments and become increasingly risky.

DIVISIONAL COST OF CAPITAL

The same type of problem with the WACC can arise in a corporation with more than one line of business. Imagine, for example, a corporation that has two divisions: a regulated telephone company and an electronics manufacturing operation. The first of these (the phone operation) has relatively low risk; the second has relatively high risk.

In this case, the firm's overall cost of capital is really a mixture of two different costs of capital, one for each division. If the two divisions were competing for resources, and the firm used a single WACC as a cutoff, which division would tend to be awarded greater funds for investment?

The answer is that the riskier division would tend to have greater returns (ignoring the greater risk), so it would tend to be the "winner." The less glamorous operation might have great profit potential that would end up being ignored. Large corporations in the United States are aware of this problem, and many work to develop separate divisional costs of capital.

THE PURE PLAY APPROACH

We've seen that using the firm's WACC inappropriately can lead to problems. How can we come up with the appropriate discount rates in such circumstances? Because we cannot observe the returns on these investments, there generally is no direct way of coming up with a beta, for example. Instead, what we must do is examine other investments outside the firm that are in the same risk class as the one we are considering, and use the market-required return on these investments as the discount rate. In other words, we will try to determine what the cost of capital is for such investments by trying to locate some similar investments in the marketplace.

For example, going back to our telephone division, suppose we wanted to come up with a discount rate to use for that division. What we could do is identify several other phone companies that have publicly traded securities. We might find that a typical phone company has a beta of .80, AA-rated debt, and a capital structure that is about 50 percent debt and 50 percent equity. Using this information, we could develop a WACC for a typical phone company and use this as our discount rate.

Alternatively, if we were thinking of entering a new line of business, we would try to develop the appropriate cost of capital by looking at the market-required returns on companies already in that business. In the language of Wall Street, a company that focuses on a single line of business is called a *pure play*. For example, if you wanted to bet on the price of crude oil by purchasing common stocks, you would try to identify companies that dealt exclusively with this product because they would be the most affected by changes in the price of crude oil. Such companies would be called "pure plays on the price of crude oil."

What we try to do here is to find companies that focus as exclusively as possible on the type of project in which we are interested. Our approach, therefore, is called the **pure play approach** to estimating the required return on an investment. To illustrate, suppose McDonald's decides to enter the personal computer and network server business with a line of machines called McPuters. The risks involved are quite different from those in the fast-food business. As a result, McDonald's would need to look at companies already in the personal computer business to compute a cost of capital for the new division. An obvious pure play candidate would be Dell, which is predominantly in this line of business. HP, on the other hand, would not be as good a choice because its primary focus is elsewhere, and it has many different product lines.

In Chapter 3, we discussed the subject of identifying similar companies for comparison purposes. The same problems we described there come up here. The most obvious one is that we may not be able to find any suitable companies. In this case, how to objectively determine a discount rate becomes a difficult question. Even so, the important thing is to be aware of the issue so that we at least reduce the possibility of the kinds of mistakes that can arise when the WACC is used as a cutoff on all investments.

pure play approach
The use of a WACC that is unique to a particular project, based on companies in similar lines of business.

THE SUBJECTIVE APPROACH

Because of the difficulties that exist in objectively establishing discount rates for individual projects, firms often adopt an approach that involves making subjective adjustments to the overall WACC. To illustrate, suppose a firm has an overall WACC of 14 percent. It places all proposed projects into four categories as follows:

Category	Examples	Adjustment Factor	Discount Rate
High risk	New products	+6%	20%
Moderate risk	Cost savings, expansion of existing lines	+0	14
Low risk	Replacement of existing equipment	−4	10
Mandatory	Pollution control equipment	n/a	n/a

n/a = Not applicable.

The effect of this crude partitioning is to assume that all projects either fall into one of three risk classes or else are mandatory. In the last case, the cost of capital is irrelevant because the project must be taken. With the subjective approach, the firm's WACC may change through time as economic conditions change. As this happens, the discount rates for the different types of projects will also change.

Within each risk class, some projects will presumably have more risk than others, and the danger of making incorrect decisions still exists. Figure 14.2 illustrates this point. Comparing Figures 14.1 and 14.2, we see that similar problems exist; but the magnitude of the potential error is less with the subjective approach. For example, the project labeled A

FIGURE 14.2   The Security Market Line (SML) and the Subjective Approach

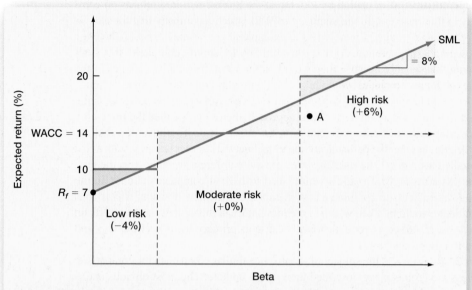

With the subjective approach, the firm places projects into one of several risk classes. The discount rate used to value the project is then determined by adding (for high risk) or subtracting (for low risk) an adjustment factor to or from the firm's WACC. This results in fewer incorrect decisions than if the firm simply used the WACC to make the decisions.

would be accepted if the WACC were used, but it is rejected once it is classified as a high-risk investment. What this illustrates is that some risk adjustment, even if it is subjective, is probably better than no risk adjustment.

It would be better, in principle, to objectively determine the required return for each project separately. However, as a practical matter, it may not be possible to go much beyond subjective adjustments because either the necessary information is unavailable or the cost and effort required are simply not worthwhile.

Concept Questions

14.5a What are the likely consequences if a firm uses its WACC to evaluate all proposed investments?

14.5b What is the pure play approach to determining the appropriate discount rate? When might it be used?

14.6   Flotation Costs and the Weighted Average Cost of Capital

So far, we have not included issue, or flotation, costs in our discussion of the weighted average cost of capital. If a company accepts a new project, it may be required to issue, or float, new bonds and stocks. This means that the firm will incur some costs, which we call *flotation costs*. The nature and magnitude of flotation costs are discussed in some detail in Chapter 15.

Sometimes it is suggested that the firm's WACC should be adjusted upward to reflect flotation costs. This is really not the best approach because, once again, the required return on an investment depends on the risk of the investment, not the source of the funds. This is not to say that flotation costs should be ignored. Because these costs arise as a consequence of the decision to undertake a project, they are relevant cash flows. We therefore briefly discuss how to include them in project analysis.

THE BASIC APPROACH

We start with a simple case. The Spatt Company, an all-equity firm, has a cost of equity of 20 percent. Because this firm is 100 percent equity, its WACC and its cost of equity are the same. Spatt is contemplating a large-scale, $100 million expansion of its existing operations. The expansion would be funded by selling new stock.

Based on conversations with its investment banker, Spatt believes its flotation costs will run 10 percent of the amount issued. This means that Spatt's proceeds from the equity sale will be only 90 percent of the amount sold. When flotation costs are considered, what is the cost of the expansion?

As we discuss in more detail in Chapter 15, Spatt needs to sell enough equity to raise $100 million *after* covering the flotation costs. In other words:

$100 million = (1 − .10) × Amount raised

Amount raised = $100 million/.90 = $111.11 million

Spatt's flotation costs are thus $11.11 million, and the true cost of the expansion is $111.11 million once we include flotation costs.

Things are only slightly more complicated if the firm uses both debt and equity. For example, suppose Spatt's target capital structure is 60 percent equity, 40 percent debt. The flotation costs associated with equity are still 10 percent, but the flotation costs for debt are less—say 5 percent.

Earlier, when we had different capital costs for debt and equity, we calculated a weighted average cost of capital using the target capital structure weights. Here we will do much the same thing. We can calculate a weighted average flotation cost f_A by multiplying the equity flotation cost, f_E, by the percentage of equity (E/V) and the debt flotation cost, f_D, by the percentage of debt (D/V) and then adding the two together:

$$f_A = (E/V) \times f_E + (D/V) \times f_D \qquad \text{[14.8]}$$
$$= 60\% \times .10 + 40\% \times .05$$
$$= 8\%$$

The weighted average flotation cost is thus 8 percent. What this tells us is that for every dollar in outside financing needed for new projects, the firm must actually raise $1/(1 − .08) = $1.087. In our example, the project cost is $100 million when we ignore flotation costs. If we include them, then the true cost is $100 million/(1 − f_A) = $100 million/.92 = $108.7 million.

In taking issue costs into account, the firm must be careful not to use the wrong weights. The firm should use the target weights, even if it can finance the entire cost of the project with either debt or equity. The fact that a firm can finance a specific project with debt or equity is not directly relevant. If a firm has a target debt–equity ratio of 1, for example, but chooses to finance a particular project with all debt, it will have to raise additional equity later on to maintain its target debt–equity ratio. To take this into account, the firm should always use the target weights in calculating the flotation cost.

EXAMPLE 14.6   Calculating the Weighted Average Flotation Cost

The Weinstein Corporation has a target capital structure that is 80 percent equity, 20 percent debt. The flotation costs for equity issues are 20 percent of the amount raised; the flotation costs for debt issues are 6 percent. If Weinstein needs $65 million for a new manufacturing facility, what is the true cost once flotation costs are considered?

We first calculate the weighted average flotation cost, f_A:

$$f_A = (E/V) \times f_E + (D/V) \times f_D$$
$$= 80\% \times .20 + 20\% \times .06$$
$$= 17.2\%$$

The weighted average flotation cost is thus 17.2 percent. The project cost is $65 million when we ignore flotation costs. If we include them, then the true cost is $65 million/$(1 - f_A)$ = $65 million/.828 = $78.5 million, again illustrating that flotation costs can be a considerable expense.

FLOTATION COSTS AND NPV

To illustrate how flotation costs can be included in an NPV analysis, suppose the Tripleday Printing Company is currently at its target debt–equity ratio of 100 percent. It is considering building a new $500,000 printing plant in Kansas. This new plant is expected to generate aftertax cash flows of $73,150 per year forever. The tax rate is 34 percent. There are two financing options:

1. A $500,000 new issue of common stock: The issuance costs of the new common stock would be about 10 percent of the amount raised. The required return on the company's new equity is 20 percent.
2. A $500,000 issue of 30-year bonds: The issuance costs of the new debt would be 2 percent of the proceeds. The company can raise new debt at 10 percent.

What is the NPV of the new printing plant?

To begin, because printing is the company's main line of business, we will use the company's weighted average cost of capital to value the new printing plant:

$$\text{WACC} = (E/V) \times R_E + (D/V) \times R_D \times (1 - T_C)$$
$$= .50 \times 20\% + .50 \times 10\% \times (1 - .34)$$
$$= 13.3\%$$

Because the cash flows are $73,150 per year forever, the PV of the cash flows at 13.3 percent per year is:

$$\text{PV} = \frac{\$73,150}{.133} = \$550,000$$

If we ignore flotation costs, the NPV is:

$$\text{NPV} = \$550,000 - 500,000 = \$50,000$$

With no flotation costs, the project generates an NPV that is greater than zero, so it should be accepted.

What about financing arrangements and issue costs? Because new financing must be raised, the flotation costs are relevant. From the information given, we know that the flotation costs are 2 percent for debt and 10 percent for equity. Because Tripleday uses equal

Samuel Weaver on Cost of Capital and Hurdle Rates at The Hershey Company

At Hershey, we reevaluate our cost of capital annually or as market conditions warrant. The calculation of the cost of capital essentially involves three different issues, each with a few alternatives:

- *Current historical book value*
  Historical book value
  Target capital structure
  Current market-based weights

- *Cost of debt*
  Historical (coupon) interest rates
  Market-based interest rates

- *Cost of equity*
  Dividend growth model
  Capital asset pricing model, or CAPM

At Hershey, we calculate our cost of capital officially based on the projected "target" capital structure at the end of our three-year intermediate planning horizon. This allows management to see the immediate impact of strategic decisions related to the planned composition of Hershey's capital pool. The cost of debt is calculated as the anticipated weighted average aftertax cost of debt in that final plan year based on the coupon rates attached to that debt. The cost of equity is computed via the dividend growth model.

We conducted a survey of the 11 food processing companies that we consider our industry group competitors. The results of this survey indicated that the cost of capital for most of these companies was in the 10 to 12 percent range. Furthermore, without exception, all 11 of these companies employed the CAPM when calculating their cost of equity. Our experience has been that the dividend growth model works better for Hershey. We do pay dividends, and we do experience steady, stable growth in our dividends. This growth is also projected within our strategic plan. Consequently, the dividend growth model is technically applicable and appealing to management because it reflects their best estimate of the future long-term growth rate.

In addition to the calculation already described, the other possible combinations and permutations are calculated as barometers. Unofficially, the cost of capital is calculated using market weights, current marginal interest rates, and the CAPM cost of equity. For the most part, and due to rounding the cost of capital to the nearest whole percentage point, these alternative calculations yield approximately the same results.

From the cost of capital, individual project hurdle rates are developed using a subjectively determined risk premium based on the characteristics of the project. Projects are grouped into separate project categories, such as cost savings, capacity expansion, product line extension, and new products. For example, in general, a new product is more risky than a cost savings project. Consequently, each project category's hurdle rate reflects the level of risk and commensurate required return as perceived by senior management. As a result, capital project hurdle rates range from a slight premium over the cost of capital to the highest hurdle rate of approximately double the cost of capital.

Samuel Weaver, Ph.D., was formerly director, financial planning and analysis, for Hershey Chocolate North America. He is a certified management accountant and certified financial manager. His position combined the theoretical with the pragmatic and involved the analysis of many different facets of finance in addition to capital expenditure analysis.

amounts of debt and equity, the weighted average flotation cost, f_A, is:

$$f_A = (E/V) \times f_E + (D/V) \times f_D = .50 \times 10\% + .50 \times 2\%$$
$$= 6\%$$

Remember, the fact that Tripleday can finance the project with all debt or all equity is irrelevant. Because Tripleday needs $500,000 to fund the new plant, the true cost, once we include flotation costs, is $500,000/(1 - f_A) = \$500,000/.94 = \$531,915$. Because the PV of the cash flows is $550,000, the plant has an NPV of $550,000 - 531,915 = \$18,085$, so it is still a good investment. However, its value is less than we initially might have thought.

INTERNAL EQUITY AND FLOTATION COSTS

Our discussion of flotation costs to this point implicitly assumes that firms always have to raise the capital needed for new investments. In reality, most firms rarely sell equity at all. Instead, their internally generated cash flow is sufficient to cover the equity portion of their capital spending. Only the debt portion must be raised externally.

The use of internal equity doesn't change our approach. However, we now assign a value of zero to the flotation cost of equity because there is no such cost. In our Tripleday example, the weighted average flotation cost would therefore be:

$$f_A = (E/V) \times f_E + (D/V) \times f_D$$
$$= .50 \times 0\% + .50 \times 2\%$$
$$= 1\%$$

Notice that whether equity is generated internally or externally makes a big difference because external equity has a relatively high flotation cost.

Concept Questions

14.6a What are flotation costs?

14.6b How are flotation costs included in an NPV analysis?

14.7 Summary and Conclusions

This chapter has discussed cost of capital. The most important concept is the weighted average cost of capital, or WACC, which we interpreted as the required rate of return on the overall firm. It is also the discount rate appropriate for cash flows that are similar in risk to those of the overall firm. We described how the WACC can be calculated, and we illustrated how it can be used in certain types of analyses.

We also pointed out situations in which it is inappropriate to use the WACC as the discount rate. To handle such cases, we described some alternative approaches to developing discount rates, such as the pure play approach. We also discussed how the flotation costs associated with raising new capital can be included in an NPV analysis.

CHAPTER REVIEW AND SELF-TEST PROBLEMS

14.1 Calculating the Cost of Equity Suppose stock in Watta Corporation has a beta of .80. The market risk premium is 6 percent, and the risk-free rate is 6 percent. Watta's last dividend was $1.20 per share, and the dividend is expected to grow at 8 percent indefinitely. The stock currently sells for $45 per share. What is Watta's cost of equity capital?

14.2 Calculating the WACC In addition to the information given in the previous problem, suppose Watta has a target debt–equity ratio of 50 percent. Its cost of debt is 9 percent before taxes. If the tax rate is 35 percent, what is the WACC?

14.3 **Flotation Costs** Suppose in the previous problem Watta is seeking $30 million for a new project. The necessary funds will have to be raised externally. Watta's flotation costs for selling debt and equity are 2 percent and 16 percent, respectively. If flotation costs are considered, what is the true cost of the new project?

ANSWERS TO CHAPTER REVIEW AND SELF-TEST PROBLEMS

14.1 We start off with the SML approach. Based on the information given, the expected return on Watta's common stock is:

$$R_E = R_f + \beta_E \times (R_M - R_f)$$
$$= 6\% + .80 \times 6\%$$
$$= 10.80\%$$

We now use the dividend growth model. The projected dividend is $D_0 \times (1 + g) = \$1.20 \times 1.08 = \$1.296$, so the expected return using this approach is:

$$R_E = D_1/P_0 + g$$
$$= \$1.296/45 + .08$$
$$= 10.88\%$$

Because these two estimates, 10.80 percent and 10.88 percent, are fairly close, we will average them. Watta's cost of equity is approximately 10.84 percent.

14.2 Because the target debt–equity ratio is .50, Watta uses $.50 in debt for every $1 in equity. In other words, Watta's target capital structure is 1/3 debt and 2/3 equity. The WACC is thus:

$$\text{WACC} = (E/V) \times R_E + (D/V) \times R_D \times (1 - T_C)$$
$$= 2/3 \times 10.84\% + 1/3 \times 9\% \times (1 - .35)$$
$$= 9.177\%$$

14.3 Because Watta uses both debt and equity to finance its operations, we first need the weighted average flotation cost. As in the previous problem, the percentage of equity financing is 2/3, so the weighted average cost is:

$$f_A = (E/V) \times f_E + (D/V) \times f_D$$
$$= 2/3 \times 16\% + 1/3 \times 2\%$$
$$= 11.33\%$$

If Watta needs $30 million after flotation costs, then the true cost of the project is $30 million/$(1 - f_A) = \$30$ million$/.8867 = \$33.83$ million.

CONCEPTS REVIEW AND CRITICAL THINKING QUESTIONS

1. **WACC [LO3]** On the most basic level, if a firm's WACC is 12 percent, what does this mean?
2. **Book Values versus Market Values [LO3]** In calculating the WACC, if you had to use book values for either debt or equity, which would you choose? Why?
3. **Project Risk [LO5]** If you can borrow all the money you need for a project at 6 percent, doesn't it follow that 6 percent is your cost of capital for the project?
4. **WACC and Taxes [LO3]** Why do we use an aftertax figure for cost of debt but not for cost of equity?

5. **DCF Cost of Equity Estimation [LO1]** What are the advantages of using the DCF model for determining the cost of equity capital? What are the disadvantages? What specific piece of information do you need to find the cost of equity using this model? What are some of the ways in which you could get this estimate?

6. **SML Cost of Equity Estimation [LO1]** What are the advantages of using the SML approach to finding the cost of equity capital? What are the disadvantages? What specific pieces of information are needed to use this method? Are all of these variables observable, or do they need to be estimated? What are some of the ways in which you could get these estimates?

7. **Cost of Debt Estimation [LO2]** How do you determine the appropriate cost of debt for a company? Does it make a difference if the company's debt is privately placed as opposed to being publicly traded? How would you estimate the cost of debt for a firm whose only debt issues are privately held by institutional investors?

8. **Cost of Capital [LO5]** Suppose Tom O'Bedlam, president of Bedlam Products, Inc., has hired you to determine the firm's cost of debt and cost of equity capital.

    a. The stock currently sells for $50 per share, and the dividend per share will probably be about $5. Tom argues, "It will cost us $5 per share to use the stockholders' money this year, so the cost of equity is equal to 10 percent (= $5/50)." What's wrong with this conclusion?

    b. Based on the most recent financial statements, Bedlam Products' total liabilities are $8 million. Total interest expense for the coming year will be about $1 million. Tom therefore reasons, "We owe $8 million, and we will pay $1 million interest. Therefore, our cost of debt is obviously $1 million/8 million = 12.5%." What's wrong with this conclusion?

    c. Based on his own analysis, Tom is recommending that the company increase its use of equity financing because "debt costs 12.5 percent, but equity costs only 10 percent; thus equity is cheaper." Ignoring all the other issues, what do you think about the conclusion that the cost of equity is less than the cost of debt?

9. **Company Risk versus Project Risk [LO5]** Both Dow Chemical Company, a large natural gas user, and Superior Oil, a major natural gas producer, are thinking of investing in natural gas wells near Houston. Both companies are all equity financed. Dow and Superior are looking at identical projects. They've analyzed their respective investments, which would involve a negative cash flow now and positive expected cash flows in the future. These cash flows would be the same for both firms. No debt would be used to finance the projects. Both companies estimate that their projects would have a net present value of $1 million at an 18 percent discount rate and a −$1.1 million NPV at a 22 percent discount rate. Dow has a beta of 1.25, whereas Superior has a beta of .75. The expected risk premium on the market is 8 percent, and risk-free bonds are yielding 12 percent. Should either company proceed? Should both? Explain.

10. **Divisional Cost of Capital [LO5]** Under what circumstances would it be appropriate for a firm to use different costs of capital for its different operating divisions? If the overall firm WACC were used as the hurdle rate for all divisions, would the riskier divisions or the more conservative divisions tend to get most of the investment projects? Why? If you were to try to estimate the appropriate cost of capital for different divisions, what problems might you encounter? What are two techniques you could use to develop a rough estimate for each division's cost of capital?

1. **Calculating Cost of Equity** [LO1] The Down and Out Co. just issued a dividend of $2.40 per share on its common stock. The company is expected to maintain a constant 5.5 percent growth rate in its dividends indefinitely. If the stock sells for $52 a share, what is the company's cost of equity?

BASIC
(Questions 1–19)

2. **Calculating Cost of Equity** [LO1] The Up and Coming Corporation's common stock has a beta of 1.05. If the risk-free rate is 5.3 percent and the expected return on the market is 12 percent, what is the company's cost of equity capital?

3. **Calculating Cost of Equity** [LO1] Stock in Country Road Industries has a beta of .85. The market risk premium is 8 percent, and T-bills are currently yielding 5 percent. The company's most recent dividend was $1.60 per share, and dividends are expected to grow at a 6 percent annual rate indefinitely. If the stock sells for $37 per share, what is your best estimate of the company's cost of equity?

4. **Estimating the DCF Growth Rate** [LO1] Suppose In a Found Ltd. just issued a dividend of $1.43 per share on its common stock. The company paid dividends of $1.05, $1.12, $1.19, and $1.30 per share in the last four years. If the stock currently sells for $45, what is your best estimate of the company's cost of equity capital using the arithmetic average growth rate in dividends? What if you use the geometric average growth rate?

5. **Calculating Cost of Preferred Stock** [LO1] Holdup Bank has an issue of preferred stock with a $6 stated dividend that just sold for $96 per share. What is the bank's cost of preferred stock?

6. **Calculating Cost of Debt** [LO2] Waller, Inc., is trying to determine its cost of debt. The firm has a debt issue outstanding with 15 years to maturity that is quoted at 107 percent of face value. The issue makes semiannual payments and has an embedded cost of 7 percent annually. What is the company's pretax cost of debt? If the tax rate is 35 percent, what is the aftertax cost of debt?

7. **Calculating Cost of Debt** [LO2] Jiminy's Cricket Farm issued a 30-year, 8 percent semiannual bond 7 years ago. The bond currently sells for 95 percent of its face value. The company's tax rate is 35 percent.
   a. What is the pretax cost of debt?
   b. What is the aftertax cost of debt?
   c. Which is more relevant, the pretax or the aftertax cost of debt? Why?

8. **Calculating Cost of Debt** [LO2] For the firm in Problem 7, suppose the book value of the debt issue is $80 million. In addition, the company has a second debt issue on the market, a zero coupon bond with seven years left to maturity; the book value of this issue is $35 million, and the bonds sell for 61 percent of par. What is the company's total book value of debt? The total market value? What is your best estimate of the aftertax cost of debt now?

9. **Calculating WACC** [LO3] Mullineaux Corporation has a target capital structure of 60 percent common stock, 5 percent preferred stock, and 35 percent debt. Its cost of equity is 14 percent, the cost of preferred stock is 6 percent, and the cost of debt is 8 percent. The relevant tax rate is 35 percent.
   a. What is Mullineaux's WACC?
   b. The company president has approached you about Mullineaux's capital structure. He wants to know why the company doesn't use more preferred stock financing because it costs less than debt. What would you tell the president?

10. Taxes and WACC [LO3] Sixx AM Manufacturing has a target debt–equity ratio of .65. Its cost of equity is 15 percent, and its cost of debt is 9 percent. If the tax rate is 35 percent, what is the company's WACC?

11. Finding the Target Capital Structure [LO3] Fama's Llamas has a weighted average cost of capital of 8.9 percent. The company's cost of equity is 12 percent, and its pretax cost of debt is 7.9 percent. The tax rate is 35 percent. What is the company's target debt–equity ratio?

12. Book Value versus Market Value [LO3] Filer Manufacturing has 11 million shares of common stock outstanding. The current share price is $68, and the book value per share is $6. Filer Manufacturing also has two bond issues outstanding. The first bond issue has a face value of $70 million, has a 7 percent coupon, and sells for 93 percent of par. The second issue has a face value of $55 million, has an 8 percent coupon, and sells for 104 percent of par. The first issue matures in 21 years, the second in 6 years.

   a. What are Filer's capital structure weights on a book value basis?

   b. What are Filer's capital structure weights on a market value basis?

   c. Which are more relevant, the book or market value weights? Why?

13. Calculating the WACC [LO3] In Problem 12, suppose the most recent dividend was $4.10 and the dividend growth rate is 6 percent. Assume that the overall cost of debt is the weighted average of that implied by the two outstanding debt issues. Both bonds make semiannual payments. The tax rate is 35 percent. What is the company's WACC?

14. WACC [LO3] Jungle, Inc., has a target debt–equity ratio of 1.05. Its WACC is 9.4 percent, and the tax rate is 35 percent.

   a. If Jungle's cost of equity is 14 percent, what is its pretax cost of debt?

   b. If instead you know that the aftertax cost of debt is 6.8 percent, what is the cost of equity?

15. Finding the WACC [LO3] Given the following information for Evenflow Power Co., find the WACC. Assume the company's tax rate is 35 percent.

Debt:	8,000 6.5 percent coupon bonds outstanding, $1,000 par value, 20 years to maturity, selling for 92 percent of par; the bonds make semiannual payments.
Common stock:	250,000 shares outstanding, selling for $57 per share; the beta is 1.05.
Preferred stock:	15,000 shares of 5 percent preferred stock outstanding, currently selling for $93 per share.
Market:	8 percent market risk premium and 4.5 percent risk-free rate.

16. Finding the WACC [LO3] Titan Mining Corporation has 9 million shares of common stock outstanding, 250,000 shares of 6 percent preferred stock outstanding, and 105,000 7.5 percent semiannual bonds outstanding, par value $1,000 each. The common stock currently sells for $34 per share and has a beta of 1.25, the preferred stock currently sells for $91 per share, and the bonds have 15 years to maturity and sell for 93 percent of par. The market risk premium is 8.5 percent, T-bills are yielding 5 percent, and Titan Mining's tax rate is 35 percent.

   a. What is the firm's market value capital structure?

   b. If Titan Mining is evaluating a new investment project that has the same risk as the firm's typical project, what rate should the firm use to discount the project's cash flows?

17. **SML and WACC [LO1]** An all-equity firm is considering the following projects:

Project	Beta	Expected Return
W	.80	10%
X	.90	12
Y	1.45	13
Z	1.60	15

The T-bill rate is 5 percent, and the expected return on the market is 11 percent.

a. Which projects have a higher expected return than the firm's 11 percent cost of capital?

b. Which projects should be accepted?

c. Which projects would be incorrectly accepted or rejected if the firm's overall cost of capital were used as a hurdle rate?

18. **Calculating Flotation Costs [LO4]** Suppose your company needs $20 million to build a new assembly line. Your target debt–equity ratio is .75. The flotation cost for new equity is 8 percent, but the flotation cost for debt is only 5 percent. Your boss has decided to fund the project by borrowing money because the flotation costs are lower and the needed funds are relatively small.

a. What do you think about the rationale behind borrowing the entire amount?

b. What is your company's weighted average flotation cost, assuming all equity is raised externally?

c. What is the true cost of building the new assembly line after taking flotation costs into account? Does it matter in this case that the entire amount is being raised from debt?

19. **Calculating Flotation Costs [LO4]** Southern Alliance Company needs to raise $45 million to start a new project and will raise the money by selling new bonds. The company will generate no internal equity for the foreseeable future. The company has a target capital structure of 65 percent common stock, 5 percent preferred stock, and 30 percent debt. Flotation costs for issuing new common stock are 9 percent, for new preferred stock, 6 percent, and for new debt, 3 percent. What is the true initial cost figure Southern should use when evaluating its project?

20. **WACC and NPV [LO3, 5]** Scanlin, Inc., is considering a project that will result in initial aftertax cash savings of $2.7 million at the end of the first year, and these savings will grow at a rate of 4 percent per year indefinitely. The firm has a target debt–equity ratio of .90, a cost of equity of 13 percent, and an aftertax cost of debt of 4.8 percent. The cost-saving proposal is somewhat riskier than the usual project the firm undertakes; management uses the subjective approach and applies an adjustment factor of +2 percent to the cost of capital for such risky projects. Under what circumstances should the company take on the project?

INTERMEDIATE
(Questions 20–23)

21. **Flotation Costs [LO4]** Goodbye, Inc., recently issued new securities to finance a new TV show. The project cost $15 million, and the company paid $850,000 in flotation costs. In addition, the equity issued had a flotation cost of 7 percent of the amount raised, whereas the debt issued had a flotation cost of 3 percent of the amount raised. If Goodbye issued new securities in the same proportion as its target capital structure, what is the company's target debt–equity ratio?

22. Calculating the Cost of Debt [LO2] Ying Import has several bond issues outstanding, each making semiannual interest payments. The bonds are listed in the following table. If the corporate tax rate is 34 percent, what is the aftertax cost of Ying's debt?

Bond	Coupon Rate	Price Quote	Maturity	Face Value
1	7.00%	103.00	5 years	$40,000,000
2	8.50	108.00	8 years	35,000,000
3	8.20	97.00	15 1/2 years	55,000,000
4	9.80	111.00	25 years	50,000,000

23. Calculating the Cost of Equity [LO1] Floyd Industries stock has a beta of 1.50. The company just paid a dividend of $.80, and the dividends are expected to grow at 5 percent. The expected return of the market is 12 percent, and Treasury bills are yielding 5.5 percent. The most recent stock price for Floyd is $61.

a. Calculate the cost of equity using the DCF method.

b. Calculate the cost of equity using the SML method.

c. Why do you think your estimates in (a) and (b) are so different?

CHALLENGE
(Questions 24–26)

24. Flotation Costs and NPV [LO3, 4] Photochronograph Corporation (PC) manufactures time series photographic equipment. It is currently at its target debt–equity ratio of .70. It's considering building a new $45 million manufacturing facility. This new plant is expected to generate aftertax cash flows of $6.2 million in perpetuity. The company raises all equity from outside financing. There are three financing options:

1. *A new issue of common stock:* The flotation costs of the new common stock would be 8 percent of the amount raised. The required return on the company's new equity is 14 percent.

2. *A new issue of 20-year bonds:* The flotation costs of the new bonds would be 4 percent of the proceeds. If the company issues these new bonds at an annual coupon rate of 8 percent, they will sell at par.

3. *Increased use of accounts payable financing:* Because this financing is part of the company's ongoing daily business, it has no flotation costs, and the company assigns it a cost that is the same as the overall firm WACC. Management has a target ratio of accounts payable to long-term debt of .20. (Assume there is no difference between the pretax and aftertax accounts payable cost.)

What is the NPV of the new plant? Assume that PC has a 35 percent tax rate.

25. Flotation Costs [LO4] Trower Corp. has a debt–equity ratio of 1.20. The company is considering a new plant that will cost $145 million to build. When the company issues new equity, it incurs a flotation cost of 8 percent. The flotation cost on new debt is 3.5 percent. What is the initial cost of the plant if the company raises all equity externally? What if it typically uses 60 percent retained earnings? What if all equity investment is financed through retained earnings?

26. Project Evaluation [LO3, 4] This is a comprehensive project evaluation problem bringing together much of what you have learned in this and previous chapters. Suppose you have been hired as a financial consultant to Defense Electronics, Inc. (DEI), a large, publicly traded firm that is the market share leader in radar detection systems (RDSs). The company is looking at setting up a manufacturing plant overseas to produce a new line of RDSs. This will be a five-year project. The company bought some land three years ago for $4 million in anticipation of using it as a toxic dump site for waste chemicals, but it built a piping system to safely discard the chemicals instead. The land was appraised last week for $5.1 million. In five years, the aftertax value of the land will be $6 million, but the company expects to keep the land for a future project. The company wants to build its new manufacturing plant on this land; the plant and equipment will cost $35 million to build. The following market data on DEI's securities are current:

Debt:	240,000 7.5 percent coupon bonds outstanding, 20 years to maturity, selling for 94 percent of par; the bonds have a $1,000 par value each and make semiannual payments.
Common stock:	9,000,000 shares outstanding, selling for $71 per share; the beta is 1.2.
Preferred stock:	400,000 shares of 5.5 percent preferred stock outstanding, selling for $81 per share.
Market:	8 percent expected market risk premium; 5 percent risk-free rate.

DEI uses G.M. Wharton as its lead underwriter. Wharton charges DEI spreads of 8 percent on new common stock issues, 6 percent on new preferred stock issues, and 4 percent on new debt issues. Wharton has included all direct and indirect issuance costs (along with its profit) in setting these spreads. Wharton has recommended to DEI that it raise the funds needed to build the plant by issuing new shares of common stock. DEI's tax rate is 35 percent. The project requires $1,300,000 in initial net working capital investment to get operational. Assume Wharton raises all equity for new projects externally.

a. Calculate the project's initial time 0 cash flow, taking into account all side effects.

b. The new RDS project is somewhat riskier than a typical project for DEI, primarily because the plant is being located overseas. Management has told you to use an adjustment factor of +2 percent to account for this increased riskiness. Calculate the appropriate discount rate to use when evaluating DEI's project.

c. The manufacturing plant has an eight-year tax life, and DEI uses straight-line depreciation. At the end of the project (that is, the end of year 5), the plant and equipment can be scrapped for $6 million. What is the aftertax salvage value of this plant and equipment?

d. The company will incur $7,000,000 in annual fixed costs. The plan is to manufacture 18,000 RDSs per year and sell them at $10,900 per machine; the variable production costs are $9,400 per RDS. What is the annual operating cash flow (OCF) from this project?

e. DEI's comptroller is primarily interested in the impact of DEI's investments on the bottom line of reported accounting statements. What will you tell her is the accounting break-even quantity of RDSs sold for this project?

f. Finally, DEI's president wants you to throw all your calculations, assumptions, and everything else into the report for the chief financial officer; all he wants to know is what the RDS project's internal rate of return (IRR) and net present value (NPV) are. What will you report?

Cost of Capital for Hubbard Computer, Inc.

You have recently been hired by Hubbard Computer, Inc. (HCI), in its relatively new treasury management department. HCI was founded eight years ago by Bob Hubbard and currently operates 74 stores in the Southeast. The company is privately owned by Bob and his family, and it had sales of $97 million last year.

HCI primarily sells to customers who shop in the stores. Customers come to the store and talk with a sales representative. The sales representative assists the customer in determining the type of computer and peripherals that are necessary for the individual customer's computing needs. After the order is taken, the customer pays for the order immediately, and the computer is made to fill the order. Delivery of the computer averages 15 days, and it is guaranteed in 30 days.

HCI's growth to date has come from its profits. When the company had sufficient capital, it would open a new store. Other than scouting locations, relatively little formal analysis has been used in its capital budgeting process. Bob has just read about capital budgeting techniques and has come to you for help. For starters, the company has never attempted to determine its cost of capital, and Bob would like you to perform the analysis. Because the company is privately owned, it is difficult to determine the cost of equity for the company. Bob wants you to use the pure play approach to estimate the cost of capital for HCI, and he has chosen Dell as a representative company. The following questions will lead you through the steps to calculate this estimate:

QUESTIONS

1. Most publicly traded corporations are required to submit quarterly (10Q) and annual reports (10K) to the SEC detailing the financial operations of the company over the past quarter or year, respectively. These corporate filings are available on the SEC Web site at www.sec.gov. Go to the SEC Web site; follow the "Search for Company Filings" link and the "Companies & Other Filers" link;

enter "Dell Inc."; and search for SEC filings made by Dell. Find the most recent 10Q or 10K, and download the form. Look on the balance sheet to find the book value of debt and the book value of equity. If you look further down the report, you should find a section titled "Long-term Debt and Interest Rate Risk Management" that will provide a breakdown of Dell's long-term debt.

2. To estimate the cost of equity for Dell, go to finance.yahoo.com and enter the ticker symbol DELL. Follow the links to answer the following questions: What is the most recent stock price listed for Dell? What is the market value of equity, or market capitalization? How many shares of stock does Dell have outstanding? What is the most recent annual dividend? Can you use the dividend discount model in this case? What is the beta for Dell? Now go back to finance.yahoo.com and follow the "Bonds" link. What is the yield on three-month Treasury bills? Using the historical market risk premium, what is the cost of equity for Dell using CAPM?

3. You now need to calculate the cost of debt for Dell. Go to www.finra.org/marketdata, enter Dell as the company, and find the yield to maturity for each of Dell's bonds. What is the weighted average cost of debt for Dell using the book value weights and using the market value weights? Does it make a difference in this case if you use book value weights or market value weights?

4. You now have all the necessary information to calculate the weighted average cost of capital for Dell. Calculate this using book value weights and market value weights, assuming Dell has a 35 percent marginal tax rate. Which number is more relevant?

5. You used Dell as a pure play company to estimate the cost of capital for HCI. Are there any potential problems with this approach in this situation?

24

OPTIONS AND CORPORATE FINANCE

After studying this chapter, you should understand:

LO1 The basics of call and put options and how to calculate their payoffs and profits.

LO2 The factors that affect option values and how to price call and put options using no arbitrage conditions.

LO3 The basics of employee stock options and their benefits and disadvantages.

LO4 How to value a firm's equity as an option on the firm's assets.

LO5 How option valuation can be used to evaluate capital budgeting projects, including timing options, the option to expand, the option to abandon, and the option to contract.

LO6 The basics of convertible bonds and warrants and how to value them.

FOR MANY WORKERS, from senior management on down, employee stock options have become a very important part of their overall compensation. In 2005, companies began to record an explicit expense for employee stock options on their income statements, which allows us to see how much employee stock options cost. For example, in 2007, Dell expensed about $436 million for employee stock options, which works out to about $4,950 per employee. In the same year, search engine provider Google expensed about $869 million worth of employee stock options, which amounts to about $51,710 per employee.

Employee stock options are just one kind of option. This chapter introduces you to options and explains their features and what determines their value. The chapter also shows you that options show up in many places in corporate finance. In fact, once you know what to look for, they show up just about everywhere, so understanding how they work is essential.

Master the ability to solve problems in this chapter by using a spreadsheet. Access Excel Master on the student Web site www.mhhe.com/rwj.

Options are a part of everyday life. "Keep your options open" is sound business advice, and "We're out of options" is a sure sign of trouble. In finance, an **option** is an arrangement that gives its owner the right to buy or sell an asset at a fixed price any time on or before a given date. The most familiar options are stock options. These are options to buy and sell shares of common stock, and we will discuss them in some detail in the following pages.

Of course, stock options are not the only options. In fact, at the root of it, many different kinds of financial decisions amount to the evaluation of options. For example, we will show how understanding options adds several important details to the NPV analysis we have discussed in earlier chapters.

Also, virtually all corporate securities have implicit or explicit option features, and the use of such features is growing. As a result, understanding securities that possess option features requires general knowledge of the factors that determine an option's value.

This chapter starts with a description of different types of options. We identify and discuss the general factors that determine option values and show how ordinary debt and equity have optionlike characteristics. We then examine employee stock options and the important role of options in capital budgeting. We conclude by illustrating how option features are incorporated into corporate securities by discussing warrants, convertible bonds, and other optionlike securities.

option
A contract that gives its owner the right to buy or sell some asset at a fixed price on or before a given date.

Options: The Basics

24.1

An option is a contract that gives its owner the right to buy or sell some asset at a fixed price on or before a given date. For example, an option on a building might give the holder of the option the right to buy the building for $1 million any time on or before the Saturday prior to the third Wednesday of January 2010.

Options are a unique type of financial contract because they give the buyer the right, but not the obligation, to do something. The buyer uses the option only if it is profitable to do so; otherwise, the option can be thrown away.

There is a special vocabulary associated with options. Here are some important definitions:

1. **Exercising the option**: The act of buying or selling the underlying asset via the option contract is called *exercising the option*.

2. **Strike price**, or exercise price: The fixed price specified in the option contract at which the holder can buy or sell the underlying asset is called the *strike price* or *exercise price*. The strike price is often called the *striking price*.

3. **Expiration date**: An option usually has a limited life. The option is said to expire at the end of its life. The last day on which the option may be exercised is called the *expiration date*.

4. **American** and **European options**: An American option may be exercised any time up to and including the expiration date. A European option may be exercised only on the expiration date.

exercising the option
The act of buying or selling the underlying asset via the option contract.

strike price
The fixed price in the option contract at which the holder can buy or sell the underlying asset. Also, the exercise price or striking price.

expiration date
The last day on which an option may be exercised.

American option
An option that may be exercised at any time until its expiration date.

European option
An option that may be exercised only on the expiration date.

PUTS AND CALLS

Options come in two basic types: puts and calls. A **call option** gives the owner the right to *buy* an asset at a fixed price during a particular time period. It may help you to remember that a call option gives you the right to "call in" an asset.

A **put option** is essentially the opposite of a call option. Instead of giving the holder the right to buy some asset, it gives the holder the right to *sell* that asset for a fixed exercise price. If you buy a put option, you can force the seller of the option to buy the asset from you for a fixed price and thereby "put it to them."

What about an investor who *sells* a call option? The seller receives money up front and has the *obligation* to sell the asset at the exercise price if the option holder wants it. Similarly, an investor who *sells* a put option receives cash up front and is then obligated to buy the asset at the exercise price if the option holder demands it.[1]

The asset involved in an option can be anything. The options that are most widely bought and sold, however, are stock options. These are options to buy and sell shares of stock. Because these are the best-known types of options, we will study them first. As we discuss stock options, keep in mind that the general principles apply to options involving any asset, not just shares of stock.

call option
The right to buy an asset at a fixed price during a particular period.

put option
The right to sell an asset at a fixed price during a particular period of time. The opposite of a call option.

---

[1] An investor who sells an option is often said to have "written" the option.

STOCK OPTION QUOTATIONS

On April 26, 1973, the Chicago Board Options Exchange (CBOE) opened and began organized trading in stock options. Put and call options involving stock in some of the best-known corporations in the United States are traded there. The CBOE is still the largest organized options market, but options are traded in a number of other places today, including the New York, American, and Philadelphia stock exchanges. Almost all such options are American (as opposed to European).

A simplified quotation for a CBOE option might look something like this:

Prices at Close June 15, 2008							
RWJ (RWJ)						**Underlying Stock Price: 100.00**	
		Call			**Put**		
Expiration	**Strike**	**Last**	**Volume**	**Open Interest**	**Last**	**Volume**	**Open Interest**
Jun	95	6	120	400	2	80	1,000
July	95	6.50	40	200	2.80	100	4,600
Aug	95	8	70	600	4	20	800

Check out these options exchanges:
www.cboe.com
www.kcbt.com
www.liffe.com
www.euronext.com

The first thing to notice here is the company identifier, RWJ. This tells us that these options involve the right to buy or sell shares of stock in the RWJ Corporation. To the right of the company identifier is the closing price on the stock. As of the close of business on the day before this quotation, RWJ was selling for $100 per share.

The first column in the table shows the expiration months (June, July, and August). All CBOE options expire following the third Friday of the expiration month. The next column shows the strike price. The RWJ options listed here have an exercise price of $95.

The next three columns give us information about call options. The first thing given is the most recent price (Last). Next we have volume, which tells us the number of option *contracts* that were traded that day. One option contract involves the right to buy (for a call option) or sell (for a put option) 100 shares of stock, and all trading actually takes place in contracts. Option prices, however, are quoted on a per-share basis.

The last piece of information given for the call options is the open interest. This is the number of contracts of each type currently outstanding. The three columns of information for call options (price, volume, and open interest) are followed by the same three columns for put options.

For example, the first option listed would be described as the "RWJ June 95 call." The price for this option is $6. If you pay the $6, then you have the right any time between now and the third Friday of June to buy one share of RWJ stock for $95. Because trading takes place in round lots (multiples of 100 shares), one option contract costs you $6 × 100 = $600.

The other quotations are similar. For example, the July 95 put option costs $2.80. If you pay $2.80 × 100 = $280, then you have the right to sell 100 shares of RWJ stock any time between now and the third Friday in July at a price of $95 per share.

Table 24.1 contains a more detailed CBOE quote reproduced from *The Wall Street Journal* (online). From our discussion in the preceding paragraphs, we know that these are Cisco Systems (CSCO) options and that CSCO is selling for $23.12 per share. Notice that there are multiple strike prices instead of just one. As shown, puts and calls with strike prices ranging from 12.50 up to 32.50 are available.

To check your understanding of option quotes, suppose you want the right to sell 100 shares of CSCO for $30 anytime up until the third Friday in July. What should you do and how much will it cost you?

TABLE 24.1

A Sample *Wall Street Journal* (Online) Option Quotation

SOURCE: Reprinted with permission from *The Wall Street Journal*, July 3, 2008 © Copyright 2008 by Dow Jones & Company. All rights reserved worldwide.

Cisco Systems Inc. (CSCO)

Last	Change	% Change	Volume	52-Week High	52-Week Low	07/03/08 NASDAQ 01:00 p.m. EDT USD
23.12	.28	1.23%	30,370,285	34.24(11/06/07)	21.77(02/07/08)	

Options Show all months

July 2008 Options: Expand | Hide   ▦ In The Money

Calls						Strike Price	Puts					
Last	Chg	Bid	Ask	Volume	Open Int.		Last	Chg	Bid	Ask	Volume	Open Int.
14.55		10.55	10.70	0	455	12.50	.01			.01	0	2,563
8.20		8.05	8.35	0	591	15.00	.01			.01	0	6,505
5.75		5.55	5.85	0	1,464	17.50	.01		.01	.02	0	4,447
4.25	-.15	4.05	4.20	1	997	19.00	.03		.02	.03	0	2,196
3.25	+.15	3.10	3.25	10	2,892	20.00	.04	-.01	.03	.04	3	27,567
2.27	+.34	2.15	2.36	44	1,727	21.00	.07	-.04	.06	.08	98	12,342
.91	+.11	.90	.93	8,310	14,005	22.50	.30	-.13	.30	.32	2,549	31,286
			LAST TRADE			**23.12**	as of 7/3/2008 1:00 PM					
.22	.00	.21	.23	967	37,460	24.00	.99	-.29	1.08	1.12	856	36,444
.09	+.01	.07	.08	336	77,919	25.00	1.85	-.38	1.92	1.97	584	55,381
.03	.00	.03	.04	21	40,294	26.00	2.70	-.44	2.87	2.93	32	27,579
.03	+.01	.01	.03	118	85,699	27.50	4.45	.00	4.35	4.45	526	50,177
.02	.00		.02	4	11,282	29.00	4.30		5.75	5.95	0	81
.01	.00		.01	10	25,560	30.00	6.71	-.17	6.75	6.95	5	630
.01			.01	0	13,965	32.50	7.20		9.25	9.45	0	50

Because you want the right to sell the stock for $30, you need to buy a *put* option with a $30 exercise price. So you go online and place an order for one CSCO July 30 put contract. Because the July 30 put is quoted at $6.95 you will have to pay $6.95 per share, or $695 in all (plus commission).

Of course, you can look up option prices many places on the Web. To do so, however, you have to know the relevant ticker symbol. The option ticker symbols are a bit more complicated than stock tickers, so our nearby *Work the Web* box shows you how to get them along with the associated option price quotes.

OPTION PAYOFFS

Looking at Table 24.1, suppose you buy 50 July 20 call contracts. The option is quoted at $3.25, so the contracts cost $325 each. You spend a total of 50 × $325 = $16,250. You wait a while, and the expiration date rolls around.

Now what? You have the right to buy CSCO stock for $20 per share. If CSCO is selling for less than $20 a share, then this option isn't worth anything, and you throw it away. In this case, we say that the option has finished "out of the money" because the stock price is less than the exercise price. Your $16,250 is, alas, a complete loss.

If CSCO is selling for more than $20 per share, then you need to exercise your option. In this case, the option is "in the money" because the stock price exceeds the exercise price.

WORK THE WEB

How do you find option prices for options that are currently traded? To find out, we went to finance.yahoo.com, got a stock quote for JCPenney (JCP), and followed the Options link. As you can see below, there were 7 call option contracts and 6 put option contracts trading for JCPenney with a February 2009 expiration date.

View By Expiration: Jul 08 | Aug 08 | Nov 08 | Jan 09 | **Feb 09** | Jan 10

CALL OPTIONS   Expire at close Fri, Feb 20, 2009

Strike	Symbol	Last	Chg	Bid	Ask	Vol	Open Int
27.50	JCPBY.X	11.20	↑1.40	10.50	10.80	4	7
30.00	JCPBF.X	8.90	.00	8.80	9.10	0	1
35.00	JCPBG.X	6.50	↑.70	6.00	6.20	5	245
37.50	JCPBE.X	6.10	.00	4.90	5.10	0	1
40.00	JCPBH.X	3.80	.00	3.90	4.10	53	380
42.50	JCPBR.X	3.50	↑.50	3.10	3.30	52	184
45.00	JCPBI.X	2.35	.00	2.40	2.55	104	328

PUT OPTIONS   Expire at close Fri, Feb 20, 2009

Strike	Symbol	Last	Chg	Bid	Ask	Vol	Open Int
27.50	JCPNY.X	2.15	.00	2.15	2.25	84	308
30.00	JCPNF.X	2.80	↓.15	2.95	3.10	30	37
32.50	JCPND.X	3.60	.00	3.90	4.10	72	73
35.00	JCPNG.X	5.30	.00	5.00	5.20	106	211
37.50	JCPNE.X	6.40	.00	6.30	6.50	20	20
40.00	JCPNH.X	7.90	.00	7.80	8.00	14	314

☐ Highlighted options are in-the-money.

The Chicago Board Options Exchange (CBOE) sets the strike prices for traded options. The strike prices are centered around the current stock price, and the number of strike prices depends in part on the trading volume in the stock. If you examine the prices for the call options, you see that the quotes behave as you might expect. As the strike price of the call option increases, the option contract becomes less valuable. You should note that all of the options have a price divisible by $.05. The reason is that options traded on the exchange have a five-cent "tick" size (the tick size is the minimum price increment). This means that any change in price is a minimum of five cents. So while you can price an option to the penny, you just can't trade on the "Penney."

Questions

1. Look up the options that are currently available for JCPenney. What is the expiration date of the longest term options available? Compare the prices of these long-term options to shorter-term options with the same strike price. What do you find?

2. Find the IBM options with the shortest maturity. How many strike prices for IBM options are available? Why do you think there are so many strike prices for IBM options when compared to some other companies like JCPenney?

Suppose CSCO has risen to, say, $25 per share. Because you have the right to buy CSCO at $20, you make a $5 profit on each share upon exercise. Each contract involves 100 shares, so you make $5 per share × 100 shares per contract = $500 per contract. Finally, you own 50 contracts, so the value of your options is a handsome $25,000. Notice that because you invested $16,250, your net profit is $8,750.

As our example indicates, the gains and losses from buying call options can be quite large. To illustrate further, suppose you simply purchase the stock with the $16,250 instead of buying call options. In this case, you will have about $16,250/23.12 = 702.85 shares. We can now compare what you have when the option expires for different stock prices:

Ending Stock Price	Option Value (50 contracts)	Net Profit or Loss (50 contracts)	Stock Value (702.85 shares)	Net Profit or Loss (702.85 shares)
$15	$ 0	−$16,250	$10,543	−$5,707
17	0	−16,250	11,949	−4,301
20	0	−16,250	14,057	−2,193
23	15,000	−1,250	16,166	−84
25	25,000	8,750	17,571	1,321
30	50,000	33,750	21,086	4,836

The option position clearly magnifies the gains and losses on the stock by a substantial amount. The reason is that the payoff on your 50 option contracts is based on 50 × 100 = 5,000 shares of stock instead of just 702.85.

In our example, notice that, if the stock price ends up below the exercise price, then you lose all $16,250 with the option. With the stock, you still have about what you started with. Also notice that the option can never be worth less than zero because you can always just throw it away. As a result, you can never lose more than your original investment (the $16,250 in our example).

It is important to recognize that stock options are a zero-sum game. By this we mean that whatever the buyer of a stock option makes, the seller loses, and vice versa. To illustrate, suppose, in our example just preceding, you *sell* 50 option contracts. You receive $16,250 up front, and you will be obligated to sell the stock for $20 if the buyer of the option wishes to exercise it. In this situation, if the stock price ends up below $20, you will be $16,250 ahead. If the stock price ends up above $20, you will have to sell something for less than it is worth, so you will lose the difference. For example, if the stock price is $25, you will have to sell 50 × 100 = 5,000 shares at $20 per share, so you will be out $25 − 20 = $5 per share, or $25,000 total. Because you received $16,250 up front, your net loss is $8,750. We can summarize some other possibilities as follows:

Ending Stock Price	Net Profit to Option Seller
$15	$16,250
17	16,250
20	16,250
23	1,250
25	−8,750
30	−33,750

Notice that the net profits to the option buyer (calculated previously) are just the opposites of these amounts.

EXAMPLE 24.1 | **Put Payoffs**

Looking at Table 24.1, suppose you buy 10 CSCO July 26 put contracts. How much does this cost (ignoring commissions)? Just before the option expires, CSCO is selling for $21.50 per share. Is this good news or bad news? What is your net profit?

The option is quoted at 2.93, so one contract costs 100 × $2.93 = $293. Your 10 contracts total $2,930. You now have the right to sell 1,000 shares of CSCO for $26 per share. If the stock is currently selling for $21.50 per share, then this is most definitely good news. You can buy 1,000 shares at $21.50 and sell them for $26. Your puts are thus worth $26 − 21.50 = $4.50 per share, or $4.50 × 1,000 = $4,500 in all. Because you paid $2,930 your net profit is $4,500 − 2,930 = $1,570.

Concept Questions

24.1a What is a call option? A put option?

24.1b If you thought that a stock was going to drop sharply in value, how might you use stock options to profit from the decline?

24.2 Fundamentals of Option Valuation

Now that we understand the basics of puts and calls, we can discuss what determines their values. We will focus on call options in the discussion that follows, but the same type of analysis can be applied to put options.

VALUE OF A CALL OPTION AT EXPIRATION

We have already described the payoffs from call options for different stock prices. In continuing this discussion, the following notation will be useful:

To learn more about options, visit www.financial-guide.ch/ica/derivatives.

S_1 = Stock price at expiration (in one period)

S_0 = Stock price today

C_1 = Value of the call option on the expiration date (in one period)

C_0 = Value of the call option today

E = Exercise price on the option

From our previous discussion, remember that, if the stock price (S_1) ends up below the exercise price (E) on the expiration date, then the call option (C_1) is worth zero. In other words:

$$C_1 = 0 \quad \text{if } S_1 \leq E$$

Or, equivalently:

$$C_1 = 0 \quad \text{if } S_1 - E \leq 0 \qquad\qquad \text{[24.1]}$$

This is the case in which the option is out of the money when it expires.

If the option finishes in the money, then $S_1 > E$, and the value of the option at expiration is equal to the difference:

$$C_1 = S_1 - E \quad \text{if } S_1 > E$$

Or, equivalently:

$$C_1 = S_1 - E \quad \text{if } S_1 - E > 0 \qquad\qquad \text{[24.2]}$$

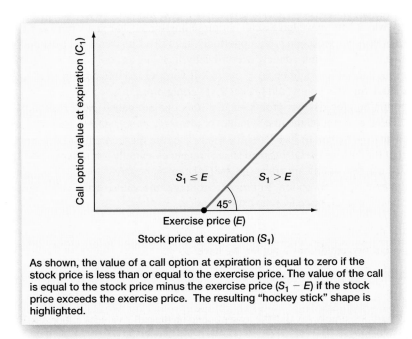

FIGURE 24.1

Value of a Call Option at Expiration for Different Stock Prices

As shown, the value of a call option at expiration is equal to zero if the stock price is less than or equal to the exercise price. The value of the call is equal to the stock price minus the exercise price ($S_1 - E$) if the stock price exceeds the exercise price. The resulting "hockey stick" shape is highlighted.

For example, suppose we have a call option with an exercise price of $10. The option is about to expire. If the stock is selling for $8, then we have the right to pay $10 for something worth only $8. Our option is thus worth exactly zero because the stock price is less than the exercise price on the option ($S_1 \leq E$). If the stock is selling for $12, then the option has value. Because we can buy the stock for $10, the option is worth $S_1 - E = \$12 - 10 = \$2$.

Figure 24.1 plots the value of a call option at expiration against the stock price. The result looks something like a hockey stick. Notice that for every stock price less than E, the value of the option is zero. For every stock price greater than E, the value of the call option is $S_1 - E$. Also, once the stock price exceeds the exercise price, the option's value goes up dollar for dollar with the stock price.

THE UPPER AND LOWER BOUNDS ON A CALL OPTION'S VALUE

Now that we know how to determine C_1, the value of the call at expiration, we turn to a somewhat more challenging question: How can we determine C_0, the value sometime *before* expiration? We will be discussing this in the next several sections. For now, we will establish the upper and lower bounds for the value of a call option.

The Upper Bound What is the most a call option can sell for? If you think about it, the answer is obvious. A call option gives you the right to buy a share of stock, so it can never be worth more than the stock itself. This tells us the upper bound on a call's value: A call option will always sell for no more than the underlying asset. So, in our notation, the upper bound is:

$$C_0 \leq S_0 \tag{24.3}$$

The Lower Bound What is the least a call option can sell for? The answer here is a little less obvious. First of all, the call can't sell for less than zero, so $C_0 \geq 0$. Furthermore, if the stock price is greater than the exercise price, the call option is worth at least $S_0 - E$.

To see why, suppose we have a call option selling for $4. The stock price is $10, and the exercise price is $5. Is there a profit opportunity here? The answer is yes because you could buy the call for $4 and immediately exercise it by spending an additional $5. Your total cost of acquiring the stock would be $4 + 5 = \$9$. If you were to turn around and immediately sell the stock for $10, you would pocket a $1 certain profit.

Opportunities for riskless profits such as this one are called *arbitrages* (say "are-bi-trazh," with the accent on the first syllable) or *arbitrage opportunities*. One who arbitrages is called an *arbitrageur,* or just "arb" for short. The root for the term *arbitrage* is the same as the root for the word *arbitrate,* and an arbitrageur essentially arbitrates prices. In a well-organized market, significant arbitrages will, of course, be rare.

In the case of a call option, to prevent arbitrage, the value of the call today must be greater than the stock price less the exercise price:

$$C_0 \geq S_0 - E$$

If we put our two conditions together, we have:

$$C_0 \geq 0 \qquad \text{if } S_0 - E < 0$$
$$C_0 \geq S_0 - E \quad \text{if } S_0 - E \geq 0$$

[24.4]

These conditions simply say that the lower bound on the call's value is either zero or $S_0 - E$, whichever is bigger.

intrinsic value
The lower bound of an option's value, or what the option would be worth if it were about to expire.

Our lower bound is called the **intrinsic value** of the option, and it is simply what the option would be worth if it were about to expire. With this definition, our discussion thus far can be restated as follows: At expiration, an option is worth its intrinsic value; it will generally be worth more than that anytime before expiration.

Figure 24.2 displays the upper and lower bounds on the value of a call option. Also plotted is a curve representing typical call option values for different stock prices prior to maturity. The exact shape and location of this curve depend on a number of factors. We begin our discussion of these factors in the next section.

FIGURE 24.2

Value of a Call Option before Expiration for Different Stock Prices

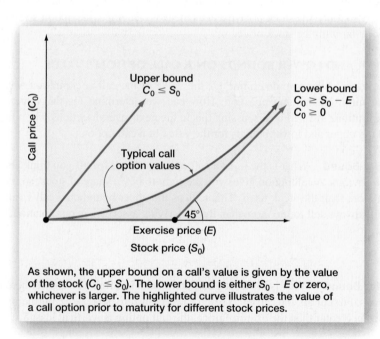

As shown, the upper bound on a call's value is given by the value of the stock ($C_0 \leq S_0$). The lower bound is either $S_0 - E$ or zero, whichever is larger. The highlighted curve illustrates the value of a call option prior to maturity for different stock prices.

A SIMPLE MODEL: PART I

Option pricing can be a complex subject, and we defer a detailed discussion to a later chapter. Fortunately, as is often the case, many of the key insights can be illustrated with a simple example. Suppose we are looking at a call option with one year to expiration and an exercise price of $105. The stock currently sells for $100, and the risk-free rate, R_f, is 20 percent.

The value of the stock in one year is uncertain, of course. To keep things simple, suppose we know that the stock price will be either $110 or $130. It is important to note that we *don't* know the odds associated with these two prices. In other words, we know the possible values for the stock, but not the probabilities associated with those values.

Because the exercise price on the option is $105, we know that the option will be worth either $110 − 105 = $5 or $130 − 105 = $25; but, once again, we don't know which. We do know one thing, however: Our call option is certain to finish in the money.

The Basic Approach Here is the crucial observation: It is possible to exactly duplicate the payoffs on the stock using a combination of the option and the risk-free asset. How? Do the following: Buy one call option and invest $87.50 in a risk-free asset (such as a T-bill).

What will you have in a year? Your risk-free asset will earn 20 percent, so it will be worth $87.50 × 1.20 = $105. Your option will be worth $5 or $25, so the total value will be either $110 or $130, just like the value of the stock:

Stock Value	vs.	Risk-Free Asset Value	+	Call Value	=	Total Value
$110		$105		$ 5		$110
130		105		25		130

As illustrated, these two strategies—buying a share of stock or buying a call and investing in the risk-free asset—have exactly the same payoffs in the future.

Because these two strategies have the same future payoffs, they must have the same value today or else there would be an arbitrage opportunity. The stock sells for $100 today, so the value of the call option today, C_0, is:

$$\$100 = \$87.50 + C_0$$
$$C_0 = \$12.50$$

Where did we get the $87.50? This is just the present value of the exercise price on the option, calculated at the risk-free rate:

$$E/(1 + R_f) = \$105/1.20 = \$87.50$$

Given this, our example shows that the value of a call option in this simple case is given by:

$$S_0 = C_0 + E/(1 + R_f)$$
$$C_0 = S_0 - E/(1 + R_f)$$

[24.5]

In words, the value of the call option is equal to the stock price minus the present value of the exercise price.

A More Complicated Case Obviously, our assumption that the stock price in one year will be either $110 or $130 is a vast oversimplification. We can now develop a more realistic model by assuming that the stock price in one year can be *anything* greater than or equal to the exercise price. Once again, we don't know how likely the different possibilities are, but we are certain that the option will finish somewhere in the money.

We again let S_1 stand for the stock price in one year. Now consider our strategy of investing $87.50 in a riskless asset and buying one call option. The riskless asset will again be worth $105 in one year, and the option will be worth $S_1 - \$105$, the value of which will depend on what the stock price is.

When we investigate the combined value of the option and the riskless asset, we observe something very interesting:

$$\text{Combined value} = \text{Riskless asset value} + \text{Option value}$$
$$= \$105 + (S_1 - 105)$$
$$= S_1$$

Just as we had before, buying a share of stock has exactly the same payoff as buying a call option and investing the present value of the exercise price in the riskless asset.

Once again, to prevent arbitrage, these two strategies must have the same cost, so the value of the call option is equal to the stock price less the present value of the exercise price:[2]

$$C_0 = S_0 - E/(1 + R_f)$$

Our conclusion from this discussion is that determining the value of a call option is not difficult as long as we are certain that the option will finish somewhere in the money.

FOUR FACTORS DETERMINING OPTION VALUES

For information about options and the underlying companies, see www.optionsnewsletter.com.

If we continue to suppose that our option is certain to finish in the money, then we can readily identify four factors that determine an option's value. There is a fifth factor that comes into play if the option can finish out of the money. We will discuss this last factor in the next section.

For now, if we assume that the option expires in t periods, then the present value of the exercise price is $E/(1 + R_f)^t$, and the value of the call is:

$$\text{Call option value} = \text{Stock value} - \text{Present value of the exercise price}$$
$$C_0 = S_0 - E/(1 + R_f)^t \qquad [24.6]$$

If we take a look at this expression, we see that the value of the call obviously depends on four things:

1. *The stock price:* The higher the stock price (S_0) is, the more the call is worth. This comes as no surprise because the option gives us the right to buy the stock at a fixed price.

2. *The exercise price:* The higher the exercise price (E) is, the less the call is worth. This is also not a surprise because the exercise price is what we have to pay to get the stock.

3. *The time to expiration:* The longer the time to expiration is (the bigger t is), the more the option is worth. Once again, this is obvious. Because the option gives us the right to buy for a fixed length of time, its value goes up as that length of time increases.

_____

[2] You're probably wondering what would happen if the stock price were less than the present value of the exercise price, which would result in a negative value for the call option. This can't happen because we are certain that the stock price will be at least E in one year because we know the option will finish in the money. If the current price of the stock is less than $E/(1 + R_f)$, then the return on the stock is certain to be greater than the risk-free rate, which creates an arbitrage opportunity. For example, if the stock is currently selling for $80, then the minimum return will be $(\$105 - 80)/80 = 31.25\%$. Because we can borrow at 20 percent, we can earn a certain minimum return of 11.25 percent per dollar borrowed. This, of course, is an arbitrage opportunity.

4. *The risk-free rate:* The higher the risk-free rate (R_f) is, the more the call is worth. This result is a little less obvious. Normally, we think of asset values as going down as rates rise. In this case, the exercise price is a cash *outflow,* a liability. The current value of that liability goes down as the discount rate goes up.

Concept Questions

24.2a What is the value of a call option at expiration?

24.2b What are the upper and lower bounds on the value of a call option anytime before expiration?

24.2c Assuming that the stock price is certain to be greater than the exercise price on a call option, what is the value of the call? Why?

Valuing a Call Option   24.3

We now investigate the value of a call option when there is the possibility that the option will finish out of the money. We will again examine the simple case of two possible future stock prices. This case will let us identify the remaining factor that determines an option's value.

A SIMPLE MODEL: PART II

From our previous example, we have a stock that currently sells for $100. It will be worth either $110 or $130 in a year, and we don't know which. The risk-free rate is 20 percent. We are now looking at a different call option, however. This one has an exercise price of $120 instead of $105. What is the value of this call option?

This case is a little harder. If the stock ends up at $110, the option is out of the money and worth nothing. If the stock ends up at $130, the option is worth $130 − 120 = $10.

Our basic approach to determining the value of the call option will be the same. We will show once again that it is possible to combine the call option and a risk-free investment in a way that exactly duplicates the payoff from holding the stock. The only complication is that it's a little harder to determine how to do it.

For example, suppose we bought one call and invested the present value of the exercise price in a riskless asset as we did before. In one year, we would have $120 from the riskless investment plus an option worth either zero or $10. The total value would be either $120 or $130. This is not the same as the value of the stock ($110 or $130), so the two strategies are not comparable.

Instead, consider investing the present value of $110 (the lower stock price) in a riskless asset. This guarantees us a $110 payoff. If the stock price is $110, then any call options we own are worthless, and we have exactly $110 as desired.

When the stock is worth $130, the call option is worth $10. Our risk-free investment is worth $110, so we are $130 − 110 = $20 short. Because each call option is worth $10, we need to buy two of them to replicate the value of the stock.

Thus, in this case, investing the present value of the lower stock price in a riskless asset and buying two call options exactly duplicates owning the stock. When the stock is worth $110, we have $110 from our risk-free investment. When the stock is worth $130, we have $110 from the risk-free investment plus two call options worth $10 each.

Because these two strategies have exactly the same value in the future, they must have the same value today, or arbitrage would be possible:

$$S_0 = \$100 = 2 \times C_0 + \$110/(1 + R_f)$$
$$2 \times C_0 = \$100 - 110/1.20$$
$$C_0 = \$4.17$$

Each call option is thus worth $4.17.

EXAMPLE 24.2   **Don't Call Us, We'll Call You**

We are looking at two call options on the same stock, one with an exercise price of $20 and one with an exercise price of $30. The stock currently sells for $35. Its future price will be either $25 or $50. If the risk-free rate is 10 percent, what are the values of these call options?

The first case (with the $20 exercise price) is not difficult because the option is sure to finish in the money. We know that the value is equal to the stock price less the present value of the exercise price:

$$C_0 = S_0 - E/(1 + R_f)$$
$$= \$35 - 20/1.1$$
$$= \$16.82$$

In the second case, the exercise price is $30, so the option can finish out of the money. At expiration, the option is worth $0 if the stock is worth $25. The option is worth $50 − 30 = $20 if it finishes in the money.

As before, we start by investing the present value of the lowest stock price in the risk-free asset. This costs $25/1.1 = $22.73. At expiration, we have $25 from this investment.

If the stock price is $50, then we need an additional $25 to duplicate the stock payoff. Because each option is worth $20 in this case, we need $25/20 = 1.25 options. So, to prevent arbitrage, investing the present value of $25 in a risk-free asset and buying 1.25 call options must have the same value as the stock:

$$S_0 = 1.25 \times C_0 + \$25/(1 + R_f)$$
$$\$35 = 1.25 \times C_0 + \$25/(1 + .10)$$
$$C_0 = \$9.82$$

Notice that this second option had to be worth less because it has the higher exercise price.

THE FIFTH FACTOR

We now illustrate the fifth (and last) factor that determines an option's value. Suppose everything in our example is the same as before except that the stock price can be $105 or $135 instead of $110 or $130. Notice that the effect of this change is to make the stock's future price more volatile than before.

We investigate the same strategy that we used previously: Invest the present value of the lowest stock price ($105 in this case) in the risk-free asset and buy two call options. If the stock price is $105, then, as before, the call options have no value and we have $105 in all.

If the stock price is $135, then each option is worth $S_1 - E = \$135 - 120 = \$15$. We have two calls, so our portfolio is worth $105 + 2 \times 15 = $135. Once again, we have exactly replicated the value of the stock.

What has happened to the option's value? More to the point, the variance of the return on the stock has increased. Does the option's value go up or down? To find out, we need to solve for the value of the call just as we did before:

$$S_0 = \$100 = 2 \times C_0 + \$105/(1 + R_f)$$
$$2 \times C_0 = \$100 - 105/1.20$$
$$C_0 = \$6.25$$

The value of the call option has gone up from $4.17 to $6.25.

Based on our example, the fifth and final factor that determines an option's value is the variance of the return on the underlying asset. Furthermore, the *greater* that variance is, the *more* the option is worth. This result appears a little odd at first, and it may be somewhat surprising to learn that increasing the risk (as measured by return variance) on the underlying asset increases the value of the option.

The reason that increasing the variance on the underlying asset increases the value of the option isn't hard to see in our example. Changing the lower stock price to $105 from $110 doesn't hurt a bit because the option is worth zero in either case. However, moving the upper possible price to $135 from $130 makes the option worth more when it is in the money.

More generally, increasing the variance of the possible future prices on the underlying asset doesn't affect the option's value when the option finishes out of the money. The value is always zero in this case. On the other hand, increasing the variance increases the possible payoffs when the option is in the money, so the net effect is to increase the option's value. Put another way, because the downside risk is always limited, the only effect is to increase the upside potential.

In later discussion, we will use the usual symbol, σ^2, to stand for the variance of the return on the underlying asset.

A CLOSER LOOK

Before moving on, it will be useful to consider one last example. Suppose the stock price is $100, and it will move either up or down by 20 percent. The risk-free rate is 5 percent. What is the value of a call option with a $90 exercise price?

The stock price will be either $80 or $120. The option is worth zero when the stock is worth $80, and it's worth $120 - 90 = \$30$ when the stock is worth $120. We will therefore invest the present value of $80 in the risk-free asset and buy some call options.

When the stock finishes at $120, our risk-free asset pays $80, leaving us $40 short. Each option is worth $30 in this case, so we need $40/30 = 4/3$ options to match the payoff on the stock. The option's value must thus be given by:

$$S_0 = \$100 = 4/3 \times C_0 + \$80/1.05$$
$$C_0 = (3/4) \times (\$100 - 76.19)$$
$$= \$17.86$$

To make our result a little bit more general, notice that the number of options that you need to buy to replicate the value of the stock is always equal to $\Delta S/\Delta C$, where ΔS is the difference in the possible stock prices and ΔC is the difference in the possible option values. In our current case, for example, ΔS would be $120 - 80 = \$40$ and ΔC would be $30 - 0 = \$30$, so $\Delta S/\Delta C$ would be $40/30 = 4/3$, as we calculated.

Notice also that when the stock is certain to finish in the money, $\Delta S/\Delta C$ is always exactly equal to 1, so one call option is always needed. Otherwise, $\Delta S/\Delta C$ is greater than 1, so more than one call option is needed.

This concludes our discussion of option valuation. The most important thing to remember is that the value of an option depends on five factors. Table 24.2 summarizes these factors and the direction of their influence for both puts and calls. In Table 24.2, the sign in

TABLE 24.2

Five Factors That
Determine Option Values

Factor	Direction of Influence	
	Calls	**Puts**
Current value of the underlying asset	(+)	(−)
Exercise price on the option	(−)	(+)
Time to expiration on the option	(+)	(+)
Risk-free rate	(+)	(−)
Variance of return on the underlying asset	(+)	(+)

parentheses indicates the direction of the influence.[3] In other words, the sign tells us whether the value of the option goes up or down when the value of a factor increases. For example, notice that increasing the exercise price reduces the value of a call option. Increasing any of the other four factors increases the value of the call. Notice also that the time to expiration and the variance of return act the same for puts and calls. The other three factors have opposite signs in the two cases.

We have not considered how to value a call option when the option can finish out of the money and the stock price can take on more than two values. A very famous result, the Black-Scholes option pricing model, is needed in this case. We cover this subject in a later chapter.

Concept Questions

24.3a What are the five factors that determine an option's value?

24.3b What is the effect of an increase in each of the five factors on the value of a call option? Give an intuitive explanation for your answer.

24.3c What is the effect of an increase in each of the five factors on the value of a put option? Give an intuitive explanation for your answer.

24.4 Employee Stock Options

employee stock
option (ESO)
An option granted to an
employee by a company
giving the employee the
right to buy shares of stock
in the company at a fixed
price for a fixed time.

Options are important in corporate finance in a lot of different ways. In this section, we begin to examine some of these by taking a look at **employee stock options**, or ESOs. An ESO is, in essence, a call option that a firm gives to employees giving them the right to buy shares of stock in the company. The practice of granting options to employees has become widespread. It is almost universal for upper management; but some companies, like The Gap and Starbucks, grant options to almost every employee. Thus, an understanding of ESOs is important. Why? Because you may soon be an ESO holder!

ESO FEATURES

Because ESOs are basically call options, we have already covered most of the important aspects. However, ESOs have a few features that make them different from regular stock options. The details differ from company to company, but a typical ESO has a 10-year life, which is much longer than most ordinary options. Unlike traded options, ESOs cannot be sold. They also have what is known as a "vesting" period: Often, for up to three years or so, an ESO cannot be exercised and also must be forfeited if an employee leaves the company.

---

[3] The signs in Table 24.2 are for American options. For a European put option, the effect of increasing the time to expiration is ambiguous, and the direction of the influence can be positive or negative.

After this period, the options "vest," which means they can be exercised. Sometimes, employees who resign with vested options are given a limited time to exercise their options.

Why are ESOs granted? There are basically two reasons. First, going back to Chapter 1, the owners of a corporation (the shareholders) face the basic problem of aligning shareholder and management interests and also of providing incentives for employees to focus on corporate goals. ESOs are a powerful motivator because, as we have seen, the payoffs on options can be very large. High-level executives in particular stand to gain enormous wealth if they are successful in creating value for stockholders.

The second reason some companies rely heavily on ESOs is that an ESO has no immediate, up-front, out-of-pocket cost to the corporation. In smaller, possibly cash-strapped companies, ESOs are simply a substitute for ordinary wages. Employees are willing to accept them instead of cash, hoping for big payoffs in the future. In fact, ESOs are a major recruiting tool, allowing businesses to attract talent that they otherwise could not afford.

See www. esopassociation.org for a site devoted to employee stock options.

ESO REPRICING

ESOs are almost always "at the money" when they are issued, meaning that the stock price is equal to the strike price. Notice that, in this case, the intrinsic value is zero, so there is no value from immediate exercise. Of course, even though the intrinsic value is zero, an ESO is still quite valuable because of, among other things, its very long life.

If the stock falls significantly after an ESO is granted, then the option is said to be "underwater." On occasion, a company will decide to lower the strike price on underwater options. Such options are said to be "restruck" or "repriced."

The practice of repricing ESOs is controversial. Companies that do it argue that once an ESO becomes deeply out of the money, it loses its incentive value because employees recognize there is only a small chance that the option will finish in the money. In fact, employees may leave and join other companies where they receive a fresh options grant.

Critics of repricing point out that a lowered strike price is, in essence, a reward for failing. They also point out that if employees know that options will be repriced, then much of the incentive effect is lost. Because of this controversy, many companies do not reprice options or have voted against repricing. For example, pharmaceutical giant Bristol-Myers Squibb's explicit policy prohibiting option repricing states, "It is the board of directors' policy that the company will not, without stockholder approval, amend any employee or nonemployee director stock option to reduce the exercise price (except for appropriate adjustment in the case of a stock split or similar change in capitalization)." However, other equally well-known companies have no such policy, and some have been labeled "serial repricers." The accusation is that such companies routinely drop strike prices following stock price declines.

For more information about ESOs, try the National Center for Employee Ownership at www.nceo.org.

An option exchange is a variation on a repricing. What typically happens is that underwater ESOs are exchanged for a smaller number of new ESOs with a lower exercise price. For example, in June 2008, LeapFrog Enterprises, maker of high-tech learning toys, exchanged options to buy 4.94 million shares for new options to buy 3.67 million shares at reduced strike prices. Frequently, option exchanges are structured such that the value of the new options is approximately equal to that of the old ones. In essence, a large number of underwater options are exchanged for a smaller number of at-the-money options.

Today, many companies award options on a regular basis, perhaps annually or even quarterly. That way, an employee will always have at least some options that are near the money even if others are underwater. Also, regular grants ensure that employees always have unvested options, which gives them an added incentive to stay with their current employer rather than forfeit the potentially valuable options.

Erik Lie on Option Backdating

Stock options can be granted to executive and other employees as an incentive device. They strengthen the relation between compensation and a firm's stock price performance, thus boosting effort and improving decision making within the firm. Further, to the extent that decision makers are risk averse (as most of us are), options induce more risk taking, which can benefit shareholders. However, options also have a dark side. They can be used to (i) conceal true compensation expenses in financial reports, (ii) evade corporate taxes, and (iii) siphon money from corporations to executives. One example that illustrates all three of these aspects is that of option backdating.

To understand the virtue of option backdating, it is first important to realize that for accounting, tax, and incentive reasons, most options are granted at-the-money, meaning that their exercise price equals the stock price on the grant date. Option backdating is the practice of selecting a past date (e.g., from the past month) when the stock price was particularly low to be the official grant date. This raises the value of the options, because they are effectively granted in-the-money. Unless this is properly disclosed and accounted for (which it rarely is), the practice of backdating can cause an array of problems. First, granting options that are effectively in-the-money violates many corporate option plans or other securities filings stating that the exercise price equals the fair market value on the grant day. Second, camouflaging in-the-money options as at-the-money options understates compensation expenses in the financial statements. In fact, under the old accounting rule APB 25 that was phased out in 2005, companies could expense options according to their intrinsic value, such that at-the-money options were not expensed at all. Third, at-the-money option grants qualify for certain tax breaks that in-the-money option grants do not qualify for, such that backdating can result in underpaid taxes.

Empirical evidence shows that the practice of backdating was prevalent from the early 1990s to 2005, especially among tech firms. As this came to the attention of the media and regulators in 2006, a scandal erupted. More than 100 companies were investigated for manipulation of option grant dates. As a result, numerous executives were fired, old financial statements were restated, additional taxes became due, and countless lawsuits were filed against companies and their directors. With new disclosure rules, stricter enforcement of the requirement that took effect as part of the Sarbanes-Oxley Act in 2002 that grants have to be filed within two business days, and greater scrutiny by regulators and the investment community, we likely have put the practice of backdating options behind us.

Erik Lie is Associate Professor of Finance and Henry B. Tippie Research Fellow at the University of Iowa. His research focuses on corporate financial policy, M&A, and executive compensation.

ESO BACKDATING

A scandal erupted in 2006 over the backdating of ESOs. Recall that ESOs are almost always at the money on the grant date, meaning that the strike price is set equal to the stock price on the grant date. Financial researchers discovered that many companies had a practice of looking backward in time to select the grant date. Why did they do this? The answer is that they would pick a date on which the stock price (looking back) was low, thereby leading to option grants with low strike prices relative to the current stock price.

Backdating ESOs is not necessarily illegal or unethical as long as there is full disclosure and various tax and accounting issues are handled properly. Before the Sarbanes-Oxley Act of 2002 (which we discussed in Chapter 1), companies had up to 45 days after the end of their fiscal years to report options grants, so there was ample leeway for backdating. Because of Sarbanes-Oxley, companies are now required to report option grants within two business days of the grant dates, thereby limiting the gains from any backdating.

Concept Questions

24.4a What are the key differences between a traded stock option and an ESO?
24.4b What is ESO repricing? Why is it controversial?

Equity as a Call Option on the Firm's Assets

Now that we understand the basic determinants of an option's value, we turn to examining some of the many ways that options appear in corporate finance. One of the most important insights we gain from studying options is that the common stock in a leveraged firm (one that has issued debt) is effectively a call option on the assets of the firm. This is a remarkable observation, and we explore it next.

Looking at an example is the easiest way to get started. Suppose a firm has a single debt issue outstanding. The face value is $1,000, and the debt is coming due in a year. There are no coupon payments between now and then, so the debt is effectively a pure discount bond. In addition, the current market value of the firm's assets is $980, and the risk-free rate is 12.5 percent.

In a year, the stockholders will have a choice. They can pay off the debt for $1,000 and thereby acquire the assets of the firm free and clear, or they can default on the debt. If they default, the bondholders will own the assets of the firm.

In this situation, the stockholders essentially have a call option on the assets of the firm with an exercise price of $1,000. They can exercise the option by paying the $1,000, or they can choose not to exercise the option by defaulting. Whether or not they will choose to exercise obviously depends on the value of the firm's assets when the debt becomes due.

If the value of the firm's assets exceeds $1,000, then the option is in the money, and the stockholders will exercise by paying off the debt. If the value of the firm's assets is less than $1,000, then the option is out of the money, and the stockholders will optimally choose to default. What we now illustrate is that we can determine the values of the debt and equity using our option pricing results.

CASE I: THE DEBT IS RISK-FREE

Suppose that in one year the firm's assets will be worth either $1,100 or $1,200. What is the value today of the equity in the firm? The value of the debt? What is the interest rate on the debt?

To answer these questions, we first recognize that the option (the equity in the firm) is certain to finish in the money because the value of the firm's assets ($1,100 or $1,200) will always exceed the face value of the debt. In this case, from our discussion in previous sections, we know that the option value is simply the difference between the value of the underlying asset and the present value of the exercise price (calculated at the risk-free rate). The present value of $1,000 in one year at 12.5 percent is $888.89. The current value of the firm is $980, so the option (the firm's equity) is worth $980 − 888.89 = $91.11.

What we see is that the equity, which is effectively an option to purchase the firm's assets, must be worth $91.11. The debt must therefore actually be worth $888.89. In fact, we really didn't need to know about options to handle this example because the debt is risk-free. The reason is that the bondholders are certain to receive $1,000. Because the debt is risk-free, the appropriate discount rate (and the interest rate on the debt) is the risk-free rate, and we therefore know immediately that the current value of the debt is $1,000/1.125 = $888.89. The equity is thus worth $980 − 888.89 = $91.11, as we calculated.

CASE II: THE DEBT IS RISKY

Suppose now that the value of the firm's assets in one year will be either $800 or $1,200. This case is a little more difficult because the debt is no longer risk-free. If the value of the assets turns out to be $800, then the stockholders will not exercise their option and will thereby default. The stock is worth nothing in this case. If the assets are worth $1,200, then the stockholders will exercise their option to pay off the debt and will enjoy a profit of $1,200 − 1,000 = $200.

What we see is that the option (the equity in the firm) will be worth either zero or $200. The assets will be worth either $1,200 or $800. Based on our discussion in previous sections, a portfolio that has the present value of $800 invested in a risk-free asset and ($1,200 − 800)/ (200 − 0) = 2 call options exactly replicates the value of the assets of the firm.

The present value of $800 at the risk-free rate of 12.5 percent is $800/1.125 = $711.11. This amount, plus the value of the two call options, is equal to $980, the current value of the firm:

$$\$980 = 2 \times C_0 + \$711.11$$
$$C_0 = \$134.44$$

Because the call option in this case is actually the firm's equity, the value of the equity is $134.44. The value of the debt is thus $980 − 134.44 = $845.56.

Finally, because the debt has a $1,000 face value and a current value of $845.56, the interest rate is ($1,000/845.56) − 1 = 18.27%. This exceeds the risk-free rate, of course, because the debt is now risky.

EXAMPLE 24.3   Equity as a Call Option

Swenson Software has a pure discount debt issue with a face value of $100. The issue is due in a year. At that time, the assets of the firm will be worth either $55 or $160, depending on the sales success of Swenson's latest product. The assets of the firm are currently worth $110. If the risk-free rate is 10 percent, what is the value of the equity in Swenson? The value of the debt? The interest rate on the debt?

(continued)

To replicate the value of the assets of the firm, we first need to invest the present value of $55 in the risk-free asset. This costs $55/1.10 = $50. If the assets turn out to be worth $160, then the option is worth $160 − 100 = $60. Our risk-free asset will be worth $55, so we need ($160 − 55)/60 = 1.75 call options. Because the firm is currently worth $110, we have:

$$\$110 = 1.75 \times C_0 + \$50$$
$$C_0 = \$34.29$$

The equity is thus worth $34.29; the debt is worth $110 − 34.29 = $75.71. The interest rate on the debt is about ($100/75.71) − 1 = 32.1%.

Concept Questions

24.5a Why do we say that the equity in a leveraged firm is effectively a call option on the firm's assets?

24.5b All other things being the same, would the stockholders of a firm prefer to increase or decrease the volatility of the firm's return on assets? Why? What about the bondholders? Give an intuitive explanation.

Options and Capital Budgeting   24.6

Most of the options we have discussed so far are financial options because they involve the right to buy or sell financial assets such as shares of stock. In contrast, **real options** involve real assets. As we will discuss in this section, our understanding of capital budgeting can be greatly enhanced by recognizing that many corporate investment decisions really amount to the evaluation of real options.

real option
An option that involves real assets as opposed to financial assets such as shares of stock.

To give a simple example of a real option, imagine that you are shopping for a used car. You find one that you like for $4,000, but you are not completely sure. So, you give the owner of the car $150 to hold the car for you for one week, meaning that you have one week to buy the car or else you forfeit your $150. As you probably recognize, what you have done here is to purchase a call option, giving you the right to buy the car at a fixed price for a fixed time. It's a real option because the underlying asset (the car) is a real asset.

The use of options such as the one in our car example is common in the business world. For example, real estate developers frequently need to purchase several smaller tracts of land from different owners to assemble a single larger tract. The development can't go forward unless all of the smaller properties are obtained. In this case, the developer will often buy options on the individual properties but will exercise those options only if all of the necessary pieces can be obtained.

These examples involve explicit options. As it turns out, almost all capital budgeting decisions contain numerous *implicit* options. We discuss the most important types of these next.

THE INVESTMENT TIMING DECISION

Consider a business that is examining a new project of some sort. What this normally means is management must decide whether to make an investment outlay to acquire the new assets needed for the project. If you think about it, what management has is the right, but not the obligation, to pay some fixed amount (the initial investment) and thereby acquire a real asset (the project). In other words, essentially all proposed projects are real options!

Based on our discussion in previous chapters, you already know how to analyze proposed business investments. You would identify and analyze the relevant cash flows and assess the net present value (NPV) of the proposal. If the NPV is positive, you would recommend taking the project, where taking the project amounts to exercising the option.

There is a very important qualification to this discussion that involves mutually exclusive investments. Remember that two (or more) investments are said to be mutually exclusive if we can take only one of them. A standard example is a situation in which we own a piece of land that we wish to build on. We are considering building either a gasoline station or an apartment building. We further think that both projects have positive NPVs, but, of course, we can take only one. Which one do we take? The obvious answer is that we take the one with the larger NPV.

Here is the key point. Just because an investment has a positive NPV doesn't mean we should take it today. That sounds like a complete contradiction of what we have said all along, but it isn't. The reason is that if we take a project today, we can't take it later. Put differently, almost all projects compete with themselves in time. We can take a project now, a month from now, a year from now, and so on. We therefore have to compare the NPV of taking the project now versus the NPV of taking it later. Deciding when to take a project is called the **investment timing decision**.

investment timing decision
The evaluation of the optimal time to begin a project.

A simple example is useful to illustrate the investment timing decision. A project costs $100 and has a single future cash flow. If we take it today, the cash flow will be $120 in one year. If we wait one year, the project will still cost $100, but the cash flow the following year (two years from now) will be $130 because the potential market is bigger. If these are the only two options, and the relevant discount rate is 10 percent, what should we do?

To answer this question, we need to compute the two NPVs. If we take it today, the NPV is:

$$NPV = -\$100 + 120/1.1 = \$9.09$$

If we wait one year, the NPV at that time would be:

$$NPV = -\$100 + 130/1.1 = \$18.18$$

This $18.18 is the NPV one year from now. We need the value today, so we discount back one period:

$$NPV = \$18.18/1.1 = \$16.53$$

So, the choice is clear. If we wait, the NPV is $16.53 today compared to $9.09 if we start immediately, so the optimal time to begin the project is one year from now.

The fact that we do not have to take a project immediately is often called the "option to wait." In our simple example, the value of the option to wait is the difference in NPVs: $16.53 − 9.09 = $7.44. This $7.44 is the extra value created by deferring the start of the project as opposed to taking it today.

As our example illustrates, the option to wait can be valuable. Just how valuable depends on the type of project. If we were thinking about a consumer product intended to capitalize on a current fashion or trend, then the option to wait is probably not very valuable because the window of opportunity is probably short. In contrast, suppose the project in question is a proposal to replace an existing production facility with a new, higher-efficiency one. This type of investment can be made now or later. In this case, the option to wait may be valuable.

The Investment Timing Decision	**EXAMPLE 24.4**

A project costs $200 and has a future cash flow of $42 per year forever. If we wait one year, the project will cost $240 because of inflation, but the cash flows will be $48 per year forever. If these are the only two options, and the relevant discount rate is 12 percent, what should we do? What is the value of the option to wait?

In this case, the project is a simple perpetuity. If we take it today, the NPV is:

NPV = −$200 + 42/.12 = $150

If we wait one year, the NPV at that time would be:

NPV = −$240 + 48/.12 = $160

So, $160 is the NPV one year from now, but we need to know the value today. Discounting back one period, we get:

NPV = $160/1.12 = $142.86.

If we wait, the NPV is $142.86 today compared to $150 if we start immediately, so the optimal time to begin the project is now.

What's the value of the option to wait? It is tempting to say that it is $142.86 − $150 = −$7.14, but that's wrong. Why? Because, as we discussed earlier, an option can never have a negative value. In this case, the option to wait has a zero value.

There is another important aspect regarding the option to wait. Just because a project has a negative NPV today doesn't mean that we should permanently reject it. For example, suppose an investment costs $120 and has a perpetual cash flow of $10 per year. If the discount rate is 10 percent, then the NPV is $10/.10 − 120 = −$20, so the project should not be taken now.

We should not just forget about this project forever, though. Suppose that next year, for some reason, the relevant discount rate fell to 5 percent. Then the NPV would be $10/.05 − $120 = $80, and we would take the project (assuming that further waiting isn't even more valuable). More generally, as long as there is some possible future scenario under which a project has a positive NPV, then the option to wait is valuable, and we should just shelve the project proposal for now.

MANAGERIAL OPTIONS

Once we decide the optimal time to launch a project, other real options come into play. In our capital budgeting analysis thus far, we have more or less ignored the impact of managerial actions that might take place *after* a project is launched. In effect, we assumed that, once a project is launched, its basic features cannot be changed.

In reality, depending on what actually happens in the future, there will always be opportunities to modify a project. These opportunities, which are an important type of real options, are often called **managerial options**. There are a great number of these options. The ways in which a product is priced, manufactured, advertised, and produced can all be changed, and these are just a few of the possibilities.

managerial options
Opportunities that managers can exploit if certain things happen in the future.

For example, in 2008, faced with dramatically higher fuel costs, US Airways announced major changes in its operations. First, the company decided to cut domestic capacity by 6 to 8 percent in the fourth quarter of 2008 and an additional 7 to 9 percent in 2009. It also planned to return 10 jetliners to lessors by 2009, and it cancelled the leases on two wide-body jets originally scheduled for its fleet in 2009. Further fleet reductions were to occur in 2010.

US Airways also planned to eliminate 1,700 jobs through attrition, voluntary leaves of absences, and furloughs. The biggest job cuts would be in Las Vegas, where 600 jobs would be lost. The company's intention was to cut the number of destinations served from Las Vegas from 55 to 31 and to reduce the number of daily flights to that city from 141 to 81.

Finally, US Airways announced increases in fees. It would begin charging $15 for a passenger's first checked bag. There would be a $2 charge for nonalcoholic beverages on domestic flights, and the cost of alcoholic beverages would rise from $5 to $7. The company also planned to charge $25 for mileage-award tickets and to increase fees for tickets purchased through its reservations line.

Contingency Planning   The various what-if procedures, particularly the break-even measures we discussed in an earlier chapter, have a use beyond that of simply evaluating cash flow and NPV estimates. We can also view these procedures and measures as primitive ways of exploring the dynamics of a project and investigating managerial options. What we think about in this case are some of the possible futures that could come about and what actions we might take if they do.

For example, we might find that a project fails to break even when sales drop below 10,000 units. This is a fact that is interesting to know; but the more important thing is to then go on and ask: What actions are we going to take if this actually occurs? This is called

contingency planning
Taking into account the managerial options implicit in a project.

contingency planning, and it amounts to an investigation of some of the managerial options implicit in a project.

There is no limit to the number of possible futures or contingencies we could investigate. However, there are some broad classes, and we consider these next.

The Option to Expand   One particularly important option we have not explicitly addressed is the option to expand. If we truly find a positive NPV project, then there is an obvious consideration. Can we expand the project or repeat it to get an even larger NPV? Our static analysis implicitly assumes that the scale of the project is fixed.

For example, if the sales demand for a particular product were to greatly exceed expectations, we might investigate increasing production. If this is not feasible for some reason, then we could always increase cash flow by raising the price. Either way, the potential cash flow is higher than we have indicated because we have implicitly assumed that no expansion or price increase is possible. Overall, because we ignore the option to expand in our analysis, we *underestimate* NPV (all other things being equal).

The Option to Abandon   At the other extreme, the option to scale back or even abandon a project is also quite valuable. For example, if a project does not break even on a cash flow basis, then it can't even cover its own expenses. We would be better off if we just abandoned it. Our DCF analysis implicitly assumes that we would keep operating even in this case.

Sometimes, the best thing to do is punt. For example, earlier we discussed the problems faced by US Airways in 2008. Other airlines faced more dire consequences. In April 2008, Ohio-based Skybus Airlines announced on a Friday that it would cease operations the next day. The company, which began operations in 2004, blamed the rising costs of jet fuel and a slowing economy for its problems. What made the situation unique is that Skybus was the third airline to cease operations *that same week*! Earlier in the week, ATA Airlines closed down when it lost a key contract for its military charter business. And Aloha Airlines blamed its closing on below-cost fares offered by Go! Airline that it was unable to match.

More generally, if sales demand were significantly below expectations, we might be able to sell off some capacity or put it to another use. Maybe the product or service could be redesigned or otherwise improved. Regardless of the specifics, we once again *underestimate* NPV if we assume that the project must last for some fixed number of years, no matter what happens in the future.

The Option to Suspend or Contract Operations An option that is closely related to the option to abandon is the option to suspend operations. Frequently we see companies choosing to temporarily shut down an activity of some sort. For example, automobile manufacturers sometimes find themselves with too many vehicles of a particular type. In this case, production is often halted until the excess supply is worked off. At some point in the future, production resumes.

The option to suspend operations is particularly valuable in natural resource extraction. Suppose you own a gold mine. If gold prices fall dramatically, then your analysis might show that it costs more to extract an ounce of gold than you can sell the gold for, so you quit mining. The gold just stays in the ground, however, and you can always resume operations if the price rises sufficiently. In fact, operations might be suspended and restarted many times over the life of the mine.

Companies also sometimes choose to permanently scale back an activity. If a new product does not sell as well as planned, production might be cut back and the excess capacity put to some other use. This case is really just the opposite of the option to expand, so we will label it the option to contract.

For example, in June 2008, Goodyear Tire & Rubber announced plans to close its Australian manufacturing plant. The closing was a result of the company's attempt to reduce operating costs. The company had previously closed plants in Texas, Canada, Morocco, England, and New Zealand.

Options in Capital Budgeting: An Example Suppose we are examining a new project. To keep things relatively simple, let's say that we expect to sell 100 units per year at $1 net cash flow apiece into perpetuity. We thus expect that the cash flow will be $100 per year.

In one year, we will know more about the project. In particular, we will have a better idea of whether it is successful. If it looks like a long-term success, the expected sales will be revised upward to 150 units per year. If it does not, the expected sales will be revised downward to 50 units per year. Success and failure are equally likely. Notice that because there is an even chance of selling 50 or 150 units, the expected sales are still 100 units, as we originally projected. The cost is $550, and the discount rate is 20 percent. The project can be dismantled and sold in one year for $400 if we decide to abandon it. Should we take it?

A standard DCF analysis is not difficult. The expected cash flow is $100 per year forever, and the discount rate is 20 percent. The PV of the cash flows is $100/.20 = $500, so the NPV is $500 − 550 = −$50. We shouldn't take the project.

This analysis ignores valuable options, however. In one year, we can sell out for $400. How can we account for this? What we have to do is to decide what we are going to do one year from now. In this simple case, we need to evaluate only two contingencies, an upward revision and a downward revision, so the extra work is not great.

In one year, if the expected cash flows are revised to $50, then the PV of the cash flows is revised downward to $50/.20 = $250. We get $400 by abandoning the project, so that is what we will do (the NPV of keeping the project in one year is $250 − 400 = −$150).

If the demand is revised upward, then the PV of the future cash flows at year 1 is $150/.20 = $750. This exceeds the $400 abandonment value, so we will keep the project.

We now have a project that costs $550 today. In one year, we expect a cash flow of $100 from the project. In addition, this project will be worth either $400 (if we abandon it because it is a failure) or $750 (if we keep it because it succeeds). These outcomes are equally likely, so we expect the project to be worth ($400 + 750)/2, or $575.

Summing up, in one year, we expect to have $100 in cash plus a project worth $575, or $675 total. At a 20 percent discount rate, this $675 is worth $562.50 today, so the NPV is $562.50 − 550 = $12.50. We should take the project.

The NPV of our project has increased by $62.50. Where did this come from? Our original analysis implicitly assumed we would keep the project even if it was a failure. At year 1, however, we saw that we were $150 better off ($400 versus $250) if we abandoned. There was a 50 percent chance of this happening, so the expected gain from abandoning is $75. The PV of this amount is the value of the option to abandon: $75/1.20 = $62.50.

Strategic Options   Companies sometimes undertake new projects just to explore possibilities and evaluate potential future business strategies. This is a little like testing the water by sticking a toe in before diving. Such projects are difficult to analyze using conventional DCF methods because most of the benefits come in the form of **strategic options**—that is, options for future, related business moves. Projects that create such options may be very valuable, but that value is difficult to measure. Research and development, for example, is an important and valuable activity for many firms, precisely because it creates options for new products and procedures.

To give another example, a large manufacturer might decide to open a retail outlet as a pilot study. The primary goal is to gain some market insight. Because of the high start-up costs, this one operation won't break even. However, using the sales experience gained from the pilot, the firm can then evaluate whether to open more outlets, to change the product mix, to enter new markets, and so on. The information gained and the resulting options for actions are all valuable, but coming up with a reliable dollar figure is probably not feasible.

Conclusion   We have seen that incorporating options into capital budgeting analysis is not easy. What can we do about them in practice? The answer is that we need to keep them in mind as we work with the projected cash flows. We will tend to underestimate NPV by ignoring options. The damage might be small for a highly structured, very specific proposal, but it might be great for an exploratory one.

> **strategic options**
> Options for future, related business products or strategies.

Concept Questions

24.6a Why do we say that almost every capital budgeting proposal involves mutually exclusive alternatives?

24.6b What are the options to expand, abandon, and suspend operations?

24.6c What are strategic options?

24.7 Options and Corporate Securities

In this section, we return to financial assets by considering some of the most common ways options appear in corporate securities and other financial assets. We begin by examining warrants and convertible bonds.

WARRANTS

A **warrant** is a corporate security that looks a lot like a call option. It gives the holder the right, but not the obligation, to buy shares of common stock directly from a company at a

> **warrant**
> A security that gives the holder the right to purchase shares of stock at a fixed price over a given period of time.

fixed price for a given time period. Each warrant specifies the number of shares of stock the holder can buy, the exercise price, and the expiration date.

The differences in contractual features between the call options that trade on the Chicago Board Options Exchange and warrants are relatively minor. Warrants usually have much longer maturity periods, however. In fact, some warrants are actually perpetual and have no fixed expiration date.

Warrants are often called *sweeteners* or *equity kickers* because they are often issued in combination with privately placed loans or bonds. Throwing in some warrants is a way of making the deal a little more attractive to the lender, and it is a common practice. Also, warrants have been listed and traded on the NYSE since April 13, 1970. In the middle of 2008, there were only 11 warrants listed on the NYSE. However, in Europe, warrants are still popular. Also in the middle of 2008, Euronext listed about 8,400 of them.

In many cases, warrants are attached to bonds when issued. The loan agreement will state whether the warrants are detachable from the bond. Usually, the warrant can be detached immediately and sold by the holder as a separate security.

The Difference between Warrants and Call Options As we have explained, from the holder's point of view, warrants are similar to call options on common stock. A warrant, like a call option, gives its holder the right to buy common stock at a specified price. From the firm's point of view, however, a warrant is different from a call option sold on the company's common stock.

The most important difference between call options and warrants is that call options are issued by individuals and warrants are issued by firms. When a call option is exercised, one investor buys stock from another investor. The company is not involved. When a warrant is exercised, the firm must issue new shares of stock. Each time a warrant is exercised, then, the firm receives some cash and the number of shares outstanding increases. Notice that the employee stock options we discussed earlier in the chapter are issued by corporations; so, strictly speaking, they are warrants rather than options.

To illustrate, suppose the Endrun Company issues a warrant giving holders the right to buy one share of common stock at $25. Further suppose the warrant is exercised. Endrun must print one new stock certificate. In exchange for the stock certificate, it receives $25 from the holder.

In contrast, when a call option is exercised, there is no change in the number of shares outstanding. Suppose Ms. Enger purchases a call option on the common stock of the Endrun Company from Mr. Swift. The call option gives Ms. Enger the right to buy (from Mr. Swift) one share of common stock of the Endrun Company for $25.

If Ms. Enger chooses to exercise the call option, Mr. Swift is obligated to give her one share of Endrun's common stock in exchange for $25. If Mr. Swift does not already own a share, he must go into the stock market and buy one.

The call option amounts to a side bet between Ms. Enger and Mr. Swift on the value of the Endrun Company's common stock. When a call option is exercised, one investor gains and the other loses. The total number of shares outstanding of the Endrun Company remains constant, and no new funds are made available to the company.

Earnings Dilution Warrants and (as we will see) convertible bonds frequently cause the number of shares to increase. This happens (1) when the warrants are exercised and (2) when the bonds are converted, causing the firm's net income to be spread over a larger number of shares. Earnings per share therefore decrease.

Firms with significant numbers of warrants and convertible issues outstanding will generally calculate and report earnings per share on a *diluted basis*. This means that the calculation is based on the number of shares that would be outstanding if all the warrants were exercised and all the convertibles were converted. Because this increases the number of shares, diluted EPS will be lower than "basic" EPS, which are calculated only on the basis of shares actually outstanding.

CONVERTIBLE BONDS

convertible bond
A bond that can be exchanged for a fixed number of shares of stock for a specified amount of time.

A **convertible bond** is similar to a bond with warrants. The most important difference is that a bond with warrants can be separated into distinct securities (a bond and some warrants), but a convertible bond cannot. A convertible bond gives the holder the right to exchange the bond for a fixed number of shares of stock anytime up to and including the maturity date of the bond.

Preferred stock can frequently be converted into common stock. A convertible preferred stock is the same as a convertible bond except that it has an infinite maturity date.[4]

Features of a Convertible Bond   We can illustrate the basic features of a convertible bond by examining a particular issue. In July 2008, solar energy company Evergreen Solar issued $400 million in convertible bonds. The bonds have a four percent coupon rate, mature in 2013, and can be converted into Evergreen Solar common stock at a **conversion price** of $12.11. Because each bond has a face value of $1,000, the owner can receive $1,000/$12.11 = 82.6 shares of Evergreen Solar's stock. The number of shares per bond, 82.6 in this case, is called the **conversion ratio**.

conversion price
The dollar amount of a bond's par value that is exchangeable for one share of stock.

conversion ratio
The number of shares per bond received for conversion into stock.

When Evergreen Solar issued its convertible bonds, its common stock was trading at $10.21 per share. The conversion price was thus ($12.11 − 10.21)/$10.21 = 18.61 percent higher than its actual stock price. This 18.61 percent is called the **conversion premium**. It reflects the fact that the conversion option in Evergreen Solar's bonds was out of the money at the time of issuance; this is usually the case.

conversion premium
The difference between the conversion price and the current stock price, divided by the current stock price.

Value of a Convertible Bond   Even though the conversion feature of the convertible bond cannot be detached like a warrant, the value of the bond can still be decomposed into the bond value and the value of the conversion feature. We discuss how this is done next.

The easiest way to illustrate convertible bond valuation is with an example. Suppose a company called Micron Origami (MO) has an outstanding convertible bond issue. The coupon rate is 7 percent and the conversion ratio is 15. There are 12 remaining coupons, and the stock is trading for $68.

straight bond value
The value a convertible bond would have if it could not be converted into common stock.

Straight Bond Value   The **straight bond value** is what the convertible bond would sell for if it could not be converted into common stock. This value will depend on the general level of interest rates on debentures and on the default risk of the issuer.

Suppose straight debentures issued by MO are rated B, and B-rated bonds are priced to yield 8 percent. We can determine the straight bond value of MO convertible bonds by discounting the $35 semiannual coupon payments and maturity value at 8 percent, just as we did in Chapter 7:

$$\text{Straight bond value} = \$35 \times (1 - 1/1.04^{12})/.04 + 1,000/1.04^{12}$$
$$= \$328.48 + 624.60$$
$$= \$953.08$$

---

[4] The dividends paid are, of course, not tax deductible for the corporation. Interest paid on a convertible bond is tax deductible.

The straight bond value of a convertible bond is a minimum value in the sense that the bond is always worth at least this amount. As we discuss next, it will usually be worth more.

Conversion Value   The **conversion value** of a convertible bond is what the bond would be worth if it were immediately converted into common stock. We compare this value by multiplying the current price of the stock by the number of shares that will be received when the bond is converted.

For example, each MO convertible bond can be converted into 15 shares of MO common stock. MO common was selling for $68. Thus, the conversion value was $15 \times \$68 = \$1,020$.

A convertible cannot sell for less than its conversion value, or an arbitrage opportunity exists. If MO's convertible had sold for less than $1,020, investors would have bought the bonds, converted them into common stock, and sold the stock. The arbitrage profit would have been the difference between the value of the stock and the bond's conversion value.

Floor Value   As we have seen, convertible bonds have two *floor values:* the straight bond value and the conversion value. The minimum value of a convertible bond is given by the greater of these two values. For the MO issue, the conversion value is $1,020 and the straight bond value is $953.08. At a minimum, this bond is thus worth $1,020.

Figure 24.3 plots the minimum value of a convertible bond against the value of the stock. The conversion value is determined by the value of the firm's underlying common stock. As the value of the common stock rises and falls, the conversion value rises and falls with it. For example, if the value of MO's common stock increases by $1, the conversion value of its convertible bonds will increase by $15.

In Figure 24.3, we have implicitly assumed that the convertible bond is default-free. In this case, the straight bond value does not depend on the stock price, so it is plotted as a horizontal line. Given the straight bond value, the minimum value of the convertible depends on the value of the stock. When the stock price is low, the minimum value of a convertible is most significantly influenced by the underlying value as straight debt.

conversion value
The value a convertible bond would have if it were to be immediately converted into common stock.

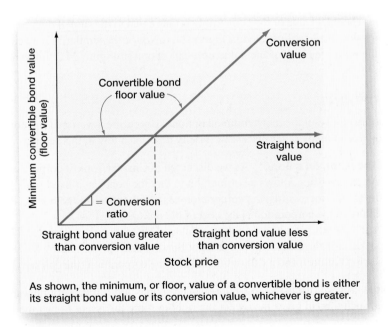

FIGURE 24.3

Minimum Value of a Convertible Bond versus the Value of the Stock for a Given Interest Rate

As shown, the minimum, or floor, value of a convertible bond is either its straight bond value or its conversion value, whichever is greater.

FIGURE 24.4

Value of a Convertible Bond versus the Value of the Stock for a Given Interest Rate

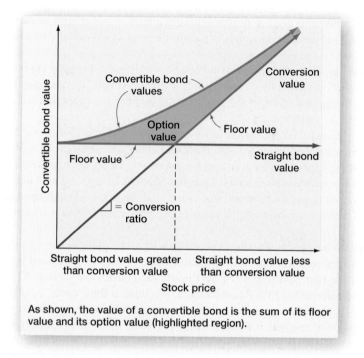

As shown, the value of a convertible bond is the sum of its floor value and its option value (highlighted region).

However, when the value of the firm is very high, the value of a convertible bond is mostly determined by the underlying conversion value. This is also illustrated in Figure 24.3.

Option Value   The value of a convertible bond will always exceed the straight bond value and the conversion value unless the firm is in default or the bondholders are forced to convert. The reason is that holders of convertibles do not have to convert immediately. Instead, by waiting, they can take advantage of whichever is greater in the future, the straight bond value or the conversion value.

This option to wait has value, and it raises the value of the convertible bond over its floor value. The total value of the convertible is thus equal to the sum of the floor value and the option value. This is illustrated in Figure 24.4. Notice the similarity between this picture and the representation of the value of a call option in Figure 24.2, referenced in our earlier discussion.

OTHER OPTIONS

We've discussed two of the more common optionlike securities, warrants and convertibles. Options appear in many other places. We briefly describe a few in this section.

The Call Provision on a Bond   As we discussed in Chapter 7, most corporate bonds are callable. A call provision allows a corporation to buy the bonds at a fixed price for a fixed period of time. In other words, the corporation has a call option on the bonds. The cost of the call feature to the corporation is the cost of the option.

Convertible bonds are almost always callable. This means that a convertible bond is really a package of three securities: a straight bond, a call option held by the bondholder (the conversion feature), and a call option held by the corporation (the call provision).

Put Bonds   As we discussed in Chapter 7, put bonds are a relatively new innovation. Recall that such a bond gives the owner the right to force the issuer to buy the bond back at a fixed price for a fixed time. We now recognize that such a bond is a combination of a straight bond and a put option—hence the name.

A given bond can have a number of embedded options. For example, one popular type of bond is a LYON, which stands for "liquid yield option note." A LYON is a callable, putable, convertible, pure discount bond. It is thus a package of a pure discount bond, two call options, and a put option.

Insurance and Loan Guarantees   Insurance of one kind or another is a financial feature of everyday life. Most of the time, having insurance is like having a put option. For example, suppose you have $1 million in fire insurance on an office building. One night, your building burns down, which reduces its value to nothing. In this case, you will effectively exercise your put option and force the insurer to pay you $1 million for something worth very little.

Loan guarantees are a form of insurance. If you lend money to someone and they default, then, with a guaranteed loan, you can collect from someone else, often the government. For example, when you lend money to a commercial bank (by making a deposit), your loan is guaranteed (up to $250,000) by the government.

In two particularly well-known cases of loan guarantees, Lockheed (now Lockheed Martin) Corporation (in 1971) and Chrysler Corporation (in 1980) were saved from impending financial doom when the U.S. government came to the rescue by agreeing to guarantee new loans. Under the guarantees, if Lockheed or Chrysler had defaulted, the lenders could have obtained the full value of their claims from the U.S. government. From the lenders' point of view, the loans were as risk-free as Treasury bonds. These guarantees enabled Lockheed and Chrysler to borrow large amounts of cash and to get through difficult times.

Loan guarantees are not cost-free. The U.S. government, with a loan guarantee, has provided a put option to the holders of risky bonds. The value of the put option is the cost of the loan guarantee. This point was made clear by the collapse of the U.S. savings and loan industry in the early 1980s. The final cost to U.S. taxpayers of making good on the guaranteed deposits in these institutions was a staggering $150 billion.

In more recent times, following the September 11, 2001, terrorist attacks, Congress established the Air Transportation Stabilization Board (ATSB). The ATSB was authorized to issue up to $10 billion in loan guarantees to U.S. air carriers that suffered losses as a result of the attacks. By mid-2004, $1.56 billion in guarantees had been issued to six borrowers. Interestingly, recipients of loan guarantees are required to compensate the government for the risk being borne by the taxpayers. This compensation came in the form of cash fees and warrants to buy stock. These warrants represent between 10 and 33 percent of each company's equity. Because of recoveries (and, thus, stock price increases) at some borrowers, the ATSB's warrant portfolio became quite valuable. According to the U.S. Treasury Department, the government earned just under $350 million from fees and stock sales.

Concept Questions

24.7a How are warrants and call options different?

24.7b What is the minimum value of a convertible bond?

24.7c Explain how car insurance acts like a put option.

24.7d Explain why U.S. government loan guarantees are not free.

24.8 Summary and Conclusions

This chapter has described the basics of option valuation and discussed optionlike corporate securities:

1.   Options are contracts giving the right, but not the obligation, to buy and sell underlying assets at a fixed price during a specified period. The most familiar options are puts and calls involving shares of stock. These options give the holder the right, but not the obligation, to sell (the put option) or buy (the call option) shares of common stock at a given price.

     As we discussed, the value of any option depends on only five factors:
     a. The price of the underlying asset.
     b. The exercise price.
     c. The expiration date.
     d. The interest rate on risk-free bonds.
     e. The volatility of the underlying asset's value.

2.   Companies have begun to use employee stock options (ESOs) in rapidly growing numbers. Such options are similar to call options and serve to motivate employees to boost stock prices. ESOs are also an important form of compensation for many workers, particularly at more senior management levels.

3.   Almost all capital budgeting proposals can be viewed as real options. Also, projects and operations contain implicit options, such as the option to expand, the option to abandon, and the option to suspend or contract operations.

4.   A warrant gives the holder the right to buy shares of common stock directly from the company at a fixed exercise price for a given period of time. Typically, warrants are issued in a package with bonds. Afterwards, they often can be detached and traded separately.

5.   A convertible bond is a combination of a straight bond and a call option. The holder can give up the bond in exchange for a fixed number of shares of stock. The minimum value of a convertible bond is given by its straight bond value or its conversion value, whichever is greater.

6.   Many other corporate securities have option features. Bonds with call provisions, bonds with put provisions, and bonds backed by a loan guarantee are just a few examples.

CHAPTER REVIEW AND SELF-TEST PROBLEMS

24.1   **Value of a Call Option**   Stock in the Nantucket Corporation is currently selling for $25 per share. In one year, the price will be either $20 or $30. T-bills with one year to maturity are paying 10 percent. What is the value of a call option with a $20 exercise price? A $26 exercise price?

24.2   **Convertible Bonds**   Old Cycle Corporation (OCC), publisher of *Ancient Iron* magazine, has a convertible bond issue that is currently selling in the market for $950. Each bond can be exchanged for 100 shares of stock at the holder's option.

The bond has a 7 percent coupon, payable annually, and it will mature in 10 years. OCC's debt is BBB-rated. Debt with this rating is priced to yield 12 percent. Stock in OCC is trading at $7 per share.

What is the conversion ratio on this bond? The conversion price? The conversion premium? What is the floor value of the bond? What is its option value?

ANSWERS TO CHAPTER REVIEW AND SELF-TEST PROBLEMS

24.1 With a $20 exercise price, the option can't finish out of the money (it can finish "at the money" if the stock price is $20). We can replicate the value of the stock by investing the present value of $20 in T-bills and buying one call option. Buying the T-bill will cost $20/1.1 = $18.18.

If the stock ends up at $20, the call option will be worth zero and the T-bill will pay $20. If the stock ends up at $30, the T-bill will again pay $20, and the option will be worth $30 − 20 = $10, so the package will be worth $30. Because the T-bill-call option combination exactly duplicates the payoff on the stock, it has to be worth $25 or arbitrage is possible. Using the notation from the chapter, we can calculate the value of the call option:

$$S_0 = C_0 + E/(1 + R_f)$$
$$\$25 = C_0 + \$18.18$$
$$C_0 = \$6.82$$

With the $26 exercise price, we start by investing the present value of the lower stock price in T-bills. This guarantees us $20 when the stock price is $20. If the stock price is $30, then the option is worth $30 − 26 = $4. We have $20 from our T-bill, so we need $10 from the options to match the stock. Because each option is worth $4 in this case, we need to buy $10/4 = 2.5 call options. Notice that the difference in the possible stock prices (ΔS) is $10 and the difference in the possible option prices (ΔC) is $4, so $\Delta S/\Delta C = 2.5$.

To complete the calculation, we note that the present value of the $20 plus 2.5 call options has to be $25 to prevent arbitrage, so:

$$\$25 = 2.5 \times C_0 + \$20/1.1$$
$$C_0 = \$6.82/2.5$$
$$= \$2.73$$

24.2 Because each bond can be exchanged for 100 shares, the conversion ratio is 100. The conversion price is the face value of the bond ($1,000) divided by the conversion ratio, or $1,000/100 = $10. The conversion premium is the percentage difference between the current price and the conversion price, or ($10 − 7)/7 = 43%.

The floor value of the bond is the greater of its straight bond value or its conversion value. Its conversion value is what the bond is worth if it is immediately converted: 100 × $7 = $700. The straight bond value is what the bond would be worth if it were not convertible. The annual coupon is $70, and the bond matures in 10 years. At a 12 percent required return, the straight bond value is:

$$\text{Straight bond value} = \$70 \times (1 - 1/1.12^{10})/.12 + 1,000/1.12^{10}$$
$$= \$395.52 + 321.97$$
$$= \$717.49$$

This exceeds the conversion value, so the floor value of the bond is $717.49. Finally, the option value is the value of the convertible in excess of its floor value. Because the bond is selling for $950, the option value is:

$$\text{Option value} = \$950 - 717.49$$
$$= \$232.51$$

CONCEPTS REVIEW AND CRITICAL THINKING QUESTIONS

1. **Options [LO1]** What is a call option? A put option? Under what circumstances might you want to buy each? Which one has greater *potential* profit? Why?

2. **Options [LO1]** Complete the following sentence for each of these investors:
    a. A buyer of call options.
    b. A buyer of put options.
    c. A seller (writer) of call options.
    d. A seller (writer) of put options.
    "The (buyer/seller) of a (put/call) option (pays/receives) money for the (right/obligation) to (buy/sell) a specified asset at a fixed price for a fixed length of time."

3. **Intrinsic Value [LO2]** What is the intrinsic value of a call option? How do we interpret this value?

4. **Put Options [LO2]** What is the value of a put option at maturity? Based on your answer, what is the intrinsic value of a put option?

5. **Option Pricing [LO2]** You notice that shares of stock in the Patel Corporation are going for $50 per share. Call options with an exercise price of $35 per share are selling for $10. What's wrong here? Describe how you can take advantage of this mispricing if the option expires today.

6. **Options and Stock Risk [LO2]** If the risk of a stock increases, what is likely to happen to the price of call options on the stock? To the price of put options? Why?

7. **Option Rise [LO2]** True or false: The unsystematic risk of a share of stock is irrelevant in valuing the stock because it can be diversified away; therefore, it is also irrelevant for valuing a call option on the stock. Explain.

8. **Option Pricing [LO2]** Suppose a certain stock currently sells for $30 per share. If a put option and a call option are available with $30 exercise prices, which do you think will sell for more, the put or the call? Explain.

9. **Option Price and Interest Rates [LO2]** Suppose the interest rate on T-bills suddenly and unexpectedly rises. All other things being the same, what is the impact on call option values? On put option values?

10. **Contingent Liabilities [LO4]** When you take out an ordinary student loan, it is usually the case that whoever holds that loan is given a guarantee by the U.S. government, meaning that the government will make up any payments you skip. This is just one example of the many loan guarantees made by the U.S. government. Such guarantees don't show up in calculations of government spending or in official deficit figures. Why not? Should they show up?

11. **Option to Abandon [LO5]** What is the option to abandon? Explain why we underestimate NPV if we ignore this option.

12. **Option to Expand [LO5]** What is the option to expand? Explain why we underestimate NPV if we ignore this option.

13. **Capital Budgeting Options [LO5]** In Chapter 10, we discussed Porsche's launch of its new Cayenne. Suppose sales of the Cayenne go extremely well and Porsche is forced to expand output to meet demand. Porsche's action in this case would be an example of exploiting what kind of option?

14. **Option to Suspend [LO5]** Natural resource extraction facilities (such as oil wells or gold mines) provide a good example of the value of the option to suspend operations. Why?

15. **Employee Stock Options [LO3]** You own stock in the Hendrix Guitar Company. The company has implemented a plan to award employee stock options. As a shareholder, does the plan benefit you? If so, what are the benefits?

QUESTIONS AND PROBLEMS

1. **Calculating Option Values [LO2]** T-bills currently yield 5.6 percent. Stock in Santa Maria Manufacturing is currently selling for $66 per share. There is no possibility that the stock will be worth less than $60 per share in one year.

   a. What is the value of a call option with a $55 exercise price? What is the intrinsic value?

   b. What is the value of a call option with a $45 exercise price? What is the intrinsic value?

   c. What is the value of a put option with a $55 exercise price? What is the intrinsic value?

BASIC
(Questions 1–13)

2. **Understanding Option Quotes [LO1]** Use the option quote information shown here to answer the questions that follow. The stock is currently selling for $85.

Option	Expiration	Strike Price	Calls		Puts	
			Vol.	Last	Vol.	Last
RWJ	Mar	80	230	2.80	160	.80
	Apr	80	170	6	127	1.40
	Jul	80	139	8.05	43	3.90
	Oct	80	60	10.20	11	3.65

   a. Are the call options in the money? What is the intrinsic value of an RWJ Corp. call option?

   b. Are the put options in the money? What is the intrinsic value of an RWJ Corp. put option?

   c. Two of the options are clearly mispriced. Which ones? At a minimum, what should the mispriced options sell for? Explain how you could profit from the mispricing in each case.

3. **Calculating Payoffs [LO1]** Use the option quote information shown here to answer the questions that follow. The stock is currently selling for $119.

Option	Expiration	Strike Price	Calls		Puts	
			Vol.	Last	Vol.	Last
Macrosoft	Feb	120	85	3.23	40	3.70
	Mar	120	61	4.41	22	5.30
	May	120	22	6.97	11	7.30
	Aug	120	3	10.20	3	9.10

a. Suppose you buy 10 contracts of the February 120 call option. How much will you pay, ignoring commissions?

b. In part (a), suppose that Macrosoft stock is selling for $134 per share on the expiration date. How much is your options investment worth? What if the terminal stock price is $126? Explain.

c. Suppose you buy 10 contracts of the August 120 put option. What is your maximum gain? On the expiration date, Macrosoft is selling for $109 per share. How much is your options investment worth? What is your net gain?

d. In part (c), suppose you *sell* 10 of the August 120 put contracts. What is your net gain or loss if Macrosoft is selling for $108 at expiration? For $132? What is the break-even price—that is, the terminal stock price that results in a zero profit?

4.   Calculating Option Values [LO2] The price of Time Squared Corp. stock will be either $62 or $86 at the end of the year. Call options are available with one year to expiration. T-bills currently yield 5 percent.

a. Suppose the current price of Time Squared stock is $70. What is the value of the call option if the exercise price is $65 per share?

b. Suppose the exercise price is $75 in part (a). What is the value of the call option now?

5.   Calculating Option Values [LO2] The price of Dimension, Inc., stock will be either $75 or $95 at the end of the year. Call options are available with one year to expiration. T-bills currently yield 6 percent.

a. Suppose the current price of Dimension stock is $85. What is the value of the call option if the exercise price is $65 per share?

b. Suppose the exercise price is $70 in part (a). What is the value of the call option now?

6.   Using the Pricing Equation [LO2] A one-year call option *contract* on Cheesy Poofs Co. stock sells for $1,300. In one year, the stock will be worth $48 or $67 per share. The exercise price on the call option is $60. What is the current value of the stock if the risk-free rate is 8 percent?

7.   Equity as an Option [LO4] Rackin Pinion Corporation's assets are currently worth $1,050. In one year, they will be worth either $1,000 or $1,270. The risk-free interest rate is 7 percent. Suppose Rackin Pinion has an outstanding debt issue with a face value of $1,000.

a. What is the value of the equity?

b. What is the value of the debt? The interest rate on the debt?

c. Would the value of the equity go up or down if the risk-free rate were 20 percent? Why? What does your answer illustrate?

8.   Equity as an Option [LO4] Buckeye Industries has a bond issue with a face value of $1,000 that is coming due in one year. The value of Buckeye's assets is currently $1,140. Jim Tressell, the CEO, believes that the assets in the firm will be worth either $920 or $1,430 in a year. The going rate on one-year T-bills is 6 percent.

a. What is the value of Buckeye's equity? The value of the debt?

b. Suppose Buckeye can reconfigure its existing assets in such a way that the value in a year will be $800 or $1,600. If the current value of the assets is unchanged, will the stockholders favor such a move? Why or why not?

9.   Calculating Conversion Value [LO6] A $1,000 par convertible debenture has a conversion price for common stock of $35 per share. With the common stock selling at $46, what is the conversion value of the bond?

10. **Convertible Bonds [LO6]** The following facts apply to a convertible bond making semiannual payments:

Conversion price	$55/share
Coupon rate	5.2%
Par value	$1,000
Yield on nonconvertible debentures of same quality	7%
Maturity	30 years
Market price of stock	$41/share

   a. What is the minimum price at which the convertible should sell?
   b. What accounts for the premium of the market price of a convertible bond over the total market value of the common stock into which it can be converted?

11. **Calculating Values for Convertibles [LO6]** You have been hired to value a new 30-year callable, convertible bond. The bond has a 7 percent coupon, payable semi-annually, and its face value is $1,000. The conversion price is $45, and the stock currently sells for $39.
   a. What is the minimum value of the bond? Comparable nonconvertible bonds are priced to yield 9 percent.
   b. What is the conversion premium for this bond?

12. **Calculating Warrant Values [LO6]** A bond with 25 detachable warrants has just been offered for sale at $1,000. The bond matures in 15 years and has an annual coupon of $45. Each warrant gives the owner the right to purchase two shares of stock in the company at $15 per share. Ordinary bonds (with no warrants) of similar quality are priced to yield 7 percent. What is the value of one warrant?

13. **Option to Wait [LO5]** Your company is deciding whether to invest in a new machine. The new machine will increase cash flow by $320,000 per year. You believe the technology used in the machine has a 10-year life; in other words, no matter when you purchase the machine, it will be obsolete 10 years from today. The machine is currently priced at $1,800,000. The cost of the machine will decline by $120,000 per year until it reaches $1,200,000, where it will remain. If your required return is 12 percent, should you purchase the machine? If so, when should you purchase it?

14. **Abandonment Value [LO5]** We are examining a new project. We expect to sell 7,500 units per year at $68 net cash flow apiece for the next 10 years. In other words, the annual operating cash flow is projected to be $68 × 7,500 = $510,000. The relevant discount rate is 14 percent, and the initial investment required is $2,300,000.

   INTERMEDIATE
   (Questions 14–20)

   a. What is the base-case NPV?
   b. After the first year, the project can be dismantled and sold for $1,500,000. If expected sales are revised based on the first year's performance, when would it make sense to abandon the investment? In other words, at what level of expected sales would it make sense to abandon the project?
   c. Explain how the $1,500,000 abandonment value can be viewed as the opportunity cost of keeping the project in one year.

Visit us at www.mhhe.com/rwj

15. **Abandonment [LO5]** In the previous problem, suppose you think it is likely that expected sales will be revised upward to 9,500 units if the first year is a success and revised downward to 4,000 units if the first year is not a success.

    a. If success and failure are equally likely, what is the NPV of the project? Consider the possibility of abandonment in answering.

    b. What is the value of the option to abandon?

16. **Abandonment and Expansion [LO5]** In the previous problem, suppose the scale of the project can be doubled in one year in the sense that twice as many units can be produced and sold. Naturally, expansion would be desirable only if the project is a success. This implies that if the project is a success, projected sales after expansion will be 19,000. Again assuming that success and failure are equally likely, what is the NPV of the project? Note that abandonment is still an option if the project is a failure. What is the value of the option to expand?

17. **Intuition and Option Value [LO2]** Suppose a share of stock sells for $65. The risk-free rate is 5 percent, and the stock price in one year will be either $75 or $85.

    a. What is the value of a call option with a $75 exercise price?

    b. What's wrong here? What would you do?

18. **Intuition and Convertibles [LO6]** Which of the following two sets of relationships, at time of issuance of convertible bonds, is more typical? Why?

	A	B
Offering price of bond	$ 800	$1,000
Bond value (straight debt)	800	950
Conversion value	1,000	900

19. **Convertible Calculations [LO6]** Rayne, Inc., has a $1,000 face value convertible bond issue that is currently selling in the market for $960. Each bond is exchangeable at any time for 22 shares of the company's stock. The convertible bond has a 6 percent coupon, payable semiannually. Similar nonconvertible bonds are priced to yield 9 percent. The bond matures in 20 years. Stock in Rayne sells for $35 per share.

    a. What are the conversion ratio, conversion price, and conversion premium?

    b. What is the straight bond value? The conversion value?

    c. In part (b), what would the stock price have to be for the conversion value and the straight bond value to be equal?

    d. What is the option value of the bond?

20. **Abandonment Decisions [LO5]** Allied Products, Inc., is considering a new product launch. The firm expects to have annual operating cash flow of $18 million for the next 8 years. Allied Products uses a discount rate of 14 percent for new product launches. The initial investment is $75 million. Assume that the project has no salvage value at the end of its economic life.

    a. What is the NPV of the new product?

    b. After the first year, the project can be dismantled and sold for $30 million. If the estimates of remaining cash flows are revised based on the first year's experience, at what level of expected cash flows does it make sense to abandon the project?

21. **Pricing Convertibles [LO6]** You have been hired to value a new 25-year callable, convertible bond. The bond has a 5.40 percent coupon, payable annually. The conversion price is $150, and the stock currently sells for $41.40. The stock price is expected to grow at 11 percent per year. The bond is callable at $1,200, but, based on prior experience, it won't be called unless the conversion value is $1,300. The required return on this bond is 9 percent. What value would you assign?

    CHALLENGE
    (Questions 21–22)

22. **Abandonment Decisions [LO5]** Consider the following project of Hand Clapper, Inc. The company is considering a four-year project to manufacture clap-command garage door openers. This project requires an initial investment of $12 million that will be depreciated straight-line to zero over the project's life. An initial investment in net working capital of $900,000 is required to support spare parts inventory; this cost is fully recoverable whenever the project ends. The company believes it can generate $9.1 million in pretax revenues with $3.7 million in total pretax operating costs. The tax rate is 38 percent and the discount rate is 13 percent. The market value of the equipment over the life of the project is as follows:

    X

Year	Market Value (millions)
1	$8.20
2	6.10
3	4.70
4	0.00

    a. Assuming Hand Clapper operates this project for four years, what is the NPV?

    b. Now compute the project NPV assuming the project is abandoned after only one year, after two years, and after three years. What economic life for this project maximizes its value to the firm? What does this problem tell you about not considering abandonment possibilities when evaluating projects?

S&S Air's Convertible Bond

S&S Air is preparing its first public securities offering. In consultation with Danielle Ralston of underwriter Raines and Warren, Chris Guthrie decided that a convertible bond with a 20-year maturity was the way to go. He met the owners, Mark and Todd, and presented his analysis of the convertible bond issue. Because the company is not publicly traded, Chris looked at comparable publicly traded companies and determined that the average PE ratio for the industry is 12.5. Earnings per share for the company are $1.60. With this in mind, Chris has suggested a conversion price of $25 per share.

Several days later, Todd, Mark, and Chris met again to discuss the potential bond issue. Both Todd and Mark researched convertible bonds and have questions for Chris. Todd begins by asking Chris if the convertible bond issue will have a lower coupon rate than a comparable bond without a conversion feature. Chris informs him that a par value convertible bond issue would require a 6 percent coupon rate with a conversion value of $800, while a plain vanilla bond would have a 10 percent coupon rate. Todd nods in agreement and explains that the convertible bonds are a win–win form of financing. He states that if the value of the company stock does not rise above the conversion price, the company has issued debt at a cost below the market rate (6 percent instead of 10 percent). If the company's stock does rise to the conversion value, the company has effectively issued stock at a price above the current value.

Mark immediately disagrees, saying that convertible bonds are a no-win form of financing. He argues that if the value of the company stock rises to more than $25, the company is forced to sell stock at the conversion price. This means the new shareholders, in other words those who bought the convertible bonds, benefit from a bargain price. Put another way, if the company prospers, it would have been better to have issued straight debt so that the gains would not be shared.

Chris has gone back to Danielle for help. As Danielle's assistant, you've been asked to prepare another memo answering the following questions.

QUESTIONS

1. Why do you think Chris is suggesting a conversion price of $25? Given that the company is not publicly traded, does it even make sense to talk about a conversion price?

2. Is there anything wrong with Todd's argument that it is cheaper to issue a bond with a convertible feature because the required coupon is lower?

3. Is there anything wrong with Mark's argument that a convertible bond is a bad idea because it allows new shareholders to participate in gains made by the company?

4. How can you reconcile the arguments made by Todd and Mark?

5. In the course of the debate, a question comes up concerning whether or not the bonds should have an ordinary (not make-whole) call feature. Chris confuses everybody by stating, "The call feature lets S&S Air force conversion, thereby minimizing the problem that Mark has identified." What is he talking about? Is he making sense?

MATHEMATICAL TABLES

TABLE A.1   Future value of $1 at the end of t periods $= (1 + r)^t$

Period	Interest Rate								
	1%	2%	3%	4%	5%	6%	7%	8%	9%
1	1.0100	1.0200	1.0300	1.0400	1.0500	1.0600	1.0700	1.0800	1.0900
2	1.0201	1.0404	1.0609	1.0816	1.1025	1.1236	1.1449	1.1664	1.1881
3	1.0303	1.0612	1.0927	1.1249	1.1576	1.1910	1.2250	1.2597	1.2950
4	1.0406	1.0824	1.1255	1.1699	1.2155	1.2625	1.3108	1.3605	1.4116
5	1.0510	1.1041	1.1593	1.2167	1.2763	1.3382	1.4026	1.4693	1.5386
6	1.0615	1.1262	1.1941	1.2653	1.3401	1.4185	1.5007	1.5869	1.6771
7	1.0721	1.1487	1.2299	1.3159	1.4071	1.5036	1.6058	1.7138	1.8280
8	1.0829	1.1717	1.2668	1.3686	1.4775	1.5938	1.7182	1.8509	1.9926
9	1.0937	1.1951	1.3048	1.4233	1.5513	1.6895	1.8385	1.9990	2.1719
10	1.1046	1.2190	1.3439	1.4802	1.6289	1.7908	1.9672	2.1589	2.3674
11	1.1157	1.2434	1.3842	1.5395	1.7103	1.8983	2.1049	2.3316	2.5804
12	1.1268	1.2682	1.4258	1.6010	1.7959	2.0122	2.2522	2.5182	2.8127
13	1.1381	1.2936	1.4685	1.6651	1.8856	2.1329	2.4098	2.7196	3.0658
14	1.1495	1.3195	1.5126	1.7317	1.9799	2.2609	2.5785	2.9372	3.3417
15	1.1610	1.3459	1.5580	1.8009	2.0789	2.3966	2.7590	3.1722	3.6425
16	1.1726	1.3728	1.6047	1.8730	2.1829	2.5404	2.9522	3.4259	3.9703
17	1.1843	1.4002	1.6528	1.9479	2.2920	2.6928	3.1588	3.7000	4.3276
18	1.1961	1.4282	1.7024	2.0258	2.4066	2.8543	3.3799	3.9960	4.7171
19	1.2081	1.4568	1.7535	2.1068	2.5270	3.0256	3.6165	4.3157	5.1417
20	1.2202	1.4859	1.8061	2.1911	2.6533	3.2071	3.8697	4.6610	5.6044
21	1.2324	1.5157	1.8603	2.2788	2.7860	3.3996	4.1406	5.0338	6.1088
22	1.2447	1.5460	1.9161	2.3699	2.9253	3.6035	4.4304	5.4365	6.6586
23	1.2572	1.5769	1.9736	2.4647	3.0715	3.8197	4.7405	5.8715	7.2579
24	1.2697	1.6084	2.0328	2.5633	3.2251	4.0489	5.0724	6.3412	7.9111
25	1.2824	1.6406	2.0938	2.6658	3.3864	4.2919	5.4274	6.8485	8.6231
30	1.3478	1.8114	2.4273	3.2434	4.3219	5.7435	7.6123	10.063	13.268
40	1.4889	2.2080	3.2620	4.8010	7.0400	10.286	14.974	21.725	31.409
50	1.6446	2.6916	4.3839	7.1067	11.467	18.420	29.457	46.902	74.358
60	1.8167	3.2810	5.8916	10.520	18.679	32.988	57.946	101.26	176.03

continued on next page

10%	12%	14%	15%	16%	18%	20%	24%	28%	32%	36%
1.1000	1.1200	1.1400	1.1500	1.1600	1.1800	1.2000	1.2400	1.2800	1.3200	1.3600
1.2100	1.2544	1.2996	1.3225	1.3456	1.3924	1.4400	1.5376	1.6384	1.7424	1.8496
1.3310	1.4049	1.4815	1.5209	1.5609	1.6430	1.7280	1.9066	2.0972	2.3000	2.5155
1.4641	1.5735	1.6890	1.7490	1.8106	1.9388	2.0736	2.3642	2.6844	3.0360	3.4210
1.6105	1.7623	1.9254	2.0114	2.1003	2.2878	2.4883	2.9316	3.4360	4.0075	4.6526
1.7716	1.9738	2.1950	2.3131	2.4364	2.6996	2.9860	3.6352	4.3980	5.2899	6.3275
1.9487	2.2107	2.5023	2.6600	2.8262	3.1855	3.5832	4.5077	5.6295	6.9826	8.6054
2.1436	2.4760	2.8526	3.0590	3.2784	3.7589	4.2998	5.5895	7.2058	9.2170	11.703
2.3579	2.7731	3.2519	3.5179	3.8030	4.4355	5.1598	6.9310	9.2234	12.166	15.917
2.5937	3.1058	3.7072	4.0456	4.4114	5.2338	6.1917	8.5944	11.806	16.060	21.647
2.8531	3.4785	4.2262	4.6524	5.1173	6.1759	7.4301	10.657	15.112	21.199	29.439
3.1384	3.8960	4.8179	5.3503	5.9360	7.2876	8.9161	13.215	19.343	27.983	40.037
3.4523	4.3635	5.4924	6.1528	6.8858	8.5994	10.699	16.386	24.759	36.937	54.451
3.7975	4.8871	6.2613	7.0757	7.9875	10.147	12.839	20.319	31.691	48.757	74.053
4.1772	5.4736	7.1379	8.1371	9.2655	11.974	15.407	25.196	40.565	64.359	100.71
4.5950	6.1304	8.1372	9.3576	10.748	14.129	18.488	31.243	51.923	84.954	136.97
5.0545	6.8660	9.2765	10.761	12.468	16.672	22.186	38.741	66.461	112.14	186.28
5.5599	7.6900	10.575	12.375	14.463	19.673	26.623	48.039	85.071	148.02	253.34
6.1159	8.6128	12.056	14.232	16.777	23.214	31.948	59.568	108.89	195.39	344.54
6.7275	9.6463	13.743	16.367	19.461	27.393	38.338	73.864	139.38	257.92	468.57
7.4002	10.804	15.668	18.822	22.574	32.324	46.005	91.592	178.41	340.45	637.26
8.1403	12.100	17.861	21.645	26.186	38.142	55.206	113.57	228.36	449.39	866.67
8.9543	13.552	20.362	24.891	30.376	45.008	66.247	140.83	292.30	593.20	1178.7
9.8497	15.179	23.212	28.625	35.236	53.109	79.497	174.63	374.14	783.02	1603.0
10.835	17.000	26.462	32.919	40.874	62.669	95.396	216.54	478.90	1033.6	2180.1
17.449	29.960	50.950	66.212	85.850	143.37	237.38	634.82	1645.5	4142.1	10143.
45.259	93.051	188.88	267.86	378.72	750.38	1469.8	5455.9	19427.	66521.	*
117.39	289.00	700.23	1083.7	1670.7	3927.4	9100.4	46890.	*	*	*
304.48	897.60	2595.9	4384.0	7370.2	20555.	56348.	*	*	*	*

*The factor is greater than 99,999.

TABLE A.2   Present value of $1 to be received after t periods $= 1/(1 + r)^t$

	Interest Rate								
Period	1%	2%	3%	4%	5%	6%	7%	8%	9%
1	.9901	.9804	.9709	.9615	.9524	.9434	.9346	.9259	.9174
2	.9803	.9612	.9426	.9246	.9070	.8900	.8734	.8573	.8417
3	.9706	.9423	.9151	.8890	.8638	.8396	.8163	.7938	.7722
4	.9610	.9238	.8885	.8548	.8227	.7921	.7629	.7350	.7084
5	.9515	.9057	.8626	.8219	.7835	.7473	.7130	.6806	.6499
6	.9420	.8880	.8375	.7903	.7462	.7050	.6663	.6302	.5963
7	.9327	.8706	.8131	.7599	.7107	.6651	.6227	.5835	.5470
8	.9235	.8535	.7894	.7307	.6768	.6274	.5820	.5403	.5019
9	.9143	.8368	.7664	.7026	.6446	.5919	.5439	.5002	.4604
10	.9053	.8203	.7441	.6756	.6139	.5584	.5083	.4632	.4224
11	.8963	.8043	.7224	.6496	.5847	.5268	.4751	.4289	.3875
12	.8874	.7885	.7014	.6246	.5568	.4970	.4440	.3971	.3555
13	.8787	.7730	.6810	.6006	.5303	.4688	.4150	.3677	.3262
14	.8700	.7579	.6611	.5775	.5051	.4423	.3878	.3405	.2992
15	.8613	.7430	.6419	.5553	.4810	.4173	.3624	.3152	.2745
16	.8528	.7284	.6232	.5339	.4581	.3936	.3387	.2919	.2519
17	.8444	.7142	.6050	.5134	.4363	.3714	.3166	.2703	.2311
18	.8360	.7002	.5874	.4936	.4155	.3503	.2959	.2502	.2120
19	.8277	.6864	.5703	.4746	.3957	.3305	.2765	.2317	.1945
20	.8195	.6730	.5537	.4564	.3769	.3118	.2584	.2145	.1784
21	.8114	.6598	.5375	.4388	.3589	.2942	.2415	.1987	.1637
22	.8034	.6468	.5219	.4220	.3418	.2775	.2257	.1839	.1502
23	.7954	.6342	.5067	.4057	.3256	.2618	.2109	.1703	.1378
24	.7876	.6217	.4919	.3901	.3101	.2470	.1971	.1577	.1264
25	.7798	.6095	.4776	.3751	.2953	.2330	.1842	.1460	.1160
30	.7419	.5521	.4120	.3083	.2314	.1741	.1314	.0994	.0754
40	.6717	.4529	.3066	.2083	.1420	.0972	.0668	.0460	.0318
50	.6080	.3715	.2281	.1407	.0872	.0543	.0339	.0213	.0134

continued on next page

10%	12%	14%	15%	16%	18%	20%	24%	28%	32%	36%
.9091	.8929	.8772	.8696	.8621	.8475	.8333	.8065	.7813	.7576	.7353
.8264	.7972	.7695	.7561	.7432	.7182	.6944	.6504	.6104	.5739	.5407
.7513	.7118	.6750	.6575	.6407	.6086	.5787	.5245	.4768	.4348	.3975
.6830	.6355	.5921	.5718	.5523	.5158	.4823	.4230	.3725	.3294	.2923
.6209	.5674	.5194	.4972	.4761	.4371	.4019	.3411	.2910	.2495	.2149
.5645	.5066	.4556	.4323	.4104	.3704	.3349	.2751	.2274	.1890	.1580
.5132	.4523	.3996	.3759	.3538	.3139	.2791	.2218	.1776	.1432	.1162
.4665	.4039	.3506	.3269	.3050	.2660	.2326	.1789	.1388	.1085	.0854
.4241	.3606	.3075	.2843	.2630	.2255	.1938	.1443	.1084	.0822	.0628
.3855	.3220	.2697	.2472	.2267	.1911	.1615	.1164	.0847	.0623	.0462
.3505	.2875	.2366	.2149	.1954	.1619	.1346	.0938	.0662	.0472	.0340
.3186	.2567	.2076	.1869	.1685	.1372	.1122	.0757	.0517	.0357	.0250
.2897	.2292	.1821	.1625	.1452	.1163	.0935	.0610	.0404	.0271	.0184
.2633	.2046	.1597	.1413	.1252	.0985	.0779	.0492	.0316	.0205	.0135
.2394	.1827	.1401	.1229	.1079	.0835	.0649	.0397	.0247	.0155	.0099
.2176	.1631	.1229	.1069	.0930	.0708	.0541	.0320	.0193	.0118	.0073
.1978	.1456	.1078	.0929	.0802	.0600	.0451	.0258	.0150	.0089	.0054
.1799	.1300	.0946	.0808	.0691	.0508	.0376	.0208	.0118	.0068	.0039
.1635	.1161	.0829	.0703	.0596	.0431	.0313	.0168	.0092	.0051	.0029
.1486	.1037	.0728	.0611	.0514	.0365	.0261	.0135	.0072	.0039	.0021
.1351	.0926	.0638	.0531	.0443	.0309	.0217	.0109	.0056	.0029	.0016
.1228	.0826	.0560	.0462	.0382	.0262	.0181	.0088	.0044	.0022	.0012
.1117	.0738	.0491	.0402	.0329	.0222	.0151	.0071	.0034	.0017	.0008
.1015	.0659	.0431	.0349	.0284	.0188	.0126	.0057	.0027	.0013	.0006
.0923	.0588	.0378	.0304	.0245	.0160	.0105	.0046	.0021	.0010	.0005
.0573	.0334	.0196	.0151	.0116	.0070	.0042	.0016	.0006	.0002	.0001
.0221	.0107	.0053	.0037	.0026	.0013	.0007	.0002	.0001	*	*
.0085	.0035	.0014	.0009	.0006	.0003	.0001	*	*	*	*

*The factor is zero to four decimal places.

TABLE A.3   Present value of an annuity of $1 per period for t periods $= [1 - 1/(1 + r)^t]/r$

Number of Periods	Interest Rate								
	1%	2%	3%	4%	5%	6%	7%	8%	9%
1	.9901	.9804	.9709	.9615	.9524	.9434	.9346	.9259	.9174
2	1.9704	1.9416	1.9135	1.8861	1.8594	1.8334	1.8080	1.7833	1.7591
3	2.9410	2.8839	2.8286	2.7751	2.7232	2.6730	2.6243	2.5771	2.5313
4	3.9020	3.8077	3.7171	3.6299	3.5460	3.4651	3.3872	3.3121	3.2397
5	4.8534	4.7135	4.5797	4.4518	4.3295	4.2124	4.1002	3.9927	3.8897
6	5.7955	5.6014	5.4172	5.2421	5.0757	4.9173	4.7665	4.6229	4.4859
7	6.7282	6.4720	6.2303	6.0021	5.7864	5.5824	5.3893	5.2064	5.0330
8	7.6517	7.3255	7.0197	6.7327	6.4632	6.2098	5.9713	5.7466	5.5348
9	8.5660	8.1622	7.7861	7.4353	7.1078	6.8017	6.5152	6.2469	5.9952
10	9.4713	8.9826	8.5302	8.1109	7.7217	7.3601	7.0236	6.7101	6.4177
11	10.3676	9.7868	9.2526	8.7605	8.3064	7.8869	7.4987	7.1390	6.8052
12	11.2551	10.5753	9.9540	9.3851	8.8633	8.3838	7.9427	7.5361	7.1607
13	12.1337	11.3484	10.6350	9.9856	9.3936	8.8527	8.3577	7.9038	7.4869
14	13.0037	12.1062	11.2961	10.5631	9.8986	9.2950	8.7455	8.2442	7.7862
15	13.8651	12.8493	11.9379	11.1184	10.3797	9.7122	9.1079	8.5595	8.0607
16	14.7179	13.5777	12.5611	11.6523	10.8378	10.1059	9.4466	8.8514	8.3126
17	15.5623	14.2919	13.1661	12.1657	11.2741	10.4773	9.7632	9.1216	8.5436
18	16.3983	14.9920	13.7535	12.6593	11.6896	10.8276	10.0591	9.3719	8.7556
19	17.2260	15.6785	14.3238	13.1339	12.0853	11.1581	10.3356	9.6036	8.9501
20	18.0456	16.3514	14.8775	13.5903	12.4622	11.4699	10.5940	9.8181	9.1285
21	18.8570	17.0112	15.4150	14.0292	12.8212	11.7641	10.8355	10.0168	9.2922
22	19.6604	17.6580	15.9369	14.4511	13.1630	12.0416	11.0612	10.2007	9.4424
23	20.4558	18.2922	16.4436	14.8568	13.4886	12.3034	11.2722	10.3741	9.5802
24	21.2434	18.9139	16.9355	15.2470	13.7986	12.5504	11.4693	10.5288	9.7066
25	22.0232	19.5235	17.4131	15.6221	14.0939	12.7834	11.6536	10.6748	9.8226
30	25.8077	22.3965	19.6004	17.2920	15.3725	13.7648	12.4090	11.2578	10.2737
40	32.8347	27.3555	23.1148	19.7928	17.1591	15.0463	13.3317	11.9246	10.7574
50	39.1961	31.4236	25.7298	21.4822	18.2559	15.7619	13.8007	12.2335	10.9617

continued on next page

10%	12%	14%	15%	16%	18%	20%	24%	28%	32%	36%
.9091	.8929	.8772	.8696	.8621	.8475	.8333	.8065	.7813	.7576	.7353
1.7355	1.6901	1.6467	1.6257	1.6052	1.5656	1.5278	1.4568	1.3916	1.3315	1.2760
2.4869	2.4018	2.3216	2.2832	2.2459	2.1743	2.1065	1.9813	1.8684	1.7663	1.6735
3.1699	3.0373	2.9137	2.8550	2.7982	2.6901	2.5887	2.4043	2.2410	2.0957	1.9658
3.7908	3.6048	3.4331	3.3522	3.2743	3.1272	2.9906	2.7454	2.5320	2.3452	2.1807
4.3553	4.1114	3.8887	3.7845	3.6847	3.4976	3.3255	3.0205	2.7594	2.5342	2.3388
4.8684	4.5638	4.2883	4.1604	4.0386	3.8115	3.6046	3.2423	2.9370	2.6775	2.4550
5.3349	4.9676	4.6389	4.4873	4.3436	4.0776	3.8372	3.4212	3.0758	2.7860	2.5404
5.7590	5.3282	4.9464	4.7716	4.6065	4.3030	4.0310	3.5655	3.1842	2.8681	2.6033
6.1446	5.6502	5.2161	5.0188	4.8332	4.4941	4.1925	3.6819	3.2689	2.9304	2.6495
6.4951	5.9377	5.4527	5.2337	5.0286	4.6560	4.3271	3.7757	3.3351	2.9776	2.6834
6.8137	6.1944	5.6603	5.4206	5.1971	4.7932	4.4392	3.8514	3.3868	3.0133	2.7084
7.1034	6.4235	5.8424	5.5831	5.3423	4.9095	4.5327	3.9124	3.4272	3.0404	2.7268
7.3667	6.6282	6.0021	5.7245	5.4675	5.0081	4.6106	3.9616	3.4587	3.0609	2.7403
7.6061	6.8109	6.1422	5.8474	5.5755	5.0916	4.6755	4.0013	3.4834	3.0764	2.7502
7.8237	6.9740	6.2651	5.9542	5.6685	5.1624	4.7296	4.0333	3.5026	3.0882	2.7575
8.0216	7.1196	6.3729	6.0472	5.7487	5.2223	4.7746	4.0591	3.5177	3.0971	2.7629
8.2014	7.2497	6.4674	6.1280	5.8178	5.2732	4.8122	4.0799	3.5294	3.1039	2.7668
8.3649	7.3658	6.5504	6.1982	5.8775	5.3162	4.8435	4.0967	3.5386	3.1090	2.7697
8.5136	7.4694	6.6231	6.2593	5.9288	5.3527	4.8696	4.1103	3.5458	3.1129	2.7718
8.6487	7.5620	6.6870	6.3125	5.9731	5.3837	4.8913	4.1212	3.5514	3.1158	2.7734
8.7715	7.6446	6.7429	6.3587	6.0113	5.4099	4.9094	4.1300	3.5558	3.1180	2.7746
8.8832	7.7184	6.7921	6.3988	6.0442	5.4321	4.9245	4.1371	3.5592	3.1197	2.7754
8.9847	7.7843	6.8351	6.4338	6.0726	5.4509	4.9371	4.1428	3.5619	3.1210	2.7760
9.0770	7.8431	6.8729	6.4641	6.0971	5.4669	4.9476	4.1474	3.5640	3.1220	2.7765
9.4269	8.0552	7.0027	6.5660	6.1772	5.5168	4.9789	4.1601	3.5693	3.1242	2.7775
9.7791	8.2438	7.1050	6.6418	6.2335	5.5482	4.9966	4.1659	3.5712	3.1250	2.7778
9.9148	8.3045	7.1327	6.6605	6.2463	5.5541	4.9995	4.1666	3.5714	3.1250	2.7778

TABLE A.4   Future value of an annuity of $1 per period for t periods $= [(1 + r)^t - 1]/r$

Number of Periods	Interest Rate								
	1%	2%	3%	4%	5%	6%	7%	8%	9%
1	1.0000	1.0000	1.0000	1.0000	1.0000	1.0000	1.0000	1.0000	1.0000
2	2.0100	2.0200	2.0300	2.0400	2.0500	2.0600	2.0700	2.0800	2.0900
3	3.0301	3.0604	3.0909	3.1216	3.1525	3.1836	3.2149	3.2464	3.2781
4	4.0604	4.1216	4.1836	4.2465	4.3101	4.3746	4.4399	4.5061	4.5731
5	5.1010	5.2040	5.3091	5.4163	5.5256	5.6371	5.7507	5.8666	5.9847
6	6.1520	6.3081	6.4684	6.6330	6.8019	6.9753	7.1533	7.3359	7.5233
7	7.2135	7.4343	7.6625	7.8983	8.1420	8.3938	8.6540	8.9228	9.2004
8	8.2857	8.5830	8.8932	9.2142	9.5491	9.8975	10.260	10.637	11.028
9	9.3685	9.7546	10.159	10.583	11.027	11.491	11.978	12.488	13.021
10	10.462	10.950	11.464	12.006	12.578	13.181	13.816	14.487	15.193
11	11.567	12.169	12.808	13.486	14.207	14.972	15.784	16.645	17.560
12	12.683	13.412	14.192	15.026	15.917	16.870	17.888	18.977	20.141
13	13.809	14.680	15.618	16.627	17.713	18.882	20.141	21.495	22.953
14	14.947	15.974	17.086	18.292	19.599	21.015	22.550	24.215	26.019
15	16.097	17.293	18.599	20.024	21.579	23.276	25.129	27.152	29.361
16	17.258	18.639	20.157	21.825	23.657	25.673	27.888	30.324	33.003
17	18.430	20.012	21.762	23.698	25.840	28.213	30.840	33.750	36.974
18	19.615	21.412	23.414	25.645	28.132	30.906	33.999	37.450	41.301
19	20.811	22.841	25.117	27.671	30.539	33.760	37.379	41.446	46.018
20	22.019	24.297	26.870	29.778	33.066	36.786	40.995	45.762	51.160
21	23.239	25.783	28.676	31.969	35.719	39.993	44.865	50.423	56.765
22	24.472	27.299	30.537	34.248	38.505	43.392	49.006	55.457	62.873
23	25.716	28.845	32.453	36.618	41.430	46.996	53.436	60.893	69.532
24	26.973	30.422	34.426	39.083	44.502	50.816	58.177	66.765	76.790
25	28.243	32.030	36.459	41.646	47.727	54.865	63.249	73.106	84.701
30	34.785	40.568	47.575	56.085	66.439	79.058	94.461	113.28	136.31
40	48.886	60.402	75.401	95.026	120.80	154.76	199.64	259.06	337.88
50	64.463	84.579	112.80	152.67	209.35	290.34	406.53	573.77	815.08
60	81.670	114.05	163.05	237.99	353.58	533.13	813.52	1253.2	1944.8

continued on next page

10%	12%	14%	15%	16%	18%	20%	24%	28%	32%	36%
1.0000	1.0000	1.0000	1.0000	1.0000	1.0000	1.0000	1.0000	1.0000	1.0000	1.0000
2.1000	2.1200	2.1400	2.1500	2.1600	2.1800	2.2000	2.2400	2.2800	2.3200	2.3600
3.3100	3.3744	3.4396	3.4725	3.5056	3.5724	3.6400	3.7776	3.9184	4.0624	4.2096
4.6410	4.7793	4.9211	4.9934	5.0665	5.2154	5.3680	5.6842	6.0156	6.3624	6.7251
6.1051	6.3528	6.6101	6.7424	6.8771	7.1542	7.4416	8.0484	8.6999	9.3983	10.146
7.7156	8.1152	8.5355	8.7537	8.9775	9.4420	9.9299	10.980	12.136	13.406	14.799
9.4872	10.089	10.730	11.067	11.414	12.142	12.916	14.615	16.534	18.696	21.126
11.436	12.300	13.233	13.727	14.240	15.327	16.499	19.123	22.163	25.678	29.732
13.579	14.776	16.085	16.786	17.519	19.086	20.799	24.712	29.369	34.895	41.435
15.937	17.549	19.337	20.304	21.321	23.521	25.959	31.643	38.593	47.062	57.352
18.531	20.655	23.045	24.349	25.733	28.755	32.150	40.238	50.398	63.122	78.998
21.384	24.133	27.271	29.002	30.850	34.931	39.581	50.895	65.510	84.320	108.44
24.523	28.029	32.089	34.352	36.786	42.219	48.497	64.110	84.853	112.30	148.47
27.975	32.393	37.581	40.505	43.672	50.818	59.196	80.496	109.61	149.24	202.93
31.772	37.280	43.842	47.580	51.660	60.965	72.035	100.82	141.30	198.00	276.98
35.950	42.753	50.980	55.717	60.925	72.939	87.442	126.01	181.87	262.36	377.69
40.545	48.884	59.118	65.075	71.673	87.068	105.93	157.25	233.79	347.31	514.66
45.599	55.750	68.394	75.836	84.141	103.74	128.12	195.99	300.25	459.45	700.94
51.159	63.440	78.969	88.212	98.603	123.41	154.74	244.03	385.32	607.47	954.28
57.275	72.052	91.025	102.44	115.38	146.63	186.69	303.60	494.21	802.86	1298.8
64.002	81.699	104.77	118.81	134.84	174.02	225.03	377.46	633.59	1060.8	1767.4
71.403	92.503	120.44	137.63	157.41	206.34	271.03	469.06	812.00	1401.2	2404.7
79.543	104.60	138.30	159.28	183.60	244.49	326.24	582.63	1040.4	1850.6	3271.3
88.497	118.16	158.66	184.17	213.98	289.49	392.48	723.46	1332.7	2443.8	4450.0
98.347	133.33	181.87	212.79	249.21	342.60	471.98	898.09	1706.8	3226.8	6053.0
164.49	241.33	356.79	434.75	530.31	790.95	1181.9	2640.9	5873.2	12941.	28172.
442.59	767.09	1342.0	1779.1	2360.8	4163.2	7343.9	22729.	69377.	*	*
1163.9	2400.0	4994.5	7217.7	10436.	21813.	45497.	*	*	*	*
3043.8	7471.6	18535.	29220.	46058.	*	*	*	*	*	*

*The factor is greater than 99,999.

TABLE A.5 Cumulative normal distribution

d	N(d)	d	N(d)	d	N(d)	d	N(d)	d	N(d)	d	N(d)
−3.00	.0013	−1.58	.0571	−.76	.2236	.06	.5239	.86	.8051	1.66	.9515
−2.95	.0016	−1.56	.0594	−.74	.2297	.08	.5319	.88	.8106	1.68	.9535
−2.90	.0019	−1.54	.0618	−.72	.2358	.10	.5398	.90	.8159	1.70	.9554
−2.85	.0022	−1.52	.0643	−.70	.2420	.12	.5478	.92	.8212	1.72	.9573
−2.80	.0026	−1.50	.0668	−.68	.2483	.14	.5557	.94	.8264	1.74	.9591
−2.75	.0030	−1.48	.0694	−.66	.2546	.16	.5636	.96	.8315	1.76	.9608
−2.70	.0035	−1.46	.0721	−.64	.2611	.18	.5714	.98	.8365	1.78	.9625
−2.65	.0040	−1.44	.0749	−.62	.2676	.20	.5793	1.00	.8413	1.80	.9641
−2.60	.0047	−1.42	.0778	−.60	.2743	.22	.5871	1.02	.8461	1.82	.9656
−2.55	.0054	−1.40	.0808	−.58	.2810	.24	.5948	1.04	.8508	1.84	.9671
−2.50	.0062	−1.38	.0838	−.56	.2877	.26	.6026	1.06	.8554	1.86	.9686
−2.45	.0071	−1.36	.0869	−.54	.2946	.28	.6103	1.08	.8599	1.88	.9699
−2.40	.0082	−1.34	.0901	−.52	.3015	.30	.6179	1.10	.8643	1.90	.9713
−2.35	.0094	−1.32	.0934	−.50	.3085	.32	.6255	1.12	.8686	1.92	.9726
−2.30	.0107	−1.30	.0968	−.48	.3156	.34	.6331	1.14	.8729	1.94	.9738
−2.25	.0122	−1.28	.1003	−.46	.3228	.36	.6406	1.16	.8770	1.96	.9750
−2.20	.0139	−1.26	.1038	−.44	.3300	.38	.6480	1.18	.8810	1.98	.9761
−2.15	.0158	−1.24	.1075	−.42	.3372	.40	.6554	1.20	.8849	2.00	.9772
−2.10	.0179	−1.22	.1112	−.40	.3446	.42	.6628	1.22	.8888	2.05	.9798
−2.05	.0202	−1.20	.1151	−.38	.3520	.44	.6700	1.24	.8925	2.10	.9821
−2.00	.0228	−1.18	.1190	−.36	.3594	.46	.6772	1.26	.8962	2.15	.9842
−1.98	.0239	−1.16	.1230	−.34	.3669	.48	.6844	1.28	.8997	2.20	.9861
−1.96	.0250	−1.14	.1271	−.32	.3745	.50	.6915	1.30	.9032	2.25	.9878
−1.94	.0262	−1.12	.1314	−.30	.3821	.52	.6985	1.32	.9066	2.30	.9893
−1.92	.0274	−1.10	.1357	−.28	.3897	.54	.7054	1.34	.9099	2.35	.9906
−1.90	.0287	−1.08	.1401	−.26	.3974	.56	.7123	1.36	.9131	2.40	.9918
−1.88	.0301	−1.06	.1446	−.24	.4052	.58	.7190	1.38	.9162	2.45	.9929
−1.86	.0314	−1.04	.1492	−.22	.4129	.60	.7257	1.40	.9192	2.50	.9938
−1.84	.0329	−1.02	.1539	−.20	.4207	.62	.7324	1.42	.9222	2.55	.9946
−1.82	.0344	−1.00	.1587	−.18	.4286	.64	.7389	1.44	.9251	2.60	.9953
−1.80	.0359	−.98	.1635	−.16	.4364	.66	.7454	1.46	.9279	2.65	.9960
−1.78	.0375	−.96	.1685	−.14	.4443	.68	.7518	1.48	.9306	2.70	.9965
−1.76	.0392	−.94	.1736	−.12	.4522	.70	.7580	1.50	.9332	2.75	.9970
−1.74	.0409	−.92	.1788	−.10	.4602	.72	.7642	1.52	.9357	2.80	.9974
−1.72	.0427	−.90	.1841	−.08	.4681	.74	.7704	1.54	.9382	2.85	.9978
−1.70	.0446	−.88	.1894	−.06	.4761	.76	.7764	1.56	.9406	2.90	.9981
−1.68	.0465	−.86	.1949	−.04	.4840	.78	.7823	1.58	.9429	2.95	.9984
−1.66	.0485	−.84	.2005	−.02	.4920	.80	.7881	1.60	.9452	3.00	.9987
−1.64	.0505	−.82	.2061	.00	.5000	.82	.7939	1.62	.9474	3.05	.9989
−1.62	.0526	−.80	.2119	.02	.5080	.84	.7995	1.64	.9495		
−1.60	.0548	−.78	.2177	.04	.5160						

This table shows the probability [N(d)] of observing a value less than or equal to d. For example, as illustrated, if d is −.24, then N(d) is .4052.

KEY EQUATIONS

CHAPTER 2

1. The balance sheet identity or equation:

Assets = Liabilities
+ Shareholders' equity [2.1]

2. The income statement equation:

Revenues − Expenses = Income [2.2]

3. The cash flow identity:

Cash flow from assets =
Cash flow to creditors + [2.3]
Cash flow to stockholders

where

a. Cash flow from assets = Operating cash
flow (OCF) − Net capital spending −
Change in net working capital (NWC)
(1) Operating cash flow = Earnings
before interest and taxes (EBIT) +
Depreciation − Taxes
(2) Net capital spending = Ending net
fixed assets − Beginning net fixed
assets + Depreciation
(3) Change in net working capital =
Ending NWC − Beginning NWC
b. Cash flow to creditors = Interest paid −
Net new borrowing
c. Cash flow to stockholders = Dividends
paid − Net new equity raised

CHAPTER 3

1. The current ratio:

$$\text{Current ratio} = \frac{\text{Current assets}}{\text{Current liabilities}} \quad [3.1]$$

2. The quick or acid-test ratio:

$$\text{Quick ratio} = \frac{\text{Current assets} - \text{Inventory}}{\text{Current liabilities}} \quad [3.2]$$

3. The cash ratio:

$$\text{Cash ratio} = \frac{\text{Cash}}{\text{Current liabilities}} \quad [3.3]$$

4. The ratio of net working capital to total assets:

Net working capital to total assets
$$= \frac{\text{Net working capital}}{\text{Total assets}} \quad [3.4]$$

5. The interval measure:

Interval measure
$$= \frac{\text{Current assets}}{\text{Average daily operating costs}} \quad [3.5]$$

6. The total debt ratio:

Total debt ratio
$$= \frac{\text{Total assets} - \text{Total equity}}{\text{Total assets}} \quad [3.6]$$

7. The debt-equity ratio:

Debt-equity ratio
$$= \text{Total debt}/\text{Total equity} \quad [3.7]$$

8. The equity multiplier:

Equity multiplier
$$= \text{Total assets}/\text{Total equity} \quad [3.8]$$

9. The long-term debt ratio:

Long-term debt ratio
$$= \frac{\text{Long-term debt}}{\text{Long-term debt} + \text{Total equity}} \quad [3.9]$$

10. The times interest earned (TIE) ratio:

$$\text{Times interest earned ratio} = \frac{\text{EBIT}}{\text{Interest}} \quad [3.10]$$

11. The cash coverage ratio:

Cash coverage ratio
$$= \frac{\text{EBIT} + \text{Depreciation}}{\text{Interest}} \quad [3.11]$$

12. The inventory turnover ratio:

Inventory turnover
$$= \frac{\text{Cost of goods sold}}{\text{Inventory}} \quad [3.12]$$

13. The average days' sales in inventory:

Days' sales in inventory
$$= \frac{365 \text{ days}}{\text{Inventory turnover}} \quad [3.13]$$

14. The receivables turnover ratio:

$$\text{Receivables turnover} = \frac{\text{Sales}}{\text{Accounts receivable}} \quad [3.14]$$

15. The days' sales in receivables:

$$\text{Days' sales in receivables} = \frac{365 \text{ days}}{\text{Receivables turnover}} \quad [3.15]$$

16. The net working capital (NWC) turnover ratio:

$$\text{NWC turnover} = \frac{\text{Sales}}{\text{NWC}} \quad [3.16]$$

17. The fixed asset turnover ratio:

$$\text{Fixed asset turnover} = \frac{\text{Sales}}{\text{Net fixed assets}} \quad [3.17]$$

18. The total asset turnover ratio:

$$\text{Total asset turnover} = \frac{\text{Sales}}{\text{Total assets}} \quad [3.18]$$

19. Profit margin:

$$\text{Profit margin} = \frac{\text{Net income}}{\text{Sales}} \quad [3.19]$$

20. Return on assets (ROA):

$$\text{Return on assets} = \frac{\text{Net income}}{\text{Total assets}} \quad [3.20]$$

21. Return on equity (ROE):

$$\text{Return on equity} = \frac{\text{Net income}}{\text{Total equity}} \quad [3.21]$$

22. The price-earnings (PE) ratio:

$$\text{PE ratio} = \frac{\text{Price per share}}{\text{Earnings per share}} \quad [3.22]$$

23. The market-to-book ratio:

$$\text{Market-to-book ratio} = \frac{\text{Market value per share}}{\text{Book value per share}} \quad [3.23]$$

24. The Du Pont identity:

$$\text{ROE} = \underbrace{\frac{\text{Net income}}{\text{Sales}} \times \frac{\text{Sales}}{\text{Assets}}}_{\text{Return on assets}} \times \frac{\text{Assets}}{\text{Equity}} \quad [3.24]$$

ROE = Profit margin
× Total asset turnover
× Equity multiplier

CHAPTER 4

1. The dividend payout ratio:

$$\text{Dividend payout ratio} = \text{Cash dividends/Net income} \quad [4.1]$$

2. The internal growth rate:

$$\text{Internal growth rate} = \frac{\text{ROA} \times b}{1 - \text{ROA} \times b} \quad [4.2]$$

3. The sustainable growth rate:

$$\text{Sustainable growth rate} = \frac{\text{ROE} \times b}{1 - \text{ROE} \times b} \quad [4.3]$$

4. The capital intensity ratio:

$$\text{Capital intensity ratio} = \frac{\text{Total assets}}{\text{Sales}}$$
$$= \frac{1}{\text{Total asset turnover}}$$

CHAPTER 5

1. The future value of \$1 invested for t periods at rate of r per period:

$$\text{Future value} = \$1 \times (1 + r)^t \quad [5.1]$$

2. The present value of \$1 to be received t periods in the future at a discount rate of r:

$$\text{PV} = \$1 \times [1/(1 + r)^t] = \$1/(1 + r)^t \quad [5.2]$$

3. The relationship between future value and present value (the basic present value equation):

$$\text{PV} \times (1 + r)^t = \text{FV}_t$$
$$\text{PV} = \text{FV}_t/(1 + r)^t = \text{FV}_t \times [1/(1 + r)^t] \quad [5.3]$$

CHAPTER 6

1. The present value of an annuity of C dollars per period for t periods when the rate of return or interest rate is r:

$$\text{Annuity present value} = C \times \left(\frac{1 - \text{Present value factor}}{r} \right)$$
$$= C \times \left\{ \frac{1 - [1/(1 + r)^t]}{r} \right\} \quad [6.1]$$

2. The future value factor for an annuity:

$$\text{Annuity FV factor} = (\text{Future value factor} - 1)/r \quad [6.2]$$
$$= [(1 + r)^t - 1]/r$$

3. $\text{Annuity due value} = \text{Ordinary annuity value} \times (1 + r) \quad [6.3]$

4. Present value for a perpetuity:

$$\text{PV for a perpetuity} = C/r = C \times (1/r) \quad [6.4]$$

5. Growing annuity present value

$$= C \left[\frac{1 - \left(\frac{1 + g}{1 + r} \right)^t}{r - g} \right] \quad [6.5]$$

6. Growing perpetuity present value

$$= \frac{C}{r - g} \quad [6.6]$$

7. Effective annual rate (EAR), where m is the number of times the interest is compounded during the year:

$$EAR = [1 + (\text{Quoted rate}/m)]^m - 1$$

8. Effective annual rate (EAR), where q stands for the continuously compounded quoted rate:

$$EAR = e^q - 1$$

CHAPTER 7

1. Bond value if bond has (1) a face value of F paid at maturity, (2) a coupon of C paid per period, (3) t periods to maturity, and (4) a yield of r per period:

Bond value
$$= C \times [1 - 1/(1 + r)^t]/r + F/(1 + r)^t \quad [7.1]$$
Bond value
$$= \frac{\text{Present value}}{\text{of the coupons}} + \frac{\text{Present value}}{\text{of the face amount}}$$

2. The Fisher effect:

$$1 + R = (1 + r) \times (1 + h) \quad [7.2]$$
$$R = r + h + r \times h \quad [7.3]$$
$$R \approx r + h \quad [7.4]$$

CHAPTER 8

1. The dividend growth model:

$$P_0 = \frac{D_0 \times (1 + g)}{R - g} = \frac{D_1}{R - g} \quad [8.3]$$

2. Required return:

$$R = D_1/P_0 + g \quad [8.7]$$

CHAPTER 9

1. Net present value (NPV):

NPV = Present value of future cash flows − Investment cost

2. Payback period:

Payback period = Number of years that pass before the sum of an investment's cash flows equals the cost of the investment

3. Discounted payback period:

Discounted payback period = Number of years that pass before the sum of an investment's *discounted* cash flows equals the cost of the investment

4. The average accounting return (AAR):

$$AAR = \frac{\text{Average net income}}{\text{Average book value}}$$

5. Internal rate of return (IRR):

IRR = Discount rate of required return such that the net present value of an investment is zero

6. Profitability index:

$$\text{Profitability index} = \frac{\text{PV of cash flows}}{\text{Cost of investment}}$$

CHAPTER 10

1. Bottom-up approach to operating cash flow (OCF):

$$OCF = \text{Net income} + \text{Depreciation} \quad [10.1]$$

2. Top-down approach to operating cash flow (OCF):

$$OCF = \text{Sales} - \text{Costs} - \text{Taxes} \quad [10.2]$$

3. Tax shield approach to operating cash flow (OCF):

$$OCF = (\text{Sales} - \text{Costs}) \times (1 - T) + \text{Depreciation} \times T \quad [10.3]$$

CHAPTER 11

1. Accounting break-even level:

$$Q = (FC + D)/(P - v) \quad [11.1]$$

2. Relationship between operating cash flow (OCF) and sales volume:

$$Q = (FC + OCF)/(P - v) \quad [11.3]$$

3. Cash break-even level:

$$Q = FC/(P - v)$$

4. Financial break-even level:

$$Q = (FC + OCF^*)/(P - v)$$

where

$$OCF^* = \text{Zero NPV cash flow}$$

5. Degree of operating leverage (DOL):

$$DOL = 1 + FC/OCF \quad [11.4]$$

CHAPTER 12

1. Variance of returns, $Var(R)$ or σ^2:

$$Var(R) = \frac{1}{T - 1}[(R_1 - \overline{R})^2 + \cdots + (R_T - \overline{R})^2] \quad [12.3]$$

2. Standard deviation of returns, $SD(R)$ or σ:

$$SD(R) = \sqrt{Var(R)}$$

CHAPTER 13

1. Risk premium:

Risk premium = Expected return − Risk-free rate $\quad [13.1]$

2. Expected return on a portfolio:

$$E(R_P) = x_1 \times E(R_1) + x_2 \times E(R_2) + \cdots + x_n \times E(R_n) \quad [13.2]$$

3. The reward-to-risk ratio:

$$\text{Reward-to-risk ratio} = \frac{E[R_i] - R_f}{\beta_i}$$

4. The capital asset pricing model (CAPM):

$$E(R_i) = R_f + [E(R_M) - R_f] \times \beta_i \qquad [13.7]$$

CHAPTER 14

1. Required return on equity, R_E (dividend growth model):

$$R_E = D_1/P_0 + g \qquad [14.1]$$

2. Required return on equity, R_E (CAPM):

$$R_E = R_f + \beta_E \times (R_M - R_f) \qquad [14.2]$$

3. Required return on preferred stock, R_P:

$$R_P = D/P_0 \qquad [14.3]$$

4. The weighted average cost of capital (WACC):

$$WACC = (E/V) \times R_E + (D/V) \times R_D \times (1 - T_C) \qquad [14.6]$$

5. Weighted average flotation cost, f_A:

$$f_A = \frac{E}{V} \times f_E + \frac{D}{V} \times f_D \qquad [14.8]$$

CHAPTER 15

1. Rights offerings:

   a. Number of new shares:

$$\text{Number of new shares} = \frac{\text{Funds to be raised}}{\text{Subscription price}} \qquad [15.1]$$

   b. Number of rights needed:

$$\text{Number of rights needed to buy a share of stock} = \frac{\text{Old shares}}{\text{New shares}} \qquad [15.2]$$

   c. Value of a right:

$$\text{Value of a right} = \text{Rights-on price} - \text{Ex-rights price}$$

CHAPTER 16

1. Modigliani-Miller propositions (no taxes):

   a. Proposition I:

$$V_L = V_U$$

   b. Proposition II:

$$R_E = R_A + (R_A - R_D) \times (D/E) \qquad [16.1]$$

2. Modigliani-Miller propositions (with taxes):

   a. Value of the interest tax shield:

$$\text{Present value of the interest tax shield} = (T_C \times D \times R_D)/R_D = T_C \times D \qquad [16.2]$$

   b. Proposition I:

$$V_L = V_U + T_C \times D \qquad [16.3]$$

   c. Proposition II:

$$R_E = R_U + (R_U - R_D) \times (D/E) \times (1 - T_C) \qquad [16.4]$$

CHAPTER 18

1. The operating cycle:

$$\text{Operating cycle} = \text{Inventory period} + \text{Accounts receivable period} \qquad [18.4]$$

2. The cash cycle:

$$\text{Cash cycle} = \text{Operating cycle} - \text{Accounts payable period} \qquad [18.5]$$

CHAPTER 19

1. Float measurement:

   a. Average daily float:

$$\text{Average daily float} = \frac{\text{Total float}}{\text{Total days}} \qquad [19.1]$$

   b. Average daily float:

$$\text{Average daily float} = \text{Average daily receipts} \times \text{Weighted average delay} \qquad [19.2]$$

2. The Baumol-Allais-Tobin (BAT) model:

   a. Opportunity costs:

$$\text{Opportunity costs} = (C/2) \times R \qquad [19A.1]$$

   b. Trading costs:

$$\text{Trading costs} = (T/C) \times F \qquad [19A.2]$$

   c. Total cost:

$$\text{Total cost} = \text{Opportunity costs} + \text{Trading costs} \qquad [19A.3]$$

   d. The optimal initial cash balance:

$$C^* = \sqrt{(2T \times F)/R} \qquad [19A.4]$$

3. The Miller-Orr model:

   a. The optimal cash balance:

$$C^* = L + (3/4 \times F \times \sigma^2/R)^{1/3} \qquad [19A.5]$$

   b. The upper limit:

$$U^* = 3 \times C^* - 2 \times L \qquad [19A.6]$$

CHAPTER 20

1. The size of receivables:

$$\text{Accounts receivable} = \text{Average daily sales} \times \text{ACP} \qquad [20.1]$$

2. NPV of switching credit terms:

   a. Present value of switching:
$$PV = [(P - v)(Q' - Q)]/R \qquad [20.4]$$

   b. Cost of switching:
$$\text{Cost of switching} = PQ + v(Q' - Q) \qquad [20.5]$$

   c. NPV of switching:
$$\text{NPV of switching} = -[PQ + v(Q' - Q)] + [(P - v) \times (Q' - Q)]/R \qquad [20.6]$$

3. NPV of granting credit:

   a. With no repeat business:
$$NPV = -v + (1 - \pi)P/(1 + R) \qquad [20.8]$$

   b. With repeat business:
$$NPV = -v + (1 - \pi)(P - v)/R \qquad [20.9]$$

4. The economic order quantity (EOQ) model:

   a. Total carrying costs:
$$\begin{aligned}\text{Total carrying costs} &= \text{Average inventory} \\ &\times \text{Carrying costs per unit} \\ &= (Q/2) \times CC\end{aligned} \qquad [20.10]$$

   b. Total restocking costs:
$$\begin{aligned}\text{Total restocking costs} &= \text{Fixed cost per order} \\ &\times \text{Number of orders} = F \times (T/Q)\end{aligned} \qquad [20.11]$$

   c. Total costs:
$$\begin{aligned}\text{Total costs} &= \text{Carrying costs} \\ &+ \text{Restocking costs} \\ &= (Q/2) \times CC \\ &+ F \times (T/Q)\end{aligned} \qquad [20.12]$$

   d. The optimal order size Q^*:
$$Q^* = \sqrt{\frac{2T \times F}{CC}} \qquad [20.15]$$

CHAPTER 21

1. Purchasing power parity (PPP):
$$E(S_t) = S_0 \times [1 + (h_{FC} - h_{US})]^t \qquad [21.3]$$

2. Interest rate parity (IRP):

   a. Exact, single period:
$$F_1/S_0 = (1 + R_{FC})/(1 + R_{US}) \qquad [21.4]$$

   b. Approximate, multiperiod:
$$F_t = S_0 \times [1 + (R_{FC} - R_{US})]^t \qquad [21.7]$$

3. Uncovered interest parity (UIP):
$$E(S_t) = S_0 \times [1 + (R_{FC} - R_{US})]^t \qquad [21.9]$$

4. International Fisher effect (IFE):
$$R_{US} - h_{US} = R_{FC} - h_{FC} \qquad [21.10]$$

CHAPTER 24

1. Value of a call option at maturity:

   a. $C_1 = 0$ if $(S_1 - E) \leq 0$ $\qquad [24.1]$

   b. $C_1 = S_1 - E$ if $(S_1 - E) > 0$ $\qquad [24.2]$

2. Bounds on the value of a call option:

   a. Upper bound:
$$C_0 \leq S_0 \qquad [24.3]$$

   b. Lower bound:
$$\begin{aligned}C_0 &\geq 0 \text{ if } S_0 - E < 0 \\ C_0 &\geq S_0 - E \text{ if } S_0 - E \geq 0\end{aligned} \qquad [24.4]$$

3. $S_0 = C_0 + E/(1 + R_f)$
$$C_0 = S_0 - E/(1 + R_f) \qquad [24.5]$$

4. Value of a call that is certain to finish in-the-money:
   Call option value
$$\begin{aligned}&= \text{Stock value} \\ &- \text{Present value of the exercise price}\end{aligned}$$
$$C_0 = S_0 - E/(1 + R_f)^t \qquad [24.6]$$

CHAPTER 25

1. Put-call parity condition:
$$S + P = PV(E) + C \qquad [25.2]$$

2. The Black-Scholes call option formula:
$$C = S \times N(d_1) - E \times e^{-Rt} \times N(d_2) \qquad [25.5]$$
where
$$d_1 = [\ln(S/E) + (R + \sigma^2/2) \times t]/(\sigma \times \sqrt{t}) \qquad [25.6]$$
$$d_2 = d_1 - \sigma \times \sqrt{t}$$

3. Value of a risk-free bond:
$$\text{Value of risky bond + Put option} \qquad [25.7]$$

CHAPTER 26

4. The NPV of a merger:
$$\begin{aligned}NPV = V_B^* &- \text{Cost to Firm A of} \\ &\text{the acquisition}\end{aligned} \qquad [26.1]$$

ANSWERS TO SELECTED END-OF-CHAPTER PROBLEMS

CHAPTER 2

2. $171,600

7. Average rate = 31.90%
Marginal rate = 39%

10. −$180

14. a. $63,745
  b. $22,100
  c. $4,700
  d. $845

18. a. $\text{Tax}_{\text{Growth}}$ = $19,870
  $\text{Tax}_{\text{Income}}$ = $2,992,000
  b. $3,400

22. a. 2008 = $1,661
  2009 = $2,142
  b. $22
  c. Fixed assets sold = $63
  Cash flow from assets = $1,896
  d. Debt retired = $180
  Cash flow to creditors = $121

26. Cash flow from assets = −$1,302.76
Cash flow to creditors = −$2,156.00
Cash flow to stockholders = $853.24

CHAPTER 3

2. Net income = $2.32 million
ROA = 13.26%
ROE = 20.71%

6. EPS = $2.88
DPS = $.83
BVPS = $25.24
Market-to-book ratio = 2.50 times
PE ratio = 21.87 times
P/S ratio = 2.94 times

10. 78.51 days

18. $194.06

22. Firm A: 18.46%
Firm B: 15.71%

26. a. 1.44 times; 1.40 times
  b. .85 times; .83 times
  c. .56 times; .51 times

  d. .95 times
  e. 8.56 times
  f. 22.08 times
  g. .39; .40
  h. .65; .66
  i. 1.65; 1.66
  j. 5.70 times
  k. 7.95 times
  l. 11.93%
  m. 11.36%
  n. 18.91%

CHAPTER 4

2. −$1,252.50

5. $1,000.14

12. 6.84%

16. 5.26%

20. 1.74 times

22. Sustainable growth rate = 16.47%
New borrowing = $14,160.64
Internal growth rate = 6.04%

28. 16.16%

CHAPTER 5

2. $6,419.51
$14,999.39
$687,764.17
$315,795.75

6. 9.68%

10. $155,893,400

14. 9.90%

18. $438,120.97; $154,299.40

CHAPTER 6

2. @ 5%: PV_X = $42,646.93
PV_Y = $40,605.54
@ 15%: PV_X = $28,629.50
PV_Y = $30,275.86

6. $411,660.36

10. $347,222.22

14. First National EAR = 15.16%
First United EAR = 15.03%

18. $28,804.71

22. APR = 1,733.33%
EAR = 313,916,515.69%

26. $34,843.71

30. 8.17% semiannual
4.00% quarterly
1.32% monthly

38. $2,235,994

42. $368,936.54

46. Profit = $7,197.59
Breakeven = 15.10%

50. $37,051.41

54. $1,364.99

58. PV of lease payments = $14,672.91
PV of purchase = $13,345.18
Breakeven resale price = $21,363.01

60. EAR = 17.65%

64. Refundable fee:
APR = 6.89%
EAR = 7.12%
Nonrefundable fee:
APR = 6.80%
EAR = 7.02%

70. 8.07%

74. 6.48%

CHAPTER 7

4. 10.15%

8. 5.97%

12. 6.30%

26. a. 30,000 coupon bonds; 315,589 zeroes
b. $32,400,000; $315,588,822

28. $7,367.76

CHAPTER 8

2. 9.38%

6. $2.45

10. $63.47

14. $48.70

18. $96.15

20. $69.55

CHAPTER 9

4. 1.81 years; 2.54 years; 3.26 years

8. @ 11%: NPV = $5,991.49
@30%: NPV = −$4,213.93

12. a. IRR_A = 20.44%
IRR_B = 18.84%
b. NPV_A = $7,507.61
NPV_B = $9,182.29
c. Crossover rate = 15.30%

16. a. PI_I = 1.267
PI_I = 1.414
b. NPV_I = $14,145.00
NPV_{II} = $6,630.35

22. a. $C = I / N$
b. $C > I / PVIFA_{R\%,N}$
c. $C > 2.0 * I / PVIFA_{R\%,N}$

CHAPTER 10

2. $403,600,000

8. $1,387,792

12. $CF_0 = -\$4,200,000$
$CF_1 = \$1,631,455$
$CF_2 = \$1,738,243$
$CF_3 = \$1,916,303$
NPV = $42,232.43

16. −$117,803.98

22. $.03163

CHAPTER 11

2. Total costs = $6,222,800
Marginal cost = $38.94
Average cost = $51.86
Minimum revenue = $194,700

8. D = 420,800
P = $69.36
VC = $37.57

12. OCF = $34,333
DOL = 4.786

18. DOL = 1.2480
DOL_A = 2.7143

22. $\Delta NPV/\Delta P$ = $148,973.62
$DNPV/\Delta Q$ = $1,226.84

30. DOL = 1.0381
ΔOCF = +2.97%

CHAPTER 12

2. R_d = 2.64%
R_c = 12.09%

6. 2.62%; 3.01%

16. R_A = 11.83%
R_G = 10.58%

20. 14.95%; 14.52%; 13.64%

CHAPTER 13

2. 13.23%

6. 12.50%

10. a. 7.64%
b. $\sigma^2_P = .02436$
$\sigma_P = 15.61\%$

14. .67

18. .0792

24. $C = \$324,074.07$
$R_F = \$145,925.93$

26. $\beta_I = 2.06$
$\sigma_I = 8.53\%$
$\beta_{II} = .63$
$\sigma_{II} = 33.96\%$

CHAPTER 14

2. 12.34%

4. $R_A = 11.47\%$; $R_G = 11.46\%$

8. Book value = \$115,000,000
Market value = \$97,350,000
Aftertax cost = 5.34%

12. a. $E/V = .3455$
$D/V = .6545$
b. $E/V = .8595$
$D/V = .1405$

16. a. $D/V = .2290$
$P/V = .0534$
$E/V = .7176$
b. 12.80%

20. Breakeven cost = \$37,943,787

CHAPTER 15

2. a. \$53; anything greater than \$0
b. 833,333, 4.92
c. \$52.16; \$.84

6. 3,186,813

8. No change;
declines by \$.69;
declines by \$1.55

14. \$38,467.41

CHAPTER 16

2. a. \$1.82; \$3.64; \$4.73
b. \$1.56; \$4.41; \$6.11
6. a. \$3.29; \$3.00; \$3.55
b. \$44,000
c. \$44,000
d. \$44,000

10. \$2,070,000

12. a. 18.18%
b. 12.66%
c. 20.01%; 16.34%; 12.66%

16. \$310,583.33

CHAPTER 17

2. a. 3,000 new shares
b. 7,500 new shares

4. a. \$54.00
b. \$78.26
c. \$63.16
d. \$157.50
e. 583,333; 402,500; 498,750; 200,000

8. Shares outstanding = 466,900
Capital surplus = \$3,410,600

10. $P_0 = \$42.08$
$D = \$25.88$

CHAPTER 18

2. Cash = \$2,035
Current assets = \$5,590

4. a. *I,I*
b. *I,N*
c. *D,D*
d. *D,D*
e. *D, N*
f. *I,I*

6. Operating cycle = 86.87 days
Cash cycle = 36.50 days

8. a. \$258.00; \$279.00; \$297.00; \$282.90
b. \$246.00; \$258.00; \$279.00; \$297.00
c. \$250.00; \$265.00; \$285.00; \$292.30

10. a. \$246,666.67
b. \$388,571.43
c. \$267,464.29
\$274,285.71
\$279,000.00

14. a. 4.89%
b. 9.63%
c. 9.52%

18. 11.76%

CHAPTER 19

2. a. \$56,000
−\$52,000
\$4,000
b. \$56,000
−\$26,000
\$30,000

6. a. \$28,620
b. 2.49 days

c. $28,620
d. $5.31
e. $17,225

10. NPV = $3,900,000
Net savings = $195,000

APPENDIX 19A

19A.2 $2,661.45

19A.4 a. Opportunity cost = $37.50
Trading cost = $266.67
b. $4,000.00

19A.10 7.68%

CHAPTER 20

2. $4,635,616

6. Sales = $444,551.28
Accounts receivable turnover = 9.359 times

10. NPV = $148,275

12. Carrying cost = $6,150
Order cost = $4,940
EOQ = 268.87
Orders = 58.02 per year

16. Net savings = $6,850

APPENDIX 20A

20A.2 a. 2/15, net 30
b. $297,000
d. NPV = −$3,023,592
Break-even price = $102.13
Break-even discount = 11.88%

20A.4 b. $77.32
c. NPV = −$74,622.27

CHAPTER 21

6. Great Britain: 3.54%
Japan: 1.04%
Switzerland: 2.07%

10. b. Krone 5.1987

12. b. 6.12%

CHAPTER 23

2. Loss = $5,075
Profit = $7,175

CHAPTER 24

4. a. $8.10
b. $5.02

8. a. D_0 = $910.60
E_0 = $229.40
b. E_0 = $288.96

12. $9.11

14. a. $360,218.98
b. Abandon if Q < 4,460

20. a. $8,499,550
b. $6,995,771

CHAPTER 25

2. $7,301.28

6. 3.90%

10. Call delta = .66
Put delta = −.34

14. $6.26

16. $5.73

20. Equity = $6,455.02
Debt = $20,844.98

22. a. $8,363,716
b. $7,636,284
c. 11.86%
d. $8,951,454
e. 11.65%

24. a. $35,234.40
b. $10,451.14
c. $24,783.26; 14.04%
d. $21,493.49; 16.89%
e. Bondholders lose $3,289.77
Stockholders gain $3,289.77

CHAPTER 26

8. EPS = $4.34
PE = 19.09

10. .4695

14. a. £26.09
b. .4821

CHAPTER 27

2. −$16,851.25

6. −$31,441.66

NAME INDEX

EQUATION INDEX

SUBJECT INDEX